THE BRIDGE

THE BRIDGE

Joining East-West Nations and Cultures
While Treading Life's Difficult Path

Mir M. Ali

Typeset by Amnet Systems

Cover design by Amnet Systems.

*Dedicated to my beloved father, Mir Muazzam Ali,
and my beloved mother, Azifa Ali, who shaped me.
Also, to my wife Dora, my two daughters Ifat and Jinat,
and my son Murad, who are all so precious to me.*

CONTENTS

FOREWORD

Mir M. Ali was a child in Pakistan, student and practicing engineer in East Pakistan (now Bangladesh) and Canada, a practicing engineer and an architecture professor in the United States, even as he has earned recognition as an international authority on Tall Buildings worldwide. He is now a citizen of the world whose life story will fascinate a wide swathe of readers in today's cosmopolitan, globalized, world. I have known him for over 35 years now, ever since he arrived at the University of Illinois, Urbana-Champaign. Mir Ali has been friend, neighbor, colleague, and mentor. I have had the pleasure of reading the first draft of his autobiography and I wish to recall some highlights. Of the many facets of such a fascinating figure, it will be imprudent of me to say more than a few introductory points. I hope to have said just enough to tease the reader into delving into the fascinating autobiography. So, I will limit myself to describing some gems from the initial chapters.

Having grown up in a small town in a backward district of Bangladesh, Mir Ali experienced a world that has long since become unfamiliar, even to the Bangladesh of today. While many of his generation are still around, it is doubtful if anyone has the accuracy and detail of his memory. Combined with this retentive memory is a literary nature that enables him to both see and express many things that pass others by. The nature of the local elites, the pervasiveness of people with religious grounding, the strong belief in civic values and the paramount degree of faith are all to be found in the introductory chapters. Also are two items: the unselfconscious manner in which Muslims and Hindus interacted with each other and the trips to a holy man, or 'pir', for advice and guidance. Of special interest from the younger days is the fascinating tale of marriage to his beloved wife, Dora, who has shared his adventurous life for over 50 years and who comes from a traditional, conservative Muslim family of Bengal. While there are several biographical accounts of Bengali Hindus from similar small-town backgrounds, I do not know of any comparable accounts of Muslims.

From the small town of Patuakhali Mir Ali went to Dhaka for college, only to face the turmoil of a country about to be cleft in two by the bigoted and unsympathetic attitude of the Pakistani elite. The turbulence of Bengali agitation, the tension and uncertainty surrounding the fight for independence, the wrenching decision to leave family and friends and go abroad to study for an indefinite period, the difficulties of finding firm ground in the new Bangladesh while he was in Canada -- all are captured in careful and absorbing detail.

The book has been arranged in a sequence that enables the reader to pick and choose among many chapters, especially, separating out the professional and technical ones, but I would suggest reading his early life in particular until the move to Canada before picking and choosing further. The small town of Patuakhali is now a humming city to be, since an international port has been set up at nearby *Payra*, and Patuakhali can host some 10,000 foreign experts and traders at any point in time. Mir Ali writes of a world that has disappeared, but he has recreated many aspects of it for us. He ends the book by illuminating the past and present of both Bangladesh and the United States.

Enjoy!

Salim Rashid
Professor Emeritus, Economics
University of Illinois at Urbana-Champaign

PROLOGUE

A bridge is the ultimate metaphor for my life. I had to bridge cities, countries, ideologies and East/West cultures. My life's work began with bridge design as a civil engineer in what is today Bangladesh. My education and varied professional experience led me to a notable academic career at a world class university in the U.S., where I spent over 30 years. This outcome is a far cry from where I began. I was born in a small coastal town in the province of Bengal (then in British India) and I made my ascent to become a naturalized U.S. citizen -- a prospect I had set my sights on decades before.

Bangladesh has a beautiful natural habitat, symbolized by the Bengal Tiger (locally known as Royal Bengal Tiger, the national animal of Bangladesh), roaming in the Sundarbans, a mangrove forest close to the Bay of Bengal. It is the symbol of my home nation. There came a time, however, when my heart called, "Oh give me a home where the buffalo roam..." The American Bison (Buffalo), the national animal of America, has its setting in the heartland prairie. Now, my love for both majestic animals, God's creations, is indelibly a part of me.

Equally indelible is the history I've witnessed. I was born during World War II and then lived through the 1947 independence and partition of India-Pakistan, which resulted in the largest population displacement in human history. So, I was an Indian, became a Pakistani and later became a Bangladeshi, after East Pakistan successfully seceded in 1971 following a bloody war. Such turbulence is a main reason so many people around the world dream of immigrating to the Land of the Free and the Home of the Brave.

My bridge from Bengal to America included scenic views of Canadian tundra mining towns, the Windy City, where I initially started my career in tall building/skyscraper design, the Lion City known for its orchids in Southeast Asia, and ultimately led me to academia in the cornfields of Midwest farm country. The story of how I achieved this end is as circuitous as it gets. It sounds cliché to say education is the key to unlocking one's future but it's mostly true, you need a skill set. What you're not taught in a classroom, however, is decision-making, courage under fire and rational approaches to deal with the curveballs that life throws!

My tumultuous journey to America includes unthinkable mega-storms, headwinds, tailwinds and near drownings which required tough mettle and crisis management. I will provide some lessons on fortitude, tenacity and audacity as mine is a story of triumph over turmoil! I hope my experiences can benefit others as I've been through more hiccups than the average person. Job loss, inadequate pay, uncertain visa status, threat of deportation, serious family illness, a cardiac event and becoming a caregiver, my latest role.

It is during this time, my retirement, that I hatched a plan to write. I am a published author but most of my work is technical and career related. I'd like to thank my dear friend Dr. Salim Rashid (retired Economics professor of University of Illinois at Urbana-Champaign) for planting the seed that blossomed into this very personal project and I'd like to thank my brother-in-law Dr. Ehsanes Saleh (retired Statistics professor of Carleton University, Ottawa, Ontario) who gave me another nudge to put pen to paper. Also, my sister-in-law Moshira Ali (Tora) and my nephew Tarek have greatly encouraged me to write this book. I am indebted to them both.

As it stands, I've personally benefitted reading about and listening to other people's life stories. Fascinating life stories should be recorded lest they become lost and unknowable.

I'd like to share my fascinating life story with family, friends, colleagues, as well as a global audience. I had a few other stories to tell. At times I considered how much detail to provide. In the end I feel I'm leaving this book for generations to come, so they can know me, my observations and life experiences years from now, perhaps at the expense of revealing a bit too much. My life is now an open book.

PART ONE:
FOUNDATIONAL YEARS

Water Lilies and Mango Trees

CHAPTER 1

CHILDHOOD IN A COASTAL TOWN
Parental Supervision is Advised

The coastal town of Patuakhali, formerly in British India, was interlaced with narrow brick roads and tin sheds with the very basic civic infrastructure needed for leading a semi-urban life. According to my mother Azifa Ali (maiden name Khatun), the setting of my birth was during the turbulence of World War II on the cold winter morning of January 9, 1944. The *muezzin* (caller for prayer) was inviting the faithful to dawn prayers from the town's minaret as my mother gave birth to me, the seventh of eight children – four sons and four daughters.

Patuakhali was the sub-divisional headquarters, administered by a sub-divisional officer, in the district of Barisal which was administered by the district magistrate. Prior to this the present-day Barisal and Patuakhali territories made up the district of Bakergonj. It was made up of forests and marshlands and was remote to outsiders. The township of Patuakhali is located about 30 miles (48 kilometers) to the north of the Bay of Bengal in present-day Bangladesh. Because of its proximity to the sea in the coastal region, it is frequently barreled by cyclones. As residents occupied tin sheds and homes that were not designed for high winds, these would, from time to time, be obliterated by severe cyclones, blurring the distinction between the municipal township and the surrounding villages. It's forests and marshlands, mighty rivers, ponds and water lilies spawned my love for Nature.

The town is bounded by *Laukathi* and *Lohalia* rivers on its two sides. These two rivers regularly encounter high tides that determine the water navigation patterns for boatmen and captains. At one time, crocodiles would frequent the rivers around Patuakhali, and stories of their attacks abounded. One legendary story involved a crocodile grabbing a man by his leg from the edge of the *Laukathi* riverbank and dramatically yanking him into the streaming water. According to accounts, the victim was frantic yet quick to react with precision in his fight for survival. Despite being seconds away from certain death, grace would prevail, and he managed to thrust his fingers hard into both eyes of the crocodile! He was thrown back to the shore, disoriented and ravaged by pain. Bystanders, incredulous, came to his aid.

Eventually, mass transit steamers, motor launches and ferries as well as many roving modes of water transport would displace the crocodiles. The aggressive creatures gradually retreated and eventually disappeared from the rivers. Rivers and natural canals were the only means of transportation in the region. There was no land transport in Patuakhali when I was a child. Townspeople would simply walk to do business, shop and make social visits. Owing to the primacy of the waterways, the district of Barisal is coined the "Venice of the East". However, this once small town has grown into a bustling city, with all the necessary amenities of life. My childhood was happily lived out against the backdrop of the town's bridges and canals that shaped me as well as my small town. Today Patuakhali boasts good schools, colleges, a university at nearby *Dumki*, a large hospital and transportation system.

My father was a lawyer, one of a few Muslim lawyers at a time when most of the eminent lawyers, doctors, and teachers in town were Hindus. The shortage of educated Muslims can be attributed to the complicated dynamics of culture, religion, language and power in British India at the time. Upon consolidating power in the region, the British were quick to replace Persian as the official language of the land. In response to this cultural incursion and loss of power, conservative Muslim religious leaders encouraged Muslims to reject English medium instruction. This led to Muslims in India falling behind in modern Western education. As an attempt to quell the influence of conservative religious leaders, Sir Sayed Ahmed, championed his "Aligarh Movement". Sir Sayed was a visionary, activist and founder of Aligarh University and Islamic modernism in India in the 19th century.

Sir Sayed advised Muslims to accept the reality of British government, embrace English and take advantage of Western sciences and modern schools. His exhortations fell largely on deaf ears, since religious leaders in small towns and villages held greater influence over the Muslim masses. Citizens continued their old attitude and were impermeable to his message. Many people think that Lord Macaulay's education policy had adverse effects on Muslims, who were the previous rulers of India. Macaulay's policy consisted of implementing Western education in the 1930s and entirely replacing the prevalent education system, which had been enacted during Muslim rule. Simply stated, Hindus readily accepted English education and became prosperous while the Muslims failed to adapt to this new political climate.

By birth order, I am the eighth child of my parents, but one of my older sisters died as child, which makes me the seventh living child of my parents. By the time I was an adolescent, my father was already a middle-aged man. Being advanced in age and naturally mellow demeanor, he never spanked me, scolded me, or even ordered me to do anything. My fond memories are of a bearded middle-aged and later elderly man. We don't have any photos of him as a young man, so I rely on the memories of my older siblings to complete the picture. Although he had a beard when I came along, I heard he was clean shaven before that.

I have long been interested in my roots and often wondered about my ancestors while imagining what they looked like, and the lives they led. My earliest known ancestor from my father's side was Syed Noor from Iraq. Syed Nader Ali, a descendent of Syed Noor moved from Khorasan to India. To preach the religion, he went to Dhaka via Delhi and other Indian cities in early 19th century. Later, Syed Nader Ali's son, Syed Nezamat Ali, moved to *Indrakul*, a rural wooded area which was then Bakergonj district and now in the Patuakhali district. He established a new settlement there for his family and became the pioneer of a new clan. Syed Nezamat Ali had three sons. He changed the family title from Syed to Mir perhaps to absolve them of the responsibility of being preachers. His oldest son was Mir Emran Ali, who visited a village called *Dharandi* in about 1900, where he met the wealthy patriarch of the well-established Khan family. The patriarch had two daughters and no son. He liked Mir Emran Ali and requested him to marry his elder daughter Jamila, thinking it auspicious that she should have a husband from the respectable Mir family of *Indrakul*. After due considerations, Mir Emran agreed and took her as his second wife. She remained however, in her parental home by agreement. Mir Emran would continue to live in *Indrakul* but would visit her from time to time. Two sons were born to Jamila. My father Mir Muazzam Ali (nickname Arzoo) was the elder of the two sons through this marriage and was born in 1901. My father was only seven years old when my grandfather died of a high fever. I can only imagine now, how my father was deprived of his own father's love, guidance and advice.

Mir Wazed Ali, an older son of my grandfather living in Patuakhali, lovingly and dutifully cared for his younger brother.
Under his care, my father was able to attend the local Patuakhali Jubilee High School. Mir Wazed was himself a *peshkar* (court
clerk). My father was always a good student. His merit as a student
was apparent as early as primary school. Owing to his excellent
performance, my father graduated with distinction at all levels
of his education. He was highly proficient in mathematics and
developed a reputation for exceling in English.

Although my father valued education, he never pushed his
children very hard in matters related to education. This was
because of his gentle and non-meddling nature. My father would
go to bed early and used to tell me and my younger brother not
to study too much at night. He advised us to be gentle with our
young brains and encouraged us to go to bed early, something
that my mother resisted. In fact, it was my mother who pushed us
in education. She was a strong woman, the motivating force and
planner behind everything in our family. A true matriarch, she
would set the goals and have my father implement the directives.
My father had a policy of non-interference, although he admitted later that he wished one of his sons would study law, become
a barrister and follow in his footsteps. In his youth, my father
aspired to go to London to pursue a prestigious credential, the
bar-at-law diploma. However, this wish never materialized. His
wish for his sons likewise did not materialize as we moved in
other directions. Despite this, he was a very successful lawyer who
was also involved in politics. He was the longtime president of
the Patuakhali branch of Pakistan Muslim League, a party that
was instrumental in the creation of Pakistan in 1947. He served
as a government lawyer for many years. He was also the secretary
of the administration on a voluntary basis for 25 years, for his
alma mater, Patuakhali Jubilee High School. In the early 1950s,
the illustrious headmaster Mr. Naba Chandra Banerjee, a Hindu

Brahmin, left the newly minted Pakistan for India resulting in a
state of instability in the leadership of the school.* Several headmaster turnovers took place in a short time. My father's dedicated
leadership and attention provided the stability and continuity
that students required. Many students were able to continue their
education, unhindered by these upheavals.

Along with his devotion to helping students, my father was
very wise and kind-hearted man who had no enemies that I knew
of. He would never hurt anybody with his words or actions. Even
when someone would hurt his feelings, he would easily forgive
and forget. He had an ideal moral character. I never saw him to
be jealous, argumentative, arrogant, bitter, or begrudging with
anybody. He was equally very kind with animals and birds and
always advised us to treat them well. He was the most nonvio-
lent person I have ever known, in fact he could not even witness
the slaughtering of chickens and livestock, although ironically,
he did love hunting birds. His compassion extended to all those
in our household, including our servants and any workers hired
to do work on our property or home. Although he was deeply
religious, he wasn't rigid and respected other views. He was intellectually inclined, above pettiness, and never vindictive. He was
exceptional in honesty, integrity and a man of conscience. I have
always wished to be worthy of the high honor of being his son.
He was a man of ideal moral character. I always hope to measure
myself by his high standard.

My most vivid memories of my father are from when I was
close to 10 years old. He allowed me grow into my unique self
without stifling my natural ways. He was an early riser, prayed in

---

* Many Muslims and Hindus migrated from India to Pakistan and vice
versa following the 1947 partition. The township of Patuakhali was populated mostly by established Hindu merchants and professionals like lawyers, doctors, and teachers. They left for India leaving a temporary vacuum
in all areas.

the morning, recited the Qur'an, and then had the endearing habit of whistling the tune of a song. He would take me to places away from Patuakhali that he'd visit. My younger brother was too young, so he would stay with my mother. Those places are still etched in my memory. Growing up, we lived in a two-story wood-framed house with tin sheathing, popular housing at the time.

If my father said something, and I disagreed, he would never push his point and force a close to the discussion. If he was disappointed about something I said, his face would show it, but he would never express it in words. He had extreme tolerance for his children and others. Although my father was not in the habit of doling out advice about what I should do or how to think, he would correct me if I said something about others that was not appropriate and tell me to rethink my stance to include the perspectives of others.

As I grew older, he would tell me stories with built-in lessons. Like the story of an unhappy man who was fixated on the apparent good fortune of a wealthy neighbor. The wealthy man, who owned a mansion and threw lavish parties seemed so happy. One day the rich man confided that he wasn't really happy at all. Unfortunately, he was impotent and could not have children. The moral of the story was clear: we should be content with who we are and what we have and not judge others outwardly.

Another story that has always stayed with me was about a mouse and a saint in a forest. The mouse felt inferior next to the size of the cats and prayed to the saint to make it bigger. The saint granted this wish. The mouse came back to the saint again and again asking for a bigger size until it morphed into an elephant. The saint granted this wish too, but the mouse was still not satisfied. The mouse returned and again requested that the saint make it even bigger. Annoyed by the insatiable mouse, the saint cursed the mouse and reverted it to its original size and drove it away. The moral again: to be content with who we are, not always clamor for more, to know our limits, and not make our ambition limitless and impractical. He was an amazing story-teller, and would tell many useful tales, but these two have stayed with me and continue to assist me through life. I would vividly recall his noble face if ever I lost my way.

Once my father retired from legal practice in Patuakhali in 1971 at the age of 70, my parents decided to move to Dhaka to our newly built house at Road No. 15 (Extension) in Rayer Bazar. Before I left for Canada in 1970, I played an instrumental role in buying the land at the behest of my mother. I was charged with planning and building the first phases of the home to sat-isfy my mother's wishes. I felt proud and relieved to know that I had helped them to settle into this new phase of life, as I also entered a new phase, thousands of miles away. Over time, my father developed a friendship with the uncle of my wife Mor-sheda Khan (Dora) who lived in Dhaka and was also retired. His name was Mr. A.R.M. Motiur Rahman living on Elephant Road, not far from where my father lived. Mr. Rahman was a likable person. The two retirees developed a strong friendship. I met him a couple of times during my visits from Canada and the U.S. to Dhaka. I developed deep respect for this incredibly wise and amiable man and enjoyed his company. After my father passed away on May 31, 1983, he wrote me a long moving letter, dated June 8; I was then living in Chicago. The letter was in Bengali. I am translating below and paraphrasing parts of the letter in English that showed the depth of his feeling for my father:

> Today I am writing this letter to you with an aching heart. Your father left us all. He was not just related to me, but he was my dear brother. He would love me so much that despite his mobility problem during his failing health in old age, he would come to my house often in the morning and leave in the afternoon. I would also frequently go to

his house to see him. I would feel good and he and your mother would be happy to see me. When I think of him now, my eyes well up in tears.

I don't wish to merely console you by saying that every-one has to die someday that includes us, so there is no need to wail about it. As it is a universal truth that man is mortal, so is a universal truth to feel sadness for the death of near and dear ones. We will always think with pain about them. Even though we may try to forget them, it will never happen, there will always be a hole in our heart. Although the sadness from the loss is very painful, you may lighten the load and feel good if you do a few things, such as praying for the departed soul, performing extra prayers, feeding the poor, and offering charity for them. You will feel better that way.

When he fell sick, I used to go to the hospital to see him every day in the evening and stay for a long time – sometimes until 10:00 or 11:00 PM. I would recite Quranic chapters, particularly the chapters of Yasin, Waqeya, and Mulk. At his request, I would recite the Prophet's prayer for him. Sometimes he was unconscious, when I would keep sitting next to him. I felt that he was a favored ser-vant of Allah. Whatever I knew about him and witnessed in him; he is now in the Paradise. Yet, I will keep praying for him every day after morning and night prayers. May his soul rest in peace!

I think of my father frequently and all he taught me; he lives on in my memory. To this day, I still feel proud to be the son of a saintly man. I still look deep in myself and hear echoes of my wise father and thereby we stay together always.

Not much is known about the ancestral history of my moth-er's side other than my mother Azifa Khatun's father Jiban Ali

Chowdhury was from a village called *Kharijjama*. He was a powerful *Zaminder* (landlord) with many subjects in the area. As was
the case with women in those days, my mother didn't have the
opportunity for studies above the primary level. That didn't stop
her from proving her academic mettle, however. She won a valuable prize in a competitive examination.

My parents got married somewhat by a combination of
happenstance and good fortune. When my father completed
his B.A. degree from Calcutta University in 1923, people
from the villages surrounding *Dharandi* where my father lived
came to see him. Acknowledging achievements was customary practice and he was the first graduate from a university
in that area. Around this same time, a soccer game was being
played one afternoon in my maternal village *Kharijjama* across
a river between the two villages. My father went to watch the
game. Noticing him, my maternal grandfather, knowing that
my father was a high achiever from the respectable Mir family invited him home for dinner. Since my grandfather was a
prominent man in that area, my father could not decline his
invitation. My grandfather might have longer term plans in
mind. At one point, my father noticed my young mother and
he told me that he was stunned by her beauty. Shortly after, my
grandfather offered his daughter for marriage and my father
accepted. Eventually, he obtained a law degree (LL.B.) from
Dhaka University in 1927 and got a lawyer's license on July 4
the same year. Initially, he took a government job. But because
of his independent nature he soon started his own practice in
Patuakhali.

My mother was a very active, outgoing and intelligent woman
with natural leadership and management qualities. Her orga-
nizational skills advanced her to a leadership position in dealing with women's welfare as well as social activities. She was a
go-getter and long-term vice-president of All Pakistan Women's

Association (APWA).* She had more than enough talent to be the President, but according to the bylaws, only the wife of the local government administrative officer could become president. Since the post of the administrative officer was transferable, she worked with several presidents. My mother stayed busy with meetings and projects at APWA's local office. She, along with others, would distribute clothing, blankets, milk powder and butter oil (*ghee*) that was sent by the U.S. to support the poor. These projects had a great impact on me in my formative years. I witnessed the magnanimity and humanitarian spirit of America and developed a great respect for the country and its people.

My mother wore many hats in her capacity as social services provider. She was the local jail visitor and checked on the conditions that female prisoners endured. She would carefully document and report those findings to authorities. Later in her life she established a primary school in Patuakhali in the area called *Char Para* (riverbank locale) near the bank of the *Laukathi* River. She was so active and confident in all her endeavors that she could meet high officials, bureaucrats, ministers, etc., and always speak freely without hesitation. She was not fond of cooking but relied on the help of our cook, Amina. She cooked only on special occasions.

My mother played a huge role making sure that her children became highly educated. Her motivation and push to education has shaped the character of all my brothers Mir Maswood Ali, Mir Masoom Ali, myself, and Mir Mosaddeq Ali. We have all obtained doctoral degrees which was a rare achievement in those days, particularly in the same family. My oldest sister, Jahan

---

* In those days APWA was a very active organization where women would participate and would work for the welfare of women and the families. Being a leader of the organization was a coveted and respected position.

Ara Begum (Jahanara) was married at a young age, as was customary then, and didn't continue with college education after childbirth.

College education for women was basically taboo in those days. But my mother, who was a proponent of higher education for women, sent our second sister, Shahid Ara (Moti) to Eden College, a women's college in Dhaka. Shahid Ara was the first female Bachelor of Arts degree holder in our area and was featured in local print media. My two remaining sisters Afroza Khanum (Jharna) and Farhad Ara Arzoo (Shelley) obtained master's degrees from Dhaka University.

I am the seventh child between Farhad Ara Arzoo and Mir Mosaddeq Ali and have been very close to them. Because all three of us were born back to back, I developed a closer bond with them than my other siblings. Occasionally during childhood, I would fight with these two, but I would always win since my brother was younger and weaker and although my sister was older than me, she conveniently had long hair that I could grab and easily pull.

I was also close to my mother and mindful to both of my parents. I could never do anything against my parents' wishes. My mother was particular about our health and always made sure that we were eating right and got us treated when we got sick. She would also take care of her own health as did my father. In addition to education and health, she was particular about making sure that we developed good moral character with her watchful eyes tracking the kind of friends we hung around.

Even the most vigilant of mothers, however, cannot stay the hand of fate. A few surprising stories that mark my early years have been well recounted in my family. Both scary events in my infant and toddler years. One occurred when I was two months old. I was sleeping inside a mosquito tent with my mother one evening. Our maid brought a flaming lantern near the bed. Very soon the curtain caught fire that spread rapidly, lighting up the house. My mother and older sister Shahid Ara started crying in fear. My father was in his office chamber with clients about 100 yards (91 meters) from our home. He heard the cries for help, ran home and managed to extinguish the fire. When I was a toddler, another accident happened. This time a decorative deer mount which hung overhead fell directly on me causing some bruising of my head. At age three I got sick resulting in swelling all over my body and I was sent to, the big city, Dhaka, for treatment.

The memory of my early years is populated by a rich cast of characters who worked and lived alongside our family. Their lives are also the source of many life lessons. They were all important parts of community life and of my childhood. Here I will share the snapshots of their faces and lives that have stayed with me over the years.

Our young maid Amina was married to Lalua, a *bhari* (water carrier), who would deliver water from reserved ponds or local water supply outlets to homes nearby. I still vaguely remember his appearance after he returned home from a long arduous day. He would carry two tin containers full of water - one in front and another behind him, hung from two ends of a length of strong but flexible bamboo across his shoulder. Despite the unwieldy load, he would walk very fast and with a bounce no less. The carrying rig was called *bharbash* (meaning a combination of weight and bamboo). He would put a *gamchha* (a locally woven towel) on his shoulder for padding. When Amina was pregnant, she was sent to my maternal uncle's home in *Kharijjama* for the delivery of her child. This young couple's story marks the very first event in my life that I can remember. My earliest memory is of a skinny middle-aged man coming from *Kharijjama*, who gave the news to my mother that a baby girl was born to Amina. I was about four years old, and perhaps owing to the nurturing relationship that

I already had with Amina who raised me I recall this occasion. Amina's daughter was named Ayena. Her father Lalua would love her a lot and, when she was a little older, would bring cookies for her.

Frequently, even in my adult life, Amina would love to talk about how she came to our home as a maid when I was six months old and raised me. I have fond memories of Amina and I feel she was like my second mother. She cooked our meals, fed me, gave me baths and took care of me. She would put up with many of my oddities and cranky behavior as a child. She was our long-time maid until my parents moved to Dhaka after my father's retirement.

The themes of young justice, politics and even animal rights, have been woven through my formative years. Sometimes as simple fond memories and sometimes as indelible lessons. When I was six, my parents were considering sending me to school. The local Patuakhali Jubilee High School was for boys, but its entry level was Class 3. The local Patuakhali Girls' High School, attended by my two sisters immediately older to me, had Classes 1 to 10. I was admitted there to Class 1 and started school. My parents bought me a bag to carry books, slate to write on and all the necessary school supplies, including new clothes and a new pair of shoes. My first day there went well. I saw the headmistress whom people would call Ranidi. She was young, slight build and pretty but had a stern face and occasionally carried a cane, which of course, she didn't use for walking.

Although I would go on to great achievements in education, my time at the Girls' High School was less than auspicious. Like the day that one of my sisters had to bring me home early. On this day at recess time, I went to admire the beautiful water hyacinth blossoming close to the shore of a large pond on campus. Although I didn't know how to swim, that didn't stop me from stretching my hand as far as I could, to pick a flower. As I tried to grasp for a gentle stem I suddenly I felt a push from behind and fell straight into the extremely sloppy winter mud. Luckily, I maintained enough balance to get out with only dirty shoes and hands to show. When I turned and saw the culprit, a little girl giggling at my predicament, my six-year old self became enraged. Not knowing what else to do, I immediately grabbed her long hair and pulled her down to the ground. She naturally started crying which drew a small crowd of girls all sympathetic to her plight. They assumed the offense was all mine. I was sent home that day.

The next day I went back to school as usual only to find out from a friend, that Ranidi had been informed and that I was presented as the sole offender. Like every young boy at the time, I immediately knew what was in store for me. I didn't wait around to be proven right, I had already seen this woman, cane in hand, on the first day of school. I snuck out of the school while everyone, including my sisters were in class. Now, I had a major dilemma; if I returned home my mother would send me back to school and I knew I would surely be caned by Ranidi. I hatched a plan. I hid my bag at the site of a deserted water supply reservoir near the school. Then, unencumbered, I roamed around until I landed up in front of a house, ironically, facing the local jail. The house was the official living quarters of a magistrate and had a steel gate at the entrance of the compound. I stood on the lower horizontal bar and held the vertical bars with my hands and started swinging the gate around to kill time until I was expected at home and stay engaged with some fun. A man, who was a servant of the family emerged, approached me and motioned to me to go into the house. I went in with him and the lady of the house asked my name and my father's name. She immediately recognized my parents, gave me some snacks to eat and sent me home with the servant. I told my mother what had happened and told her I would never go back to that school.

Luckily for me, my parents disapproved of corporal punishment in school and my mother began to consider other options. In Patuakhali there were some *Pathshalas* (small private schools that would cater to the educational needs of very young children). However, as I heard later, my oldest brother Mir Maswood Ali went to a *pathshala* but also left after seeing the caning of children. I suppose that could be the reason why my mother decided to educate me by hiring home tutors. She tasked my father with finding the best teachers. Since my father was the Secretary of the Board of Patuakhali Jubilee High School, a prominent role in the school system, and being a lawyer, he had many clients and connections. He didn't have any problem to find new tutors from among his many networks. The first tutor started me with lessons on reading, writing, and memorizing the Bengali alphabet from a book titled *Adarsha Lipi* (Ideal Writing). However, he and two more tutors who were successively hired were let go as I didn't like them for different reasons. Finally, my father found a home tutor by the name Shukhoranjan Das. He was a teacher of *Hindu Shamaj* (Hindu Society), a local *pathshala*.

I called him Sir as was and still is the custom in Bangladesh. He was a very good teacher and taught me how to start reading and writing. Like other teachers he was a poor man and every morning he would request a simple breakfast of raw rice to chew on and a glass of water. My mother offered him instead a breakfast that he would savor. Shukhoranjan Das was basically destitute like many teachers, yet they planted the seeds of our basic education. This was a predicament for which I always felt bad. Very soon I picked up on my reading. I remember the first story from a book that I could read on my own was about a king and a boy. The boy was in prison for some offense. The king made a surprise visit one evening to the prison to check its condition. The boy didn't know it but at the time he was praying for the health and longevity of the king, a benevolent ruler. The king overheard the boy's prayer and was pleased. He immediately ordered the release of the boy.

Once I started reading and writing, my father took me to the boys' school, Patuakhali Jubilee High School. The headmaster, Naba Chandra Banerjee, briefly interviewed me with some questions and then by asking me to read a paragraph from a children's book, which I did without much difficulty. I was admitted to the school immediately in Class 3 at the age of 7. I continued my studies there until Class 10 and matriculated with distinction in 1958 at the age of 14. Because I skipped two classes, my immediately older sister, Farhad Ara Arzoo, became my year mate albeit in the Girls' High School.

Outside of the classroom I also got a rich education from the world around me. I was a wandering child. Sometimes when very young I would go to my father's office chamber near our house for no particular reason. I recall people there were still talking about World War II in its aftermath, Hitler, Churchill, the Japanese, and the atomic bomb dropped by the U.S. on Hiroshima and Nagasaki, etc. They would also talk about the perennial India and Kashmir problem. I also heard about the assassination of Pakistan's Prime Minister Liaqat Ali Khan, which left Pakistan in political turmoil. The first American president's name that I heard and could remember was President Dwight Eisenhower. I would listen to these conversations intently. Hearing such discussions made me politically conscious right from my childhood.

When I was about eight years old, I had another unique encounter with local custom and the law, this time it was a truly traumatic experience. We had a cow which provided us milk. One day our cow trespassed onto government property. The consequence was that the cow was impounded far from our home at the outskirts of the town near the *Eidgah*, where Eid prayers were held. My mother gave our servant some money to get the cow released and sent him to take care of the matter. Because of my curious nature, I wanted to go with him on that late afternoon; he obliged.

It was rainy season so there was mud and water everywhere as it started pouring. He told me to stand on the roots of a large tree near the street to avoid mud and rain while he went to handle the errand. He returned to tell me he needed extra money since a "late fee" had been applied. Surely a ruse on the part of the cow's impounder to get more money. I was told to stay put while he quickly went back home to get the extra money. Time stretched endlessly and soon it was pitch dark, I could find nobody nearby. It was still raining. I developed an eerie feeling.

Suddenly, I was gripped by the legendary tale of someone who had committed suicide by hanging himself from the very tree I was standing on and his "golakata bhoot" (headless ghost) was still thought to be present in the same spot.

I looked up, terrified. I could not take it anymore and started running as fast as I could in the deserted street. I don't even remember what happened next. All I know is I found myself tightly embracing my mother hollering with tears as I told her what happened. My dear mother felt sorry since she was the one who delayed the servant's arrival by sending him on some quick errand rather than directly back to me. She did not realize I was waiting for him and he clearly didn't inform her either. That night I had chills and developed a high fever. The fever continued for a few days when I had strange nightmares in my sleep. These haunted me for some time, but I eventually recovered.

During the earlier years of my childhood my parents lived near the town's business center. Many stores flanked the sides of a major east-west street, parallel to *Laukathi* River. Most of the stores were established by migrants from other places outside Patuakhali district. Toward the east, on the river side the area was mainly occupied by Bihari merchants, migrants from Bihar, India. They lived behind their shops, on the river's edge with their families, on simply constructed wood deck floors supported by posts. They were native Urdu-speaking but also spoke fluent Bengali with an accent. They assimilated well into the local population. To the west there were a large number of migrants from Dhaka, some of whom were engaged in the hotel business on the river side of the street and others mainly in the bakery and book-binding businesses on the other side. Our house was located near this area. Moving further west, the area was mainly populated by local Hindus who were engaged in fabricating tin suitcases, trunks, and safes, while others were involved in selling clothes, music related items, sweets and a myriad of products. There was a market called *Notun Bazar* (New Market) and close to it was a movie theater named *Light House,* owned by a rich businessman. Further west across the street were blacksmith shops operated by Hindu welders.

Near our house in the midst of some bakery shops and stores was a welding shop. Kader, the son of the welder, was known as *Nawshir Bap* (Nawshi's father). In the countryside and small towns, many people are simply identified by their relation to a child or parent. No one knows their actual names. I used to play marbles with Kader who was a challenging opponent. I'd go to his welding shop to watch his father's work. He used to do *jhalai* (welding) using zinc or some kind of alloy. A skinny and short man with a cap on his head, he was known as a *karigar* (technician). He used his left hand to intermittently press the bellows laid on the ground. Then he would place the tip of a long iron tool with a flat head on one side there to heat it up that he would use for welding. I was fascinated by his skill and craftmanship. Nearby there was a popular bake shop selling bread, cookies, and treats. I would watch how they made breads and cookies after preparing and placing the dough in the nearby large kiln. The delicious aroma of the fresh baked bread and cookies filled the air.

In winter, a Bihari man and his brother known as *dhunkars* (quilt-makers) would make thick *leps* (quilts or comforters) by stuffing processed cotton into a fine bag of cloth and I enjoyed watching the technique of preparing a quilt in a shop. They would use a large special device with strings to refine the raw cotton into an increasingly softer and thinner consistency. Continuously hitting the thick string with a unique hand-held, wooden tool shaped like a dumbbell, would produce interesting sounds like those from musical instruments. The images of the refining process stay with me until today. Whenever I got involved in a research problem or attempted to solve a complex engineering problem, I would use the analogy of refining raw cotton. Delving into finding the solution to the problem was for me, analogous to the dumbbell turning the raw cotton into processed cotton. Once the cotton was refined, the two men would stuff it inside a large bag of soft cloth, customarily red in color and turn the whole thing over. With their hands they leveled the cotton inside by tapping and pressing, then sealed the open end of the bag by sewing with a long, thick handheld needle. They would continue quilting with the large needle in a delicate and well-designed pattern. I would frequently go to the workshop and just sit there to witness the entire step by step process.

I lived fairly near the courthouse. This is where civil lawsuits were deliberated by *munsifs* (lower court judges for civil lawsuits). In the large yard, peddlers would sell herbal medicine and tooth powder in the shade of a large banyan tree. Usually someone started with a card game or quasi-magic to attract the mostly rural folks who were in town for business or court. Once gathered, the "doctor" would deliver a rousing and convincing stump speech to the crowd and try to sell his concoctions. I used to attend some of these when I could because it was so entertaining. He would sell tooth powders and would occasionally even extract teeth. He would also sell "medicines" to increase vitality and male libido.

Kite-flying was an iconic pastime in my childhood. I spent much of my free time with friends flying kites on the riverbanks; it was a favorite pastime along with playing games with "latims" (spinning tops). One evening my adult cousin saw me playing with a friend. He grabbed my hand and took me to my father's office chamber where he was busy with his clients. He told my father that I was playing with some questionable boys who could be bad influences. My father, who was a very calm person, replied, "Don't worry. I trust my son and I'm certain he will not be influenced by those boys." But, in keeping with her no-nonsense, vigilant demeanor, my mother was not so sure. Because of some of the offenses for which I had already been caught, together with my younger brother who would just follow me, my mother had already hatched a plan that she executed later.

I recall one incident that even upset my usually calm father. When I was in Class 5, my mother gave me two rupees to pay my tuition fee at the school. Under the influence of a friend, I snuck away from school without paying the fees and the two of us went to play lottery at a *mela* (fair) and used the money there. We spent all day there and came home in the evening. The school reported my absence to my father who had no clue where I was. As soon as I came home, I realized my mother was worried; so, to comfort her I handed her the soap that I won at the fair and told her where I was. That didn't help. My mother realized that something needed to be done. She sent our servant to get my father from the office chamber where he was dealing with his clients near our house. She then admonished my father for being too lenient and tolerant, since clearly, I was out of control. So, my father, who was an incredibly kind man and could never lay a hand on his children, instead punished me with an unpleasant detention – the only real punishment I ever got from him. I was unceremoniously held in detention in our family's poultry coop. I was stuck in there with the startled chickens and ducks until my mother came to my rescue.

My livestock cellmates were not scary enough for me. My detention didn't serve to deter other wayward offenses for which I also got caught. These included smoking with a few friends and my younger brother after climbing through a narrow spiral stair to the top of the minaret of a mosque. This last infraction was too much and my parents finalized their decision to move to a new neighborhood. Granted, they had been considering a move already, but this incident led them to a firm decision. They purchased a large plot of land in a prime location away from the commercial area, demolished the existing one-story home and built a new two-story home for our family. Typical housing at the time was wood-framed construction with tin sheathing for the walls and roof. The kitchen in the back was detached from our new home and my parents made a new pond by excavating the land behind the kitchen. There were many fruit trees everywhere, especially in the back. Soon we happily moved to the new house.

As mentioned, the school went into a turbulent period following the departure of an excellent headmaster Naba Banerjee. It created a vacuum, and no one was capable of filling his role immediately, although some tried. The first replacement was called Quaid-e-Azam (leader of the people) a title given to him by students because of his resemblance to the founder of Pakistan Mr. Muhammad Ali Jinnah, who was called Quaid-e-Azam by Pakistanis. He didn't last long and was replaced by another who would always wear a specially made white cap covering his ears. Yet another new replacement followed whom we called Imran Sir, a competent teacher. He was however extremely strict.

He would walk around the verandah of the school with a cane in hand and if he spotted a student in class talking to friends, he would cane the student.

Fortunately, he would use a strong and distinctive scent which would alert us of his presence nearby. Eventually, his stern measures made him unpopular among students and he was forced to resign. A new headmaster by the name Abdul Awwal Khondker came next. He was very wise and capable and brought much-needed stability to the school. He taught us English when I was in Class 9. Among other things he taught us Abraham Lincoln's Gettysburg Address which left a deep impression on me about Abraham Lincoln. I was impressed with how great a person he must have been, to express such deep thoughts in a very short speech. I was all the more impressed when I realized that his casual musing became the textbook definition of democracy.

I remember with fond reverence some other teachers who wholly impacted my future education. Rahman Sir had a long beard and he taught us Bengali literature. Once he was ill and a few of his students and I went to see him in a nearby village called *Jainkati*. He had a small hut-like home which we found by asking villagers. He developed a high fever and some cold water was dripping on his head from a hole at the bottom of an earthen pitcher hung from the roof as he was lying flat on his back. The abject poverty of the household didn't go unnoticed. I didn't know what to do about it, but in his story, I found yet another example of how our schoolteachers were so poorly paid even though they shaped who we are today.

There were some other teachers like Kalikanta Sir who taught us English at lower levels and had beautiful handwriting we could see on the blackboard; Sachin Sir who taught us Bengali grammar; Siraj Sir teaching us science occasionally with small experiments including one to demonstrate how metals expanded under heat. This was something that impressed me greatly and made me interested in science. Ganesh Sir was loved by students because he was a great storyteller. A favorite story was about his encounter with a wild elephant somewhere near Darjeeling, a hilly terrain in India north of Bangladesh, which he repeated a few times at the request of students; Hamid Sir, who was the assistant headmaster, wore a Rumi cap (fez) and taught us geography. He advised us to learn one new word every day; Sattar Sir taught history; and Emdad Sir taught mathematics, among many others. I fondly remember another teacher, Chitta Sur, who led students in extracurricular activities. We rehearsed songs and recited poems for special cultural events, which he directed. He led the school's boy scouts. We had a class for physical drills and exercise. Athletic instructor Mr. Tofazzal Hossain (nicknamed Tofada, meaning Brother Tofa) taught us well how to march and make other moves in drills. He led all our sports and athletic events.

We had two teachers teaching us Urdu and Arabic. We called them by the honorific, *Huzurs* (teachers graduating from *madrassas*); one Huzur taught Arabic and another Huzur, Urdu. To make a quick distinction between the two while referring to them we called one *Dhola* (fair) Huzur and the other *Kala* (dark) Huzur, respectively. In the former Huzur's class we were not allowed to wear shorts even though we were kids. He insisted on full length trousers. Any violators were ordered to sit on a back bench. The latter Huzur would enter the classroom and usually hoist himself on top of the desk and sit there on his bottom dangling his legs and sometimes squatting on the desk. He was a character. Often, he would call someone bigger and stronger in class to massage his neck and shoulders from his back for a while. He would look around and suddenly ask a student to read a passage from an Urdu essay or story or recite a stanza from an Urdu poem assigned in the previous class. If in his judgment the student failed, he would get down from the table and ask the student to lower his head, so he could throw light punches on the student's back that wouldn't hurt. But nevertheless, students liked his relaxed personality. Sometimes he would dismiss the class abruptly and told us to go home early as his was the last class of the day. He would teach part time as he also taught at the Girls' High School.

A third Huzur joined the staff later to teach Urdu. Since he was short, students called him *Baytay* (short) Huzur. One day after a class, while he was relatively new to school, he gave the class a homework assignment. He looked at the son of the local sub-divisional officer (the chief administrator) of Patuakhali sub-division, addressed him by name and assigned the lesson to him. This didn't sit well with me and I stood up and asked him,

"Huzur, is the lesson for him alone or for the entire class?"

He replied, "For the entire class."

I countered, "But that's not what you said."

He said, "You are right. I should have said that."

After finishing school that day when I was leaving for home in late afternoon, he sent a peon to tell me that he wanted me to see him in the teachers' room. When I saw him there, he took me to the students' boarding house next to the school where he resided in a small suite. He motioned to me to sit on a chair and brought me a glass of warm milk. He explained that he was new here and repeated that I was right to ask him the question and told me not to hold any bitterness against him for it. I immediately knew he was a decent man and developed respect for him.

Meanwhile, Shukhoranjan Das, who started tutoring me at my old house continued to do it at our new house for a little while but expressed his inability to continue when I was in Class 7. Since the subject of mathematics got more complex, particularly with the introduction of Algebra, he only continued to teach my younger brother who was in Class 4. One day my father brought a new teacher named Emdad Ali, whom I called Emdad Sir. He looked like a white person as his complexion was extremely fair and had light-colored eyes. He was a brilliant student who just received a B.Sc. degree with top distinction. But because he came from a very poor family, he didn't have the means of furthering his education. Perhaps he needed immediate income and joined the Jubilee High School as a mathematics teacher. I became his first student to receive home tutoring. He was also my mathematics instructor at school. He was an exceptionally good no-nonsense teacher. Organized and quick, he kept his students continuously engaged. He was instrumental in my eventual proficiency and ease with mathematics. I enjoyed dealing with the logic and the symbolic language of mathematics, particularly algebra. Because of his discipline, efficiency and good interpersonal skills he became the long-time headmaster of the school later in his career.

Even as I continued my educational career, the backdrop of political unrest following partition loomed over our daily life. The Pakistani rulers in West Pakistan misread the deeply held sentiments of the Bengali people regarding their attachment to the Bengali language. On February 21,1952, the students of the University of Dhaka and other political activists organized a protest defying the law against the imposition of Urdu as the only state language of Pakistan. Following the brutal killing of some student demonstrators and bystanders by police near the Dhaka Medical College that day, a general protest movement started throughout East Pakistan. This barbaric killing shocked the Bengalis and widespread public grief ensued. Although I was only eight years old going to Class 4 at the time, I can recount a meeting organized by the older students. It was held soon after in front of our school. I still remember the face of one lead speaker who was of fair complexion and wore a white shirt. Unbeknownst to me at the time, this violent event sowed the seed for the eventual secession of East Pakistan from Pakistan. After much upheaval and loss of life, finally an independent, sovereign country called Bangladesh was formed, following a bloody civil war.

In addition to Emdad Sir who taught me, another tutor Mazharul Islam was hired to teach me and my sister Farhad Ara when we were in Class 9. He taught us humanities courses such as literature, history. Further, to strengthen our command of written English my mother retained Hem Chandra Sen, the elderly headmaster of Patuakhali Girls' High School for both of us. We would walk together to his house after school to take lessons. Hem Sen was such a pleasant person that I would feel good and motivated in his presence. Each time we saw him at his home he would assign me and my sister an English passage which we translated into Bengali. He would check our Bengali translation, and then ask us to retranslate it back into English. He would review our translations and retranslations and correct any mistakes. He was very open-minded. Even though he was a Hindu, he would say that Prophet Muhammad was a truly great man and he loved to read the Qur'an from time to time. When he felt that we had developed enough proficiency in English, he told my father of our achievement and so we no longer needed to go to him. I feel his teaching method really helped both of us gain good writing skills in English. I always remember him with reverence for his influence on me.

My parents' commitment to education included a commitment to supporting the many teachers that helped us learn. My parents felt the need to give me an Arabic education, so I could read the Qur'an. My father brought home a teacher proficient in Arabic and Urdu. Since East Pakistan was still part of Pakistan, we had to learn Urdu side by side with Arabic starting from Class 7. We had to learn Arabic much earlier at home for religious reasons. For this reason, a tutor was retained to teach me Arabic when I was living in our old house. The new teacher was from *Sandwip*, an island in the southeastern coast of Bangladesh.

He was a teacher in the Girls' School. His family would live in *Sandwip* and he was given free lodging and meals at our house. We would call him Moulavi Saheb, a common title for religious teachers. He also became the imam of a nearby mosque.

He moved to the mosque to sleep but would eat his meals at our house. He placed his bed next to a window overlooking a small burial ground to get the southern breeze. I would sometimes wonder how he could sleep there without any fear. He moved with us to our new house when we moved and continued to teach me. He was always nice with me, never scolded me for anything, although I heard he was quite strict at school with the girls and rebuked them for minor offenses from time to time. He was very likeable and moderate in his outlook and would tell me stories. On occasions, he would go home to see his wife and children. Sadly, I assume that he likely perished in a major cyclone and tidal wave from the Bay of Bengal in November 1970, when I was overseas, as he went home but never returned. He taught me well. When I was in Class 10, I won an Urdu essay contest at the district level held in Barisal. I thank him for his efforts with me.

Being the seventh child shaped my relationship with both my immediate and extended family. I was witness to much of my parents lives across middle age and beyond. I came from a middle-class family as was the case with most professional families in those days and knew that my father spent a lot of money on my elder siblings' education. I saw the chronic illness of my mother from ulcer and colitis and occasional severe illnesses of my father. Thus, I developed a deep love, admiration, softness and respect for my elderly parents and watched over a few of our family crises. Seeing this phase of their lives, made me appreciate small things and simple pleasures.

I had always been reluctant to ask anyone, including my parents, for anything let alone gifts. However, I admit to a great fantasy about getting a bike, blue in color. I would see a merchant's son by the name Mujibur frequently riding the bike of my dreams, but never asked my father to get me one. I didn't want him to spend a large sum of money just on my entertainment.

Also, as the result of being the seventh of eight brothers and sisters, I didn't have a chance to see my grandparents from either paternal or maternal side as they already passed away. I was unfortunately deprived of their love and affection. Most of my uncles were also middle-aged or elderly and were detached from me. Moreover, the last four of the siblings grew up together. The older ones left home for their college education in Dhaka as there was no college in Patuakhali until 1958.

Overall, I feel I had a very good education and solid nurturing relationships. I always enjoyed reading and could read with full concentration. Books became my constant companion when I was alone or when I felt miserable. I even enjoyed the smell of new books. Every year when I would get new textbooks, I felt so happy and proud to carry them around guarding them as a precious treasure trove. I had one problem though -- I spent less time on my academic books and much more time on reading books for pleasure, a habit that continued all my life. I loved novels, detective and mystery books, adventure books and any other books I could get hold of including history, politics, religion or any subject. I had a large reserve of books at home collected from those that my older siblings and parents bought. I read all of them. Whatever books or magazines I came across I loved to read.

There were a few books at home that drew my special attention: *Bishwa Porichoy* (Introduction to the World); *Cheena Golpo* (Chinese Stories); and *Manusher Dhormo* (Religions of Mankind); *Gulistan* and *Bustan* (translated to Bengali from famous Persian

Sufi poet and writer Sheikh Saadi), *Islam and Communism* (in Bengali), among others. The wise writings by Saadi deeply influenced me as these were full of morals and practical lessons for life. Several stories dealing with animals had some parallel to *Aesop's Fables*.

Another book *Aborodhbashini* (Confined Women) by Begum Rokeya Shakhawat Hossain, commonly known as Begum Rokeya deeply influenced me. It contained many stories of how Muslim women were poorly treated by male-dominated society and kept under their thumbs. Begum Rokeya was a pious Muslim and had the intellect to decipher that extreme forms of restriction as mandated by men were not reflective of the teachings of Holy Qur'an. She made a spirited attack on the prevailing society. She vehemently protested such maltreatment of women in the name of religion, such as imposing unfair and extreme forms of the veil and social stigmas against female education, thereby stifling their thoughts and derailing fulfillment of their aspirations. She advocated that both men and women should be treated fairly and equally, and that lack of education was the main reason for women lagging behind men.

In a fictional book, *Sultana's Dream*, she wrote about a feminist utopia *Naristhan* (Ladyland), a land ruled by women portraying a role reversal of men and women in which men were subservient to women. She was a prolific writer, activist and social worker fighting for women's rights and girls' education by establishing the Bengali Muslim Girls' College in Kolkata, a school that she administered until her death. Begum Rokeya lived from 1880 to 1932, a rather short life. I still don't know of any feminist of her stature in the Indian sub-continent. My mother was also a promoter of women's education as she allowed my sisters to attend college in Dhaka, although the pursuit of higher education for women was uncommon in those days.

I was strongly influenced by Begum Rokeya's work as well as my mother and remain a dedicated proponent for women's education. I encouraged my own daughters to pursue education and enlightenment.

Another great mind advancing equality of men and women was the renowned Bengali rebel poet Kazi Nazrul Islam, who expressed his thoughts eloquently in his poems and songs. I will quote here the opening lines of his poem *Nari* (Women). He was later honored with the title of Bangladesh's National Poet. Here is the opening of this poem:

Shammyer gaan gai ---
Amar chokhhay purush-ramani kono bhedabhed nai!
Bishhay ja-kichhu mohan srishti chiro kalyankar,
Aurdhek tar kariachhay nari, aurdhek tar nawr.

Translation:
I sing the song of equality ---
In my eyes no difference exists between men and women!
Whatever are the great creations made for perpetual human welfare,
Half of them were done by women, half by men.

I was surrounded by all forms of writing and public discourse. My parents subscribed to a daily Bengali newspaper called *Azad*; my mother and I used to read it daily from start to finish. Staying on top of the latest world news remains a passion of mine.

Once I was engrossed in an island adventure book titled *Bombaytay Dwip* (Bombaytay Island). It was time for school, but I was reading a most interesting part of the book and I wanted to know what happened next. I carried the book with me, and the first class of the day was on English taught by the headmaster. I deliberately sat in the back with the open book on my lap and began to look down and read from time to time when I thought he was not looking. But he noticed it and approached me, took the book away from me, and scolded me. He returned it after the class, and I finished reading it at home later. My mother also rebuked me for reading story books instead of preparing for my exams ahead.

My love of reading extended to the fine arts and poetry. I started drawing figures and writing poems at a young age. With a group of my friends I organized a literary club we called United Stars. I spearheaded the establishment of a private lending library where each member brought some books from home that the other members could borrow. The venue for the club and library was a vacant outdoor shed beside a government police official's quarter. The official's son was a friend of mine and got involved in this. This was a short-term project for fun but could not be carried out long term as we moved on to other things and I got busy with studies. I also started writing a short Bengali novel in later years which I never finished because I left for overseas in 1970.

On the social front, I had quite a few friends. Despite my mother's watchful eyes over my choice of friends, I associated with, and met with friends of all different backgrounds. Since I had skipped two levels, I was always younger than my classmates. This meant that from an early age I learned to bridge the age gap in my social life. With my older classmates I related at one level, but I would play outdoor more often with students of my own age and from lower level classes. In some cases, I had two brothers as friends. The older one from my class level at school and the younger one from a couple of classes behind. I had another group of friends who were not connected to my daily life in any way, but I found them active, fun-loving and like-minded and so we got close. Most of my amusement and adventurous explorations were with this third group of friends. I loved the outdoors. We would play hide and seek from one end of town to the other. We would risk jumping over fences of private homes, hid in backyards, got yelled at by ladies who could see us from their homes, or chased by the man of the house. So, we ran.

Occasionally, I would go to a pond to bathe with my mother's permission. Once in a while, I would go to the nearby *Laukathi* river to swim without telling my mother so I would not scare her. Together with my friends we would on occasion temporarily get some boats that were tied to wood poles with ropes. Villagers would leave their boats when they arrived at town for business. We would row the boats in the river and would even go further away from the bank. For fun, occasionally one or two of us would jump into the river, swim a distance, then return to the boat or to the shore. We would eventually bring the boats back to the place we got them and tie them back to the poles.

It was these childhood games and having the freedom to roam the town that shaped my character and my spatial understanding.

I would often visit the local Patuakhali Dramatic Club where dramas and cultural shows were a mainstay. The club was located on a busy business strip next to a busy street and close to many stores, restaurants and the *adalat* (civil courthouse). The front was a cemented verandah and I remember a man selling ointments for earaches and skin rashes and boils. Another man would sell lemonades, peanuts and other edibles. On Pakistan's Independence Day on August 14, I sang a song there. I rehearsed under the coaching of a music teacher known as Buddha Master. An unknown lyricist wrote a Bengali song critical of the British colonialists. These are the first four lines that I remember:

Baniker beshay esheschhilo jara khulachhay taader chhaddabesh
Chhalana mukhosh porachhay khoshia nafar poraychhay nababi besh.
Hawo bir hawo aguan; rakho Bharat Matar maan.

Sagarparer doshyu esheche, esheche lutitay moder desh.

Translation:
Those who came as merchants, their disguise has been revealed
The mask of deception has fallen off and the servant has put on
    the garment of the master.
O hero come forward; keep the dignity of Mother India.
The pirates from across the ocean have come, have come to loot
    our land.

Next to the Dramatic Club was the store and studio of Mr. Gopal
Dutta, an artist and photographer. He was a mild-mannered
bespectacled man with a pleasant demeanor. I would go to his
studio and watch him work with the utmost concentration on pictures and portraits spread all around him on the floor, table and
hung on walls. While the club building was being renovated, the
main entry door was kept open. This provided a perfect opportunity for me to frequently observe the progress of a series of
large paintings being created directly on the walls around the
auditorium. The depictions of multiple colors portrayed the history of Patuakhali stage by stage starting with a wooded settlement on the bank of *Laukathi* River infested with crocodiles until
the most contemporary time. As the paintings were close to the
ceiling, to gain height he would climb to a wooden platform on
scaffolds, sit there and keep painting with the attentiveness of a
Kingfisher. I enjoyed watching him in action and the smell of the
paint. I would wonder how he could do such an intensely difficult job, so flawlessly, and I developed a deep respect for him and
an interest in art. Now I know what a gifted gentleman he was!

Since childhood, I have been a lover of Mother Nature. During my time in school and later college, I'd stare at the blue sky
on clear days and at imagined shapes in floating or dark clouds
on rainy days. I watched the sky during rainfall and loved occa-

sional rainbows. I liked to look up at the night sky dotted with stars -- some of them blinking -- and the moon. All these made me wonder about Nature.

I would often stroll in our large, tree filled backyard and enjoy the pond. A bevy of birds would visit the yard like *Masranga* (Kingfisher), *Kaththokra* (Woodpecker), *Kokil* (Cuckoo), *Choroi* (Sparrow), *Tuntuni* (a small Sparrow always flying from one branch to another of trees) and a few others like *Tia* (Parrot), *Shalik* (Robin), *Bou Kotha Kao* (Bride Please Talk), *Bawk* (Flamingo), *Holdi Pakhi* (Yellow Bird), *Dahuk* (a rarely seen Flamingo of gray color) and more.

Of particular interest to me were the little Woodpeckers drilling into hard tree trunks with their beaks, and how the Kingfishers would spot a moving fish under water and suddenly dive and come up with a fish by instinct, without any complex mathematical calculation. The focus and concentration of these two birds were very impressive. I would birdwatch and think about how happy they seemed. They could fly in the air and see everything from above! In the early morning *Doels,* local singing birds, would sing in their ultra-sweet voice sitting on our rooftop. I would also watch birds in other places. I heard that there were some *Harials*, rare colorful local birds, in the two Banyan trees in front of the court building. I would go there and stare at the branches of the trees for a long time to see them but never could. At night, sometimes hoots of *Pecha* (Owl) could be heard from our garden. The hoots sounded scary. Many superstitions abounded about them from bad luck to omen for death in the family. These birds were also called *Bhutum Pecha* (Ghostly Owl) to make them sound even more scary.

I would often go bird hunting, using slings, with a few other friends. I had a friend by the nickname Jhilu who had very good aim for birds with his sling. He would lead a small group of us to different places, usually the surrounding villages. Before the day of our planned trip we would get together at his house to help him mold wet clay into small balls, sundried later and used for the sling. I immensely enjoyed the pastime and view of rural Bangladesh (then East Pakistan) for its green landscape and natural beauty. When Jhilu successfully hit a bird some of us would run to get it. On one occasion my nephew Akhtaruzzaman, who came to visit us, was so excited he jumped into a pond and swam to retrieve a maimed Flamingo.

On one occasion my liking for birds and my eagerness got the best of me. I became too adventurous. A few younger friends, my younger brother and I planned a trip to a village called *Balai-kathi*, about 5 miles (8 kilometers) from Patuakhali. I heard that there were many good Flamingoes there, so the village seemed to me like a utopic wonderland where I could get my hands on these birds. The idea to go there was thrilling and fascinating. Even though I was the leader and organizer at the age of 11 or so, I had no idea what it entailed to get these birds.

One day in the early morning as planned, we snuck out of our homes all at the same time, without any breakfast. We gathered at a designated meeting spot to set out on our mission to this unknown place. I heard that this village was somewhere along the route beyond the Number 2 Bridge. Of the few bridges in town, there were two popular bridges that were considered landmarks. The first bridge called Number 1 was over a creek way which was part of a drainage network and a mile (1.6 kilometers) from the post office and the second bridge was a mile (1.6 kilometers) after that over a natural canal branching from *Lohalia* River. I often would go to this latter bridge to visit friends in the afternoon there and play in the wilderness and to view the nearby *Chandmari*. A raised concrete structure for shooting target practice was used by the police and *Ansars,* who made up a local paramilitary force. They were employed and trained by the government. We would sometimes lean against the railing of the bridge and watch the natural landscape and the passing boats and ducks swimming under the bridge. Never did we dare to venture beyond the second bridge unattended at that age.

On this fateful morning however, we started walking in a small group and crossed Bridge Number 2 to into uncharted territory. The road was all mud and we forged ahead until we reached a riverbank. By this time, we were very hungry and ate the bananas and *Muri* (rice cereal) we had just purchased with the little cash we had brought along. Now we faced a problem, unexpectedly, we encountered a ferry which we needed to take across the river. There was a cost and wait. Once we got on the boat, we were tired and nervous not knowing where we were going. Seeing our condition and realizing we were in over our heads, without enough money, the boatman let us go for free with a few other passengers. Some passengers on the boat told us that *Balaikathi* was very near that gave us hope and renewed energy.

After we reached the other side of the river we started walking again and soon saw a cluster of homes. We went there and asked a bearded man in front of a house to help us figure out where we were. He told us that we were in *Balaikathi.* He told me he was the head of his household and immediately recognized my father after hearing his name saying he was my father's client. He took us inside and gave us lunch and fresh coconut water to drink. After we rested, he arranged to get some baby Flamingoes from the nearby trees and gave us homemade cages of bamboo sticks to house the birds. We left for home very happy since we were leaving with the birds we came for.

Our smiles faded however, when we reached Patuakhali. It was dusk and I realized my brother and I were due for punishment. Some of the birds were already dead. I had a couple of birds as our share and one was barely alive. My brother and I went directly to the detached kitchen at the back of our house to assess the situation. Our maid Amina saw us and announced to my family that we were back. To my surprise we got royal treatment, were given shower and a decent meal. I realized then that my parents and sisters were extremely worried and incredibly happy that we had returned intact. For us, it was a youthful adventure, but I learned that it was announced in the town everywhere that a few boys went missing, and parents needed help locating them.

My father would often take me with him when traveling. He would not take my next younger brother since he was very young compared to me and my father would have difficulty managing two of us away from home. Occasionally, my father would take me with him and a servant to villages near our hometown Patuakhali for hunting trips. He had a good aim and we would bring home hunted birds that were eventually cooked, and savored.

My father once took me to our ancestral village *Indrakul*, the home of my grandfather. My father, however, was raised in his native village of *Dharandi* because his mother -- my grandmother -- lived there as my grandfather's second wife. This was the earliest trip I remember when I was very young, about seven or eight years old.

My father and I went first to a place called *Bagabandar* from Patuakhali by steamer. In those days, steamers would anchor to a barge on the riverbank as the water was deep. From the steamer, my father and I along with a few other passengers descended to an open roofless boat. The strong water current made the boat unstable and wobbly as both boatmen and passengers were trying to steady it against the edge of the steamers high floor. Because I was so small, I was totally under the black hull of the steamer. When I looked up, I saw the underside of the hull, I became nervous. But soon the experienced boatman got us out of there and came to a *ghat* (a wooden dock), where we disembarked. Coincidentally, my first home tutor was on the same boat. Even though I was not his student anymore and he taught me only for a few days, he was elated at seeing me. He quickly bought some candies there and handed me those to show his affection. I was so delighted that he acknowledged me with such warmth. From there we took another boat to a nearby place from where my father and I walked to *Indrakul.*

Once there, I met many new relatives. I remember feeling uncomfortable in the new setting unless my father was with me. I had several uncles who lived with their families in different houses all in a cluster. The cluster and surrounding areas were collectively called *Mira Bari* (home of the Mirs) in the region.

My constant curiosity helped me to explore the village, just as I would explore my small town. I would occasionally slip out alone and go through backyards. The village was a wooded area filled with wild trees. Occasionally, I got so enmeshed in the jungle that it appeared dark since only a scant amount of sunlight penetrated through the trees. I got nervous and retreated. Later I continued to go as I got accustomed to the thrill of being there. One day, I saw a wildcat that was staring at me as if I was unwelcome trespasser in its territory. Being a little boy myself, the animal looked large to me and I felt threatened. I quickly backtracked and ran away until I made it home.

Another memory from the village is still vivid today. My father took me for a walk, and we stopped at the bank of a nearby pond. My father told me this was his father's grave. He stood next to it, recited a few verses from the Qur'an, and prayed for my grandfather in reverence with outstretched hands. I stood next to him imitating him knowing he was doing something solemn. This brief stop had a profound effect as I thought about death and dying for the first time. My father lost his father. Someday I would lose my father. In my childlike mind, I marveled that even though my father and grandfather were so physically near each other, they could not speak to each other.

My father occasionally took me to villages where *pirs* (spiritual guides) would hold *mahfils* (religious gatherings). People travelled from distances to listen to the sermons. In keeping with tradition, I wore local rural clothing called *lungi* (an ethnic skirt) and *punjabi* (an ethnic shirt). I would not fully understand the lecture, but realized he was asking people to practice religion to avoid hellfire and achieve paradise after death. Occasionally the *pir* would get very emotional and burst into tears about our fate in the afterlife if we sinned. Many people would join him in weeping. The speech ended with a long-spoken prayer in Bengali with everyone's outstretched hands slightly apart in a typical Muslim supplication. Then dinner was served. Usually these gatherings took place in an open field during harvesting season next to a residential madrassa where some young students lived.

Occasionally, I fancied to be a madrassa student just to live with other students in freedom away from my mother's watchful eyes. I assumed madrassa students were very happy, as they had many friends who lived together in a community. On one occasion, my father took me on a large green boat where the famous *pir* of *Sharshina* was present. My father became a disciple of the *pir's* father who had a great reputation of piety. He counseled my father at times of illness and crisis. The *pir* that I met was a handsome bearded young man dressed in green leaning against a *takia* (bolster cushion) in a very luxurious environment inside the covered boat. There was a man fanning him with a large decorated fan. My father asked him to bless me. The *pir* did so by holding the back of my head, lowering it and blowing on me.

On another occasion a *Jainpuri pir* from India visited Patuakhali and came to our home. When he and his associates left, I followed him to a nearby place where he embarked a *paalki* (closed overhead carrier), which was lifted and carried by four men on their shoulders at its four corners walking along. I observed the inside of the *paalki* when he was boarding, which was nicely crammed with luxury amenities. After seeing the *pir* of *Sharshina* and this *pir*, both of whom were beyond a healthy weight, I concluded that they were well fed and had a comfortable lifestyle. I contrasted them to the poor masses who were not as fortunate.

I had a couple of other trips with my father. One trip I remember was to a village called *Kestokathi* for a wedding. The groom was a cousin from my father's side; we called him Jhiluda (Brother Jhilu). We traveled by steamer and disembarked at a place called *Gournadi*, from where we took a boat to a village called *Natoi* where my father's brother-in-law (sister's husband) lived. My uncle was widower, and very respected for his piety. His house was near a mosque and the adjacent village pond. Ponds were customarily created near mosques so people could readily use their water for ablution before prayer and bathe. I spent most of time with my father as there were not too many people in the house at the time.

My father took me to a *mela* (fair) which was going on in the nearby village called *Goila*. I recall walking with my father and a guide to accompany us as there was no transportation available. This is a very fond memory I have of my father, who took me there just for my entertainment. I enjoyed the fair. He and I later went to *Kestokathi*, the bride's parental village, to attend the wedding of my cousin. My father and I were seated next to my cousin. A lavish wedding dinner was placed in front of him which I savored. The fish Korma (a curry with sweetened yogurt) was the standout. I remember a few other locations with memorable sights during this trip. All these places and scenes left a deep impression on my mind about rural Bengal.

In Patuakhali there was a large reserved pond where no fishing or public use of water was allowed. Water from this pond would be treated in a treatment plant. The plant was located on its east shore with an elevated water tank was situated next to it. Every afternoon a mechanical pump was activated, pumping treated water up to the tank. I remember a skinny man of fair complexion, wearing khaki shorts and carrying a small tool, would climb the steep ladder attached to the water tank.

As our sources of recreation were limited, I would enjoy seeing the man doing his official duties. After he climbed down, he would go into the plant and then manually start a machine. I can still remember the loud noise that would continue for a long time until the tank filled. I vaguely realized that I was witnessing an important water distribution process. Water was distributed and delivered by gravity, in late afternoon at some selected public spots in town where people would collect their drinking water.

I recall hearing an interesting story about an incident happening before my time. A tall, red iron pole stood in the town. It had a tall ladder attached that extended all the way to the top. On one side, there was a field and on the other side there were many trees and bushes. The pole was likely used for telegraphic transmission. Telegraph as a means of long-distance communication is now extinct and a lost art. When I went to the post office, I loved to hear "tore tokka" sounds and see equipment with small moving parts on the postmaster's desk. Other kids and I would enjoy climbing the red pole since nobody would prevent us. I would test my mettle by climbing up as far as I could to see when I would get scared.

In a village or small town, simple landmarks like the tall red pole, often had lasting stories associated with them. The tall tale I heard was about a developmentally challenged man who once climbed the tall ladder to its apex on a windy day -- truly a dangerous feat. He fearlessly held onto a rung of the ladder and screamed to show off his achievement. Stunned by his loud screams, people gathered in the field under the pole apprehensive of what disaster might befall him.

They urged him to come down slowly, but he ignored them. Suddenly, he uttered the words "*Allahu Akbar* (God is the Greatest)" and "*Pakistan Zindabad* (Long live Pakistan)" and jumped. Nobody could ever survive from a fall through such height. People nervously ran away to avoid seeing a mangled dead body on the ground. After a few moments, the same words were heard as he walked off with only a limp to show for his dramatic fall. Clearly, he fell on the trees and bushes on the other side and so escaped with his life.

Along with the occasional life-threatening adventure, in our home we knew how to entertain ourselves. My siblings and I were all fond of music and could sing modern, folk, Tagore's, and Nazrul's songs. We inherited this from my father who could sing and was proficient at playing the flute and harmonium (a local version of keyboards). But under the guidance of the *Pir* of *Sharshina*, he gave up all these pursuits after falling ill. Although I never learned how to play musical instruments as they were absent in our home, I could sing like my siblings and the love of music stayed with me.

I was fond of animals as well. I had many pets including a dog, two cats, a few chickens and roosters, and ducks. I first met my pet dog when he was a little puppy who followed me on my way back from my uncle's house next to the local jail. He appeared abandoned and looking for a home. When he followed me all the way to our house, I asked my mother if I could keep him with us as a pet.

I started to call him *Bhokka*. He grew big over the course of time and became my constant companion. One day he came home in pain and near death. It appeared that he had been bitten by a snake. Unfortunately, he didn't survive, and I felt very sad losing him.

Of the two cats, one was well behaved, whom I named *Kudu* and the other was a bit mischievous, whom I called *Budu*. I don't recall how I got these strange names for my dog and cats, probably it was just random.

After school, the cats would run to me raising their tails and rub against my legs in happiness. At night *Kudu* would manage to jump up to my bed and sleep outside my mosquito tent near my feet. Once she had a litter of kittens which my mother gave away. I felt sorry for *Kudu* and the kittens and asked my mother not to give them away, but she didn't want so many cats at home.

I had chickens and ducks that I raised. Watching the ducks swim in a pond was fun and so was watching them hatch their eggs. I would keep checking until the day the chicks and duck-lings burst out of the shell! I monitored how they grew into their adulthood.

We had a gray cow who provided us milk. She was very gen-tle and nice. Once she grew older, my father bought a younger hornless dark brown cow – a rather violent one – and sold the older cow. I vividly remember the scene when the buyer came to take her away. I was so sad. Incredibly, I saw the cow in a very depressed mood with teary eyes. Who says animals don't have emotions? I saw her tear up the moment she was carried away by her new owner.

Barisal was a much larger town than Patuakhali and the headquarters of Barisal district. I had been there before, mostly accompanying my ill parents, going to the Barisal Sadar Hospital for treatment. I can't forget the gory scene of the crowded hospital and the smell of disinfectant from the floor. I didn't feel good in that environment. Patuakh-ali didn't have qualified doctors or a good hospital in those days.

I vaguely remember the details of those trips. I remember though that on one occasion we stayed in a large rented boat on a canal called *Bhatar Khal* connecting to the *Kirtonkhola* River. Next to our boat there was another boat in which a *Mog* family lived. The *Mog* community was from southern Patuakhali; they were Buddhists who had Mongolian features. I noticed two pretty teenage girls wearing decorative *lungis* (ethnic skirts) and short colorful shirts would occasionally come out of the boat and stroll in open air while smoking *bidis* (locally made cigarettes).

During another trip we stayed in a relative's home near a cemetery. The home was located in a remote area at the outskirts of town. We arrived there by horse carts drawn over a rugged unpaved road. I would feel scared occasionally at night because of a spooky feeling.

My mother used to make all these living arrangements for our trips to Barisal. On one trip we lived on the ground floor of a building. The cemented floor had a smooth finish and was painted in red. I was so young but still recall visiting the hospital and a dentist's clinic on that trip. The dentist was treating me and simultaneously yelling at me to shut up when I screamed in pain.

I remember a particular trip when I was in Class 9. I went to participate in a district wide Urdu essay competition. Our head-master Abdul Awwal Khondker took me and a few other students to Barisal. The trip in the rivers from Patuakhali to Barisal took about five to six hours in a motor launch (a motorized large boat carrying many passengers). The competition was held at Barisal Zilla School where I was one of the many students from different schools in the district. There were some Bihari students from other schools, children of Muslim migrants who were native Urdu speakers. I was somewhat nervous to compete against them but when the results came out, to my surprise, I learned that I was a winner.

At an early age I won another student competition. It was a school literary competition in Bengali in which I was awarded a book prize entitled *Rangila Nayer Majhi* (boatman of a colorful boat) with the picture of a boat and a lovely rural woman in a sari carrying a pitcher on her waist with her head tilted toward the pitcher. I was delighted I won a book as a prize.

Unlike many students, I was not particularly good at memorization. I would have ideas in my head and write answers in my own language as I had good command of writing and some proficiency in Bengali and English. I also developed a clever technique in which I would memorize some key words to help me answer questions, instead of reading everything from the books for Board examinations. Using old questions available for purchase, I would guess what might be asked in different subjects and prepare for those. It worked well for me.

When I was in Class 10 and ready to graduate from high school, I was ready for the matriculation examination conducted by the East Pakistan Secondary Education Board. Later, when I went to Canada and the U.S., I noted from my children's class assignments that school students were assigned projects and encouraged to be analytical. This stood in contrast to the emphasis placed in East Pakistan on memorization. Also, the matriculation exam was controlled centrally by the Board, a system introduced by the British colonialists, whereas in Canada and the U.S. such exams are held at the school where the students were enrolled.

We had a few very bright students in my class. In the test exam held before the matriculation exam, I had to face stiff competition with another student. There were conflicting rumors that I was at the top of the class versus him at top of the class. When the results came out, to my relief, it was me. In March 1958 at the age of 14, I took the matriculation examination and passed in the first division with distinction. That year there were eight students who got first division and two with distinction – a long standing record at the school. Our headmaster and teachers were very excited about this and expressed their pride in us as did the townspeople.

As always, my risky adventures had no end. After the matriculation examination my nephew Akhtaruzzaman, who also matriculated the same year, came to Patuakhali to spend some time with us. We went on a vacation to my maternal uncle's home in *Kharijjama*. My nephew, whose father was a police officer, came to Patuakhali for a visit with my sister and her other kids. From there we decided to go to *Kharijjama* to relax before college.

One day, following my old habit in Patuakhali, we took a boat that was anchored to the shore of a canal next to my maternal uncle's home and started rowing it in the canal towards a river between *Kharijjama* and the village of *Dharandi*. This was just to have some fun. We reached the river and turned right into it along its shore. Our plan was to go some distance and return along the same path. Suddenly I noticed our boat had started moving faster along the river and drifting away from the shore.

Patuakhali is a coastal district and *Kharijjama* is even further south of the township of Patuakhali. The river that we were in led to an even mightier river and eventually headed for the Bay of Bengal. I realized that the downstream tide was pulling us towards the sea. We panicked and wondered how we could return. We started rowing at an angle towards the shore and eventually reached the shore. I took the *baitha* (oar) and pushed it in the mud but it was getting harder to stay in place as the strong water current had been pulling us downstream and the oar got dislodged from the mud. It was difficult for us to navigate through the strong currents. We could only manage to come near the shore but could not hold the boat under control near the bank. We cried for help.

Fortunately, two farmers were tilling the land in a nearby paddy (rice) field. They heard our cries and rushed to where we were and rescued us. Once again, my father's good standing, family name and broad networks helped us out of a pinch. I told the two field workers my father's and uncle's names and they immediately recognized us. They told us we were about 2 miles (3.2 kilometers) away from *Kharijjama*. We sighed in relief as one of them walked us back to my uncle's home.

Despite being curious, I was not particularly courageous by nature in my young age. I believed myself to be adventurous rather, in a foolhardy way. It was this experience that taught me something new about myself. Although I was afraid of getting lost and drowning in the river, in a dangerous situation, I realized I had inner courage that somehow allowed me to think calmly push through the fear and not to panic under the frightening situation.

Time for college quickly arrived and along with it, the time came for me to leave my parental home. Although a new Patuakhali College was established right when I matriculated, my parents wanted me to go to a good junior college for my two-year intermediate education. I went to Dhaka, the capital of the province of East Pakistan, to get good education.

CHAPTER 2

ADOLESCENT IN DHAKA

Coming of Age Unattended

The City of Dhaka was not totally unfamiliar to me before I went there for studies. Dhaka is an ancient city and was at one time called Jahangirnagar after Mughal Emperor Jahangir. It was known for its textile industry which produced *muslin* fabric of the finest quality. Under Mughal rule, the production of this ultra-fine woven fabric became a worldwide industry. The British East India Company could not compete with local *muslin* production. British colonial rulers were unsuccessful to increase their own export of cloth to India, so they suppressed local production. Eventually, craft and weaving knowledge was eradicated. In a few horrific instances, the *muslin* weavers were allegedly rounded up and their thumbs chopped off. Consequently, the quality of the fabric diminished and the art of producing this fine cloth was lost.

In 1952, my oldest brother Mir Maswood Ali, who was a lecturer in Statistics at Dhaka University, was heading for London, England for higher studies. He used to live with some friends at 7 Bonogram Road in old Dhaka. I went with my parents to Dhaka to see him off at the airport. I vaguely remember the details as I was only eight years old but one memorable event stayed with me.

In those days, there were many urban monkeys in old Dhaka. One day, I was left alone for a short time in the house with the servants, one of whom had likely left a door open. A monkey somehow entered the house. I was near the kitchen and suddenly I saw it approaching me. The monkey went into the kitchen looking for food. I felt like it was almost of my size and was moving freely without fear since he realized that I was a kid and could do him no harm.

Failing to find any food he became disappointed and started making faces at me and baring his teeth in frustration. I was scared and didn't know what to do. Fortunately, to my relief, a servant appeared on the scene. He held my hand to keep me safe, chased the monkey back out the door with a stick.

My next visit to Dhaka that I recount was for my medical treatment. In 1957, I went to Dhaka accompanied by my second oldest brother Mir Masoom Ali. My health-conscious mother wanted me to get the best treatment for a slight urinary problem. My brother and I stayed at Salimullah Muslim Hall. He was a student of Statistics at Dhaka University at the time. Since I was older this time around, I had a better understanding of the city. The roads were dusty. I noted a lot of manually driven rickshaws and few cars. Having a car there was a great luxury. The few cars were compact in size. There were also quite a few horse-carts. I felt bad seeing these poor horses looking undernourished, being repeatedly whipped and forced to move on. I had the experience of riding these in Barisal also.

I was checked by Dr. Nandi, a famous physician in Dhaka in those days, whose office chamber was in Wari, an old part of the city. For my return home, my brother arranged for me to travel with a lawyer friend of my father from Patuakhali who was also traveling the same day. I was in the inter class of the steamer, which was a room with wide benches for sleeping, whereas the first and second classes had beds and were secluded at the front. The cheapest third class was on the deck.

During lunch time the lawyer, who was supposed to take care of me, forgot all about me instead. Hungry, I asked him how I could have my lunch. He pointed to the dining cabin for inter- and third-class passengers. When I went there, I was told they had just stopped serving meals a few minutes ago. Frustrated, hungry and to kill time I went to watch people coming in and getting out at a station where the steamer anchored. Suddenly I saw my much older cousin, Mir Alauddin Ahmed. He was a businessman who later became a wealthy industrialist in Dhaka after starting a business fabricating tube-wells that pumped drinking water from the underground aquifer. He would expand the business to other manufactured products.

Upon seeing me, he asked if I had my lunch. When I answered no, my waiting at the deck to watch people paid off and he invited me to accompany him to the first-class dining room. Once settled in, the two of us had a great lunch with chicken curry, vegetables and a pudding as dessert. The food was delicious. It tasted all the better since I was very hungry.

The butler and server were dressed in white uniforms as was customary in British colonial days. The custom continued past colonial days and they were very courteous. I remember this event because I felt my cousin was godsend that day. I always admired him for his charming personality, and I remained in touch with him in Dhaka until his death in June 2019. He was the longest living cousin of our Mir dynasty.

For admission to college in Dhaka, I was interviewed by a couple of professors at Dhaka College. This was a prestigious government college with an excellent academic standard. The campus was totally new in Dhanmondi area and so were the two hostels within the campus. I liked the large galleries used as classrooms.

Each was individually attached to the departments of Physics, Chemistry and Biology and the respective labs. Arts and literature classes were also held there.

Typically, good students, strong in mathematics would choose to study science in those days. So, when asked by a committee member what my intention was, I opted for Intermediate Science (I.Sc.), which was a two-year program before entry to undergraduate education at a university. I said this instantly, even though I liked liberal arts and literature also. One professor noted that I also had high marks in History and literature and asked whether I would reconsider. I replied, "But I have high marks in mathematics and science also." After some discussions between themselves the committee recommended me for admission to I.Sc.

Meanwhile, I heard that Notre Dame College had a better reputation in science than Dhaka College. I met the Principal, Father Martin and showed him my mark sheet. He commented, "We always welcome students like you. I hope you will come here." I was inspired and thought this was the right place for me to study. So, I decided to have a look at the accommodations at the hostel called Baptist Mission. The hostel was in Sadarghat, a very crowded area in old Dhaka next to the Buriganga River. Students would have to take the bus or rickshaw to get to college. I specifically checked the bathrooms there because I would judge the standard of a building and living conditions from its bathrooms.

I didn't like the building, the living conditions, and the surrounding environment when I compared them with those of Dhaka College. A friend of mine Anwarul Karim Chowdhury (Joy), a classmate from the high school, was admitted to Notre Dame college and had already moved in.

During that time Patuakhali was a sub-division under Barisal district; later it became a district of its own. Joy was the son of a sub-divisional officer of Patuakhali. Later he joined the Pakistan Foreign Service and held high positions in Pakistan and later in

Bangladesh. I met him at the hostel and talked with him about the place. But I was not impressed and the newly built glistening buildings of the new campus, the newly built New Market and other nearby structures in the new part of the city pulled me to attend Dhaka College. I confirmed my decision and decided to accept admission to Dhaka College, which also had a good reputation.

Before classes started, I left home for Dhaka to pursue my student life there. I lived in Room 211 of North Hostel with a roommate by the name of Shah Hussain Imam (Buli). He was the son of the sub-divisional police officer at Patuakhali and my classmate at school. He was an arts student. I started the college in good spirts. I was 14 and at least two years younger than most of my classmates in both science and arts. This meant I had a small circle of friends, primarily my two school friends, Syed Mahtab Kabir and Shah Hussein Imam, my classmates from high school. In one Chemistry class Harunur Rashid Sir asked me, "Where are you from?" I replied, "From Patuakhali." He remarked, "You are so young! Did your mother let you go away from her?" I didn't know what to say but felt a bit embarrassed as all the students in the large gallery stared at me.

Apart from being misfit in social life with classmates I had another problem which was in athletics. In Patuakhali I used to play soccer and cricket with kids of my age who were at lower-level classes than me. Here I had to play with classmates older and bigger in size than me as I was not fully developed physically. I had no choice other than getting hurt. So, my athletics ended there, and I never did pick it up again. The gated New Market close to us had many well-lit stores and a few restaurants. In the afternoon, for leisure time, I would go there for a stroll and occasionally eating snacks at the restaurants.

⋟⊹⊹⋞

The founder of Pakistan, Mr. Muhammad Ali Jinnah, died of natural causes in 1948, soon after the independence of Pakistan in 1947. Shortly after, the capable first Prime Minister Liaquat Ali Khan of Pakistan was assassinated in 1951. Liaqat Ali Khan could have provided stability to the country but instead his assassination created a political vacuum. In October 1958, amidst political instability in Karachi, the capital of Pakistan at the time, General Ayub Khan staged a military coup against the civilian government, abrogated the constitution, and sent the sitting President, Major General Iskandar Mirza, into exile in the U.K.

Being fed up with politicians squabbling with each other, the people of Pakistan welcomed the new military ruler with the hope that he would give political stability to the country. The coup was generally accepted by East Pakistanis although some people thought that it killed democracy and might perpetuate military rule to the detriment of the country. There was a declaration of Martial law and that decree brought order back to the country for the duration of strict military rule. Ayub Khan abrogated the previous constitution that prescribed a parliamentary system of democracy.

In 1959 General Ayub Khan introduced a new constitution prescribing a presidential form of government that included a new system called Basic Democracies. In this system, people would vote for members of the union councils representing various local constituencies. These would elect council chairmen, who would in turn form an "electoral college" and elect the president from the list of candidates running for president. Although quite different in the details, this had a faint resemblance to the electoral college system of the U.S. where the president is confirmed by an electoral college, and not automatically by popular vote. People didn't like this indirect form of presidential election and preferred an election based on popular vote.

In a widely publicized election, Ms. Fatima Jinnah, the sister of Mr. Muhammad Ali Jinnah ran against General Ayub Khan and lost. Clearly, the system was set up to favor the incumbent president Ayub Khan. If Ms. Jinnah had been elected president, she would have restored full democracy. The union council chairmen would lose their privileges. They were elected by popular vote for a fixed term and they formed the electoral college. Needless to say, they had considerable local judicial and executive power. Therefore, the assumption was that they had voted for Ayub Khan to protect their own power. Ayub Khan ruled for 10 years as a generally benevolent dictator and eventually stepped down under populous pressure.

Amid the tumult of regional politics, at my hostel, I used to go and watch movies at a theater with one my friends. There was one movie called "Black Sleep" in which a doctor would do research on human brains illegally. I don't remember the full details, but what I remember is that his victims, whose faces became disfigured and scary, were kept in the basement of a large building supervised by a brutal guard by the name Maangoe. After coming back to my hostel, I had difficulty sleeping, the frightening mangled faces were haunting me. That continued for a few days. I guess I was too young to watch a horror movie. I never told my friends about it, so they didn't think of me as a coward. These were among the ongoing pitfalls of being the youngest of the class.

I enjoyed my classes at Dhaka College and learned new subjects. I very much liked English and Bengali literature, Physics, Mathematics, and Biology, but not Chemistry so much as the odor of chemicals in the lab would bother me. I would always like to attend class lectures and listened intently to the teachers[*].

---

[*] Our English literature teachers at different times were Abu Rushd Matin Uddin (prose), Enamul Karim (prose), Kabir Chowdhury (prose), and Noman Sir (poetry). Our Bengali literature teachers were Shawkat Osman

Since I was in the college for two years there were probably some more teachers whom I can't recall. Their names are worth mentioning. They were all good and dedicated teachers and students revered them highly.

Each teacher had a unique style of teaching and they generally taught us in a warm manner without intimidating us and they motivated us to study. Ashwini Kumar Sir who taught college algebra invited us to his home if we had questions and wanted to learn more. He lived in the old part of Dhaka. Accepting his invitation, I visited his home a few times. He would not charge anything for the extra lessons. We also had the laboratories for science classes. Overall, I feel I had a very good education at the college.

Rashid Sir had a strong interest in cultural matters. Somehow, he came to know that I could sing. So, he contacted me and asked me if I could sing at a cultural show at the college. Because of my love for music, I readily agreed. He gathered a few more students and organized rehearsals at his house in old Dhaka. He selected two Tagore's songs for me. The songs in celebration of the arrival of spring season. These are some beginning lines from each song:

Rodonbhora ay basanta shokhi, kokhono ashayni bujhi agay.
More birohobedona rangalo kingshukraktimragay.
Kunjodaaray bonomallika shejeshay poria nobo patralika,

(prose), Hishamuddin Sir (novel), Idris Mullah, (drama), Monsuruddin Sir (prose), Abdur Rashid (poetry), and Rowshan Ara (prose). Mathematics teachers were Aswini Kumar (algebra), Bodruddoza Sir (algebra), Monzur Sir (calculus) and Shamsuddin Sir (analytical geometry). Our Physics teachers were Nasimuddin Ahmed and Zohurul Huq and Chemistry teachers were Harunur Rashid, Abdul Jabbar, and Serajul Islam. For Biology, we had Bhuiyan Sir (Zoology; he wrote a book on Biology that was our textbook), Mustafizur Rahman (Zoology), Talukdar Osman Haider (Botany).

Sharadin-rajani onimikha kaarpoth chayay jaagay.

Translation:
A spring such as this replete with tears my friend, perhaps never
  came before.
My agony of being separated has been colored in bloodred hue
  of scentless red flowers.
At the garden gate the wild jasmines are dressed in new leaves,
They stay awake waiting day and night for something.

Ora okaranay chanchal
Daalay dolay bayuhillolay nabopallabdal.
Batashay batashay pranbhora banee shunitay payechhay kokhon
  ki jani,
Mormorotaanay dikay dikay anay koishorkolahol.

Translation:
They are restless for no reason
On the tree branches new leaves swing along jubilant wind.
Scattered winds are laden with hearty words; they have heard
  these sometime,
Their rhythmic murmur brings forth euphoric commotion
  everywhere.

After the few rehearsals, I sang those songs at the college function. As I mentioned before, since I lost interest in athletics at
that time, this was a good outlet for me to express myself in some
form.

Monsuruddin Sir, who was an elderly man and an admirer
of Rabindranath Tagore, had long hair and a beard mimicking
Tagore. He had a special interest in folklore. He liked me a lot
and once told me I should write, he thought I would be a good
writer when I grew up.

Before the summer vacation, Monsuruddin Sir told all the students to collect local sayings and proverbs from our home-towns and surrounding villages. He asked us to keep them and share with him when classes resumed.

When I went to Patuakhali, I told my mother about the assignment. Being an ardent promoter of education, she earnestly helped me in collecting these and I dutifully recorded them. When I returned after the vacation and saw him in class, I expected him to ask for the assignment. However, I noticed that he didn't mention anything about the proverbs. I realized that he forgot what he said before the vacation. I really felt bad about how much effort my mother had put towards the task. She meticulously collected the material for me from different sources. At the end of the class, when I took the material to him, he seemed a bit flustered, but took the material from me anyway. In order to show his appreciation, he affectionately hugged me but sadly I don't know what he did with my work. To this day, I regret not saving the submission, as it meant so much to me and my mother. I don't remember those sayings anymore.

I used to travel from Patuakhali to Dhaka and back by launch or steamer. Since they were slow, I would carry story books and novels with me and read them throughout the journey. Once one of my father's clients was near me in a steamer. This friend would marvel to my father about my reading stamina and expressed his surprise at how I managed. I would genuinely enjoy the endless reading that made travel feel short. Along with reading I have always been a curious observer of people and would watch what was going on. Some people would discuss contemporary politics, religion, foods, or some other issues. Others would play cards and just gossip. I would never get bored. Even today, I don't know what boredom is, because I always find something interesting to do that keeps me engaged.

Toward the end of the first year in Dhaka College, I moved to a house to live with my brother Mir Masoom Ali and his wife. My brother was recently married and rented a house conveniently close to the college. Soon however, I realized that it was better for me to move back to the hostel, so I could focus on my studies without as much distraction. In my second year in Dhaka College, as there were no vacant seats left in the popular North Hostel. I moved to the South Hostel instead, next to the large Azimpur Cemetery. I stayed in a room on the third floor with two roommates. I needed to study with complete concentration and no distractions, a habit that has remained with me throughout my life. To avoid the noise from my roommates and their occasional visitors, I created my own isolated microenvironment by surrounding my desk with bed sheets which also attached to the bed posts. This makeshift space included the mosquito tent around my bed. I would sequester myself inside, turn on the light and focus on my work. I knew this was weird, but it was a good option in my crowded setting.

In late 1959, during a short college vacation when most students left for home, I decided to stay back to prepare for some exams. I finally had the room to myself. One warm and breezy night, shortly before midnight. I was startled by unusual sounds outside my window. I looked out and saw a few people in the cemetery down below next to our hostel burying a body. They were holding a bright lamp and chanting religious verses. The eerie, pitch dark scene really scared me. All I could do was close the window, lay down, and start calling on God to give me courage. Eventually fatigue overtook fear and I fell asleep.

⸎

In 1960, I appeared in the final I.Sc. examination in April and passed in the first division with distinction. Surprisingly, I got high marks in English and Bengali comparable to some top students in arts even though I was a science student. The time had come for me to consider university for undergraduate studies, I had an important choice to make. Our college was administered under auspices of the University of Dhaka. All colleges in those days were under the jurisdiction of either University of Dhaka or Rajshahi University. Since I was a good student all around, I had many options and I was forced to do some soul searching.

Deciding what to study in Dhaka College had been easy, since I had only two options: arts versus science. Now that I had myriads of choices, I realized I loved both arts and science and their many subdisciplines. It was my love of the subjects that drove my decision process, rather than job opportunities or future prospects.

I prepared a mental list in order of my preference: History, English, Physics, Engineering, and Medicine. I always loved history and do so even today. English was my other love. In science Physics a clear choice. I found Physics to be the foundation of science and a mystic discipline. I was deeply influenced by Newton's laws of motion and of falling bodies. I developed a dislike for the odor in Chemistry labs, so that option was easily eliminated. I did enjoy the theoretical part of Chemistry since it was so fundamental in nature. Studying Engineering was not particularly on my mind, but it was an applied science based on Physics and Mathematics, so a real option. Engineering at the time was very popular and competitive and being a keen student, that also attracted me.

At the time, I liked the idea of Medicine quite a lot, since I would be able to help people in a noble profession. I was attracted to medicine for several reasons including the lifestyle, independent practice and the ability to treat people with care, attention and sincerity. In my hometown, our family physician, Dr. Shailen Babu would visit me if needed, on house calls. He was a refined gentleman with a good understanding of health and medicine even though he was not a medical degree holder. He was a licensed medical practitioner with a diploma in medicine. I admired his personality and his personal touch. Seeing him, I sometimes cherished the idea of being a doctor. I was also influenced by my mother's crucial lessons about health and wellness. However, not getting into the medical college at that time didn't bother me much as I had a phobia of blood. In later life in the 1970s, I realized once again, however, the importance of being a physician after I had recovered from the phobia, a significant story in itself.

To help guide this important decision, I needed more information. I decided to meet the department heads of the various disciplines. I met the Head of the History department, whose name I can't remember, and then of English, Dr. Syed Sazzad Husain. Based on my marks, both advised that I should study engineering since I would be able to secure jobs immediately upon graduation. The burgeoning country needed many engineers. I went to see Dr. Abdul Matin Chowdhury, Head of the Physics department. He was happy to see me and set up a date for an interview. I had to wait for Engineering since student selection for the incoming class was not complete. In the meantime, I went to see the Principal of Dhaka Medical College. My brother-in-law, Dr. Muhammad Anwarullah was a senior medical student there at that time. He was the husband of one of my older sisters, Afroza Anwar. I saw him there. He took my mark sheet to the Principal of the College and reported back that the latter also advised me to study Engineering for the same reasons as the other Heads.

So, after some legwork, my choices had been narrowed to Physics and Engineering. In those days engineering was a coveted field and most strong science students went on to study Engineering. For admission to Ahsanullah Engineering College (AEC), the only engineering college at that time affiliated with the University of Dhaka there was a drawing test that required intensive preparation. Drawing was not my forte, so I practiced engineering drawings rigorously, even while I continued to explore other possibilities.

AEC candidate selection notice came out during the summer vacation of 1960. Although more than half a century has elapsed, to me it feels like just the other day. Someone told me that the results were posted on the notice board near the main entrance. Selection was based on the combined results of science subjects of I.Sc. exam and the drawing test. I was never great with drawing, so I was most curious to know how I did after that grueling drawing test. I rushed to the college to check the list.

There were hardly any people in the building at the time. I went to the principal's office, saw the long list of 242 selected students under the title Admissions List and was trying to locate my name. The names were not apparently in alphabetical order. Since the college was out of session, it was very quiet. Suddenly I heard footsteps and turned to see a man, short to medium stature, bearded and unassuming, wearing a simple white Hawaiian shirt. He had a bunch of keys in a key-ring dangling in his hand. I thought he was a staff member of the college. He stood next to me and asked, "I guess you are searching for your name; what is your name?" As I told him my name, he quickly spotted it on the list, pointed his forefinger to where my name was, and opened the padlock of the principal's office door.

I wondered who this simple, unpretentious, mild-mannered man was and I thought he was probably a clerical staff member coming to check something in the principal's office. To my surprise, he went around the table and sat in the principal's chair and asked me about myself. He then said, "I am Dr. Rashid, the principal. Engineering is a great field; there is a great demand for it in the country. I would like to see you here after the vacation." He was persuasive and humble, I appreciated both traits. I thought he must know something that I didn't. So, I got fired up by his persuasive words and said "Yes, Sir, I will be here."

I also learned a lesson that day: never judge a book by its cover. Later, I came to know what an august personality he was, despite his unassuming demeanor. He was the face of the college and subsequently the university. I immediately canceled my forthcoming interview with the Physics Department and left for my home in Patuakhali. Even today, half a century later, I feel a tinge of embarrassment knowing that I prejudged the late Dr. M. A. Rashid simply based on his appearance. Dr. Rashid contributed so much to the college and later, to East Pakistan University of Engineering & Technology (EPUET). He remains an iconic personality and a legend in the field.

As I reminisce about the four years spent at AEC, now forever in the past, I remember the many faces, places, events and incidents that shaped my (mostly happy) days. By the time I returned to Dhaka to begin studies at AEC, I was a little late. To my dismay that all spaces at Plessey Hostel, residence for first-year students, were already taken. Latecomers like me were placed at the Main Hostel alongside the second-year students. My roommates and I were placed in a five-seated room next to the bathrooms, the worst accommodation in the old building and one of my worst memories. The other much hated component for me was a mandatory, early morning physical drill, held in the nearby playground.

For the second time in my school career, I found myself mismatched by age and class level. This largely cut off my social life and stunted my interaction with classmates. I mainly interacted with my four roommates, and a few students in the Main Hostel, all of whom were in first year. One day I went to see the movie "A Woman Like Satan" starring Brigitte Bardot with some of my classmates at the local Gulistan Theater but was denied because I was not an adult. My friends convinced the gatekeeper that I was their classmate and therefore mature enough to watch the adult-rated movie. He reluctantly let me in after looking at me from my head to toe, I felt really embarrassed. Of my four roommates, one of them, Hemayet Uddin Ahmed, became a close friend of mine, we knew each other from Dhaka College days. We remained roommates throughout and even after my graduation, we remained good friends. Sadly, while working in Nigeria, he was killed in a car accident at a young age. He was my good friend and I was saddened by his tragic death.

Initially, I was very excited about being an engineer some day in the future. I began my studies in earnest but was jolted to realized that first year training included hands-on workshops. I had to study carpentry, blacksmithing, foundry, pattern making, and machine shop in addition to my theoretical courses and associated laboratories. The study program was intense and rigorous, which I didn't mind. I soon found however, that I was not a good handyman and had difficulty with the workshops. I particularly hated the machine shop, shaping metal pieces with very noisy machines. The foreman was a stone-faced, emotionless man with a demeanor to match the shop environment. One day he came to my machine and saw I was not shaping the piece of metal properly. Instead of being patient and teaching me how to do it right, he amplified the screeching noise of my machine by screaming and rebuking me.

This one gruff instructor shaped the class experience in lasting ways. Returning to my hostel, I was in a bad mood and thought perhaps I should have studied Physics. One of my classmates and close friend Syed Mahtab Kabir, from high school and Dhaka College, had similar feelings. He left for the Punjab University in Lahore, West Pakistan to study Physics. Another roommate, Moazzem Hossain, also left for other reasons, to study

Naval Engineering in Japan. My small circle of friends shrank again.

Later I learned that my oldest brother also left AEC after experiencing the same thing. He eventually went to Dhaka University to study Statistics. Over the course of my factfinding endeavor, I talked to some senior engineering students. They said the workshops and harsh standards were meant to teach engineers how to supervise technical staff. This would pass after a year and they advised me to hang in there. I took their advice and by second year I did feel better. Happily, I was allotted a seat in the newly built New Hostel (renamed Ahsanullah Hall later) with the third-year students along with several other classmates of mine. I enjoyed learning the basic engineering courses.

Unlike Dhaka University, AEC used a semester system for the four-year B.Sc. Eng. program. The system and curriculum were modeled in collaboration with professors from Texas A & M University. The first three semesters had a common curriculum for all students. In the fourth semester students would move on to different disciplines of engineering of their choice. Towards the end of the third semester we chose which discipline to pursue for the remaining five semesters. I was contemplating Mechanical Engineering as I had always been fascinated by how machines and engines worked. During trips between Patuakhali to Dhaka, I would spend time watching the steamer and motor launch engines, wondering how they worked. However, later in my third semester, some events occurred to change my mind.

During the summer of 1962, as we wrapped up our semester final exams, there was some student unrest taking place against the education policy of the government. After several skirmishes between police and Dhaka University students, some students from EPUET also joined the protest movement.

A student procession (protest march) was passing through the street on one occasion, next to the New Hostel where I lived.

The police and soldiers of the East Pakistan Rifles chased and arrested some of them. Many of them ran into our hostel for cover. My room was near the main entrance on the ground floor and as it was daytime, the door was unlocked. I was in the room with my roommate Mahbub, popularly known as Golla, a nickname assigned to him by his classmates. Our third roommate Hemayet was away at that time. In the chaos and confusion, a soldier entered our room and arrested me and Mahbub despite our pleas to clarify that we were not in the demonstration. The officer led us to an open truck on the street. All of the students, who had been arrested in their rooms were driven to Ramna police station, a building under construction.

We huddled in a large crowded hall and sat on the concrete floor. It was past nightfall and by then we were hungry. Some students started raising slogans demanding food and threatening a hunger strike. Finally, around midnight we were given rice and buckets of beef curry. I don't remember how we managed to eat but being hungry, we just did.

The long night dragged on and I could not sleep on the concrete floor. Early the next morning someone from AEC came to tell us that our release had been negotiated with the government. The terms for release included signing a bond stating we would not participate in any political activities in the future. Some students continued to pursue political engagement with the government, including our classmate Serajul Majid Mamoon. He later became a news anchor at Radio Pakistan, Pakistan TV and then Bangladesh TV.

Students went on strike, Mamoon took a leadership role and the bonds were canceled by the governor of East Pakistan, Lt. General Azam Khan. General Khan was considered very warm and benevolent in his manners. The elite and common people alike, felt he could level with the Bengalis. These traits made him very popular. I may mention here that unlike Dhaka University, we had no political student parties or any political activities. So, the restrictive terms of release were irrelevant, and in my case, I was not even in the procession. I signed and was released, relieved to be out of my dilemma. Later, General Khan visited AEC and at the request of students promised to tear off the bond papers.

━━◁┼┼▷━━

We had a subject called Heat Engines in the third semester. We missed the final semester exam because of the prevailing political turmoil and thereby technically failed the course. A supplementary exam was held later. By regulation if we failed in one course, we had to repeat the entire year, a harsh rule indeed!

The teacher who taught this course was somewhat unconventional. I heard that he was telling students their marks and rumors were flying that many students had failed. I rushed to the campus and went to his office. There was a long queue. The student in front me approached him, and he said "You failed. Next one." My heart started beating hard as this teacher was so unpredictable. He said "You passed. Next one" and returned the graded exam to me. I said, "Thank you, Sir." He said, "Don't thank me, thank God." After exiting the line, I reviewed my exam and to my surprise, I didn't do very well. I found one question for which I wrote something totally wrong. Instead of giving me a zero or a low mark, he gave me a negative mark for that question, lowering my overall mark in the exam.

Being a diligent student, I met the professor to discuss the mark, he told me why it was wrong. Knowing his eccentric behavior, I didn't pursue the matter any further. I was afraid he might find something else, lower my marks further, get angry or even fail me if I questioned his judgment. I was glad I passed. Unfortunately for many, it was a bloodbath as he flunked 69 students.

These were all good students who rose to their admission into AEC through a rigorous screening process. Nevertheless, they had to repeat the entire year according college rules, delaying graduation by one year. This volatile behavior from the Mechanical Engineering professor, as well as my poor performance in his course and the bad memory of the temperamental machine shop foreman all turned me off. I started rethinking my earlier plan of choosing Mechanical Engineering.

Chemistry was not my favorite subject, so Chemical Engineering was ruled out. I was good in the Electrical Engineering, but I liked the Civil Engineering courses too. I thought, unlike electrical engineers, civil engineers had a good amount of interaction with the public and their work was more visible. So, at the end I opted for Civil Engineering. My education at AEC went well. In 1962, it was upgraded to an independent university and renamed East Pakistan University of Engineering & Technology (EPUET). Dr. M. A. Rashid, the former Principal of AEC was appointed the Vice Chancellor of the new university. I liked the rigorous nature of the courses in various years and the discipline. I also liked the interdisciplinary courses like English, Sociology, Economics, and Accounting included in the curriculum.

I was taught by many professors over the four years, many of them were excellent teachers. I can't remember all names now[*].

---

[*] Some names that pop up in my mind at random, in no particular order, are: Abul Kalam Azad (Mathematics), Harunur Rashid 1 (Estimating), Nazmul Huda (Planning; Geodesy), Hari Prasad (Electrical Engineering), Abdul Matin Patwary (Electrical Engineering), Nani Gopal Bhowmik (Structural Design), Bhupati Biswas (Highways), Mosharef Hossain (Railways), Harunur Rashid 2 (Structural Analysis), Khondakar A. Rahman (Irrigation and Flood Control), Kamini Saha (Physics), Mumtazuddin Ahmed (Accounting), M.A. Hannan (Hydraulics), Wahiduddin Ahmed (Structural Analysis), M.A. Naser (Fluid Mechanics), Hamid Shah (Mechanics), Abu Taher (Mechanics), M.A. Aziz (Geology; Engineering Materials), Haidar Azam (Structural Analysis), Jahedul Alam (Structural Analysis), Rafiqud-

One reason why I can't remember the names is that students gave some of them nicknames and we would know them by those names.

One teacher who stands out is Dr. Wahiduddin Ahmed, whom we called Wahiduddin Sir. He was the Head of the Civil Engineering Department. After I asked him an insightful question in class about a structural analysis problem and we solved the problem together later on having occasional discussions at his office. He admired the incident and I became well-liked by him. All these professors left an indelible impression on me. Each was unique in his style of teaching.

During this period, I traveled from Dhaka to Sylhet where my oldest sister and her family lived for some time; my oldest brother married a girl from there. Sylhet is known for its tea gardens, oranges and pineapples, and of course its scenic beauty. It has a hilly terrain unlike much of Bangladesh which is plain land. One notable exception is Chittagong Hill Tracts which I visited much later in 1999. The town is known for a highly respected Sufi saint and mystic originally from Konya, Turkey, called Shah Jalal, who settled there with his followers during the late 13th to early 14th centuries. His mausoleum is a site of many visitors. I visited that site, a solemn place. Dhaka's International Airport is at present named after him. I also visited a place called Jaflong a few miles away near the border with India. It is a hilly area of exquisite natural beauty.

I can trace my interest in travelling to the childhood trips I took with my father. In a way, I believe we are travelers, walking

---

din Ahmed (Mechanical Engineering), Subodh Das (Foundation), M.A. Rauf (Soil Mechanics), among others.

the earth for some time and then we are gone. Traveling can broaden our horizons and transform us. Through exploring the earth, we can better narrate the anthology of our experiences and share these with others. In countless ways, big and small, we change the world while it reciprocates and changes us in turn. I was fortunate enough to travel to many countries and cities. A number of these trips were to present papers at academic conferences, employment consultancies, and professional committee meetings. Most were made possible because of my long academic career. Others were private travels, too many to recount, except the ones that left lasting memories.

A major unforgettable trip away from East Pakistan took place while I was an engineering student. In November 1963 I had an opportunity to visit India and West Pakistan. The university administration for the students arranged a voluntary study tour to West Pakistan via India. I jumped at the chances. M. Shah Jahan, our Civil Engineering professor, was slated to lead the tour. The tour was organized into groups of four students. The other three in my group were Golam Fariduddin Akhter (Farid), A.K.M. Rafiquddin (Rafiq), and Kabir Hossain (Kabir). Each group was supposed to stay together during the entire trip. We set out on our journey from Dhaka to Calcutta (now called Kolkata) by train. When we reached the crowded Chitpur Railway Station in Calcutta, the sight of crowds lying down all over the platform was jarring, I was appalled.

We stayed at a low-cost place called Tower Hotel and spent much of our time going into the city to view lively street scenes. Some local customs were new to me. For example, lunch and dinner at the hotel was served on a brass platter. It would be served with a mound of rice in the middle and other dishes in small brass cups set around it. I was not used to such arrangement of meals. I also noticed that the quantities of food were scanty compared to what we were used to in East Pakistan.

I was struck by the relative level of poverty. People were very thin looking undernourished. Both men and women were dressed in plain clothes. People traveled into the city via two-wheel human rickshaws pulled by a man walking in the front. These rickshaws were different from those in Dhaka, which were three-wheeled bicycles pedaled by the driver sitting on a cushioned triangular seat. For fast travel, people used street trams. Interestingly, unlike the bus in Dhaka, where women sat in a reserved area, men and women in Calcutta sat together in the tram. There were a few notable differences between Calcutta and Dhaka when it came to women.

We visited a shopping market called New Market, where I noticed a few girls standing in a group. One of the girls saw us and made an audible comment saying teasingly "Look, these guys are so excessively well dressed." Of course, we were nicely dressed but such comments from girls about boys were unthinkable in Dhaka. It was usually the other way around.

Among other sites, we visited the famous Howrah Bridge, a cantilever bridge with a suspended span on the Hooghly River.

We witnessed the historic visit of female Russian astronaut Valentina Tereshkova. She was the first woman to have flown in space on June 16, 1963. The huge reception at the Rabindra Sarobar Stadium caused terrible traffic gridlock. Some of us tried to attend anyway. After waiting too long in a jam, our Sikh taxi driver snapped "What is the point of this crowding just to see a woman astronaut? If she was a film star I would understand." Because of the traffic congestion we could not make it to the stadium.

My most memorable experience in Calcutta during the entire trip was a visit to the residence of renowned Bengali poet Kazi Nazrul Islam who is known as the Rebel Poet. He was a multifaceted man from West Bengal. He was a poet, a storywriter, playwright, composer, novelist, actor, journalist, and a political revolutionary activist. He lived in a small apartment with his eldest son Kazi Sabyasachi Islam and his family. He is the only Bengali poet comparable to Rabindranath Tagore in stature.

When a few of us, led by Professor Shah Jahan visited the apartment, Kazi Sabyasachi Islam, a tall hefty man greeted us at the door. I saw the great poet in the front room sitting on a bed looking at us with a blank look. He had developed a very rare neurodegenerative disease that damaged his mental power in 1942 at the age of 43. A stack of newspapers was placed next to him, and he was tearing the paper into small pieces. The poet's wife Prameela Devi was deceased. His daughter-in-law would take care of him. I saw two little girls Khilkhil Kazi and Misti Kazi, the poet's granddaughters.

I felt bad to see such gifted and renowned person like him, revered by all Bengalis, living in such squalid conditions in India. We were told that he received a monthly allowance in equal amounts from the Indian and Pakistani governments. Once Bangladesh became an independent country in 1971, he was transferred to Dhaka and given a bungalow. He was appropriately honored by the Bangladeshi government and named the National Poet of Bangladesh. He died at the age of 77. No doubt, had he retained his mental capacity, he would have continued to climb the heights of his intellectual acumen. Even what limited amount he left is enough to sustain us for many generations. His Islamic songs are unparalleled by any standard. His contribution to a new vocabulary in his writings resulted in the major transformation of the Bengali language.

From Calcutta, we took the Toofan Mail, an express train going to Delhi. When the train was passing through Agra, we got a glimpse of the Taj Mahal not too far from the train. In Delhi, unlike Calcutta, I noticed men and women were nicely dressed. It was cold. We stayed at the newly built Pakistan Embassy in New Delhi. The building was not commissioned yet and was vacant. We visited the Red Fort, the main historic site in Delhi. It was built by Emperor Shah Jahan in 1639. It got the name from its massive exterior walls of red sandstone. It was the residence of Emperor Shah Jahan and all subsequent Mughal emperors. We took a tour inside and saw the place from where Queen Mumtaz Mahal could view a court presided over by Emperor Shah Jahan. We also saw the luxurious marble Hammam or the royal baths. We visited a few other sites, particularly Emperor Humayun's Tomb and the 240-feet (73-meter) tall Qutub Minar. We then visited the Delhi Jama Masjid, the largest mosque in India built also by Mughal Emperor Shah Jahan. When I saw these colossal structures, my mind marveled at how these structures were conceived, designed and constructed, considering the time they were built.

Another place we visited in Delhi was the mausoleum of the renowned Sufi saint Nizamuddin Awliya, who preached that love was the key to realize the presence of God. Side by side near it was the tomb of Jahan Ara, Mughal princess and daughter of Shah Jahan. We also visited the famous Chandni Chowk, an old shopping market. We took a trip to Raj Ghat where we visited the tomb of Mahatma Gandhi, the saintly man and India's foremost politician who preached non-violence and against communal feelings and hatred. It appears now that his teachings have taken a back seat in present-day India.

From Delhi, we took a train for Lahore in Pakistan. It stopped at Amritsar in East Punjab, a border city home to the Sikh's holiest shrine, the Golden Temple. From Amritsar, we headed for Lahore in West Pakistan by train after crossing the border at Wagah, a small town on the Pakistan side halfway between Amritsar and Lahore. Soon after we were on the streets, we found healthy men and women around us. In buses women sat separately from men. This city was the center of Pakistan's film industry. In Lahore, we stayed in a dormitory of the West Pakistan University of Engineering & Technology. We were warmly received and treated well by the faculty and students there. In one student gatherings I sang a Bengali song by request of West Pakistani students.

We visited a manufacturing plant called Ittefaq Foundry owned by the Sharif family. Nawaz Sharif became the Prime Minister of Pakistan much later. We were treated with a lavish dinner after our tour of the plant. One of the items I remember was a fried fish caught from the local Ravi River. The head of the company gave a speech welcoming us and mentioned spreading his two arms "East and West Pakistan are just like the two wings of a bird." That sentiment unfortunately didn't represent that of Pakistani politicians. They instead espoused policies of political, social and economic control over East Pakistan, as well as cliquey aspirations of power. Ultimately this resulted in the birth of an independent Bangladesh, through a bloody Liberation War in 1971.

We also visited the famous Badshahi Mosque built by Mughal Emperor Aurangzeb in1673. The mosque's architecture was similar to Jama Masjid in Delhi. We visited Empress Noor Jahan's Tomb in Shahadara Bagh where we saw the famous epitaph asking visitors not to light a lamp or place flowers at the grave of this wretched woman. She was buried alongside her deceased husband. We reflected upon her sad life after the death of her husband Emperor Jahangir. She was a gifted and powerful woman of exquisite beauty and wielded enormous power in administering the empire. But once she became a widow, following a power struggle, Prince Khurram (later Emperor Shah Jahan) placed her in confinement in a luxurious mansion.

Leaving Lahore, we went to Rawalpindi, a garrison city and the Pakistan Army Headquarters, as well as the nearby new transitional capital city, Islamabad. The new capital was planned to replace the port city of Karachi, the major business center next to the Arabian Sea.

From Rawalpindi, we went to a hill station and summer resort town to the north called Murree, about 35 miles (56 kilometers) away. We had a very pleasurable experience there even though the weather was very cold. I remember there was a long main road, a lot of stores and a few restaurants. This town was the gateway to Pakistan-controlled Kashmir, known as Azad Kashmir. We traveled to the Mangla Dam named after the village Mangla. It is over the Jhelum River in Mirpur District of Azad Kashmir and is the seventh largest dam of the world. The terrain was barren, and the dam was in the initial stages of construction. The engineer-in-charge explained the project to us. Although I didn't understand everything about the project, as an engineering student I felt proud that civil engineers could design and build such mammoth edifices for the benefit of mankind. Our hospitable host treated us with an opulent lunch.

From Rawalpindi we headed for Peshawar, the main city of the Northwest Frontier Province or NWFP. It is an ancient city and the oldest city of Pakistan. It is the provincial capital, administrative center and economic hub for the federally controlled tribal region. A semi-autonomous zone, it is located about 30 miles (48 kilometers) to the east of the historic Khyber Pass. Unlike Lahore where we saw many young women in the street, to our surprise, we didn't find a single woman in this city's streets during our short stay for a day or so, signaling that Peshawar was a deeply traditional, ultra-conservative city. In those days, most Muslim women in Dhaka, Lahore and elsewhere would not usually wear hijab (head scarf) in cities. Wearing hijab has become a common practice worldwide these days. I also remember an outstanding lunch at a restaurant in Peshawar. The meal was a well-cooked mutton dish served with naan bread, fresh and hot from the oven, expertly crafted to be soft and the perfect thickness. I was very hungry and relished the meal so much that I still remember the taste.

The next fascinating leg of our trip was to the historic Khyber Pass and a nearby town called Landi Kotal at its western edge. It is a very rugged mountainous area with an arid climate. The Khyber Pass remains the only land route from Afghanistan to the Indian Sub-continent. This was the only route for past invaders from Afghanistan and Central Asia. When we reached the area, I saw some armed locals strolling around. I heard, unlike the rest of Pakistan, these tribal people were autonomous, somewhat lawless and allowed to openly carry guns. I remember one young man carrying a gun asking me in Urdu where I was from. I replied in the broken Urdu that I learned in high school, "I am from East Pakistan speaking Bengali and can't speak in good Urdu." He rebuked, "You must know and speak in Urdu as it's the language of the country." Seeing the attitude of the armed man, I didn't continue the discussion to either correct or educate him about Bengali being the native language of East Pakistan. Instead, I left him quickly.

We reached Landi Kotal, a high point of the region, bordering Afghanistan; it was a totally different experience. There was a market called Landi Kotal Bazar where we found all sorts of inexpensive merchandise. I bought a few things and a cigarette lighter as I would very occasionally smoke after a decent meal or when traveling; smoking was a common practice among young men in those days and to a large extent it continues even today. I gave up the habit when I lived in Chicago in the early 1980s at the insistence of my four-year son Murad, who didn't like my smoking even occasionally. We had lunch at a restaurant, which was really an open food stall as there were no walls. Tables were set under a roof and some out in the open. Along with some of my friends I sat outdoors and ordered their famous *bhuna gosht* (well done meat curry with little gravy). Once again, I noted the slight difference in food culture between East and West Pakistan. The simmering meat was placed on the table in the same pot used for cooking it. So, savoring the large naan placed beside it, I ate directly from the pot. The meat was amazingly delicious and being a good eater, I enjoyed it immensely.

After our visit to the Khyber Pass, we proceeded by train from Peshawar to Karachi, a long way almost 900 miles (1,440 kilometers). We took a stopover at Sukkur, about 600 miles (960 kilometers) from Peshawar, to see the famous Sukkur Barrage also known as Lloyd Barrage. It had been built on the Indus River by the British. This was a striking place to visit and the Barrage was a majestic civil engineering structure worth visiting. The area was very arid with sandy soil totally in contrast to East Pakistan, which was full of rivers and lakes as well as lush green. For lunch, some of us went to a restaurant. We had been missing our typical Bengali meal of plain boiled rice, *dal* (lentil), vegetables, and fish or meat curry.

Thinking that the province of Sind might have some rice, we ordered rice and some other dishes. We ended up somewhat disappointed since there was no plain boiled rice, but a type of fried rice. We satisfied our hunger anyway. We took another train from Sukkur to Karachi, the largest city of Pakistan. As the train passed through desert-like areas, our compartment filled with sand and dust that had been seeping through window cracks. Finally, we reached Karachi. This city began as an old settlement which the British later developed. It was the original capital of Pakistan, before Islamabad. During the partition of India in 1947 many Muslims migrated from India to Karachi. There wasn't much to see as it was not really an historic city. It is the birthplace of Pakistan's founder Muhammad Ali Jinnah. We visited his tomb to pay our respects and I vaguely remember that we visited the famous Clifton Beach and Gandhi Gardens.

A very fascinating side trip was to the historic archeological site of Mohenjo-Daro in the province of Sindh. Built in the 26th century BCE, a UNESCO World Heritage site, it is one of the major ancient cities of the world. It is the site of a highly developed society representing the Indus Valley Civilization. I observed the city's layout was very well planned. Remains of most buildings revealed they were built mostly of fired bricks with some sun-dried mud-brick buildings as well. The city had a provision of public buildings and facilities including public baths and a well-organized wastewater drainage system including covered drains lining the main streets. Clearly, the city had great social organization. There was another ancient city called Harappa in the Punjab province, but we didn't get the chance to visit it.

It was time for us to return to Dhaka. We took a train from Karachi to Lahore about 770 miles (1,230 kilometers) away northeast. From Lahore, we took the return trip to East Pakistan. Traversing India, we reached Calcutta on November 22, 1963 and stayed overnight at the same Tower Hotel, returning with broadened horizons.

The next day, I went for a haircut at a nearby barber shop. I may not have remembered this small detail but that while there, I came to learn that U.S. President John F. Kennedy had been assassinated in Dallas, Texas on November 22, local time, while he was riding in an open car. I was startled to hear this. People at the barber shop were speculating about who might be behind it. One person suggested Pakistan might be behind it since Kennedy was favoring India over Pakistan during the Indo-China War of 1962. The U.S. asked Pakistan to support India, an unthinkable proposition. At the time there was anti-American feeling prevailing in Pakistan as a result.

Continuing our trek towards home, we took a train to Dhaka. While in Benapol, a border town in East Pakistan we went through customs and immigration, the officials there were also talking about Kennedy's assassination. Finally, we reached Dhaka and I felt delighted to be back. After returning to Dhaka I needed a few days to rewind the many memories and reminisce. Eventually I got back into my normal student life. I took no more major trips until going to Canada for higher studies in 1970.

The fourth (final) year flew by in a rush of studies for upper level courses and the final exam. Before the final exam, in the eighth semester, Wahiduddin Sir taught us a course on structural analysis. I briefly alluded to this before. He was teaching us the column analogy method to analyze structures. In structures there are three types of supports: fixed, hinged and roller. In this method, all the structures with fixed and hinged supports were treated in the analysis but not roller supports. So, I asked him in class how rollers are treated in this method. He didn't have an answer, but welcomed the question, and he invited me to his office to discuss it. With his guidance, I found the answer. He was very impressed and when he left for an overseas conference, he asked me to substitute for his third-year class of structural analysis. I enjoyed lecturing without any nervousness even though I was speaking in front of a class for the first time in my life.

CHAPTER 3

YOUNG ADULT IN DHAKA

Finding Life's Trajectory

I graduated from EPUET in 1964, although the results were published in January 1965. I graduated in the first class with my rank near the top. Soon after graduation, Wahiduddin Sir invited me to his office and said, "I would like to have you as a lecturer here, but this year we are not hiring right now. We will hire you as teaching assistant for our new master's program. As soon as we can hire, you will be the first to be appointed as a lecturer. It should not take long. In the meantime, we will give you an independent office and a lecturer's residential flat." I was happy for the opportunity. I moved into my new independent office and nice apartment in a building next to the main entrance of the university. I felt life was treating me very well. My love for books and reading and the confidence I developed in lecturing convinced me that academics was my destiny. I was excited about the prospect of being a lecturer at this prestigious engineering university, the only one in East Pakistan at the time.

Suddenly, in early April, things took a wrong turn for me. One day, I was sitting in Wahiduddin Sir's office and someone by the name of Abdus Salam entered the room. His name had been mentioned before as a graduate from the famous Shibpur Engineering College in West Bengal, India. He had, however graduated in second class. Since he didn't meet the stringent qualifications set by EPUET, he wasn't hired as a lecturer. He was sufficiently qualified to be an instructor at the Dhaka Polytechnic Institute (DPI), governed by the Directorate of Technical Education. At the time, it was headed by Dr. Waqar Ahmed.

I don't recount the full details but based on what I heard around the office, where I was seated with Wahiduddin Sir, he liked Mr. Salam, an engineering graduate of Shibpur Engineering College in West Bengal, India, from where Wahiduddin Sir also graduated before, and had reached out personally to the director of DPI, Dr. Waqar Ahmed requesting help with Mr. Salam's employment. He requested that despite Mr. Salam's second class standing at Shibpur, he be given full salary at DPI with benefits similar to that of an EPUET lecturer, since the pay scale for instructor was low. Mr. Salam went to see Dr. Ahmed, but the request was turned down. Disappointed, Mr. Salam reported this to Wahiduddin Sir in my presence and said, "Sir, you've done enough for me, that's okay, please leave it at that." Wahiduddin Sir, however, was enraged that his request was not honored by Dr. Waqar Ahmed and felt embarrassed in front of Mr. Salam. He impulsively said, "I will hire you as a lecturer here. I will talk with the Vice Chancellor and make it happen." Mr. Salam left the office thanking Wahiduddin Sir.

I was quiet and dumbfounded. I had been promised to be hired as the first lecturer. Wahiduddin Sir sensed it looking at me and said, "I had to do this. We can't hire two people at the same time as the Vice Chancellor would not approve it. But I will hire you very soon and send you to a foreign university for a Ph.D. degree before anybody else." Although I understood the situation, my spirit was somehow broken. I started doubting that I could trust his promise anymore. I left the room and decided to look for a job in the industry, which was very easy to find those days.

I walked into the office of Ammann & Whitney, a renowned international consulting firm. They dealt with transportation systems and had an office at Motijheel Commercial area. I got a job offer the next day. I saw Wahiduddin Sir and told him about my decision and told him I would resign because I wanted industrial experience and the money was good. I didn't feel comfortable confronting him about the real reason I was leaving. He persuaded me to rethink my decision, but I already made up my mind. I joined the firm immediately. Although things worked out well for me later in life as eventually, I did embark upon an academic career, I often thought I had probably taken a wrong turn early in my life.

Unfortunately, my experience at Ammann & Whitney was not good. This firm had separate bridge and highway sections. My employer placed me in the highway section working on the Dhaka-Chittagong under an authoritarian and unfriendly engineer of East Asian origin. I was working on the alignment and layout design of the highway to determine the curves, elevations, exits, ramps, etc. He was a pipe smoker with a stern face and he never smiled. Instead of coaching and training me as a new young professional, he was impatient and expected me to do things right the first time. My workstation was a stool with a drawing board in front of me. He would frequently look over my shoulder to check on my work. Being an accomplished, independent worker by nature, I felt belittled and intimidated. I started resenting and hating his behavior. I missed my nice office room at EPUET, and the dignified, collegial environment of professors.

I became unmindful at work and started thinking of finding another job. I was second guessing my decision to leave EPUET and wondered if I had made a mistake in my haste. Some of my classmates were placed in the larger bridge section and they told me they had nice and friendly American bosses and they enjoyed their work. This made me even more frustrated. At this point, only after a few days of work, my employer told me that my immediate boss was not happy with my performance and they could not keep me anymore.

I told him, "I was not happy with him either and was seriously thinking of leaving this firm as he was rude and treated me very unfairly. Can I be in the bridge section? I enjoy dealing with structures."

He said, "There is no opening there. You should have told me about your preference before."

I didn't pursue it knowing it was useless but still said, "I was not given a choice. I was just placed under this engineer."

In a way, I was relieved and happy that I didn't have to be in that unpleasant environment anymore. Immediately, the same day, I walked into a larger American engineering firm called Louis Berger Inc. It was nearby and had an international reputation. The allied local firm was Consulting Engineers (Pakistan) Ltd. I met Mr. Moqbulur Rahman, Managing Director of the local firm, who, I heard later, came from an aristocratic family. He had a poised personality and treated employees with affection and respect. The firm had a Building Division and a Highway Division. The Building Division was administered by Consulting Engineers (Pakistan) Ltd. and all the employees and supervisors were local. The Highway Division had only one local engineer Abdus Salam, a nice guy. He was working on the layout and alignment design, like what I had briefly done at Ammann & Whitney. He worked under a senior American transportation engineer, but besides him, the rest of the engineers and the supervisors were Americans. Only all the draftsmen were local. I remember the name of one of them; he was called Mr. Sardar, the chief draftsman, a very experienced man with a pleasant personality and leadership qualities.

The entire team was working on the Dhaka-Aricha Highway project. I was placed in the bridge section working on bridges and culverts under the supervision of a senior bridge engineer named Roman Kowalski from the company's East Orange, NJ office. Hank Jongsma was the Chief Bridge Engineer. Mr. Kowalski was a very pleasant and experienced man. Much older than me he treated me as a work friend rather than a subordinate and would occasionally tell me jokes. He was patient and taught me how to design transportation structures. He never failed to give me encouragement when I made mistakes and appreciation when I was right. Once he invited me for an American-style dinner at his large house that he shared in Gulshan area. He lived there with other American engineering colleagues. None of them had their families with them.

Occasionally, I interacted with Mr. Jongsma. There were a few other engineers, all nice people. Mr. Kowalski taught me how to design long span bridges, including some challenging ones. I learned a lot from him. Sometimes he assigned me complex problems which I managed successfully. He was impressed and happy with me and arranged to give me an early raise. I enjoyed the work, liked the people and the environment. My self-esteem went up and I was fully engaged in my work. I also started liking Americans. I liked bridge design so much that I began to think of building my career around it.

I also designed some culverts under Mr. Kowalski's direction. I worked as well for another bridge engineer, Jose Cosio, an equally nice man. He was originally from Peru who joined our office later from the company's East Orange, NJ office. He treated me like friend, and I felt very comfortable with him. Once he had difficulty solving a problem related to the slope of the three-dimensional backfill soil around the wing walls of a culvert. He asked me to do it and he was greatly impressed as

I was able to solve it in a short time that another engineer was struggling with.

I also realized I was most fond of structural design. I knew this even as a student and during my short tenure at EPUET when I taught a structures class. Beyond the technical problem solving, I liked to think about the mystical nature of invisible internal forces that developed in a structure. I was fascinated by the deformations that occur in response to external forces and how these can be captured by mathematical modeling. The intersection of my favorite subjects, namely, Physics, Mechanics, and Mathematics are applied to finding the internal forces and deformations of a real object.

Those happy days didn't last long. In 1965, a war broke out between India and Pakistan. Prior to that, there was a war in 1962 between India and China over disputed territory in the Himalayan region. While world's attention was on the Cuban Missile Crisis, China attacked India that year. While China was winning in the war, President John Kennedy wanted President Ayub Khan to help India against the communist country. Ayub Khan was surprised at this unusual request as the U.S. knew full well that India was Pakistan's arch enemy owing to the Kashmir issue. So, he refused. In 1965, the U.S. stayed neutral that also displeased Pakistanis. Following that in 1967 he published a political autobiography entitled *Friends Not Masters* in which he made a reference to his meeting with President Kennedy. He argued that Pakistan considered America a friend not a master that gave orders for its foreign policy.

His thoughts influenced the sentiments of Pakistani citizens. Pakistan was an ally of the U.S. through two pacts called CENTO and SEATO. The relationship between the U.S. and Pakistan became strained, and Pakistan started questioning the sincerity of the U.S. as a true ally. Meanwhile, China and Pakistan became friendly with India as their common enemy, a position that remains in place until today. Against this backdrop, the 1965 Indo-Pak war became a litmus test for the true nature of the relationship between Pakistan and the U.S. Popular perception in Pakistan was that the U.S. had given tacit support to India by staying neutral.

Under these circumstances, Americans in Pakistan began leaving to return to the U.S. The Highway Division of our office was empty except for me, the other highway engineer Abdus Salam and the draftsmen. I was asked to take charge of the bridge section temporarily.

I moved to the chair of Hank Jongsma and became the interim Chief Bridge Engineer reviewing and continuing all the work. Despite being a junior bridge engineer, I was the only one in the entire office who knew about the bridges and culverts being designed for the ongoing Dhaka-Aricha Highway project. Once I even met with a senior highway engineer from the government to explain the project.

The departure of the American engineers created a financial crisis for Consulting Engineers (Pakistan) Ltd. There was not much work to be done, so I was given an assignment for a project from the Building Division. Projects from this division were led by senior local engineers. Even though a few American engineers returned eventually, the damage was done. I found that out the hard way when the paycheck bounced one month. I showed it to a director of the firm who dealt with such matters. He looked embarrassed and wrote me a personal check telling me this was just a temporary thing. I thought it was time to get back to the job hunt. While checking the newspaper employment section, I found a prominent advertisement for Assistant Executive Engineer at the State Bank of Pakistan. The position was considered a Class I officer. Since it was the central bank of Pakistan the job was secure and stable. I applied but did not get an interview letter.

One day in late May of 1966, a friend of mine came to see me at my office to socialize during lunch time. He told me he had just come from an interview with the State Bank of Pakistan. He wondered why I had not been there since he saw my name on a list of interviewees. I told him that I never got an interview letter. He said they were still interviewing. Since their office was nearby, I rushed there and told the receptionist at the front desk about my situation. He told me that the committee just finished the interviews and were now deliberating. I requested that he go in and tell them I was there. He did so and came out with good news, would grant me an interview.

I went in and found a few people, mostly senior bank officials and two engineers – Mr. M. M. Hossain, Director of Engineering from the Bank headquarters in Karachi and Mr. Abid Reza Choudhury, local Resident Engineer. They asked me some technical questions that I was able to answer. At the end, they wanted to know how much my present salary was. They said since I worked for a private firm, my current salary was more than the fixed scale that the Bank could offer. Without thinking much, I replied as an idealist, "Money is not everything in life." I learned much later in life that money might not be everything but was an important thing to have in order to live a comfortable independent life. I didn't know how to negotiate a salary at the time. I was given an offer, accepted it and joined the Bank. Mr. Rahman was disappointed but graciously told me to come back anytime if I wanted to.

I was given the responsibility of supervising the construction of the large two-story Deputy Governor's bungalow in Gulshan. A small office was built on the construction site. I reported to Mr. Abid Reza Choudhury, Resident Engineer, who was a retired, well-respected engineer in government service. He was the father of Dr. Jamilur Reza Choudhury, a professor at EPUET and later, a prominent structural engineer in Bangladesh.

Construction of the main six-story State Bank building designed by architect Saleem Thariani was nearing completion. It was being supervised by Abdul Majid Khan, Executive Engineer, a refugee from Bihar, India, and his team. I interacted with Mr. Thariani on many occasions and found him to be a very competent architect as well as a fine and smart man with a friendly and gregarious personality. I was living in a wood-framed, tin shed home employing cemented floor at 109 Rayer Bazar, Road No. 15 (extension) bordering Dhanmondi. At the persuasion of my mother I was instrumental in buying the property and supervising the construction as a temporary structure to ensure possession of the land. My mother felt we should have a piece of land in Dhaka as she liked the City of Dhaka very much. I used to go to my job site from that house.

My second brother Mir Masoom Ali had already left for Canada to pursue post-graduate studies at the University of Toronto, leaving behind his wife Firoza Ali (Lina) and their three very young daughters. They all joined him later, once my brother got settled. My sister-in-law was spending time shuttling between my parents' home in Patuakhali and her parents' home in Rangpur. To make life easier before leaving for Canada, she asked if she and her daughters and a girl servant could live with me in the Dhaka house. I agreed to her request although there was not enough space in my house. In an effort to make everyone more comfortable, I tried to get a larger apartment in the newly built staff quarters in Banani near my job site. The quarters were exclusively for married Class II officers of the Bank, so I was disqualified since I was a bachelor. I talked to my boss and some senior officials and argued that if I could live at Banani quarters, near where I had a site office, I could avoid a long commute and readily supervise the construction of the bungalow. To my relief, I did get an apartment at 4F-3 State Bank Officers' Quarters, Banani and moved there with my brother's family. We lived there together for a few months before they left for Canada.

The construction of the bungalow in Gulshan was completed on time. I was moved to the Bank's main office at Sadarghat. Once the Bank's new office building was completed in Motijeel Commercial Area, I moved to that building on the third floor in the engineering department. I headed a large technical staff who were involved in maintaining the bank's buildings, residential quarters, etc. The Bank would subsidize employees rent if employees preferred to rent privately. Employees also qualified for loan if they wished to buy plots of land to build homes. In all such cases, they needed certification from me. I was also in charge of renovation, repairs and general maintenance of all the Bank's buildings. Although I enjoyed a great deal of authority and felt like a "boss" the position was overly bureaucratic. I found no creative outlet in the position and felt like the job was too easy. My only task was to oversee the work of a large technical staff. I would report to the local Manager of the Bank. The good part was that the bank gave free living quarters and bonuses before the two Eid festivals including other monetary and medical fringe benefits.

A multistory Annex Building was being planned near the new Bank building. I felt that my skills would be put to better use on that new construction project. The Resident Engineer who was dealing with new construction was no longer my boss, the manager was my boss now instead.

I put in a request for working on the forthcoming Annex Building. He directed me to Mr. Abdul Majid Khan, the Executive Engineer, a very sly man with a silver tongue. I approached Mr. Khan, who was lukewarm to the idea and told me I was hired to oversee maintenance of buildings, rather than new construction since he didn't need an additional engineer.

The Director of Engineering from the head office in Karachi would come to Dhaka from time to time. I approached him about the new construction position, but he also told me to talk with Mr. Khan, which I did. He declined a second time, to add me to his team. I realized he had also overseen the main office building construction. Over the course of that project he had developed his own team. As such, he didn't want to insert a newcomer or outsider like me into his well-knit team. They were a hand-picked few and loyal to him. Clearly, I was not very happy about it.

When my sister-in-law left for Canada to join my brother, I had the entire large apartment to myself. I lived with my servant in the quiet neighborhood of Banani, a suburb far from Dhaka city proper. I had plenty of free time spent on reading books about Bengali and English literature, History, Geology, politics, etc. and socializing with visitors.

It was at this time that I began to consider going to the U.S. or Canada for higher education. I thought I should get married before going. As was the custom there, my mother and sisters were looking for a suitable match for me. I realized that if I would spend the time, I could find quite a few suitable matches. Although arranged marriages (I prefer to call them negotiated marriages as there are a few steps in the process) were common in those days, I had a quixotic mind because of my love for beauty, music and literature. I had some emotive attributes in my personality, and inexplicably, I found some girls attractive but not others, despite each being equally pretty. I heard the famous adage: "beauty is in the eye of the beholder," the universal truth of which I experienced firsthand.

Beauty truly can't be measured; it emanates from a face in an incomprehensible way. I didn't know then what beauty really meant other than seeing and feeling it. Later in my life when I was writing about aesthetics of buildings for a book, I studied the subject of beauty. Philosopher George Santayana defined beauty as "pleasure objectified." Thus, beauty is something that gives us inherent pleasure in our mind and soothes our eyes when we see an object, a scenery, or a living being. It is therefore subjective. It is uncertain what will give us pleasure, although the associated pleasure once achieved, is objectified. Poets and composers of lyrics write about the beauty of women and artists draw them in many different ways. No wonder there is something called beauty contests for women, but not for men. Philosopher David Hume aptly made the argument that beauty, "is no quality in things themselves: it exists merely in the mind which contemplates them; and each mind contemplates a different beauty."

The question I asked myself was, "Can I find true love with someone, who would love me too, enough that we could stay together, in constant love throughout our lifetime?" I knew if I stayed a bachelor for long enough, I probably could find a soul mate along the way. But the probability of finding the *one and only* soul mate was very slim. It could be an endless search. Even if I was immensely attracted to some girl, I might never know if she would be my ultimate soul mate until I married her, had children, raised them until we became empty nesters.

I was perplexed by internal questions. When our love would be unaccompanied so much by lust, would we still be bound together by love like before? Or even more? Another indication of true love was mutual understanding, faithfulness, and loyalty. At the time of marriage, how could we know all these untested attributes? Ideal soul mates were not guaranteed in life, despite what some may think, it was a gamble. Perhaps the answer is to marry and patiently work and nourish love to be soul mates and kindred spirits. It was too much to think about for a young man like me. So, I decided to marry whoever came to my mind.

When I was about eight years old, one day some kids and I were trying to pluck fruits off a tree at a friend's house in Patuakhali. I saw a little girl standing on the front steps of her parents' house next to my friend's house. I had a clear view of her.

For some reason, I liked her face and posture. That scene stayed with me. I knew her name was Dora. But that was it. When I was in the final year of my engineering degree program in Dhaka about 12 years later, I had a captivating dream. I saw and recognized the same girl, now a beautiful adult, standing on a boat out at sea, facing me and approaching the shore towards where I was standing. She was dressed beautifully as a bride and looked stunning. I was standing on the sandy beach and she came very close to me looking down bashfully. I woke up in the middle of the night and wondered why I saw her as I had not really been thinking at all about her. When, in late 1967, I was wondering whom I might marry, I remembered that dream and realized she was dormant in my heart, but I missed her in the outside world. I decided that I should marry her. I told my mother about my intention.

In March 1968, my dream literally came true and I married that girl from Patuakhali. Her name is Morsheda (Dora), the fourth child of Mr. Serajuddin Khan and Mrs. Umme Bilkis Khorsheda Banu. My father-in law hailed from an aristocratic family in *Kaunia* in Barisal district. He was a mild-mannered handsome man and a good friend of my father. The tale of his ancestry goes as follows... Prince Shah Shuja, the son of Emperor Shah Jahan of India, fled to Arakan (now called Rakhine) in Burma, over a power struggle with his brother Prince Alamgir (later known as Emperor Aurangzeb). The fraternal dispute was for the throne of the Mughal Empire in Delhi. A close friend of Shah Shuja by the name of Niamat Ali Khan decided to stay back near the Shuzabad Fort in *Nolchiti*. His descendant, Nuruddin Khan visited *Kaunia* where the local people liked him so much that they requested that Nuruddin stay there. He complied with their request and decided to settle and eventually built a brick mansion. His son Kutubuddin Khan built more buildings and a mosque. The family established a *Zamindary* (landlordship) in the village and came to be known as *Mian bari* (home of the Mians).

My father-in-law had a successful law practice in Patuakhali. He was involved in many social activities, and especially facilitated women's education through his engagement in various capacities, particularly the role of Secretary of the local girls' school administration. My mother-in-law was the daughter of a police officer hailing from *Shailakupa* in Jessore district. She was a widely respected housewife of Patuakhali who raised seven daughters and two sons. She was an excellent cook and was renowned in the town for that and for her many recipes.

My marriage with Dora was solemnized at Dhaka's Paribagh Mosque on March 3, 1968. As was the custom, she went back to her father's home in Patuakhali immediately following the betrothal. I went there and on July 7th after a wedding reception, hosted by her parents, she and I came away together to Dhaka. Our new married life had commenced. I soon found that she was a good homemaker and a great cook, as well as a pious girl.

On April 8, 1969, we were blessed with our first child, a beautiful daughter. We named her Ifat Maqsuda Ali. Later, while in the U.S. her nickname became Eve. When she grew a little, she would see me off from her seat in her mother's lap when I left for work in the morning. When I returned, she would wait for me and stretch her tiny hands towards me to climb into my lap. At night when I was lying in bed on my back, she lay on my chest comfortably facing me. It was an exhilarating feeling of being a father for the first time. Around this time, I was given a very nice and spacious apartment at Bank Quarters on Minto Road, a posh area of Dhaka, which was for Class I officers.

In 1969, an important world event took place symbolizing a major milestone in human achievement. Apollo 11, landed to deliver the first humans on the Moon, American astronauts Neil Armstrong followed by Buzz Aldrin 20 minutes later, on July

20, 1969. As part of NASA's efforts to publicize the accomplishments of the Apollo program the three Apollo astronauts were dispatched on a goodwill tour of 24 cities across the world. On October 25, 1969, the crew arrived in Dhaka.

People everywhere lined up along streets and building tops, anywhere they could stand, to catch a rare glimpse of them. I was in my office in the Bank building facing the street. I saw them in the open convertible car and could see them clearly approaching our direction. Their car slowly made its way along the street with the three men and their wives waving. It was a memorable sight and is one of my most enduring memories. Mr. Armstrong was a reserved man and stayed out of sight since his landing on the moon. He was an alumnus of Purdue University at West Lafayette, Indiana. As a member of a Phi Delta Theta he would often visit that campus. Many years later in late 1990s my son Murad, who was a student at the same university and a member of the same fraternity met and chatted with him at a fraternity event.

Toward the end of Field Marshall Ayub Khan's rule, (he was self-promoted from General) in 1969, the political turmoil reached its peak. Before this, after defeating Ms. Fatima Jinnah in the presidential elections of 1965, his standing began to decline amid allegations of widespread electoral fraud. His peace agreement to end the 1965 war with India was entered into without any visible gain. Many Pakistanis took this as softness and a perplexing compromise. It was generally viewed unfavorably by the people. Consequently, popular discontent coupled with rising food prices resulted in widespread social and political unrest. Massive countrywide demonstrations began and increased dramatically from 1967 onwards. To quell this, in 1968, Ayub Khan promoted a "Decade of Development" campaign to bolster support for his rule. Ironically people perceived this campaign as a manifestation of his plans to remain in power longer, as a life-long president.

Around the same time, the Pakistani government filed an Agartala conspiracy case. The case, brought in early 1968, charged Sheikh Mujibur Rahman, the leader of the Awami League party and 34 others with conspiracy to begin an armed rebellion for East Pakistan to secede from Pakistan. The government also charged that there was collusion from India. The group was arrested and jailed. The Bengalis however, viewed this as an attempt by the Pakistani government to suppress the ongoing autonomy movement through a six-point demand in East Pakistan and started protesting in the streets against it.

Amidst all this chaos the conspiracy case was withdrawn in February 1969. Later in the same year, over political unrest in Pakistan, Ayub Khan resigned and handed power to General Yahya Khan. Ayub's legacy remains mixed. He is credited with ushering in ostensive economic prosperity but is also criticized for overseeing the first incursion by the army into civilian politics. He is criticized for concentrating corrupt wealth in a few hands and for introducing policies that would lead to the break-up of Pakistan. Once Sheikh Mujib was released, the Agartala case was viewed as a vindication of a concocted attempt to suppress Bengalis. New political slogans of "Joi Bangla" (Victory to Bengal) emerged. To maintain order, General Yahya Khan declared martial law in the country. The political disturbance and instability made me think hard about the country's future and my own future in it.

In late 1969, I decided to pursue higher studies. I thought this might be a good time for me to satisfy my aspirations and go abroad without delay. I recalled how I had enjoyed my short stint as a teaching assistant in EPUET and longed to join academia again.

Throughout my stay in Dhaka, I would frequently go to the United States Information Service (USIS) at Segunbagicha, the British Council on Fuller Road near EPUET campus, and the Dhaka Public Library at Nilkhet. The USIS and British Council had excellent libraries that would bring the West close to me through newspapers, magazines, and books. The Public Library also had a large collection of books in Bengali and English that opened the world for me. At USIS I had access to resources related to several American universities. In those days, it was hard to find information about foreign universities.

I spent most my time researching different universities and their Civil Engineering departments. I came up with the short list of Stanford University, University of Illinois at Urbana-Champaign, Carnegie-Mellon University, University of Pittsburg, and a few others. I applied to all of these. Not having the benefit of internet at the time, it was difficult to do the research accurately. In Canada I had my oldest brother, Dr. Mir Maswood Ali, who was a professor of Statistics at the University of Western Ontario, London, Ontario and my brother-in-law (second older sister's husband) Dr. Ehsanes Saleh, who was a professor of Statistics at Carleton University, Ottawa, Ontario. So, I also applied to a couple of universities in Canada and got accepted at Carleton University, Nova Scotia Technical University in Halifax, Nova Scotia and University of Manitoba in Winnipeg, Manitoba. My first letter of admission came from Professor Alan Strehler of Carnegie Mellon University in Pittsburg. I also was accepted by other U.S. universities like University of Pittsburgh and Stanford University. My applications for admission in the U.S. and Canada were all accepted, except the University of Illinois at Urbana-Champaign where ironically, I later became a professor and built a career.

My problem was that I had no assurance of a full assistantship. Some universities offered a small amount of funds which would be inadequate for me. I realized later that after arriving on campus it was easier to arrange financial support, immediately or after a semester. My brother-in-law had a friend in the Architecture department who told him that once I went to Carleton University, he would be able to support me from his grant money. With such assurance in mind and comforted by the fact that my sister was there, I decided to attend Carleton University.

I applied and was granted study leave from the State Bank of Pakistan to pursue higher studies. It came towards the end of September 1970. I was getting ready to leave for Canada, but ran into some obstacles, both practical and emotional. I realized I had to get a student visa from Islamabad, the capital of Pakistan, where the Canadian High Commission was located. There was no consular office in Dhaka. This meant I had to fly there and apply in person. In addition to the cost involved for the trip I was running out of time as classes started at Carleton University on September 21 and I was already late. Instead, I decided to take a risk and enter Canada as a visitor and apply for a visa once there. This was a route taken by some others that I knew. By then I had a wife in advanced stage of pregnancy and a one-year old baby, whom I would be leaving behind with the expectation that they would join me soon when I got settled in Canada.

Most difficult of all, was leaving my elderly parents behind, knowing they didn't want me to go since I was taking care of them. I saw the disappointed looks on their faces as they felt another son was slipping away from them. I always had a deep love, obedience and close emotional tie with my parents. I had looked after them like an elder son catering to their needs as my two other older brothers were already abroad. I was particularly attached to my dearest mother who was in Dhaka at the time of my departure. She discouraged me but also perhaps understood my mind as she always promoted education. I realize now how far-sighted she was as she cautioned me that it was not a good idea to be a minority member in a foreign country. I was torn and felt bad inside for Dora and for my beloved elderly parents. I also knew that to be a happy person in my future life, I had to attain my cherished goal, achieve higher degrees all while I was still young. I had three sisters and a younger brother still there*.

Seeing my passion my parents realized they couldn't stop me and reluctantly agreed. I told them -- and I was sincere about it -- I would return after finishing my education overseas. But the looks on their faces haunted me then and later. When I visited my father in Patuakhali where he was by himself at the time, he pleaded with me to stay saying that I could do just as well in my life staying in my own country. I remained unconvinced and held on to the burning desire to go to Canada. My father was a soft-hearted person and told me he didn't want to go to the motor launch station to bid goodbye to me. I knew he didn't want to see me off there, in public, because of the agony he was feeling inside. Instead, my uncle who was there at the time, accompanied me to the station by rickshaw. It was a bright and sunny autumn morning. My father stood solemnly in the front verandah of the house with a gloomy face, staring at me as the rickshaw was leaving. He looked helpless. I really felt bad. I was torn thinking to myself how I could be so callous to leave my parents who depended on me just to fulfill my selfish desire. While on the rickshaw I continued to remember the scene of my father standing looking at me sadly that haunted me even many years later. Once I reached the station, I was seated in the upper level cabin of the launch; soon after unexpectedly I saw my father entering the cabin. He could not bring himself to stay at home while his son was leaving for a distant foreign country. He wanted to see me one more time while I was still nearby. He stayed for a short time and left with my uncle after a while, after lovingly hugging me.

---

* One sister and my younger brother also left for North America later after I left.

In Dhaka I got a jolt about my forthcoming trip to Canada at a wrong time. Because I planned to go to Canada as a tourist, I had to buy a two-way ticket from Swissair, departing on Friday, September 25 for Ottawa via Montreal. The night before I left for Canada, I got a telegram from my eldest brother in Canada telling me not to attempt entry without a student visa. He was just being cautious and meant well, but it was too late for me to stop the process. His message only served to increase my tension. Things seemed very uncertain moving from my known world to uncharted terrain.

My mother, who was in Dhaka at that time, my wife, my servant Kader, and a few relatives and well-wishers came to see me off at the airport. I looked at my mother, my wife and my baby daughter one last time before entering through the gate not knowing when I would see them next as overseas visits were expensive particularly for students and not as convenient those days like now.

I proceeded to the airplane, black suitcase in hand with its repaired lock that I had got from my younger brother in haste who left it at my apartment before joining his job in Chittagong. I had quickly gotten it repaired, filled it with my clothes and a few belongings and only 20 Canadian dollars in cash in my pocket, the State Bank limit allowed at that time to be taken out of country. I boarded the Pakistan International Airline (PIA) flight to leave for Karachi en route to Montreal, my port of entry in Canada. I still have that suitcase for its sentimental value, and I showed it to my children. That suitcase and the $20 were all I had with me when I came all the way from East Pakistan to the distant shore of Canada. I was burdened with all the anxieties of separation and felt a piercing emotional pain in my chest when I left.

PART TWO
O CANADA

Maple Leaf Land

CHAPTER 4

OTTAWA AND LONDON, ONTARIO

Separation Anxiety; Wandering Life

Once the airplane started moving on the runway, I felt the pang of separation anxiety. I had not ever flown before this. Within minutes the plane took off and I looked through the window from my window seat. As the plane was ascending, I saw the landscape, the *Buriganga* River, lakes, ponds, buildings, slums, and streets of Dhaka gradually diminishing in size. In addition to leaving my near and dear ones, I felt the additional pain of separation from my dear motherland. I realized how much I loved my country. Soon the plane was flying over the countryside and then over India. My eyes became watery with tears for leaving my old parents who were so dependent on me, my pregnant wife, a baby daughter and my country, and I tried to suppress it. The stewardess came to ask me what I would like to eat and drink. I declined as I was not in any mood for eating, even though I was a good eater.

By the time I got to my hotel room in Karachi, I was very hungry. I went to have my dinner served outdoor under tents. I saw a blonde Caucasian girl singing an English song on a stage using a microphone to entertain the diners. I loved the music and felt boost in my mood. The next morning, I boarded a Swissair flight headed for Montreal via Zurich. I had to disembark from the aircraft at the airport for a short time.

This marked the first time I had stepped on the ground of a western country. I sat on a bench at the airport and looked around. I was struck by the discipline of people and cleanliness of the airport and its surrounds. I boarded the plane again. Soon we were flying over the Atlantic Ocean. Seated next to me was a man and his wife. I started a conversation once he told me that he didn't like flying and the noise of the plane made him uncomfortable. He also told me he was a car mechanic from Greece and was going to Canada looking for more high-paying jobs. In the plane high above the ocean, Dhaka became more and more distant in my mind but didn't totally fade away.

I landed in Montreal's Mirabel International Airport on the same date, Friday, September 25 as I gained a day traveling west and crossing the International Dateline. I went through immigration and customs with the fear that I might be sent back. However, the immigration officer, a young lady, who took me to her office room, was very nice and warm. After briefly hearing that I had a job in Dhaka, was on leave and would like to spend time with my brother and sister who lived in Canada, she immediately stamped my passport without further questions and told me, "Welcome to Canada, I am giving you a visa for six months. Enjoy your stay here. You will like this country." I thanked her and felt relieved. After I went through customs, I came out through the gate trying to figure out how to get my connecting flight to Ottawa to join my sister. To my pleasant surprise, I found my brother Dr. Mir Maswood Ali and my sister Shahid Ara and her husband Dr. Ehsanes Saleh were waiting for me outside the gate!

While walking through the airport I looked around and viewed the same kind of discipline and cleanliness as I saw in

Zurich. On our way to Ottawa from the airport we stopped at a service center to take a bite. I was hungry, so I tried a hamburger and french fries. These were new foods for me, but I liked them.

While my brother was driving his large car, popular at that time because of cheap gasoline, I was looking outside, making my first impressions of the new world around me. This was a totally new and different landscape than I was used to in East Pakistan. Miles and miles of empty space was traversed at high speed. There were hardly any other cars on the highway driving at high speed like my brother's. I could see very little sign of people or habitation on either side of the highway. It was late September-- autumn or fall as it's called there; all the trees assumed beautiful hues of orange and crimson, very delightful and soothing for the eyes. It all looked awesome and surreal to me. The picturesque landscape around me gave me an exhilarating sensation. The highway surface was so smooth, and the car had such a great shock-absorbing system that I felt like I was in an airplane flying in the air with occasional gentle bumps.

At my sister's house in Ottawa I rested a little and had dinner of chicken curry. My sister wanted to know if the farm-raised chicken was palatable to my taste as we had only pasture-raised organic chickens in East Pakistan in those days. I said "Yes. It is delicious." I was never picky with food and generally enjoyed eating any kind of food. Also, I always liked and still do like meat, fish, vegetables and fruits, as well as yogurt, ice cream, and other desserts. Once I was settled, my two favorite desserts were cheesecakes and apple pies. All my life I have been a good eater, but not an overeater. After dinner my brother took me out to a restaurant for coffee. Later, I found out he was fond of going out for coffee, a habit he developed when he was in London, England. At the restaurant he gave me some advice about how to adjust to the new environment and to student life since I had been working before for a few years. He drove from London, Ontario to

Ottawa to receive me at Montreal. He left for London the next day. I didn't sleep well at night due to jet lag.

My sister had a teenage daughter Isme, who was born in Patuakhali and two sons Resve and Bab. I liked them a lot. It was good to see them. After resting over the weekend, my brother-in-law drove me to the Carleton University campus Monday morning, where he was a professor, and left me off at the Civil Engineering department. I met my adviser Professor Gary Suter, who assigned me my courses. I told him my visa situation and requested that he give me a letter confirming that I was admitted to the university and was eligible to get a student visa. Later I went to the immigration department in Ottawa and handed in the letter with anxiety about how they would treat it. A female elderly officer went through my passport and read my adviser's letter. She issued me a student visa without asking any question and told me, "This is a beautiful country. Settle down here after you finish your studies; you will like it." I was taken aback to see how welcoming Canadians were. I recalled I had experienced the same treatment at Montreal airport.

I started living with my sister in her home. At one point I heard the beautiful Canadian national anthem "O Canada." I liked its lyric and tune. I also liked the Canadian flag with a maple leaf. My sister was very social and had a few good friends. She would occasionally throw dinner parties at her home and the place would be lively which I liked. Isme could sing and has a beautiful voice. Occasionally she would sing which I really enjoyed.

Soon my short spell of tailwinds and buoyed mood was overtaken by headwinds that started blowing and my jovial mood changed. I found out that the verbal commitment for financial support was no longer available to me since I arrived late. No funding was in sight in my department that semester as all assistantships were already allocated. My delayed arrival hit me hard.

So, my brother-in-law co-signed a bank loan for me. I was committed to pay it off, which I did later. I also realized that by missing one week of classes, I really missed a lot as things moved fast here. I felt all the more behind since I had been out of touch with studies for about six years. I already got some homework assignments which I didn't know about, one of them in a course on computers, which I never learned anything about at EPUET. And to top it all off, I still had some jet lag.

I also experienced culture shock. I noticed that in the post-hippie era, local male students had long hair and all, male or female, wore bell bottom jeans. It was a totally different social environment. On top of all this, I was preoccupied with thoughts of my parents, my wife with advanced pregnancy and my baby daughter. I was not feeling very well. I started asking myself: did I make a mistake by coming here hastily and unprepared? Should I go back to Dhaka? I could still do so before getting too engaged here, I had the return ticket anyway, maybe I should come back at a later time when I was well prepared? I could tell my relatives, friends, and co-workers that I didn't like it there in Canada, so I came back.

But then, I also asked myself the following questions: can I face everybody there when I return? Wasn't this a defeatist attitude that I might regret later? What if people thought that although I was a good student I couldn't cope with the pressure of study in Canada? Wouldn't it hurt my self-esteem and pride? I passionately loved studies and the academic environment, but my mind was in turmoil as if there was a storm raging inside and I could not concentrate on anything. I remembered my past boss Roman Kowalski in Dhaka who taught me practical bridge design, who was at East Orange, NJ near New York City, and who liked me so much. I thought perhaps I could get a job there, get settled and then go to school after that. So, I wrote a letter to him seeking a job with the firm. He promptly replied that because of a mild recession the firm was not hiring now and asked me to contact him after six months.

Despite my internal doubts and struggle, I was a risk-taker and adventurer by nature. I decided to go to East Orange and meet Mr. Kowalski there anyway. I called him beforehand since by now I had his phone number and told him about my plan. He was surprised but didn't discourage me. I told my sister and brother-in-law with whom I was staying and boarded a greyhound bus for Montreal en route to New York. During the trip my mind was wandering but I also enjoyed the night journey and stops at different places. I reached New York in the morning and took another bus, much later to East Orange. Mr. Kowalski came to the bus station to receive me and put me up at a Holiday Inn. The next morning, he came again to pick me up and took me to his office, where I met a few engineers whom I knew from the Dhaka office. I went around the office but could not secure a position despite Mr. Kowalski's efforts as there was simply no opening.

Disheartened, I returned. On my way back, I went to the Empire State Building and took a brief tour inside it. The tall skyscrapers in Manhattan were awe-inspiring. I took in a panoramic view of the skyline and felt uplifted. Upon my return to Ottawa, my soul-searching started again. I was attending classes, working on assignments but could not fully devote myself up to the task at hand.

In October, some political unrest started in Canada. Tension between French and English Canadians had been brewing for a long time, since the end of the 19th century. The province of Quebec was almost totally French, distinct in its language, traditions, and culture. They always felt like a vanquished people and fostered some degree of resentment against the political and economic domination of the English Canadians. This came to a head almost at the same time I came to Canada from East Pakistan, where, ironically, similar tensions were smoldering, although of a different nature and scale. In the traditional parties, opinions ranged from a demand for a special status for Quebec to support for separation and independence. An active minority of leftist Montrealers broke with the Liberal Party and began promoting total independence as a first step to social change. Their efforts resulted in the establishment of the Parti Quebecois, which advocated secession from the confederation. Under Rene Levesque, this party won a quarter of the popular votes.

Other extremist social revolutionaries resorted to terrorism. Bombings began in 1963 and continued sporadically. Most French and English Canadians vehemently disapproved of these actions. In October 1970 a terrorist group, the Front de Libération du Québec (Quebec Liberation Front), kidnapped the British trade commissioner, James Cross, and Quebec's labor minister, Pierre LaPorte who was subsequently murdered. Quebec's government asked for federal intervention, prompting enactment of the War Measures Act, which suspended the usual civil liberties. Subsequently some 500 people were arrested, and the Prime Minister, Pierre Trudeau, ordered troops into Quebec.

The Canadian public generally approved of the bold act, but there were very few criminal convictions, apart from those accused of the murder of LaPorte. Trudeau showed great leadership during the crisis. I watched this strong and charismatic leader on television; he left a long-lasting impression on me. A strong federalist and a member of the former Prime Minister Lester Pearson's cabinet, he was elected leader of the Liberals after Pearson led the party to a decisive victory in Canada and Quebec. Trudeau's rule was greatly personal, his ideas clear, precise, and inflexible. Trudeau dominated the political history of Canada through most of the period from 1968 until the early 1980's. Quebec remains an autonomous province of Canada to this day due to his and his successors' capable leadership. I could not help comparing this with the situation in Pakistan where the short-sighted and incapable leadership of the military and politicians eventually led to the secession of East Pakistan.

My brother from London, Ont. came to know of my vacillating mental state. He came to Ottawa as any loving brother would, to persuade me to stay and forget about returning home. He told me he would arrange to bring Dora thinking that it would give me some mental peace and stability. But that didn't help. My heart was not there anymore. After a lot of fretting, I finally decided to withdraw from my degree program and return home. I told my adviser, who was surprised and advised me to rethink. But nothing could stop me at that time. So, after a lapse of about a month since my arrival to Ottawa, I withdrew and became a visitor again.

My second brother Dr. Mir Masoom Ali in Muncie, IN in the U.S., who was a professor of Statistics at Ball State University there, invited me to go there for a change before I returned to Dhaka. So, I boarded a greyhound bus once again for a long trip and went to Muncie. My brother came to receive me at a small bus station at night in a dark desolate location. I had many good times there with my brother and my sister-in-law as well as their kids. My brother had several friends and he would take me to their homes for social visits. As I had made a firm decision to return home, I didn't have to deal with my vexing anxieties any longer.

Since I had no longer any studies and no office to go, I had a plenty of free time. To overcome my lack of activity and the associated indolence, I used to go to the library of Ball State University. I enjoyed being there, it felt so peaceful in the quiet environment of the library; I felt at ease. Occasionally, I would look up at things pinned on the notice board near the ground floor lobby. These were mostly about graduate degree programs at other universities, jobs for graduating students, and short courses. The last item caught my attention. One day I saw an ad for a short course of few weeks at another university, related to building construction. I thought it might not be a bad idea to take the course, at least I would return home with some credentials from the U.S. I called them and found out all I had to do was to attend classes and there was no examination. That didn't sound good to me as there was no challenge in it. I asked my brother about it, who told me that this might be an easy way out, but I should actually pursue a master's degree. I agreed and quickly dropped the idea.

〜✛✛〜

Some historic events were taking place in East Pakistan during this time. On November 13, 1970, tidal waves and storm surges hit the shores of the Ganges Delta, wreaking fatal damage on the people of East Pakistan. A 100-mph (160-km/h) tropical cyclone spurred the deadly tidal wave of ocean water causing catastrophic flash floods that washed over scores of coastal islands and destroyed the densely populated delta region. It was the worst natural disaster in the region's recorded history and 20th century's worst calamity by cyclone. It made landfall on November 12 and raged the strongest on November 13 with the resulting storm surge of more than 20 feet (6 meters) high topped by huge tidal waves, washing over offshore islands carried ocean water many miles inland. The storm and flood destroyed the entire infrastructure of the country's southern coast and killed an estimated 500,000 people, though some researchers estimated that the death count was more than a million.

This catastrophe happened when the autonomy movement was in full swing in East Pakistan. President Yahya Khan was passing through Dhaka Airport from a trip abroad in the wake of the disaster. When asked by a reporter if he would go to the devastated areas to see his people's condition, he declined. This lack of empathy for his fellow countrymen and the subsequent failure of the Pakistani government to respond quickly to the crisis galvanized the Bengali people. They understood that their nationalist movement, based on the six-point autonomy plan, was in fact correct as the Pakistani government didn't care for them. This made Sheikh Mujib, the leader of the movement, even more popular.

On December 7, 1970, a general election was held in Pakistan. Most of the East Pakistanis voted for the Awami League securing 160 seats, whereas Mr. Zulfiqar Ali Bhutto's Pakistan People's Party secured only 81 seats out of the total of 138 seats from West Pakistan allotted for the National Assembly. This was the first democratic general election of Pakistan based on adult franchise, since its independence from British rule. Bhutto's votes were from West Pakistan, and the votes there were divided among some other rightist parties, lowering the vote count for his party. The election was an indication how divided the nation was. Although the election results were not to Bhutto's liking, General Yahya Khan initially declared that Sheikh Mujib would be the next Prime Minister of Pakistan. However, a highly ambitious Bhutto and some others in West Pakistan were not comfortable with the results, leading to some confusion and political instability in the country.

Meanwhile, in early January of 1971, while still in Muncie I got a letter from my sister-in-law Moshira (Tora) that Dora gave birth to another beautiful daughter in Patuakhali on December 23, 1970. My father-in-law named her Jinat (nickname Jinni). I was delighted but felt bad that I could not see her immediately and didn't even know when I would see her. It was a holiday season in the U.S. and Canada due to Christmas and the New Year.

Ball State University didn't have an engineering program. So, I felt I could go back to Ottawa and perhaps take some technical courses there before returning to Dhaka. I left for Ottawa via Toronto, where a friend of my brother, Satyendra Kalra, was working on his Ph.D. in Aerospace Engineering at the University of Toronto. Following my brother's instructions, I stayed with them at their apartment.

During the daytime Mr. Kalra took me with him to his office in the Space Research Institute. I went to the library and found a lot of books on Mathematics, Physics, and engineering. Although these were not meant for light reading, I enjoyed reading them anyway. I started reading with concentration in the quietness of the library and learned some advanced mathematical topics. It was good mental exercise. I felt myself engrossed in these books on Aerospace Engineering -- something new for me. Mr. Kalra asked me later if I was bored in the library. I said, "Not at all. Actually, I enjoyed being there and reading books that I never saw before."

The Kalras had a little son Vinay. At night I went to watch a Hindi movie at a local theatre. After a short stay and enjoying the curry-like vegetable dishes prepared by his wife Kusum Kalra (Mr. and Mrs. Kalra were vegetarians) and the hospitality of the Kalras, I was ready to return to Ottawa. In Toronto, I visited the University of Toronto campus, went to the Civil Engineering department and talked with a professor about their program out of curiosity. Because of the holiday season there were very few people there. I also visited some buildings in Toronto and was amazed by the several skyscrapers and Toronto City Hall, not a tall building but a remarkable architectural masterpiece.

Upon my return to Ottawa I thought as I had a one-year leave, it best not to travel due to the political turmoil back home. I might spend the winter in Ottawa, take some courses here and earn credentials that would be useful in Dhaka. So, at the very least, I didn't go back without any academic achievement. At Algonquin College in Ottawa I took a short course called "Effective Supervision in Construction." I realized I had no background in computers, so I enrolled in another course called "Computer Programming" at the same college. It was cold Canadian winter. My brother-in-law Dr. Saleh would drive me to and from the classes on cold winter nights. Despite the cold weather, I liked looking at the snow-covered landscape, a different face of the earth that I never had seen before. I would also enjoy seeing the many tall, upright evergreen trees surrounded by snow.

While I was taking the courses at Algonquin College, political unrest reached a high point in Dhaka. History was unfolding there. Mr. Bhutto was vehemently opposed to a Bengali becoming prime minister, and he began a campaign of ethnically charged speeches across West Pakistan to invoke fear of Bengali domination. Bhutto pressured Yahya Khan to take a stance. Yahya Khan fell under the spell of the manipulative Bhutto. On March 3, 1971, the convening of the National Assembly was postponed until March 25, leading to an outcry across East Pakistan.

Violence broke out in several cities, and the security forces killed dozens of unarmed civilian protesters. There were open calls for Sheikh Mujib to declare independence from Pakistan, and the Awami League called a large public gathering at Dhaka's Ramna Racecourse on March 7th to respond. In this historic speech Mujib declared at the end "Our struggle, this time, is a struggle for our freedom. Our struggle, this time, is a struggle for our independence." He of course did not yet formally declare independence hoping that a political resolution was still possible.

Negotiations started in Dhaka between Mujib who came to be known as *Bangabandhu* (Friend of Bengal) and the military rulers from West Pakistan to find a solution to the crisis. The Pakistanis were not doing this in good faith as they really used it as a cover. The time between March 7th and March 25th was used by the military to transport thousands of soldiers by air from West Pakistan to Dhaka. The *Ottawa Citizen,* a daily newspaper and the radio and television news, however sketchy, were the sources of my information. In the late hours of the night of March 25th, the Pakistan Army lodged a massive campaign in Dhaka resulting in the massacre of civilians and other unspeakable atrocities.

Bangabandhu was arrested and sent to a prison in West Pakistan. The brutality of the Pakistan Army and the carnage enraged the Bengalis who formed the *Mukti Bahini* (Liberation Force). Later, India gave support to the movement against its archenemy Pakistan. After a long war of liberation and a brief Indo-Pak war, in which the Soviet Union was an Indian ally, and the U.S. backed Pakistan for fear of the spread of Soviet influence in the region, the Pakistani Army surrendered in Dhaka on December 16th and the imprisoned soldiers returned to Pakistan by an agreement. The liberation war left a deep scar on the Bengali psyche and is remembered every year along with the Language Day of February 21, and reflected in music, movies, dramas, and literature. During the turmoil, I attended a demonstration by Bengalis in Ottawa in front of the Parliament building. The new nation of Bangladesh was born of Bengali nationalism.

In the meantime, after I finished my courses at Algonquin College, the spring of 1971 set in. Because of the civil war in East Pakistan, Dora, who was already in Patuakhali, left for her village home in *Kaunia,* with her family, along with our two baby girls as it was not safe anymore in Patuakhali. I was totally disconnected from her as there was no telephone there and postal service from a rural area was not as operative. I would rarely get letters from her. My parents also left for my mother's rural home. I was wondering if I should return now to Dhaka not knowing the full extent of the situation there because of lack of communication. My older brother from London asked me to stay back, enjoy the beautiful Canadian summer and then return in September when my leave of absence expired. I agreed, thinking that by that time the political stability of the country might be restored. I moved to London, Ontario and started living there with my brother and sister-in-law. They had a few small children and the house was always lively. My sister-in-law's brother Mr. Momin Chowdhury, a decent and amiable personality, who recently immigrated was also living there. Like me, he also left his wife behind and planned to bring her after he got settled. Soon the two of us became good friends, as both had plenty of free time and were unemployed.

To spend my time constructively, I took two undergraduate computer courses titled "Computer Science" and "Computer Simulation" at the University of Western Ontario in the city and took a summer job as a Space Survey Technician, a nice job title. Mr. Chowdhury took a job at the university's bookstore. My job was to measure all the rooms of the different buildings and record them. I had a Canadian student as my partner. I was able to go into all the nooks and corners of the buildings and enjoyed the work. A young person needs to stay mentally active and busy since as the saying goes, an idle brain is the devil's workshop. It has been a mantra for me throughout my life.

Somewhat aimlessly, Mr. Chowdhury and I visited restaurants, took bus rides, strolled in London's downtown sidewalks, and occasionally went to the local Hyde Park, sat there and reflected on our lives. The landscape was utterly beautiful everywhere. I liked the cleanliness of the city wherever I went. At home, we would talk about the political crisis in East Pakistan in company with my brother, who kept track of news and was very disturbed by atrocities back home committed by the Pakistani Army. My brother was a night person, and we would often stay late beyond midnight carrying on conversations. Mr. Momin Chowdhury would also join us. His younger brother Aziz Chowdhury, a librarian, who lived in Windsor, occasionally drove to London and would join us.

As was my habit, I would find time to read books. One book was an autobiography by Maulana Abul Kalam Azad, a devout Muslim and a close disciple and associate of Mahatma Gandhi, that I found fascinating. In this book, he wrote against the partition of India and predicted the break-up of Pakistan, which surely happened later in 1971 fulfilling his prophecy; he gave some strong arguments supporting his forecast.

While in London, I got a telegram from home that my father-in-law sadly passed away. Although my time was passing well, I felt adrift as I was not in my own home and at times felt like a wanderer without purpose. As summer was ending and I finished my courses and summer job, I started to get restless again as I didn't have any tasks to occupy my mind. I was still determined to go back as planned, even knowing full well that East Pakistan was in turmoil, although my brother kept telling me to reconsider my decision.

All I could think of was my secure job in Dhaka. I had the return ticket. I could reunite with my aging parents, who were unhappy when I left, and take care of them. And, of course, I would have my wife and baby daughters with me. Opposing thoughts also came across my mind. After many months of absence from home, could I piece my life together again with my family still being in rural areas in East Pakistan? Was it safe for me to return there when a bloody civil war was raging? Was I overly emotionally attached to my near and dear ones, so much so that I needed to sacrifice a higher goal? Above all, would I regret it later once I returned? I was torn inside me as if two opposing forces were pulling me in two directions. I realized that there was no point in asking for my brother's advice as he would tell me again to stay. I had to make that decision myself. At that young age, I wasn't so spiritually driven that I might seek God's help to guide me and show me the correct path.

A few days passed like that. Then came a memorable September night. I was talking with my brother in the family room. He was wise and high-minded and would say things that I liked hearing, although occasionally I disagreed with him, not fully comprehending his point of view. This was because of my young age and lack of worldly experience. However, later I found most of his perspectives to be true. Like me, he loved music and would constantly listen to the radio or stereo music in the family room. He would also keep track of the news about the liberation war in East Pakistan.

I was not feeling well mentally that night, so I left for my bedroom upstairs and lay down to get some rest, calm my restive mind, and try to sleep. But the currents of opposing thoughts, the contradiction from outside telling me to return home and the inner voice asking me perhaps to stay here were plaguing me. I wondered at the terrible emotional pain in my chest. I felt my whole chest was constricted and a very strong inexplicable feeling as if losing my consciousness. My eyes were closed, and I felt terribly rigid, as if my body was changing into a hard rock. A storm was swirling around me. I thought to myself, was I losing my mind? Was my body trying to resist a nervous break?

I thought of the faces of my dear parents and my dear wife, my dear baby daughter, Ifat, whom I left behind, and my dear newborn daughter, Jinat whom I had not even seen yet. I wondered how they were doing in my absence in a rural area during this horrible liberation war. Instead of sleeping I became more awake and began trembling with a strange and incomprehensible sensation flowing through my chest and spine. I felt as if a tempest was tearing me apart inside. To avoid facing this furious internal gale, I totally submerged my consciousness, deep into my inner self to figure out who I really was and what I wanted out of my life. I yearned to find the reason why I was sent to this world by the Creator, who gave me the gifts of thinking and questioning. If there was a purpose -- and I felt, there was a purpose -- I must fulfil it. While trying to understand myself, I plunged into my subconscious passing through the layers of my mind and stayed at the farthest depth almost in a trance.

Suddenly I woke up. Calmness enveloped me. I felt that my stiffness had melted away and all my discomfort vanished. It was as if someone woke me up from my mental slumber and whispered in my ear that I should stay here and complete my higher education. It was the reason that I had come to Canada. Without looking behind, I must look forward after breaking the shackle of my tender feelings for my country and family. This was now more important than anything else if I wanted to be a happy person for the rest of my life. My destiny lay in uncovering, nourishing, and improving myself. I felt relaxed, determined and joyful. Who was telling me this? I felt confident and convinced and decided I would not waiver anymore. I had finally reached a decision that I would stick with no matter what. I immediately thought I had to tell my brother. I came out of the bedroom, heard music downstairs. Knowing that he was a night owl, I thought he would be there. Sure enough, he was resting on the sofa enjoying his music. It was about 2 AM.

When I told him about my decision with firmness and determination, he was elated, got up from the sofa animated, and told me that the University of Waterloo located about 70 miles (112 kilometers) away had a great engineering school and asked me to get ready, so he could drive me there and find a professor who might accept me as a student. That's how he was; he would do things in his often-unplanned way and go out of his way to help others, in this case his brother. He drove to Kitchener-Waterloo -- a twin city, after stopping at a service center on the way to have coffee, a favorite pastime for him.

We reached the university campus at Waterloo at around 4:30 AM. There I started looking up the names of professors and their areas of specialty on the notice board of the Civil Engineering department. I liked Structural Engineering as I liked the undergraduate courses in structures because they were mainly based on Physics, Mechanics, and Mathematics and I had the practical experience in buildings and bridges in East Pakistan. After sorting some names of the structural engineering professors, I found the name of Professor H. Leipholz in the area of structural stability who had very strong credentials and a great reputation. I liked reinforced concrete and found a couple of other names. But being a curious person and not knowing what structural stability entailed, I decided to meet Dr. Leipholz to explore it. We waited until people started arriving, then went to his office upstairs and knocked on his door. He was not there.

Suddenly, a tall young man with long hair and bell bottom jeans (this was fashionable even at the end of the hippie era) appeared on the scene. His office was just across Dr. Leipholz's office. He was Dr. Donald E. Grierson, Assistant Professor, was written on his door. Seeing the two of us there at that early hour he asked us if he could help. My brother told him that I was looking for a professor to work with. He invited us inside and talked with me for a few minutes asking some questions, looked at my mark sheet and degree certificate, and accepted me as his student.

He helped me get admitted the same day and granting me a research assistantship.

There was one problem though -- to qualify for that grant I needed to be a citizen or landed immigrant. The graduate office advised us to approach the local member of the parliament requesting a waiver of the rule. On our return to London my brother wrote a letter to Mr. Judd Buchanan, M.P. requesting that the regulation be waived for me by citing the raging civil war in East Pakistan to support the case. The request was honored, and I got the financial support. I felt very fortunate and decided to do my level best and make any sacrifice to realize my goal. I now experienced tailwinds in my favor. I may add here that, unlike the U.S., the Canadian government was fully sympathetic to the Bengali cause.

CHAPTER 5

KITCHENER-WATERLOO, ONTARIO
Back on Track; Found My Path

After completing the two computer courses at London, I moved in late September of 1971, to Waterloo to start my M.A. Sc (Master of Applied Science) degree in Civil Engineering at the University of Waterloo. My recent experience at Carleton University and Algonquin College in Ottawa, as well as at the University of Western Ontario in London, helped me quickly adjust to the new academic environment. I was mentally prepared to focus on my studies until I achieved my goal.

Kitchener and Waterloo are often called "twin cities" and referred to as Kitchener-Waterloo, located in southern Ontario, only 60 miles (96 kilometers) from Toronto. There are two universities in Waterloo near each other: University of Waterloo and Wilfrid Laurier University. The University of Waterloo's focus is on engineering, mathematics and computer science whereas the latter university is primarily an arts college. The University of Waterloo was established in 1956 as a public research university to educate engineers and technologists. Subsequently, it expanded and added many other disciplines. The campus was very attractive with new buildings including a beautiful library building and well-maintained landscape. I liked the campus very much.

I also liked the courses that I took. I realized that there were a lot of things I could learn beyond what I learned at the under-graduate level. I rented a room in an old house near the down-town area of Kitchener. Cooking lessons that my sister in Ottawa gave me, came to be useful as I would cook some dishes for my dinner, I had lunch at the university cafeteria. I tried different kinds of hot meals there and savored them. My wife Dora and my two children as well as my elderly parents were on my mind, but I tried to compartmentalize those thoughts and concentrate on my mission since it was not possible to bring them to Canada at that time. The liberation war and unstable political condition in East Pakistan as well as my family temporarily being in a rural area kept them from joining me.

My room, on the second floor, had cooking facilities which I shared with my floor mates, a white Canadian young girl and a young man from Trinidad. This marks the first time I was living alone in Canada, which gave me an opportunity to study without distraction. I devoted myself to studies and got good result in my first semester. My adviser praised me once and told me that his first impression of me was confirmed.

Winter was harsh but I kind of liked it as the white blanket of snow made me look at the world differently. During snowstorms, I would watch the fury of nature and recall the cyclones in my native town in East Pakistan and even composed some poems about snowfall. I had a poetic bend of mind and I composed poems while I was back home as well as when I was in Ottawa, Muncie, and London. When writing a poem, my mind would trek to a different emotive wonderland where things were sub-lime and surreal. I enjoyed that feeling. The ferocity of nature during storms and nature's beauty in different seasons made me reflect and gave me food for thought.

One day, following an overnight snowstorm, I was coming out of the house in the morning using the front stair which was several steps high and very slippery. Having no prior experience with such terrain, I fell on my back and skidded all the way to the edge of the street. My young body took it well. I realized I had to be careful in the future. It was around Christmas time and the homes were lit up with holiday lights. On Christmas day I stayed home as everything was closed and thought about Jesus Christ, whom Muslims also revere, about whom I read a book in Bengali back home titled *Premabatar Jishu Christo* (Avatar of Love Jesus Christ). I reflected on Jesus's life and how he suffered at the hands of the Romans. I always had and still have admiration of Buddha and Jesus for their teachings of love and non-violence.

I made some friends at the university. One of them was Aminur Rahim from East Pakistan. He and I decided to move to a large home called International House close to campus. I made more friends there as well. The place was noisy, so in fall Rahim and I moved to a house closer to campus, moving in to the second floor; the ground floor was a barber shop. Mr. Botos, a barber from Hungary, owned the house. I liked the place although its heating system was very poor. Around this time, I got a letter from my father, who urged me to return to Dhaka when I was done with my studies. East Pakistan was liberated from Pakistan on December 16, 1971 and became the new country called Bangladesh. Once that happened, I was hopeful that Dora and my two children would soon be able to join me in Canada. With that in mind, I applied to rent a two-bedroom apartment in the Married Students Housing Complex of the university. I moved there, to 155 West University Avenue, Apartment No. 225 the following year.

I had been checking with the local immigration office frequently about Dora's visa application status. Her case had been dragging because of the instability during the early stages of formation of the new country. I came to know from the local immigration office that immigration and visa matters were being handled at the Canadian High Commission in New Delhi. After a while I heard that her file had been transferred to Hong Kong for processing. I was getting impatient and didn't know what to do other than wait. Although my wait was agonizing, I benefited from the time doing my own soul-searching and extensive reading.

Around this time, I got a letter from Bangladesh Bank (former State Bank of Pakistan) in Dhaka to urgently return and report for duty as my leave expired and the Bank had no senior engineer to supervise the Bank's engineering projects. I was still thinking of finishing my master's degree and returning to serve my country, which would also make my parents happy. So, I secured a letter from my adviser stating that my study and work on my master's thesis would be completed in a few months and requested my employer to extend my leave on that basis. But the extension was not granted, and my services were terminated by the Bank. I also got another letter from the Bank headquarters in Karachi asking me to report there for duty. I wrote back that since I was the citizen of a new country, Bangladesh, I didn't want to return to Pakistan. They wrote me a letter thanking me for my services, telling me they understood my predicament, and accepted my resignation. Now that I had cut my career ties with my native country, I had only one choice -- continue the course without vacillating about whether to go back or not.

⊷┼┼⊷

While my academic studies were going well, I could not be without books; reading was enjoyable and would always delight me. It also made me think out-of-the-box. All my life I had been searching for something to keep me content and happy, perhaps searching for the truth behind everything. I found it elusive though. I always felt something was missing in my life. While on hiatus from graduate studies during 1970-71 and wandering through life in Ottawa, Muncie, IN, and London, Ontario, I was not a strictly practicing religious man as I would always question what I heard, read or learned about religion and I was never satisfied. I realized no one else could do it for me. So, I looked deep within myself to find the imperceptible me.

Although I was generally a believer in a Higher Power and creationism, I always wondered how humans originated on this planet from an alternate scientific viewpoint. So, I ordered a 16-volume Time-Life Book series called *Emergence of Man* published during 1972-73 that described all I wanted to know. The books arrived successively, and I continued reading until I finished all 16 volumes. It was a treasure trove of knowledge to enlighten me and I still keep them on my bookshelf as a reminder of a time of solitude and reflection.

Through reading these volumes, I was naturally drawn to books on Anthropology and evolution. I also borrowed some books from the university library. Alone in the quiet apartment, I would play soft music on the radio in the background while I read. Often, I enjoyed closing my eyes and imagining myself living in the prehistoric times. An Indian visiting professor once came to my apartment, saw the books on my living room shelves and asked me, "Are you a student of Anthropology?" He was surprised to hear that I was a student of Civil Engineering.

I read about evolution, which I was first exposed to through a course in biology at Dhaka College. I decided to read the original books written by Charles Darwin. I borrowed his book *The Descent of Man, and Selection in Relation to Sex*. I still remember his writing, "We must, however, acknowledge, as it seems to me, that man with all his noble qualities... still bears in his bodily frame the indelible stamp of his lowly origin." I pondered over this idea and what he was suggesting, again and again.

I used to visit the university bookstore frequently. One day I saw Darwin's famous masterpiece in paperback entitled *The Origin of Species by Means of Natural Selection: Or, the Preservation of Favored Races in the Struggle for Life.* I decided to read the whole book. Darwin proposed the biological notion that the form to leave the most replicas of itself will survive in successive generations. This concept of natural selection led to the well-known term "survival of the fittest" coined by philosopher Herbert Spencer. I read with delight until past midnight without looking at the clock. Because I had taken biology in higher secondary class and because of my readings in Anthropology and the other Darwin book, I grasped his argument well. The more I read the more I wanted to explore the concepts further. Two words did stick with me: strength and adaptability. I realized that one had to be strong but also able to adapt to changed circumstances in order to survive. I learned in the process that Darwin traced some of his ideas to a French naturalist Jean-Baptiste Lamarck who had offered the first coherent theory of evolution based on a complex biological force and an adaptive feature in the species. His original writings were in French so I could not read those writings but did learn more about his theories from other sources.

While reading about evolution, I learned about Charles Lyell, a foremost geologist of the 19th century who wrote a classic called *Principles of Geology.* Lyell's interpretation of geologic change as the steady accumulation of small changes over enormously long spans of time influenced Darwin immensely. "The present is the key to the past" was a principal theme summarized in Lyell's work. Darwin read this book and extended the ideas of change to biology. I went to the university library and located the book. It was a rare, old book, exclusively for reference. I was not allowed to take it home. So, instead, I went every night and read the voluminous book with awe and wonder from cover to cover. I learned how the large mountains and oceans originated, how Niagara Falls was created, and about the past of such other natural wonders. At the beginning of the book Lyell acknowledged the work of Arab geologists who initially proposed the idea of changes in the earth's composition and structure happening over time. This gave me the impetus to read about the large number of Arab and Muslim scientists during the Golden Age of Islam. I came to this reading later as finding the relevant literature at the time was not easy.

I felt the urge to understand human nature, since we had to deal with human beings at every stage of our lives. I found my alternate space in the library and my voracious appetite for knowledge spanned many disciplines, each important in its own way. I wanted to embrace different facets of our human life, in pursuit of a complete and well-rounded understanding. Once I learned enough about the theory of evolution, I turned my attention to psychology. I have been always curious about the human mind and human nature. I read some primers and introductory books on psychology. But I wanted to know the subject better and in more depth from the top authorities.

I heard about Sigmund Freud, the father of psychoanalysis, and found several references to him in books. His formative book was *Interpretation of Dreams*. I read the entire book almost nonstop except for sleeping and working hours. Freud went deep into our unconscious mind and the symbolism of dreams. It was one of the best books I have ever read. It opened my intellect to the inner chambers of my mind. I then bought and read Freud's book titled *A General Introduction to Psychoanalysis* (translated in English by Joan Riviere) that took me further into this subject. I proceeded to read more books on psychology especially on Freud and learned about his concepts of id, ego, and superego. I learned in detail about Oedipus complex, libido, mania, narcissism, and a few other things. Then I got a book from the library that was a collection of Freud's papers and lectures and read a few of these papers.

After reading his writings I came to believe what he proposed as a universal truth, that we are not really in full control of our mind. This is so because there are several layers of our mind and unconscious factors influence how we think and act. The unconscious can lead us in the wrong direction to a destructive path if we are not aware of it. We must endeavor to control it and divert it to a constructive path by careful work and deliberation. Overall, among other things, I came to realize how childhood experiences shaped our behavior and mental state in later life. I benefited from this notion and cured myself of the blood phobia that I had for many years. The mere sight or even mention of blood or bleeding would produce a panic attack, to the point that I was thinking of getting professional help some day. Instead, taking a cue from Freud, I traced an eventful experience back to my childhood.

When I was in school, I was playing soccer with a few kids in a field one afternoon. At one point the two opposing teams started pelting broken bricks and stones at each other. One of the sharp-edged pieces hit me hard on my head causing profuse bleeding that spilled over my face and chest. Seeing it I fainted. When I woke up, I was at home in bed with my head bandaged. Later I learned some older kids playing nearby heard my playmates scream and took me to the hospital nearby. I saw who threw the broken brick but never told anyone about him since I knew it was playground accident, but I still remember his face and that day. I had no doubt that this was the incident that produced my panic attacks. I took control of the phobia, knowing it was not an inborn problem but had an eventful origin and so, curable. Knowing the root cause of my problem, I gradually conditioned myself to unravel it. To my pleasant surprise, I found I was cured, and I have no more fear of blood. I learned that guidance from the right literature could help solve many of my life's problems.

I read a few other books of psychology as well as articles to get other viewpoints. I started with Carl Jung, a follower of Freud who later disagreed with Freud over the latter's excessive emphasis on human sexuality. While Freud believed in cause and effect like a scientist, Jung believed that certain events happened without any real scientific explanation. Later, I also read from Ivan Pavlov about conditioning, Abraham Maslow and the hierarchy of needs, and some more. I always held high regard for Freud as I feel no one else had probed human psyche as deeply. I also read the thought-provoking book *Eros and Civilization: A Philosophical Inquiry into Freud* by philosopher Herbert Marcuse. Of particular interest to me was the difference in male and female psychology and behavior as I observed they behaved differently. Over the course of my readings I found the reference to a seminal book called *Psychology of Sex* by Havelock Ellis. I borrowed this thick book from the library and read cover to cover. Later, I read a book titled *Games People Play* by Eric Berne, a very interesting read about day-to-day human interaction and behavior.

I then turned to history, my favorite subject. I bought a very thick book *Columbia History of the World* from the university bookstore and started reading it. I still have this comprehensive treatise in my collection. Next, I bought a book on philosophy and studied, Avicenna (Ibn Sina), Rene Descartes, Frederick Nietzsche, Baruch Spinoza, Jean-Paul Sartre, Herbert Marcuse, Bertrand Russell, and so on. Of course, I also read about Socrates, Plato, and Aristotle. In these readings, I found a reference to God. I read about the European Renaissance and the Age of Enlightenment, as well as some of the great thinkers of that time. I tried to read the original writings but found them too ethereal for a young mind like mine as I had more of a scientific than philosophical bend. However, I continued reading such books when I was more mature later in life, whenever I found time.

I also read *The Arabian Nights* replete with thrilling stories and *Gulliver's Travels* retelling fascinating stories of voyages for entertainment. After reading as much as I could I turned my attention to spirituality, an abstract human faculty generally discussed in organized religions. After being enlightened in different areas of learning and information, I realized I needed to understand the nature of God and the mystery of creation from a spiritual perspective. Although I was born a Muslim and was taught the tenets of the faith and how to pray, I would not practice my faith regularly. This stemmed perhaps from youthful indifference and seeing that most boys of my age did not pray regularly. I was, however, a believer despite asking many perplexing questions about religion that others could not answer. I thought about the nature of God and I felt no one could prove or disprove the existence of God. There are thinkers, philosophers, and scientists who were religious, agnostic, or atheists, but millions of human beings have believed in the existence of God over the ages; could all of them be wrong? This fundamental human need for spirituality might just be proof that God does exist. But skeptics might say spirituality arose out of human consciousness of nature, fear of the unknown, and the environmental surroundings. The focal point of spirituality became the invention of a supreme entity or deity who controls everything.

I had never been one to accept things at face value, I had to be rationally convinced. I thought most people accepted the religion they were born into because of their upbringing and conditioning. I was inquisitive about other religions but only had a cursory understanding from my earlier readings. I was curious to see how mine related to other religions. This was not out of any crisis of faith regarding my own religion. I always believed that there must be a creator, a higher supreme power who is a grand designer and maintainer of the unfathomable universe. But my concern was how to connect to Him? Simply believing in a creator but not knowing how to connect to Him would make me lean toward being agnostic, a prospect I didn't like as it struck me as half-hearted or mental limbo, suspended in confusion.

Great sages, who were clearly and immeasurably smarter and wiser than me, had already done this and some succeeded through founding or adopting a religion. I felt I needed to study other religions to pursue this thought. So, I studied Hinduism, Buddhism, Sikhism, Judaism, Christianity, Islam, Baha'i faith and some other faiths like Mormonism, Zoroastrianism and Shintoism.

My reading of the book *Religions of Mankind* (in Bengali) during my high school years at home was helpful and acted as a springboard. I could not finish reading all of them fully during this short time in Waterloo but continued reading later and throughout my life.

Later in life, I read the Qur'an together with commentary several times. I still do read a volume of the Qur'an translated by Abdullah Yusuf Ali, published in 1938. It was the third edition, and its first edition was published in 1934. After my father's death, I inherited this rare volume. One early morning when I was awake and still in bed, I heard my father who finished reading the Quran say to my mother, "I will give this holy book to my son who has the strongest faith." My father never decided to give it to anyone during his lifetime.

After my father's death, however, having overheard what my father said to my mother, knowing he wanted one of his sons to have it, I felt I should cherish it regardless of how strong my faith was compared to my brothers. Much later, when I went to Patuakhali during a visit to Bangladesh with my family in 1984, following my father's death in 1983, I found this rare volume in our home where a cousin of mine was residing. I brought it to the U.S. I still recite verses from it chronologically and read the accompanying English translation and commentary regularly. Such readings give me enough food for thought and I tried to imagine and explore the inherently abstract ideas of faith and spirituality hidden behind the external rituals. I have also been wondering about the external rituals to which the vast majority of people are attached. Many seem focused on outward rituals rather than on an internalized understanding of the faith itself. Many indulge in inexplicable superstitious thoughts. My explorations also led me to contemplate the vastness of creation and silent universe of which the earth is only a tiny element and the mystery associated with it.

Later, I also secured a Bible (King James version) that I have read thoroughly. The Quran and the Bible (containing the Old and New Testaments) have many common themes. Judaism, Christianity, and Islam are all Abrahamic faiths and Islam is preceded by the other two.

Unless it was a miracle, how did an unlettered man like the Islamic prophet, living in a very ignorant and backward society, utter countless words of faith, law and spiritualty -- all while using the elegant and rhythmic Arabic found in the Quran? The nature of an invisible omnipotent and omnipresent God, the total absence of anthropomorphism in Islam, and the notion of equality of all and universal brotherhood are important aspects that drew me closer to the faith of my birth.

While keeping myself busy with books and articles as a hobby to expand my knowledge about all faiths, I would continuously check with the immigration department about Dora's immigration status. I was told her file was being processed in Hong Kong as there was no Canadian High Commission in the new country of Bangladesh yet. Finally, she got the visa and arrived by Swissair with our two daughters to Montreal on December 23, 1972, auspiciously on the same day that my daughter Jinat turned two. Dora was meant to arrive in Toronto so I could go there and pick her up. But there was a severe snowstorm, and I got a call from Swissair that she was stranded in Montreal. It would take a long time by road from Waterloo to Montreal, so I requested my brother-in-law in Ottawa, to receive her.

I boarded a bus from Kitchener and went to Ottawa. After an overnight stay in a hotel in Montreal, Dora and my kids came to Ottawa the next morning and joined me. Finally, I was reunited with my family – a happy time for me indeed! We took a train and left Ottawa for Waterloo. It was a big relief for me to finally have my family with me in my apartment. The next couple of months was spent dealing with my family's adjustment in the new environment. Looking back, I was too young myself, and having been away from them for more than two years, I was not the best father as I knew little about how to deal with them. After leading a bachelor's life for more than two years, I also needed to adapt to this new environment.

I was working hard, paying full attention to master's thesis. My research was in the area of optimization of reinforced concrete structures using the limit design method. In May 1973, I received my M.A.Sc. degree in Civil Engineering with concentration in Structural Engineering. It was time now to decide what I would do next -- take a job or proceed to a Doctor of Philosophy (Ph.D.) degree. Taking a job was tempting. I heard my classmates debating job versus Ph.D., and many of them opted for jobs. They liked the prospect of immediate earning, gaining experience and seniority in the industry. Another pitfall was that firms might not even hire Ph.D.'s as they might be considered overqualified. I thought seriously about joining the work force as I had a wife and two children to support. It would be a very good thing for me financially, particularly since engineering was in demand as a highly professional and technical discipline. I thought, after gaining some Canadian experience I could return to Bangladesh.

While I was trying to make a decision, one day my adviser asked me, "Are you thinking of going back across the ocean or continuing for a Ph.D.?" After giving a lot of thought I opted for a Ph.D. as I thought that would be more in line with my aspirations and based on what my adviser proposed to me. He was happy with me and my work, so he offered me a research assistantship if I did my Ph.D. with him. I was also a teaching assistant, so I felt financially secure, and agreed to stay there. He and I agreed that I should continue my research in the same area and extend the work that I had been doing to a new and higher level. My research problem involved extending the initial design method that I developed in addition to developing an alternate method with an entirely original concept.

I continued with studies my new research project while enjoying Dora's excellent cooking. I started eating well and we socialized with other families. My kids were learning to speak English and were making new friends. It was a period of tailwinds blowing in my favor. I enjoyed my teaching assistant work and my research was very stimulating. I was venturing into uncertain conceptual territory with excitement and curiosity. I truly enjoyed this intellectual exercise.

From time to time, famous Indian singers would host concerts in nearby Toronto. I was so immersed in my studies, that despite my love for music, I wouldn't accompany my family on these entertaining trips. I avoided any distractions. I always felt, and still feel, that I should give endeavors my full attention to succeed with a good outcome. My sense of urgency was heightened since I had taken some time wandering through life for a year. Also, I had a responsibility to Dora and the kids. In summer, when it was green and beautiful, I would take my family to a nearby park. The kids really enjoyed it.

When I was doing my doctoral research, my adviser suggested I attend the CANCAM-75 (Canadian Congress of Applied Mechanics) conference in May 1975 with my family in Fredericton, New Brunswick, a remote eastern maritime province of Canada. Because he noticed how hard I was working, he recommended a vacation. Not only that, he said he would fund my trip from his grant money. This was the first time I drove long distance, about 900 miles (1,440 kilometers) on major Canadian highways. Although it was a great opportunity for me to relax and explore, I was a little nervous about making the long drive myself. Particularly since I would be passing through large cities like Montreal. Finding the courage, I drove to the outskirts of Montreal and stayed in a hotel overnight.

The next day, we set out early in the morning and passed through Montreal when the traffic was light. We were well on our way to Fredericton 500 miles (800 kilometers) away. After driving some distance, I noticed the fuel level in the car was low but thought I would fill up at the next station. The next station was nowhere in sight in the sparsely populated, remote area. I became concerned, as I had two small children with me, but outwardly I maintained my calm. In those days, there was no easy way to communicate if one was stranded on the highway. Usually a motorist would have to wait for a passing police officer come to the rescue. I heard many horror stories about stranded drivers especially in winter. When my gas tank almost ran dry, I finally saw an exit to a small village. Driving a few miles, I spotted a gas station next to a ramshackle store, which to me was a beautiful sight. The man from the store came out and filled the tank. I thanked God and left relaxed.

With the radio playing music in the background, I enjoyed the scenery of Mother Nature around me. The changing terrain was picturesque as we entered a hilly area. In some locations, the uphill slope was very steep, the car, an old Ford Mercury Montego, had some trouble making the climb. My inexperience was only a slight hinderance, I remembered shifting gears and was able to make it. Finally, we reached Fredericton and checked into a hotel. After a good night's sleep, I drove around to explore the small city of Fredericton. Besides the bridge connecting the two halves of the city which is bisected by St. John River, there wasn't much else that interested me.

I gained a lot from the CANCAM conference itself like new insights into how conferences were held and listened to academic paper presentations.

On the return trip, as planned, we stopped in a small town called Arvida to visit a friend of mine, Dilip Sen, and his wife. Dilip completed his Ph.D. from the University of Waterloo and got a job in this remote town in Quebec. Arvida was founded as a settlement in 1929 by the Alcoa aluminum company. After driving through a picturesque but isolated tract bursting with natural beauty we reached the town, about 360-mile (576-kilometer) drive from Fredericton. On the way I learned many lessons about long distance driving in unknown territories, including the importance of being attentive.

I got a serious jolt while driving through the hills. The highway was moderately sloped, and the signs were inadequate. I encountered a sharp left turn along the edge of a large river or lake. The waterfront was hidden behind a row of trees and difficult to see in the distance. Fortunately, I was driving slowly downhill and managed to brake and navigate the turn instead of driving headlong into the water. I was greatly relieved to reach my friend's apartment, where we were hosted graciously. There wasn't much sightseeing nearby so Dilip and his wife took us for a short ride to the city of Chicoutimi. It was a nice, memorable trip.

Once we got back to routine in Waterloo, I continued reading for pleasure and learning, albeit to a lesser degree. I developed a deep respect for Socrates, Plato and Aristotle. Socrates for his wisdom, Plato for his thoughts on a political system, and Aristotle for his earliest scientific notions. Some other significant readings were Bertrand Russell's *Unpopular Essays* and *The Conquest of Happiness,* Khalil Gibran's *The Prophet,* Hans Selye's *Stress Without Distress,* and John Kenneth Galbraith's *The Affluent Society.* I've taken great life lessons from each great mind. Russell's books are very thought-provoking and testify to his independent thinking. His book on conquering happiness is a great read for anyone who wants to be happy in life.

Khalil Gibran famously wrote: "Are you a politician asking your country what your country can do for you or a zealous one asking what you can do for your country? If you are the first, then you are a parasite; if the second, then you are an oasis in the desert." Much later, President John F. Kennedy famously said "Ask not what your country has done for you. Ask what you can do for your country." I found this out in 1972 and thought: "Great minds think alike."

Selye coined the term "Stress" and Galbraith popularized the expression "Conventional Wisdom." I could relate to Selye's thesis that stress in life was natural and inherently harmless, but what was harmful was distress. Applying an analogy from structural engineering, I knew that a structure needs stress in order to remain stable under its own weight and any other gravity load on it. However, when it is overloaded with gravity or lateral load causing overstressing, the structure is distressed beyond the carrying capacity. That's when the structure fails or gets damaged.

After reading Galbraith's book I developed some interest in economics. I read parts of The *Wealth of the Nations* by Adam Smith to learn more about capitalism as well as the English translation of *Das Capital* by Karl Marx to understand socialism. Since money and finance were not my favorite subjects, I got bored after reading the introductory parts of the books and later preferred to read some secondary sources to understand the subject matter of these books in depth.

Even though I had taken the requisite undergraduate course in accounting and another in economics, I never studied them seriously, considering them peripheral to my focus on engineering. I must admit my interest in economics and finance grew out of much more practical considerations, years later in the late 1990s. I had been a bit inattentive with my money but Dora, thankfully, was good at accounting and had a keen sense of money management. She taught me the steps of money management. Now, I know how important it is to understand the art of saving, spending, investing, refinancing a home, shopping for loans, etc. early on in life. I came to a late appreciation of the role of economics and finance, both in everyday life and as a powerful engine driving global progress.

During this period Akhtaruzzaman, my nephew, immigrated from Bangladesh. We were back-to-back in age and were like friends. I suggested that he live with me until he got established and he lived with us for four months. He had a master's degree in philosophy from Bangladesh, but he was unsure about what to do in Canada. Having been through this grueling decision process myself, I persuaded him to apply for a Master of Arts (M.A.) degree program in the subject of his choice at the University of Waterloo. He was soon admitted to the Political Science department. Given my varied subject interests, I was happy to engage with his studies from time to time.

He sought my help to write some papers, the first was on Bangladeshi nationalism. The assignment came on the heels of a national tragedy, when the founding leader of Bangladesh, Sheikh Mujibur Rahman, was assassinated along with most of his family, in Dhaka on August 15, 1975. A short period of political turmoil and instability followed, but soon Major Ziaur Rahman, an army official, took over as the president of the new country. The topic of Bangladeshi nationalism was thus an interesting and new one. Another paper was on the role of charisma in leadership. I studied the literature on nationalism to work on the first paper and charisma separately from leadership, then blended some ideas together for the second paper. I learned a lot from my readings and enjoyed working on the papers with my nephew.

While my doctoral research was in full swing, in 1975 my adviser left on a sabbatical leave at the University of Liege, Belgium. He left me in the capable hands of Professor M. Z. Cohn, an authority on limit design of concrete structures. Since I was also working on optimum limit design, I felt good about being under his wing, sure that I would learn a few things from him. Since I was not his regular student, his supervision of my work was somewhat cursory. He gave me the freedom to continue my work with my own independent thoughts without giving me too much direction. I also worked, on an hourly basis, with Professor Eric Burnett who hired me to conduct research related to my area. The understanding was that I would use the research results for my thesis, and he would use the results to write a publishable paper, which he did.

During the same time period, a Bangladeshi friend of mine, Farrukh Mohsen, a Ph.D. student, told me that Dr. Fazlur Rahman Khan, a structural engineer from Bangladesh working in Chicago had been getting attention and recognition for his work on tall buildings. Fazlur Rahman Khan was the lead engineer for the iconic John Hancock Center and Sears Tower in Chicago. For many years, the latter tower held the prestigious distinction of being the tallest in the world. I was proud of my fellow countryman and engineer.

While the tallest tower in the world was under construction using complex calculations, you may be very surprised to learn that it was only in 1975 that I first laid eyes on a calculator. The sharp mathematical minds of engineers were the main tools for study and innovation in the field. It was Professor Neil C. Lind who got a calculator and showed us how it worked. Today, it is hard to imagine any field without it's corresponding technology, but at the time, I was not yet ready to embrace it. In fact, I was comfortable with my slide rule that I had with me brought from Dhaka. In my opinion, the slide rule was a wonderful and smart tool that could be used to solve arithmetic, algebraic and trigonometric operations. I still consider it a cool object and brilliant tool. I preserved it as a memento for a long time but unfortunately misplaced it during my many moves.

I would communicate regularly with my adviser in Liege through letters. Of course, there was no email, cell phone or Skype those days. Although in general he had agreed with me, my ideas and propositions, at one point he suggested an alternate procedure to the formulation of the problem and derivation of the design equations. He thought his would be a better way to approach the problem. I did attempt his procedure but after working on the problem for a long while, my gut instinct was that his idea would not work, which I politely let him know. He didn't push it and instead told me to complete my work as quickly as possible and start writing my thesis. Once I had found the solution of my research problem and sorted out the ideas and since I already had written a master's thesis, writing this one was not a major undertaking.

In the meantime, my adviser returned from Liege. While he was busy settling down in Waterloo, he advised me to complete writing my thesis, so I could defend in the winter semester of 1976. He got busy with his other students, particularly the new ones. In February 1976, I finished writing and wanted him to review it before I submitted it formally. He told me that he had confidence in me, and I could go ahead and submit it and he would read it later before my defense. I was a bit surprised and apprehensive, but also felt good about the obvious trust he had in me. So, I submitted my thesis and a defense date was fixed.

Anticipating my degree soon, I started applying for jobs. Things, however, took a turn for the worse, much different than the immediate future I was envisioning. I felt the happy days of my life were ending, as turbulence began that turned into a storm.

For my thesis defense, my external examiner was Professor Herbert Sawyer, a very senior faculty member from the University of Florida at Gainesville, selected by my adviser with my consent. Although he didn't reject my thesis, he did ask a few challenging questions. Specifically, he mentioned that he could not understand the mathematical expressions I had developed for my work. The expressions he questioned were defining two critical variables. These variables and their derivation had been approved by my adviser early on in my work, long before he went to Liege. His letter discouraged my adviser, who was young and inexperienced as a researcher. His motivation was to get my thesis accepted by someone like Professor Sawyer with name recognition. Many years ago, Professor Sawyer had developed a limit design method and was, in my opinion, somewhat archaic in his thoughts. Moreover, he was never particularly involved in structural optimization. My formulation was more on limit design and mathematical optimization using nonlinear programming. This was not his cup of tea.

One day, just a few days before my defense, my adviser called me to his office. He told me that he himself didn't understand the mathematical derivation of another key equation fundamental to the validity of my design formulation. I reminded him he approved it through our written correspondence while he was in Liege. Influenced by Professor Sawyer, he started doubting my work. Then came the bombshell. He was not moved, and he bluntly told me "I think you have fabricated this mathematical derivation. I have cancelled your defense. I can support you for one more semester in fall, until you convince me that your derivation is correct."

I felt hurt and a chill ran through my spine. I also remembered what he did for me when he first accepted me as his student. I felt bad that I let him down. I said politely, "Professor, I can tell you from the bottom of my heart that I have done all my work conscientiously and I didn't fabricate anything in my thesis." He looked at me but didn't respond and asked me to go the registrar's office to check out something. I don't recall what it was. With a destroyed spirit, I left his office, with my gloomy face down and headed toward the registrar's office.

There I met Faizur Rahman, a graduate student of sociology and a Bangladeshi friend of mine. Seeing my dejected face, he wanted to know what happened. I told him and he said, "You look depressed. Let us go to my house and chat." I needed that support at that moment, so I went with him to his apartment near the campus. His wife Sabiran, a fine woman from Pakistan, made some tea for us. We talked and then I left for my nearby apartment. I told Dora the bad news. Being a very calm person and a comforter throughout my life during difficult times, she gave me encouragement and called my nephew Akhtaruzzaman to come and give me company. He came, stayed for a short time, but seeing me so disheartened he left, thinking I needed some time alone.

That night I was wondering what to do. The only thing I could think of was to calm my restless mind and focus entirely on my research with renewed vigor. I decided to give up the position of teaching assistant. The next day I told my adviser, who was surprised and told me to reconsider, but I didn't change my mind. When I told Professor Cohn that I no longer wish to be his teaching assistant, he was initially a bit annoyed, since it was the middle of the semester. Recognizing my resolve, he quickly accepted it. Clearly, the loss of pay was a big sacrifice for me and my family, but it had to be done. Fortunately, I still had the research assistantship and Dora had a low-paying job with that kept us going. For the next few months, I was detached from my adviser as I had nothing new to report and didn't know how to convince him regarding the validity of my work. The following summer my adviser was away once more. I labored over my derivation of the equation again and again. It was fundamental for my thesis and without it my proposed design method became invalid. I was consumed with thinking how to better present it with no clue, nor even a glimmer of hope in sight.

I would occasionally tell Dora, often as late as midnight that I had to go to the university. On my way I would climb a high embankment close to our apartment and lie on the grassy flat expanse at the top. I would look up at the starry night sky and think about what to do next. I thought I must do the Ph.D. that I set my mind on. I couldn't take a defeatist attitude and drop my studies after coming this far. Should I go to a different university? It might not be that simple now. Should I go for a different field like psychology or history that I liked so much? I could not find a way out, as if all the doors were closed around me. I felt depressed. I heard that people in such a desperate situation lost interest in this world and had even suicidal thoughts. But I knew I could never do that as I was not a coward who couldn't face the challenges of the world. Moreover, I had a responsibility to my wife and two minor children.

By now I realized life was difficult, or to put it in Shakespeare's words: "Life is not a bed of roses." I felt I had a mission on earth but was at a low point. I was admittedly troubled by strange thoughts that were creeping through my mind. As I learned from my readings of Darwin, strength and adaptability were the key to the survival of the fittest. So, I thought to myself that I needed to be strong and adapt to the situation rather than worrying too much. My readings of psychology taught me to explore human minds. Recalling how I cured my phobia of blood by studying psychology, I decided to read some books on psychology again to resolve the problem of unrest plaguing my mind.

One late night, I went to the university library and walked directly to the section on psychology. I sorted a few books and journals on very melancholy topics like death, depression, suicide, psychotic disorder, etc. Since I myself was in a depressive mental state, I glanced through some of them but didn't find anything to shed light on how to overcome depression and start living again. Suddenly, a doctoral thesis drew my attention. The title of the thesis intrigued me. I don't remember it, but it was about some psychological aspects of suicide. I pulled it off the shelf. I read through it quickly and towards the end I found something interesting. Some sketches at the end caught my attention. In a nutshell, the diagrams illustrated that when one was depressed and suicidal, it was as if one dropped into a low valley and were trapped there. One could easily lose all hope of not getting out of there and commit suicide. On the other hand, if one could overcome the lowest point, roll uphill on the other side using an inertia force to get out of the valley, one would experience a rebirth and resurgence.

The thesis and diagram helped me set my coordinates. I knew that I was simply at the lowest point in a valley, not a dead end. I could overcome the depression and suicidal thoughts and be a much better and stronger person. I finally found some light in the tunnel; I had to be strong, determined and energetic enough to cross the lowest point and reach the other side to renewal.

I felt like I reconnected to my true self. I came home content and confident with a sense of renewed inner strength. I deeply believed that negative emotions could be redirected to make a person stronger and more fit to handle the seemingly insurmountable challenges of life. I promised to myself I would fulfil my intended goal, of achieving a doctorate degree and this was just a detour in my roadmap.

I liked psychology so much that I thought I would apply for a Ph.D. in psychology, and that might be what suited me best. I shared this thought with Dora, who advised me against it and told me to continue what I was doing as I had already invested so much time. She told me to see my adviser and ask him again what he could do for me as he had been indifferent to me for so long. I contemplated what I should do, but now with a clear head.

The summer of 1976 just flew by. I would spend time doing different things including watching the TV series Star Trek with my daughters. Ifat would enjoy watching with me, Jinat would also join but she was too young to fully grasp things. I would go to the nearby park with Dora and the little girls to entertain them. One late afternoon, in fall semester, I was sitting quietly on a sofa in my living room. My two daughters were playing outside in the playground, and Dora was at work. I was totally absorbed in my thoughts and as if in my imagination, I heard a voice telling me, "Go, see your adviser and talk with him confidently about your predicament. You will get your degree." I wondered who was telling me this. The next day, I knocked on my adviser's office door and told him that I needed to talk with him. I sat facing him and said,

"Professor, I tried my best. Whatever I did for my thesis I am confident about it. Look, I can't go on like this in an uncertain way. I have a family to take care of."

He looked at me and said,

"But I don't understand it. I can't let you put it in a doctoral thesis if I don't understand it as your adviser. Remember, I wrote to you from Liege about an alternate way to formulate this problem. You said it was not right, but I think it is the way to go. If you do this now, my way, I will allow you to submit your thesis again."

I was happy inside me for two reasons: first, he was giving me another chance and second, he was telling me to do it his way, which I knew in the back of my mind was wrong. I told him that I would consider his suggestion thoroughly and get back to him soon. I left his office content at the thought that I now had a road forward. All I needed to do was to prove the fallacy in the logic of his proposition. I felt confident enough that I could do it.

The next few days were most crucial for me. I totally immersed myself in trying to prove the proposal of my adviser was erroneous. I worked on it to develop a mathematical model viewing at it from different angles since explaining to my adviser in words would not do it. It had to be scientifically proved with mathematical equations. The problem was constantly on my mind and spent many hours brooding over it. One night while I was working on it in my study room attached to my bedroom, I had the Eureka moment that I needed! That night I lay in bed thinking about how to present it to my adviser in a polite way without offending him. The next morning, I called him and told him that I had some new developments in my work and would like to see him. He told me to see him the following day at 10 AM. He sounded eager to hear my results.

I prepared myself well for the meeting and knocked on his door the next day. He led me to a nearby conference room. Taking a seat, he asked me to use the chalkboard to show my findings. When I reached the last stage of my presentation, having written all the mathematical derivations by his method, he sensed that something was not working. He stood up, took another chalk and tried to figure it out himself. I stayed quiet and respectful and let him do the thinking so that he didn't feel embarrassed. He went through my derivations for his method slowly and eventually realized for himself that they landed nowhere and produced an illogical and faulty outcome.

In despair, looking down at the floor he sat down and seemed to carry out some quick introspection. Shortly, he gathered himself and told me, "Okay, now show me on the chalkboard your method of the formulation." Now, he was receptive and in fact refined my thought process by collaborating with me. I continued my work on my thesis, addressing some of the questions Professor Sawyer raised. Although he agreed with my fundamental thinking about the new design method, one crucial change he demanded before approving my thesis was that I should derive the key formula by removing one of the variables I had introduced. He thought I had too many variables and this one was unnecessary. After much hard work, I met his demand and submitted the revised mathematical derivation for his review. He told me to see him the next morning.

The next day, as I approached the Civil Engineering building some nerves kicked in. My heart rate went up thinking about what would happen if he said he couldn't approve it? In nervousness, I uttered the words, "God, you help me." When I entered his office, he greeted me with a smile and told me, "Mir, I am happy to report that I am prepared to approve your work. You have crossed the hump." He, however, showed me that he had made some minor changes and refinements in what I did to make it even more clear. I didn't mind as I realized he was now on my side and trying to help me. I thanked him profusely. He set a new date for my defense, March 3, 1977. Coincidentally it was my wedding anniversary day. Heeding the advice of his senior colleague, he invited Professor Fred Moses of Case Western Reserve University as my external examiner. Professor Moses had the necessary expertise and was more up to date on structural optimization. This storm that raged through my life was now losing strength, and when I successfully passed my defense without any required change sought by the committee members including Professor Moses, it was finally over. Brighter days were waiting for me ahead.

During the last year of my doctoral studies, Dora was pregnant and at the time of my defense, the pregnancy was in advanced stages. I decided to be at Dora's side at the hospital during the delivery to experience it since I never faced it before. Despite my good supportive intentions, I could not bear it. During the agonizing delivery, when Dora was in great pain, the doctor saw my facial expression and said, "The father has to leave now." I waited outside feeling completely tense when the doctor finally came and gave me the good news. Dora gave birth to our son, on April 5 at Kitchener-Waterloo Hospital. A nurse invited me to the room where I saw them washing a blood-soaked baby in a large bowl. The scene was new and wonderous. Once she cleaned him, she handed him to me. Extending my arms, I felt exhilarated holding him. We named him Murad.

Although I was pleased at the thought of a boy after two girls, I was equally happy with either a boy or another girl. All I wanted was for them to be decent people, with good education and character, who cared for others but having a son after two daughters was a welcome change. His birth came at a good time in our lives, I had just completed my defense a month before and finally received my doctoral degree.

Now, I had to decide whether I would return to Bangladesh or stay in Canada. Both options had their pros and cons. My thinking leaned toward returning as the country was now in peace and needed engineers to reconstruct after the liberation war. After all, I got almost a free education there with government scholarships that I received and paying very low tuition fees. Much of the educational expenses were subsidized by the government. My engineering education prepared me for what I became then. It would also satisfy my elderly parents. Moreover, I could live with my own people and raise my children in my own culture. However, I thought instead of returning immediately it would be a good thing for me to work in Canada in the industry for a short time to gain some practical experience in the West before I returned. Engineering is a professional discipline and I thought it would be good to hone my professional skill in Canada so I could better serve my native country.

The dilemma I faced was a common one for foreign students. In fact, someone wrote about it and used the title "Trapped in Paradise." Here how it went in general sequence –

1. Go to the West for higher education; 2. Stay on to get Western job experience; 3. Earn a decent salary, buy a home, get comfortable; 4. Watch the children grow in affluence and get a good education; 5. Postpone returning to native homeland until children get established and tell yourself that you'll return home after retirement; 6. Retirement comes but health problems arise and you need to be close to children; and finally 7. Settle in the West for good.

These days this paradox is less prevalent as young people come to the West with the intention of settling, fully encouraged by their parents. The world has also become a "global village." People can move more freely back and forth between East and West.

CHAPTER 6

TIMMINS, ONTARIO

Gold Mine in the Canadian Tundra

O ne day, I received a telephone call from Mr. Barry H. Martin, the engineering partner of the architectural/engineering firm Martin & Martin located in Timmins, Ontario. He was responding to my application for a job advertised in the newspaper. He invited me to Toronto International Airport for a dinner interview. We dined together, he treated me well, and I found him very likeable. He offered me a job and invited me to visit Timmins before accepting the offer.

I recalled the turbulence I experienced when first flying from Dhaka to Karachi, then again when flying from Zurich to Montreal. I developed a fear of flying and really didn't like it. My adviser once told me he was afraid of flying too. This might have inadvertently encouraged the irrational fear in me. I explored the option of driving to Timmins from Waterloo, but realized the city was about 430 miles (690 kilometers) north of Toronto and I would have to drive through a lot of wilderness. Once again, I employed my engineering training to work out a personal dilemma. I thought to myself that the airplane was mechanically and structurally designed with a high margin of safety. That single rational thought was enough to help me to overcome my fear.

I was received in the evening at the Timmins Airport by Barry Martin himself, who drove me to his house. There I met Jim Martin, the other architectural partner in the company along with their wives. After enjoying a meal of beef stew cooked by Barry's wife Shirley, we chatted for a bit before Jim dropped me off at a local hotel.

The next morning, a staff member picked me up and took me to the office where I met other employees and looked at some ongoing projects. The multi-faceted company did architecture, structural engineering and municipal engineering. It was housed in a new modern building and I liked the people and the facility. Even though this was my first offer, I knew I immediately needed to get my foot in the door and gather experience. So, I didn't care about seeking other jobs or about the remote location. After all, I was about 8,000 miles (12,800 kilometers) away from my own country anyway, so a few hundred miles more really didn't matter. My career mattered more, and I was comfortable knowing that I could change jobs later if needed.

Upon returning to Waterloo, Barry Martin sent me a written offer which I accepted. On Saturday, April 30, 1977 I drove to Timmins with my family and belongings. Our baby son Murad was less than a month old. A family friend of ours, M. Mustafizur Rahman and his wife Barbara, followed us with another car to help us out. I joined work without delay on Monday, May 2. Since I hadn't held a full-time job since 1970, I really felt delighted and excited that day to be back in the work force. After initially staying at an apartment that my employer arranged, we moved into an apartment at 641 North Cedar Street and settled in.

Timmins is basically a mining city in Northern Ontario with a long history of mining dating back to 1912, when gold was discovered there. The city that had a very large land area despite its small population, which at the time was about 45,000 people. The city mined different types of mineral resources that originally included silver and cobalt. Subsequently, large gold mines were discovered, attracting several mining companies, such as Dome Mines and McIntyre Mining Co. etc. In the 1960s Texas Gulf Sulphur Company started mining for copper and zinc, and when I was there, their presence was still felt.

My first assignment was to deal with an eight-story masonry apartment building known as Chartrand Apartments owned by one Mr. Chartrand, reportedly richest man in town. It was designed by Martin and Martin and condemned by the City of Timmins even before its construction was completed. Unfortunately, my engineering predecessor made a design mistake on this project, most likely through oversight. The floors and roof of hollow concrete, precast planks were supported upon walls of hollow masonry blocks. The problem came to light when a structural engineer, who was an expert on masonry structures, came to Timmins to give a seminar on masonry. He wanted to see a few masonry buildings in the city. The visiting engineer inspected this building, the tallest in town, and discovered a major problem in the structure.

As built, the design caused overstressing of the narrow masonry piers between the vertical rows of the door and/or wide window openings between the living rooms and balconies. Following engineering ethics guidelines, the problem was reported to the Association of Professional Engineers of Ontario (APEO). This caused a rift between Mr. Chartrand and Martin & Martin and eventually led to a lawsuit. My predecessor realized that he made a mistake and sensing trouble, he reportedly resigned and left. This also led to a misunderstanding between the two Martins as Jim, the architect, blamed Barry's lack of supervision for the mess. Incidentally, around this time I received a practicing license as P. Eng. (Professional Engineer) from APEO.

Barry asked me to thoroughly analyze the building structurally to see if there were any other areas of concern. This was a major challenge for me as I never had taken a course in masonry structures nor had I designed a building using structural masonry. The firm was depending on me to resolve and coordinate with others about this issue. I relied on my practical experience from East Pakistan where I had developed problem-solving skills. My post-graduate education gave me additional problem-solving abilities through research. I went ahead and started to tackle the task.

Since Timmins was a rather small city population wise, there was only one other structural engineering firm there. There was a community college called Northern College, but the resources were limited. I could not get hold of any books on masonry. Instead, I reviewed Canada's National Building Code and found some information there. I carried out a simple analysis, based on my common sense and technical skill and found that the piers were overstressed. I also checked a few other things following Barry's request, but found no major mistake. I suggested to him that while a simple analysis could reveal a problem, a different more detailed analysis, called finite element analysis, which considered the wall as a whole, including the piers, might yield different results.

I had taken a course on this subject at the University of Waterloo, taught by Professor G. McNiece. I told Barry I could consult Prof. McNiece and ask him to analyze the building. I thought it would be worth doing and could save a large sum of money if we could demonstrate that piers were not overstressed after all. He was excited about the possibility and asked me to see Professor McNiece. So, I went to meet the professor and he agreed to do the work.

However, when I came back and told Barry, he balked. He was afraid, as he told me, that the professor might find additional problems putting him into more trouble. I believed at the time, and still do, that the finite element analysis would actually help him demonstrate that the system as a whole was not over-stressed. My opinion was that the inherent, untapped strength of the adjoining wall could be exploited to show that the walls were fine, except for some possible overstressing, at the corners of the wall openings, which would relatively be a minor fix. My confidence came from knowing that an ordinary analysis by practitioners was only approximate. It considered the piers between the openings as separate, which they were not. This analysis exploits the reserve strength of the entire wall segment, in which the loads from above are distributed throughout the walls, thereby reducing the stress on the piers. I explained this to him, but my academic reasoning of structural logic and load path could not move the needle of his professional mind. I thought perhaps he wanted to stay the course since his firm had already hired a large structural firm in Toronto, Farkas Barron Jablonsky Ltd., to recommend the repairs needed. I don't believe the Toronto firm did any finite element analysis as I later visited their office and talked to engineers, all of whom were unfamiliar with such sophisticated method of analysis for masonry walls.

The Toronto firm prepared the structural repair drawings for wide-ranging repairs from the foundation up. A local contractor was hired to implement the work. I was assigned to be the resident engineer supervising the work. To unload the existing loaded elements and then transfer the loads to the newly installed columns, a new steel vertical framing system along with steel beams in affected areas were installed after placing shores throughout the building. Supervision of the sequence of work was extremely important to avoid damage to already built structures made of brittle concrete masonry and reinforced concrete beams over the lower-level garage and ensure the required load transfer to new added elements. Many unforeseen field problems needed on-the-spot decisions. I had to resolve these issues in consultation with the Toronto consultant. The repair work continued for six months and I had been sitting in a temporary office room this entire time. I had my construction boots and hard hat and would go out on inspections for other jobs from time to time. I kept a daily journal logging all activities and events at the job site. It was quite an experience for me.

While the initial discussions on the Chartrand Apartments project were ongoing, I was also asked to look into another interesting and challenging project. It was the existing South Porcupine Arena in South Porcupine, a few miles from Timmins. The story went that one Mr. Hippel, who was not an engineer, sold the large Hippel trusses in timber to many townships and cities in Ontario for the arena roofs in the 1940s. These arenas somehow survived blizzards. However, a severe winter blizzard in the mid-1970s caused the roof collapse of a few arenas that employed these trusses. As a result, all buildings with these trusses were condemned by the Ontario government. The cities and towns were ordered to fix these trusses before getting permission to reopen.

I visited the South Porcupine arena that remained vacant for a long time, leaving the local community without a recreational facility. I met the city officials at a prescheduled meeting at the arena led by one Mr. Davis. They were really angry with my predecessor who delayed the project, and with Barry. They expressed to me in unflattering language, that nothing had been done for a long time. They were also upset that Barry was not there with me. Barry was a likeable gentleman and my boss; I felt bad and somehow these words crossed my lips, "Don't worry. Since this is in my hands now, I will find a solution and it will be done very soon." Seeing my confidence, they liked it and felt reassured. Mr. Davis commented, "If you can do it, we will always remember you as the engineer from the south who came and fixed our problem." He told me to find a cheap solution as the city didn't have much money. Upon returning to the office, I reflected on what I said not knowing how bad the problem was. Barry wanted to know how my visit went. I replied that it went well, and I would find a solution to the problem. I had never taken a course in wood structures, nor designed any wood structures before. I realized this was a big challenge for me and I must succeed. I wanted to keep my word and good reputation.

I dedicated myself to the arena project. Referring to some books in the firm's small library, I found by calculations, that the trusses spanning 120 feet (37 meters) and spaced at 14 feet (4.2 meters) were highly structurally inadequate at their joints. I decided to talk with some experienced engineers in other cities who had solved this problem. I found out that most of them used several glulam rivets to reinforce the truss joints. There were numerous joints in each truss in the large arena and there were quite a few trusses. The cost of such repairs was very high and way out of the small budget of the city. Other cities had to do it to comply with the government's order or otherwise close down their arenas. So, I had to try and keep my promise and find a much cheaper solution.

Along with this challenge, I was working on other wood-framed homes and apartment buildings and gaining experience in wood design. I learned through self-study about plywood web beams. The beam's top and bottom were provided with wood along its length and its depth was sheathed in plywood nailed to the wood at the assembly's top and bottom. As it happens, I found a clue to the solution for the trusses. The repair involved a novel technique of nailing plywood sheets on both sides of the trusses and reinforcing the high shear zones at the supports with steel plates. This changed the structural function of the elements essentially from truss members to components of plywood web beams. The cost of this repair was only 25% of cost of the conventional repair technique with glulam rivets for similar Hippel trusses in Ontario. I submitted the drawings and calculations to the government engineers in Toronto, who approved my solution. The work was completed under my supervision. Mr. Davis was satisfied with the outcome and informed Barry of it. Barry was very happy with me and immediately gave me a raise in my salary telling the business manager Elaine in my presence "Mir has proved his mettle, so I am giving him a raise."

Jim Martin left the firm as his relationship soured with Barry over the Chartrand Apartments debacle. Another architect, John Osborne, closely associated with Jim also left soon after and started his own practice in Timmins. He took some other architects from the firm with him. Now, the firm was totally an engineering company, renamed B.H. Martin Consultants. I was moved to the nice office vacated by Jim Martin and was given full responsibility over the engineering section. A junior structural engineer, Robert Falcioni, was hired later to assist me. I was involved in a few more interesting projects involving new design and investigation.

One interesting project I can think of was an existing building in a place called Moosonee, a remote town further north of Timmins in Northern Ontario on the Moosonee river a few miles south of the James Bay, an extended part of the Hudson Bay. Being the northernmost settlement of Ontario, it is known as "The Gateway to the Arctic." The experience lives on in my mind, not so much the project, but as personal experience associated with it. Nearby Moosonee is the Moose Factory Island, which is linked to Moosonee by water taxi in summer and ice road in winter. In the winter of 1977, I went by a small plane to Moosonee to investigate a two-story building formerly used as an Air Force Officers' Mess. The building was burnt down by a fire and abandoned. Moosonee authorities decided to remodel and upgrade this building to make it a young people's club, an amenity which was badly needed in this solitary town.

It was a bitterly cold day and the building had no heating. I managed to survey and gather the information that I needed to analyze the existing structure and redesign the building as needed. When I returned, I boarded a really tiny plane which had four passenger seats with hardly any partition between the pilot and passengers. There was only one other passenger. The pilot carried our luggage and loaded it on the plane. Once the plane ascended, I noticed water below, and the wind started shaking the plane badly. I had never flown such a little plane. The cockpit was only a few feet away and I saw the pilot maneuvering the plane, seemingly unconcerned. Suddenly, the plane went into a dive and tilted, frightening me. My fellow passenger saw my face and reassured me saying "I fly regularly in this plane. It is as safe as a jumbo jet and there is no need to be scared." I felt better, tried to maintain my composure and had counted the minutes before I would land in Timmins.

My professional experiences are often the backdrop for some personal memories I hold today. One that stands out is my first new car. A few days after we moved to Timmins, I bought a Ford Custom 500, to replace my old Ford Mercury Montego that looked pretty tired. I took my family for rides around Timmins and enjoyed driving a totally new car for the first time in my life. Two days after I bought the large eight-cylinder car, my office got a call from a mortician, who was the funeral director in town. He told me that the sloped ground behind his funeral home bordering the town's most luxurious hotel had eroded badly after a heavy rain and was very unstable and needed to be retained to avoid collapse. Coincidentally, I had stayed in that hotel, while interviewing.

He wanted us to take a close look at it and design a retaining wall to hold the soil. I jumped into my new car and happily headed for the site. Reaching the site, I saw there was a gateway for the entrance to the building. I had never been to a funeral home before, and had an eerie feeling about going in. I was a bit distracted and my car hit the brick pillar of the gate as I turned in. My car, brand new, was damaged on the passenger side. I was upset and thought this was not a good start to my relationship with the new car. The funeral director took me to the site. To the best of my recollection I noticed there was a very old wall in dilapidated condition and already badly tilted under the soil's lateral pressure. I could not design a wall with its foundation encroaching into the hotel's property and the mortician wanted to build the wall exactly on the property line, so no land was lost to the other side. With these design constraints, I came back to the office and designed an L-shaped retaining wall with the entire footing inside the property line avoiding any encroachment.

One other project was dealing with the collapse of a heavy plastered ceiling in an adult movie theater. Barry asked me to investigate the collapse of the ceiling. It had occurred shortly after midnight following a heavy rainfall. I went to the site to inspect and found many seats totally or partially crushed and scattered over the floor along with the debris from the ceiling. I heard the collapse happened immediately after a show was over. I shuddered at the thought of what a tragedy it would have been had it occurred during the show. The plastered ceiling was 30 feet (9 meters) above the floor. The contractor for the project placed a tall upright ladder attached to a scaffold. I didn't have any experience climbing such a height. Although I disliked being at great heights, I took it lightly as I thought it was only 30 feet (9 meters). However, after I climbed to about mid height or so, I looked around in the open space of the large movie theater and people down below staring at me, I felt spacy and was thinking I had better go back down before I got more lightheaded and lost control. But, my rational mind and sense of dignity prevailed. I thought about the people on the floor, who were looking up to me as a professional to investigate and resolve the problem. What would they think of me – a cowardly structural engineer! That gave me a rush of adrenalin. I managed to go to the top where a worker was waiting for me. He grabbed my right hand and lifted me up to the platform.

I viewed the failed area of plaster up close as well as underneath the roof, before climbing down. I concluded that water was dripping from the leaky roof at about 20 feet (6 meters) above the ceiling. Repeated impact resulted in a dent on the top face of the plaster. Over a prolonged period of time, the dent became a partial hole, not visible from below. The plaster was reinforced with a steel mesh. Water seeped through the damaged plaster and spread out, causing rusting and weakening of the mesh and sagging of the ceiling. After a heavy rainfall, water accumulated above the sagged ceiling and the weakened plaster and mesh could no longer carry the weight of the water pond and collapsed. I offered a technical explanation to the insurance company. As with many old buildings, the roof is rarely inspected or monitored and usually leakage occurs though deteriorated flashings at joints, recesses and corners. I've investigated many such failures in Timmins and always enjoyed solving the mystery behind the real cause. I always felt like a detective trying to find the culprit in a crime or a physician trying to diagnose the disease in a patient.

While employed by B.H. Martin Consultants, word spread that I was a well-qualified structural engineer. Timmins is a mining town mainly known for mining carried out by Texas Gulf, an American company, at that time, of which Mining Corporation Canada Ltd. was the local subsidiary. Texas Gulf contacted me to design some of their mining structures. I sought Barry's consent to see if I could consult outside my regular working hours.

He told me, "Go ahead, Mir. In this community, we all need your expertise." I was encouraged and excited about having the opportunity, as mining was a totally new area of endeavor for me. Working in the industry allowed me to explore and learn new things.

During my stay in Timmins, I worked on several mining projects that entailed many structures that I had never heard of. I came to really appreciate the breadth of my structural engineering education. The training helped me apply universal truths about structures to any design solution. Regardless of the type of structures, the fundamental structural principles are the same, only the loads, functionality and relevant codes for the structures are different. I noticed that unlike commercial and residential buildings, the mining industry wasn't as concerned about the quantity of materials nor the cost of the structures. They just wanted structures that would perform without problems. There was no need to optimize structures; playing safe and conservative was the key to design in the mining industry. I enjoyed designing bulkheads, buried storage structures, unusually tall and heavy retaining walls, the foundation of a jaw crusher building, and many more. I studied the subject of mining structures as much as possible. I wish I had the opportunity to design a head frame, another important mining structure, but it was not to be as I left Timmins for another city after some time.

I had fond memories of my brief role as a teacher in Bangladesh at EPUET. So, I sought out an opportunity to teach part time, at Northern College. Northern College was a local community college for applied arts and technology serving northeastern Ontario. When I lectured at EPUET as a senior student, on a structural engineering course as a substitute for my professor, I discovered my liking and ability to teach. I got positive feedback from a student who commented on my lack of nervousness throughout the class. I contacted the Principal of Northern College and offered to teach a diploma level course in technology called "Structural Design & Technology" for one semester. I developed the syllabus and taught in the evenings.

I thoroughly enjoyed this and my interaction with the students. Before the final examination, I got a call from the Principal, who wanted to review the questions I set. I met him and shared the question set with him. Although I didn't like the interference at the time, I complied with his request. Considering I didn't have much teaching experience, I realized he might teach me something new. He pointed at two questions and said "These questions will be too hard for them. Can you change them? Also, you set too many theoretical questions. Since this is a professional field, students should learn more problem-solving skills. Can you set more practical problems for them and cut down the number of theoretical questions?" I took his advice to heart instead of getting offended and thanked him sincerely. He taught me something valuable and later when I entered my full-time teaching career, I put his good advice to practice.

I had been working on several projects of varied nature ranging from industrial buildings, skating rinks, to large concrete swimming pools and a new museum building in Timmins, as well as other projects in surrounding smaller towns. I relished the opportunities to learn new things in a developed, Western country. A museum building was one such memorable project. The museum was located on a deep fill of loose material. To stabilize the structure, I used timber piles, and since the perimeter columns were very closely spaced, I employed a continuous concrete footing underneath as a cap to the 60-foot (18-meter) long piles. I supervised the foundation construction and encountered some unexpected surprises. I was called from the site on two occasions.

One was when a pile, while being driven, suddenly disappeared into the ground. The other one was when a pile hit something hard like rock or boulder at its tip and could not be driven. I had to make on-the-spot decisions to resolve these field problems.

I truly enjoyed working with focus on the tasks at hand as well as the adventure of doing different things during the same period. It was a welcome change for me to work on practical projects in the real world after spending years in the academic environment. My research training during master's and Ph.D. prepared me to dig deeper into each project, an attribute that I retained in my later career. I also called on earlier practical experience in Bangladesh to deal with practical problems in Timmins despite the differences in construction methods and practice. This experience also exposed me to Canadian engineers, architects, contractors, developers, owners, building officials, and public at large. I could better understand their customs, manners, and *modus operandi*. I found them to be very logical, impressively professional and well-mannered people. Since I loved my work, I had been absorbing the lessons I learned from each experience like a sponge.

In 1978, I acquired Canadian citizenship. I felt more established in the country but also felt a pang of despondence that perhaps I no longer formally belonged to my dear native land. Bangladesh was where I was born, raised and educated. I remembered with renewed emotion that my native country had given me so much. Most especially, an almost free education. I was able to pursue becoming an engineer, only to end up in service of another country. The tug of guilt was relieved when I considered that Canada had also given me a lot. All people are basically the same in their hearts, only slightly distinguished by race, language, culture, and religion. Moreover, both Canada and Bangladesh allowed dual citizenship, so I was consoled knowing that I was still a citizen of Bangladesh.

On other fronts, there wasn't much there in terms of entertainment or recreation for the family. In the summer of 1978 an American musical film, *Grease*, an adaptation of the hit Broadway musical, came to movie theaters. Starring John Travolta and Olivia Newton-John, it featured songs like "Sandy" and "You're the One That I Want." The film depicted the lives of two high school seniors Danny (John Travolta) and Sandy (Olivia Newton-John) in the late 1950s. The movie was a cultural flashpoint of the era and critically and commercially successful. The whole family enjoyed the movie and I always associate it with my short stay in Timmins.

One trip that flashes in my memory during my stay in Timmins is a visit with my family to Moose Factory. In late summer of 1978, with Dora and the three kids we drove to nearby Cochrane, and boarded the Polar Bear Express, a tourist train traveling to Moosonee. We were joined by our friends Subrata and Leena Barua, who came from Waterloo, to visit us. Subrata was a doctoral student at the University of Waterloo. We witnessed unbelievable wilderness and natural beauty. We were surrounded by pin drop silence during our round trip. The area seemed starved for visits by humans or any life forms. As the train hurtled through the wilderness, I enjoyed the abundant number of trees, lush shrubbery, swamplands, and tall weeds all around us. The whole natural landscape was as if untouched by anyone. Along the way we saw masses of logs floating on water presumably as part of the seasoning process for lumber. We had some American tourists on the train as well. I remember one chatty woman who sat across the aisle and became friends with us. She eventually gave me her home address and telephone number and kindly invited us to visit if we ever traveled to the U.S.

The first stop on our visit was to a place called Moose Factory on Moose Factory Island. The island is near the mouth of Moose

River, at southern end of the James Bay. A guide explained the history, as I recall we visited a small museum there. From Moose Factory to Moosonee, we were ferried across the Moose River by a boat, also called water taxi. There wasn't much startling to see in this small community and the train returned the same day. Overall, it was an enjoyable day trip. Despite the toil of traveling with three kids, including one who was just a year old, we relished the trip. The kids were all well behaved as usual and liked the adventure. They were also happy to see our friends Subrata and Leena, whom they knew and loved.

To entertain my children, I would frequently drive around the city and often take my family to the nearest town of Porcupine, where a sea plane was anchored in a lake. Texas Gulf had a few buffaloes and the kids would enjoy seeing them. Once a circus party came to Timmins and performed at the local McIntyre Arena; my family and I went to see it and we all enjoyed the evening. There were a few Indian Hindu families in Timmins. Most of them were engineers in the mining industry but we were the only Muslim family in town. Sharing a culture and minority connection, we soon became friends with some of them. We would even attend their religious festivals. Eventually, one young Muslim couple moved to town. I also became friends with some of my co-workers in the office.

I would occasionally go south with my family to visit places for short vacations. Hunting and fishing were popular in the area surrounding Timmins. I never had a good luck with fishing, and I would get bored after some time waiting for a nibble at the hook. As I grew older, I didn't like the idea of shooting or killing innocent birds and animals for pleasure. My father was fond of hunting and was a good shooter. But somehow, I didn't inherit that trait. In fact, I found this out rather early in my life, in Dhaka, when I tried shooting some birds in a nearby village while I was working there as an engineer.

One day Barry invited me to go hunting with him. He shot some pheasants and instead of taking them home he brought them to my apartment. Neither me nor Dora had ever done much serious manual work in our native country, let alone butchering and skinning an animal. We lived in a traditional service economy, where home help was cheap and there was plenty of labor. From my demeanor Barry perhaps sensed that; so, instead of leaving them to us he asked for a knife. He cleaned the feathers off the pheasants on our back patio, skinned and washed them, and gave these to us. Later Dora roasted them. The next day I took some cooked meat and rice pilaf to Barry's house. Shirley and the kids weren't home. Barry invited me to eat with him, but I declined saying I had food at home. He warmed up the food in a microwave oven. He had just bought this new gadget. This was the first time I had seen a microwave oven. He ate while we chatted and enjoyed the meal. He thanked me and conveyed his thanks to Dora as well.

The climate and wilderness in Northern Ontario, made the province and ideal place for moose, but not deer. People would go out moose hunting to get recharged and escape the stresses of life. Moose was also considered a hazard since in spring and summer, these animals would wander across the highway and frequently cause accidents. I heard stories of accidental deaths in the area. My family and I had a very close encounter while returning to Timmins from Sudbury, 180 miles (290 kilometers) south of Timmins.

It was a summer evening, and darkness was falling. The highway was desolate, with forests all around and no signs of other humans or cars. Suddenly, I saw a large animal about the size of a buffalo cross the highway in front of me. Then I saw another one following it a short distance away. I was traveling at a high speed, about 60 to 65 miles (96 to 104 kilometers) per hour. If I braked to save it, I would lose control of the car. If I didn't, I would certainly hit this large animal. Either way, it would be the end of me and my family in this deep, no-man's land of forest. The second moose suddenly stopped approaching and stood still on the highway, its eyes were dazzled by the headlights. I guess God was taking care of me that night. Instead of me avoiding it the moose avoided the car, it backed off and my car flew by. I clearly saw its large head a few inches to my left from my car window.

I was shaken but didn't want to stop in this scary location. With a pounding heart I spontaneously shuddered at what just happened. Had my fast-moving car hit the large animal, my entire family and I might have been killed. Still shaken, I reached a small settlement with a population of a few hundred called Gogama, 70 miles (112 kilometers) from Timmins and thought of stopping to recover from the shock. But it looked very bleak at nighttime, so I decided to continue driving and return home. It was a truly harrowing experience which I've never forgotten.

I had been relishing my work and stay at Timmins, with Barry who was very friendly and affable. He treated me fairly, like a friend and not an employee and with respect, and had I decided to stay there for some time, he would most likely have made me a partner, as he was already treating me like one. The weather was very cold; the winter temperatures were sub-zero for the duration and people there called it dry cold. The snow didn't melt, and the ground was usually covered with snow all season. When I walked on the snow it would make a tell-tale crunchy sound. My car, like all others, had to be plugged in to an electric outlet so the battery wouldn't freeze overnight, and the car could start in the morning. Cars needed snow tires in winter. If ever I was out for a long time, visiting job sites, I wore full-length thermal underwear, a down-filled jacket, hefty winter boots, and heavy-duty caps and gloves. I liked the natural beauty of the landscape throughout the year. In summer, it was enjoyable to visit lakes that had calm and clear water. These lakes were usually caused by heavy, molten glaciers. The surroundings were extremely peaceful. Even today when I meditate, I imagine that I am there in that calm setting.

⚔

It was the December 1978 holiday season of Christmas and the New Year. In those days, it was not simple to visit my native country, which I missed all the time. It was expensive for a student with a family to afford a return trip. At that point, with the benefit of fulltime employment, I was finally able to afford the trip to see my elderly parents. I had really missed them and my other relatives, after a lapse of eight years. I decided to go to Dhaka adding a few weeks to the regular leave, making it a month-long vacation.

When we landed in Dhaka on December 8 and exited the airport, all along the street, I saw big crowds and distant memories of the noisy environment came back. It was bit of a shock at first going from a quiet place like Timmins, but I soon felt back at home in my original, natural setting. I found my parents looking much older but felt ecstatic when I hugged them warmly after so many years. They were living in a residential area called Rayer Bazar that had some stores and a fresh market. It was in the home that I built when I was there was later expanded by my younger brother, Mosaddeq. I heard the *Azan* (the Islamic call for prayer) from the minaret after many years. I visited my oldest sister Jahan Ara Hossain and third sister Afroza Anwar and my younger brother Mosaddeq and his wife, Moshira (Tora). Tora was also Dora's sister and therefore my double sister-in-law. I met my nephews and nieces. My youngest sister Farhad Ara Arzoo and her husband, Mr. Amanullah Bhuiyan, a mechanical engineer, and their children had since immigrated to Canada. I did meet my in-law's family and some of my old classmates. Soon I felt like

I had been living there all along and the memory of Canada, a distant country across the ocean, was less in the forefront of my thoughts. Dora and the kids also enjoyed it there. The kids were exposed to a new environment. My parents were happy to see their grandchildren. It was a joyful experience for all of us.

Dora always wanted to return to our native land. I also felt very connected to that land and the environment. I knew that with my Western education and practical experience, I could serve my country and look after my elderly parents in their advanced age. My children were still very young, and they would adjust very quickly. They would get the love and affection of their grandparents and our other relatives which they missed living isolated in Canada. Also, Bangladesh was a new country; there were many opportunities for engineers. Amidst this busy and pleasurable time, I recalled how my parents wanted me to stay with them and not go overseas. They only reluctantly let me go after sensing my burning desire, and I told them before I left for Canada that I had no intention of settling in a foreign country, as I loved my own native country and culture very much. Also, my father had written me a letter when I was in Waterloo asking me to return after finishing my studies. So, this was the time to fulfil that promise and my wish. I had to find a good job while I was in Dhaka.

First, I went to meet the Vice Chancellor of Bangladesh University of Engineering & Technology (BUET, formerly EPUET), who was the administrative head of the university. It so happened that Dr. Wahiduddin Ahmed was the Vice Chancellor. He was the same professor, who was the head of the Civil Engineering department when I left EPUET. I was not very comfortable seeing him ever since he had impulsively hired someone ahead of me, breaking his promise to make me the next faculty hire at the time. But I respected him as my one-time teacher who liked me, and I tried to understand the predicament he was in when he broke his promise. I recalled the favors he bestowed on me by giving me a nice office and an apartment. Thus, I buried any grudge or bitterness against him.

I expressed my intention to return to Bangladesh and join BUET as a faculty member. He replied, "Good to see you. We can hire you, but we have a very rigid hiring system. Since you have no teaching experience and will start here as a new faculty member, you must begin your career as an assistant professor even though you have a Ph.D. and practical experience. Those who are now assistant professors will have seniority over you and will be promoted before you even though you graduated before them. You may not like it but if you are willing to accept that, we will be happy to hire you." This didn't sound very appealing to me and I was disheartened.

Next, I went to see Mr. Moqbulur Rahman, Managing Director of Consulting Engineers Ltd. I was uncomfortable seeing him as well, since I left his firm for the State Bank of Pakistan despite his request that I stayed with his firm. However, I knew he was a gentleman and probably didn't remember that or care about it as he had been dealing with many employees and many bigger issues over the years. He welcomed me heartily and heard my story. He told me, "You came at the right time. We have a few bridge projects and we need a structural engineer as qualified as you are. With your credentials I can offer you the position of Director. It is a good idea to raise your children in your own culture. I hope you can join us." I may add that he had a master's degree in Civil Engineering from an American university, so he knew enough about America and its culture to make the recommendation.

This offer appealed to me and I was elated at the thought of returning to my beloved native country. I also had early experience in bridge design when I worked in his firm in the 1960s. I told him I would think about this and decide quickly. So, now

I had to give the good news to my elderly parents who always wanted me near them. I assumed they would be very happy especially since my ambitious younger brother, who was in Dhaka, was planning to leave for America soon, to pursue advanced studies. His departure would leave them without any son nearby in their old age. In Bangladeshi culture, sons were primarily responsible for taking care of their parents. I also had two sisters there, but in those days, women in Bangladesh had limited opportunities. They were constrained from taking care of same things outside the home that men would do. Of course, things have changed much at this writing.

I returned home excited at the pleasant thought of how my parents would rejoice over the job offer and the prospect of having me back near them. I told them "I have a decent job offer here. You always wanted me to return after I finished my education abroad. I can now return to Dhaka." My wise father replied "Look, we have a few years left of our life. You have a long life ahead of you. You seem to be doing well in your job, and happy and successful there in Canada. I also see Dora and your kids look so healthy and happy. Bringing them here is not a good idea. This country is going through an uncertain and unstable period." My mother sitting next to him was quiet, and I felt she was agreeable with my father's advice.

The country's founder, Sheikh Mujibur Rahman, was assassinated in August 1975 and the country was still going through an unstable period. I had one consolation since I had two sisters there along with their husbands. My brother-in-law (oldest sister's husband) Mr. Altaf Hossain, who was a police officer, was a very caring, responsible and affectionate person. He was like our elder brother with a towering and pleasant personality and admirable human qualities. I saw him on many occasions, through thick and thin while I had been living there. I assumed in my mind he would take care of my parents during emergencies. Moreover, I had another brother-in-law (my other sister's husband) Dr. M. Anwarullah – a physician and a gentleman – who would also take care of them. Also, a maternal cousin, Mofiz Chowdhury (Mofee), who was a student, was staying with my parents. With such reassurances in my mind and based on what my judicious father said, I returned to Canada.

Before I returned, I had the land of our Rayer Bazar home surveyed, filled up the low-lying areas with new soil fill, and engaged a contractor to build brick walls around the property. My parents were concerned about how to secure the ill-defined property line, but ill-equipped to deal with the many aspects of the project. This project took up much of my vacation time. My father was very appreciative and thanked me profusely for this effort. I realized that even if my life was across the ocean, I could still help my parents and give them the security and peace of mind they needed in their old age. But it was not to be as life is difficult and full of constraints.

It was hard to leave Bangladesh this time. Unlike 1970 when I first headed for Canada, with the hope of returning, this time I knew I would most likely live in a foreign land for an unforeseen duration. I was leaving knowing that I would not be the one to care for my elderly parents or even visit them frequently. But by now I also learned that being too emotional didn't help or serve any purpose, it only clouded my rational thinking. As much as I had an obligation to my parents and my country, I also had obligations to my wife and children. Our children were totally dependent on us for their future and I knew I must move on with my own life. So, even though this time I had my father's blessing to go, it was with a heavy heart and with suppressing any emotion that I took leave of my old parents. I asked for their forgiveness for any time I hadn't lived up to their expectations or hurt their feelings in any way, through my actions or words. I sought their blessings, not knowing when I would see them next. My father was about 77 and mother 74 at the time, both were in poor health due to advanced age and loneliness.

When we returned to Timmins, it was early January 1979 and it was a shock to see the white snow-covered land. A stark contrast to the mild climate, din and bustle of Dhaka. I quickly got readjusted to the utter quietness and bitter cold environment in Timmins and I got back to work.

The solitude and isolation of Northern Ontario inspired a sense of deep introspection and spirituality. Some places were very picturesque and amazingly tranquil that made me automatically relax into a reflective mood. I had already encountered some bumps and bruises in my life's pathway, but for me this was a time in which I felt stronger and more confident. Over the course of my musings about religion, I came to believe that they all taught the same values. For instance, distinguishing between right and wrong, being good people and developing a moral compass to guide actions. People born in one faith can sometimes criticize other faiths and develop a bias toward their own faith. Agnostics, skeptics, and freethinkers could criticize all faiths. So, even without comparing between religions and other viewpoints, I felt that there must exist an intelligent higher power that controlled our lives and set up universal laws. To connect to that supreme power, religion became a necessary vehicle.

I was born a Muslim, and others could find fault in my faith as I could in theirs if I wanted. In my opinion, it would be an endless debate to try and determine which faith was true, or the best, since adherents would most likely stick with their own beliefs. The resolution was to shake off our ignorance and simply respect one another's faith. In fact, the Quran states that there is no compulsion in religion. Despite feeling the confidence that comes with age and experience, I had a habit of worrying in those days, a trait I inherited from my father. I read the classic book *How to Stop Worrying and Start Living* by Dale Carnegie in my younger years. He referred to the concept of total surrender to God in Islam as an approach to happiness. With the acknowledgment that our life is controlled by Almighty God who decides our destiny, ultimately, we need to surrender to God for the outcome of everything after exerting our own best efforts. A belief based upon the latter could free us from the burden and agony of life's worries.

In Islam, we are urged to live a face-to-face life with God without an intermediary, and if we remember and call upon Him sincerely, He will reciprocate. Thus, in times of crisis we should remember to connect with Him and seek His help. This direct communication distinguishes our relationship with Him. With these notions in mind, I started prayers on a regular basis. This line of thinking allowed me to face the world calmly, with courage, strength, and confidence. I felt confident that as a believer, if I submitted to the will of God, He always would have my back. What could be more reassuring than this to achieve mental peace and keep stress and depressive thoughts at bay? The reassurance of my religion helped greatly when I needed to overcome calamities throughout my life.

After I learned to deal with many smaller projects of varied nature in Timmins, I decided that I should attempt larger projects and challenges. So, I needed to move to a bigger city. I had a typewriter that I used for typing job applications while I was still in Waterloo. I brought it out of storage and left it on a desk in the living room. A close Indian friend of mine, Dr. Jay Pathak, a mining engineer, and his wife Madhuri, saw it while visiting us. He quipped, "You want to leave Timmins and apply for jobs in the south right? I and many others like me are mining engineers, so we have no opportunity there, but you have." I remained quiet as he read my mind and figured me out.

I applied to a few places in and around Toronto and got interview calls. The first interview was in Peterborough, 85 miles (136 kilometers) north of Toronto. My job was to assist a senior structural engineer in the design of water retaining structures. The job was not very appealing to me and my interviewer, sensing my hesitation and perhaps to entice me, said "If you join us, this place is so close to Toronto, you can eventually move there."

On another occasion, I went for three separate interviews with three engineering firms. The first one was in St. Catherines, a town near the Niagara Falls region about 30 miles (48 kilometers) from Toronto. I drove to St. Catherines. I learned the firm was primarily engaged in building repair, renovation and remodeling projects, which didn't excite me. I think the interviewer sensed that and he and I mutually felt this would not be a good fit.

Next, I went to a hotel in Toronto where I met a principal of a firm. He explained to me that they needed someone who take full responsibility for the structural design of a 20-story concrete building in Edmonton, Alberta. I told him that while I didn't have that specific experience, I could manage the task, given my background in reinforced concrete research during graduate studies and my proven ability in dealing with new challenging projects. I also mentioned that I designed reinforced concrete buildings and bridges while I was in Bangladesh. He didn't seem all that impressed. He was looking for an engineer experienced in the design of high-rises, one who needed no supervision. I was also a bit wary since he had a point about my needing some supervision. I never designed a multistory concrete building of that size. Moreover, I didn't want to go to Alberta. It seemed a bit too far away from Ontario, where I had developed some roots and had my siblings and some friends. Our personal chemistry was not very positive either and we shared a mutual lack of enthusiasm.

At the end of the interview, he told me he would contact me later, which he never did. But this interview had one positive effect on me. I discovered my professional limitations. If I was ever going to work on the sort of challenging projects that would satisfy my inquisitive nature and analytical aspirations, I needed more experience. More experience would help me find a good job with a major company, in a large city. I came to the definitive realization that I needed to gain experience doing larger projects.

My third interview was with a large company dealing with nuclear structures. I was interviewed by a senior engineer presumably with hiring authority. He was likeable and a friendly person. He said his firm did the work for a large American company. I don't recall the nature and extent of the position, but what I got from his explanation was that I had to do a lot of computer analysis of nuclear structures. This was totally unknown territory for me, but I showed a lot of interest as it was something new and the job was in Toronto. Moreover, he was a likable person and would be my boss. If I didn't like the work, I could always find some other job in the large metropolitan city. He also recognized that I would need some degree of training and orientation for the job.

He saw my passion and seemed to like me. He told me he knew about Timmins and offered me a job saying, "We can hire you right now if you want to come here immediately." I was not prepared for this, as I was thinking of my pending commitments in Timmins. So, I said "Can I go back home and get organized there and get back to you soon?" He agreed and told me to make up my mind and let him know within a month and gave me his contact information. Having secured a verbal offer and the prospect of moving to Toronto, a big city with many engineering opportunities, I felt delighted when I returned to Timmins. Although I got the offer and was happy about moving to Toronto, in the back of my mind I was also thinking of whether the job would be a suitable match for my background and interest. I knew I would enjoy working on buildings or bridges since I had experience in those structures. So, I decided to sleep on it as I had one month to decide.

After a couple of weeks, I decided that I should accept the offer if I wanted to move to a metropolitan city like Toronto where there would be many better opportunities. I called my contact, but his secretary said, "He is out of the country. He had to go to Europe on urgent business and will be there for an extended period of time." I told her I was returning my decision about a job he had offered. She said she would check it out and let me know. I got a call back and she reported that there was no record of the offer he made as it was verbal, and I had to wait until he came back. I realized my mistake in not accepting the offer immediately, I got disheartened and gave up.

A few days later, responding to an advertisement, I applied for the position of senior structural engineer at a firm called Albery, Pullerits, Dickson (APD) & Associates in Sudbury. The job was a good match for me, and I thought I could move closer to Toronto. I got an interview call and job offer after I was interviewed by an engineer, Mr. David H. Smith. He was the Northern Ontario Division Manager. I decided to accept it right away and soon joined the firm on June 11, 1979.

The local Indian community in Timmins organized a farewell party for my family arranged by Ramesh Mandal, a mining engineer and his sociable wife Manju. Barry also bid me goodbye with a brief office party and a nice gift on June 8, my last day with the firm. Barry was bit disappointed and said, "I am sorry that you are leaving us. I knew we couldn't keep you here too long. Someone like you with your credentials belongs in the south. If you ever decide to come back in the future, our door is always open for you." I had developed a good relationship with Barry, and he treated me like a friend. I also had close relationships with other employees. Timmins was a very nice small-town environment and saying goodbye to everyone was hard for me. But I had to move on.

CHAPTER 7

SUDBURY, ONTARIO

Hard Knocks in the Nickel City

S udbury is the largest city in Northern Ontario. It is known for nickel and copper mining. The city has a long history of mining dating back to the 19th century, throughout which different companies conducted mining operations. In the 1960s or so INCO had been carrying out nickel mining operations. Parts of the city looked dismal with no vegetation and the surface looked like that of the moon. Some people said it was because of all the mining operations and the chemicals and acids emitted from chimneys. In fact, there was a very tall chimney emitting gases that were alleged to have caused acid rain. Somewhat oblivious or at least unmoved by any health risks, my family and I settled in soon after renting a townhome at 20 Brookview Gardens. I was quickly ready for work.

The office of APD had several employees and was administered by a soft-spoken manager, David Smith, gentle in manner. I had to report to another experienced senior structural engineer who was heading the structural engineering section. His name was Arturo (Art) Abrera, originally from the Philippines. He helped me get oriented and I soon found out he was a very friendly person but liked to micromanage. I heard that my predecessor left, and Art mentioned him in unflattering terms. I suspected he probably left because of Art's perceived penchant for interfering. I noted that he soon became somewhat respectful to me although he would still like to look over my shoulder and give me unsolicited advice about my work. Of course, I didn't like that because in Timmins, I worked independently, and Barry always trusted my work and judgment. Regardless of that I soon discovered that Art was a very capable and experienced engineer with perfectionist tendencies. In a way, I liked that, and thought I could learn more from him about the profession. So, my respect for him developed as I found him to be careful and conscientious in his work. He could anticipate any possible problem in structural design or investigation by looking at it from different angles. After some time, I noticed he found me to be a serious worker too and started giving me more and more independence in my work. I also liked his otherwise friendly demeanor. Everything was going well for me and my family.

I started my work with some small projects. We used to get frequent requests from insurance companies to investigate cracks in buildings caused by rock blasting in the mines. It was our job to figure out if the claims were genuine. Even though I worked in a mining town, I never had any experience with investigations dealing with rock blasting. First, I would go to the building site to view the cracks in the damaged foundation walls in the basement. With a magnifying lens I would check to see if there were any dust particles in a crack. This would prove it was an old crack and not caused by recent rock blasting. I could identify other cracks that were not due to rock blasting. I studied the literature and figured out the formulas and analysis methods soon enough. I would use analysis and calculations to assess the cracks that might be caused by rock blasting. I would prepare a report on my findings and deliver it to the insurance companies. On one occasion, I visited the home of an elderly lady to check cracks in her basement. She led me to the basement and after checking the cracks, I asked her, with her permission, "Do you live here alone?" She said, "Yes." I told her "This is unthinkable in the culture I'm from. Children keep their older parents with them and take care of them."

"I know. We are independent-minded people and don't depend on children in the West. I have a daughter living on the other side of town. When I can't handle things, she comes to help me," the woman replied. I was impressed by the woman's spirit, particularly the way she told me.

I was asked to work on a small but challenging project in Sudbury. An apartment building with foundations on the steep slope varying from 20 to 45 degrees of a rocky hill developed cracks in masonry walls retaining backfill under the floor. Some tie rods and anchors holding these walls ruptured requiring complete evacuation of the building for fear of the building's collapse. A large steel truss was fabricated in a 24-hour round-the-clock operation, to temporarily support the floor system on the down-hill side of the building. As a permanent solution, I designed a reinforced concrete wall around the existing foundation walls by doweling the new wall to the sloped rock and fastening it to the existing wall with anchors. I supervised the work during construction and resolved many unforeseen field problems.

I also was charged with supervising the construction of a new 14-story concrete apartment building in Sudbury. This project kept me very engaged for quite some time. It gave me the opportunity to deal with the foreman and crew, and coordinate with the architect and city officials. It also exposed me to new construction of a mid-rise building. With hard hat and construction boots on, I felt more down-to-earth, like a hands-on engineer. I used to go to the site every day and stay at the site office to oversee things. Then I would go around the building under construction accompanied by the foreman. I resolved some of the field problems. I can still remember the images I saw and the smell of the newly poured concrete. A memorable scent that I loved since childhood.

I got involved in an interesting project related to a 10-year old row house apartment building called Apollo Terrace, owned by the Government of Ontario. It consisted of a series of apartments contained in a continuous long building with basement in each unit. Several units developed cracks in the basement walls, notably in the units in the middle section of the building. In the past these cracks were repaired, but they continued to progress and open wider, and in a couple of cases the crack width was wide enough that a penny could be pushed in through it. My previous experience with fact-finding projects dealing with existing buildings and my training in research gave me the confidence and the tools needed to handle such projects.

After inspecting the crack patterns, I immediately realized that they were caused by foundation settlement. This led me to explore into the history of the building's construction and study, in-depth, the soil conditions of the site. The problem was caused by a soft clay layer; high ground water level; and deep fill on the front of the building, used for creating a parking lot. The building was very long, and the design didn't provide a separation joint or any breaking up in the length the building. After thorough investigation and analysis, I prepared a detailed report for the Ontario Ministry of Housing recommending upgrading of the structure including shoring and underpinning of the foundation.

Another interesting project I worked on was a senior citizens' apartment building in North Bay, Ontario, a city about 90 miles (144 kilometers) east of Sudbury. It entailed the investigation of an existing 14-story reinforced concrete apartment building that tilted at one corner. The City of North Bay condemned the building and all occupants were evacuated. The building was founded on compacted gravel piles. A soil engineer's investigation revealed that settlement of some corner piles, caused inadequate compaction during construction, was the reason for the tilting. I completed the analysis of the building and investigated means and methods of repair to upgrade it. Because it was a concrete building, attempts of shoring and underpinning would disturb the stress distribution and might cause stress reversals of the concrete floor system. This would lead to extensive cracking. Although it was not impossible to do this, the cost of repair would be prohibitive. I recommended the demolition and reconstruction of the building.

In Sudbury, I remained very engaged and busy with work. There were several other projects I worked on including the design of a concrete slab bridge. I enjoyed that project since it reminded me of working with Louis Berger Inc on bridge design for the Dhaka-Aricha Highway in East Pakistan in the 1960s. Each time I worked on any practical project I faced a different type of challenge and found a way to problem-solve. I dealt with different people in different situations and tried to understand and appreciate the diversity of people's mindsets, their agonies, greed, rudeness, insensitivity, callousness, cooperative spirit, and gentleness. My extensive self-study in psychology helped me enormously in understanding people's behavioral complexities, motivations, frustrations, etc. This helped me deal with people of varied personalities in professional and personal life.

I particularly remember one situation with a new construction project in Sudbury. It was a steel structure for a new shopping mall. During the construction of the building, when the steel framing was completed, during a routine inspection, the city's building inspector found some defects in the open web steel joists employed in the roof. The defects were in their bearing detail, at their supports, over the perimeter steel beams. Our firm was hired by the City of Sudbury to review this and any other possible construction defects in the structure. The project was assigned to me. During the inspection of the structure, in addition to the defect found by the inspector, that was relatively minor, I found a major deficiency in the construction.

Next to the one-story flat-roof shopping mall, I found an existing multistory office building. The distance between the two was only a few feet, whereas the difference in height between them was substantial. I knew there was a code requirement regarding this and based on my previous study of the National Building Code of Canada, I found out that Canadian snow load regulations were very stringent. In Timmins, I worked on a few projects and I had to learn the Canadian code regulations on snow. Just a few weeks prior, the roof of a large one-story garage collapsed under heavy snow load after a blizzard. I investigated that, which made me very conscious of the snow loads in this cold country.

I made the necessary measurements of the shopping mall at the construction site, returned to the office. I checked the building code to determine the additional snow load, if any, that would land on the low roof if drifting snow was dumped from the higher roof onto the lower roof. I concluded that the mall roof would experience a much higher snow load than assumed, over a large area on the side of the office building, and the roof joists as designed and installed were structurally inadequate to carry the anticipated snow loads. Once the city officials got my report, they set up a meeting with the architect, my manager Mr. David Smith, myself, the owner, the contractor, and some building officials together with them. The city building director presided over the meeting. I was asked by him -- a very dominant and intimidating personality – to present my findings to the group. At first, I got a little nervous as I was sitting with very professionally seasoned people, and much was at stake.

As I gained my composure and overcame my tension quickly, I gave my presentation. The meeting didn't go very well for the architect who was facing the building officials and the owner with a somber face upon hearing what I found out from my investigation. He was an experienced and well-respected architect in Sudbury who had designed many important buildings there. I felt bad seeing his disappointed look. My uneasy feeling was exacerbated when the building director, a hefty man with a thick and loud voice, looked at the architect and exclaimed, "You tried to work as a structural designer which you are not and now see what you got us into! If this happens one more time, I will blacklist you from practicing architecture in this city." In many cities in Canada and the U.S., architects were, and still are at this writing, allowed to do structural design for buildings up to a certain floor area. Cautious architects usually hire structural engineers for complex projects or when they don't want to take a risk. Others take a risk and do the structural work on their own to save money from the design fees. I realized the legal and financial implications of this for the architect and the predicament he had gotten into. I felt bad for him, but I had to do what my conscience and professional ethics dictated.

The next day, I got a call from the architect. He invited me to his office to talk about the dilemma. After courteously receiving me like the gentleman he was, he wanted me to show him in the code, where this item on snow loading was mentioned. Once I showed him the relevant clause, he checked this with numbers to satisfy himself and found that my observation was correct. I was very polite and respectful, not wanting to embarrass him any further, and said as politely as possible, "I was asked by my employer to investigate the entire building. Once I found this omission in the structural design of the roof framing, it was my professional responsibility to report it, as it was related to public safety. I am sorry that this has affected you negatively." He invited me to a restaurant for lunch. We chatted, I ordered a baked trout following his suggestion and we parted ways amicably. In the next few days I worked on the project and redesigned the roof structure by adding more structural elements to the roof framing to compensate for the additional snow loads.

We were also socially active in Sudbury. The city had a larger community. In addition to my friends at the office, we became friends with several Indian, Pakistani, and Arab families. They were mostly professionals, like professors, lawyers, doctors and engineers. The local Laurentian University had a small engineering program. Because of my liking for teaching I was planning to teach part time there once I got more settled. My heavy workload at the new job and family life kept me busy, however. My children were growing fast, and I realized I needed to spend more time with them. Some Muslim leaders organized religious discussions over the weekend in a room at the university.

A lasting memory from Sudbury was of a smelt-fishing trip organized by the office. I gladly agreed to join this new experience. We drove several miles from town to a waterfront, arriving at a culvert in which water was flowing fast from one side to the other. With fishing boots on and large nets we entered into shallow waters near the culvert to trap fish swimming against the current. To my surprise all I needed to do was hold the net and swarms of jumbo, bright, silver smelt got trapped. I had eaten Canadian smelt before, and they were very delicious but much smaller in size. I was excited to catch such a bounty of fish, they continued to swim into my net. I caught so many that they filled a full-sized garbage bag, which was so heavy, I couldn't lift it. To lighten the load, I offered some of my catch to coworkers, but no one was interested because they were all in the same predicament. So, I returned many fish to their natural habitat. It was their lucky day.

When I returned home, I thought Dora would be happy with such a huge catch. But we realized soon it was impossible to handle such a quantity. So, I called Mr. Mahadev Chakrabarty, an Indian friend from West Bengal and a longtime resident in the city, to help us out. He took most of the fish and distributed them among his friends. Dora cooked a delicious meal with the freshly caught fish, which we savored for days.

In the late summer of 1979, I took a few days off for a family vacation. We went to Waterloo to visit some friends of ours, and then headed for Muncie, Indiana to visit my brother Dr. Mir Masoom Ali. Subrata Barua, and his wife Leena Barua, whom I mentioned before, accompanied us to Muncie. After spending some time with my brother and his family, we headed for Chicago. There we visited another friend from my Waterloo days, Dr. S.K. Ghosh, who was employed by Portland Cement Association. He took us around and I had a glimpse of this large city.

One day he took us to the downtown and drove along Lakeshore Drive next to Lake Michigan. I was greatly impressed with the tall and supertall buildings, including the John Hancock Center and Sears Tower. I was so inspired after seeing the skyline that it left a deep unforgettable impression on me. I had already seen the tall buildings in New York and Toronto before, but I was not in the best state of mind then, so these seemed even more exhilarating. At that point in my career, I felt academically qualified to venture into finding the opportunity to work in a firm where such majestic buildings were designed. We returned to Sudbury after dropping off Subrata Barua and his wife at Waterloo on the way.

After returning to Sudbury, I reflected on my trip for some time. I thought how exciting it would be to design the structure of tall buildings that looked like urban giants! But to do that I had to first move to a large city like Toronto, Chicago or New York. America came to my mind first. After working for a few months at APD, I realized that even if I was content with my work, perhaps I needed to move to a bigger city, so I could work on larger projects with more challenges or to a university to teach. I realized that America had the most inventors and innovators of the 20th century and this trend would likely continue. It had the best movies and musicians from around the world; it had the largest banks and financial institutions and the best universities, best researchers in most fields, the best engineers and architects, it sent a man to moon, and frequently was at the forefront of technology. It had a great Constitution that ensured freedom, equality and happiness for all.

I read the American Declaration of Independence, which was drafted by very thoughtful, wise, far-sighted individuals like Thomas Jefferson and it was supported by the founding fathers of the country. The U.S. was the land of opportunities where people from all over the world flocked. I had also heard the unique expression "American Dream". The Declaration of Independence was the genesis of the American Dream. Although the notion of an American Dream was a bit vague to me, I liked the broad meaning and could relate to it as I had always been a dreamer myself. I read about George Washington, the founding father and first president of America, who stepped down voluntarily after two terms so future presidents didn't stay in power more than two terms using his example as a precedent. I realized that power did not spoil him, a rare example amongst politicians all over the world. I read Abraham Lincoln's life and his famous Gettysburg Address. How concise, yet so meaningful it was! It could only come from a great mind. Who else could give the best definition of democracy in just a few words, now taught in school textbooks all over the world? And, being a white man, despite many people disagreeing with him, who could have the audacity and greatness of heart to fight people of his own race? Although causing massive casualties on both sides of the American Civil

War, he chose to abolish slavery because he felt that it was the right thing to do to keep the nation together. In my estimation, a country that produced leaders like that must be a great country.

I was seriously thinking about the possibility of moving to America, a large vibrant country. It had many large cities and major companies providing ample opportunity for someone with my technical skills and qualifications. So, I started to send job applications to American employers. I got a response from a firm in St. Louis. But their work was mostly with industrial structures. The idea of moving to a major city in America was exciting enough, but my primary interest was still in buildings and bridges, so I wasn't enthusiastic about the position. While I was still conducting my job search from Canada, there came an unexpected occurrence and my wish was suddenly fulfilled. The future course of my life was changed forever.

At about the same time that I was dreaming of moving to America, following my visit to Chicago, APD appointed a new junior structural engineer named Guido Mazza. He was working with and assisting me. One fine day in October, Guido brought a book into the office. It was about structural engineering, published in the 1970s. Always curious about books, I started browsing the pages. The name Dr. Fazlur R. Khan jumped out. Along with his associates at Skidmore, Owings & Merrill (SOM) in Chicago, he was a pioneer in the development of groundbreaking structural systems for tall buildings. I recalled that while I was a doctoral student at the University of Waterloo, I heard his name from Farrukh Mohsen, another Bangladeshi doctoral student. Dr. Khan's native land was Bangladesh, as was mine. I was delighted and proud to see that someone in my field from Bangladesh could achieve so much success and get wide recognition in America for his work in his field. With Dora's encouragement, I decided to write him a letter, describing my desire to work on tall buildings and floating the possibility of working with him.

These days, we call it networking, I sent him a letter dated October 29, 1979.

After waiting for a few days and getting no reply I almost gave up hope. I assumed he must be extremely busy, and likely disregarded my letter as one of many requests. Surprisingly, he responded to me in a letter dated November 20, 1979 suggesting that I meet him at his office if I happened to visit Chicago. Meanwhile, my younger brother Mosaddeq came to the U.S. for higher studies in the fall, 1978 with his wife Tora. He enrolled in an M.S. program in Mechanical Engineering at the University of Missouri-Rolla. We decided to visit them and continue together to Florida for the Christmas and New Year holiday. I had another reason to visit Florida, as I had bought some land in Melbourne, FL and I was going to see it. Dr. Khan's letter came at the right time and we included Chicago in the travel plan. I was going to meet Dr. Khan in person. I got an appointment with him from his secretary, Jane Quinn, on Monday, December 17 at 3:00 PM at SOM's office in the Inland Steel Building at 30 West Monroe St. in the heart of downtown Chicago. He was scheduled to go overseas soon after that and fortunately for me, his schedule and my travels matched up.

We started from Sudbury on Saturday, stayed overnight at a friend's apartment in Waterloo. Then on Sunday I drove to London, Ontario to visit my oldest brother Dr. Mir Maswood Ali. After spending some time with him and his family, we headed for Windsor, Ontario to visit Mr. and Mrs. Aziz Chowdhury. Aziz Chowdhury was a librarian and a relative and friend of mine. He was the younger brother of Mr. Momin Chowdhury whom I met when I stayed in London in 1971. That same evening, I started for Chicago hoping to reach there by midnight so I would have enough time to rest before I met Dr. Khan. It was snowing, but due to my risk-taking and perhaps occasional imprudent nature I ventured onto the highway with Dora and three small children at night. I drove slowly and found the snow-fall got worse, turning into a storm and many cars had skidded off the highway. I thought of stopping and staying at a hotel on the way but realized that I wouldn't be able to see Dr. Khan. I couldn't risk losing such an opportunity especially since I lived so far from Chicago.

I continued and reached Gary, IN to the southeast of Chicago in the early Monday morning. After resting in a motel and eating lunch, I headed for downtown Chicago. The snowfall had stopped by then. I had never driven in a large city like Chicago, so I was apprehensive and careful to go to SOM's office after parking my car safely in a parking garage. I asked Dora and the kids to wait in the lobby, as I thought the meeting would take only a few minutes. Surely, Dr. Khan, a partner in a large internationally known architectural/engineering firm, must be a very busy man.

When I arrived, Jane met me and soon ushered me into the office. As I approached the door to the office, I saw Dr. Khan waiting at the door to greet me with a smiling face. He shook my hand and escorted me to a chair next to his office desk. His warm and informal demeanor made an immediate impression. Someone of his stature didn't need to receive me that cordially but he made me feel at ease. We talked about professional topics, high-rise buildings, and about Bangladesh. Although he didn't mention this to me, I later came to find out that he provided leadership to Bengalis during the Liberation War by holding meetings at his Chicago home. I heard later he was affected by the gruesome war images from overseas. During the conversation, he offered me tea and we shared some familiar jokes from back home. An office holiday party was going on at the time which Jane came to remind him of. But he was enjoying our conversation so much that we continued talking until about 4:00 PM.

At the end of the meeting, which was really an interview, Dr. Khan led me to the door and handed me an application form for employment and asked me to send it to him directly. We shook hands and he bid me goodbye after saying "I have a soft heart for my Bengali brothers."

I was elated for two reasons, first, I was able to converse with him privately for an hour and second, he seemed to appear genuinely interested in having me work with him. My longtime dream of designing tall buildings under the mentorship of someone like him felt closer to realization. Also, moving to a large skyscraper city like Chicago would be a great boost for my career, and I could someday fulfil my American Dream. I was fired up. I came down to the lobby where Dora and the kids were waiting patiently for so long and told her the good news. I told her my meeting went well and Dr. Khan treated me warmly. I asked Dora how the three kids behaved during the long wait, to which she replied, "They were fine." After the meeting, I hit the highway and headed for Rolla, Missouri, enroute to Florida.

We reached Rolla before midnight. We appreciated the dinner my sister-in-law Tora had prepared, despite the odd time. After staying there for a couple of days we left for Florida. I drove through the highways all day and continued driving at night, reached our motel in Melbourne late at night. On the way, we passed through Atlanta and Jacksonville and included Plains, Georgia among our stops so we could see the hometown of Jimmy Carter, the 39th U.S. President. We visited the local museum and drove around the peanut farms. This was our first time in Florida. I enjoyed the picturesque landscape which was totally different from Northern Ontario and the U.S. Midwest. The abounding coconut and palm trees reminded me of my native country, particularly my home district in the coastal area. We visited Melbourne, Orlando, Miami and Key West. At Melbourne, a GDC (General Development Corporation) employee showed us from a distance, the wooded land I bought and told me it would be developed in the future. I did not feel very good about it as it looked like a forest to me. We all enjoyed the rides at Disney World in Orlando and the view of the ocean at Miami Beach.

The drive to Key West was beautiful. Miles of highways connected sparse islands over long bridges surrounded by a vast expanse of water. Driving in this setting was a unique experience for me. The surrounding water produced a calming effect on me. Arriving in Key West, we went to the furthest point where we saw a sign pointing in the direction of Cuba, only 90 miles (144 kilometers) away. We stayed overnight at a hotel in Key West. After enjoying the Florida vacation, we headed back for Rolla early the next morning. The three kids never complained throughout the entire trip, they were thrilled to see and experience new things. Surprisingly, even my two-year old son Murad was looking around, attentive to the new things and scenes around him. I drove in a 24-hour marathon stretch, without sleep, only taking occasional breaks for gasoline, food and bathrooms. When I reached Rolla the next morning, I just hit the bed and slept like a baby for many hours. I still marvel at why I did that foolish thing and abused my body. Perhaps my youth, adventurous nature, and imprudence of the moment played a role. I do not, however, recommend that anyone do this.

On our way back, we visited Memphis to tour the house of Elvis Presley and also visited the motel site where Dr. Martin Luther King Jr. was assassinated. This trip marked the first time I had driven long distance through America. I got a sense of the vast country and the many well-planned and well-built cities. I felt the richness of the country and its people. I've always enjoyed driving and road trips didn't tire me out. Throughout the long rides, I talked with my brother while Dora talked with her sister, time passed very quickly.

The delightful trip to Florida has an unusual postscript, one that came to light many years later, when we were planning a trip to Bangladesh in 1988. We were living in Champaign, IL at the time. The GDC fund for my Florida property had accumulated a few thousand dollars. I had been a bit skeptical about the property after my visit it in 1978. I recalled that an attorney, Tony Ciccone in Timmins had also given me cautionary advice about the investment. Years went by and I got busy with my life, the property was only in the back of my mind. When we decided to go to Bangladesh on a visit, years later, I decided to go ahead and take the money out of the GDC fund and sell the property. I invoked the cancelation provision in the contract and the company graciously sent me a refund check after I completed some paperwork. My experience with them made me think perhaps they had been genuine after all. A few years later, however, I came to learn that GDC was indeed a fraudulent organization and had declared bankruptcy after taking all money collected from buyers. The scheme was hatched by a couple of people at the top, even the employees didn't know about it. I was so glad to get my money back in good time.

Upon our return to Sudbury after the New Year, we settled in quickly and I went back to work. I felt relaxed after the vacation and was in a joyful mood hoping to hear good news from SOM. I got a call from Mr. John Zils, Associate Partner at SOM, soon after. He verbally offered me a job of project engineer with SOM but asked me to apply for H1B visa on my own. Out of modesty and not wanting to trouble anyone with logistic matters, I did not contact Dr. Khan. I wasn't familiar with the visa system of the U.S. So, when I got a written offer letter, I contacted an attorney, Mr. Dobkins practicing in Detroit, Michigan, to help with the process. I got his name from an advertisement in a Canadian newspaper. A few months elapsed, and I remained busy with my work, family and social life. I was content with the idea of moving to Chicago once my visa application was approved and I just kept my fingers crossed. I had no idea that a new terrible storm was forming on the not-too-distant horizon.

In May 19, 1980, on Victoria Day in Canada, a national holiday, we took a vacation that week combined with the long weekend. We decided to visit my sisters Shahid Ara Saleh in Ottawa and Farhad Ara Bhuiyan in Montreal. It was a nice drive on a beautiful sunny day. We went to Ottawa first and stayed a couple of days. We enjoyed our stays in Ottawa and Montreal, where we visited some interesting tourist spots. Toward the end of our stay in Montreal, Dora could not sleep well one night as her left eye had been itching badly. In the morning, she found her left eyelid swollen and the fair skin around her eye had turned blue; she also felt some numbness there. I thought it was an allergic reaction to something and would go away soon, and if it continued, she could see a doctor in our hometown. The next day towards the end of the week, we left for Sudbury and returned home.

Soon, I noticed some change in her mobility and she complained that she felt weak and had difficulty going up the stairs of our townhome, unusual given her normally fast speed. Her condition started deteriorating and despite being a very active person she was sluggish and would lie down on the sofa in the living room downstairs. We realized that something was very wrong when one day, as she was brushing her teeth, she could no longer control her brush on the left side of her mouth. I immediately set up an appointment with one Dr. Takach. He prescribed penicillin. After a day or two she developed a severe rash in reaction to the penicillin. The doctor suggested that she might have a viral infection, so no antibiotic would help and thought the sickness would go away given some time. I noticed slowly and gradually she was feeling more and more fatigued.

While this was going on, I had an unforeseen problem of my own. On an earlier occasion, I went to inspect the high foundation wall of a building under construction. The soil backfill to the foundation was not in place. The contractor placed a ladder between the top of the foundation wall and the regular ground plane. I used that to go to the top of the foundation and walked around at that that height to check the quality of the construction. When I was done, I wanted to take a shortcut to the spot where my car was parked. I unwisely jumped from the top of the foundation wall onto the ground, and when I hit the ground, I felt a major impact on my back. I was in my mid-30s and somehow my body seemed to absorb the initial shock and my back healed with some subsequent minor aching.

When Dora was coping with her illness, I got a renovation/ remodeling project for a large abandoned hospital in Sudbury, which would be converted to a new occupancy type. I needed to physically inspect and survey the building. Accompanied by an assistant, I went there one day and found the building in decrepit condition. Even though it was daytime, it was dark inside as there was no power and the windows were boarded up. My assistant had a powerful flashlight and guided us inside. The building looked like it had been abandoned for many years and there were stray and crumbling materials all around. It seemed haunted. Strange thoughts came to my mind about this place, and my imagination took flight, how many sick people agonized in this hospital? What kind of doctors and nurses roamed the halls? How many people had been in pain, comatose or died here? A chilling cast of characters came to mind.

While looking around on the second floor I saw a large piece of cardboard lying on a shelf with some writing on it. Out of curiosity, I pulled it up to reveal the following words in large hand-written letters, penned with a red marker: I am Death and You are Next! It momentarily shook me, I showed it to my assistant and said, "Look, someone left this here to scare people." I put the cardboard facedown, back on the shelf and proceeded.

As we walked and surveyed, I looked at the structural condition and my assistant exposed the ceiling. He took measurements of the steel beams and other structural elements. At one point, we entered a room which looked different than the rest. There were large metal drawers in the wall. My assistant opened one of the drawers and seeing the size of it, immediately closed it, backed off and said to me, "This is where I guess they would keep the bodies." We didn't like being there and quickly left the room.

We surveyed the entire building and at the upper floor we found a vertical ladder leading to the roof. I told my assistant that we should go to the roof to check its condition. He went first, opened the access hatch and got close to the roof. I followed him up. The roof opening was small, and the top of the ladder was much lower than the roof opening, he had difficulty lifting me up. I told him not to try since I thought he might drop me accidentally. So, I placed my elbows on either side of the opening and hoisted myself up. I finished the inspection and we came down.

After spending a couple of hours there, we were struggling to find our way out of the large building. We found a staircase leading to the ground floor. We sensed that we were at a different location from where we entered. Suddenly we heard a woman wailing. Both of us jumped, alarmed and thought perhaps some unhappy spirit in the building was moaning from the dead. Inexplicably, we decided to move in the direction of the sound to investigate. As we approached, the sound got louder and louder. Eventually we reached an exit door and found the source. Instead of finding the ghostly spirit of a wailing woman, we found an intoxicated hobo with a bottle of alcohol in his hand leaning against wall. I was struck by the sight of a fellow human being in this state but didn't know what I could do to help.

When I returned home, Dora noticed that I looked tired and was stooping. I ignored it, took a warm shower and had dinner.

Even though she was weak, she managed to cook some meals, so we could eat. She was so good and efficient at cooking and other household work that she would never let me do any work at home. The next morning, I woke up with severe back pain and could not get out of the bed. I realized that climbing and hoisting myself to the roof the previous day had probably exacerbated my back. I called Dr. Takach, whose receptionist gave me an appointment for a few hours later. Dora was already weak due to her sickness, so my eldest daughter Ifat, who was only 11 years old at the time, helped me to the car. She accompanied me to the appointment and again helped me to get to the doctor's office.

After taking some painkillers, my back pain subsided and eventually went away after a couple of days. Dora's condition, however, deteriorated further and soon she lost total control of her facial muscles on the left side. Her face became partially paralyzed and deformed to the left. She had difficulty in eating and drinking. Seeing the malformation of her face and continued weakness, I was alarmed and consulted an Indian doctor friend, Dr. M. Iqbal Ali, who examined her at the local hospital, the St. Joseph Hospital near Ramsey Lake, which was the largest in the area. He referred her to a neurologist, and she was admitted to the hospital for thorough medical examination.

In the meantime, while Dora was under the neurologist's treatment, I heard from my attorney that my H-1B visa was approved and I should expect written notification soon from the U.S. Immigration and Naturalization Service (INS). I was happy about the news, but Dora's illness was worrying me. I got the written letter a few days later from the INS. The letter indicated a time limit for me to enter the U.S.; I was expected to enter by the end of July. I didn't have much time to decide what to do. Should I stay in Sudbury until Dora recovered and ask for an extension of my visa? Should I ask SOM to indefinitely delay my joining or should I move my family to Chicago and grab the once in a lifetime opportunity? Remembering the last time that I had delayed acceptance of a job offer in Toronto, I was reluctant to get into unforeseen complications.

Through my friend Dr. S.K. Ghosh, I rented an apartment in Palatine, a Chicago suburb, where we were set to move in on August 1. In the meantime, the neurologist at the hospital told me that he failed to come up with a diagnosis of Dora's illness and suspected it could be a very serious disease of the brain or the neurological system. She had to be checked out and treated at a good hospital in a large city like Toronto. It was late July and I had already resigned from my APD job, with July 28 as my last day of work. After a lot of thought, I decided to move to Chicago and continue Dora's treatment there once I had a foothold. I reasoned that she would get better treatment in a large American city with advanced healthcare facilities. I got hold of all the medical records from the hospital, so I could share them with her new doctor in Chicago.

I informed my oldest brother Dr. Mir Maswood Ali of my decision. He and his wife Suraiya (Ira) immediately drove to Sudbury. Our friends Mustafiz Rahman and his wife Barbara had come earlier to help us out and were with us.

My brother advised me to take Dora to Toronto General Hospital instead of Chicago. The tremendous stress ensuing from Dora's illness, coupled with our impending move to a new city, in a different country, my resignation from my job, and my need to support the family financially was quite overwhelming. My brother's wise counsel appealed to me and I immediately agreed. He told me that he would take our three kids to London, Ontario, where they would stay until Dora felt better and I was settled in Chicago. Mustafiz and Barbara would look after Dora at the hospital in Toronto, allowing me to meet my visa requirements and enter the U.S. before the deadline. The immediate, generous and selfless help that our friends and family provided in my moment of crisis can never be repaid. It made all the difference.

Accordingly, after our dinner, leaving my sister-in-law and Barbara behind with the kids, I left for Toronto with Dora, accompanied by my brother and our friend. Our three-year old son Murad sensed that we were going somewhere and taking his mother, so he panicked and came to the front lobby with his shoes in hand, insisting that he would go with his mom. He was held back, but that image is still stuck in my mind. I heard later that the next day he wanted to be with his mother but was told that I took the car away, to which he replied he would walk there. We reached Toronto after midnight and went straight to the Emergency Department of the Toronto General Hospital. Dora was immediately admitted to the hospital.

We returned to Sudbury starting from Toronto in the morning. It was Monday, July 28, my last day of work. I went to the office for a short time, quickly completed my pending work, cleaned up my desk, and said goodbye to all. After resting for a day, my brother and his wife left with the kids and so did my friend, who drove my car and Barbara drove theirs back to Toronto. They lived in an apartment complex and left my car in their parking lot. I decided to take a bus to Detroit from Sudbury to enter the U.S. to validate my visa and then go to Toronto also by bus. I planned to take the car back from my friend's parking lot on my way to Chicago after seeing Dora at the Toronto hospital. This way I could avoid driving long distances by myself under stressful conditions.

My brother coordinated this part of the plan for me. I had notified my landlord earlier and arranged a mover, who would come later that week to take my belongings to Chicago. I gave a duplicate key to Mahadev Chakrabarty, who would coordinate with the mover and return the key to the landlord. In the evening, I was all by myself. I felt miserable as I was recollecting the events of the last few days. I was scheduled to leave for Chicago via Detroit and Toronto next morning. I booked a taxi to take me to the bus stop. I got a call from Mrs. Chakrabarty, who had muscular dystrophy and had some difficulty walking, who also knew what was going on with us. She kindly invited me to dinner at their house. I was hungry but was in no mood to go anywhere and eat. So, I politely declined. After that I got a call from an old friend from Timmins, Dr. Jay Pathak, a mining engineer who wanted to know about Dora's condition. Finishing the conversation, I lay down on my bed to rest and try to gather my thoughts peacefully.

Shortly, I heard my doorbell ring. I had turned off all the lights, so the house was totally dark except a faint light from a bathroom upstairs. I was hoping the dark would help calm my mind. I ignored the doorbell, as I was alone and not expecting anyone. I heard it a second time and ignored it again, hoping whoever it was would go away. Finally, after a third time I went down and took a peek through the side of a window. To my surprise, I saw Mahadev Chakrabarty standing outside. I opened the door and let him in. He told me, "I came to take you home for dinner. My wife talked with you earlier and sensed you were depressed. So, she sent me over. She told me you left your car in Toronto, so you must be in. That's why I repeatedly rang the doorbell."

I could not say no to a gentleman and his wife who clearly cared for me so much, and so got into his car. When we arrived at their home, I saw Mrs. Chakrabarty was cooking. She greeted me. I had a good time with them and their son who was studying at the Royal Military College at Kingston, Ontario. He was home for a visit. I realized I was very hungry and enjoyed the hot meal. I was uplifted by the company and chatting with such decent people. Around 10:30 PM Mr. Chakrabarty dropped me off, wishing me good luck and assuring me he would take care of my affairs with the movers the next day.

Getting home, I went to the bedroom and decided to sleep immediately since I had to get up early the next morning. The dismal, dark and solitary environment brought my spirits down again and I just lay on my back, in bed, without even changing my clothes or even taking off my shoes. I found myself ruminating over the recent events of my life. Soon my thoughts drifted to the Higher Power. I realized that we were not in control our lives and the Supreme Power pulled the strings and determined our fate. This led me to communicate, from my heart for the first time in my life, directly with God. I spoke of my sorrows to God, asking Him what I did wrong to get this punishment and why He was so harsh with me and my family. Obviously, I didn't get a verbal answer, it was a one-way conversation. I was feeling helpless and despondent; with my eyes closed I kept repeating my grievances directly to Him in words. I felt that this was coming from the bottom of my heart. At some point, I got drowsy and went into a trance-like state.

I was not fully asleep, but in a transitional state of sleep and wakefulness. Suddenly, I felt a bright light in my eyes. I opened my eyes and saw my entire bedroom engulfed in a bright white light. I thought I might be dreaming, so I pinched myself, feeling the pain I realized that I was awake. I sat on my bed, looked at my wristwatch and saw it was midnight, exactly 12:00 AM. I looked at the large window behind my bed, the only window in the room, to see if the light was coming from there. There were a large open field and a street that ran across at a great distance. I couldn't see any cars. Even if there was a car on the street, there was no way any headlight could be so bright, nor focus directly through my window as the car would be driven across, not toward, my townhome. I was dazed by the light and looked on in awe. I pinched myself on my arm again to check if I was dreaming and felt the pain. I was flustered and lay back down on the bed to experience the light enveloping the room. Shortly, the light became dimmer and dimmer, concentrated on the white wall ahead of me. It turned sort of light orange in color, then into a thin ray, like the light from a doctor's otoscope. Soon the ray turned dense orange and turned off. I felt relaxed.

I never had such an experience in my life, nor could I remember a time when I ever saw anything so mysterious or paranormal, so clearly, with my conscious mind. I tried to find the meaning of this. The only thing I could think of was that God had listened to me expressing my agony and shown me a light of hope because of my sincere and fervent appeal to Him. I went into deep sleep until the alarm woke me up in the morning. I woke up feeling calm and confident that Dora would recover from her illness. I took a shower, ate a light breakfast from the food that was left in the refrigerator, and got ready to leave. My taxi arrived to take me to the bus station.

From Sudbury, I took a bus across the border at Sault Ste Marie, Michigan some 200 miles (320 kilometers) away, where my visa was validated. It was Tuesday, July 29, 1980. Now I could go back to Toronto via Detroit to see Dora at the hospital and get my car from my friend. I boarded a Greyhound bus in the late afternoon for Detroit about 350 miles (560 kilometers) away. The Detroit-bound bus stopped several times in different towns to drop off and pick up passengers, as well as at service centers on the way. We reached Detroit around midnight. At the bus station, I changed buses and boarded another Greyhound heading for Toronto, which was 245 miles (392 kilometers) away. It was another long overnight journey with stops at cities and service centers. At the Canadian border immigration, I explained why I entered the U.S. hours before and was returning to Canada again so soon. Thankfully, the officer didn't give me any hassles.

I could not sleep at all in the bus in a seated position and on top of that, getting interrupted by the frequent stops. A lot of stray thoughts came to my wandering mind. I thought about my predicament -- Dora in a hospital in Toronto and my three dear children in London, Ontario without their parents. Who else can give so much love, warmth, and affection to children other than parents? And, what would happen to me alone in an apartment in Palatine, Illinois, a new place, without my wife and children? What if God forbid, Dora could not survive her serious illness, the Toronto doctors had given up treatment? But I remembered the white light in my bedroom in Sudbury for a reason and felt reassured that this storm of my life would also be resolved.

Finally, in the early morning of Wednesday, July 30 I reached Toronto. The bus stopped at the Greyhound terminal on Bay Street in downtown Toronto. The Toronto General Hospital was less than half a mile away from there. So, I walked towards nearby Elizabeth Street and kept walking along until I made it to the hospital. I walked into Dora's room and found a nurse with her. Once the nurse left, I held Dora's hand to comfort her and said, "Don't worry, you will be fine. Everything is going to be OK. I saw an intense bright light last Monday night in my bedroom. I think it is a divine sign of hope as I can't find any scientific explanation of what happened." I narrated the whole miraculous event to her.

She was very weak and could not eat because of her facial paralysis. I stayed with her for a few hours and left. I got a taxi and went to Mustafiz and Barbara's apartment complex to get my car. I was very tired due to lack of sleep and anxieties, so decided to get the car key from Barbara and drive to London, 120 miles (192 kilometers) from there, and rest peacefully at my brother's home. I arrived at Barbara's apartment and she opened the door to let me in. I asked for my car key, saying that I planned to drive straight to my brother's house. She told me to sit on a sofa and wait for Mustafiz who was at work. Because she was alone in the apartment, it was not customary that I should stay. Seeing my state, she insisted and kindly said, "You look very tired. You relax there, I will make a sandwich for your lunch." When I said she didn't need to take this trouble for me, she replied, "What are friends for?"

I thought to myself, she could have just given me the key and let me go, particularly as her husband was away. Mr. Faizur Rahman, a Muslim, took me to his home when he saw me despondent after my doctoral thesis was postponed in Waterloo, Mr. Mahadev Chakrabarty, a Hindu, took me to his home and his wife, cooked and fed me a delicious dinner when I was in distress and felt hopeless in Sudbury, and now Barbara, a Christian, was treating me like this in her apartment, even though her husband was at work as she saw how worn-down I was.

These were the times I needed comfort and help from others. People are good and decent regardless of their religious beliefs. I thought goodness of heart was an inherently godly attribute, a quality found in all people of good character. I thought it was true that people often acted in self-interest but when endowed with the quality of altruism, they were able to empathize and help others selflessly. Once I finished eating, Barbara showed me to the bedroom, showed me the attached bathroom, and told me to rest. She then left the room closing the door. I was so tired that I don't remember if I took a quick shower, probably I did, and soon went into deep sleep once I hit the bed. When I woke up, I heard some muffled conversation outside the bedroom. I realized Mustafiz had returned from work. To the best of my recollection, they asked me to have dinner and stay overnight with them and go to London the next morning, I gratefully accepted.

When I reached London, my three children were overjoyed to see me even though my separation from them had only been for a couple of days. Ifat and Jinat had good company with my brother's daughters, so they were fine. It was baby Murad who was clinging to me lest he become separated again. I stayed there overnight and left the next morning for Chicago. My brother took Murad, diverting his attention from me, so he wouldn't see me leave.

PART THREE
LAND OF THE FREE & HOME
OF THE BRAVE

CHAPTER 8

CHICAGO

Windy City Blues

After a long drive I finally reached Chicago, the Windy City as it is popularly known. I drove straight to Palatine in the late afternoon, to the housing office and after signing the lease I got my apartment key from the lady at Deer Grove Apartments. I moved into the empty and spacious apartment with my skimpy luggage. I wished my family were here with me. Despite all my troubles, I was thrilled that I was finally in America -- the "land of the free and home of the brave." It is the richest, the most advanced, and most powerful country of the world, a land of op-portunities. I got a morale boost from being employed by SOM, a prestigious firm, internationally renowned, in this skyscraper city of Chicago.

I was on my way to realizing the American Dream, starting from my humble beginnings in a small coastal town, without elec-tricity and no car. Even while studying at the bigger city of Dhaka, I hardly saw any high-rise buildings, since few existed. I could remember clearly how I came to Canada from East Pakistan with an old damaged black suitcase, that I hastily got repaired before my departure and only $20 in my pocket.

I settled down soon after unpacking, prayed and thanked God for His favors on me. I was ready to join my new job on Monday, August 4. I felt excited and went to a nearby restaurant to eat. My new life in America had started. That night, when I threw my physically and mentally tired body into a sleeping bag on the floor, I fell immediately into a deep sleep, feeling relaxed. I somehow felt my family would be with me soon, counting on the vision of light that I experienced in Sudbury. I slept on the floor for the next few days until all furniture and other belongings shipped from Sudbury.

After spending the weekend familiarizing myself with my surroundings, on Monday morning I took a commuter train from a nearby train station, headed for downtown Chicago about 30 miles (48 kilometers) from Palatine. This was a new experience for me. I walked into SOM's office on Monroe Street and reported to the person in charge of new employee orientation. After the orientation, I reported to John Zils, who had earlier sent me the official job offer. He took me to a large open space where many engineers and architects were working on a project on Mecca University campus. I was introduced to one Dr. Mohammed Salem who was leading the project. He was a very nice man originally from Syria. I was assigned some design work on one of the buildings. Many of my coworkers were younger and junior engineers. There were a few senior engineers like Mr. Hadi and Mr. Pandya, with whom I soon became familiar. I also made friends with some junior engineers as essentially, I was learning new things just like them. The Mecca University project had many buildings and ancillary structures, mostly in concrete. I worked on a few of these isolated items.

I didn't initially like the bustling environment with so many people working in a large open hall. I was used to having my own office even as a doctoral student in Waterloo and as the chief structural engineer in Timmins. The new setting took some time getting used to, but I adjusted easily. I recalled Dr. Khan mentioned that SOM used a shared working space and I would be with junior co-workers in the beginning. I told him it didn't matter. I realized that I was hired as a project engineer and this was only temporary as I needed time and experience to work up the ladder. I needed to work hard to prove myself in SOM's very competitive environment. The private office, or my perceived stature, was of little concern. Of greater concern was learning and familiarizing myself with the American and Chicago building codes and regulations. In a matter of days, I got used to the new environment and enjoyed my new work. I kept personal matters, about my wife's illness to myself at this very early stage of my employment, not wanting to signal that my concentration might be divided. Throughout my student and working life I have been always good at compartmentalizing my work life from my personal life.

Shortly after I joined the firm, I met Dr. Khan in his office as a matter of courtesy. He gave me some important advice about how to work in the office and handle myself in this competitive environment. This is what he told me, "I would like to give you some unsolicited advice. When dealing with other professionals and colleagues, be aggressive, but not offensive. This is what is needed in America. When you talk with them be sure of what you are saying and don't be speculative. Learn architecture well as it is very much connected to structural design of buildings and one must deal with architects. Utilize weekends to do research and write papers documenting the projects that you work on." These few words were invaluable to me and showed me a path to success directly hearing from a very successful man.

He also told me that there were a few Bangladeshi families in the Chicago area who had recently formed an association and made him the president. He encouraged me to join it and attend their next cultural function, which I later did.

When I returned home, sometimes I cooked dinner or occasionally went to a restaurant. Every night I called Dora to see how she was doing. On occasions, I called my brother in London and enquired about the kids too. Dora was under the treatment of Dr. Humphrey, a senior neurologist. A biopsy of her lymph nodes revealed some inflammation. Mustafiz and Barbara were there at the hospital for the procedure. I felt bad that I couldn't be there because of my new job and the distance involved. But I trusted the couple, our reliable friends.

A diagnosis was soon made. She had developed an uncommon disease called sarcoidosis which was caused by an allergic reaction born from a virus that she might have inhaled from air or ingested from food. Electric shocks were applied on occasions to stimulate and arouse her facial nerves. After a few weeks, I contacted Dr. Humphrey and asked him about the prognosis. He said that, although the entire medical team wanted to prescribe steroids to treat the disease, he would not prescribe such medication as she was so young and if I wished I could bring her to the U.S. He mentioned to Dora earlier that the medication could have serious long-term side effects and might not even work. Even if it did work, she had to take it for many years and if she stopped taking the symptoms would likely return again. He assured me that Dora could travel for a few hours despite her physical weakness. So, I decided to go to Toronto to bring her to the U.S.

I took time off from work, telling my supervisor that I had to bring my family from Canada. I drove to Toronto one day starting early in the morning, went straight to the hospital and saw Dora. I was saddened to see her turning almost into a skeleton. I met with Dr. Humphrey. Dora was also present at the meeting. I liked his personality and will always remember him. He was tall and thin with grey untidy hair, looking like a thoughtful scientist. He was unpretentious and dressed very plainly with worn-out shoes. His mind was focused on his patients and their treatment rather than how he looked. He seemed to be a thinking and analytical man with only his patient's wellbeing in his mind. He narrated to me in detail what he found and why he was against any treatment that included strong drugs.

He found that Dora's nerves were recently responding to electric shocks. So, he was hopeful that she would recover eventually if she could start eating healthy foods and gain strength. He preferred that her body fight off the illness without medical intervention. Being with the family in her own home would make her feel better. She had a long way to go and had to be careful about possible future lung or kidney disease, since this disease could stay in a dormant state and attack those organs in the future. There was also the possibility that she might develop diabetes later. After coming to know that I was a structural engineer, he looked at Dora and quipped, "You see, your husband might not know much about how the human body functions, but he knows how a bridge works, which I don't understand at all." I felt deep respect for him and found that he thought outside the box. He was not a pill-pushing doctor like some in his profession, but someone who believed in the natural healing capacity of the body. It was an important lesson for me that day that I took to heart. He advised me to keep in touch with a doctor in the U.S. I gathered her medical records before I left to carry with me.

After Dora was discharged, one of the nurses brought her via wheelchair to the front of the hospital and got her settled into the back seat of the car. Even though she was sick and extremely weak, I felt good to be with her again after almost a month of her stay in the hospital. It was almost evening. I drove to London and reached there in about two hours. Dora was happy to see the kids and so were the kids seeing us. We stayed there overnight and left for Chicago next morning. After crossing the border at one point I drove through Interstate Highway 94. When I reached the south side of Chicago in the afternoon, I suddenly saw smoke coming out from under the hood. This was the worst possible time in the afternoon with heavy traffic on the highway and at the worst possible location. It was near the confluence of interstate highways I-65, I-94, and I-90.

I got nervous, as I had a sick wife and three small children with me and if the car broke down, I would be in trouble in this unfamiliar place. I tried to be calm and thought this too would pass, I had gone through much worse circumstances before. I stopped in my lane, in very heavy traffic and raised the hood. I saw steam coming from the radiator. In the tension of the moment, I didn't realize I had blocked the lane on the busy highway. I created a massive traffic gridlock behind me. An angry white police officer, appearing in a bad mood approached me and told me from a short distance, somewhat rudely, with a loud voice, to start the motor. He was big, and his face looked scary. I showed him the leaking radiator. He looked inside the car and saw Dora and three minor children including a baby. That calmed him down. He told me to move my car to the extreme right lane and then to the next shoulder, and he would help me. He directed the traffic accordingly.

After pulling over to the shoulder, fortunately I found an exit ahead. I took that exit not knowing where I was going. I rolled ahead slowly and found a car repair shop. I talked with the mechanic who had a gentle demeanor. He told me that they were closing soon and couldn't fix the car right away, there were other cars waiting to be fixed. After having a look, he assured me that I could reach Palatine without any danger and advised me to go to a garage the next day. He also very kindly gave me directions to Palatine, avoiding the busy highway.

To my great relief, I reached my apartment with the family. I was unhappy about the officer's rude behavior, something astonishing that I never experienced in Canada during my 10-year residence there. But I was in no mood to analyze him then. Later, I thought he should have known from the car's license plate that I was from Canada, not a local, and I had a car problem. I expected he would be nice to me and extend his help rather than scaring me. I thought of complaining against him to the city's mayor or chief of police. But then I thought this was Chicago, a large city with a reputation for crime and murder, and these officers had to deal with tough situations day in and day out. Moreover, the location where I got stranded was very busy with heavy traffic. I gave him the benefit of the doubt, maybe he wasn't a bad guy, it was just his tough job that made him rude and insensitive. I advised myself to focus on my newly arrived family, sick wife and the three children who had been deprived of the love and care of their parents for some time.

I had arranged for my brother Mosaddeq and Tora, to get the door key from the housing office and meet us in the apartment. They were there when we arrived. They drove all the way from Rolla, Missouri. Mosaddeq was a graduate student at the time. They were shocked to see Dora's skeletal physique. My brother left after a couple of days and Tora stayed behind to help us. She cooked for us, but Dora could not eat. However, Tora made small amounts of food for us, to her sister's liking, in an attempt to revive her taste buds. Dora started eating in small amounts. Tora stayed for a whole month. I dropped her at the Union Station Bus Depot in downtown Chicago for her return trip to Rolla.

Life was not easy for me after Tora left. Dora was very weak; she could not do much at home. She still couldn't eat much of anything as she had hardly any taste in her mouth. Even if she tried to eat our own familiar ethnic food, that I cooked to suit her taste, she would not be able to hold it down. But being a good cook, she could not go too long without cooking. She started by boiling some rice and prepared a simple lentil dish. During weekends, I cooked other meals, including meat and vegetables. I cooked enough so that we could eat throughout the week. I fancied myself a pretty good cook. I had learned from my sister in Ottawa and I used to cook my own meals as a student before Dora came to Canada. Despite this she still couldn't eat full meals. It was a grueling time for me since I had to do all household work and look after the kids. And of course, I had a full-time new job in downtown Chicago, a serious commute. Despite my positive outlook and optimism that things would be eventually fine, to play safe I noted the telephone number of the United Way, in case I couldn't handle the pressure and needed to seek their help.

Meanwhile, I took Dora to one Dr. Michael Stocker, an internal medicine physician for checkup. After reviewing her medical records, he said the same thing as Dr. Humphrey said, "Mrs. Ali, you will need a long time to recover. You have to start eating whatever tastes good to you." I remembered a few high school lessons about vitamins so asked, "Can she take some vitamin supplements that might give her some strength and help in her speedy recovery?"

He replied "Vitamin supplements are useless. If you take them, they come out with the urine. Instead, if you eat a hamburger that will give you a lot of vitamins."

I paused to think. Even though he was a medical doctor and his observation might be true, I didn't like his response. I decided to study the subject of vitamins.

The following day, I went to a health food store. I saw a few books on the shelf and of course any time I see books, they attract me like a magnet. The book titled *How to be Healthy with Natural Foods: Renew your Vitality and Live Longer with Wholesome Natural Foods* by Edward E. Marsh caught my attention. It was first published by Arco Publishing Co. in 1967, then reprinted as fourth edition in 1978. Surprisingly, the price of the book was a meager

$1.50. I remembered the adage - the best things in life are free. I looked up the book's Table of Contents, speed reading through the Preface and Chapter 1 and thought this was what I needed for Dora.

The author was not biased or bound by his profession. He was neither a physician nor nutritionist and wrote the book guided by self-study and research. He had suffered through a debilitating illness that forced him to quit his job. The book's Foreword was written by an Dr. John P. Urlock, Jr., M.D., President, Maryland Academy of Medicine and Surgery, who endorsed the book. I bought the book in no time, read the whole thing. By the time I had finished, I had a totally new perspective on health and wellness. The book opened a new horizon of learning. I remember vividly, Chapter 4 Vitamins -- Nature's Spark Plugs. To me, the very cheap book was a priceless introduction to a new wonderland of lifelong learning: treating food as medicine leading to self-healing.

I tried to maintain this practice throughout my life, albeit with occasional lapses and deviations. Many of Mr. Marsh's ideas espoused back in the 1960s, like low carbohydrate and high protein and fat, eating natural and wholesome foods, were at one point debunked. But with the advent of the Atkins diet, as well as the prevention and treatment philosophies of naturopathic medicine, integrative medicine, functional medicine, and even lately segments of mainstream medicine, his ideas and nutrition concepts are being embraced and finding revival at this writing. I have kept the book as a souvenir for about four decades now.

Dora had been steadily gaining strength and started eating in very small quantities. Her facial paralysis started to go away slowly and gradually. But she was still very thin and weak, so I continued to do all housework, take care of kids, cook and go to work. This lasted a few months. Then my oldest daughter Ifat contracted chicken pox, which was going around at school. One fine day, blisters showed up on her face. Things became a little harder with her illness, as she would normally give us a hand, we relied on her as one does with the oldest child. By the time she recovered, I developed blisters and realized I had chicken pox as well. This grounded me at home. I slept in a separate bed applying calamine lotion to minimize itching. I remember during this time of my sickness, President Ronald Reagan was shot on March 30, 1981 and the news was continuously broadcast over the radio in my room.

Although I loved reading, my physical discomfort just didn't allow me to do it, nor could I sleep well. So, I spent my time instead, listening to the news and music on the radio. My illness had one silver lining. Since I was now inactive, Dora was compelled to start cooking and pushing herself to do minor household work. By this time, she had gained a bit strength and weight. She was eating healthy foods and the vitamin supplements which I introduced to her diet. She could not still fully retain the foods that she ate. She had to do things now for our children, for herself and, ironically, for me. I needed her help applying the calamine lotion. By the time I recovered, after a week or so, she had reclaimed charge of the kitchen. I could finally focus on my work and other pending matters.

At the office, in early 1981, I was transferred from the Mecca Campus project and assigned a challenging project by my boss John Zils, at the instruction of Dr. Khan. It was a 60-story steel office building called Pacific Plaza in Los Angeles. I started working on this project while I was taking care of Dora and before my illness. For me, it was a dream project, since now I would be working on a tall building, in a severe earthquake-prone zone. The structural design of very tall buildings, and earthquake-resistant design, were both uncharted territory for me.

I was the Project Engineer for the 60-story office tower. There were other segments of the project that were assigned to other project engineers, like a five-story low-rise steel structure at the base of the tower, and a 14-story separate concrete parking garage. Others involved in the project were Sarv Nayyar, the senior project engineer, and John Zils, who reported directly to Dr. Khan. He was the partner-in-charge of the project and led the entire team. He would periodically review all our work. We posted the drawings on the wall of the conference room. I saw how easy it was for him to assess the structural system and determine the discrepancies, areas of concern, and inefficient use of structural material. We worked on several different options for a structural scheme during the initial stage of the project for the building with a pentagonal footprint.

Dr. Khan's signature innovation in tall buildings was Tubular design. I read the theoretical papers he wrote, explaining the mechanics of the system. I studied the Chicago building code to determine the wind loads for the structure. I also studied seismic design concepts and the associated code requirements of the Uniform Building Code. Dr. Mahjoub Elnimeiri, a structural engineer with experience in computer analysis of tall buildings, tutored me with my analysis. I also conducted investigations for the most optimum floor framing and lateral load-resisting systems. I was assisted by a few junior engineers in the project. One of them was Joseph Burns whom I found very talented and helpful.

One day I saw a small computer on Mahjoub's drawing board. He told me that it was called a personal computer (PC) and he demonstrated a bit of how it worked. I marveled at how technology had progressed since the mainframe computer. I remembered two things. First, when I was doctoral student working late at night in the computer labs, my little daughter Ifat asked me why I couldn't have a computer of my own at home, so I could be home more often. That wish had now become a reality. Second, I recalled the day when Dr. N.C. Lind at the University of Waterloo showed us a new digital calculator and demonstrated how it worked.

During the design process, I developed an approximate method of dynamic analysis of tall buildings that could be used in the preliminary design stages. It could be used to design tall buildings subjected to seismic forces. The method was subsequently published. Under Dr. Khan's direction, we investigated different possibilities to improve the efficiency of the tubular system. I also worked on a huge 8-ft. (2.4-m) thick concrete mat foundation supporting the building. Unlike New York and Chicago, Los Angeles, in general, didn't have rock close to the surface. There was no surface rock on our project site so we could not use the typical large concrete caissons. The design of the mat by itself was a major project to deal with. Despite my worries about Dora's health condition at home, I enjoyed my work at the office, immersed in these design adventures. Notwithstanding my hard work on the project, for financial reasons it was never built in its original form. It was revised later, for a shorter building after I left SOM.

I developed professionally while working on the Pacific Plaza project. Before, I was unaware of the problem of "quartering wind", which comes from the diagonal direction of a building. This phenomenon was faced by renowned structural engineer William J. LeMessurier, for the Citicorp Center in New York, which he designed. His firm inadvertently overlooked this wind force the result was a design flaw in lateral bracing system. LeMessurier only discovered his conceptual error in 1978, after the building was already built and occupied. He did subsequently repair the deficiency. The problem came to light after a graduate student at a local university found it. The student was using Citicorp Center as a case study for his project. LeMessurier's reputation was on the line and he didn't initially know what to do. He became so dejected that he had suicidal thoughts. Eventually he recovered, admitted the mistake and faced the consequences.

Ours was a large project in a severe seismic zone. Neither I nor the other engineers were aware of the problem of "quartering wind". During the wind load analysis, I considered the wind forces only from the two principal directions. As part of conventional wisdom, while analyzing building structures, engineers do not normally apply wind loads diagonally, on rectilinear buildings. The rationale behind this is that for a regular building, if the structural framework is adequate for wind load in the principal perpendicular directions, it is taken to be acceptable for any other direction of the wind. But this pentagonal building had a long diagonal face, with a 45-degree angle to the principal perpendicular directions. It was narrow in plan across the diagonal. For this building, structural members were sized for wind load applied in the principal perpendicular directions alone. However, wind load should have also been applied for the analysis on the diagonal face which had a much wider sail than that of the principal directions. Later when I analyzed the tower applying the wind on the diagonal face, the load had critical design consequences. When looking at earthquake load, however, a similar analysis showed that it didn't affect the design.

When this omission in the analysis was initially detected by Dr. Khan during the review, I was shaken and embarrassed. I tried to explain my case during a discussion in his office. John Zils and Sarv Nayyar were also present. Dr. Khan listened intently, noting that I was young and inexperienced in tall building design, he never expressed the slightest frustration or anger. Construction drawings were not yet prepared, although preliminary design and drawings were completed, and total steel quantities were already communicated to the developer. Dr. Khan suggested an innovative design approach to resolve the problem and keep the total quantity of steel used in the preliminary design the same, while satisfying the building code. To my great relief, the problem was easily overcome, and Dr. Khan had once again demonstrated his vast experience and sharp engineering mind.

After staying in the apartment at Palatine for a year, in August 1981 we bought a newly built home in Bartlett, a Chicago suburb, and moved there. My family was happy to move to our new home. This was the first home of our own in North America. We made some friends in the neighborhood. Things in my family had turned for the better and I felt I was going in the right direction to fulfil my American Dream. I used to commute to work by train, and in hindsight, our decision to buy it was hasty. Perhaps we should have rented because the interest rate was very high at that time and an unforeseen calamitous event took place shortly after. I had been moving from place to place with my family, so I wanted to settle down. But that was not to be.

In March 1982, a terrible, unexpected event shook SOM. In late March, Dr. Khan prepared to go on a trip to Korea and Saudi Arabia. He included a side trip to Bangladesh to visit his elderly mother. A few days before his trip, as busy as he was, he gave me some time and candidly told me a few things – mostly in the form of advice and encouragement, and especially about his plans to do more research on tall buildings with my help. He told me: "I am going on an overseas trip soon. I got a good report about your performance from John Zils. I don't have as much energy as I used to. I was able to work until late hours at night in my younger years. You are young and energetic. I would like you to work on two research projects. To do well in anything you have to like it. We will discuss these things further when I return. Meanwhile, think them over, I will give you a research account to which you can charge your time."

He used to carry a small notebook in his coat pocket, which he pulled out during this conversation to show me some sketches of a tubular building. The examination entailed how he might increase the column spacing at lower floors, to facilitate architectural planning. He told me that the close spacing of columns at lower floors were disliked by architects for functional and aesthetic reasons. He was also thinking of energy savings in buildings, which was a hot topic in those days after the energy crisis of 1973. He didn't explain to me what he had in mind about this latter topic. I realized his mind was always active and he would continuously think about how building design could be improved. He also requested that I prepare some slides of the Pacific Plaza project for him. He encouraged me to write a few papers on the project, without revealing the name of the project and other basic identifying information about the architect or developer. I did subsequently write those papers. I felt good about this conversation, realizing he had developed some trust and confidence in me.

After he left for Korea, a military coup d'état took place in Bangladesh. When his wife Liselotte heard about this news, she immediately informed him upon his arrival in Hong Kong. Because of the ongoing political turmoil in the new nation of Bangladesh-- exacerbated by the coup -- Dr. Khan cancelled that wing of his trip, and went directly to Jeddah, Saudi Arabia. He arrived there on the evening of March 26. In the afternoon of Saturday, March 27, after attending a meeting in Jeddah about the implementation of the Master Plan for the King Abdul Aziz University, he was walking with two others. At about 3:30 PM he collapsed after suffering a fatal heart attack. He was immediately taken to the nearby University Teaching Hospital. After being admitted to the hospital, he briefly recovered but died soon after. A full team of qualified doctors were attending him, but the heart attack was just too massive. He was only 52 years old.

I heard the news on Saturday at SOM's office, several of us were working overtime on the Pacific Plaza project. Several members of the project team were present, Sarv Nayyar came and broke the news. Instead of announcing it he approached me to ask, "Did you hear anything about Faz?" His face was gloomy, and gaze lowered. My first reaction was that Dr. Khan was involved in some accident or that he had fallen ill during the trip. Even when I last saw him, he looked so sporty. I replied, "No, all I know is that he is out of the country." Sarv murmured a few words but could not find it in himself to tell me. I insisted on hearing it. He said, "I heard the bad news...Faz suffered a heart attack in Saudi Arabia...and they are saying he passed away. I hope it isn't true."

In shock, he and I agreed it must be a false rumor. Other team members overheard our conversation and gathered around us. Everyone was shocked and speechless. We all lost our focus on work and wondered what to do next. Gloom and silence prevailed. One person in the group tried to motivate us by breaking the silence and said, "Let's continue what we are doing. If he were alive that's what he would expect us to do anyway." But our spirits were destroyed completely. We began to leave. Before I left, I called friends of Dr. Khan whom I knew, confirming the same news. I finally began to accept the grim fact that it was true and not a rumor. On the train ride home and at home all day I felt very distressed. His loss was both personal to me and professional. I was so honored and privileged that someone like him, of his stature touched my life. I found a great mentor but only for such a short time. I thought, I could still look up to him as a role model, even in his death and follow his last words of advice.

His remains were flown from Saudi Arabia to Chicago. The Saudi government offered to honor him with a burial at a sacred site in the holy land of Islam. But at the request of his wife he was buried on April 2, 1982 in Chicago's Graceland Cemetery, the peaceful, serene, permanent resting-place of a constellation of famous people including many renowned architects and engineers of Chicago. I was present at his eulogy and burial at the cemetery along with his relatives, friends, and co-workers. I realized that nobody could escape death. His accomplishments in structural design over 25 short years were almost unparalleled by any account. Yet, he could not withstand the ruthless clutches of death that snatched away his vitality and spirit, so abruptly, without notice, at the premature age of 52 – when he was responding to the call of his profession. If such was the fate of a man who was sent to earth with a clear mission of serving society, of contributing to urban civilization, where did the average man or woman stand in the grand scheme of things?

As the SOM office coped with the loss, we started working on the Pacific Plaza project again. After some time, however, the project was put on hold due to funding problem and then at some point discarded. It was revived later as a much smaller project. This was quite common in the building industry for such major projects when circumstances changed, usually when an unexpected financial crisis emerged. I was disappointed that I could not have the satisfaction of finishing the project fully and seeing the tower built. But I also thought that I learned a lot from this project, things that I could never learn from reading books or technical papers alone.

I was assigned to another smaller but interesting project called Dearborn Park Apartments (renamed South Plymouth Court in Dearborn Park) in Chicago. The site was in a neglected neighborhood on the south side of State Street. The City of Chicago decided to implement a beautification program by building new buildings and other development projects. The 11-story apartment building was designed in concrete with step-backs creating roof terraces at each floor level. It was intended to house young couples or young urban professionals (Yuppies, a term introduced in the 1980s) who worked in downtown Chicago. It had a large spread-out low-rise base for parking and accommodated a few wood frame townhomes on the roof of the low-rise structure. The floors were designed as flat slabs. In some areas the columns were not on the building's gridlines, thereby creating a geometrical irregularity which posed a challenge for floor slab design.

I came up with an innovative approach to resolve this problem by adding concealed wide beams in the slabs. Another challenge was posed by the temperature difference between the floor slab of the unheated, two-level parking garage which supported the heated townhomes at the upper level. I anticipated a problem with this, and I decided to carry out a thermal analysis to determine the effects on the structure. I found some corner columns were overstressed and so added additional steel reinforcement. I enjoyed working on this project and was content that I could face the design challenges squarely. I also occasionally supervised the construction of the building. The contractor made a major mistake in not precisely locating all the caissons for the foundation with respect to the columns they were supporting. Following John Zils' guidance, I worked on a solution to the problem and sketched the corrected design for each caisson.

While I worked on parts of some other projects, another major project came my way. This was the 38-story Chicago Exchange Center on Congress Parkway in downtown Chicago. I worked with another competent senior engineer, Ray S. Clark, and our team was headed by Mr. Hal Iyengar, a structural partner and a close associate of Dr. Khan. Mr. Iyengar was a great engineer in his own right and had worked with Dr. Khan on major projects. He came up with innovative techniques for simplifying the computer analysis of tall buildings. He played a prominent role in some of Dr. Khan's innovations, particularly in mixed steel-concrete structural systems for tall buildings. We utilized a tubular system with vertical trusses at the elevator core to resist wind loads for this 38-story steel tower. I carried out the computer analysis of the tower for gravity and wind loads, using what I had learned from the Pacific Plaza project. Together with Ray, I worked on all the beam-to-column and other connection details. I also worked on a five-story low-rise portion, built over an abandoned railroad bridge over Congress Parkway. I investigated the existing heavy bridge structure to check its structural adequacy and determined its strengthening requirements. The building was built in 1984 after I left SOM.

It was during Ronald Reagan's presidency around this time in the early 1980s that the U.S. was hit by the worst economic recession since World War II. This affected the construction industry badly. While the design work for the Stock Exchange Center was nearing its end, there was a brutal layoff. Many engineers and architects at SOM, including several senior people and even an associate partner from another department had to pack their belongings and leave. The office looked half empty. I was still working on my project and wrapping it up. Seeing the office environment around me, I felt somewhat anxious. I was still on the H1 visa which had been extended twice in 1981 and 1982 by SOM's attorney Joanne H. Saunders. I was still waiting to get my green card approved, based on the sponsorship of my brother in Muncie. I was told that I could reside in the U.S. with the H1 visa for up to three years. I was wondering what would happen if I got laid off and became unemployed. It would lead to the loss of my legal status and without legal status, it would be very difficult to get another job especially during the ongoing construction slump.

Once the structural design of the Chicago Stock Exchange Center project was completed, there was no work for me. Despite all these uncomfortable thoughts, I tried to think positively. I was told that since there was no work for me, I would be conducting some R & D (research and development). I realized that this was a temporary arrangement. With the demise of Dr. Khan, who led research activities, there were not too many research-minded people left there, and if there were, I was not aware of them. As I had always been a workaholic, I felt bad about not doing much at the office. I sensed that some dark clouds were forming on the horizon and soon headwinds could perhaps start blowing. Normally engineers would not deliver drawings between offices, however, in the slump, we didn't have delivery personnel. One day I was delivering drawings and I found out that this office had a bridge design section. I met someone at a higher level there and told him that I had bridge design experience with an American firm called Louis Berger Inc. in Bangladesh as well as in Sudbury, Ontario, so if they were looking for a bridge engineer, I was available. I didn't get a good response to my proposition. I was told they were fully staffed at that time.

Soon my worst fear came true. Sometime in mid-February of 1983, I heard my name called on the intercom one Friday asking me to see John Zils in his office. Once I was in his office and took a seat John said to me, while holding a pink slip in his hand,

"You probably know this firm is going through a period of downturn. So, we must let you go. I had nothing to do with this decision. I am just conveying the information. You will get two weeks' pay but you don't need to come to the office on Monday." It was a bombshell for me. Having weathered some past storms, I didn't panic, but stayed calm. I had been mentally preparing for this news.

I asked him "You have other offices in other cities; is it possible for you to transfer me to another SOM office in another city?" He replied that they already factored that possibility into their evaluation.

I immediately realized that this was not going to be pretty for me. Unless I found a job immediately, I would have to leave the country. I had no chance of unemployment benefits since I was neither a green card holder nor a citizen. My source of income would be cut off. I spent my savings for the down payment of the new home. So, I would be completely without money. It didn't take long for these thoughts to flash through my mind, while sitting in John's office. I told him these concerns of mine and requested some time as this was too drastic for me to digest. I told him "I understand you don't want me to hang around here and I have no intention of hanging around here anymore either, after news like this." John was a decent man and a protégé of Dr. Khan and grasped my situation well. He said, "Okay, let me talk to some people and I will let you know on Monday."

After spending an anxious weekend, the following Monday I saw John. He said there was no change in my situation. I should leave the office as soon as possible. Then I decided to meet Hal Iyengar, the structural engineering partner, whom I met before a couple of times before, over the design of the Chicago Stock Exchange Center. While in his office, I passionately explained my situation to him and requested that they keep me longer. Initially he was resisting but I realized I had nothing to lose by being forceful in my plea. I made my case accordingly. Seeing I was not giving in and I was vigorous in my narrative, he backed off and told me, "Let's end the conversation here. I will see what I can do. Until you hear from us you keep working." I called my home mortgage lender that day and asked what I should do if I didn't have a job. I was told I could pay a nominal amount of $100 per month until I found a new job. I thought that was a very nice gesture on their part.

After a couple of days John called me in to his office. I was of course apprehensive. But I was prepared for facing any even-tuality. I continued believing in my destiny and that sometimes things were not in our control. I was ready to accept anything I heard as God's plan. I comforted myself by thinking that all headwinds and tempestuous days eventually passed and sunny days reappeared. We were meant to experience cycles of head-winds and tailwinds. I had to accept reality and try to withstand the headwinds and enjoy the tailwinds while they lasted. With this resolve I entered John's office and took a seat. He said, "We are giving you two months to find a job. Try to find something by then. But we won't let you go until you find one, we are by no means executioners." I came out of his office relieved at the breathing space. I continued my work on R&D and bits and pieces of some other ongoing projects. But I felt uncomfortable there now, on borrowed time, unwanted and only there by their favor.

During this time, it was Dora who gave me the encourage-ment that I needed and told me that things would be alright. I was even thinking of going back to Bangladesh, but she told me not to go now under these circumstances, with bad memo-ries. She said I could go if I wished, from a position of strength, not weakness. I started a serious job search and jumped on the phones. Because of the slump in construction activities, it was not easy to find work. I called my old employer, Barry Martin in Timmins, Ontario and told him my situation. He was gracious enough to offer me a job at his firm again and even mentioned the salary. I kept that as a backup in case I had to leave the U.S. but didn't feel good about returning to the old place in a remote location.

One day I saw an advertisement for a Chief Structural Engi-neer in the *Engineering News-Record*, a construction magazine. The job was advertised by a small firm in Tampa, Florida. The quali-fications for the job were not too demanding in terms of experi-ence. The firm was involved in the design, manufacture, delivery and installation of a special type of precast concrete floor system called Filigree Precast Floor Slabs. It was not very attractive to me as it was a proprietary material with a narrow scope. Yet, under the circumstances, I applied. I got a call from the president of the firm who told me, "We are looking for someone like you. Your track record looks great, particularly your experience with SOM, which is a great firm. I can offer you the position, but I would like to meet you and perhaps you also want to see what we do. When can you fly to Tampa?" I told him about my visa situation. He said, "That's not a problem. We can help since you have good credentials. Also, I notice you have a Ph.D. If you want, you can teach part time at the local University of Southern Florida. The cost of living is low here compared to Chicago and there is no state tax." Things looked good to me, but I thought I would be dislocated from Chicago and lose my connection to the tall buildings that always fascinated me. I told him to give me some time to think it over and I would get back to him soon.

At the same time, I saw an advertisement from a large Chicago firm called Sargent & Lundy (S&G), who designed power plants, especially nuclear power plants. Their office was located just a couple of blocks to the east of SOM's office on Monroe Street. I went there and filled out an application form and gave it to the personnel department. Someone called me and asked for my visa status. I told them my situation and that my brother had sponsored me for a green card. I had an H1B visa that would expire next August after being asked about it.

I was told since I didn't have a green card and my H1B would expire shortly, they could not hire me. I spent the next few days thinking what to do. Upon the suggestion of a friend named Shah Jahan, I decided to write a letter to Mr. Thomas Longlais, Head of the Structural Engineering Division at S&G. I wrote a detailed letter explaining my situation and attaching my resume. I didn't hear anything for a couple of days. Then while at work, doing some routine task and ruminating over my uncertain future and seeking God's help in my mind, I got a call from the personnel department of S&G. They asked me to join the firm.

I met John and Hal Iyengar and gave them the news. I thanked Mr. Iyengar for going out of his way to keep me in consideration of my circumstances and immediately resigned from SOM. Friday, February 25, 1983 was my last day there.

I joined S&G the following Monday on February 28. I went to see Mr. Longlais to thank him. He said in reply, "I saw your qualifications and experience and didn't want to lose you just because of the technicality of a visa issue." I was placed under the supervision of Mr. Hingorani, a very senior engineer, on the first day. Later, I was working with Mr. Robert Tso, a very nice man. I started working on new types of structural components for nuclear structures. I started to get adjusted to the new environment of many structural engineers. I went through orientation and a series of in-house lectures on the engineering aspects of structural design of nuclear power plants. I enjoyed those technical lectures and started to think that S&G would be good place to settle down. It was a large firm with many engineers, offered a good salary. It was in fact known as "paymaster" and I heard that layoffs were rare. One could build a full-time, long-term career there.

The projects I worked on were new, but with my experience in the design of building, bridge, mining and now nuclear structures, I realized my education in structural engineering was a big asset as I could apply this knowledge to any type of structure. I enjoyed the time in the office as I got busy with a large nuclear power plant project called Marble Hill Nuclear Power Plant-Units I and II at Saluda Township near Hanover, Indiana. The construction of the project started in 1977 and when I joined the project, I didn't know that it's future was tenuous.

The Three Mile Island Nuclear Plant accident in March 1979 caused a meltdown and sent panic across America about nuclear plants. The plant that I was working on was totally built, but in view of the Three Mile Island accident, the Nuclear Regulatory

Commission (NRC) developed and issued new design regulations. Therefore, as part of the design team, I mostly worked implementing these new regulations. I worked on the modification and upgrading of containment buildings that housed the reactor and auxiliary structures. I spent much of my time on steel beams subjected to seismic and thermal loading and their special connections to resist twisting. While working on this project, rumors started about the possible closure of the plant, under mounting public pressure. Toward the end of 1983 there was no work left for that project. The project was totally abandoned, together with scores of other nuclear plants that closed around the country.

The next project I was assigned to, was the Clinton Nuclear Power Generation Station. This project was under construction as NRC imposed the more stringent regulations for the project. I carried out investigative analysis of the existing cable tray hangers to meet the new NRC requirements. I resolved many field problems involving fit-up difficulties of steel beams at their supports during erection. Sketches and concerns of field problems were being faxed to us by the field engineers. Facsimile (shortened to Fax) technology, which was in its up-and-coming stages and later peaked in the late 1980s, was amazingly useful for long-distance written and visual communications. I visited the construction site once, which was a great experience for me.

While working on these two projects I realized that most of the work was repetitive and NRC regulations were very stringent. So stringent that there was hardly any room for creativity or innovation on the part of the engineers. I started getting somewhat bored once I gained enough mastery of the work.

I got comfortable at this firm despite my boredom and the realization that I couldn't do this all my life. Soon headwinds started blowing again. While I had been working on the Marble Hill project, my H1B visa was set to expire in August as it would be three years then, but I still hadn't heard anything about the renewal application, filed in 1982 by Attorney Joanne Saunders while I was at SOM. I assumed that perhaps Immigration and Naturalization Service (INS) had accepted it and eventually I would address a possible extension for a fourth year. The visa issue was somewhat out of my purview, as Ms. Saunders had been dealing with INS about it.

On account of the Three Mile Island accident and the ensuing public reaction to it, the nuclear industry had come under scrutiny. Because of the uncertain nature of my visa status and the dullness of my routine work, in the early summer of 1983, I decided to look around for academic jobs. I liked teaching and the academic environment including the independence and job security that a teaching job at a university allowed. I liked the idea of eventually settling down in an academic setting as my long-term career. Factoring all these aspects into my consideration, I started applying to a few universities in the U.S. and overseas in case I had to leave the country suddenly.

I got a response to my application from the School of Architecture at the University of Illinois at Urbana-Champaign (UIUC) seeking a tenure-track faculty member for its Structures Division. I saw their advertisement earlier and it attracted me because it was in structural engineering -- my profession, and it was in an architectural school. I had come to like architecture through my experience in building design, particularly at SOM but also liked art and architecture more generally. I thought I would enjoy a teaching career which engaged both the analytical and artistic sides of the brain. Soon, I was invited by Professor James Simon, chairman of the Structures Division for an interview at the UIUC campus.

I prepared well for the interview by posing questions to myself and creating my own best answers. Also, I reviewed my SOM projects and took the drawings that I could show the search committee. I enjoyed the company of the professors who interviewed me. It was more of a conversation than an interview as they didn't ask me the tough questions that I anticipated. But my methodical preparation helped as they perhaps perceived me to be well prepared and confident.

I found out there were seven professors in the Structures Division, and they were looking for one more. At the final meeting with the School Director, Professor Alan Forrester, I asked for an Associate Professor position because of my professional experience. After the interview process, I left Champaign with a good feeling. A few days later, to my delight, I was offered a position of tenure-track Associate Professor, which I accepted. They subsequently sponsored me for a green card and applied for my labor certification to the Department of Labor, which was approved in a couple of months. They expected that I could join in the fall semester starting in late August. But because of the visa process they realized this might be delayed.

Around this time, I got bad news from Bangladesh. My 82-year old beloved father, who was ill for some time passed away on May 31, 1983. Because of my unsettled immigration status, I could not go to see my father to pay my last respects. Fortunately, two of my sisters living in Bangladesh and my oldest brother flew from Canada to be there. For the first time, I felt how hard it was to lose a parent. I spent a day at home mourning and reflected on my days with my saintly father. I sensed the truth of mortality and the pain associated with the loss of a dear one. I wondered if I could have been a better son to him. I felt I couldn't measure up to his many virtuous qualities. I prayed for my father's departed soul, so he might rest in peace in his eternal afterlife.

While still grappling with this personal loss, I got an offer, through a telegram, for a faculty position in Civil Engineering at the University of Benghazi in Libya. Almost at the same time I got another offer from Nanyang Technological Institute (NTI) in Singapore (later renamed as Nanyang Technological University (NTU). I was holding these two offers and took some time to decide. It was already fall of 1983. My three-year H1B visa term had already expired, but I hadn't heard anything back from INS. I thought I might hear back much later and by that time I would get my green card. UIUC had sponsored me and got the labor certification from the Department of Labor. It was a very confusing time for me as things were so fluid. I was just hoping that I would get the green card by the end of the year and start teaching from January 1984. However, things turned out differently.

In late 1983, I got a letter from INS that notifying me that my H1B visa could not be extended and I would have to leave the country. They gave me a couple of months to leave. This was an unexpected blow. I immediately contacted Mr. Ling Sing Wang, a musical name to me, the registrar of NTI, who arranged for an interview with someone at the Singapore Consulate in Chicago. Following the interview my appointment as Senior Lecturer was confirmed. I decided to go to Singapore. The prospect appeared promising because of the progress the country made after its independence from Malaysia. I declined the offer from Libya.

Meanwhile, I realized I needed a new lawyer to deal with my case rather than the one from SOM. I saw an attorney in the Chicago downtown area to discuss my situation. At the front desk, the secretary told me, "You have to pay the consultation fee in advance now." I wrote a check. When I saw the attorney, he heard my story, and told me about the immigration law. When I mentioned my predicament at a personal level, he curtly said, "I advise on legal matters, not your personal problems." He was both insensitive and of no use to me. I considered going back to Ms. Saunders, who dealt with my case at SOM. I met her and told her about the INS letter. After reading the letter, she told me, "You have an offer at UIUC where you can have a career, not just a job. You aren't going anywhere outside the U.S. I will apply to INS for your extended stay here and you should get your green card in the meantime."

I said, "I don't want to stay here in an uncertain predicament. I have decided to go. I can get the green card while there and return after that."

She said, "Okay, if that's what you want. I will do all the paperwork for you from here. I have all the necessary papers. If I need anything else, I'll call you."

I replied, "I will pay the fees for your services when I come back. But you have spent time on me today. How much should I pay you for that?"

She looked at me and told me, "You don't have to pay anything now or in the future. I got paid enough from SOM while dealing with your case."

I was dumbfounded. Lawyers were expensive, but she seemed like a selfless human being or even an angel to me for a minute. I felt she was kind and empathetic about my lingering hardships and therefore wouldn't accept money from me. But I had my pride and self-esteem, I felt that even in dire straits, I could not be a subject of her pity.

So, I said, "I will feel better if you accept some money from me."

She said, "Fine, if that's what you'd like, give me $200."

I wrote a check, thanked her and left. Once again, I realized that a person's goodness of heart did not depend upon one's race, religion, ethnicity, skin color or gender.

I notified Professor James Simon of my plans. He was surprised but said, "I am sorry INS put you through this. But don't worry, we want you here and will wait for you. Stay in touch." After getting this assurance I started preparing for my departure to Singapore. Mr. Wang and I negotiated a time in late February 1984 to join NTI which was before the deadline INS gave me to leave the country.

For a few reasons I decided to go to Singapore. First, I didn't want to remain in the U.S. under any shadowy circumstance, even though my attorney said she could help me stay. I guess that was my personality, I inherited it from my father who was very conscientious. This was an easy value to uphold since I knew that I could eventually return to the U.S. with proper legal status. If I didn't have this assurance, I might have stayed back following Ms. Saunders' advice. Secondly, if I went to Singapore, I would be close to Bangladesh and could visit my elderly mother who was a widow now. Thirdly, by living in another country we could experience a different culture, which might allow my children to develop a fuller world view. Fourthly, this was a teaching job that I loved, which would prepare me for UIUC. Finally, as I mentioned before, I was getting bored with my routine work. The person I was working with on the Clinton Nuclear Power Plant project was very impersonal and stone-faced, in contrast to Robert Tso, with whom I worked on the Marble Hill Nuclear Power Plant project.

I felt like my time was being wasted, and honestly, the prospect of teaching at a university in Singapore excited me. I studied the island city-state of Singapore and was impressed by the progress the country had made under good political leadership despite being a third-world country. It was approaching a quality of life and standard of living comparable to many developed countries. NTI was a new engineering university where I could make positive contributions and be a trend-setter. In addition, the salary offered was comparable to that in the U.S. and the cost of living was reasonable. They offered good fringe benefits and topping all was the fact that faculty members were provided with free accommodation. This would allow me to save enough to make up for the financial loss I might incur selling my home, if I couldn't sell it before I left.

Selling the house was a serious undertaking. I had invested a large sum of money as down payment, which I wanted to recover. I realized it would be hard for me to oversee things from Singapore. Even after my return I would be in Urbana-Champaign. I didn't have the financial flexibility to keep it unoccupied indefinitely. I thought of renting and contacted some known people, but nobody wanted to take the responsibility, which was quite understandable. In such a short time, it was imperative that I find a tenant or a buyer. It was around December-January, a slow period for home sales. On top of that the interest rate was high, discouraging potential buyers. Since none of the choices were good, I took the chance anyway and put the house on sale in early January but didn't get any offers. I contacted the mortgage company who came to an agreement with me to take back the home under a deal called "Deed Back." They assured me that they would not report this to the credit bureau, and this would not affect my future credit rating since I didn't default on any payment and they got the house back.

Just a few days before my departure for Singapore, the engine of our car broke down. A friend of mine Abu Chowdhury gave me his old second car which allowed me to travel in the city. Meanwhile, I resigned from S&L. On the last day of my work on February 17, 1984 I went to see Mr. Thomas Longlais to thank him again for facilitating my employment at his company. I was excited about travelling across the ocean.

A few days later on February 24, we left Chicago and took a flight out of O'Hare Airport, with destination to Singapore. Dora was not as fully energetic as before although she had recovered a lot. I was concerned about the long flights, particularly over the Pacific Ocean. Ifat was 14, Jinat 13 and Murad was 6. I had many concerns about the distant land and about my children, particularly my two beautiful teenage daughters, how would they react to a new culture in a developing country after living in the West? My two daughters were aware of my situation, and likely used to my several moves. Yet the question remained lingering with me: I might like adventure, but would they?

CHAPTER 9

SINGAPORE

Orchids in the Lion City

Once we were in the air for a few minutes after the airplane took off from Chicago, I felt some separation anxiety. I was going to a different country, far away across the ocean after living in the West since 1970. It was known for its orchids and called the Lion City. When would I return? Or what if I liked it, could I live there longer? Our flight from Chicago was bound for Los Angeles with a stopover at St. Louis. After we left St. Louis, Dora soon complained of serious nausea after her in-flight dinner. The flight attendant was very helpful. She arranged for Dora to lie down, stretching herself across a few empty seats. Because of Dora's weak health and her previous health history I was already prepped for a tough flight. I comforted her by saying that she would like the new place, and everything would be fine once we were there.

At Los Angeles International Airport, my nephew, Dr. M. Rafiquzzaman, who was a professor of Electrical Engineering at the California Polytechnic Institute at Pomona, California and his wife Reba and son Tito came to see us. From there we took a flight to Singapore via Honolulu and Taipei operated by

Singapore Airlines. The airplane took off from Los Angeles Airport in the evening; we were soon flying over the Pacific Ocean. The bright distant lights of Los Angeles became dimmer and dimmer and then faded away in the horizon behind us over the ocean. I kept thinking about the distant shore of Singapore. It surely felt like an adventure! Accustomed to changing course in life, I enjoyed it and took it in stride. My separation anxiety subsided, and my mind was occupied with the suspense and excitement of going to a new country and teaching at a university, as a full-time faculty member for the first time.

The stopover in Honolulu was brief, before a very long flight, about 11 hours over the Pacific Ocean. We reached Taipei, Taiwan and had a four-hour layover there. We waited in the airport's waiting room. It was a sizeable hall with large open space. Being a structural engineer, I could not avoid looking up at the ceiling above. I noted it was a two-way concrete grid-beam system that allowed long spans over the hall, a concept that I later used for a large consultancy project. After a long flight this break allowed us to rest for a while. We boarded another plane for the last leg of our journey. Finally, we landed in Singapore's Changi National Airport. At the arrival gate, someone was holding a poster saying, "Dr. Ali." He welcomed me and took us to a hotel.

In the hotel room my 6-year old son Murad wanted to watch TV, so I turned it on. He tried to get his cartoon channel there but couldn't. I told him we were in a different country, so he wouldn't get his favorite channels there. Then he tried to call his friend Derrick in Bartlett from the phone but found out it didn't work. He looked frustrated and I felt bad for him. My daughters were older and understood. The following day someone came to take us from the hotel to a Guest House on the NTI campus. It was a comfortable place and the housekeeper Madam Ng, an elderly woman, was very nice. I went to see the Dean of Engineering, Professor Chen and the Registrar Mr. Ling Sing Wang. I was told that there were a few professors there also originally from Bangladesh. They were Dr. Jahedul Alam (my former teacher at EPUET in Dhaka), Dr. A. Jabbar and Dr. Rezaul Karim, all of them hired on contract like me.

We stayed at the Guest House for a few days before being allotted an apartment on campus. These were old buildings. The apartment was spacious but somewhat rundown. I was told a new campus and faculty residences were being built nearby on a vast tract of land. We got settled, found shopping places and grocery stores. There was a good public transportation system and efficient taxi service. The weather was warm and humid, typically fluctuating very little, between 75- and 95-degrees Fahrenheit (24- and 35-degrees Celsius) throughout the year. Singapore is close to the equator. Singaporean society was very disciplined, the city was clean and orderly. At taxi stands people queued and drivers picked up a passenger who came first. Slum housing was being replaced by government subsidized apartment buildings, to accommodate low income residents

We got fresh foods and meat from the farmer's market. There were many restaurants in the city catering to the palette of a cosmopolitan population. The government, under Lee Kwan Yew, was totally free from corruption and their social, economic and education policies were very praiseworthy. Soon all three of our children were enrolled in school and started to make friends. Interestingly, at the schools my two daughters had a course called "morality education." It was mandatory for students to wear school uniforms. Girls were not allowed to wear jewelry, lip stick, or makeup of any kind at the schools.

My son Murad was admitted to a primary school in Boon Lay. On the first day of school, Murad was greeted by two little girls, Nimmi and Barsha. They were the daughters of Dr. Jahedul Alam and Dr. Abdul Jabbar, respectively. Nimmi and Barsha held his hands on either side as they walked through the hallway telling the other students, "He is my friend." The teacher was called *Chegu* (not the teacher's name but how they were addressed by students), who would use a cane to discipline the children. Because of the language barrier, one day Murad didn't understand the teacher's instruction and failed to comply. The teacher took Murad by the hand and pulled out his cane. Nimmi, was nearby; she ran to Murad and told the teacher, "Don't hit him. He is from America. He doesn't understand your words." The teacher resisted. When I heard about the incident, I went to school, met the teacher and asked him not to try hitting again. I reported the incident to our dean's secretary, who began looking into an alternative school for Murad, Henry Park Primary School, a prestigious school. Murad was placed on a wait list but by the time a seat became available, we were ready to leave Singapore. I thank the brave girl Nimmi, for protecting her little friend.

Concern for morality permeated through the society. Even though it was a very secular society, pornographic literature and magazines were banned. One would never come across such books or magazines in the bookstores or any stalls or shopping malls. All religions were accepted equally, with national holidays observed during the main festivals of Buddhism, Christianity, Islam, and Hinduism. There was hardly any crime. I recall asking an employee of NTI who arranged our move to the apartment if there was any crime in Singapore. He looked at me in surprise and retorted, "Did you not come from Chicago, a city of high crimes, and you are asking me about crime here? No, we don't have any crime here. You can walk safely on the street at any time of the day or night."

Once I joined NTI, I was given a nice office. A few days later, I had lunch at the university cafeteria with some of my Chinese colleagues and another Bangladeshi faculty member, Ahmedul Amin of Mechanical Engineering. A very nice man, he had settled in Singapore and lived in his own home. I saw some of them ordered something called "Thousand Year Egg", a Chinese deli-cacy. I was feeling adventurous and wanted to taste it. The egg was dark in color and looked somewhat strange to me. I was told it was cooked in a very special way. I didn't like the look of it, but since it was already in front of me and the others were enjoying it, I ate it hoping it would be fine. I didn't suit my palette, but I finished eating it despite my revulsion. Returning to my office, I felt nau-seated and started vomiting violently every few minutes. It got so bad that one of my colleagues in a neighboring office physically helped me into his car and drove me home. My condition was so terrible that he went to the university's health clinic and sent a doctor, who came to see me and gave me some medicine that helped. I learned my lesson about eating something new without trying a little of it first. I should "trust" rather than "test" my gut!

In 1956, Nanyang University was established, before Singa-pore became independent from the British. It was merged with National University of Singapore in 1980. NTI was formed in 1981 as an engineering university with the ambitious plan of producing top-notch engineers at the vacated campus of Nan-yang University. In 1982 NTI started as a functioning university consisting of three engineering departments with an enrollment of only 582 students. When I joined its Civil Engineering disci-pline in February 1984, the new university had been experienc-ing growing pains. Some of the planned courses were not devel-oped and laboratories not yet fully set up. It has come a long way since those days. At this writing, the student population at NTU is almost 35,000 and it has many departments with graduate pro-grams offering master's and doctoral degrees.

I was assigned two courses to teach, none of them on struc-tural engineering. The dean told me that there were enough faculty members to teach the structures courses. I was assigned the two lecture courses with the rubrics Civil Engineering Construction and Civil Engineering Practice. These were both new courses with no syllabus in place yet. The onus therefore fell on me to develop these course syllabi. I never took these courses as a student. In Ottawa, Canada I took an introductory evening course called Effective Supervision in Construction at Algonquin College. The only real asset that I had was my practical experience and the dean was counting on that. I started studying the subject of construction, so I could develop a syllabus to teach from.

In addition, I was assigned a laboratory course called Civil Engineering Construction Laboratory. I had to develop a program of laboratory tests for several materials and elements and write up the test procedures for the students. These were difficult challenges that I had to accept. But my attitude was never to be cowed by hard tasks. In fact, I looked forward to learning new things along the way. So, instead of feeling pressured, I happily started doing what I needed to do.

The same thing happened with the Civil Engineering Practice course. The dean told me to include Human Resource Management, following the Japanese system of management and referred to my professional experience in Canada and the U.S. as enough to make him think I was up to the task. They like the Japanese model, since the oriental country was an economic success, despite its utter ruin in World War II. The Pacific Rim countries were impressed and started emulating its management style. Again, this was an uncharted territory for me, but I gladly accepted the challenge as I thought I would learn something new by teaching this course. He said that this was mandated by the government. Two other items that were part of the course were the In-house Practical Project and Industrial Attachment.

The Human Resource Management segment of the Practice course was an eye opener for me. First, I studied the Japanese style of management. After Japan was vanquished by the U.S. in World War II, Americans introduced their management system and offered aid to help develop the country's infrastructure. The proud Japanese didn't like it for too long. Despite the merits of the American system and aid, they wanted their own system, fitting their own culture and heritage. To the best of my recollection, the intelligentsia and businessmen got together and developed a multi-point manifesto.

The first point stated that Japan was a proud nation and would not like to be known as a beggar nation. Then it went on to propose numerous steps about how to achieve self-sufficiency and progress by adopting these propositions. They presented this to the government which embraced the ideas. The ideas were focused on increasing the productivity of workers in various settings. Some of the basic concepts were that a corporation was like a family. It should provide lifetime job security and would get loyalty and commitment in return from the employees. It was essentially a large clan pulling for each other. Employers would take care of workers if there was downturn in the company. Another important topic was how to manage time. I taught and benefited myself by implementing the notions presented there. I used *The Time Trap* by Alec Makenzie and Pat Nickerson for the course.

I also simultaneously taught a course on Engineering Materials, temporarily, until a regular instructor was available for it. Yet another new course at the school and for me. As far as I recall the regular instructor had a medical issue. I developed the syllabus as I went and taught it for some time until the designated instructor took over. It was a course for all students across engineering disciplines. So, I had to include materials related to other disciplines, which was quite a challenge. Teaching this course was one of the hardest classroom challenges I faced there at NTI.

The In-house practical training project was another exciting one for me. Students would build an actual concrete pavilion for the playground from the ground up. The concrete structure had a few columns on one side that supported an overhanging canopy. The foundation was designed to stabilize the structure above against overturning. They carried out the excavation and began the project. I found them very diligent and committed to their tasks. They placed the steel reinforcing bars and poured the concrete. The whole process took a few weeks. I would supervise the work very closely.

Regarding the Industrial Attachment Program, I led a group of students in a construction project at the dockyard site of the Port Authority of Singapore. I would go there frequently on certain weekdays to see what the students were doing and how they were learning from their experience. Two students also successfully carried out two Independent Study projects under my supervision. Overall, I found the students at NTI very serious and attentive in and outside the class. It was a pleasure to teach them. While teaching full time there I realized that I held an important role as a teacher, a noble profession. I could influence young students' minds and practices, so they could shape the future society in a fitting manner.

One other important development kept me preoccupied almost throughout my stay in Singapore. Early on, Dean Chen called me to his office and asked me if I would be willing to do some consultancy work on tall buildings. He found my experience on tall buildings at SOM Chicago in my resume, and that's why he chose me for this opportunity. I immediately agreed to do it. The dean suggested that I should partner with Paul Ang a local junior faculty member. I was retained by National Iron and Steel Mills Ltd. who would manufacture reinforcing steel for concrete. I met the executives and found out that it was an investigative project. Like many Asian countries, Singapore traditionally used concrete in construction and most of their high-rise buildings were in concrete. The Japanese steel manufacturers were trying to penetrate the construction market in Singapore with the supply of structural steel. The goal of my investigation was to find out if either steel or concrete would be a suitable material for tall buildings in Singapore. The project was a unique consultancy opportunity.

To celebrate the completion of our consultancy project, Paul arranged a dinner for me and my family in a posh Chinese restaurant. His wife also joined us. He invited a few other professors. He was happy that I had an opportunity to work on the project, which also benefited him financially. However, the day before the dinner, I got the sad news that my elderly mother in Bangladesh was very ill and could not take care of herself any longer. Although I was quite glum, I didn't want to cancel the engagement and affect schedules of the many invitees since I was the guest of honor. Also, Paul ordered Peking duck especially for Dora and me since we had heard a lot about it but never tried it. It was on the order menu, but what we got was not what we expected. The dinner didn't go very well for us although we enjoyed the company of my Chinese colleagues.

I have a few recollections from life off the NTI campus. As mentioned before, there were a few Bangladeshi families with whom we would socialize. In addition to those mentioned before Dr. Abdul Aziz, a Bangladeshi professor at the National University of Singapore, and a former teacher of mine from EPUET became our good friend. A few European professors were also there on contract. In addition to some Chinese and Indian professors, I developed friendship with some of these Europeans.

Some interesting places to visit were the Singapore Zoo, the Jurong Bird Park, and Sentosa Island. I visited these tourist attractions with my family. In the zoo there was a section for snakes of different kinds, housed behind glass boxes, clearly visible from outside but very close to the sides. The Bird Park was an immensely interesting place. Different kinds of birds were encased in a huge net covering the vastness of the entire park. A natural habitat was created for them inside. The different colors of birds and their chirping coupled with their beautiful habitat offered serenity and calmness to visitors. An artificial waterfall on one side of the park added to the relaxing setting.

The Sentosa Island was a place of fun and exploration. There was large expanse of woods and forest, hiking paths, a museum, and many fun activities for children. One could easily spend a day there. Transportation the mainland was via ferry or overhead cable car. We took the cable car while going and the ferry on the way back. These were some of my favorite experiences and stay with me till today. Occasionally I picture those soothing scenes of Jurong Bird Park and Sentosa Island during meditation. The shopping area on Orchard Road was another place to visit as there were many stores and shops. Because of the open market policy any and all commodities were readily available. Tourist would crowd this delightful and brimming place.

I lived with my family in Singapore from February to November of 1984. My nephew, Dr. Kaisaruzzaman, the son of my oldest sister, lived in Malaysia with his wife Suraiya. Both were medical doctors. They lived in a town called Kota Tinggi, the capital of Kota Tinggi district, Johor, Malaysia. The town was about 40 miles (64 kilometers) from Singapore. He and his family would visit us from time to time. On one occasion on April 7 my nephew took us to his home.

Singapore is connected to Malaysia by the Johor-Singapore Causeway that was built in 1923 over the Straits of Johor. The bridge spans between the small township of Woodlands in Singapore to Johor Bahru, the capital city of Johor state. The ride from Johor Bahru to Kota Tinggi was very fascinating. Large tracts of land containing palm trees lined both sides of the highway. On the side of the highway vendors were selling coconut water from fresh green coconuts. The ride to Kota Tinggi was a very peaceful experience, with green forests all around.

My nephew took us to Desaru Beach. It is a well-known beach in that region. It was truly soothing to look at the vast body of water there. We stopped at a local resort hotel and had some delicious pineapple drinks. We also visited the Kota Tinggi Waterfalls with near-vertical falls and cascades of water. It was a very serene place of sparkling beauty and ideal for relaxation. These scenes have never left my memory and I still picture them during meditation. We stayed overnight and returned to Singapore the next day. We visited my nephew a second time on November 2, when he invited us to attend a dinner party to celebrate his gaining citizenship. He invited many local Malaysians and a minister of Johor state. It was interesting to see that the minister's driver sat in a chair at the same table next to him and his wife, who was an Egyptian. My nephew's presence in nearby Malaysia was a great source of pleasure for me and my family.

While I was preoccupied with my teaching and social life, I got a letter on July 31, 1984 from Attorney Joanne Saunders advising me about my immigration status. She mentioned that I should be hearing from the U.S. Embassy in Singapore about the date of an interview in August. I would be granted an immigrant visa to enter the U.S. Also, Professor Jim Simon sent me the rubrics of two courses that I would be teaching in the winter semester of 1985 at UIUC. I was elated by these developments and finally got the much-anticipated interview letter. At the interview, I was granted the coveted visa along with my family. I resigned immediately surprising the dean and my colleagues and friends there.

I had to keep this matter confidential so NTI did not come to know of it, perhaps to my detriment.

After fixing a date for departure I purchased air tickets for Chicago via Dhaka, Bangladesh so I could visit my motherland. It had been six years and I wanted to see my ailing mother. Secure now in my visa status, I was able to make the trip and gain re-entry to the U.S. Before I left Singapore, I had to get an exit permit from the police department and collect my money from the government office from the provident fund in which NTI deposited money every month as a fringe benefit. Both offices gave me a time when I could collect the permit and the check. At each place, at the appointed time, I was promptly given an envelope containing the permit and the check. I was very impressed at the efficiency and competence of the Singapore government at both offices. We departed from Singapore on November 8. My nephew Dr. Kaisaruzzaman came to the Changi Airport to see us off.

We boarded the plane heading for Dhaka. I felt some separation anxiety when the plane took off from Singapore. In the few months we had been there, we started liking the place and the people. I felt a tinge of sadness, even though I was heading for my motherland, where I would see my beloved mother in a few hours. Also, my eventual destination was the land of opportunities where an academic position at a reputed university was waiting for me, but I must admit I had developed an affinity for Singapore. Among its many positive points, this city state was lacking crime and corruption, disciplined, had forward-thinking leaders, efficient and competent government, showed respect for all religions, had an acceptance of multiculturalism, and despite being exceedingly secular society I found its moral compass to be better than many religious societies. I liked it and perhaps I might have settled permanently but it was not comparable to America in terms of its scope and reach. It didn't have the elastic-ity that America had. While I could envision a bright future for country itself, I didn't think I could stay and meet my own aspirations. Looking back, I was right. As the island vanished from my view, I wished the country and its people well.

In the airplane, I saw Mr. Kamal Hossain, a renowned attorney from Bangladesh, a politician, and one of the authors of the famous six-point plan for autonomy of East Pakistan. It was a document that contributed to the eventual independence of Bangladesh. Since I missed the liberation movement of Bangladesh, I wanted to talk with him. With his consent I sat next to him in a vacant seat for a few minutes. He was a fine gentleman. I talked with him about the political condition of Bangladesh during the liberation war. After the conversation, I returned to my seat and started imagining what Bangladesh would be like, after my six-year absence. So much had changed there; I would not be seeing my dear father who passed away in 1983 and I had to prepare for seeing my mother very ill. The thoughts didn't sit well with me. My younger brother was in Dhaka in 1978 when I visited last. I would miss his company since he was in the U.S. I tried to uplift my mood by thinking positively about my impending return to the U.S., and my new life at Urbana-Champaign. It was only a four-hour flight, our plane landed in Dhaka shortly.

From the airport, I went straight to see my mother. I noticed she was lying in bed and didn't initially recognize me; she mistook me for my father. I realized she had been missing my father, her life-long partner. I corrected her saying that I was her son. The next day, we moved to my other sister-in-law's home. Her name is Munira (Gora). She is the most hospitable clear hearted and generous person that I have ever known. Her main pleasure had always been to make others happy even to this day. She would cook delicious meals for us and make sure we were comfortable in her home.

We had a good time with our relatives and friends in Dhaka. In November we visited Patuakhali to see my mother-in-law and another sister-in-law Maksuda Khan (Daisy). Back in Patuakhali, my birthplace, I felt nostalgic seeing the old places, buildings, structures, and sites. This was the first time I visited it since I left for Canada in 1970 and I found plenty of changes.

Many new buildings and many cars on the streets. The city expanded west beyond the town's cemetery to the village of Kalikapur where administrative offices and the court had been built. I visited the court building and found one of my classmates, now a lawyer. In our youth he used to bully other students at schools but changed when he went to local Patuakhali College. He was elected the vice president of the student association. I met a few others there whom I knew before and who had become lawyers. I remembered the old court building in the old part of the town that was built by the British where my father would practice. I visited my parental home where I grew up. My cousin Manirul Islam was living there with his family. He entertained me and my family with an opulent dinner. I met some of my relatives who were living there and old friends from my school days. While in Patuakhali, I decided to visit my father's village home *Dharandi* and my mother's village home in *Kharijjama*.

Manirul arranged a speedboat and accompanied me for the trip by the rivers. I visited *Kharijjama* first as many of my cousins were still living were there but most of my uncles had since expired. After visiting the village, I went to *Dharandi* on the other side of the river. My uncle Mir Mohsen Ali was deceased, but my aunt was alive and living there. I was treated with great hospitality at both villages. I went to the family graveyard in *Dharandi* where my father was buried next to his mother and brother according to his wish. Before my father's death, he instructed my cousin Mir Alauddin Ahmed, a wealthy businessman in Dhaka whom my father loved very much to take his remains to *Dharandi* and bury him there next to his mother whom he loved dearly, and next to his younger brother whom he also loved very much. He had died earlier and was buried next to her. I solemnly performed the *ziarat* (visiting and praying at the gravesite) standing next to the grave. Even though I could not reach my father and talk with him, I felt so connected standing next to his grave and remembering my noble father with reverence and with a heavy heart. I prayed for him to the Almighty, to forgive his sins and grant him the highest level of the Paradise. I recalled the day when my father prayed at his father's gravesite while I was a child and accompanied him. I didn't know when I would come to this remote village and pray for my father again. With that thought I felt saddened when I left the site.

In Dhaka I would spend much of my time with my ailing mother. Seeing her physical and mental condition I knew I may or may not see her again. During my stay in Dhaka she got very sick and was admitted to a health clinic. After some time, she was released, and a nurse was hired to attend her at home around the clock for a few days. I stayed there for a few days while Dora and the kids were at my sister-in-law's home.

One night I decided to sleep next to her and saw firsthand how she was suffering and how old age and sickness had affected her body, mind and spirit. I witnessed her physical discomfort, infirmity and utter frailty, and was thinking of my failure of not being able to do anything about it, other than patting her on the head and trying to comfort her. Despite this, I felt good to be lying next to my beloved mother, after having missed her company for so many years. I recollected some of my experiences with her as a child and felt bad seeing her like this. She had been such an outgoing, intelligent and street-smart woman. I wished I could stay there to take care of her during the last years of her life. But I was in a state of transition myself, still unsettled and soon moving back to the U.S. As a father I had obligation to my two minor daughters and my son in addition to my wife. We had experienced so many moves that affected all of us. It was painful to leave her, but the lack of any solid foothold there in Dhaka, my financial and other immediate and long-term responsibilities and family obligations, as well as my own search for stability in life, prevented me from staying there. I felt life was so full of difficult choices and decisions.

It was time to return to the U.S. Before leaving my mother, I hugged her and took a last look at her. Before exiting through the bedroom door, I looked back to see her one more time and noticed that she was staring at me. I was deeply saddened to leave her in this condition. When I made eye contact with her, she said, "Do you have money? I can give you some if you need." I knew this was my original mother, disoriented now, but still thinking about her son's wellbeing. I politely replied, "Ma, I have money. Don't worry about me." That was my last conversation with her. To avoid being overwhelmed by my intense emotions, I quickly left the room without looking back.

When we had visited Bangladesh from Canada in 1978, we had a long layover at the airport in London. Despite having time, I didn't venture out with the girls and my one-year old son Murad. However, this time, on our return trip, we decided to visit London for a couple of days as tourists. We left Dhaka for Chicago on December 17, 1984 and gaining day arrived in London. We stayed in a hotel for two days and visited many places. We got a feel for this historical city, once the capital of the British Empire, upon which "the sun never sets".

London, an old city with a significant history warrants some review. Londinium was founded by the Romans in about the year 43 on the bank of the Thames River as the capital of their remote outpost. The original city lasted for 17 years before it was burnt down. The new London was built after that. The Great Fire of London in 1666 lasted three days and destroyed the whole city.

The city was rebuilt on the existing foundations. In the mid-19th century London's population grew significantly, and following the Industrial Revolution, this growth expanded into the suburbs. Eventually, London became a world leader in both business and tourism.

From our hotel, we took an iconic double decker bus on a sightseeing tour of the historic and landmark sites and buildings. A running commentary explained the brief history and importance of the places and structures. It was a great spectacle. The bus carried us through Piccadilly Circus, Trafalgar Square, London Bridge (now called Tower Bridge), Big Ben, Tower of London, and Buckingham Palace, among some other London attractions. I knew the names of many of these places. Piccadilly Circus, a famous road junction and bustling public space, was a very busy site. We disembarked at Trafalgar Square, a historic landmark site and public gathering space used for special events. There was a public speech going on at the time of our visit. I noticed many city pigeons roaming around unafraid of people. While traveling I was marveling at how the British were able to rule a large empire from this small island nation.

The Tower of London is an ancient castle and fortress, notable for housing the crown jewels and keeping many notorious prisoners. Throughout its history, the tower has served many purposes. The tour guide on the bus mentioned that the tower had a dungeon where some people had been imprisoned and tortured. The Tower of London has an important place in London's history. The London Bridge is another important structure. This was the one built in the early 1970s and is also known as Tower Bridge. I enjoyed watching Big Ben clock and its tower, a popular icon. To the best of my recollection, the highly recognizable chiming clock was being repaired at that time. Another attraction was, of course, Buckingham Palace, the administrative center and the residence of the British monarch. The palace, a majestic building with a very large compound, caught my special attention.

While experiencing this remarkable spectacle, I was thinking of the glory days of the British Empire. Although the empire was no longer there, the royal traditions had been maintained and still revered. The attachment to history demonstrated the people's admiration of their past and their willingness to maintain ties to days gone by. The Queen's guards at the palace were another enlivening sight, in beautiful bright and colorful uniforms, some of them on horses and others standing still dutifully near the gates of the palace. I wanted to see the Cambridge and Oxford University campuses and Westminster Abbey, the burial sites of luminaries like Isaac Newton and Charles Darwin as well as British monarchs but these were not included in the tour. Because of my tight schedule, I missed those sites. We departed from London for Chicago on December 19 and arrived in Chicago the same day in the evening.

CHAPTER 10

BACK TO THE U.S.

Home of the Fighting Illini

When we landed at Chicago's O'Hare International Airport, I felt great relief. I was entering with a permanent resident visa and the opportunity of realizing my American Dream was closer to certainty. I was heading for Urbana-Champaign, the home of the Fighting Illini, UIUC's athletic team. I was on my way to an academic job that I would often cherish. I finally found my niche.

At the airport in Chicago, after we were cleared by immigration and customs, we came out of the arrival gate. We met my brother Mosaddeq and his wife Tora. After exchanging our greetings, Mosaddeq, Tora, their son Tarek and our three kids got into their car. I rented a car and Dora and I drove together. Mosaddeq was a doctoral student in Mechanical Engineering at Purdue University in West Lafayette, Indiana. It was about a two-hour drive, mostly on Highway 65 from Chicago. While driving, I recalled, before leaving for Singapore, Mosaddeq urged me not to go but to stay and continue with S&L and work out the offer at UIUC. I sensed that he thought it was risky and I might not get a chance to return. I explained my situation and thought process, but he still had some misgivings and thought I should stay in Chicago. He felt that I should take the attorney's suggestion which assured that I could stay in the U.S. Mosaddeq and I had grown up together, extremely close, like brothers and best friends. We could always talk freely, heart to heart with each other. He cared for me as I did for him.

Soon we reached West Lafayette and parked near his apartment on campus. We stayed with them until January 2, 1985, when we moved to university housing called Orchard Downs on campus It was a semi-furnished apartment for married students in Urbana. Interestingly, I felt like I was in a familiar setting. The twin cities of Urbana-Champaign, home to a renowned university in the U.S. reminded me of the twin cities of Kitchener-Waterloo home to the University of Waterloo, a renowned university in Canada.

UIUC is one of the largest, world-class universities in the U.S. with emphasis on research. It was established in 1867 following the American Civil War. It was initially called Illinois Industrial University to reflect the growing need for technical education covering engineering, agriculture, and business. This industrial focus was considered a departure from the liberal arts education prevalent at that time. Initial enrollment was in engineering and business, based on student interest, to be followed later by agriculture. It was renamed the University of Illinois to satisfy the aspirations of both faculty and students, who preferred to continue building the university with a broader scope and gradually add other disciplines.

UIUC started its world class architecture curriculum in 1870, the fourth program in the U.S. following three other universities: MIT, Cornell University, and University of Pennsylvania, MIT being the first in the country to offer this curriculum in 1868. The first student in architecture at UIUC was Nathan C. Ricker, who graduated in 1873. He became an instructor and the head of the program. He toured Europe and introduced the German Polytechnic method of architectural education that emphasized the applied and practical aspects of architectural education rather than architectural design alone. In 1890 Ricker introduced a four-year curriculum in Architectural Engineering, thereby creating a new discipline combining architecture and engineering specifically focused on buildings. This was the first in the country and other institutions followed suit.

Over the second half of the 19th century there were many advances in building construction practices that originated in Chicago. It was truly the outstanding engineers and architects of Chicago whose vision, creativity, led to the building construction innovations which still resonate globally. After the Great Chicago Fire on October 9, 1871, that destroyed some 18,000 buildings it was imperative to rebuild much of the downtown with non-wood construction. The fire, disastrous as it was, provided both impetus and space. Chicago was already a vibrant business hub, contributing to the urgency to rebuild. Rapid technical and architectural developments ensued, making Chicago the birthplace of skyscrapers. The building boom also facilitated the growth of a new academic field of building engineering. Under the direction of Nathan Ricker, UIUC developed the innovative interdisciplinary field which came to be known as architectural engineering. This curriculum, with occasional modifications, continued to be taught until the 1970s. It was revised again and renamed the Structures Division, under the School of Architecture. The Architecture School consisted of four distinct divisions with architectural design being the largest. I joined this historic Structures Division as a faculty member.

Once we settled, I contacted Professor James Simon and met him in his office. He welcomed me and said, "I am relieved that you've finally come to Urbana-Champaign to join us." My official starting date was January 6, although classes started later in January. In those days, the official joining date for the winter semester was January 6, changed later to January 16. He explained to me what I would teach every semester, both an undergraduate and a graduate course in structures. I felt glad to know that I would be engaging in structures courses again, after having taught non-structural courses in Singapore. He introduced me to some faculty and staff members.

I also met the school director Professor Alan Forrester, originally from Scotland, a fine gentleman. For the spring semester I was assigned to teach a section of Statics, a foundational undergraduate course in structures required by all students, and Advanced Steel Design, a graduate course required in the M.Arch. program. Since both courses assigned to me were new to me, I started focusing on developing my lecture notes and handouts.

Soon classes started. My most recent teaching experience in Singapore helped me during this transition. I was brushing up my old knowledge and learning new materials, particularly in the graduate course, since to teach effectively I had to know the subject well. I wished to be diligent and serve the students, rather than falter in class and lose their respect. I brought my abundant real-world experience to the classroom, which students liked.

A brief article presenting my biographical sketch was published In the School's student newsletter *Rickernotes*, the week of February 11, 1985, and I was welcomed to the School. My interviewer Scott Bloom, asked me to talk about my teaching philosophy, I replied "I want to transfer my knowledge and experience to the students through courses and projects." This was quoted in the article. I mentioned that despite my personal inclination towards art and architecture, I liked my practical engineering background too. It provided a lens to understand how the physical world with its many manifestations, acts and reacts. I liked using the fundamentals of Physics, Chemistry, Mechanics and Applied Mathematics to solve practical problems.

Soon after, in a letter dated February 22, Dr. Stanley O. Iken-berry, President of the University of Illinois sent me a letter in which he and Chancellor Dr. Thomas E. Everhart welcomed me to the university. Although this was standard practice for incoming professors, I felt good about joining this professional, collegial setting. I soon got adjusted to the new academic environment and was very well treated.

While I had been adapting to my new teaching job, I also had to address the needs of my family. On the social front, we met some local Bangladeshis one of whom was Dr. Azizul Islam, a researcher in agronomy and his wife, Hosne Ara Islam. My brother Dr. Mir Masoom Ali in Muncie, IN knew Dr. Islam and gave me his telephone number. When I called him, he immediately invited us to his home for lunch next day. I thought that was such a great gesture. He had a daughter Rebecca and a son Rizvi, both adults. He also invited Dr. Salim Rashid, an Economics professor, and his wife Zeenet Rashid whom we met for the first time in his home. The Rashids had three little sons Shahid, Sabir, and Imran. The Rashids invited us to their home next. Later, Monzur, a graduate student, and Ranga also invited us to their apartment. We were very happy to meet them. We met a few married graduate students of which Monzurul Hoque and his wife Ranga Monzur became close friends with us. Also, Shamsul Huda and his wife Julie invited us for dinner then.

We didn't know anybody there when we arrived and were wondering if we would have friends of our ethnic background. But with such welcoming invitations, we felt good knowing we had warm, friendly and hospitable people around to socialize with, from our own and other ethnicities. Soon after we moved to the twin cities, the Rashids had a baby daughter. They named her Suraiya. Another graduate student Ashfaq Hossain, joined UIUC and arrived in Urbana-Champaign. While there, he married Izzat, an engineer from Bangladesh. The couple became good friends with us.

We stayed at Orchard Downs for a month and then moved to the Champaign side of the twin cities. I heard the school district of Champaign was good, so we decided to move there, and get the three children admitted to schools. They easily adjusted to yet another new setting and soon engaged in their education, outdoor life and friendships. We had some adjustments to make as well.

Our first cultural shock came when our two daughters wanted to go to their school Prom. We had never heard of this before. After we learned more about it, we were hesitant, wondering if we should allow them to experience this. When I felt that they really wanted to go along with all of their classmates, I realized we had to relent, adjust to a new social reality and give our children some slack. Since we chose to stay in the U.S., we should not be too strict with them but instead help them assimilate to a different and new cultural environment. Adaptability and integration are important in this melting pot setting, and we felt these could be embraced while adhering to our own values.

Immigrants from other countries frequently face this dilemma as their kids grow up in an environment foreign to their parents. It was true before and is true now. Children get confused if they hear one thing at home about cultural values and another message outside their home. Navigating a conflict of native values and managing assimilation is hard on both parents and children.

On the 14th day of February 1986, I got the sad news of losing my dear mother. I already knew that her health was failing. Something inexplicable happened that day. On my way to McKinley Church in Champaign for Friday congregational prayer, as no mosque existed there at the time, I was feeling very miserable for no reason. I didn't teach on Fridays, so I returned home after the prayer. The whole day was depressing for me. After the afternoon prayer, I felt as if I had no energy and just sat on the prayer rug. Evening set in while I was still sitting on the prayer rug. I had just completed my evening prayer when I got a call from my elder brother in London, Ontario. He gave me news of my ailing mother's death. It was hard on me. I felt bad that I could not be at her bedside when she passed away. I comforted myself thinking at least I had spent time with her in 1984. With the demise of both my parents I felt that a great emptiness surrounded me. The next few days were difficult.

In late October 1986 I attended a conference on prestressed concrete at Purdue University, West Lafayette, Indiana, where my brother Mosaddeq was still a student. I went alone as Dora stayed home with the kids in Champaign. As all expenses were covered by the sponsors of the conference, I decided to sleep at a hotel overnight in the outskirts of the city, while spending most of my free time in the evening with my brother and his family. It was Halloween Day. In the evening, as usual I had dinner at my brother's apartment. Then later we watched a horror film appropriate for Halloween. Shortly before midnight, I hit the road to go to my hotel. West Lafayette is a small university town and roads were eerie at that time of night. It was also raining lightly. While driving, I noticed I missed the approaching street of the hotel. It was on the other side separated by a wide strip of grass from my side, and I needed to make a U-turn somewhere. I found a traffic light ahead and decided to turn. The light was red so instead of waiting, I quickly decided to take a right turn on the cross-street and turn back to take a left turn on the green light from that street.

Once I took this right turn, I noticed it was a narrow gravel road with mud on the left side and a very short, about 3 to 4 feet or (a meter) high wall on the right. Upon closer look, I saw a few tombstones and realized it was a cemetery. There was pin-drop silence, with not a single soul around. I got scared having just seen a horror movie at my brother's place, in which zombies were crawling out of their graves in a cemetery. I could feel my heart beating faster. I looked at my watch; it was 12 midnight. I saw a small home, probably a farmer's, with outside lights on, at a distance ahead of me but decided not to go there at this odd hour. I quickly made up my mind to do a three-point turn, very slowly, so I didn't accidentally hit the cemetery wall or get my car stuck in the mud on the other side. If I hit the cemetery wall and damaged it, that would be a bad omen. On the other hand, if I got stuck in the mud, I would be in a predicament with no help available.

There was no mobile phone in those days. Instead of getting panicked, I maintained my calm and gave full concentration to driving while at the same time praying to God to get me out of there. I was reciting verses from the Qur'an for courage and confidence. I succeeded in making a 180-degree turn and approached the traffic light. It was red and illegal to turn left, but with my heart pounding, I turned anyway as fast as I could. If an officer came to give me a ticket, I actually would not mind; at least I would have the company of a living human being after my encounter with a cemetery past midnight. I got to the hotel and went to sleep after I thanked God for protecting me from any potential hazard.

At UIUC, I devoted myself to teaching and research. I started writing papers knowing that in my chosen profession I had to play the game right. I was assigned to a research committee, which at some point I chaired, and then to the library committee. Of course, I enjoyed what I was doing. In 1986, I got a consultancy project with the U.S. Army Corps of Engineers working on development of an evaluation procedure for emerging technologies. I focused on my work. Dealing with family issues was a distraction for me, and I couldn't spend quality time with them. My two daughters were doing well at school, so I didn't need to worry about them. Murad was still young. In hindsight, I should have spent more time with them as those times never returned.

Professionally, my hard work paid off. I was considered for tenure in 1987. Director Forrester reviewed my tenure documents and told me that he was impressed by the number of publications I had in such a short time. The tenure process went smoothly to completion. I felt secure in the permanency of my job and after having made so many moves, so I decided to settle there.

I liked my colleagues in the Structures Division. They were Professors Albert Bianchini, Bill Erwin, Lloyd Leffers, Jim Simon, Ingvar Schousboe, and David Wickersheimer. They were all experienced people and very friendly and welcoming to me. In addition, there was another junior faculty member Lou Surr, in structures, sent from our school to teach in Versailles, France, where we had a Study Abroad program. I developed good relationships with my colleagues, and it seemed they also liked me. After joining the School in 1985, Professor David Wickersheimer invited me to do consulting work at his structural engineering firm, Wickersheimer Engineers in Champaign. It was a good way for me to stay engaged in professional practice and to make some extra money. I would spend a few hours a day working at the firm. The School encouraged such professional activities, so I could bring my real-world experience into the classroom.

In September 1986, I went to Nanjing, China to present a paper and chair a session at an international conference at the Nanjing Institute of Technology. I was excited to go to this large communist country for the first time. In my childhood, I read a book called *China Golpo* (Chinese Stories) that had a few nice stories touching upon Chinese culture. I read about the history of China – a seat of ancient Chinese civilization, the Kingdoms and Dynasties, and the revered sages Lao Tzu, the founder of Taoism and Confucius, the greatest philosopher and teacher of China, and of course about Mao Tse Tung and his Cultural Revolution. In 1984 when I lived in Singapore, I came into close contact with Chinese culture through my interaction with students, colleagues, professionals and the public at large.

First, I flew to Beijing. I was received at the airport by a Chinese gentleman who told me that he was my host and drove me to a dormitory where many other participants were staying. He told me to rest and he would come back to take me out touring the next morning to show me some important places around the city. He also asked me I wanted to see any specific sites. Without a second thought, I mentioned the Great Wall. He was initially hesitant as that site was about 50 miles (80 kilometers) away from Beijing. Then he said "I know you would not leave Beijing without seeing the wall. I will take you there." My visit to the Great Wall was a special experience for me. I had been reading about it as one of the seven wonders of the world since my childhood. This wall was seen by the astronauts from space.

Perhaps the most recognizable symbol of China and its long and glowing history, the Great Wall of China measures 13,247-mile (21,196-km) long. It consists of numerous walls and fortifications, built and rebuilt in different eras to protect the land from marauding invaders. I was able to see only a section of the wall, but it gave me the idea of its nature and size. I saw the construction was solid, and the structure was very stable. I was trying to figure out how the builders were able to design and construct such a mammoth structure in ancient times, without the benefit of sophisticated architectural concepts, complex engineering calculations and the intricate means and methods of construction that we have at our disposal today. I walked along the wall for some distance to get a feel for it. Upon my return to Beijing, my guide took me to a few interesting sites in the city including the Forbidden City.

From Beijing, I flew to Nanjing (previously Nanking), my destination for the conference. I stayed in a luxurious hotel there with many other delegates. The main organizer of the conference, Professor Ding Dajun, a Structural Engineering professor, was a great host who received us and gifted us art pieces that he made himself. I later hung this on my office wall in Champaign. We were given an outdoor reception close to the campus next to a 200-year old tree. We enjoyed the nightly entertainment in the hotel by musicians and dancers. I became friends with three professors from Yugoslavia, Portugal, and Hawaii. One night following a banquet, we witnessed a delightful acrobatic show in an arena. The Chinese are known for their acrobatics and I certainly could see why and agree.

At night, we went out to experience the city, randomly walked through the streets. There was not much to see. We saw some statues of war heroes of World War II. We were taken to Shanghai from Nanjing for a visit. The city of Shanghai, located at the mouth of the Yangtze River, is a port city. It enjoys proximity to the Pacific Ocean via the East China Sea. It is a truly cosmopolitan city. People of different cultures and religions that later helped shape the city's international and multi-cultural orientation. It was once known as a city of crime but had since evolved under communist rule. When I visited, the city was not yet developed into the modern skyscraper city of today. Today, there are many sky huggers in the Pudong district, which I have written a book about, called *The Future of the Cities,* which I will discuss later.

I also went on a group bus tour arranged by the conference organizers to a few historic sites that flash into my memory even now. I can't recall all the details as I didn't keep any journal of any of my trips. What I remember is that I visited some eye-catching and attention-grabbing places including imperial palaces and large temples with large idols of Buddha and some of his disciples. At one point, we crossed a bridge over the Hwang Ho River. It was dusk and the large beautiful orange-to-red setting sun, sinking into the river at a distance, left a permanent stamp on my mind.

In large cities, particularly in Beijing, we saw scores of bikers traveling to their destinations. There was hardly any building taller than 10 stories, mostly hotels. I noted a disciplined society. I also sensed the emphasis on education at the university, particularly the advanced level of mathematics that the students were learning. I also noticed the devotion of Chinese students was the same as that of students in Singapore in 1984. Seeing the discipline, commitment and aspirations of the public, I commented to some of my Western colleagues at the conference that China was soon to become a very advanced country. All agreed. My observations and prediction proved accurate, as we can see today.

About a year later in1987, I took a memorable trip to Reno, Nevada, a gambling and casino city. I went there to present a paper on architectural engineering education in June. The conference was organized by the American Association for Engineering Education (AAEE). There I met up with Mr. Aminul Karim, an electrical engineer, and educator, whom I knew from my Chicago days in the early 1980s, but not very intimately. We quickly drew close to each other. He is a very bright, friendly, and likeable person. We spent time together during the conference sessions. At the hotel, which was huge, I was surprised at the abundant quantity and variety of food available at an incredibly low cost. I soon found out that the hotels did this to keep guests inside, so they would spend time indoors and gamble at the slot machines. One evening, we attended an amazing dinner show.

Another day, we watched a circus at night which was also spectacular. Meanwhile, I was invited to the house of a friend's sister, whose husband Dr. Abul Khair was a professor at the University of Nevada, Reno. I enjoyed my dinner with the gracious couple. At one point, Aminul Karim and I decided to visit the famous Lake Tahoe and Virginia City. We rented a car, drove from Reno to Lake Tahoe. It was a rough ride. I remember at one point along the highway, at a great height, I saw a cautionary roadside sign posted next to a sheer vertical cliff. I looked down and felt somewhat dizzy but maintained my calm and composure while driving. Finally, we reached Lake Tahoe.

Lake Tahoe is a large freshwater lake in the U.S. Lying at 6,225-ft. (1,900-m) high, it overlaps the state line between California and Nevada, west of Carson City, the capital of Nevada. Lake Tahoe is just behind the five Great Lakes as the largest by volume in the U.S. Its depth is an incredible 1,645 feet (500 meters) making it the second deepest in the U.S. When we visited one segment of the lake and noted the large mass of water looked dark. Some people swam at a shallow spot with a few boulders. Numbers of hotels were visible along the bank of the lake. We drove around the lake for some time to get a sense of the place and returned. We also visited Virginia City, a city that retains an authentic historic character with boardwalks, and numerous restored buildings dating to the 1860s and 1870s. Virginia City is home to many attractive and informative museums. Known as "The Last One Standing", the Fourth Ward School Museum brings Comstock history to life in interactive displays, and a restored 1876 classroom. The four-story wooden school is the last one of this type left in the U.S. We visited the museum and surroundings and walked along the boardwalks downtown. The city became a boomtown in 1859 after silver deposits were discovered in the area, the first in the U.S. The famous and popular cowboy western TV series, *Bonanza*, was based on the story of the rich Cartwright family living in this area around 1860. The show ran on NBC and was the second longest running series in U.S. network television from 1959 to 1973. When I lived in Canada, I watched this show regularly.

At the university, one day in in late 1987, I met Professor Albert Bianchini in the front hallway of the Architecture Building. He complimented me on an article I had written on Gustave Eiffel, the designer and builder of Eiffel Tower in Paris. It was published in the Discussions section of the *ASCE Journal of Structural Engineering* in response to a paper published in its September 1987 issue. He suggested that I should seek a promotion, to the rank of full professor. I reminded him that I had just started at the School in 1985, just got tenured earlier part of 1987, and asked him whether this was too early for me. He told me in reply that there was no time frame to be promoted to full professor; it all depended on one's accomplishments. He thought I was ready for this and encouraged me to proceed. He also told me that timing was important and since I was very active in my research and publications, this could be a good time to try. As he was a very senior, full professor, I took his advice to heart and thought it was worth a try. A full professor had to nominate me for the promotion. I realized he would gladly nominate me, but I decided to ask David Wickersheimer, since I worked as a consultant to his firm and he knew me and my work best. To my surprise, he readily agreed to do so.

Then I talked to James Simon as he was the chairman of the Structures Division. He resisted initially and told me there were many senior professors in the School who still held the rank of associate professors and might resent my early promotion. I told him that both Albert and David, who were full professors, felt

I was ready for it, and seniority didn't matter since the promotion criteria for full professor were based on accomplishments, not seniority. He quickly agreed and graciously told me that he would support my case. The School asked me to prepare promotion documents per the university regulations. My promotion papers were reviewed and deliberated by the School's promotion committee and then College promotion committee, and finally the Campus promotion committee. I felt my promotion process seemed to go smoothly without any hurdles as I didn't hear anything in the negative, nor was I approached by anyone for further clarification or additional information. But the outcome was slow to emerge, and I remained in suspense.

In 1988, something positive happened to me, quite by accident, that had a lasting impact on my career. I was planning to participate and present a paper at a conference in Jakarta, Indonesia. At the last minute, I got a telegraph from the conference organizing committee that this conference was canceled. I had already bought the plane ticket and prepared to leave. I prepared my presentation material and spent time writing the paper for the conference proceedings. I felt somewhat dejected at this turn of events. Furthermore, although I had been in Singapore and Malaysia before, I was hoping to see a larger country in the region, as I enjoyed traveling and experiencing different cultures, I was looking forward to that opportunity.

The cancellation, however, opened my schedule for another opportunity. I got a call from Mr. Aminul Karim, President of the Bangladesh Association of Chicago, asking me if I could attend a meeting with Dr. Lynn S. Beedle as the chief guest. Dr. Beedle was a prominent internationally known structural engineer, professor emeritus and University Distinguished Professor at Lehigh University, who founded the Council on Tall Buildings and Urban Habitat (CTBUH. Dr. Beedle appealed to the Bangladeshi community in Chicago to help fund a Chair at Lehigh University in honor of the late Dr. Fazlur Rahman Khan. I decided to go for this noble cause and to meet Dr. Beedle in person. At the meeting, Mr. Karim, an accomplished and fine gentleman, gave me the honor of introducing Dr. Beedle before his speech. This interaction led to a long and lasting relationship and friendship with Dr. Beedle. I remain grateful to Mr. Karim for extending the opportunity that led to a new important dimension in my career.

In December 1988, I visited Bangladesh with my family, we stayed on past the new year. This was our third visit since leaving in 1970. I felt the absence of both my parents on this trip. In Dhaka, I visited my mother's grave in the Banani Cemetery and prayed for her departed soul. I visited many relatives and some old friends in Dhaka. In January 1989, I met Mr. Abul Faraz Khan, Superintending Engineer of Public Works Department (PWD) of the Government of Bangladesh in Dhaka. He wanted to see me after hearing about me from Mr. Nazrul Islam, a diploma engineer and an employee of PWD. I had never met Mr. Islam but apparently, he had come to know of my achievements from certain sources. My meeting with Mr. Khan was very cordial and we discussed a few engineering issues. He arranged a trip to Comilla where I gave a seminar on earthquake-resistant design to a group of engineers. In Dhaka, I visited BUET and met Dr. Jamilur Reza Choudhury, head of the Civil Engineering department and Dr. Mosharraf Hossain, the Vice Chancellor of BUET. I gave a seminar at BUET on structural systems for tall building at the invitation of Dr. Choudhury.

In February, soon after our return to Champaign in January 1989, I got a call from Professor Ingvar Schousboe, who was the acting director of our School at the time, congratulating me on my promotion to full professor. I was delighted. I also felt gratified that the university recognized my accomplishments by promoting me in an unusually short time. Rather than feel complacent after this, I felt invigorated at the thought of having many years left in my career and much to accomplish.

In the summer of 1989, I visited Bangladesh once again as a Fellow of the United Nations program TOKTEN (Transfer of Knowledge and Technology by Expatriate Nationals). I gave a series of seminars in Bangladesh, on several engineering topics and held workshops. I will discuss this TOKTEN mission in a later chapter. During the visit, my sister Afroza Anwar living is Dhaka, who was very devout in her faith, gifted me a book on the biography of the Muslim Sufi saint Abdul Qadir Jilani. She used to give me religious books during my visits to Dhaka. Upon my return to Champaign, I found time to read it, as I had known this highly revered, saintly figure's name since my childhood.

He was born in Neef, a village in the Jilan province, Iran. At the age of 18, he wanted to go to Baghdad, a prodigious seat of spiritual learning in those days, to be a student under renowned teachers. But he was concerned about leaving his elderly, widowed mother alone. He asked his mother's permission to go to Baghdad and expressed his concern about who would take care of her in his absence. She gave him permission as she wanted her son to be a man of knowledge and learning and told him not to worry about her as God would take care of her. I wondered that even a saintly man like Abdul Qadir Jilani had left his mother alone in his search for learning. When I visited my parents in 1978, I received my father's blessing to continue my living in Canada. But I could identify with the anxieties of Abdul Qadir Jilani, a young man with a passion for learning. I could have had a good job in Dhaka and was often torn by the pressures of life, compelling me to leave my parents behind in their old age. After I read the life story of Abdul Qadir Jilani I felt reassured and relieved that perhaps I had done the right thing after all, to leave Dhaka in 1970.

The next couple of years I was busy with my academic work and consultancy. In 1989, severe flooding took place in Dhaka and its surroundings. After seeing the images, I was moved; so, I talked with some of my friends in Champaign and Chicago, and we formed an organization called Bangladesh Environmental and Flood Committee in America (BEFCA) to work from abroad to alleviate this problem in whatever way we could do. I remained engaged in setting up, coordinating and conducting meetings and developing plans of action in consultation with my friends. I will tell this story in a later chapter in detail. During this time, I bought a newly built home in Savoy, a suburb of Champaign after renting a townhome for a year and then a house. We moved to the newly built home in November 1989. My children were happy to be in a house with more space. Our two girls stayed with us there for less than three years.

We were very happy in the small university town environment. In addition to our friendship with Dr. Salim Rashid and Zeenet Rashid, and Dr. Azizul Islam and Hosne Ara Islam, whom I mentioned before, we developed friendship in Champaign with Dr. Motiur Rahman, a chemist working in the food industry and Aparna Rahman. I found a teacher of mine from EPUET in Dhaka, Dr. Nani Gopal Bhowmik, who was working at the Illinois Water Survey Department, which was affiliated with UIUC. We developed friendship with him and his wife Krishna Bhowmik. We also became friends with Dr. Mushfequr Rahman, a senior Mathematics professor and Bilkis Rahman, Dr. Belayet Khan, a Geography professor and Moushumi Khan, Dr. Abu Wahid Chowdhury, an Economics professor and Bithi Chowdhury, Dr. Asit Basu, M.D., a practicing medical doctor and Manju Basu, all of whom lived in Charleston, Illinois a small city about 60 miles (96 kilometers) south of Champaign, where Eastern Illinois University is located. We had another couple living in Mattoon near Charleston, Mr. Golam Mustafa working in the culinary business and his wife Dr. Iffat Ali, a Chemistry professor at Lakeland College.

We also became friends with Dr. Baker Siddiqi and Nazma Siddiqi, and Dr. M. Shahidullah and Daisy Shahidullah living in Springfield, the capital of Illinois located about 90 miles (144 kilometers) west of Champaign. Dr. Siddiqi was a professor of Economics at the then Sangamon State University, which in 1995, became the University of Illinois at Springfield. Dr. Shahidullah was a statistician and worked for the government. At Effingham, a small town also about 90 miles (144 kilometers) south of Champaign, we had friendship with Dr. Ekramul Kabir, M.D., a radiologist and Gulshan Kabir. Also, Mr. Musharef Husain, a businessman, whom I knew from my Bangladesh days in the 1960s, was another friend who lived in Rantoul, a town near Champaign and owned a motel there. Since we were living in a university town, we had developed friendships with many families of graduate students, such as Shawkat Ali, Faridul Islam, Abdur Rauf, Rezaur Rahman, Nazmul Hasan, Shahid Rashid, and several others too numerous to mention.

Later, several professionals also moved in and the size of the Bangladeshi community grew steadily. We would have frequent social visits and dinners at different homes and would invite others to dinner parties at our own home. Since Dora enjoyed cooking and we enjoyed the company, this was a frequent occurrence. We would also include undergraduate and single graduate students in our dinner parties. We organized annual picnics and occasionally, we would go to Chicago for shopping and social visits. In addition, we had friends from communities other than Bengalis. I once invited my colleagues for dinner at our home. I always believed in integration with the other communities. My colleague David Wickersheimer and I became close friends. His wife Hanna had a very warm personality. Once when Dora was in Bangladesh, knowing that I was alone, they invited me for dinner. Among others, I became a close friend of another colleague Kathy Anthony. I would frequently go to lunch with each of David and Kathy. Overall life was hectic and enjoyable on the social front.

On another front we used to hold cultural events at the Orchard Downs Community Center. I used to sing songs as a participant. We would have rehearsals at different homes including ours. Manju Basu would enjoy music and could sing and occasionally I would sing at her home at dinner parties. Gulshan Kabir, wife of Dr. Ekramul Kabir was another patron of music and could also sing well. They visited us a few times at our home for rehearsal for cultural functions. There were some students and mostly their wives who could sing as well. Early during my stay in Urbana-Champaign I organized a cultural program at the Urbana Civic Center. It was intended to jointly celebrate the birthdays of the Bengali poets Rabindranath Tagore and Kazi Nazrul Islam. I invited the local West Bengalis to join the Bangladeshi community. They responded to it and we held the cultural function together.

A remarkable experience of mine was my participation in the Tagore festival which would be held every year in the Channing Murray Foundation Chapel in Urbana. The Festival observed was in honor of Rabindranath Tagore. He was a poet, dramatist, musician, philosopher, thinker, and humanist, who became the first person of Eastern heritage to earn the Nobel Prize for Literature in 1913 for his body of literary work, most notably for his book *Gitanjali,* a collection of poems and lyrics of songs. The festival commemorates the Nobel Laureate's visit to the UIUC campus in 1912 when he delivered a series of lectures at the Channing Murray Chapel. Tagore's genius had been celebrated here over the years with a banquet and presentations of music, art, literature and his overall philosophy, which naturally attracted me. I started attending it in the early 1990s. Dr. Nani Bhowmik lead the organization of the festival with the help of West Bengalis. No one from the Bangladeshi community would, to the best of my knowledge, participate in it. I was at one point invited to sing there and take an active role in it. So, I brought along some of our Bangladeshi singers.

I met a Bangladeshi musician by the name Shahab Latif, who was involved in the festival's musical events. He used to show Bengali movies from time to time in his building's basement on Goodwin Avenue. Before the movie started one day, he was making tea for the few viewers. He offered me tea and began a conversation. I liked him and saw that he was a gentleman and a very private person. Because of his involvement in the Tagore festival, run by West Bengalis all his friends were from West Bengal. I noticed no one was from Bangladesh, so he was elated to meet me, and a deep friendship ensued. One day in my office he opened up about his past and shared what he was going through. I empathized with him. I sensed he liked me and considered me a friend.

Mr. Latif, a dedicated instrumental artist and a lover of music, requested that I orchestrate efforts with the Bangladeshi community to participate in the forthcoming Tagore festival. We prepared and hosted a sumptuous dinner for the festival with rich Bangladeshi cuisine and a major musical performance. I invited him to my house for the rehearsal dinner before the forthcoming festival. Dora took the lead in cooking and organizing the dinner along with some Bangladeshi women from the community.

It was a stellar event in which the Indian Ambassador to the U.S., who was from West Bengal, was the keynote speaker. Dora recited a poem at this event. She did this very well as she won prizes in her high school and college days. The Bangladeshis including the Rashids and the Islams also participated in the festival. I continued to attend these festival events and sing from time to time, although in later days I could not keep up with it due to my other commitments. It was more difficult to keep pace after the departure of Mr. Latif from Urbana-Champaign to Chicago. I had the pleasure of meeting him there for another music session a few years later. The last time I participated, after a lapse of a few years, was in 2010 when Sunil Ganguli, a Bengali novelist and writer, was the keynote speaker. I gave a speech on Dr. Mohammad Yunus and his Grameen Bank at the request of Dr. Anil Bera, an Economics professor at UIUC, who organized the festival that year, and also sang a Tagore song along with some other Bangladeshis.

I also got involved with the Central Illinois Mosque and Islamic Community (CIMIC). My involvement began in 1985, just after I moved to Urbana-Champaign, when the first phase of the mosque was being built. Mr. Waleed Jasim was leading the efforts. Because of my professional background I was introduced to him by Mr. Omar Zaka, a local resident so I could help with my technical knowledge. I found Mr. Jasim very energetic and active and liked his personality. He urged me to be on the CIMIC Board through election, which I did and continued for many years. I met several others from the Islamic community in leadership roles, particularly Mr. Mohammad Al-Heeti. I worked with these two gentlemen and many others too numerous to mention on several CIMIC projects dealing with new construction, remodeling, property management, new land purchase, and cemetery land purchase, until I left Urbana-Champaign when I retired.

In November 1990, I participated in the Fourth World Congress on tall buildings in Hong Kong, organized by CTBUH. Hong Kong was still a British territory and not part of China. My paper was on structural form and its integration with tall building architecture. My visit to Hong Kong was quite thrilling to me for a few reasons. First, it is a skyscraper city where some remarkable buildings were designed by renowned architects and engineered by prominent structural engineers. Second, it is an island city state like Singapore, and when I was in Singapore, I heard interesting stories about Hong Kong. The two cities had cultural similarities as they were populated by the Chinese people. Third, at the time it was still a British colony, this is before rule ended in 1997, when it was handed over to China. I wanted to see a British administered territory, something I had never witnessed. Hong Kong consists of Hong Kong Island, the Kowloon Peninsula, and the New Territories. British colonization and control of Hong Kong remained uninterrupted for 150 years, except for the short Japanese occupation during World War II. Hong Kong's architectural style, therefore, had been impacted by British and Western culture and influenced by both Eastern and Western cultures. It has often been referred to as a place where "the East meets the West."

When, after a long flight, the plane approached the Kai Tak Airport, also known as the Hong Kong International Airport (now defunct) around midnight, I didn't realize the difficulties I would face for being at the wrong place at the wrong time. It took some time going through immigration and customs. When I came out of the airport building, I was tired and sleepy. The place was totally desolate. Some hawkers were asking me to go to their hotels. I declined saying I had already a reservation. No taxi driver wanted to go to Hong Kong city which was some distance away from there at that time of night. I must admit I had no idea of the geography of the region then.

I got worried in this new and strange place. I could not trust the hawkers, as I would be at the mercy of these strangers, at this hour in this unknown place. Finally, a kind-hearted driver approached, seeing my tired and anxious look he told me he could just take me to the other side of the river where I might find taxi drivers willing to drive to the hotel where I had my reservation in downtown Hong Kong. He drove me to the other side of the river and parked at a taxi stand. On my behalf, he talked to some reluctant drivers and finally found a willing one. I thanked him profusely supplemented by a generous tip. He was a godsend for me. Good people are everywhere. It transcends nationality, race, and religion. To my great relief the new driver brought me to my hotel. I promised myself that I would never again go to a city, particularly in a foreign land, late at night. I was so tired that I slept like a baby that night.

The next day, I attended the Congress, which was my first since becoming an active participant in CTBUH activities. The Congress was attended by delegates from all around the world. I met Dr. S.K. Ghosh there. I also met Bungale S. Taranath, who wrote a couple of excellent books on the structural analysis and design of tall buildings. Dr. Ghosh was staying at the same hotel as me. He is an accomplished structural engineer in Chicago. I knew him from the University of Waterloo in Canada from where we received our Ph.D. degrees in the same general area of research. When I and my family first went to Chicago from Canada for a trip, we stayed at his residence with them.

We immediately bonded in this foreign land again and became constant companions at the Congress, the hotel and in the city. We toured the city together to visit some interesting sites that included a trip to Kowloon City, where one could go from Hong Kong by ferry or subway. We took the ferry there and subway for returning to Hong Kong, experiencing both modes of travel. We visited the Kowloon market and bought jewelry for our wives. The store was guarded by armed security staff at the entrance and was full of shiny stones, pearls and other kinds of dazzling jewelry. The place was historically known for its pearl, so we bought pearl necklaces. Dr. Ghosh later founded his own consulting firm S.K. Ghosh Associates in Chicago area.

Hong Kong had some notable, unique qualities. We toured the crowded mountainous city, where only about 3% of Hong Kong's total area is built up. The remaining areas occupied by forest, grassland, cropland, wetland and water bodies. Consequently, its topography influenced its vertical architecture. Most of the buildings were located along the less steep coastline, resulting in dense, tightly packed buildings. I observed that the entire population lived in an urban setting, and the built environment in Hong Kong was totally urban. There was limited land available for expansion. Thus, the city was at its maximum carrying capacity, driving the land costs to exorbitant levels. The only solution was to build higher for both residential and commercial occupancies. I enjoyed seeing the many famous tall buildings and realized why Hong Kong was a great skyscraper city, in the league of New York and Chicago.

We were invited to a banquet hosted by the British governor of Hong Kong. There was a dress code stipulated for attending the lavish dinner. One had to wear black shoes, black belt, and a black bow tie. I had black shoes and belt, but no bow tie. I had never worn a bow tie. By nature, I was never snobby, and I didn't feel like dressing in a fancy manner or in conformity with an exclusive dress code. Even if I did, I did it reluctantly to "be a Roman in Rome." Dr. Ghosh cared for it even less, didn't feel like buying anything for the banquet and passed on the invitation. Reluctantly, I bought a bow tie, since I wanted to experience this event, as a leader of CTBUH by then and the chairman of the Committee on Architecture. It was a festive event and I met some new people, particularly, Mr. Sabah Al-Rayes, chairman of Al-Rayes Group, from Kuwait, who was a leader of CTBUH and a wealthy Kuwaiti businessman, with whom I developed friendship. I still relish the experience of my trip to Hong Kong.

On January 4, 1991 we applied for naturalization to the U.S. Department of Justice. I was granted citizenship on January 14,

1992 after taking the oath of allegiance in a ceremony conducted by the United States District Court for the Northern District of Illinois at Chicago, IL. It was a memorable day for me, and I had deep emotion and inner conflict, figuratively severing my connection to Bangladesh, my native country, in favor of a new country. But I wanted to live here and felt comfortable with living in America. I could overcome any negative feelings about it. I felt that I was officially attached to this adopted country. Dora obtained her citizenship later, on June 26, 1992 by the United States District Court for the Central District of Illinois at Danville, Illinois.

Although I was a full professor, I was not happy with what I was being paid by the school, so I went into the job market looking for a higher salary. I had a mortgage loan to pay, I had two young daughters in their late teens and a son for whom I had major expenses to meet. I married at an early age and by the time I was fully settled in Champaign, the girls were already in their late teens. I felt bad that perhaps they weren't happy with what I could provide. I could not fully cater to the popular hobbies and attractions that teenagers usually have at that age. I also felt financially stressed and got worried about financial security. To make matters worse, at that time there was no work in consultancy because of a slump in building construction in the area. Dora took a job at a nursery for a short time but didn't like it and quit. I mentioned my financial needs once in 1989 to Director Forrester. He did augment my salary but not to my full satisfaction. I decided to go back into the job market.

In early 1992 I applied for the position of the Head of the Department of the Department of Architectural Engineering with the California Polytechnic University (Cal Poly) at San Luis Obispo, California. The reputed architectural engineering program there has a long history. I was interviewed twice, first by the Search Committee and then by the Dean of the College of

Architecture and Environmental Design, Professor Paul Neil. San Luis Obispo is located very close to the Pacific Ocean in a very scenic landscape. The Dean drove me southward towards Santa Barbara along Highway 101 and took me to lunch at a restaurant at a resort next to the ocean. He treated me to a salmon lunch. We had a good conversation there about the university, the place, and the architectural engineering department. We exchanged ideas and stories. I liked his personality and I felt he also liked me. The picturesque landscape all around impressed me.

Meanwhile, my two daughters were very close to the completion of their undergraduate degrees at UIUC. Ifat started her undergraduate studies with architecture but didn't like the long and irregular hours of studio work, occasionally working overnight to meet project deadlines, and so she switched to geography. Because of the switch, she and Jinat, who enrolled in urban planning, graduated in the same year in 1992. They wanted to go to a different university for graduate school. They enrolled at universities in Chicago. Eventually Ifat graduated in Urban Planning and Policy Studies from the University of Illinois at Chicago and Jinat graduated from Northwestern University's Medill School of Journalism, in Broadcast Journalism. Jinat first completed a degree from Columbia College in Chicago, achieving a second bachelor's degree in Broadcast Journalism. After preparing well, she later applied and enrolled in the highly reputed, Medill School of Journalism in Evanston, a north suburb of Chicago. In the summer of 1992, I rented an apartment for them on Sheridan Road near Lake Michigan in Chicago and helped them move there. I arranged for them to move early on, so they had enough time to adjust to the new large-city environment. My friends Faridul Islam and Monzurul Hoque helped me with the move.

We realized once the girls left home, our house would be quiet, and they would not live with us again as they had before.

Also, two of our three kids were leaving at the same time. It was hard on us. The night before we moved them, Dora and I slept together with them on the floor. I couldn't sleep well and was reflecting on how quickly they had grown up into two beautiful women, from two little girls and their time to take off from home had arrived. I wished I could spend more happy times with them showering more fatherly love on them, as now I could never go back in time to do that again. After we came back from Chicago our house looked and felt empty as the two girls would keep us busy and the house lively. We felt depressed but soon realized that this was how it was meant to be. We consoled ourselves for the time being, with the thought that at least Murad was still at home in high school but even he wouldn't be with us for long. Dora and I visited our daughters a few times, so they could feel comfortable in their new place and environment.

Soon after my daughters moved to Chicago, I got an offer letter, dated September 16, 1992 from Dean Neil of CalPoly. I was offered the job of department head with a generous salary, almost twice my salary then, to my satisfaction. It was quite exciting, particularly being the head of a department with a long history, in a scenic setting, with beautiful weather. I had a major career and life decision to make. I noticed Dora was not very happy thinking about another move after having made so many, including to Singapore. We had many relatives and friends in the Midwest and moving so far would isolate us from them. We would be far from our daughters in Chicago. Our son, still in high school, would lose his friends. Although the salary was great, the cost of living was high in California, particularly home prices. I decided to talk with Director Forrester. I met him and showed the offer letter.

After congratulating me he said, "Great! This is usually a political appointment, but you got it. We don't want to lose you though. Let me know what you would like to do. If you decide to stay, I will see if we can match the offer." After a lot of considerations, I was leaning towards declining the job offer from Cal Poly. I called Dean Neil and after thanking him told him some of the issues I was facing. He suggested that I could go there on a leave of absence for a year or two and see how it went.

I went back to Director Forrester and asked to what extent he could match the offer. I decided if the match was not satisfactory, I would most likely go to San Luis Obispo. I knew after all, no matter what, Dora would accept my decision, as she had been always supportive of me throughout our life's journey together. After Director Forrester consulted with higher authorities, he came back to me with a figure much lower than the amount in the offer. But considering I had a nine-month appointment at UIUC, and the cost of living was much less, I accepted his offer. After I told Dean Neil about my decision, he seemed a bit upset but said that he respected my decision. However, shortly after this I got a call from the Chairman of the search committee who said "You rejected us! We were hoping you would come, we all liked you so much. Will you reconsider?" Despite my mixed feelings, at the end I decided to stick with my decision.

The year 1992 is a memorable year for me although not for happy reasons. After coming to U.S., we started celebrating Thanksgiving Day. An American harvest festival of sorts, families gather to feast on roast turkey and stuffing, mashed potatoes and gravy, cranberry sauce and pumpkin pie. As the story goes in November 1621, the Native Americans and the newly arriving Pilgrims from Europe joined together to celebrate. The Europeans commemorated the celebration every year thereafter, calling it Thanksgiving Day. It falls on the last Thursday of November. In Canada, it is celebrated in October, as the harvest and winter, arrive earlier than in the U.S. In 1992, it fell on November 28.

Dora and I had planned to celebrate it on that day as usual and wanted to have our daughters living in Chicago with us. My sister Shahid Ara and her husband Dr. Saleh from Ottawa, Canada were also scheduled to join us on this occasion at Urbana-Champaign. In the late morning on Wednesday I started driving and hit Highway 57 North toward Chicago two and a half hours away. The route is mostly rural, through the middle of corn and soybean fields dotted by villages, small towns and a small city called Kankakee. While I was near Rantoul, which is about 20 miles (32 kilometers) from Urbana-Champaign, I felt a discomfort in my chest. I felt as if some rays of mild pain were radiating from the center of my chest. I never had such feeling or experience before. I had a dinner invitation the previous night at a party thrown by a friend. I thought this could be heartburn from indigestion, although I never remembered having heartburn before.

I stopped at a gas station in Kankakee, to rest a bit and freshen up, splashing water on my face. But it was of no help. I thought I should perhaps go to the local hospital and see a doctor. But then I thought of Dora, alone at home with Murad, waiting to see me back with my daughters, who were also waiting for me in Chicago. All our plans would be ruined. I had no idea what was going on. It was snowing lightly, and Chicago was only a little over one hour away. So, I decided to hit the road again. The highway was somewhat crowded with cars and trucks that evening because of the holiday traffic. I thought I could push through the pain and discomfort and make it to my daughters' apartment.

Once I entered the apartment, Jinat was not there. Ifat told me that I looked pale. I thought I might have been going through a heart attack, so I asked for an aspirin, but she didn't have it and I was not surprised as the girls were too young to need medicine like that or keep it at home. Sitting on a sofa, I was waiting for Jinat. Soon she arrived. We were ready to leave. They took some light luggage with them. I took a handbag in my left hand and as we stepped out of the apartment, I felt I had no strength in my hand and the bag fell on the floor. I was feeling some dizziness and more discomfort in my chest. I managed to get to the car, parked under the front porch of the building.

To her surprise, I asked Ifat to drive the car. I never ever gave my car key to anybody except Dora, when I was in my car. I asked Jinat to sit in the front passenger seat next to Ifat and decided to lie down in the back seat as I felt weak. Soon I started sweating even though the inside of the car was still cold. I took off my shoes and then my shirt. I still felt uncomfortable. Soon after, I felt a stronger pain in my chest that was spreading to my left shoulder and jaw. I concluded something serious was going on. My daughters were discussing my condition in the front although I couldn't concentrate on what they were saying. My daughters could not clearly see what was happening with me in the back. I asked Ifat to take me to the nearest hospital immediately.

Fortunately, there were two major hospitals nearby close to the Dan Ryan Expressway: Rush Presbyterian Hospital and Cook County Hospital. The former one was better known for heart disease treatment. Ifat drove me there to the Emergency Room, where she temporarily parked on the ramp and both my daughters walked me to the receptionist counter. I was barely managing to hold myself up. After I told her about the chest pain, shoulder and jaw, the receptionist at the front desk asked me, "How severe is your pain on a scale of 1 to 10?" I replied, "9."

She was going to ask me another question, but I felt like fainting and told her I needed to lie down. She immediately called for help on her pager. Then I fell unconscious.

When I regained consciousness, I found myself on a hospital bed in an open area with people and powerful lights around me. They were all medical professionals. On my left was a physician who said, "I am Dr. Chablani, a cardiologist here. Dr. Ali, you had a heart attack." He went on to explain that his friend's son was also a mutual friend of my daughter Jinni. My daughter contacted him. Dr. Chablani was in the hospital at the time but preparing to leave when he got the call. He told me not to worry, "…we will take good care of you. I heard you are a professor living in Champaign and you came here just today. You could have lost consciousness in a rural area on your way to Chicago. Clearly, God was with you. I have already called your wife." From his soothing words, I felt he was a good man and a compassionate doctor.

I felt solace but must have been in shock and my judgment was certainly clouded, as I foolishly asked him "Will I be able to go back to Champaign tonight or tomorrow and get treated there?"

He replied "No, we have to keep you here for some time until you are out of danger."

I was hooked up to machines and equipment and a male nurse on my right side told me that they gave me a clot-buster and I would soon be taken to the Intensive Care Unit (ICU). I recall another female nurse was standing next to him. I remember being wheeled to the ICU.

The news of my heart attack spread like wildfire. Dora was planning to come that night but could not because of bad weather and hazardous roads. I don't recall what was happening that night except faded glimpses of nurses frequently coming in and checking my vitals and the equipment surrounding me. The following day, that is, Friday, Dora and Murad came. Dr. Salim Rashid, Dr. Azizul Islam and Mrs. Islam accompanied Dora from Champaign with Dr. Rashid driving. My brothers Dr. Mir Maswood Ali and his family from London, Ontario, Dr. Mir Masoom Ali and his wife of Muncie, Indiana, along with Dr. Mir Mosaddeq Ali and his wife and son from Cincinnati, Ohio came to see me. Also, my sister Shahid Ara and her husband Dr. Saleh visited me. A few of my Chicago friends came to visit me that day and the next day.

Because of the holiday, nothing was being done other than monitoring my condition. I was feeling very miserable all day because of the turn of events and my predicament. I was still in the ICU. At night, the hospital was desolate, with only a few nurses attending the patients in the ICU. Of course, the ICU was isolated from other segments of the hospital. I recalled that my older brother Dr. Mir Masoom Ali had undergone angioplasty, an invasive cardiac procedure, before my heart attack. Alerted to this health risk, I saw my primary care doctor at Carle Clinic in Champaign and requested a stress test. He declined my request and said I was still too young, I looked great, and I had no major marker for heart disease. Two months later, this unthinkable thing happened.

On that Friday, several tests were performed. Some of these were for research purposes, for which I gave my consent. Since I was lying in bed all day, at night I felt restless, unable to get any sleep. I didn't know what was going on, my treatment was going very slowly because of the holiday. I was thinking about how this had happened. I began to delve into my past, present and future. I questioned myself: Did I do something wrong with my body or morally? Am I going to survive? Did I work too hard and push myself beyond what my body could take? My body felt like an ominous stranger to me. It had turned against me at the young age of 48, unbelievable as I was not even 50 yet. I felt betrayed. Even if I survived, I would still have this indelible episode with me, and I would always feel that I carried a repaired heart – not my original healthy heart. How could I trust it again? It had tried to kill me once already. I faced my own mortality. Death could be waiting around the corner for me. It would mercilessly get everybody, following its own schedule, not giving anyone a pass. When it found someone, it would snatch away the soul whether the victim was rich or poor, courageous or coward, uncivil or decent. I thought how it would be to be put into a casket and buried underground. I thought of Dora and my three children: what would happen to them if I had died. I felt scared but realized that I was not indispensable, and life would continue for them even if I left this world for good, albeit in a different way. I felt helpless despite the doctor's best efforts. I plunged into a deep, mindful, introspective state.

Later that night I experienced an unusual vision. I was fully awake and saw the nurses walking outside my room through a large transparent glazed window with a see-through white drape just in front of me. The place was very quiet. My room was dimly lit. Suddenly I saw a few black images of human skeletons, flash in a horizontal row on the wall above the large window. I started wondering what these were, and what they meant. The images merged with each other and became like a dark cloud flying out of the wall towards the interior of the room. The cloud gathered into a rounded solid circle and slowly floated towards me on my right side. It looked like a large round head with two large round red eyes, black upright hair on its head and an open mouth with a red tongue sticking out, it gradually moved towards me.

The thing looked terrifying. Indeed, I was terrified and started shuddering. I thought this must be the Angel of Death approaching to get me. In a panic, I started praying passionately with the following words: "Oh God, please save me from him. I have children who are still students not yet established. Dora will not be able to handle them in my absence. I am still young and have yet to accomplish many things in my life. I beg of you to save me from him. Please save me … I beg of you my life … I beg of you …please!" I started reciting verses from the Qur'an and asked God again and again feverishly to save me.

The specter was slowly approaching but suddenly stopped, about a foot (one-third of a meter) away from me. I looked directly at it, it remained motionless for a while staring at me, then started moving backward. It morphed back into a flying cloud and went back into the wall above the window from where it originated.

There the dark cloud began to coalesce and develop into a well-defined form, and to my utter surprise changed into a replica of the Kaaba, in Mecca. It stayed there for a while, then gradually dissipated and eventually vanished. I felt ecstasy in my heart and took it as a sign from God that I was spared from a catastrophe. All this happened when I was fully awake. I felt it was a clear vision and not a dream and still feel that way to this day. I came to learn in later days that according to my religion once God orders the Angel of Death to take out somebody's soul, the angel never fails in his duty. I checked later in the Qur'an and found a verse stating that. But then I also realized that if God retracts the order, the angel would no longer carry it out.

While I was still trying to reconcile what had just happened, a female nurse entered the room and asked me "How do you feel?" I said "Fine. What is the time now?" She said, "It is 12 midnight." A grin and happy tears came from my eyes spread across my face. She saw the tears in my eyes. She handed a tissue to me to wipe my eyes. The swell of emotion was due to the inexplicable occurrence followed by a feeling of elation, and newly developed confidence and comfort in the thought that I would come around soon. I felt great relief and soon fell asleep. People might say it was a hallucination, that I was under the influence of drugs or perhaps just a nightmare. I'm not bothered by the opinion of others, who have not experienced it or anything like it. To me, the vision was and will always remain, a reality and not delirium.

Over the weekend, I was transferred from the ICU to a regular room. It was a two-patient room separated by a screen. I could hear everything from the other patient's side. Some friends came to see me. Sunday night a surgeon came to talk to the other patient about his bypass surgery next day. The patient was scared, and the doctor gave him reassurances. I didn't like the conversation and I didn't know yet what was in store for me. A research professor wanted to do some non-invasive tests on me, free of cost to see the condition of my heart. I asked him "Will I be able to lead a productive life in the future?" He replied, "Of course you could if you pursue a healthy lifestyle."

On Monday, Dr. Chablani came to see me and said that he would determine what needed to be done after some invasive tests. However, later in the afternoon, he told me that Health Alliance, my insurance company in Urbana, Illinois, wanted me to be sent by an ambulance to the Carle Hospital in Urbana. Clearly, the idea was to minimize the cost for any invasive procedure that would be needed. Dr. Chablani told them that he would not allow me to be sent by ground ambulance; it must be air ambulance. This was agreed upon. In the evening, I was taken by helicopter ambulance on a very cold and windy day. The helicopter took off with me and a nurse sitting next to me, periodically checking my vitals. It landed on the roof of the Carle hospital. I was taken to a room. The hospital was quieter and more peaceful than the large Chicago hospital.

Dr. Salim Rashid was there at Carle Hospital to receive me. Seeing my good friend and being in my hometown, I felt reassured. The next morning, Dr. Nelson, my cardiologist, came to see me and apologized, saying that he had nothing to do with bringing me there; the insurance company told him to contact Dr. Chablani and arrange my transfer from Chicago.

After a day of carrying out some tests, Dr. Nelson told me that since I survived the heart attack, the clot was busted and there was no lingering angina (chest pain) now, it meant the damage to heart muscle was already done. This damage was irreparable. So, nothing could be done now, and he would discharge me from the hospital. I was delighted to know I could return home. However, the delight was short-lived as a day later Dr. Nelson called me home to say that Dr. Chablani in Chicago got the results of the advanced tests performed there and found that my heart muscles were intact without any damage. This meant that although the clot was busted, the original blockage was still there and if not treated I might suffer another heart attack in the future. I was taken to the hospital immediately by my daughters, on Thanksgiving Day, and quickly I got medical attention. The fast decision probably prevented any damage to my heart muscle. Dr. Chablani also called me and explained why I should go back to the hospital in Urbana and undergo angioplasty. As desired by the two cardiologists, I went back to the hospital prepared for angioplasty, also known as balloon procedure, or a more invasive bypass, if needed. Stenting was still not available at that time.

Accordingly, Dr. Nelson performed the procedure late in the afternoon. I was not allowed to have any food or drink all day which weakened me very much. I felt some natural anxiety but was basically confident that everything would be fine as I remembered the vision I had in the ICU in Chicago. During the procedure, I felt some chest pain even though I was sedated. After the procedure was done, I heard Dr. Nelson say to me "You will not remember anything as you since you were sedated but I will explain what I did later." Then I was moved to a recovery room. It was early evening and I was not feeling very well and saw on the monitor that my systolic blood pressure was rapidly dropping. It went dangerously low as I felt more and more feeble. The attending nurse got panicky, gave me some water to drink to increase my blood pressure, and called other nurses and the doctor. Soon, I went into a state of semi-consciousness. At one point during the melee, I overheard that I would be moved to the catheter lab again and vaguely felt that I was being transported to some place. I could not remember anything after that.

Th next morning, as reported by Dora, Dr. Nelson called her and told her "Your husband had another heart attack in the recovery room, and I got very nervous. But we treated him. He is not fully conscious, but his vitals are okay. Everything is under control now. He is so young; we don't want to do a bypass right now and want to see what happens." I was in that state of semi-consciousness for a couple of days during which Dr. and Mrs. Salim Rashid, Dr. Azizul Islam and other local friends and students took turns staying in my room watching me. I faintly remember glimpses of some of them sitting in a chair in the room. Once I regained full consciousness, I was moved to a regular room.

One Dr. Handler came to see me in the morning and said "As Dr. Nelson was not on duty the night you had the second heart attack, I carried out another catheterization on you and found that the 90 per cent blockage in the Circumflex artery collapsed and totally stopped blood flow to the Right Coronary Artery (RCA). Therefore, there is no need to do anything now. The good thing is that the collateral arteries have taken over supplying blood to the affected areas." The same afternoon Dr. Nelson came to see me and repeated almost the same thing that Dr. Handler said and urged me to do regular exercise to keep the collaterals active.

Director Alan Forrester and some other colleagues including David Wickersheimer and Lloyd Leffers came to see me. My students sent me a bouquet of flowers with a note wishing me a speedy recovery. A counsellor saw me the next day and gave me some advice. One piece of advice she gave me did stick. She said "If someone's words or actions hurt you, don't get upset. Take it like this: it's his or her problem, not yours." I have tried to follow this as a motto for the rest of my life and benefited from it.

I was discharged from the hospital soon. Before the discharge, the head of the cardiology department came to see me and quipped to Dora who was there with me, "Tell your husband to cut branches off trees. Boil the leaves and let him eat those." I got the message by translating it to "Tell your husband to exercise and eat vegetarian foods." Once I returned home, I felt relieved that I survived once again.

I was still in a trancelike state at night and I thought Dora was a nurse, walking around, as I had seen so many nurses of late. In early morning at about 4:00 AM a powerful light broke through the windows near our bed waking Dora. She saw the light behind us, woke me up and asked me what was going on outside. It was a cold night in December. The light was so powerful that our whole bedroom was lit up. It appeared to me that the sky was red, and we heard human voices. It appeared to be happening on our driveway. I got up and took a close look and saw the office building across the creek adjoining our home was on fire. Firefighters were on the scene. The entire area surrounding it was lit up. I got concerned as the fire might spread to the nearby offices and homes. I took it as a bad omen. I thought to myself: was it a sign that I had to go through some more troubles? Fortunately, there was no blowing wind. We spent a tense hour or so before the fire was brought under control. I felt relieved after all the recent trauma and certainly didn't need any more.

When I had my heart attack, it was near the end of the semester. So, my students didn't suffer much. In my absence, my two remaining classes were handled by my colleagues. I went on a prescheduled sabbatical leave in the spring semester. This gave me an opportunity to read half a dozen books on heart disease that I had borrowed from the Carle Hospital Library and UIUC Library and some that I bought. Surviving a heart attack made me more health conscious. I tried to learn as much I could about human health and wellness. Simultaneously, I spent my leave carrying out research on earthquake-resistant design of foundations. The research was supported by the Portland Cement Association located in Skokie, a suburb of Chicago. It was a new topic for me, and it kept my mind stimulated and occupied.

The leave was followed by a three-month summer vacation, which gave me enough time to recuperate as I had no teaching duties for about eight months. I went through a cardiac rehab program in January and February at the local Carle Hospital to rejuvenate my heart. The program introduced me to formal physical exercise as a prescribed routine. In the lectures, we were told that generally heart attack survivors would relapse within five years, with new heart problems. On the day of my discharge I shook hands with Tony, the lecturer, I told him: "I like you Tony, but I would like to see you again in a shopping mall or restaurant, and not here." The heart attack was a hard blow for me, yet a blessing in disguise, as it gave me a whole new perspective on life. I got a taste of the meaning of mortality and vulnerability. I realized if I didn't take care of my God-given body, the same body could turn against me again. It was like a rebirth. It made me stronger but mellow and jovial. I developed a love for exercise and started a heart-healthy diet. Such efforts kept me free from heart problems for the next 16 years – the most productive period of my career.

My parents Mir Muazzam Ali and Azifa Ali, Dhaka 1978. We visited that year from Canada, my first time back since I left Dhaka in 1970

Me as an engineering student, Dhaka 1961

Newlyweds, Dhaka 1968

Dora and me with our firstborn child Ifat, Dhaka 1969

The beat-up suitcase I still keep from 1970 when I left East Pakistan

At Niagara Falls 1973

Dora and me with the girls at University of Waterloo campus near
Library building, May 1974

Ifat and me, Waterloo, Ont. 1974

Giving a seminar on Dhaka's city planning and high-rise
developments, Dhaka 1989

Working with Chief Draftsman Mr. Sardar on a bridge project at the
office of Louis Berger, Inc., Dhaka 1965

My brothers (L to R: Me, Mir Maswood Ali, Mir Mosaddeq Ali,
Mir Masoom Ali), Muncie, IN 1986

On the job at Singapore dockyard 1984

With Professor Ding Dajun at Nanjing Technological University,
Nanjing, China 1986

At the Great Wall of China 1986

North American Association of Muslim Professionals and
Scholars (NAAMPS); I was its first chairman; inaugural
conference in Chicago, April 1993

American Association of Bangladeshi Engineers and
Architects (AABEA) sponsored a fundraiser event in New York, NY for
establishing Fazlur Rahman Khan Chair at Lehigh University, with
Dr. Lynn S. Beedle as the Guest Speaker, November 1997

Enjoying snack and drink at Dhaka Local Government
Engineering Department (LGED) after my seminar there.
Its head Quamrul Islam Siddique is to my left, Kasem,
an employee there and my friend, to my right, 1989

Dharandi (my ancestral village) inhabitants came to see me off
after my visit there, 1984

My back-to-back siblings Farhad Ara Arzoo to my right and
Mir Mosaddeq Ali to my left, Champaign, IL 2000

CHAPTER 11

URBANA-CHAMPAIGN

Executive Decisions

I went back to my regular teaching schedule in the fall semester of 1993. It was a great feeling to finally get back to normal life after about nine months. As if I got a new lease of life, I appreciated the opportunity of teaching again and viewed my office, the campus and the students with fresh eyes. On the first day of class, although I felt a bit weak physically, I felt mentally vigorous in the classroom, ready to take off like a plane, once stuck on a runway waiting for air traffic control.

In late summer of that year, I got a call from Director Forrester asking me if I would be willing to accept the position of chairman of the Structures Division. Jim Simon resigned earlier, as he felt he was overworked and was then replaced by Lloyd Leffers. Division chairmen were expected to teach courses and were paid an allowance for the added administrative responsibilities. This could be overwhelming. Lloyd resigned from the position. I asked for some time to think this over. I thought about the pros and cons of this position. I realized that as an administrator I could have prestige, additional compensation, and a bit of clout to shape the policies of the Division.

On the other hand, it demanded additional time dealing with routine bureaucratic matters like meetings, curriculum issues, scheduling, deadlines, advising graduate students, and dealing with faculty members and student problems. A commitment like this was sure to take time away from the scholarship and teaching that I loved. In addition to this, I was just recovering from the near-death experience of two successive cardiac events. The extra workload and the stress might negatively affect my health. Finally, after some soul-searching, I decided to accept the appointment. My health and stress concerns were outweighed by my natural love for challenges and new experiences.

As chairman, I led the group of professors in structures. All of them were older than me except the one teaching in Versailles. Both Jim and Lloyd were helpful in my transition. Initially, I didn't change things much, as the policies for the Division were quite well established by my predecessors and I thought they were generally good. Soon I started feeling comfortable in my new position.

As days passed, I discovered a "turf war" going on in the School. I had an inkling of it before but to maintain our morale in our divisional meetings, neither Jim nor Lloyd explicitly described their ordeals. The Design Division being the largest division of the school wanted administrative oversight over the smaller Architectural Communications & Technology, History & Preservation, and Structures Divisions. The Design Division controlled the design studio -- the heart of any architecture school. While most design professors were understanding, a few vocal ones were somewhat hostile to structures and would openly say that the Structures Division belonged to the Civil Engineering Department and was taking resources away from the Architecture School. They were not proponents of the divisional structure of the school, although this was mandated, by university regulations, for large schools. Many of them were not aware of the history of the school or disregarded it.

Nathaniel Ricker, the founding father of the school, envisioned the school as one that would embrace science and technology side by side with design. The word "architecture" itself originates from art and technology. Ricker's vision was inscribed on a plaque in front of the school. The difference between a Civil Engineering Department and the Architecture School was that the courses were framed for different audiences. Whereas civil engineering taught structures for all types of applications, such as buildings and bridges, the architectural curriculum was focused exclusively and extensively on buildings. The battle of opinions continued, between several of the design faculty some of whom were outspoken and sat on important committees. With dwindling resources available from the State of Illinois, things were getting harder to fund and growth was difficult to anticipate.

I soon faced some staffing challenges. Some of the faculty members in my division were nearing retirement. Ingvar Schousboe was the first to retire, followed by Albert Bianchini. It was very difficult to get replacements for these positions since any time there was a search for a new faculty position, Design Division got the priority. To fill one of the vacancies, we hired a new, experienced faculty member from another department, where her temporary position had become redundant. She had a doctoral degree in structural engineering from outside the U.S. I used the computer program she developed, called PLATO, to solve assignment problems for my Statics course, a foundational course in the structures program. I knew her well because of my frequent interactions with her when I used PLATO. She was a very nice person and well qualified.

Before approaching me for the full-time position in our division, she taught at the school as a substitute when one of our faculty went on sabbatical leave. After considering the pros and cons, and particularly, the shortage of structures faculty and the low probability of hiring new ones, I recommended her full-time appointment on a contract basis.

Due to faculty shortage, I was tasked with searching for part-time instructors to teach the courses. I was definitely unhappy with this. In addition to staffing, I dealt with scheduling classes. I came to find that some faculty members were unwilling to teach new courses, while others wanted only the time slots that suited them, and so on. Juggling conflicts of time and venue, working around graduate teaching assistants' own class schedules and their undergrad tutorial responsibilities was cumbersome. I had to struggle with the logistics every semester.

I sat on many academic committees at different levels and had to deal with multi-faceted tasks and problems. These included the sensitive matter of student complaints related to poor teaching by some faculty members. I had to deal with student advising, orientation, miscellaneous complaints, as well as student admissions, awards, scholarships, and assistantships. I helped many students with job placement. Most firms looking for graduates would contact me and take my recommendation. I also had to deal with our alumni, many of whom were in Chicago and were in high positions as presidents or partners of companies. The position was quite demanding.

Despite all this, I still loved teaching, particularly new courses. As always, I would gain additional insights in new areas. I taught a total of 15 courses, 13 in the School and two campus level courses. Of course, I felt I could teach better if I had more time to prepare. My administrative duties took away much of my time. I envisioned and developed a seminar course called "High-Rise and Habitat" in collaboration with my colleague Paul Armstrong from the Design Division. I introduced two new graduate courses called "Soil Mechanics and Foundations" and "Seismic Analysis and Design of Structures."

Although we already had a course on foundation design, we didn't have a course on soil mechanics. The Illinois Board of Regulations that controlled the various professional licenses, wanted an additional course on soil mechanics as a prerequisite for foundation design. Since there were no resources to add a new course, I created the new course combining the elements of soil mechanics and foundation design by truncating some of the topics of the existing full course called "Foundation Engineering." This was acceptable to the Board of Regulation. We introduced the other course as well, since earthquake-resistant design was assuming new importance, due to repeated seismic events around the world. I developed the syllabi of both these courses. We also had a graduate course entitled "Advanced Structural Planning" acting as a capstone course in which a complete building project was assigned. Later, I converted it to a studio course in structures, still as a capstone.

In addition to teaching, I also volunteered at the School. For example, I worked with the Tang Committee in Chicago. It was established by the alumni in honor of the late Steve Tang, a previous chairman of the Architectural Engineering Concentration who was revered by his students. The committee wished to offer a seminar course where a guest speaker from our pool of alumni would come weekly. I developed a syllabus and called it "Integrated Design and Construction of Buildings." I assigned the course to a newly hired assistant professor, Abbas Aminmansour. His job was to coordinate with the guest speakers and host these seminars. He has been teaching this course annually ever since. When the search for his position was underway, I was instrumental in hiring him, noting that he had good computer skills, was eloquent and might be a good spokesperson for the Structures Division after I quit as chairman.

Some of our students would need my approval to take structures courses in the Civil Engineering Department, to get a second degree in Civil Engineering. Noting the trend, I decided to develop a double degree program of M.Arch. and M.S. and met the chairman of the Structures Program, my counterpart in the Civil Engineering Department, Dr. Robert Dodd, to discuss this matter. After several meetings between me and some other civil engineering professors for about a year, we came up with the syllabus of the joint degree program. I was very overworked at that point, so I delegated the task to the newly hired assistant professor at the very end. I wanted to groom him in such matters of curriculum, so he could succeed me in the leadership position. I found that he was very engaged and was happy to see it. Around the same time, I initiated an online journal titled *CTBUH Review Journal* for CTBUH of which I was the founding editor. I appointed the new faculty member as managing editor and Paul Armstrong the assistant editor to work with me.

Earlier in the summer of 1992, I met a group of Muslim professionals and scholars from around North America at Macomb, IL where Western Illinois University is located at the behest of Dr. Mohammad Ahmadullah Siddiqi, a faculty member in Journalism and Public Relations and Dr. Mohammad O. Farooq, a faculty member of Economics at Iowa Wesleyan College, Mt. Pleasant, Iowa.

We felt that there were many Muslim scholars and professionals in the U.S. and Canada who didn't know each other personally nor through their work projects. A new organization was conceived to build professional bridges and connect over a collective vision and shared goals. The idea was to develop a common understanding of the challenges facing Muslims in North

America as well as the global Muslim community. The organization called North American Association of Muslim Professionals and Scholars (NAAMPS), would encourage cooperation and coordination among interested Muslim professionals and scholars to promote an unimpeded, nonpartisan, non-dogmatic environment of understanding, tolerance, devotion, and pursuit of professional and academic excellence.

It would focus its efforts in North America. These were indeed lofty goals for the group. The emphasis would be on cultivating independent thinking free from financial contribution from individuals or groups with vested interests to avoid external pressures. My experience with CTBUH and BEFCA, as well as the enthusiasm of the group in the meeting, gave me hope and I felt optimistic about the success of this new endeavor.

The first meeting was well attended, and an ad hoc committee was formed. I was unanimously elected the chairman of the committee of eight members. This inaugural meeting was followed up with others in Chicago and Urbana-Champaign. Meanwhile, we planned for a conference in Chicago in April 1993. The purpose of the conference was to bring together prominent Muslim professionals and scholars to discuss various issues related to academia and industry facing Muslims domestically and the global Muslim community in general.

The new organization was taking shape while I was still recovering from my recent double heart attack in late 1992. Within months, I got busy again with the BEFCA's international conference, held in Urbana-Champaign, the first week of April,1993. I was also working on the book *Architecture of Tall Buildings*. I was on sabbatical leave in the spring semester and working on a research project at Portland Cement Association in Chicago in collaboration with Dr. S.K. Ghosh. I had been also reading many books on heart health. All these activities kept me engaged, and occasionally I felt weak and drawn.

Yet, I participated in the first largely attended NAAMPS conference in Chicago and made my inaugural speech short so as not to stress myself. After the conference, the NAAMPS committee held a meeting elsewhere in a suburb of Chicago. I felt somewhat exhausted and tried to excuse myself. But they reminded me that as I was the chairman, my presence at the meeting was much desired. So, I decided to attend and chair the meeting.

Meanwhile, NAAMPS was introduced to Muslim communities by members, particularly, by Dr. Ahmedullah Siddiqi. After a year had elapsed it was time for a new leader. After some private discussions, it was agreed that I would step down. Dr. Mohammed Fathi Osman, an academic, editor-in-chief of the *Arabia: The Islamic World Review* during 1981-1987 and a resident scholar at the Islamic Center of Southern California, Los Angeles since 1987, took over as president.

I felt relieved as I realized that our emphasis on financial independence, although noble in concept, was too idealistic, and that no organization could operate without enough resources to fuel it. The conference was funded by small donations, contributions from NAAMPS members, and conference registration fees. Despite having no major donors, the organization was still active.

My thought was to create monographs on different topics, seek grant funding and major benevolent donors. This was not, however, what others felt. They wanted to be totally financially independent. I knew in the back of my mind that to have an impact, NAAMPS needed reliable funding sources to support its mission.

We held a meeting of the Executive Committee, August 6-8, 1993 in Macomb. Because of my health, Dora didn't want me to go alone from Champaign although these cities were only 140 miles (204 kilometers) apart. So, a graduate student in accounting, Nurul Amin, accompanied me. Over the course of the weekend, we discussed many issues including the April 1993 conference in Chicago. I proposed that we not let the excellent oral presentations get lost and instead ask the participants to submit written papers and publish the proceedings.

After some discussion, we agreed to publish a book. Dr. Siddiqi took the initiative to compile and edit. In May 1994, the book entitled *Islam: A Contemporary Perspective* edited by Dr. Siddiqi was published by NAAMPS Publications (ISBN 0-9641624-0-7). There was a total of 16 papers by 16 contributors covering various issues facing Muslims, primarily in the U.S. as well as the world at large. The title of my paper was "Resurgence of Islam: Dream or Reality?" In my paper, I examined the scope and possibility of an Islamic resurgence while the Muslim world was in chaos and turbulence. I argued for focusing on the development of one Muslim country at a time, to stimulate an intellectual, moral, and scientific reawakening after the Islamic Golden Age. The clue to Islamic resurgence lies in the revitalization of the socio-political structure and the education system at a grassroots level.

NAAMPS published newsletters outlining its activities and mission. At the Executive Committee meeting in Macomb, a decision was taken to hold our next conference in 1995. Many people, including me, gave oral presentations. To the best of my recollection, no written document of the conference was compiled or published. The organization continued for a year or so after me under the chairmanship of Dr. Fathi Osman and was then discontinued, although we started with a lot of zeal.

Reflecting on why this initiative lost its steam and eventually died, I believe timing played a part. I was looking at this up-and-coming organization as a place where Muslim professionals and scholars could exchange their ideas through conferences and publications, in the form of proceedings and monographs. Creating such a platform would take time. My sudden illness slowed me down for a while and also, I was already involved in other

projects that demanded my time and attention. I found that committee members coming from different backgrounds had diverse
interests. This was voluntary work, and most had only marginal
interest as they had full time jobs or business.

Although we had a mission statement, it was in my opinion
open-ended and unclear. We didn't have the funding sources to
meet expenses nor maintain financial sustainability. We needed
to spend time contacting donors nationally and internationally
and explain why our organization was important. While people
didn't mind donating for humanitarian causes, we met resistance to the idea of donating to an organization with a mission
like ours, its value was not immediately easy to understand. We
had trouble convincing people of the importance of sustaining
an organization such as ours, for the long term. I could see these
challenges clearly and repeatedly emphasized this point to the
committee. We needed major funding sources and paid employees to deal with fundraising, explaining our mission, and other
support activities.

I found the general lack of interest in the group to address
core issues and as a result I lost interest myself. Dr. Siddiqi, as the
convener, had been doing a tremendous job, but I guess eventually he might also have become tired of doing the heavy lifting
by himself. Above all, a dedicated and strong leader with paid
helpers who could devote enough time to it was needed to run
this organization. Many such organizations like ours later vanish
because of similar reasons after their initial short-term agenda is
fulfilled and their mission starts slithering that can be labeled as
"mission creep."

In May 1995, I participated in the Fifth World Congress of
CTBUH held in Amsterdam, ironically, a city that hardly had any

tall buildings. The 35-story Rembrandt Tower built in 1994 was the only notable building adoring the city's skyline at the time. Although more tall buildings were built after my visit. Amsterdam is the largest city in the Netherlands and the official capital of the country, although the seat of government and administrative offices are located in The Hague. It is also the cultural center of the country. In my teenage years I read that Holland (often used interchangeably with Netherlands, although there is a subtle difference between the two), was under or close to sea level and was protected by dams and embankments. I tried to imagine what it looked like and thought the dams were an amazing feat by Dutch civil engineers.

This was my first time traveling overseas since my heart attacks. I still felt somewhat weak, presenting my work in a European city had been a wish of mine. My younger brother Mosaddeq cautioned me against going and suggested I should rethink whether my body was up to it. Dora preferred staying home with the kids if I ever I travelled for conferences and meetings. I decided to stick with my decision. Once again, I was compelled by my adventurous and curious nature and the pleasure of seeing different countries and experiencing the other cultures.

I flew a commuter flight from Champaign to Chicago, and then overnight from Chicago to Amsterdam. I reached Amsterdam in the early morning. When I went to check-in, I was told that my check-in time was noon. I booked the hotel through my travel agent and didn't pay attention to the check-in time. I requested a vacant room as I was very tired and needed sleep. There was nothing available, but I could check in early at 11 AM. I asked her if there was any other place I could rest for a while. Following her advice, I went to the hotel restaurant which had just opened, so it wasn't very crowded. I took a seat in corner and started napping. Soon other people started coming in for breakfast. I was hungry, so I had my breakfast too and felt somewhat refreshed and energized. But time was passing slowly for me. The restaurant music was enjoyable, but it was all American and British songs in English. I asked the waitress "Don't you have local Dutch music and songs?" She replied, "No. These are more popular for hotel customers. They like English songs."

Finally, I got my room, surprisingly small, unlike what I was used to in North America and Asia. It was a rather expensive hotel. I headed for the showers. The bathroom was also small, and it was difficult to move around in it despite me not being a big man. After the shower, I fell into a deep sleep.

I walked around one afternoon and realized that Amsterdam was still a bit chilly in May, but I didn't have a jacket with me. I wore two T-shirts under my dress shirt before going to the conference the next day. I met Dr. Lynn Beedle, the founder and director of CTBUH and some others like Dr. Shankar Nair, a reputed Chicago engineer and Mr. Mehta, a professor from India. Mr. Mehta was a likeable fellow and we quickly bonded, spending time together throughout the conference. While there, I chaired a workshop session on tall buildings. A brief discussion on a possible bulletin, became a catalyst to launch the *CTBUH Review Journal*, of which I became the founding editor, with support from Mr. Shankar Nair.

Mr. Mehta and I toured the city, visiting its historic, well known canals, among other sites. The conference arranged a group tour to The Hague and Rotterdam. In the Hague, we visited the administrative offices and buildings of the International Court of Justice. I could not visit Rotterdam because of a time constraint, but it would have been great to visit. On my return flight, I reflected on the congress and mused over how to establish a journal, framed and formatted for CTBUH.

In the summer of 1995, I was in Dhaka to participate in a conference on floods in Bangladesh and the Mississippi River Basin. Before I left for Dhaka, Rizvi Islam, a lawyer, the only son of our retired friend Dr. Azizul Islam, had been suffering from a terminal disease. It was an unexpected blow for Dr. Islam. He had been enjoying his retirement with his son's family and little grandson Mikhail, and it was a tumultuous time for our community. I remember when he called to tell me the bad news about his son, he uttered the words, "This is also my end." We were all deeply saddened by this tragedy and realized that as a grieving father, he was devastated. During my stay later in Dhaka, my daughter Ifat, who was visiting Urbana-Champaign from Chicago, called to let me know that Rizvi had passed away at Carle Hospital. I was shocked. Upon my return, I came to know all the details and tried to console the family. Soon afterwards the Islams moved to California to be with their daughter Rebecca. Dr. Islam fell ill there and was hospitalized. I called him, and I sensed how heartbroken he was. In distress he told me, "I can't forget my son and I always see his face." Unable to withstand the overwhelming burden and pain from the loss of his only son, he too died shortly after. It was a sad event for our community.

Soon after, in mid-1990s, Dr. Taher Saif accompanied by his wife Shahneela Chowdhury moved to Urbana-Champaign as a new faculty member in the Mechanical Engineering department. They were a very young couple and we soon became close friends. They came from Ithaca where Taher completed his Ph.D. degree from Cornell University. We shared a few social connections, they knew a childhood friend of mine at Cornell, Dr. Rafiquddin Ahmed, a historian and his wife. Shortly after, when Dr. Jamilur Reza Choudhury, a BUET professor, came to Champaign for a visit, I hosted a dinner for him and invited Taher and Shahneela. Taher was a student of Dr. Choudhury. Two children were born to the couple in Champaign, Farzad, a son and Faaiza, a daughter.

In the 1970s when I was living in the freezing city of Timmins, I would hear about people going to Acapulco, Mexico in the winter for vacation. Even later I heard about it many times as a popular vacation spot. So, I was curious about experiencing the city and Mexican culture. Fortunately, I had the opportunity to go. I went as a presenter and attendee of the 11th World Conference on Earthquake Engineering during June 22-28, 1996. My paper was on tall buildings in earthquake zones. The city is located on the Pacific Coast of Mexico and is a major port and tourist destination owing to its nice weather, attractive large beaches, restaurants, and resort hotels. It is a great get-away place for tourists from the U.S. and Canada to escape the cold winter. I stayed in a hotel next to the Acapulco Bay with only a street between the hotel and the waterfront.

I spent much of the daytime at the conference and made some acquaintances there. In the late afternoons and evenings, I strolled in the area near my hotel and enjoyed the wind and the sound of waves from the bay. I immediately noticed the cosmopolitan nature of the city's population, many of whom were tourists. I went to dine at some fancy restaurants and open-air food courts and enjoyed the cuisine. The conference organizers arranged a cultural show in which young Mexican girls dressed in fabulous Mexican dresses performed dances on an open-air stage. As with all conferences, a lavish banquet was thrown for the participants. The food was excellent and different from what we normally find in Mexican restaurants in the U.S. I was told by some Mexican participants that the food was a mix of local, Spanish, and Arab cuisines, reminding me that Spain was ruled by Arab's for centuries and their cuisine was influenced by Arab foods. I visited the Mayan Resort at Acapulco and spent half a day in that beautiful setting. I thought of possibly coming back for a resort experience with Dora, but this wish never materialized.

I booked a coastal cruise in the evening, a day before my departure scheduled for June 28. Little did I know that Hurricane Boris was about to hit the area on June 27, with its full fury. During the day I noticed that it was very windy and water waves were striking the shore hard. The place where the cruise ship was supposed to dock was within a walking distance from my hotel. Before the check-in time I went with the hopes of enjoying the cruise but looking at the water it looked doubtful. Soon after I learned that they were expecting a hurricane strike, and the cruise was canceled. Disheartened, I came back to the hotel and consoled myself with the thought it was better to miss the panoramic nighttime view of Acapulco from the sea, than sail through inclement weather. I went to bed, prepared for my morning flight, and booked a taxi hoping everything would be fine the next day. I went into a deep sleep as I often did and still do.

In the early hours of the morning, the next day before sunrise, I woke up to the spluttering sound of the wind striking and shaking the two-story hotel. I opened the backdoor of my ground floor room and watched the wrath of Nature. High wind and rain were violently battering the whole area, helpless trees were swinging back and forth. I was born and raised in the coastal district of Bangladesh, which was prone to frequent tropical cyclones; I had seen this dramatic weather before. It was dark outside, only flashes of lightening illuminated the city from time to time. I could see that the land was covered with water from the tidal waves. The water was close to the hotel's raised ground floor level. I got worried and thought of going upstairs to avoid inundation. I tried to turn on my room light, but there was no electricity. I closed my door and made my way along the dark hallway to the front desk. Nobody was there.

I came back to my room, picked up the phone to call the hotel authority, but found the phone was dead. I decided to stay vigilant and not to go upstairs unless the situation got worse. The best thing would be to stay calm and see what happened next as it was impossible to contact anyone. While waiting in my room helplessly I was just praying to God to end the storm, so I could go to the airport as scheduled and go home. Fortunately, the storm appeared to weaken and subsided after daybreak. I looked out the rear window to see the water receding. With great hope I got ready for the taxi I had arranged but I wasn't certain it would come. I may add here that mobile phones became common in about 1997. At the time, the land lines were out and there was no way to contact the driver.

Hoping against hope, I got ready and waited at the front lobby. Suddenly, I saw a taxi at the appointed time and the driver got out and asked my name. I got in. There was still some standing water on the streets but as we moved away from the coast, the streets were just wet. The driver told me the airport was still open. Once we reached the airport, I found there was water, knee-deep, at the entrance of the terminal. The scene was chaotic. Passengers were trying to wade through the water since the steps and ramp were flooded. I was discouraged but did what I had to do. I took off my shoes and rolled my pants above my knees. Holding my shoes in one hand and my suitcase in the other I stepped into the water and made my way to the terminal. Upon entering, I got my boarding pass and waited for my flight with relief. After about an hour or so, to my disappointment, I heard an announcement that my flight was cancelled. I went to the counter and asked them to re-book me for a later flight. They declined my request saying no bookings were available and asked me to call later giving me a telephone number. I decided to go back to my hotel and call from there.

Outside many disgruntled travelers were waiting for taxis on the raised platforms, which were few and far between and everyone was vying to get on. While I was wondering what to do next, a taxi suddenly came in and ignoring the clamoring crowd, he drove right towards me and told me to get in. We chatted on the way back to the hotel. He told me that his name was Jesus and the other drivers knew him well said I should call him if I needed a ride, now or if I ever visited Acapulco again. When I asked him why he picked me up rather than anyone else from the crowd, he said that I stood out to him as a foreigner and he wanted to help me. His name, demeanor and willingness to help made me think he was a godsend. I thanked him profusely.

Once in the hotel, I asked the girl at the front desk if the hotel phone was working. She said, "No. but there is a public phone booth at the street corner nearby that might work." I went and found two people trying to call but the lines were out. After they left, I tried those two phones anyway hoping against hope, and found them without any ring tone. Then I looked around and found a third phone, hidden from view from the street side. I picked that one up and lo and behold, to my pleasant surprise, I heard a ring tone. I called the number I had been given at the airport and booked my flight for the next morning. I thanked God from my heart for His repeated favors to me.

The next day, I safely returned to Chicago via Mexico City. While enjoying the panoramic view from an upper floor of the Mexico City airport, I couldn't help thinking of the catastrophic earthquake the city had experienced on September 19, 1985. It had a magnitude of 8.0 on the Richter Scale and the major aftershock on September 20, had a magnitude of 7.5. About 5,000 people lost their lives in that earthquake. As a structural engineer with research, teaching and practical experience in earthquake-resistant design, having lived through catastrophic storms, the destruction was well known to me.

In 1997, I got the bad news from Dhaka that my sister Jahan Ara Begum, my oldest sibling, had passed away. She was about 70 years old. I knew she wasn't in good health, but nor was she in any critical health condition. Her second son Dr. Kaisaruzzaman a practicing physician in Malaysia died earlier, quite prematurely. My sister had been grieving this loss and could not overcome it. I witnessed that when I visited her in Dhaka in 1995. Her death was the first in our family after our parents' demise. I had difficulty accepting it. Although I never had close contact or relationship with her because of our age difference, I recalled the many good times I had with her and my brother-in-law. He was like our alternate older brother, and a towering personality in our family. I had always considered my sister like my mother as her oldest son was only a year older than me. I felt very sad. It was a sad time across the globe in fact, since around the same time, Princess Diana was killed in a car accident in Paris, at a very young age, and an international outpouring of grief ensued.

In the fall of 1999, I took a sabbatical leave. I was working on a book, which was eventually published, *The Art of the Skyscraper: The Genius of Fazlur Khan*. I decided to go to Bangladesh to do some research. I also wanted to research the problem of traffic gridlocks on Dhaka's streets and think of solutions. Dora and I visited Dhaka in October and stayed for a few weeks with my brother-in-law (Dora's brother) Salahuddin Khan, a district judge. I was busy meeting people and friends. As our children were all adults and either working or studying, this time, we left them behind. Our daughters were in Chicago. Murad was going to Purdue University in West Lafayette, Indiana.

We took a trip to Chittagong where my second brother-in-law Col. Ziauddin Khan, an army officer, was posted. He lived in the

Chittagong Cantonment, a secluded and quiet area. I developed a bad back ache soon after arriving. Chittagong is a port city and the second largest city of Bangladesh. This was my first visit. It was an interesting place, much less crowded than Dhaka. We spent a few days there and despite my back pain went on sight-seeing on a few occasions. We visited a nearby tourist spot called *Patenga*, a sea beach next to the Bay of Bengal. This was the first time I had seen this sea even though my hometown Patuakhali itself was so close to the Bay of Bengal. There is another place to the south of Patuakhali called Kuakata with a sea beach.

At *Patenga* I saw many ships anchored offshore. My back pain prevented me from going to some other places like *Teknaf* and *Bandarban* by road. But I didn't want to miss *Rangamati*, a small town in a remote area. It was one of a few hilly places in that region of Bangladesh other than Sylhet. So, I saw a doctor, got treated for the pain and soon felt a bit better. I may mention here that the doctor gave me an injection to relieve me of my pain, yet I didn't want to go too far from Chittagong where good medical facilities might not be available.

In any case, we set for the famous little town called *Rangamati*, in the Chittagong Hill Tracts District (now a Division). This is a region where the *Chakma* tribe, belonging to the Buddhist diaspora, forms a large segment of the population. The car ride from Chittagong to *Rangamati* was challenging as the narrow winding roads didn't have any guard rail in most places. We drove care-fully up the rolling hills. I was amazed to see how large and high some of the hills were. In my opinion, the steep slopes would qualify to be called mountains. I noticed they were covered with green vegetation and an abundant number of banana trees with large hanging bundles of bananas.

On our way, we stopped at an army rest house for lunch. We arrived at *Rangamati*, a small place, with not much to see in the town itself. We visited the nearby Kaptai Lake, which is the largest man-made lake in Bangladesh. The lake was created as a result of building the Kaptai Dam on the *Karnaphuli* River, a part of the *Karnaphuli* Hydro-electric project. It was a splendid sight, the immense body of calm water and the green landscape, tall trees and verdant bushes surrounding it. I saw a Buddhist monk working on a garden near the temple. At my request, he took us inside the temple where I found a mammoth gold color statue of Buddha in his usual sitting position, in meditation. Even today I relish the memorable experience of my trip to this region of exquisite natural beauty. From Chittagong we came back to Dhaka and stayed there for a few days.

After spending a pleasurable time in Bangladesh and accomplishing some professional work, we headed for Jeddah, Saudi Arabia on the way to Mecca and Medina, the two holy cities of Islam. This was part of our travel plan. We performed the Umrah, also known as the "Little Hajj" in Mecca. When we landed in Jeddah, I was thrilled to be in the Holy Land of Islam.

The number of pilgrims performing Hajj has always fluctuated. Lately, due to Muslim population growth and increased transportation opportunities, including air travel, the number of pilgrims has soared to about 2 to 3 million compared to about 30,000 in the1930s.

To meet the increased demand from air travelers, the Saudi government invested about $5 billion in developing the new King Abdul Aziz International Airport near Jeddah. It occupies an area of 35 square miles (90 square kilometers), larger than the international airports of New York, Chicago, and Paris. The airport's most spectacular feature is the Hajj Terminal. It consists of vast tented halls, making up the world's largest fabric structure and enclosing its largest covered space. Viewing the scene from the airplane, as it was landing, I could see the bright tents of the Hajj Terminal glow in the desert sunshine. This structure was designed by the prolific, late, Dr. Fazlur R. Khan of SOM, Chicago.

A doctoral student in economics at UIUC, Shahid Rashid, and his wife Kushnar became our family friends in Urbana-Champaign. Shahid offered to help facilitate our trip to Mecca. His two brothers lived in Saudi Arabia, one in Jeddah, who came to receive us at the airport, and the other in Mecca, who helped us with our hotel arrangements as well adjoining us in the rituals of the Umrah.

The first time I saw the Ka'ba in the evening, I was fascinated by it, as I have read so much about it and seen its picture so many times. I recalled my vision in the ICU of Rush Presbyterian Hospital in Chicago in November 1992, where I saw the image of the Ka'ba at one of my life's darkest moments, fighting for my life. A strong emotional feeling touched me, and I moved close to it and touched its walls. I thanked the Almighty who had saved me from the clutches of death after my earnest appeal to Him on that fateful night.

The next morning, I hired a taxi and it so happened that the driver was from Bangladesh. I asked him to take me and Dora to all the holy sites in and around Mecca. One of the sites was the Hira Mountain, a few miles away from Mecca, where Prophet Mohammad (peace be upon him) would meditate in a cave at the top. I was stunned to see the height of the mountain and the approximate location of the cave, at a great elevation. I marveled at how the Prophet could climb this great height and stay in the cave for prolonged periods, including nights, to meditate.

The next day, we went to Medina by bus, 270 miles (432 kilometers) to the north of Mecca. We went through arid and rugged desert and it took all day, as the bus stopped at a few service centers, holy sites and mosques. It was a tiring journey. Again, I marveled at how the Prophet managed to cross such a harsh desert environment and rugged landscape. All the while avoiding assassination attempts by the Meccans, in his famous migration from Mecca to Medina.

This migration, known as Hijrah (Hegira), is an important event and turning point in the history of Islam. It auspiciously marks year 1 of the Islamic calendar.

In Medina, we stayed at a nice hotel next to the Prophet's Mosque where we prayed. We hired a taxi to visit the holy sites and important mosques in the city. It was a great experience as many of the sites had historic significance and I had read about them earlier. After our visit in Medina we returned to Jeddah and stayed overnight at our host's home. The host and his wife were very gracious. With all these good memories of Bangladesh and Saudi Arabia, we returned to Champaign spiritually charged. Eight years later in 2007 Dora and I went to performing the Hajj from Urbana-Champaign.

After I started teaching in fall, I got back to my normal routine at the university. In the meantime, in 1999 Alan Forrester moved to Versailles, France as Director of the overseas program there. His change of position was unexpected. Mike Andrejasich was appointed Interim Director until a new director was appointed after a national search. Although he wasn't experienced in administration, he performed reasonably well.

The National Architectural Accrediting Board (NAAB) team visited our school every few years. During the tenure of Director Alan Forrester earlier, the visiting team met with some design faculty members about the divisional structure of the school. These faculty felt the divisions caused a lack of integration and encouraged a "turf-protection mentality" amongst faculty members of the different divisions. This was reported in the Architectural Program Report (APR), submitted by the team to the school. In the next visit, the issue was brought up by some professors who reminded the visiting team again. The result was a recommendation from the visiting team, that since the different divisions created a territorial attitude among the faculty, divisions should be made permeable. The administrative borderlines of the divisions should blur. This, however, could not be changed easily, as the university mandated the divisional structure for all large schools.

This issue had been gathering steam for a while but not all design faculty were concerned about it. There were a handful of vocal ones, who were not as appreciative of structure and technology and were instead more focused on architectural design. Some of them admitted to me they had difficulties and poor grades in structures courses as students. There were some who were theoreticians or creative designers and were indifferent to the significance of technology overall. Although the other smaller divisions had concerns about this, it was the Structures Division that had the utmost concern of being diluted. Structures had the most technical and mathematical courses. Therefore, it would be most impacted if the divisional structure was minimized or reorganized. Some design faculty members argued that the School's rankings were more affected by the strong reputation of the structure and technology programs rather than design program. As chairman of the Structures Division, I had to face this challenge squarely in meetings and defend our structures program whenever resources were being cut because of budget deficits.

I always strove to maintain the quality and national reputation of our century-old program. The program had produced countless graduates over the years, many of whom were in high positions in industry and were responsible for the structural design of major buildings around the country and overseas. With the basic knowledge of structures under their belts, some graduates were successful in other industries as well, like nuclear structures, mining, construction, among others. It was a series of constant stress-inducing battles for me to protect the structures program in the face of unyielding opposition in the school. I tried not to take it personally and I told the people I debated, that my position was in support of the school's programs and nothing personal about it. I avoided confrontation with others in order to avert creating enemies in the School. The status quo held while the debates raged, but nothing changed under the tenure of the interim Director.

The year 2000 went well without major changes. Earlier, a search was carried out during 1998-1999 academic year for the Director's position. I was on the search committee. We interviewed several well qualified candidates who were short-listed but we still could not identify someone for the position. One problem in attracting well reputed people was that they preferred large cities, where they could also practice or consult. Architecture is a highly professional field and practice is always valued, even for academics.

On a personal level, I remained very busy with writing another book, that I will discuss in a later chapter. Before the year 2000 was over both our daughters were married: Ifat to Michael Boles, a regional manager in the pharmaceutical industry, and Jinat to Dr. Byron Johnson, M.D., a radiologist. I was awaiting the new century and the new millennium on January 1, 2001. Very few people in human history have witnessed these two historic milestones occurring simultaneously, only once in a thousand years. It was an exhilarating moment and I felt fortunate to experience it and share it with a few billion people around the world. By this time, the world had changed so much politically, culturally, and technologically. With the collapse of the Soviet Union, the Cold War was over. But that didn't help to promote world peace as new tensions along ethnic, racial, political, and religious lines started taking shape.

CHAPTER 12

URBANA-CHAMPAIGN

The Dearly Departed, 9/11, and More

The year 2001 was tempestuous for me. I experienced tragedy at a personal level, and witnessed a catastrophic, world-shaking event. The new millennium started, however, with great joy and hope for me. My younger brother Mir Mosaddeq Ali, a mechanical engineer at General Electric Company in Cincinnati, started a real estate business there in the early 1990s and had been doing well in it. He even resigned at one stage from his full-time job to fully concentrate on his business, self-employed and independent. He was overworked but making good progress. In 1996, I advised him to be careful about not moving too fast to expand. He was an ambitious and optimistic person willing to take risks. In late 1990s he started to note cash flow problems and soon discovered that his property manager, whom he trusted, was being dishonest. So, he decided to liquidate his assets and go back to his old job after an absence of one year. Because of his good work ethic and reputation, he was re-hired by his former employer. The associated stress, however, perhaps took a toll on him.

He experienced some breathing problems and occasional discomfort in the chest in 1997. His cardiologist ordered a stress test
which he failed. The doctor wanted a to do an angiogram to see
the exact nature and extent of any possible blockage. My brother
called me, and I strongly urged him to undergo the procedure,
as heart disease seemed to run in our family, at least those of us
living in North America. He also talked with some others, but
finally, he decided not to do it, probably wary of the invasive procedure and associated risks. Instead he decided to improve his
lifestyle with better eating habits and regular exercise.

The doctor allowed him this option and asked him to follow
up in six months. However, because of his busy work schedule
and family life, he procrastinated and didn't follow up. In January 2001, while on the phone with him, I sensed that he sounded
despondent. I immediately thought of visiting him to see for
myself if he was alright. My spring semester had not yet begun,
so I could have made the trip to comfort him. However, I was tied
up with a few pressing things other than classes, and assumed
he was not in major danger. I decided to stay home, planning
to see him in summer during vacation -- a decision that I later
regretted.

On Friday, April 6, after I came home from work, I was feeling somewhat tired and in low spirits for no apparent reason.
Normally I don't lie down during the daytime. But that day I
lay down on my bed and soon fell into a brief slumber. I saw a
strange dream. The entry door at the corner of the bedroom
was wide open. The house had a small vestibule next to the door
and the adjoining staircase. I saw my sister-in-law Tora, through
the open door, standing there with her two sons, twenty-year old
Tarek and seven-year old Khaled. All of them were looking very
sad and their eyes were cast down. I asked Tora "Where is my
brother?" She didn't reply. The entire scene was eerie to me in
my dream.

I woke up and felt an inexplicable sadness. I decided to call him after dinner. Then I realized that he might not be home as it was Friday evening (it so happened that he was at a dinner party at a friend's home that night) and decided to call him the next day. I went to bed at night as usual but could not sleep. I always slept well and usually fell asleep almost immediately. But that night I couldn't and was feeling deep emotional pain for some reason. Dora had already fallen asleep. The discomfort in my chest became intense and I sat up in bed. I knew it was not a heart attack as I had experienced that before and knew the nature of chest pain. It was something else. I looked at the clock and saw that it was about 2:00 AM. Dora also woke up and seeing me sitting up, asked me what was going on. I replied "I have no idea. I just feel very bad." She told me to lie down, keep my eyes closed and try to sleep. I lay down again on the bed. After a while, my tired body started feeling sluggish.

Then came the fateful call. At about 5:00 AM the telephone rang. The phone ringing at this odd time was unnerving. It was my nephew Tarek. He was crying. I knew that my elderly mother-in-law was in a critical condition in Dhaka and thought something probably happened to her as we were anticipating getting bad news about her anytime. I asked him why he was crying. He said "My dad stopped breathing and they have taken him to the hospital. Please inform our relatives of this." I asked him, "Where is your mother?" He said that she went with them in the ambulance. I immediately called my brothers and sisters in the U.S. and Canada.

Later that morning I came to know the doctor was trying to revive him at the hospital. Then I heard the doctor's effort was futile, as he was not responding.

I hit the road in the early morning as soon as I could, for Cincinnati, still in a state of denial thinking he might be alive. When I reached his home, I saw a few people on the front porch.

One of them named Habib, a friend of my brother, approached me to say, "He is no longer alive." I felt like lightning had struck me. Dora and I rushed into the home. I started weeping and moaning at this terrible news and the personal loss of my dearest brother and best friend. Dora's nephews, Sajjad and Mehdi had to hold me up. Dora and I both cried profusely.

I saw my sister-in-law Tora sitting on the sofa in the family room with several women sitting around her. Her face was emotionless, hiding deep anguish inside. Tora is Dora's younger sister and I've known her since our days in our hometown in Bangladesh, during my teenage years when she was a little girl. I consider her my younger sister. In the absence of my beloved brother, she was the closest family I could have. I fell on my knees next to her with tears in my eyes, not knowing how I could overcome my own grief to comfort her. The event was so traumatic for her that she was at a loss, surely unable to process her future with two young sons, one an undergraduate college student and the other a minor with special needs who needed his father badly. Who would take care of him and protect him like his father? Tora, who was a homemaker, burst into tears and said, "What should I do now, where can I go now, who will take care of us?" I felt her feelings of despair, of being without an anchor, and helplessness. I just murmured "Don't worry, you will not be left alone, we will take care of you." I remembered the conversation I had with my brother after my recovery from the heart attack in 1992, when I told him "I thought I was going to die and at that moment I was concerned about Dora and my children; I wondered what would happen to them in my absence. But I knew and felt somehow reassured that you would take care of them." In reply, he said "Of course I would. But I also know if something happens to me, you will take care of my family." That conversation continued to ring in my ears.

All my brothers and sisters and their spouses in Canada and the U.S. immediately came to his home. Also, Tora's two sisters and their children from Dallas and Indianapolis came immediately. My brother's friends came to pay their last respects. The next few days were full of sadness and activities. As I said, he was very close to me, my best friend. He was a very unflappable and energetic man. I was deeply affected by the entire episode beginning with his sudden death, seeing his body lying so still in the funeral home, and then watching his body being lowered into the deep grave. He was buried in a large cemetery in Cincinnati, I was watching while they covered him with soil and dirt, this affected me deeply. It was hard to see his older son Tarek wailing at the grave site for his father, and his younger son Khaled, a small child, during the burial. At the funeral home when I saw his face, it looked as if he were sleeping peacefully, I could not leave him. I wondered if he could be brought back to life. It was so surreal.

When we were leaving the funeral home for my brother's burial, the family, and his friends were at the front lobby, Murad came to me and said, "Let's see him one last time." We walked back, passing through several dark hallways and creepy open spaces. After reaching the half dark room, Murad stood on one side of the narrow bed on which his body was placed, and I stood on the other side. We joined our hands over him, and Murad asked me to say a prayer for him, which I did. When we left the room, we had difficulty locating the lobby, and nobody was around. Fortunately, we heard some muffled voices of people and guided by those sounds, we reached the main lobby. We found many people had already left for the burial. At the cemetery, after everybody was leaving and at some distance from the grave site following the burial, Murad asked me, "Dad, can we go there once more?" The two of us went there and I offered a prayer once more. That was a bit of closure for my grieving heart.

After the funeral, we held a gathering of family and friends to mourn his death, talk about his life, and offer prayers for him. My siblings and I discussed who would take care of Tora and her children. Remembering my conversation with my departed brother, I volunteered to take responsibility. I knew it was a major responsibility, but I had to do it. After all my visiting relatives left, I began to sort things out for Tora. To get started on all matters related to a deceased person, I needed to get the death certificate first. Simultaneously, I invited an estate and financial planning expert to the house to deal with my brother's estate. I realized that many daunting tasks needed to be undertaken once someone died. Leaving Dora behind with Tora in the house, I left for Urbana-Champaign to take care of my teaching and administrative duties at UIUC.

I drove back to Cincinnati on Thursday, in the evening as I did not have any classes to teach on Fridays. I spent Friday visiting all the offices in Cincinnati, together with Tora to take care of a multitude of things. My brother left a few incomplete tasks related to his investment properties, so I consulted with his attorney. I also met people from General Electric to figure out my brother's retirement funds and other financial matters. Clearly, my brother was not expecting this would happen to him, and therefore, many issues were unsorted, still needing resolution.

When I was alone or in bed at night at my home in Savoy -- a suburb of Urbana-Champaign – memories and images of recent events would flash before my eyes and produce miserable thoughts. I had never witnessed the death of someone so near and dear, someone so routinely involved in my everyday life. I was in the U.S. when my parents and my oldest sister died in Bangladesh. I felt a void inside me and the futility of life. I felt death could snatch someone away without notice. Once a person dies it was as if a ship had sunk in a sea never to be seen again. It takes so much time to construct a building, yet minutes to demolish.

After the death of my parents, even though I was living far away, I had feelings of emptiness, but consoled myself at the thought of their full lives, living to their elderly years. Yet I still wondered why I hadn't told them how I felt about them. I hadn't told them how well they raised me in my childhood and adolescent years and how much I loved them. How could I overcome the grief of losing my brother, younger than me? I realized that dying was not just a nominal malfunction of our body. It was definitive, a feature predictable at birth, that would certainly happen in an unpredictable way. It took a while for me to get out of this mental state. Tora and I met a grief counselor in Cincinnati, assigned to us by my brother's employer, who explained the ideas of mortality and death, and gave Tora and me some tips for coping.

I had been going back and forth from Urbana-Champaign to Cincinnati, occasionally accompanied by Murad, to deal with the many issues facing Tora in the aftermath. I realized this travel was not sustainable. Also, I realized it would not be possible for Tora to deal with her affairs by herself. So, I decided, in consultation with her, to move her and her two sons to our home in Savoy. Fortunately, summer was approaching, and I had some free time during the summer vacation. I could stay in Cincinnati with occasional visits to Urbana-Champaign, while coordinating the move.

I started the task of sorting belongings in the home. While checking my brother's home office, I found quite a few things. One was a collection of Bengali poems that he had composed. I knew he would write poems, as he shared a few with me when I was in Dhaka. I found he had a poet's mind. I appreciated that because I would also write poems but later gave up while I was in Canada. I found that he had written quite extensively. I read some of these and liked them. I had no idea if he had any plans for the poems, but I felt strongly that I should have them published, otherwise, they would be lost forever. Later in 2003 when

I visited Bangladesh, I took it as a project and got his poems published in a book that I edited and entitled *Kabitamala* (Necklace of Poems). My brother, like me, was an avid reader, and had a large book collection. With the help of my daughter, Ifat, I catalogued all the books, arranged for their disposal and donated those on Mechanical Engineering to the University of Cincinnati. We put her home up for sale after clearing most of Cincinnati's official and unofficial requirements. In June, Tora and her children moved to our home in Savoy, and they settled in there.

While in Cincinnati, I noticed Khaled's restlessness and anguish after his father's death. He could sense that something had happened to his father and was missing him. Khaled was upset and agitated. My brother loved him dearly. He would routinely spend plenty of time playing with him after work. He would take his son to stores, to show him things and do whatever his young son wanted him to do. In Urbana-Champaign I started treating him like my son. He liked to call me *Abba* (Dad) for a while even though he was eight years old, he took me as his father. Gradually I taught him to call me *Chacha* (Uncle). Tora and my two nephews soon adjusted to the new environment. My nephews started going to school. I would frequently drive to Cincinnati, a four-hour drive, to visit my brother's grave along with the family. Meanwhile, Tora's home in Cincinnati was sold. Tora was still trying to overcome her grief, hard though it was. Nevertheless, things at home became somewhat more stable. The family stayed with us for a few years.

In the fall semester, I got back to teaching and my administrative duties at the university. Soon after, we were shaken by the tragedy that came to be known as 9/11. It was the late morning of September 11, and I had just finished teaching a graduate class.

Once I stepped out of the classroom into the hallway, a female student approached me and said, "Did you hear the big news? Terrorists attacked the World Trade Center in New York and the towers are now on fire!" I didn't digest this unexpected information quickly and asked her if she could repeat and elaborate. She said that she didn't know the full details. Ironically, I just finished teaching the subject of fire protection of buildings. I was struck with awe and wonder. My heart started beating faster. I rushed to my office to settle down. Once there, I picked up my phone to call Dora at home if she knew anything. But I found there were several voice mail messages from journalists, TV stations, and news media.

It was because of my association with CTBUH and my publications on tall buildings, that they contacted me. I called one of them back, who sounded very eager to talk with me. He told me that two planes hit the WTC towers and they had collapsed. He started asking me questions. I was disoriented from the news and told him that I had just come out of class and couldn't answer any questions without knowing more details. My heart started pounding and wondered who could have done this? Some Arab terrorist attacked a tower earlier in 1993 with a Ryder truck. But this was a much more extensive and sophisticated attack. I couldn't believe the Arabs were technologically savvy enough to plan and execute this. My initial thought was that this might be the deliberate attack by some other terrorist groups, which later I found out was not true.

Over my life, I had engaged in extensive self-study of both Western and Islamic histories. My interest in Western thought, in all its dimensions of literature, politics, science, and intellectual developments, was shaped by a love of learning. By virtue of living in the West and interacting with western people for three decades by then, I felt I could understand the Western mind. On the other hand, my upbringing in an East Indian and Islamic culture, and my living through some seminal world events, characterizing the East-West relationship, also allowed me to understand the Eastern mind. I recounted the West's past resentment against Muslim Arabs and Ottomans, for their perceived incursions into the heartland of Christendom in Europe. I recalled the historical events of the Crusades and the Spanish Inquisition, as well as the colonization of Muslim lands by Europeans. America's prevailing foreign policy in the Middle East, including the creation and continuing support of a new Jewish state in the Muslim heartland, all contributed to a sense of anti-Western feeling in Muslim lands, particularly in the Middle East.

While all these complex dynamics remained somewhat dormant during the Cold War, I thought the recent rise of religious fundamentalism and the West's fear of a resurgent Islam caused an enhanced bitterness. Also, the West was perceived as having military domination over Muslim lands and apathy towards them. Maybe after this attack, old wounds had been opened. I feared a clash of civilizations in which nobody would be a winner. But I also knew that no Muslim country could match America's military might. All these rambling thoughts crossing my mind made me very uncomfortable. I could foresee renewed misunderstanding and tension between the West and the Muslim world that might continue for a long time.

I went home and looked up the information about the collapse in some detail. Having first-hand professional experience, years dealing with structural design of very tall buildings, including editing and writing a book about tall buildings, I took great interest in understanding just how exactly these robust towers could so totally and easily fail simply because two planes, albeit loaded with jet fuel, crashed into them?

The telephones at my office and home were inundated with messages from journalists, TV reporters, radio hosts, and all types of news media. I had to prepare some answers as I was suddenly being recognized as an expert on tall buildings by the media. I very quickly analyzed the failure of these two urban giants, WTC 1 and 2, followed by WTC 7 and put together my preliminary thoughts. I came up with a technical explanation of how the towers might have failed although without detailed investigations my thoughts were presumptive. During this time, I was approached by many media outlets and I gave a large number of interviews.

The School of Architecture arranged a forum in a town hall format on October 18, with the title "Rebuilding a Way of Life in the Face of Disaster" in which I was a guest commentator on a three-person panel. The other two were Carol Ross Barney (architect of Oklahoma City Memorial) and Francis Halsband (Visiting Plym Professor at the School of Architecture and a New York architect.) It was reported on local Channel 3 Television News the same day and the local newspaper *The News-Gazette* on October 19 in an article ""Building Experts Say Skyscrapers Will Rise Again." In this forum and all other interviews, I reiterated that skyscrapers would continue to be built. They are a necessity to deal with land shortages in urban centers, accommodate the growing world population and the massive migration of people from rural areas to cities.

A few months later, at the Chicago book signing event on November 14 for my book *Art of the Skyscraper: The Genius of Fazlur Khan*, I was expecting questions about the book. But to my surprise, all the questions were about the WTC collapse, as the event was fresh on everybody's mind. Long after, I continued to be interviewed by phone and email. In my seminar at Champaign's University YMCA, I explained the collapse, how to build better, terror-proof tall building, and what the future held for tall building construction. I got calls from conspiracy theorists, who were also writing books and articles. I realized the raging controversy. There were those who doubted the FEMA and NIST Reports and the findings of the 9/11 Commission, appointed by the U.S. government.

A few respectable professionals and scholars declared that 9/11 had rung the death knell for the future of tall building construction. I was asked this question by some reporters and at some meetings. My answer was always that tall building is here to stay, and more buildings, even taller will be built in the future.

The most well-known proponent of the idea of the downfall of skyscrapers was Henry Petroski, a professor of Civil Engineering at Duke University and a prolific writer. In a letter entitled "Fall of the Skyscraper" published in the January-February issue of the esteemed *American Scientist* magazine, he made the case that the destruction of the WTC towers had effectively made it impossible for the skyscraper typology to be built in future.

I was struck with awe and surprise that someone with his reputation would so quickly rush to such mistaken judgment. I assume he had, to my knowledge, no background on tall buildings. I immediately sat down to write a rebuttal, vehemently opposing his contention as I strongly believed that his assertion was incorrect. I wrote a letter titled "The Future of the Skyscraper" and sent it to the magazine. The letter was published in its May-June 2002 issue.

I argued in the letter that tall buildings were not built as a whim but out of necessity, in areas of high population density. The undeniable truth is that when lands become scarce and expensive, it is necessary and logical to use the available vertical space. In the future, urban populations will grow alongside the global population increase. As more people move to cities from rural areas for employment opportunities and better facilities and amenities, more tall buildings will be the natural solution. I argued that occasional terror attacks, as horrific as they are, will not prevent future construction of tall buildings, as the market demands it. I gave other technical arguments in favor of tall buildings despite some of their drawbacks.

In layman's terms, I also argued that people did not stop driving cars because of the many accidents or stop flying planes after crashes or even hijacking. My professional position held and today, we see more supertall buildings have been built in the decade following 9/11 than in the decade before, at a higher rate and a one-kilometer tall, Jeddah Tower in Saudi Arabia, is under construction at this writing. The tall building phenomenon and the height race continue with full force.

In Kuala Lumpur, in October 2003, I presented a paper at an international conference on the topic of tall buildings, organized by CTBUH and CIB covering the topic in a comprehensive way. Although I had been to Malaysia before while living in Singapore, I visited Malaysia again this time in connection with my paper on the safety and security of tall buildings in the wake of 9/11. I was charmed to see the modern airport. Then I was impressed by the many tall buildings and parks, the most remarkable one being the Petronas Towers. These twin towers were the tallest buildings in the world for some time until Taipei 101 toppled the record. The architect, Cesar Pelli was an alumnus of the School of Architecture at UIUC where I taught. As a reputed alumnus he visited our school and I had a dinner meeting with him once in Champaign along with a few other senior faculty members.

As part of the conference program we visited a place called *Putrajaya*, a planned city and the administrative center of the federal government since 1999. Spearheaded by Prime Minister Mahathir Mohamad, the city was built to avoid congestion in the former location, although Kuala Lumpur remained the capital of the country. I remember the ride there from Kuala Lumpur. It was interesting for me to see how women wearing hijab in this Muslim country managed the check points. The new city was designed with as a mix of Middle Eastern, with European over-tones, and modern architecture, as well as Islamic arts.

We were given tours of the city and saw it still in development. We were taken to a large impressive mosque in red color, appro-priately called the Red Mosque. It was very beautiful and could accommodate 15,000 worshippers. It had a man-made lake next to it. The Malaysian Prime Minister's office was close to it too. I offered an optional prayer there.

The main part of our visit was a mammoth convention cen-ter where a meeting of the Organization of Islamic Conference (OIC) was once held. I remember I had a scary experience there. There was a huge raised platform like a spacious deck in the front of the building. I wanted to take a picture of the building's front facade. So, standing on the platform, I faced the building and started walking backward to capture a good image of the building and as much background as possible. As I continued to walk, I heard a loud voice saying, "Don't move." I turned my head and saw a man below cautioning me not to proceed any fur-ther as I was near the edge of the platform. I noticed there was no guard rail or high parapet around the platform to prevent a fall to great depth. I could have been either killed or severely injured. Living in North America for decades where safety regu-lations were very stringent, I could never imagine a huge deck at a great height, without a sufficiently high perimeter barrier. I felt the man who saved me was another godsend. I thanked God and the man abundantly.

Following 9/11, Muslims in the U.S. had been feeling uncom-fortable, but they also knew that this was a country of law, that had a great constitution that outlawed discriminating against people of different faiths, races, and ethnicities. People of all faiths could worship freely in their houses of worship here. They also knew that the majority of American people were decent fel-low human beings. Although new immigrants needed time to assimilate, subsequent generations eventually began to assimilate easily, going to schools and interacting with local people. This feeling of integration with the local communities gave them faith and loyalty to their adopted country.

In April 2003, I had an unexpected health problem. It was a hectic and stressful time for me at work. The pressures of teaching, administrative work, writing, as well as struggling to protect the structures program at the School from attrition and eventual demise, weakened me mentally and physically. At one point, I thought something was not right with me, I felt as if my body was shutting down under stress and I couldn't take any more. I told a doctor friend about this at a dinner party. He said, "This does not sound good." I thought of taking a short respite, but I faced too many deadlines and it was not in my nature to submit to overpowering stresses.

One Sunday, I developed a mild fever and was not feeling good. I was hoping it would go away with some rest and if necessary, over-the-counter medication. On Monday, I noticed I was having some difficulty in urinating. I thought the fever had perhaps dehydrated me, so, I drank plenty of water. But that caused me to go to the bathroom more frequently. I noticed it was becoming more difficult to urinate as the evening progressed. Around 10 PM I went to the bathroom with an urge to urinate but could not do it at all. My nephew Tarek and Dora accompanied me immediately to the Emergency at Carle Hospital.

I was treated for prostatitis, an infection of the prostate, which was now an additional health woe for me. I had to be under the care of a urologist. When I saw the urologist, Dr. Richard Wolf, his procedure showed that I had an enlarged prostate and my

PSA test result showed an abnormally high number. He wanted me to undergo a biopsy under sedation. A few days later the doctor called me and told "I got the biopsy result. You don't have cancer. That is the good news. But the bad news is they found some cells that have a chance to turn malignant in the future. Since I only took a dozen cells, I want to get more. Checking a few is like searching for needles in a haystack." I underwent the procedure a few weeks later under full anesthetic, so the doctor could collect more specimens.

I got a clean bill of health this time that relieved me of my anxiety. He suggested that the high PSA number was because the test was done immediately after the prostatic infection. Just like the cardiologist I started to see the urologist annually. A year later, my PSA test result showed a quite high value in the abnormal range. My urologist ordered another biopsy; the result came out well. I told him I did intense exercise in the gymnasium the day before my blood test. He told me that exercise, particularly biking or exercise in a sitting position could raise the PSA value and, in the future, I should avoid exercise for a couple of days before the PSA test.

The year 2003 was also a critical year for me as Professor Lynn S. Beedle, founder and long-time director of CTBUH died at the age of 85. After the death of Dr. Fazlur R. Khan, Dr. Beedle had become my mentor. I worked with him closely for many years. Through my continuous contact and work with him, I knew what a special person he was. The first thing that attracted me to this august personality was his modest and charming behavior. His attitudes, conversations, and manners as well as his hearty welcome and words of greeting told me that he was a perfect gentleman. Whenever I talked with him on the phone, I never found him patronizing, irritated or angry, he never cut me off or took my words the wrong way, and never rushed me through the conversation. He would treat me like a friend, although I was much younger than him, and he was a giant in the field of structural engineering. I found him flexible when we had a difference of opinion and he was respectful of my opinion and suggestions. All these and other faculties in him made me respect and admire him. He inspired me in more ways than one. I must admit I became a better person because of my association with him. His passing was a great blow to CTBUH, the tall building professionals around the world and a personal loss for me.

In my other academic efforts, assisted by my colleague Paul Armstrong, I voluntarily introduced a graduate seminar course titled "High-Rise and Habitat" that I mentioned previously. That course continued for many years until about four years after my retirement. We also offered a discovery course to undergraduates on the same topic. After I gave a keynote presentation at our school on Hurricane Katrina in August 2005, I became interested in natural disasters. Amongst others, I taught an undergraduate discovery course titled "Architectural Response to Natural Disasters" that covered wind, floods and earthquakes. In addition, I participated in the honors course "Reducing Earthquake Consequences" offered by the Civil Engineering Department.

One important aspect of architectural education is the design studio. Students at different levels carry out studio projects administered by the Design Division. The studio culture has been a vital component of architectural education. Students would be assigned a building project that they would design from start to finish. Throughout the semester, they would work very hard and their work would be critiqued by a group of professors and outside professionals, twice during a semester, at mid-semester (midterm review) and immediately before the final exam (final review). The course instructor would give the final grade after reviewing assessments by the review team members. Critiques were often severe and nerve wracking for students.

When I joined the School, the review team was called the Design Jury. This, however, carried a harsh connotation; students were on trial and the jury judging them. Later, the term "Design Jury" was replaced with "Design Review." I had been on review teams regularly and enjoyed the review sessions. They were mutually beneficial, good for learning other reviewers' viewpoints. I always felt this was a great practice as students knew how to prepare, organize, and present their work, and of course take criticisms. It also helped them develop good oral communication. This being an important skill in every profession, but especially in the architectural profession, when working with clients. These reviews broadened my horizons to include the artistic and aesthetic design considerations along with the function of buildings from an architect's perspective. This is good design training that many structural engineers miss in their academic settings. Based on the "High-Rise and Habitat" seminar course that we developed, Paul Armstrong, developed a "High-Rise and Habitat Studio" that continues to this day at this writing.

When I decided to relinquish my position of chairman of the Structures Division, to reduce work-related stress, I recommended Abbas to take that role to the interim director, Andrejasich Aminmansour. Abbas had just been promoted to associate professor and I thought he was up to the job. Shortly after this, in 2004, we hired a new director, Professor David Chasco. I was on the Director Search Committee with David Chasco, an alumnus of our School who had been the Head of the Department of Architecture at the Lawrence Technological University in Detroit. The new director appeared to be laid back, personable and a good listener. He had many policy ideas, one of which was to demolish the divisional structure, a position for which he had a few supporters from the Design Division.

Soon the new chairman of the Structures Division got into a disagreement with the new director on some curricular issue. This strained their relationship, continued for some time and got worse. David Chasco re-appointed me as the chairman of the Structures Division in 2007. I reluctantly accepted. I knew he was counting on my experience and I felt I would be able to retain the Structures Division through my efforts and good relationships.

Although I enjoyed teaching all along, returning to the position I once left, was giving me stress again. The main stress was over the new director's vision of centralization of the School administration, where the power and authority of the divisional chairmen was reduced. I was used to Director Alan Forrester's style. He delegated much of the authority in terms of curriculum, staffing, etc. to the divisional heads. At that time, all the divisions were autonomous, and Forrester would rarely tell the division chairmen what to do. This style engendered a sense of mutual respect and trust. Division chairmen were independent to consider what was best for the divisions. I enjoyed working with him.

The new director had vision for a more blended and seamless, shared interdivisional administration. This was a serious deviation from the long-standing tradition of the School. At the same time, as our role in the School was being diminished, my structures colleagues were thinking that I was not doing enough to prevent it. At my end, I was trying my best to protect our structures program in its full form.

I always cherished the idea of seeing the Pyramids in Egypt. As a child I read about the Seven Wonders of the World. I read about the history of the pyramids and why and how they were built. Although many theories have been proposed, so much mystery still lies in how they were built. I read *Chariots of the Gods;* a fascinating book authored in 1968 by Erich von Daniken. It hypothesizes that the technologies and religions of the past in several ancient civilizations were brought to earth by extraterrestrial beings from outer space who were welcome as gods. They were technologically advanced and helped build the structures and artefacts on earth including the pyramids. As a structural engineer the unique shape of the pyramids impressed me. When a vertical structure is subjected to gravity or lateral wind or earthquake loads the minimum stress occurs at the top and the maximum stress develops at the base demanding the minimum and maximum amount of material at the top and bottom, respectively. Thus, a pyramid is an optimum structural form.

My longtime fascination with the pyramids was finally satisfied, when I went to Cairo to present a paper at an international conference held during May 29-31, 2007. The paper was on low-cost housing for megacities in developing countries. As Cairo was an exotic destination and Dora shared my interest in seeing the pyramids, we went on this trip together. We were met by a driver and escort and taken to our hotel, in a beautiful setting next to the Nile River. On the way, our escort, who was an engineer with the housing department of Cairo explained the places and artifacts to us. He pointed to a mansion visible from the highway and said, "This is where our president Mubarak lives." When I asked him a question about the president, I noticed he avoided it and diverted the conversation. I realized this was not a democratic country where people could express their opinion freely. Even the driver could be a secret spy for the government.

After participating in the daily conference sessions, Dora and I visited a number of sites in Cairo by taxi in the afternoons. We visited the Egyptian Museum of Cairo in Tahrir Square, a treasure trove of frozen Egyptian history dating back to the Pharaonic days. The museum is the home of a huge collection of ancient Egyptian antiquities. We retained a paid commentator who we found at the entrance gate who gave us the tour inside the museum and explained the brief history of the artifacts, paintings, mummies, and much more. One early evening we took a cruise down the Nile River. The hotel manager was nice enough to arrange it but neglected to tell us that dinner was served on board. So, before going to the dock we had dinner at the hotel restaurant. After embarking on the large ferryboat, we joined other tourists, and found that an extravagant buffet dinner was being served, but we couldn't enjoy it as we were full. Soon after the boat started cruising, a belly dancer appeared and started dancing between the dinner tables entertaining the tourists. Once she stopped dancing, and as dinner was being served, we left as we were not hungry and moved to the upper level to view the coastline. It wasn't totally dark, so we could see the many buildings and other structures. We saw the famous Cairo Tower from a distance and some major bridges spanning over the Nile River. Even today I cherish the memory of the Nile cruise. As our boat was cruising, I watched the crimson red sun setting on the Nile and took in the wide-ranging view of the city segment. Standing in the dim twilight as night fell, the star-studded nocturnal sky lit up. Cairo is a crowded city, humming with sounds and noises of different kinds. The cruise provided us a degree of tranquility in this city of din and bustle, a city that never sleeps.

Our next visit was to the much-anticipated Pyramids of Giza on the outskirts of Cairo. It was a guided tour in which a female guide accompanied us with a male driver. After reaching the site I noticed a few pyramids of different sizes scattered over a large area. It was really a wow moment for me. I read so much about the pyramids since my childhood days and now I was right there. Our guide gave us a running commentary as we visited different spots in the area, with quite a few pyramids. When I saw the awe-inspiring pyramids, I was thinking about the motivation of the Pharaohs to build these colossal structures. I marveled at the well-defined geometric form more than 4,500 years ago, the large number of workers who built these and how these were built. It was mind-boggling to contemplate. Theories and speculation by Egyptologists abound, but nobody truly knows the answers, prehistory has no written record. The largest of the pyramids is the 456-ft.(139-m) tall Great Pyramid of Giza built by Pharaoh Khufu, which is one of the Seven Wonders of the Ancient World. Of course, I couldn't leave Egypt without taking a ride on the iconic, "ship of the desert." I took a ride around the complex on the lofty back of a local camel.

Next, we visited the Great Sphinx of Giza. It is a massive lime-stone sculpture representing a mythical creature with the body of a lion and the head of a man. The face is believed to be that of pharaoh Khafre. It is located within Khafre's Pyramid Complex. Although the timeline is controversial, it is believed to be built during the same era of the Old Kingdom when the Great Pyramid was built. The lion's body is intended to display the pharaoh's courage and power. I spent some time there and reflected on ancient times when emperors, kings and rulers as well as millions of visitors visited the site. The Sphinx suffered the ravages of time but was still there in its majestic posture. When Napoleon arrived in Egypt in the year 1798, it is reported that he found the Sphinx without its nose. Following this elating experience, we visited some relics of a few ancient temples in the area.

On our way back home, our guide took us to a large store for a stopover. It was part of the tour program, but the purpose was not revealed to us. After reaching there we were offered cold drinks and we gladly accepted. Soon we were taken to a place inside the store where they sold perfume and a very high-pressure salesman started a sale pitch. The pressure was so intense,

I bought some perfumes just to get out of there. I was annoyed with the guide but being in a foreign land didn't express my feelings. On another occasion, Dora and I were strolling along the bank of the Nile near our hotel in the late afternoon. A gentleman approached us and asked, "Are you from India?" I replied, "No, we are from Bangladesh, but we live in America." He started a very friendly conversation and told me that he had been to Bangladesh and went to Dhaka on business and liked the city and the friendly people there. He invited us to his "office" nearby, but I was in no mood as we wanted to walk on the bank of the river. But he requested us so passionately that we accompanied him to his office which was in fact a store. I made it clear that I wasn't interested, but he insisted. He said if we didn't, he would feel bad and he would like to just chat with us. To make the long story short, he was able to sell two perfumes, one for Dora and one for me. Once I stepped out, I realized I should avoid strangers in this city.

Cairo, known as the "City of Minarets," is a city of endless numbers of mosques. We visited a few famous one with a tour guide. The most well-known was the Muhammad Ali Mosque. The full name of the mosque is the Great Mosque of Muhammad Ali Pasha. It was designed by an architect from Istanbul, who emulated that city's famous Blue Mosque. It was built on the premises of Cairo's Saladin Citadel. The campus includes Saladin's Mosque built by Saladin Ayubi in the 12th century, and a few other mosques and museums. The Muhammad Ali Mosque's construction was completed in 1857. Muhammad Ali Pasha was buried in a tomb in the courtyard of the mosque the same year. The mosque was constructed with a central dome surrounded by four small semi-circular domes. Two tall graceful, rocket-shaped cylindrical minarets, of Ottoman style, are located on the western side of the mosque. The interior of the mosque is nicely elaborated with decorative attention-grabbing embellishments. The underside of the dome was fabulous and aesthetically elegant. We spent a lot of time visiting different segments of this magnificent mosque.

Adjacent to the Cairo Citadel we visited another historical mosque called Al Rifai Mosque. We also toured inside this mosque and visited the graves of King Farouk of Egypt and Reza Shah Pahlavi of Iran in the same area. We also saw the Amr Ibn Al-Aas Mosque from outside but didn't tour inside. The original mosque at this site was built after the Islamic General Amr Ibn al-Aas conquered the city in the 7th century and was rebuilt much later. It is historically significant as it was the first mosque of Egypt and Africa. Similarly, we saw from outside the Al Azhar University and Mosque Complex but could not fit a visit into our schedule.

Cairo, being an old city, is known for its many bazaars. However, our guide took us to the famous Khan Al-Khalili Market, a loud, busy, crowded, and exciting place with winding alleys and walkways. The market dates back to 14th century, although it was expanded in different phases later. At the entrance to the market our tour bus parked in a very busy place next to the tomb of some past rulers. The market had almost everything. There were several stores selling eye-catching, shiny trinkets for tourists. Because of limited time we didn't go deep into the market as the guide didn't accompany us and we didn't want to get lost in the labyrinth.

I must admit I had never been good with my sense of direction in an unknown place and occasionally got lost. Vendors had been constantly inviting us to visit their stores. I recall one young man who literally chased us passionately to sell us shoes. He called Dora "mom" and requested that she buy some shoes which she could not turn down. During our return we stopped at an open café to have some tea and relax. This trip was an interesting experience for us and while inside the market I felt transported to an ancient past.

I also wished to visit the City of the Dead, a large slum district. But due to time constraints, we could not go in too far. Our guide just drove around it, giving us a glimpse of the place. On some evenings we walked around our hotel and had dinner at a restaurant outside instead of the hotel, to experience the local food and street life. Cairo has a rapid transit metro system. I saw an underground metro station but was unable to take a ride on the metro. On the whole Cairo was an amazing city to visit.

While in Egypt visiting Alexandria is a must. Our hotel authorities arranged a day trip from Cairo to Alexandria, a historical city about 110 miles (176 kilometers) from Cairo by road. A driver and a guide were with us. It was an interesting trip for me as I was able to see a fairly decent stretch of rural Egypt. Alexandria is the second largest city and a major commercial center along the coast of the Mediterranean Sea. The history of this city dates back to 332 BCE when Alexander the Great founded an ancient town. It became an important center of Hellenistic Civilization. Subsequently, the Romans and finally the Muslims ruled the city. During the Hellenistic period it became known for the 330-ft. (101-m) tall Lighthouse of Alexandria, one of the Seven Wonders of the Ancient World, which no longer exists. I remember a long, major road along the coastline that offered a panoramic view of the ocean and the surrounding areas. Then our guide took us to a few historic sites, the memories of which I always cherish.

Our visit started with the King Farouk Palace, the summer home of the king who was considered the most controversial king of Egypt. The palace is spread over a vast expansive property located near the seashore. Our taxi driver drove through a beautiful garden, adorned with rows of roadside trees and numerous flowers. The landscape was simply fabulous. The scene was so serene that I still use that scene in visualization during my meditation to calm myself.

Soon we arrived near the shore. But just before that we saw the gated, unoccupied mansion that was once the King Farouk Palace. I got out of the car to have a glimpse of the palace from nearby. I found the architecture spellbinding and intriguing. The massing of the building, its color scheme, the arches, the varied roofline, the large number of windows and wall openings, exterior twin columns, and the intricate craftmanship throughout the building, was all spectacular. It is a combination of monumental and Islamic architecture with regal overtones. It seemed to stabilize the scenic setting with its grandiose presence and clearly made a royal statement and communicated majesty. There was a dock built nearby for people to enjoy the view. We went there and coincidentally met a young Bangladeshi couple with whom we started chatting. They were students at the Alexandria University and invited us for dinner in the evening. We politely declined as we would go back to Cairo the same day.

Our next stop was the Citadel of Qaitbay. It is a 15th century fortress situated on the Mediterranean Sea coast established by Mamluk Sultan Qa'it Bay. He was a great patron of art and architecture and ordered the construction of many spectacular buildings in the cities of the vast Mamluk Empire including Mecca, Medina, Jerusalem, Damascus, Aleppo, Cairo, Alexandria, and more. The Qaitbay Citadel is considered one of the most remarkable strongholds for defense along the Mediterranean Sea coast. The fortification was designed to withstand any naval attack against the Turks of the Ottoman Empire. The Citadel was renovated in the 19th and 20th centuries. Our guide gave us a tour outside and inside the fortress. The front entrance was very impressive. Upon entering the enormous structure, I noticed a spacious foyer which was open above. Soldiers would pour hot oil over intruders if ever the attacking army broke through the massive front gate. We visited the place where the soldiers would have their meals. At a higher level we saw a place where watchmen would keep an eye through a window overlooking the sea. I took a peek through the window and noticed that a very wide expanse of the sea was clearly visible from that vantage point. Sultan Qa'it Bay would occasionally visit the fort; a special location was earmarked for his stay, when he visited the fort. The fort was overwhelming to tour. During the tour as I often do in such cases I imagined the lives of soldiers and others, keeping a state of preparedness amidst their daily routine.

We visited the Catacombs, a major historical archeological site in Alexandria, considered one of the Seven Wonders of the Middle Ages. This ancient underground site consists of a series of tombs, statues and objects of Pharaonic funeral rites with Greek, Roman and Egyptian influences. After entering the Catacombs through the visitor's entrance, we were led by the guide, with running commentary, throughout the eerie place filled with statues and atypical things. The site was used as a burial chamber from the 2nd to 4th centuries. The catacombs were rediscovered in 1900 when a donkey accidentally fell into the access shaft, hidden under loose soil. A stone staircase descended to the second level an area jarringly alive with sculptures. We climbed down the circular staircase, which was often used to transport corpses. There are a few burial chambers, including some for royal horses. The catacombs were well designed and built by cutting into solid rock. As the surroundings of the place were very desolate, ghastly, and depressing, we decided not to go any further into the extended areas. Nevertheless, through our short visit I gained enough insight into this awe-inspiring place, dating back to antiquity.

Our other important visit was to The New Library of Alexandria. Near the entrance of the Library we found the statue of Alexander the Great. This national library was built in 2002. However, the initial concept of building this modern library dates back to 1974 when a few people from the Alexandria University decided to build it between the campus and the shoreline of the Mediterranean Sea. The idea was to revive the spirit of the ancient Great Library of Alexandria, which was one of the largest and most significant libraries of the ancient world. It flourished under the patronage of the Ptolemaic dynasty and acted as a foremost center of scholarship since its construction in the 3rd century BCE. The library was eventually destroyed in 270. Construction of the new library started in 1995 and completed in 2002 with funding from different sources.

I talked to the library staff to find out detailed information about the library as our guide just asked us to tour inside on our own. The library contains books in Arabic, English and French. Parts of the collection were donated by different countries. The library is huge and has 11 cascading levels. I noticed many of the bookshelves were empty waiting to receive more books. The library's architecture is very arresting. The main reading area stands below a large, greatly elevated roof made of glass panels tilted out toward the sea. The stone walls are of gray color carved with scripts of different languages. The library had a few museums and galleries for art. We took tours through these spaces. Some of these tours were guided by the courteous staff there. I was immensely enlightened by the numerous historical objects and exhibits from the past and felt delighted seeing the artwork. I could not make it to Luxor, known as the World's Open Space Museum because of a time conflict, but I regret not working into my schedule, as such opportunities don't come frequently.

In December of 2007, after I finished the semester final exams, I went on to perform Hajj, the pilgrimage to Mecca, together with Dora and my sister-in-law Tora and her son Tarek. Although Dora and I performed the optional Umrah in 1999, the Hajj or "Greater Pilgrimage" is obligatory for every able Muslim who can afford at least once in a lifetime. One of the richest aspects of Islamic religious contemplation and practice is that of Hajj, which epitomizes a Muslim's sense of identity as a distinct community of faith. The Muslim community has developed a strong sense of its literal and symbolic centrality through the international annual gathering in Mecca. Perhaps more than other basic religious traditions, Hajj highlights the notions of community and the equality of every individual before God. The gathering reflects the aspirations that many Muslims have for a humanity healed of ethnic tensions and divisiveness. It embodies a metaphor for return to the center. It is one of the five "pillars" of Islam. For the devout, it is an occasion when people suspend their worldliness and totally focus on God and His love and mercy and seek His forgiveness for past shortcomings and sins.

We went to the Hajj with a travel agency called Dar es Salam. We flew to Dulles International Airport near Washington D.C. from Indianapolis, and on to Medina. Upon arrival in Medina, we visited the Prophet's Mosque and prayed there. Our travel agent arranged a bus tour to holy sites. We had visited some of these sites before during umrah in 1999. After finishing our stay in Medina, we flew to Jeddah. We successfully completed all the steps and rituals of the Hajj. I noticed the large crowds everywhere and some new facilities and structures for crowd control. I performed some of the rituals in Mecca before in 1999, so it was not new to me.

The most significant time was my full day's stay at the Mount of Arafat. I spent the entire time in contemplation and prayer. The travel agent made it very convenient for us to fulfill all the requirements of the Hajj. We were also given sumptuous foods. The pressure of the crowd was too much for me and chances of infection were high. I got sick with mild fever and cold. We had a very nice and comfortable hotel near the Ka'ba. The hotel doctor came and treated me. I got back on my feet. After being spiritually recharged we returned to Urbana-Champaign before the New Year with the distinctive, life-long memories of the Hajj.

I had been reading and hearing about the progress being made in Dubai. It was fast developing into a full-blown modern city and an international commercial hub. I wanted to visit and was able to in March 2008. I went there to present a paper on sustainable tall buildings at the CTBUH 8th World Congress.

The Emirate of Dubai is one of the seven emirates of the United Arab Emirates. Dubai is the capital and principal city of the emirate. The emirate is located south of the Persian Gulf coast on the Arabian Peninsula. The City of Dubai provides an interesting story for architects and urban designers. In the early 1990s it was an unnoticeable small town, originally a fishing village. Today it's evolved into a major world city with many tall, innovative buildings, commercial and infrastructure developments. This emirate didn't have as much oil resources as some other areas of the Middle East. So, the visionary ruler of the emirate wanted to put the city on the world map by building spectacular skyscrapers to draw the international community's attention and announce to the world that Dubai was a key global city, an international financial hub.

This garnered more international recognition, and investment. It boasts of the Burj Khalifa, the tallest building of the world at this writing. To attract foreigners to it, Dubai seems to have slackened its strong cultural roots and opted for an immigrant-friendly cosmopolitan city. It has an open-door policy with financial enticements welcoming all cultures and people. Thus, the planning and design of the city reflect this new, globalist agenda, eschewing the image of its simple heritage. The city's glistening and relaxed nightly environment reminds one of Las Vegas.

For my flight to Dubai, Professor Paul Armstrong, my colleague, collaborator and co-author of some books and many research papers, accompanied me. After we landed at Dubai International Airport and entered the premises, I met and talked with Ken Yeang, a renowned architect known for his pioneering innovations in bioclimatic architecture. It is a type of architecture that connects the building to Nature. It considers climate and environmental conditions to help achieve maximum thermal comfort inside while avoiding total dependence on mechanical systems, which are included only as secondary support systems. He had sat on the CTBUH Committee 30: Architecture, that I had chaired, and he wrote a wonderful Foreword for the book *The Skyscraper and the City: Design, Technology and Innovation* which I co-authored.

During my stay in Dubai, I took a bus tour of the city arranged by CTBUH. A large number of skyscrapers were being built at the time as evidenced from numerous cranes soaring high in the sky. Among others, I saw the Burj Dubai (later renamed Burj Khalifa) under construction but it was not open for visits yet. So, we saw it from outside. It was poised to be a spectacular landmark in the middle of a growing complex of skyscrapers, quite a big jump from what was once a desert landscape. This megatall tower along with other tall and supertall buildings had dramatically changed the cityscape of Dubai.

On the bus a former student of mine sat next to me and we chatted along the way about the construction scenario in Dubai. She was actively involved in the construction of the Indigo Tower where we took a full tour. This was a 35-story, multiuse tall building with an iconic design accommodating offices and apartments. The construction was just completed but the building was still unoccupied. A representative of the contractor gave us the tour explaining the details of the construction. After the incredible growth that Dubai experienced on all fronts, the rumblings of a global economic recession were being felt beginning in 2006. Construction of some of the buildings was put on hold. The actual financial market collapse happened in September 2008 when Lehman Brothers declared bankruptcy.

One evening we were bused to the existing Burj Al Arab Tower, built in 1999. A 60-story luxury hotel building and the city's earliest and most recognizable landmark, located in Dubai's Jumeirah Beach strip. It is a unique forerunner of tall buildings in Dubai, Abu Dhabi, Saudi Arabia, and other neighboring areas. It drew world attention when it was built because of its iconic form and symbolic character inspired by the traditional shape of fishing boats. It was an early attempt to provide a representation of the future hoped for in Dubai. It stands offshore on an artificial island linked to the mainland by a curved bridge. The entire area along the shore and the tower itself were flamboyantly lit when we visited. Staying in this hotel is very expensive and it is known for excessive degree of affluence. It is considered a 7-star hotel. I had a chance to meet some of my domestic and overseas colleagues that I didn't get a chance to meet during the huge conference.

I hired a taxi to take me to some other interesting sites that were not covered by the bus tours. I saw a few spots but can't recollect the details. One place I remember is a large shopping mall. Several shopping malls in Dubai were built at different times. I don't recount which one this was, but it was a huge, bustling and fun place. I spent a good amount of time there and visited the many shopping zones and other ancillary facilities and venues. I noticed shoppers were of various ethnicities, ranging from Western tourists to locals; some women were in conservative Islamic garb while others were not.

During the closing of the congress I attended the official banquet. While I was eating my dinner and chatting with others in the table, Sabah Al-Rayes, a wealthy Kuwaiti businessman whom I knew well, approached me and told me that he was taking a few key people of CTBUH by helicopter to Kuwait. He invited me to join them. Because I hadn't planned for this and would lose a day while my classes were going on, I politely declined. I regret it now as such opportunities don't always come along. I could have adjusted my schedule for a day if I wanted. It was a missed opportunity to see a different country and city in the Middle East and enjoy Sabah's well-known hospitality while having a good time in the company of my CTBUH colleagues.

I got a Fulbright Award from the Fulbright Foundation to study the feasibility of constructing new tall buildings in Malta. In the summer of 2008, I traveled to Malta accompanied by Dora. At the Malta airport, a representative of the U.S. Embassy came to greet us. Also, Joseph Scalpello of Malta Environment and Planning Authority (MEPA), who was my contact person, came to welcome us and escort us to an apartment. Our third-floor apartment was in an old building in the old part of the city close to the seashore. The building had no elevator and above this floor there was a roof terrace overlooking the Mediterranean Sea. The stories were very high making the third floor at the same elevation of five floors by modern standard.

Mr. Scalpello and I carried the luggage to our apartment. The next morning, I developed a back strain. I had back problems in the past, but this time it returned with a fury. The back pain stayed with me throughout my stay in Malta and beyond for some time. Buying our groceries and carrying them upstairs became difficult. After I complained to MEPA, a few days later, we were transferred to a modern apartment with elevators in a really nice location next to the sea in another part of the city with shopping, restaurants, a park, and recreational facilities all around us.

When we were in Malta the local currency had just changed from the Lira to Euro. My professional visits took me to sites all over the island. There were beaches, hilly areas and many scenic places. The Maltese were very conservative in their way of life and proud of their heritage. Dora and I would often walk to the coast of the Mediterranean Sea near our apartment and sit on the boulders in the shore. It was very soothing to experience the panoramic view of the city and the sea at the same time and hear the sloshing sound of waves hitting the coast. We would also frequently go out to eat in the restaurants, savoring pizzas and sea food within walking distance of our apartment. I still cherish the pleasant memories whirling around in my mind.

While I was preparing to leave for Malta, I got an invitation from the Jordan Association of Engineers to present a keynote paper on tall buildings at the Fourth Architectural Conference on High-Rise Buildings in Amman, to be held June 9th -11th. I accepted the invitation before I left for Malta. I chose the topic of the integration of cities and tall buildings to create a better urban life. During my hectic work schedule in Malta as I was trying to wrap up my work and prepare a detailed report, I took time out for only two days to visit Amman with Dora. Once we reached there, an engineer received us at the airport. We were placed in a luxury hotel. I heard that a terrorist attack took place at a wedding reception in this hotel not too long ago. I remember there was another old hotel across the street that had unique and distinguishable architecture. It was a sharp contrast to the surrounding built environment.

After I gave my keynote speech at the beginning of the conference, I met a number of local and international delegates. The speech was held in a large auditorium and the city mayor also attended. The next day Dora and I took a comprehensive tour, arranged by the organizers. Along with its interesting sites, first and foremost I wanted to see the city as a consultant for tall buildings. I wanted to tour the major construction sites so I could provide analysis and meaningful recommendations to the City of Amman about how to proceed with tall building construction.

The city had about four million residents and also accommodated many Palestinian refugees. I sensed that -- and this was my personal observation -- there was a geopolitical and regional interest in what was going on in Dubai, Abu Dhabi, and Saudi Arabia and the anticipation that building a landmark skyscraper might be beneficial for Amman. When I had been intensely deliberating the case for Malta, I noticed that it was a very conservative society and the people didn't want to change their way of life by building "intrusive" tall buildings. But I also found that they didn't have a population density problem and their financial resources were limited. I couldn't fully justify the construction of tall buildings without proper master planning and other socio-economic and environmental considerations. In Amman, I noted some similarities and therefore I wanted to see firsthand what was going on in this city.

During the day tour I visited the downtown area, bustling with shoppers and outdoor cafeterias. The sidewalks were crowded. The driver took us to various places including large mosques and hotel buildings. Amman is an ancient city where inhabitants had been living for 7,000 years. It was built on seven hills, still a feature of the terrain. There were hardly any tall buildings over 20 stories, and these were mostly hotels. At one location two tall buildings were being built that were still close to foundation level but above ground; I went around the construction site to see what the local construction practice was. I also visited some nice and affluent residential areas in the suburbs, with single-family homes. Among others, I saw from the car, the royal palace of King Abdullah on top of a hill. Also, I saw a very large number of densely built homes on the hills where many of the Palestinian refugees lived. I noticed that large areas of land were available on the outskirts for new developments.

At night the conference organizers hosted a sumptuous banquet. Next day, there was a special meeting attended by local architects, engineers, urban planners, building officials and other stakeholders in a large hall of the Engineers' Club. I realized that the engineers in Jordan dominated the building industry. I delivered a short speech explaining the problems of urban growth and when tall buildings were needed. There was a panel discussion following. I answered several questions but my responses could be summarized as: Jordan did not have enough wealth to build spectacular tall buildings; Amman was an ancient historical city and its heritage and historical character would be disturbed by introducing tall buildings; if tall buildings were to be built they should be built on the outskirts, by developing those areas; tall buildings demanded a well-functioning infrastructure which Amman lacked at that time; and the problem of population density justifying tall buildings didn't exist.

I suggested, as I did for Malta, that a good master plan should be drawn. After hearing from comments one engineer in the audience remarked that the way I described Amman's urban issues showed as if I lived there. The next day in the morning they wanted my written recommendations. As I was ready to depart, I prepared a brief handwritten report giving my recommendations.

Because my mind was focused on my work in Malta, I didn't pay much attention to sightseeing during my brief Amman visit and hurried my return. I needed time to put together my findings and prepare a detailed report with my recommendations before I was scheduled to leave. Clearly, I didn't plan my schedule well and as a result I could not go to see the many archeological sites in Amman. I particularly wanted to pay visits to the ancient city Petra and the Dead Sea. Like the missed chances in

Egypt and Dubai, I missed another opportunity here in Amman. Upon my return to Malta, I started working on the report of my findings. Towards the end of our stay in Malta, our daughter Ifat joined us her company making our stay more enjoyable.

We planned a trip from Malta to Sicily, Italy. Ifat organized the booking for our trip. We boarded a large catamaran (ferry ship) moored at the Malta Harbor bound for Sicily and set sail across the Mediterranean Sea. The weather was good, facilitating literally, smooth sailing. It was a new experience for me as I never cruised across a sea before. The catamaran was full. Once we reached the shore of Sicily, I saw a bus waiting for us. The bus took us on a long ride through some towns. The island's landscape was extremely picturesque. The driver explained the history of Sicily and the places we were passing through in a running commentary. While passing by some agricultural fields he explained that the Arabs, when they ruled Sicily, taught the locals about innovative irrigation methods and introduced other techniques and means to boost agriculture in Sicily.

While the bus was passing through some rural areas, the driver stopped at a place with a few tourists and a small hill. People were climbing the hill to its peak to view a fertile valley at a distance. I was curious and started climbing when both Dora and Ifat told me not to do it particularly as I had back pain. My curiosity compelled me to try anyway. I was accompanied by Ifat. While near the top I lost my balance on the slope. I reflexively caught on to Ifat's clothing but started pulling her backward with me. A lady, another, godsend, saw the scene and came to my rescue from behind. Thank God, that saved me from being severely injured and needing immediate medical care in this unknown remote place. The lady disappeared in the crowd before I could thank her. I reminded myself of the adage: Be careful when you travel. We saw a small street-side market near the foot of the hill where vendors were selling famous Sicilian honey. I sampled some, liked it, and bought a couple of small bottles that I later enjoyed at home. The honey was different than any other I had tasted before, but it was enjoyable.

A visit to Sicily is incomplete unless one visits Mount Etna and another historic tourist town called Taormina (also known as Tower Mina). A main attraction of the trip was our stop at the famous Mount Etna, an active volcano on the east coast of Sicily between the cities of Messina and Catania. It is the highest peak in Italy standing at 10,900 feet (3,322 meters). On the bus on the way to the mount we saw black ashes on both sides of the steep uphill road. The bus took us to a gently sloped area at a high elevation. We stopped at the only restaurant, had our lunch and rested. The building complex atop the surrounding panorama contained a nice restaurant and a gift and souvenir shop. Later, I walked around to get a feel for the place. While walking I grabbed a piece of burnt rock to take home as a memento.

After returning from Mount Etna we headed for Taormina. The town was first established by the Greeks, and subsequently conquered by Romans, Arabs, and Normans, who all left remarkable art and architecture permanently stamped on the town's face. Alighted on a serene, rock-strewn promontory, elevated above the sea, Taormina has been the most popular tourist destination in Sicily for some centuries. Many famous people including royals, poets, authors, politicians and celebrities had visited and stayed. A few gardens with flowers added to the relaxed and soothing setting. After reaching Taormina the driver gave us a couple of hours to stroll. We were hungry, so we found a restaurant, washed ourselves, then ordered pizzas. I still remember the taste of the pizza, it was delicious. After lunch the three of us started a walking tour.

We saw buildings impressively restored from mediaeval times and awe-inspiring sights around every corner. There was a network of winding streets on every slope, scattered with shops, bars and restaurants. The place makes for a perfect tourist destination and vacation spot. We visited the ruins of a mammoth Greek Theater built about 2,500 years ago, and later rebuilt by the Romans. It was an awe-inspiring site and I stood there and wondered how the builders conceived of and build such a grand theater two and a half millennia ago. Because of the limited time of only two hours we could not see many other historical sites in the town. When we returned to our gathering place at the appointed time, I walked to the edge of the elevation and watched the blue sea below, surging at a great depth beside the rugged terrain and the lush green trees. It was an unforgettable dramatic view that I still vividly remember. No wonder Taormina is aptly called the "Pearl of the Mediterranean Sea."

After completing my Fulbright mission in Malta, I left the island state with lasting memories and flew to Rome. At the Rome airport, we had problems with our luggage as they were sent to a different building nearby. After some hassles, we were finally able to get our luggage and then we headed for our hotel in the downtown area. The hotel was an old building with a primitive elevator. After resting overnight, we set out to see the city. Ifat is an urban planner and is inherently very good with site locations and directions. She was an excellent guide for us in this ancient city.

First, we went to the area called the Roman Forum, or just Forum, also called *Forum Romanum*. It sits at the center and is surrounded by the ruins of several ancient government buildings. This space was originally a marketplace, and was known then as the *Forum Magnum*, or simply the Forum. We walked through the narrow streets and alleys and saw the ruins of many ancient buildings. I noticed in the structures the mark of the ancient Romans, who were known as great builders.

We visited the Colosseum to the east of the Forum, or what is left of it. It is the one of the most remarkable and most visited, ancient monuments. Meticulously designed, the amphi-theater could hold an average of 65,000 spectators. It was built between the years 70 and 80. Many events would be held in it, notably ferocious gladiator fights and mock battles to entertain audiences in the Republic of Rome and throughout the Roman Empire. Events involving wild animals and condemned criminals took place here. I never liked the brutal nature of gladiator fight-ing, even in the movies. When I saw the site, I thought of how many miserable men had been there risking their own lives for entertaining the audience. It reminded me of the disturbing vio-lent side of human beings.

Another important historic site was the Pantheon which is a former temple. The building is circular with a front porch of large granite Corinthian columns. It is one of the best-preserved of all ancient buildings of Rome. This is due in large part to the fact that it has been in continuous use throughout its history. Since the 7th century the Pantheon has been used as a church. The square in front of the Pantheon is called Piazza Della Rotonda. A rect-angular vestibule links the porch to the rotunda, which is below a coffered dome, with a round opening to the sky. We stayed for some time at the Rotunda to relax and viewed the Pantheon from outside to relish the enchanting and lively surroundings crowded with tourists and visitors.

We visited a few other fascinating places. But I really wanted to visit the house and museum of British romantic poet John Keats near the Spanish Steps, as I had a deep fondness for his poems. Keats was one of the three romantic poets of his era, the other two being P.B. Shelley and Lord Byron. All three died at young ages, of which Keats died the earliest at the young age of 25 of tuberculosis, a deadly disease of the time for which only primitive and speculative treatment was available. Sadly, Keats languished in this house for some time before his death. The "Spanish Steps" is a monumental, steep stairway of 135 steps with a church at the top. We went there and sat on the steps. I decided not to climb the lofty stair and overexert myself as I already visited a few other sites that day and was mindful of my back.

Leaving Dora and Ifat at the steps, I entered the house and museum of Keats. To the best of my recollection the house was on the second floor, and I climbed the stairs where I met a receptionist near the entrance. I asked her if I could tour inside and see the place. I was particularly interested in seeing the place where Keats took his last breath. She told me I could. I went in and saw and read a few things but then noticed that it was not easy for me to go further. I came back and asked her if she could accompany and guide me inside the building as the place was dark and ghastly. I must admit I was not brave enough to do it alone as I was getting an eerie feeling in the dimly lit place. It seemed to be haunted, particularly when I thought about the unhappy and grueling way that Keats died almost two centuries ago. Even if I developed enough courage, it was hard for me to navigate in the dark. The woman politely declined by saying that she was the only staff member there dealing with incoming visitors and could not leave the front desk. That made sense, and I took some comfort in knowing that at least I was there, so I wasn't disheartened that I didn't see the actual spot of Keats' last breath. I returned to the Spanish Steps to join Dora and Ifat.

Another climax of my visit to Rome was the Vatican City, a large sovereign enclave in Rome with the status of a country with the Pope as the head. We took a guided tour of this vast and crowded complex. Our guide led us through this complex, we heard her pleasant voice and Italian accent narrating the surroundings, through the tour headphones provided. We saw a few things here and there but the most memorable tour there was the Sistine Chapel.

The Sistine Chapel ceiling, painted by Michelangelo between 1508 and 1512, is a seminary work of High Renaissance art. It is the large papal chapel built within the Vatican and is the venue for papal conclaves and many other important services. It was a long walk in the Chapel, but I enjoyed it as the surrounding space was so graceful. The ceiling's various painted elements form part of a larger scheme of decoration within the Chapel, which includes the *The Last Judgment,* a fresco painted on the sanctuary wall, also by Michelangelo, wall paintings by several leading painters of the late 15th century, and a set of large tapestries by Raphael, another famous Renaissance painter. Central to the ceiling decoration are nine biblical scenes of which *The Creation of Adam* is the best known. The complex design includes several arrays of individual figures, both clothed and bare, which allowed Michelangelo to fully reveal his skill in creating a great diversity of forms and postures for the human figure. This set the standard for future generation of artists to emulate. Our guide told us that Michelangelo would paint on the ceiling using a platform on scaffolds at a rather advanced age for that time. I paused and tried to imagine how this great artist lay with his back on the scaffold to draw extensive artwork on the ceiling – a rather daunting and exceptional task.

We also visited the graves of a few popes in one area. While touring inside I had been taking pictures at places where photography was allowed. At one point, after visiting a spot the commentator left with the group, leaving me behind in a crowded place, as I was busy taking a few additional shots. When I finished, I could not find my group. I had no cell phone with me as I was in the country for a short time; I realized it would have been helpful. It was a crowded place with other tour groups walking around. I got worried and didn't know how to reconnect with my group, find my wife and daughter in this busy and jam-packed place. I rushed to around but still couldn't find anyone. I never told my wife and daughter -- which I should have -- where we should meet if we were separated. I frantically searched all around knowing they were not too far from me and I should not stray too far-off lest we got further separated.

Suddenly, I heard a faint voice in my earpiece, of a woman whose voice sounded like our guide's. I immediately moved in different directions to locate the origin by gauging the volume of the sound. I was able to find it and suddenly found my daughter moving with the group. I felt relieved and joined them. Soon after we came out of the building to the large square and experienced the delightful fresh air and sunshine. Our guide told us that the pope came to the balcony on the upper floor above the main entrance daily at a certain time to greet visitors from there. We didn't see him during our visit.

In my earlier years, I read about the life and profound sayings of Socrates, Plato and partly read his classic book *Republic,* and a book on Aristotle and his multi-faceted works. He was a philosopher, thinker and scientist. These three great men and thought masters, represent the triad of the earliest Western philosophical tradition. I developed a deep respect for all three, but the deepest is reserved for Socrates, for his wisdom, moral philosophy, ethical conduct, and courage. I was thrilled to read Plato's widely read dialogue the *Republic,* in which the main character is Socrates, with brilliant thoughts about justice and politics, and about Aristotle for his pioneering notions in multiple fields, particularly in logical and scientific thoughts. Aristotle had great influence on subsequent Islamic philosophers and scientists who considered him "The First Teacher." Socrates was known as a street-corner philosopher in Athens. His student Plato established the Plato's Academy in Athens where he wrote the *Republic* and his student Aristotle studied under him for 20 years. So, l always cherished the idea of a visit to Athens whenever I could.

On September 23, 2008 I went to Skiathos, a Greek island to present a paper on the role of tall buildings in sustainable cities in a conference on urban regeneration. I grabbed this opportunity to combine my trip to Skiathos with a visit to the historical city of Athens. First, I flew to Skiathos airport, a small airport via Athens. This beautiful island in the Aegean Sea was a setting for the Hollywood movie Mamma Mia. I stayed at hotel on a hill next to the sea, which was the conference site. From the hotel, I could see the picturesque scene of the sea, the beach and the adjoining hilly, green landscape. It was so soothing just to see it from a distance! One day I climbed down the steps built alongside the hill to the beach. On my way back to the hotel, I realized I had to climb as many steps uphill or walk uphill along a steep and winding road. I opted for walking uphill along the winding road, and when I reached the top my heart was pounding fast, and my knees started aching. I got concerned about my heart for the first time since my heart attack. I rested to calm my heart and headed for the hotel.

Following the conference, I flew to Athens. I already bought a ticket for a group tour. The bus took us to a few interesting sites. The high point of the tour was the Acropolis, the word generally means a citadel usually built on a hilltop. It is an ancient fortified rocky mount located above the City of Athens and contains the remnants of many ancient structures with great architectural and historic importance. These include the Parthenon, which is the most famous and a great tourist attraction. Although the term acropolis is generic and there are many other acropolises in the country the significance of the Acropolis of Athens is such that it is simply referred to as The Acropolis.

Arriving at the site, crowded with tourists, I looked around and got a bit worried as it was a major climb using steep stairs to see the Parthenon. I paused and considered if I should go up considering my heart health. If I had a heart attack here, nobody knew me, and I was by myself. Moreover, this was a foreign country. However, I read and heard so much about this famous historic temple of Athena. I saw other tourists going up and felt if I didn't, my trip to Athens would remain incomplete. I remembered climbing the hill walking on a steep road to the hotel in Skiathos without any problem. I gained the confidence I needed and climbed the steps slowly, taking occasional breaks and finally reached the peak. I walked around the site and saw the statue of the Greek goddess Athena, for whom the city Athens was named. The large tall columns along the perimeter of the temple gave it a majestic expression, inspiring awe and wonder. I thought of the wonderful designers, engineers, builders and the craftsmen who built this signature historic structure so far back in human history. Even now I am 'wowed' by the feeling. I also looked at the ruins of some other temples at the site. I looked down to the city from there and had a panoramic bird's eye view of the cityscape. It was an exhilarating experience for me.

From there we were taken to the ancient Agora of Classical Athens near the Acropolis. Agora is a Greek word meaning a gathering place. The driver slowed, and the commentator pointed to a site where Socrates spent much of his time and spoke to young people about his philosophy, asking them to gain knowledge, stand for truth and justice and against tyranny and corruption in the society. People became so enamored of him that ultimately his popularity irked the rulers, who ordered his execution on the charge of corrupting the youth. We were not given the time to disembark from the bus and walk around. This was not the tourist package I was expecting, what a pity! As Plato's Academy was outside the city the bus didn't take us there either. Aristotle studied under Plato but taught at his own school in a different location. We didn't see the site of that school either. Inexplicably, based on my short visit and quick observations these sites didn't seem to be that important to locals nor the tourist department of the government. I asked myself: I wonder how many people are interested like me in seeing these spots after all? I don't know the answer.

The other important element of my visit was the Olympic Stadium. The Panathenaic Stadium is a multi-purpose stadium in Athens. A main historic attraction, it is the only stadium in the world built entirely from marble. A stadium was built on the site of a simple racecourse in around 330 BCE. It was subsequently rebuilt in marble. By the year 144, it had a capacity of 50,000 seats. In the 4th century, however, it stood mostly abandoned. The stadium was excavated in 1869 and rebuilt and it hosted the Zappas Olympics in 1870 and 1875. After being renovated, it hosted the opening and closing ceremonies of the first modern Olympic Games in 1896. It was used for various other purposes in the 20th century and was once again used as an Olympic venue in 2004. We were given some time to spend there. I reflected on the stadium's history, marveling at how much was etched there. Now, the Olympic Games are an international event that owes its roots to Athens. After my stay of a few days in Skiathos and Athens I returned to Urbana-Champaign on September 29 with all sorts of pleasant memories.

CHAPTER 13

URBANA-CHAMPAIGN

Bittersweet Days; Goodbye to Urbana-Champaign

Classes at UIUC started in fall. I found that efforts in the School to eliminate the divisional structure to exist as an independent or autonomous entity were in full swing. My struggle to preserve it in its original form increased, aggravating my stress level, but my efforts were succeeding. The NAAB team was scheduled to visit the School in the winter semester of 2009. But the preparatory work started in 2008. Being a member of the NAAB Committee, I got busy with the related activities and meetings.

In March 2009, something happened with my health. I noticed that when I walked to my office from the parking lot, I felt some discomfort in my chest. Since I had been doing fine with my heart since my heart attack in 1992, I ruled out the possibility of any new heart issue as the medical check-up the previous year revealed normal heart function. I assumed that this was probably some temporary thing when the weather changed from winter to spring. Usually I got allergies or cold symptoms around this time of the year. Dora had been suffering from some health problem at the time as well. I called the scheduling office of Carle Hospital to set up an appointment for her with her doctor. While I was talking with the nurse on the phone, by the by I mentioned that I was feeling some discomfort in my chest when I walked a long distance. She looked up my medical records and suggested that I should see my physician Dr. Connor as I had a history of heart disease. With my consent, she set up an appointment.

Sitting with my long-time doctor, I asked him if it could be seasonal allergies. He replied, without mincing words, "If it's allergies, you'll survive but if it's a heart problem, you could be dead any minute. I wouldn't wait". Instead of delegating to a nurse, he picked up the phone himself, right then and there, to make an immediate appointment for me with the cardiologist.

Accordingly, I saw the cardiologist the next day on March 20. I had an angiogram done where they found a few blockages in a cardiac vessel and placed four stents. I thanked God that I was lucky enough not to have a heart attack during my many recent travels. I had been climbing, walking, touring and traveling via every mode of transport and between foreign countries, many for the first time. All the while not knowing I had blockages in my arteries. Instead of coming home with many fond memories, my story could have ended very differently, I was grateful to be back home in the U.S. where my treatment was fast and in good hands.

The NAAB Team was visiting our School right at that time. Before I fully recovered, I decided to participate in the visit on the day when all the divisional areas were presented. Since I was on the School's NAAB Committee and organized the exhibit materials for the Structures Division, I was confident that my presentation would be thorough, accurate and relevant. It wasn't stressful to prepare. Although as requested, my presentation was during the morning session, as I answered questions from the visiting team, I felt weak and occasionally leaned against the wall behind me. In the afternoon, the visiting team met the entire faculty group. I didn't want to miss this important meeting. It was a large meeting, so I needn't talk much, rather listen and observe. So, I decided to go.

The team leader wanted to know about the historical changes in the School's curriculum and the direction it is going. There was radio silence. I was surprised since there were a few senior faculty members there who could have responded. Someone had to break the silence. So, I addressed the faculty members asking any one of them to share a reply. Immediately, the team leader pointed toward me and requested that I do it. This was a challenge, I wasn't expecting to be the one to field these questions, nor was I feeling up to the task of giving an impromptu, articulate answer. I thought better of it, but I was on the spot.

So, I gave a rundown of the School's activities and transformation in terms of curriculum and other challenges which we successfully mitigated. I emphasized the digitization of teaching methods and the rapid use of educational technology in architectural education. Students no longer drew on drawing papers but used the computer for their studio projects. Professors used PowerPoint presentations, rather than chalkboards and transparencies with overhead projectors. I also talked about the changes in curriculum content to keep pace with the evolving building profession to meet the demands of the marketplace. I stopped when I felt I was losing energy and getting tired. Thankfully, this overview set the direction of the discussion and opened further exchange in the meeting. The NAAB report was positive. By fall, I recovered and felt invigorated and ready for the new semester.

In July 2009 me and Dora got an amazing opportunity to travel to six cities in Turkey. A Turkish cultural student organization in Champaign arranged the trip for a few Americans. The students took care of our logistics and hosted the trip in all six cities of

Turkey. The only cost we had to bear was for flights. These cities are Istanbul, Izmir, Bursa, Konya, Cappadocia, and Ankara. On our own we wouldn't have been able to travel so extensively inside the country. Our daughter Ifat joined us as well.

Out of my many travels, I cherish this one for the extensive tours. I got the consent of my cardiologist before I decided to travel. I was also concerned about Dora who had been suffering from kidney disease and not in good health. But she was very eager to go and encouraged, actually insisted, on it despite her health condition. The three of us flew from Chicago to Istanbul by Turkish Airlines. After reaching Istanbul we were escorted to the hotel by a Turkish student where we met the others in our group. I must say we had so many experiences, I can't remember all the places and events, but I enjoyed every moment of it.

Rising again after the fall of the Ottoman Empire, I found Turkey to be a great progressive country with cultured people. Istanbul is a historic city with many tourist attractions. We stayed at a hotel near the famous Hagia Sophia and the Blue Mosque. In fact, they were at walking distance. The Hagia Sophia was built in 537 and served as Eastern Orthodox Cathedral. In 1453 Ottoman ruler Mehmed the Conqueror converted it into a mosque and it remained so until 1931 when it was secularized and converted into a public museum. Its architecture is spectacular and changed the course of architectural history. The building exhibits multiple architectural elements. Spires and rounded arches, which are common features of Byzantine buildings, are used throughout. The spacious nave of this monumental structure is covered by a huge central dome supported by massive columns placed on the four sides of a square. The style is a blend of Ottoman and Byzantine effects under the huge dome. There are two half domes on the east and west ends of the structure. The roof is supported by two rounded arches situated at the south and north exteriors. The Hagia Sophia is a great tourist attraction.

We spent plenty of time exploring inside and around this magnificent historical monument.

Near the Hagia Sophia is the famous Blue Mosque, which is considered the last Great Mosque of antiquity. It was built on the orders of Sultan Ahmet I and is also known as Sultan Ahmet Mosque, although popularly it is known as the Blue Mosque. It has five main domes, eight secondary domes and six minarets. Its architecture is a combination of Byzantine, as seen in the Hagia Sophia and traditional Islamic architecture. The interior employs iconic Turkish ceramic tiles at the lower level and at the piers in various decorative design. There are many intricate stained-glass windows allowing in natural daylight. The upper levels of the interior are awash in classic blue paint.

The large prayer area under the main domes was awe-inspiring. Our group visited the mosque once. It was an exhilarating experience for us to feel the place. Subsequently, I went there for a prayer at one of the scheduled prayer times. I also wanted to visit the Suleymaniye Mosque, another great mosque in Istanbul but it was being renovated at the time and closed to the public. There are also many Ottoman era palaces in Istanbul. We were able to visit two of the most popular tourist attractions, the Topkapi Palace and the Dolmabahce Palace.

Construction of the Topkapi Palace was ordered by Mehmed the Conqueror in 1459 after his conquest of Constantinople in 1453. In 1924 a government decree was issued converting the palace to a museum. It's located where the Bosporus Strait and Marmara Sea meet. It functioned as the main residence and administrative headquarters of the Ottoman sultans. We toured this interesting palace and learned about its many important components with a guide. It went through several modifications and expansions following a 1509 earthquake but keeping the basic layout intact. In 1574 following a great fire that destroyed parts of the palace, Mimar Sinan, the most well-known Ottoman architect and civil engineer was retained by Sultan Selim II to rebuild the damaged areas, and also the Privy Chamber, Harem, baths and shoreline pavilions. There are a few gates to the palace and The Palace complex has a few courtyards. The Imperial Gate is the main entry to the First Courtyard. The palace complex is so huge that we could not cover it in its entirety in one visit. It was a great experience for me to be there, and the palace spoke volumes about the greatness of the Ottoman rule.

Dolmabahce Palace is the largest palace of the Ottoman sultans. At the time, the Topkapi Palace from the medieval period, became old and was lacking contemporary style, luxury and comfort. So, Sultan Abdulmecid I built the Dolmabahce in1856 next to the Bosporus. It was a blend of European and Ottoman architectural styles. The opulent palace was built at an enormous cost and crippled the country's finances. Our guide took us through the various rooms, hallways, foyers and large open spaces. The palace was residence to six Sultans till the fall of the Caliphate in 1924. Kemal Ataturk, the first President of the new Republic of Turkey, used the palace as a presidential residence during summers. He died on November 10, 1938. We visited the well-preserved bedroom that he used during his last days and saw the bed where he breathed his last.

The world-famous Grand Bazaar is an important historic market of Istanbul. It is one of the largest and oldest covered markets in the world with 61 covered streets and more than 4,000 shops. It draws from 250,000 to 400,000 visitors daily. It is also considered one of the earliest "shopping malls" of the world. Construction of the market's core started in 1455, soon after the Ottoman conquest of Constantinople and was a part of larger initiative to quicken economic growth and bring prosperity to the city. We visited the market by tram accompanied by a student guide. Once inside the market, vast space opened up. We went to a few shops and at one point as I focused on something too long,

I got separated from my family and the guide in the huge crowd. I started looking around, but they were nowhere to be found. I decided to go back to the place where I last saw them, hoping they would come back and find me. I went back and found them waiting for me there already.

After completing our stay in Istanbul, we headed for Izmir, the third largest metropolitan city of Turkey after Istanbul and Ankara. Izmir is an important port city, located at the western extremity of Anatolia on the coast of the Aegean Sea. It boasts almost 4,000 years of recorded urban history and even longer as an advanced human settlement. So much history is imprinted there. In ancient times it was called Smyrna but renamed in1930. It was a mercantile city acting as an important trade route.

To get to Izmir, we boarded a large ferry that took us through the Marmara Sea. The ferry was nice, spacious with food stalls and clean bathrooms. I loved the trip, relaxing as I watched the sea through my window. The ferry docked and we continued to Izmir by land. In Izmir we checked into a nice hotel and got ready for our next days of touring. I particularly enjoyed the awesome view of the sea from the coast, where I discovered a very long and wide paved walkway for strolling. I recall some boys were diving into the water right from the walkway.

A family living in a village in the outskirts of the city invited our group for a lunch. The husband was a teacher and owned an expanse of farmland, where they had a beautiful home, in a peaceful setting. We sat outside for the lavish meals cooked by the lady of the house herself. The hosts were most generous and hospitable and few of us took a tour of the farm. I recall seeing a large number of sunflower plants.

In the evening, a few of us took a walk along the coast of the Aegean Sea, looking for a place to eat. It was a pleasant evening for a walk, and I relished the views and the gentle, soothing breeze. We spotted a restaurant at the harbor and went in. While having dinner we overheard some people speaking Bengali at the next table. Naturally I introduced myself and came to know, they were two families on vacation from Bangladesh. They soon left for the ship anchored nearby, taking them and many other tourists, on an excursion to Greece.

A major part of our stay in Izmir was a half-day visit to the historical ancient city of Smyrna near modern Izmir. It is a Greek city dating back to ancient times. The city's origin is associated with Alexander the Great and it reached metropolitan status during the Roman Empire. Most of the remains today are from the Roman era. Our group visited this fascinating archeological site for many hours. It was a hot day, but the excitement of seeing this ancient city made me forget the discomfort. Time had surely devastated this ancient site with a brutal assault, but it was still hanging on. We saw the ruins of the central market square, the heart of the ancient city, we were told that one building was a library and another belonging to the oldest profession, an ancient brothel. Columns reaching up commemorated the progress of days past, some still at full height, others only of partial and some with inscriptions. They tell the tale of the passage of two millennia.

The Theater of the Archaeological site of Ephesus was a major attraction. It was built during the Hellenistic era and became the focus of many activities including gladiator fights during the Roman era. The theater's awesome size is able to accommodate about 24,000 spectators. St. Paul preached there, among the people of the Christian faith. The theater is an architectural and engineering marvel. I was impressed by the design and construction of this mammoth structure. It was actually exhilarating to see the level of design and technical dexterity of the builders. They produced a masterwork, all by hand, during an ancient period.

Next, we left Izmir for Bursa by air. Bursa is the fourth most populated city of Turkey situated in northwestern Anatolia within the Marmara Region. It is one of the most industrialized metropolitan centers in the country and the administrative center of the Province of Bursa. Bursa holds a special significance in Turkey as the first major capital city of the early Ottoman Empire. This was following its capture from the Eastern Roman Empire in 1326. As a result, the city witnessed a considerable amount of urban growth throughout the 14th century. It is a nicely planned city, marked by greenery as well as parks and gardens. It has many museums, bazaars, and other historical monuments. We visited several interesting sites. As I didn't keep any journal, I can't recollect now many of the spots we visited. As with other cities of Turkey, Bursa has many Ottoman-era mosques. On Friday I prayed the congregational prayers, most likely at the Bursa Grand Mosque. I noted the mosque was full, indicating that a large portion of the people were practicing Muslims.

Our next stop was Konya. It is a major city of Turkey with a few universities and colleges. This city's importance comes from being the home of Jalaluddin Rumi, the Sufi, mystic poet and scholar, better known simply as Rumi. He is widely known and venerated around the world and I admire him greatly. Rumi was a Persian living in Afghanistan and during the Mongol invasions he moved to Konya, settled and resided there until his death. His famous work is the *Mathnawi* consisting of six books of poetry.

He was a devout Muslim who believed most genuinely in the human connection to God from the heart. He sought solace and the overpowering love of God rather than thoughtless adherence to outward ritualistic practices. This is what he taught his students. Rumi developed the habit of turning around and round while reciting his poetry. This circling dance formed the basis of the practice in the Mevlevi Order, or Whirling Dervishes, after his death. The dance is believed to be a mystical gateway between the earthly and heavenly worlds.

We had the opportunity to see the Whirling Dervishes in person. I remember seeing a visiting troupe of the order, in the UIUC's Foellinger Auditorium, some time before. Seeing this now, in the city where this dance was born, was a wonderful experience. I noticed some young boys performing along with adults. I was amazed at seeing how they continued for such a long time, so disciplined, without feeling dizzy or losing their balance, nor frankly, becoming nauseous. As a kid, I remember spinning for fun (without any knowledge of the Whirling Dervishes) but I couldn't keep my balance and laughed at how dizzy I felt, seeing the world seemingly spinning in the opposite direction. We visited the place where Rumi would sit with his students to teach. Even though it was about 600 years since he taught, I tried to recapture the scene of his activities in my mind and feel his presence with his disciples.

We also visited the mosque and museum complex where Rumi was buried. In the museum, we saw the manuscript of Rumi's *Mathnawi* and a few other artifacts. We saw his grave, stood beside it and prayed for him. I saw an American Christian woman in our group who was so emotionally overwhelmed, she also raised her hands with outstretched palms as in a Muslim prayer and prayed with us. The religious influence of Rumi was everywhere. It was noticeable, with many women wearing the *hijab* in public places, stores, and shopping malls. In no other city in Turkey I have seen so many women in *hijab* as in Konya. We visited a market and a shopping mall there. We also visited a university and saw young students, both boys and girls. The students looked well dressed, healthy and affluent, with the classically attractive features of the Turkish people. Our tours were extensive and fast paced. I remember souvenir shopping, museum hopping and generally absorbing all the sights and sounds around me. At this point, it's hard to remember all the specific names and places we stopped.

After Konya, we traveled to a very ancient historical city, with exceptional landscape called Cappadocia. This part of my trip was amazing and most memorable. We stayed at a unique hotel near the woods. The general landscape was barren, with countless rocky crests as if the whole region was a different planet. I had never seen anything quite like it. I took my time enjoying the panorama at length. The setting was a rare sight and I knew it was a once in a lifetime opportunity.

Although mindful of my recently installed heart stents, I decided to climb an ancient, not-so-tall tower, which was inscribed with writings about the Christ. A major part of the trip was our visit to a cave-like underground city carved out of the rocks. We were told that such cities were built with vast defense networks, with traps at different levels for protection against invaders. These traps were very creative, including devices like large round stones to block doors and holes in the ceiling to allow ventilation. As we crawled through the tight tunnels, I imagined the people living in the congested spaces trying to perform their day to day tasks. It was, and still is mind-boggling for me. My structural engineering mind wondered about who built these tunnels, without the tunneling technology that we have today. The planning was also unbelievable. Who says our ancestors were less smart than us? What humans have achieved now has come from an evolutionary process whereby the innovators of one generation stood on the shoulders of those of the past.

The last leg of our trip was the capital city of Ankara. To the best of my recollection, we took a bus for this long trip with frequent stops. I was impressed by the clean, elegant, and organized bus terminals. The food and other services were also good. I looked through the window of the bus, enjoying the countryside scenery with rows of fruit laden apricot trees on both sides of the highway, running for miles. Finally, we arrived at our destination and checked into the hotel. The city was well maintained being the country's capital. We visited a few places, mostly government buildings and parks. One memory stands out. We went to a tall round tower where with an elevator to get bird's eye view of the city and the parliament building. The main gate of the parliament building was closed, so we couldn't take a tour of the building nor premises.

Soon we flew back to Istanbul. We relaxed there and didn't do too much besides going to the European side of the Bosporus Strait. The two sides were connected by the Bosporus Bridge. There we had a lavish lunch hosted by a couple in their home. In the evening, our group went to an outdoor eating place by the waterfront. It was a delightful venue and I relished the gentle evening breeze, watched the setting sun, crimson over the Bosporus. Another UIUC professor and I gave a short talk, reflecting on the trip, we thanked our hosts and enjoyed our last evening in Turkey.

We reached Chicago on July 30, concluding one of my best and most memorable trips. I was able to see several cities, the interior and rural areas of the country. I found the people everywhere to be friendly, refined and hospitable.

Meanwhile, a major storm was gathering once again over the sea of my life. Since her major illness in 1980 in Canada, Dora had been steadily recovering. When we returned from Singapore, she was totally healthy and looked beautiful. But in the 1990s she developed high blood pressure. At one stage of her treatment the physician noticed a high level of creatinine in her blood and referred her to a nephrologist. Soon we came to learn that her kidneys were functioning at a 50 percent filtration rate meaning the kidneys were already damaged. Fortunately, her condition remained stable for several years. The doctor assured her that she could function well if her kidneys were not gradually deteriorating. This relieved us. There were no apparent physical symptoms, and she didn't feel any loss of energy. Her kidney function was being monitored though and was found to be gradually decreasing. I was hoping for the best. The nephrologist, Dr. Abdel-Moneim Attia, an excellent and caring physician at Carle Hospital with good bedside manner, was an eternal optimist. He would always use encouraging words to boost our spirits.

Nevertheless, I was concerned deep down, as I remembered what the neurologist, Dr. Humphrey at Toronto General Hospital, said when she was there in 1980. He said that sarcoidosis was a disease that could lead to diabetes and damage any part of the body, particularly the lungs and kidneys. Dora was very careful and health conscious and had been generally at her ideal weight; but a preexisting, dormant condition could certainly hurt her health in the future. The doctor also predicted that she could be diabetic later in her life. This came to be true as in 2005 she was diagnosed with Type 2 diabetes.

In late 2009, the doctor was somewhat concerned and told us that her kidney function was further deteriorating and was approaching a critical level. If the filtration rate reached 20 per cent, she would need to be listed for a kidney transplant at a major hospital. This was a wake-up call for us. She was being more closely monitored with more frequent, advanced and comprehensive blood tests. In July 2010, our son Murad married Rashmee Nayab from Dallas. Her parents were immigrants from Bangladesh. She worked as a marketing analyst with a major American bank. To prepare for the wedding, shop and visit our relatives and friends, we visited Bangladesh that summer before the wedding, after clearing the trip with Dora's doctor. It was not an easy journey for us as Dora had significant swelling in her legs due to her kidney problem, sitting too long on her seat, and airplane cabin environment. In Bangladesh, we restricted our stay to Dhaka only and canceled a planned trip to Jessore, where Dora's brother was a district judge.

After our return from Bangladesh, the wedding was solemnized in Dallas. We arranged a wedding reception in November around Thanksgiving Day in Champaign. Until then we never mentioned Dora's advancing condition to our children, never mentioning that she would soon need a kidney transplant. Right after the reception, I told them about their mother's state of health. All of them were willing to donate a kidney. But I told them that we would try to get a donor kidney through the hospital.

Things got worse in early 2011 as fluid was accumulating in her legs causing them to swell; she lost energy and could not walk too far nor do household chores; and she was losing taste for food. Her blood creatinine level increased. Then her blood hemoglobin level began to decrease. The doctor ordered blood and iron infusion immediately. I took Dora to Barnes Jewish Hospital in St. Louis and Indiana University Hospital in Indianapolis for evaluation as her filtration level fell below 20 percent. She was enlisted and put on their waiting lists. I heard many horror stories about how patients died while waiting for a match. I heard from well-wishers that kidneys were available in India, Singapore, Pakistan, Bangladesh, and Canada more readily. I checked out some of these and found there were many constraints. None of them appealed to me. My best hope was she would find a donor in America. Her nephrologist continued to give us assurances and hope.

My attention turned to care for Dora. She was losing her strength by the day as her kidneys failed to process the protein being lost profusely through the urine. Moreover, the volume of her urine production continued to decrease as the kidneys were failing to produce urine resulting in accumulation of fluid in her feet, ankles, and legs. I studied the subject to enlighten myself and realized what a devastating disease it was that sapped the body of its energy and vitality. So, I decided to retire in May. But because of my love for teaching, I continued teaching part time without any other official responsibilities. Director Chasco requested that I continue as a chairman of the Structures Division since I would still be teaching and associated with the School. I declined as I thought it would not be appropriate for me to do while I was retired, nor did I want to bear the stress related to it when my hands were full at home and already. I anticipated what was coming. Also, following my Fulbright project in Malta, I started writing a book based on my work there. I invited Dr. Kheir Al-Kodmany, a former student at our School, to co-author the book with me. After my heart procedure in 2009, I was not feeling well and decided to drop the book project. It was a lot of work. Since the ideas and experience in Malta were uniquely mine, I thought I was the only one who could write the book. I also had previously written books and had that experience as well. When I told Kheir about my intention, he assured me he would work hard and take the lead in developing the manuscript. I agreed. I wrote a few chapters and was working on the overall manuscript in terms of layout, editing, and other components.

In September 2009, I presented a paper in Las Vegas, Nevada at an engineering and construction conference. Dora accompanied me there even though her health was declining. Actually, she insisted that we should go to see the Grand Canyon from there. This was the first time I visited the place known as the "sin city." We visited a number of major hotels in the glitzy area of the city and watched some shows. I knew some Bangladeshi students living there, one of whom was a doctoral student in Civil Engineering. He invited us to his house for dinner. We met his wife and some other Bangladeshi students and families there.

We also had a relative there, Salma Chowdhury, who was born in Kitchener-Waterloo Hospital. I was the one who brought her home from the hospital since her father's car broke down that day. She is the daughter of Aziz Chowdhury, a relative and my friend while I was a student living in Waterloo, Ontario. Now all grown up, she invited us for dinner with her family too.

Dora and I took a tourist bus to the Grand Canyon via the Hoover Dam. It was a memorable trip through small towns and wilderness. First the bus took us to Hoover Dam, an engineering marvel and an example of extreme engineering. Hoover Dam was originally known as Boulder Dam from 1933 to 1947, before it was officially renamed Hoover Dam by a joint resolution of Congress. It is a concrete arch-gravity dam in the Black Canyon of the Colorado River, on the border between Nevada and Arizona. It was constructed between 1931 and 1936 and was dedicated on September 30, 1935, by President Franklin D. Roosevelt. Its construction was the result of a massive effort involving thousands of workers at a cost of over one hundred lives.

Hoover Dam holds Lake Mead, the largest reservoir in the U.S. by volume, at its full capacity. The dam is located near Boulder City, Nevada, a municipality originally constructed to accommodate workers on the construction project, about 30 miles (48 km) southeast of Las Vegas, Nevada. The dam's generators provide power for public and private utilities in Nevada, Arizona, and California. Hoover Dam is a major tourist attraction; nearly a million people tour the dam each year. The Hoover Dam Bridge over the river was built later since the main travel route over the dam itself, is a long and high massive arch bridge, comprised of a 1,060-foot (323-meter) long, 277-foot (84-meter) high arch. I was thrilled to see the dam and its setting as well as the mammoth bridge as if floating in the air. The tourist bus stopped there for a while giving us time to view this dam and the bridge under the open sky. It was a spectacular sight!

We boarded the bus and it started rolling along the high-way to the Grand Canyon. The bus stopped at a rest area near a large store and restaurant. Dora and I lunched there. An Indian professor from India and his wife joined us, and we had some interesting conversations. We admired the landscape and reached our destination. Over 270-mile (432-kilometer) long, up to 18 miles (29 kilometers) wide and about a mile (1.6 kilometer) deep, the Grand Canyon is known throughout the world for its overwhelming size and its intricate and colorful landscape. Located in northern Arizona, the majestic vista is geologically important. The layers of beautiful ancient rocks preserve a timeline of our planet's geological history. Its origin dates back to millions of years.

In the early 1800s, expedition teams sent by the U.S. government began to explore and map the Southwest, including the canyon. Although first afforded Federal protection in 1893 as a Forest Reserve and later as a National Monument, the Grand Canyon did not achieve National Park status until 1919, three years after the creation of the National Park Service. Today Grand Canyon National Park encompasses more than 1 million acres (405,000 hectares) of land and receives close to 5 million visitors each year. We went to a spot near the borders of Nevada and Arizona states. It was only one segment of the huge expanse of the Grand Canyon. The terraced walls of the canyon were created by a natural process of weathering, leading to differential erosion. We visited a few spots and looked down to the bottom of the canyon at a dizzying depth. I had never seen anything like it. It was a thrilling experience. The view is unforgettable. For me it was a great place for contemplation and reflection on the geological wonder of our planet. So much pre-historic history was frozen there!

We returned to our Las Vegas hotel and the following day we left for Champaign with the memories of Las Vegas, the Hoover

Dam, and the Grand Canyon. I treasure the experience and the indelible images of the Hoover Dam and the Grand Canyon even today with great exultation.

Around the beginning of March 2010, the founder of the Grameen Bank in Bangladesh visited our UIUC Campus. Nobel Laureate, Dr. Muhammad Yunus, is an economist, social entrepreneur, banker, founder of Grameen Bank and pioneer of Microfinance and Microcredit. He is a world-renowned Bangladeshi who worked hard to alleviate poverty in Bangladesh. In addition to the Nobel Peace Prize, he has received the highest possible awards from organizations and institutions around the world. When he visited Champaign, he was given a grand reception by the university and the local Bangladeshi community.

He particularly champions the needs of rural women, who fall behind men in education, self-fulfillment, and economic prosperity because of social restrictions against them. He left his academic job in the U.S. for a similar job at Chittagong University in Chittagong, his hometown. He was driven to answer an inner clarion call urging him to look after the poor and downtrodden of society. He began visiting poor people in rural areas there to get a sense of their problems first-hand. Although I knew about him and his work, I first came across his name in an economics textbook in 2001. There was a section on microfinance. He became friends with many important people around the world including President Bill Clinton. In a way, he put Bangladesh on the world map. If anyone came to know I was from Bangladesh, they brought up his name and their admiration for him.

I first met him at UIUC campus in the open atrium in the newly built state-of-art building of the Business School. It was built using the latest green design technologies. Dr. Irfan Ahmed, a friend of mine and an admirer of Dr. Yunus, led me to him and we had a brief conversation. On March 1, he delivered an inspiring speech at the university's large Foellinger Auditorium that was fully packed. The university's interim President at the time, Dr. Stanley Ikenberry, bestowed university's most prestigious award by garlanding him with the Medal of Honor. He was honored the same day in the evening with a dinner reception at the Ball Room of the local I-Hotel. At this gala event, all the university's top administrators and invitees including distinguished faculty members, his friends and admirers, local businessmen, and the Bangladeshi community members were present. Dr. Salim Rashid, also an economist like Dr. Yunus, took an active role in organizing the event together with university authorities and others. He gave me the honor of making an introductory welcome speech for Dr. Yunus.

In April 2010, I was invited to present a paper titled "Sustainable Urban Life in Skyscraper Cities of the 21st Century," at the 6th International Conference on Urban Regeneration and Sustainability in La Coruna, Spain. The conference offered me the opportunity to visit this historic European country. Spain has historical linkage to Islamic and Arab history, and the history of North and South America, especially the latter.

La Coruna is a busy port located on a promontory of a large gulf on the Atlantic Ocean. It provides a distribution point for agricultural goods from the region. The conference was held at a hotel overseeing the ocean where the delegates also stayed. Despite my desire to do so, I didn't include a visit to Alhambra in Granada, Andalusia and Cordoba. I simply couldn't, as my classes were going on and Dora was weak and needed me with her.

My plane landed in Madrid on April 13, 2010. From there I took a flight to La Coruna. My visit to La Coruna was not pleasant. After I checked in at the hotel, I was given a choice to have room on the top floor with a view of the ocean or a room in the second floor. I opted for the top floor to have a decent view of the ocean. Heading to my room with all my luggage, I found a spiral stair to the top floor and had a bad feeling. I already had mild back pain embarking the flight from Chicago. I remembered that when I was in Malta, I had bad back pain and the doctor told me to avoid spiral stairs and any twisted movement. I went up anyway carrying my luggage. The room was very isolated which I disliked. I changed rooms and checked into a regular room on the second floor. During the second day of the conference, while getting up from tiny, classroom style seat and desk, I twisted my right leg. Suddenly I felt as if an electric current shoot through my leg. I got out to stretch and walk, but I felt intense pain in my right knee, almost immobilizing me. I started limping but managed to walk.

The next day, we were given a welcome reception by the city administrator at a nearby venue within walking distance. Despite my penetrating knee pain, I limped over, determined not to miss the event. It was an interesting place and the food was good. A British delegate by the name of Raymond approached me and started talking to me warmly. We became friends quickly. After the reception we walked back together. He invited me to join him for sightseeing the next day. I reluctantly declined despite my burning desire to see new places as I realized it would demand a lot of walking. I was taking a painkiller but didn't get relief. With the help of the hotel's front desk I went to a local clinic. I walked in and realized that no one spoke English. Frustrated, I called the hotel and explained my predicament. I was told to go to a private hospital, and she arranged a taxi for me. There, I was able to see a doctor and get an X-Ray of my knee. The result revealed that I had no arthritis but might have torn something that could only be diagnosed with an MRI or ultrasound. He advised me to get it checked by a doctor after my return to the U.S.

Despite my misery, I participated in all the sessions and had a breakfast meeting with Dr. Carlos Brebbia on the book *The Future of the City* that I co-authored with Kheir Al-Kodmany, to be published by WIT Press. I also participated in a committee meeting at a waterfront restaurant as I was a member of the conference International Scientific Committee. Although I was staying at a nice upscale hotel, and was not a picky eater, the hotel offerings didn't suit my palette. I found one vegetable sandwich on the menu, and simply ate that every night for dinner.

With my continuing knee pain, I was confined inside the hotel and counting my remaining days before going home. But my travel saga was far from over. A volcanic ash cloud had been sweeping through northern and western Europe, from April 14-25. The volcanic eruptions originated from Iceland and caused enormous disruption to air travel for a period of six days. Spain was initially spared from this event.

However, the night before my departure, I was watching TV and they said the ash cloud was entering Spain. I hoped this wouldn't delay my departure. The next day I went to the airport and checked in. When I was in line ready to board the plane bound for Madrid, I heard an announcement in Spanish and noticed that many passengers looked flustered. I asked someone nearby what happened and was told that the flight had been canceled because of the ash cloud. In the din, I missed the English announcement but noticed that passengers left the line and were dispersing.

Seeing me dispirited, a girl approached and said, "Professor Ali, I am a Brazilian student. I heard your presentation at the conference. I am headed for Brazil. Now, I don't know what to do."

I suggested, "Maybe we can go back to the hotel and stay there until the cloud clears since we don't know how long that may take."

We considered the options, but then she said, "Why don't we stay here and see what happens?"

So, we did. She was by herself too and I felt better that having company to bide my time. We chatted and at one point I told her that I had a heart condition, and this was stressful for me. She comforted me by saying, "Professor, you look fine; nothing will happen to you." Some people left the airport, but many remained.

Around dusk we heard another announcement saying that the flight was cleared to go to Madrid. Jubilantly, we lined up for the flight. I felt so relieved. I realized I would miss my connecting flight from Madrid to New York but decided to go anyway and leave this remote port city, hoping I could get any other flight out of Madrid.

We reached the Madrid Airport almost at midnight, it was completely desolate. I lost that Brazilian girl in the crowd. Probably she was trying to figure out her own flight home. By then, I was exhausted, almost lost and there were no airline officials on duty to help. Suddenly, I sighted some people and a well-lit counter at a distance. I rushed to get some information or help. They were with Iberian Airlines, my carrier. There were two ladies at the counter, helping a few passengers. One checked on any flights to Chicago or New York, but she told me, "Sorry, I can't find anything for you. The authorities are allowing only a very few outgoing flights tonight. You have to stay in Madrid overnight."

I desperately told her, "Look, I'm 65 years old with a heart condition and an aching knee, and I am very tired. I don't know where I can go at this hour in Madrid. Please keep looking. I don't have to go straight to Chicago, any American airport will do including Hawaii." But she didn't change her stance.

I noticed the young lady at a counter next to her was listening to our conversation. She called me and motioned me to her counter. She said, "Don't worry sir, I am trying to find something for you." She said, "A flight is leaving in a few minutes for New

York. You will have to run to catch it. Do you want it?" I replied in the affirmative.

She worked on it and gave me a boarding pass and said, "I have booked you to Chicago via New York. Good luck!" The flight was at a different terminal and I had to catch a shuttle train. She quickly gave me the directions. I felt she was another godsend and thanked her profusely and told her "May God bless you." Once again, I found decent people were everywhere.

Of course, I couldn't run with my bad knee and the carry-on luggage I was pulling. But I forgot my pain and walked as briskly as my knee and my tired body permitted. A driverless train was just approaching the platform.

Realizing I must catch this train or miss my flight, with a burst of adrenalin I started running and limping at the same time, frantically, and just barely reached the open door. A kind man, another godsend, extended his hand and pulled me in fast. I pulled in my carry-on with my other hand just as the door closed a split second later and the train started moving. I was breathing fast, and my heart was pounding, and I thanked the man for his help.

Finally, at the terminal, I realized the gate was the furthest one, and the boarding time was almost passed. I continued running, breathing faster, heart beating at top speed. When I reached the gate, I noticed only a few people straggling at the gate ahead of me, I was the very last person to board. I boarded immediately and the gate closed. I was assigned a seat next to the emergency exit, glad for the extra legroom. I sat next to a passenger who was a professor at the University of Cordoba and was going to New York for a conference. He told me that he had restless leg syndrome and that's why he was assigned this seat. Come to think of it, perhaps the nice lady who booked my flight requested this for me because of my knee pain. I will never know.

While waiting on the runway to get clearance, I was still anxious about being turned back in case the ash had worsened. Even after takeoff my concern remained. It was only after the we gained altitude, left the land mass and began flying over the Atlantic Ocean that I was fully relieved. As the lights from the city were becoming more and more distant, I realized I was somewhat traumatized by the long ordeal.

My flight went well, and I chatted with the amiable professor about Spain, Cordoba, and the academic system and culture in Spain. Once the plane landed at Kennedy International Airport in New York on April 18, after checking through immigration and customs, I sat on a chair waiting for daybreak and for my departure to O'Hare International Airport in Chicago. I reflected upon my ordeal in Spain like a nightmare. Once dawn broke, I left the airport to get some fresh air and felt buoyed by the fact that I was back in America, my country. Once I reached Chicago and exited the airport, I saw Jinat and Dora, waiting for me. I emotionally explained to them what had happened to me during the last few hours. They told me they were worried as I didn't return to Chicago at the scheduled time. I felt great when Jinat started driving us home.

Dora's declining health was becoming a great source of anxiety and worry. She was very weak. Around this time, I got an invitation from Dick Brandt, Director of Iacocca Institute to participate in their program, Global Village for Future Leaders. The institute was established by automotive icon and Lehigh University alumnus, Lee Iacocca, in partnership with Lehigh University. I was requested to get involved with the organization as well as offer a few weeks course on building construction, as a learning experience for the global attendees. Although I felt very tempted to accept the invitation, I politely declined, citing my wife's poor health. He asked me to contact him again if my family situation improved and I wanted to participate in the future. I never did contact him as Dora's condition worsened with time.

The time was approaching for her to need the much-dreaded kidney dialysis. I had heard about the process but had no idea what it would feel like for the patient. I thought she could live without dialysis for some time and just hoped for the best. Eventually in May 2011, her kidney's filtration rate dropped to a level so dangerously low that she needed immediate dialysis. The doctor who usually had a sunny disposition gave us the bad news with a grim face. He recommended a type of dialysis called peritoneal dialysis instead of the conventional hemodialysis.

For hemodialysis, a patient must go to a dialysis facility three to four times a week and stay seated while his or her blood is drained, filtered and recirculated back to the body through a port in a vein of the arm. The peritoneal dialysis can be carried out at home every night either manually or aided by a digital machine.

We went to a dialysis center in Urbana for orientation and training. The environment was very depressing. When the nurse showed us how to conduct the manual peritoneal procedure Dora was totally turned off. I told the doctor, so he sent her to a vascular surgeon for a venal map to find out if hemodialysis would suit her. After examination, the surgeon concluded that hemodialysis would not be possible for her as her veins were too thin. The only choice therefore was the peritoneal dialysis. Dora went through a surgery in which plastic flexible piping was inserted into her abdomen. The tube was used for infusing medication for dialysis. She needed a couple of weeks to recover from the surgery.

During this period, I had been working intensely on two CIMIC expansion projects: one related to the remodeling of the mosque and the other on a new Cultural Center Complex with student dormitory, gymnasium and classrooms. This was planned on a large site, on other side of Busey Street, across the mosque premises. Earlier I was involved in the purchase of the land. Around the same time of Dora's illness, hearings with the Urbana City Council for the Cultural Center project were being held.

Some of the neighbors in the area vehemently opposed the project, citing many reasons. On a very crucial day of public hearings, Dora was very sick, but I felt my presence at the meeting was essential. No one else had been as intimately involved with the project, right from the beginning. I had been directly and continuously involved, meeting the architect, city officials, the city mayor, CIMIC Board, CIMIC Expansion Committee, and other stakeholders. Together with my CIMIC colleagues Moham- mad Al-Heeti, for whom it was a passion project that he initiated, Waleed Jasim and few others. Waleed Jasim was instrumental in conceiving, leading and building the mosque. Al-Heeti and sev- eral others including me were also involved throughout that pro- cess as well. Knowing all the technical and architectural details for the new expansion project I thought I could confidently answer all the questions.

I felt I would like to see the project materialize and it was very important to me, as I had invested so much time and energy already. I asked for Dora's consent to be away for about two hours in the evening after explaining the matter to which she of course, graciously agreed. At the hearing I defended the project vigorously; others from CIMIC also participated. The project was approved by all Council members except one who cast a dissent- ing vote. Alas, the eight-million-dollar project did not material- ize as the funds could not be raised. However, the remodeling of the mosque was partially completed with donor funds after I left Urbana-Champaign in 2015.

On June 11, 2011, Dora began manual dialysis. It had to be done every few hours daily and continued for a few days. Soon a dialysis machine arrived and a truck with medical supplies and many bags of the liquid medicine for infusion. The nurse from the dialysis clinic, Emilda, a very nice Filipino lady, demonstrated the whole process for us at home. She showed us how to set up and operate the machine, which was placed on a small table next to the bed. I was trained to set up the machine every day and the dialysis was performed all night. That night, as usual I lay down next to Dora. There was hardly any room for me to sleep as she needed much more room because of the tubing and equipment. I had to be careful not to touch her to avoid interrupting the dialysis.

The machine would make some occasional noise, which got louder when the medicine was infused and then drained out to empty bags. The machine was very sensitive. Whenever Dora would toss and turn, the infusion or drainage process was disturbed, and the machine would sound an alarm. I would get up to set it up again. This happened a few times at night. Both of us had difficulty getting sound sleep. Because of my inexperience with the machine, occasionally I didn't know what to do and called the dedicated a 24-hour hotline, set up by the machine provider. I talked with them and on occasions I had to cancel the setup, throw away the bags and set it up again. One night I remember the machine sounded the alarm nine times. In the morning, I would take the bags collecting to the bathroom and drain them out into the bathtub. We retained a part time helper who would help change the dressing daily to avoid infection.

Sometimes we were without a helper and I did it myself. Because of her weakness, Dora could hardly cook. Tora by this time had moved to Indianapolis. Dora's other sister, Munira Khan (Gora), came from Bangladesh with her retired husband, to live with their son and family in Indianapolis. The two sisters occasionally brought food, which was of great help along with their love and bigheartedness for us. Some of our local friends occasionally cooked for us too. I used to do the groceries and laundry and any chores that Dora would normally do. Our daughters in Chicago would visit us but could not do much because of the distance. They tried to find helpers. The pressure of being a constant caregiver sometimes became overwhelming.

I found out early on, that Medicare, to which we were entitled, did not pay for the expense of hiring a nurse. I looked into hiring someone at my own cost. We initially hired some help, but it didn't work out long term. The first helper Elizabeth, an African, would come for a short time to help drain the bags, cleaning and changing the dressing. Then we found Eunice, a Filipino young woman who stayed for a long time.

It so happened that in July 2011, almost a month after starting dialysis I got a call from Barnes Jewish Hospital in St. Louis, telling me that a kidney transplant was planned for a lady that day but if for any reason, it didn't work out, they needed a backup patient and selected Dora. I decided to go and take the chance. We knew a friendly couple, Mr. and Mrs. A. Mannan in the city. They were very helpful. At the end, the surgery for the lady was successful and we returned. We didn't mind even though Dora didn't get the kidney because at least someone's life was saved.

After Eunice left for family reasons, I was without a helper and on my own. It was a heavy burden on me, but I realized that I must remain strong and in control of the situation. There was no choice. I remember reading Charles Darwin's observation that the species that were strong and adaptable ultimately survived. That's what he meant by "survival of the fittest." I further remembered the maxim that in times of crisis "organize, don't agonize." Above all, I knew prayer helped, and trusting the Higher Power, asking Him to give us the strength to face catastrophes. Submitting to Him for our destiny gave us true bliss. I decided to do my best to help Dora, literally the woman of my dreams. I had dreamt about her and decided to marry her. She had always been a steadying force for me and kept me stable in times of crisis all throughout my life. Her calm disposition had always a calming effect on me. This time was no exception.

We decided at one point that we needed to sleep separately so each of us could sleep. I had tried in vain to manage around the machines and tubes, to stay close to her, but none was comfortable. Yet I slept like that with her for a few months. Finally, I moved to a different bedroom. She had a spacious bed and so did I. Initially I thought of sleeping in a sleeping bag on the floor of our bedroom so I could be near her. But she felt sorry for me and asked me to move to an adjacent room. We kept our mobile phones on all night so when she needed me, or the machine sounded alarm, she could call me. I would keep mine on round the clock anyway, with the hope that I would get a call from one of the hospitals where Dora had enrolled, to give me the good news of a matching kidney.

I slept alone, without hearing the machine pumping and draining, or Dora's moaning in discomfort; I was getting some sleep. It was occasionally interrupted when Dora called. The alarm from the machine was so loud that more often than not, I heard it from my bedroom and would rush to her room even before she called. During this period, I forgot the scale of time, hours became almost indistinguishable to me as I woke up, then slept, then woke up, then stayed awake, then slept in a seemingly endless cycle.

One day, I noticed that because of my distress and overwork, I was not feeling very good. I checked my blood pressure and it was very high. I waited a couple of days, but there was no change, so, I saw a doctor who told me to relieve my stress by yoga and meditation. I was also prescribed some blood pressure medication, which helped. I used to meditate for a few years after my heart attack in 1992 but had given it up after getting busy with the demands of life. I knew about yoga since my student days in Bangladesh. I liked the peaceful practice of meditation, being immersed in contemplation. I found temporary solace from the many chaotic pressures of daily life.

I joined a yoga and meditation class at the UIUC athletic center. Most of the participants were young female students and I, as a 68-year old man, felt somewhat awkward being there. But I decided to continue and learn the techniques from a professional. I knew yoga as an ancient Indian practice meant for yogis and associated with Hinduism. It has become now a worldwide practice, owing to its many physical and mental benefits. Some religious scholars from all three Abrahamic faiths question its permissibility, because of yoga's connection to polytheistic Hindu beliefs and occasional use of Hindu mantras. I, however, felt that yoga, the way it was universally practiced was secular without the mantras. As a Muslim I felt that the postures in our own prayers: standing, bending, sitting, prostrating, etc. resembled the various yoga *asanas* (poses).

A Hindu yoga teacher whom I knew and who authored a book on yoga once told me that when Muslims prayed five times a day, that was as good as performing yoga. That was reassuring. At any rate, this debate would continue but I separated the religious associations from the physical benefits and never felt any contradiction when performing yoga. Lately, yoga has been combined with many stretching exercises as part of physical therapy regimens, making it a more secular health-based practice in many countries. I have always enjoyed doing it.

The instructor, a middle-aged man with a deep and calming voice would conduct a meditation session after yoga, which I thought was very good. He would read from a book and the passages were always soothing. I got the name of the book from him and bought it. The book is *Wherever You Go There You*

Are by Jon Kabat-Zinn. He was influence by mindful meditation, practiced by Buddhist monks, and is himself a meditation guru.

At first, I simply read the book, as even reading the passages
gave me solace and reduced my stresses. It gave a practical guide
for meditation of different kinds. I liked some of the mindful
meditations in the book. The Mountain Meditation, The Lake
Meditation, Tree Meditation, Standing Meditation, and Lying-
Down Meditation, as described in the book, appealed to me and
I started practicing them regularly. I felt it was beneficial and
calmed the storm going on inside and around me on the outside. I even bought some CDs by the author and used them, but I
must admit that I felt that his voice was not as calming as my yoga
instructor's, but it was a good start. After hearing the CD a few
times, I memorized the words. Mindful meditation can be done
for only five minutes or over a longer period. Overall, it was good
for me during these rocky days.

Dora was getting weaker although the dialysis kept her alive.
She also developed some major skin problems probably as reaction to the dialysis medicine. I kept my cell phone on and with me
all the time, even in my classrooms, telling students my situation
with the hope that a call for transplant would come soon. One
day our daughter Ifat told me that she had a friend whose father
was a well-known nephrologist affiliated with the University of
Chicago Hospital. Her friend told his father, Dr. Gary Toback
about Dora's condition, and asked him to help us. I sent Dora's
medical records to him. After he reviewed them, he called me.
We talked for about half an hour. He commended the nephrologist who was treating Dora at Carle Hospital and gave me some
advice about Dora's illness. At the end, he suggested that Dora
should enroll at the University of Wisconsin Hospital in Madison, which had a great transplant program and the waiting time
was shorter. I have been always grateful to him for this sugges-

tion. Very sadly, in 2016, Dr. Toback was killed by a speeding car, on his morning jog.

Heeding his advice, I drove Dora to Madison, about 250 miles (400 kilometers) from Urbana-Champaign for her evaluation and enrollment. I liked the way this hospital coordinated between specialists. They each came to see Dora at one place as opposed to Barnes Jewish Hospital where we had to go to different places, which was hard for a weakened patient like her. The evaluation process at the hospital in Indianapolis was not very appealing to me either. In both St. Louis and Indianapolis, we were unable to meet the surgeons. At Madison, however, a surgeon came to see her himself and explained things well, answered our questions and made us feel comfortable with the procedure. I also noticed Madison is a beautiful city. While approaching the city from the highway the large lake and Capitol Building on its shore produced an amazing panoramic view from a distance. At night, the lights of the Capitol reflected in the lake producing an even a more astounding sight.

During the second year of Dora's dialysis, that is, in late 2012, I started getting calls. I got a call one evening from Madison, in November 2012 when I was in the middle of a yoga session at the UIUC gymnasium. I told the instructor early on that this might happen. I left and talked with a transplant nurse who said that two donor kidneys were available from a man in his 60s. If both were transplanted, they could function at the rate of a young person's single kidney. This was adequate as one could live with a single kidney.

It was not ideal, so I called Dora's local nephrologist, who told me to go ahead as kidneys were hard to get. So, I asked Taher, our family friend to accompany us as it was nighttime, and I had to drive through rural areas for about four hours. I drove to Madison and reached there at about midnight. Our daughter Ifat and her husband Mike also drove from Chicago to join us there. Dora was admitted to the hospital and assigned a room. The nurse prepared Dora for the surgery and told us to wait. Dora was without food and drink since we started from home for Madison. A few hours later, we were told that the donor kidneys were of poor quality and the surgeon declined to use them for transplant. We stayed in the hospital room overnight with little sleep. Th next morning, we returned home somewhat tired and disheartened.

Days later I got a second call from Madison. I was told that although the kidney from the donor was fine there might have been a case of HIV in that family. The caller didn't elaborate. I said no to that offer. Days later I got a third call from Madison in the evening. We went there, and Dora was admitted and assigned a room. She was prepped for surgery and again, was not allowed any food or drink since leaving home. Nothing was happening. The next day, a surgeon together with a few of his students came to see us. He told us that the potential donor had been on a ventilator for a long time but still alive. The doctor didn't want us to wait indefinitely and asked us to return home. It was disappointing. I was told later by the transplant coordinator that Dora was at the top of the waiting list and her blood type was common and it would be easier to get a good match. Since I was getting these calls frequently it gave me hope that someday very soon Dora would get a kidney.

The fourth call came one late evening, asking me to bring Dora to Madison right away. We drove and arrived at about 2 AM. Our daughter Ifat and her husband Mike also came to join us. As a matter of fact, she and Mike came on every occasion to all hospitals. Once we checked in at the receptionist desk in the transplant section of the hospital, we were told that they just were notified that the donor kidney was of poor quality. Since Dora was not admitted we could not stay there and went to a hotel near the Capitol Building.

The hotel was not easy to reach as some repair work was being done to the Capitol Building and therefore the area was barricaded. And of course, it was late at night. The streets were very quiet, and our GPS wasn't working properly because of the barricades. Finally, at about 4:00 AM we checked in at the hotel to get some sleep. Because of the tiredness, anxieties, and frustrations, I could not really sleep but just lay down in the hopes of getting some rest. In the early morning, after having a quick breakfast, we left Madison. I felt tired and realized I should not drive in this condition; so, I stopped at a service center on the highway and parked. Both Dora and I took a short nap in the car. After recharging ourselves we headed for home. This was the third failed attempt to get a kidney in Madison. But I was still optimistic, and my gut instinct told me that we would be lucky soon.

I got a fifth call, (but fourth viable option, as we rejected the one offer), in late December. During that holiday time, our son Murad came to visit us from Washington, DC. He drove us to Madison. After a four-hour drive, just as we were ready to take the exit, I got a call from the transplant clinic telling me that the kidney was not of good quality. We got disheartened and turned back.

After that for some time I didn't get any more calls but still didn't give up hope. I checked with Barnes Jewish Hospital to find out how she was doing on their wait list. I was told she was near the top of their list and should get a kidney in about six months. Dora was getting weaker, didn't have taste for food and her bodily fluid level was increasing, raising her weight by about 30 pounds (14 kilograms), unusual as she was a slim person to begin with. My two daughters were not eligible as donors. I thought if things got worse, Murad would have to donate one of his kidneys. He was already under evaluation at Barnes Jewish Hospital as a possible donor. His blood type matched his mother's. I didn't prefer that extreme outcome and was torn between my love for both of them. He was focused on his studies in a part-time MBA degree program at the University of Maryland while working. I didn't want any interruption in his studies. I just kept my fingers crossed and waited for another call from one of the hospitals.

Although I had gotten all these calls in fairly rapid succession, I didn't get any others for some time. Then, on March 12, 2013 at about 5 AM I got a sixth call from Madison. By then, I knew that a call at such an odd hour was most likely from the hospital. That night, like many other nights, I didn't sleep much and was feeling bleary. But I was alert when I heard the phone and picked up in anticipation, but cautious not to get my hopes up, as we failed five times before, including one attempt at Barnes Jewish Hospital. Once the nurse told me about the offer I said, "We went to Madison four times but failed to get a good kidney. If we go, this will be the fifth time."

She said, "This is a very good kidney and the match is excellent. I saw the blood test reports. Don't you want to come?"

I replied, "We will go of course. I was just telling you about our frustration. We go a long distance and my sick wife can't eat or drink until the transplant surgery is done, and this long-time fasting makes her so weak. But we will go without question, and start out as soon as we can, possibly in an hour."

We always had a suitcase ready for overnight stays. I got up from my bed and went to the other room where Dora was staying. Once I gave her the news, she told me, "I didn't sleep much last night. Let's skip this one as I am not feeling well, and we have been sent back so many times."

I replied, "We can't miss any opportunity, this is too important. Let's get ready, I told them we would leave in an hour."

We reached Madison in the late morning and Dora was admitted to the hospital promptly. I was praying that this one would be a success and kept my fingers crossed. We stayed there all day and Dora was prepared for the surgery. We were kept informed of the developments, several blood tests and x-rays were done to make sure she was up to it. I was told that they were waiting for a vacancy in the operating room. It appeared that this time it would work. Our daughters came from Chicago. Dr. Joshua Mezrich, the surgeon and a fine gentleman, saw us in the afternoon and told us that everything looked good; the transplant operation was expected to take place; and he assured us by saying that he had done hundreds of such surgeries before.*

Finally, a medical staff member came and wheeled her to a preparation room around 9:00 PM. We accompanied her to that room. While were waiting, the surgeon came to see us as Dora was being sedated by the anesthesiologist and told me that the donor kidney was of good quality and he was almost ready to proceed. It would take a few hours. Soon after, Dora was wheeled to the operating room. I returned to her hospital room and both our daughters coming from Chicago waited in the nearby lounge. I was in suspense, knowing that Dora was very weak, and the surgery was grueling.

I was sitting on a chair in the patient room when suddenly the phone rang at about 2:00 AM. I was told the operation was successful and Dora was in the recovery room and they would contact me again updating her condition. I felt very excited and gave the good news to my daughters waiting in lounge. I came back to the room and sat on the chair and felt some relief. I was somewhat drowsy and suddenly heard a voice asking me, "Are you awake Mr. Ali?" I stood up and answered in the affirmative. It was the surgeon. He explained the surgery to me, "She got a very good kidney. The blood profusion was good. Her blood creatinine level has come down and will continue to do so. Everything

---

* Dr. Joshua Mezrich later authored a book titled *When Death Becomes Life.*

looks good. The kidney should last for many years. Your wife will be brought to the room soon."

I must say I didn't know what "blood profusion" meant in this context. I learned later, in the seminars which I attended over the next couple of days. In fact, those seminars on several topics related to post-transplant stage were very educational and helpful for patients and caregivers. After the doctor left, I looked at my watch and found it was about 4:00 AM. Right after sunrise Dora was brought into the room. Several medical professionals including a fellow, a resident, a nurse, medical students, and Dr. Mezrich came to see Dora soon afterward. Our son Murad flew from Washington, DC to see his mother. Dora's two sisters and their families later came from Indianapolis to see her also. Things went well under the circumstances.

There was one major complication during this time that made me nervous. Fortunately, after I prayed hard overnight for God's mercy the complication subsided. At night, she could not urinate, and a catheter was placed to help her. Thankfully, the problem resolved itself and she wasn't discharged with a catheter. I was worried about being able to help her with it at home.

I had stayed by Dora's side the entire time on a little foldout "bed". I came to admire the nurses and nursing assistants, and truly felt a deep sense of appreciation for what they did. They had a difficult job, yet they were so graceful and did their occasional unpleasant tasks so cheerfully. I realized just how noble their profession was and how much of God's blessings they deserved for their dedicated service to humanity.

Once Dora was discharged, we left for home accompanied by Ifat and with the doctor's follow-up instructions. She was prescribed a very large number of medications out of which three were immune-suppressant, anti-rejection drugs. After we returned home, a home healthcare nurse visited Dora initially every day, then three times a week for six weeks to check on her and draw her blood for lab tests. After this period, she needed a monthly blood test, on a permanent basis to monitor her condition. We had to visit Madison frequently early on, when the possibility of rejection was very high, that eventually became once a year. In addition, she saw the local primary care physician and the nephrologist. From time to time, her medicines were adjusted. Throughout this ordeal, I learned a lot about kidney disease, transplant, and a host of other related issues that I never thought I would have to experience.

Dora wrote a letter to the donor's mother thanking her and recognizing that her child's kidney gave her a new life, although nothing could compensate for the loss of her child. The mother sent a nice reply thanking Dora and saying her son, whose kidney was transplanted, enjoyed outdoor life and advised Dora to enjoy her new life and go into the outdoors to experience fresh air and sunshine. This correspondence was facilitated by the University of Wisconsin Hospital.

While Dora was on the verge of undergoing dialysis in 2011 and I decided to formally retire in May, the Structures Division was still intact at the School. After my formal retirement, I continued teaching advanced graduate courses part-time at the school. During my entire academic career, I felt that whatever course I taught – undergraduate or graduate – it was important to me. I enjoyed every course and attempted to pass my passion for the subject on to my students. I advised them in lectures that every subject was important, as each represented one segment of the vast gamut of knowledge. I planned to continue teaching part-time as long as I could. I continued to teach even when I was going through probably the toughest time of my life. As a matter of fact, my love for teaching kept my mind preoccupied with intellectual pursuits, and somewhat diverted my attention away from the agony of the period. With Dora's recovery, I was happy that she got the gift of a renewed life.

Soon after my retirement, while I was no longer involved in the School's administration, the Structures Division was eliminated. The structures courses were retained and placed under a newly created, Performance Division, that had a few other technical areas. I was sad to know about this as I had worked so hard to prevent it. The long-standing Structures Division had survived against great odds, with the support of our distinguished alumni for so many years, during my tenure as its chairman. I was occasionally aggressive but tried to resolve disputes and occasional assaults on the structures program as tactfully as possible, in a non-confrontational manner. Although early on, my relationship with Director Chasco was less than cordial because of his anti-technology outlook, towards the end, our relationship improved, and we could work together, and became good friends. I took some satisfaction, however, that at least the elimination of the division didn't happen during my chairmanship.

We made more new friends with people who moved to Urbana-Champaign. These were Dr. Muhammad Al-Faruque, a librarian working at UIUC and his wife Parul; Dr. Zahirul Islam, a post-doctoral fellow in agriculture and his wife Rukhsana; Ruhul Hoque, a businessman and his wife Nazma Hoque; Sharif, a civil engineer working for Champaign County and his wife Rushi, a medical doctor; Dr. Shah Jahan Ali, a researcher at UIUC and his wife Nargis; Dr. Tareq Islam, an oncological physicist at local Carle Hospital and his wife Luna; Mizan, a businessman and his wife Rani, a medical doctor; Wahidul Islam, a mechanical engineer working for Caterpillar in Decatur and his wife Rumana; Dr. Mizan Mehtab, M.D. and his wife Rumana (Rumki), a law professor at UIUC; Dr. Nadim Ahmed, M.D. and his wife Rita; Dr. Chandra Nath, a post-doctoral fellow and his wife Tanwi, as well as a few others. The medical doctors were all working at Carle Hospital. We socialized with them on a regular basis. Many of them were helpful during our difficult days, in addition to our older friends. However, because of Dora's illness our mutual social visits became fewer and fewer.

The remainder of the year 2013 and much of 2014 went well for us compared to what we experienced in the previous few years. But one night in the middle of November 2014, I saw many black flying particles called floaters in my right eye. I had no idea what they were. I checked on the internet where I read that they were generally harmless. That was music to my ears. The following night, I saw some flashing lights, almost looking like lightning, in that same eye. I waited and thought these things would heal on their own and go away with some rest. The next morning, I felt as if some dark screen was blocking my peripheral vision when I turned my head. I realized something was getting serious and called the doctor's office. The receptionist told me to go and see the doctor that afternoon. I had a class to teach at that time and didn't want to miss the class. The content of that lecture was the last segment of a topic and was crucial for the students to learn before their approaching final exam.

I went to see an ophthalmologist Dr. George Panagakis the next day at Carle Hospital. Upon checking my eye, he told me that I had a detached retina and told a nurse to accompany me and take me to Dr. Mike Tsipurski, a retina surgeon in the same floor. My eye was immediately checked by the surgeon who told me that I had two retinal tears and one third of the retina was detached from the eye wall and any further delay would have caused more detachment and would damage the macula that would lead to permanent loss of vision. He treated me with an injection in the eye, infusing some gas bubble inside, after numbing it, instructed me to lean my head on one side, and told me that that he would check it the next day; if this didn't work he would have to do a surgery on my eye. Salim Rashid, with whom I had long-time friendship and his wife Zeenet Rashid, were always available to help us out; they came to take me home.

The next day he said there was still a problem and I should see him again the following day in the morning and come prepared for surgery. The following day, after checking my eye he decided to operate.

When he explained the procedure, it was scary to hear how he would cut across my eye sparing the lens. I realized he had to work on a very small area inside my eye and realized I would have to trust him, just as I had to trust a pilot if I was flying. Being a technical man myself, I trusted my own training and calculations when assessing the performance of any structure.

I liked the surgeon, he appeared to be very professional and caring. I stayed calm and prayed to God to keep me strong and make the surgery successful, so my vision was restored. A nurse came to see me for some paperwork and told me I was scheduled for 5:00 PM and I could not eat or drink anything. I went for pre-op tests when a call came to tell me that a spot was available, and the surgery would be done at 1:00 PM, and I should report to the outpatient surgery department immediately. Soon after that I was put to sleep. I woke up as the anesthesia wore off. My real suffering, unexpected, began after that.

As soon as I woke up in my hospital room, I found myself sitting on a chair with Dora holding my head down. A nurse told me not to look up or around as I was trying to see the people around me. The retina surgeon explained to Dora and the Rashids following the surgery, that I had to keep my head down continuously for 24 hours, for seven days with a 10-minute break every hour. When I went home Ifat had arrived from Chicago. Ifat made all the arrangements to rent a special chair and bed.

The first night I sat on a regular chair with my head down on a desk, and when it became unbearable, I sat on the floor leaning against the side of the bed with my head down. I could hardly sleep. The chair had a headrest in the front with a hole for breathing. The bed was like a massage table, I lay on my stomach. It was quite a depressing experience being cut off from the world, it was like torture for a workaholic like me. My right eye was bloodshot and was covered with a bandage initially. My habit of meditation helped me through these days, reflecting upon my past life and seeking God's help and forgiveness for my shortcomings. Despite my distress I felt connected to God and counted on His help and protection.

I went to see Dr. Tsipurski as instructed for regular follow-ups and he assured me I would be fine, but it might take up to two months to regain my vision. He also told me that he found a third tear in my retina during the surgery that he hadn't see the first time and that could be a reason why his first attempt to treat it with an injection didn't succeed. After the seven-day period, I could return to my normal life, except without vision in my right eye. Occasionally, the frightening thought crossed my mind: what if my vision did not come back? By now I was battle-hardened and resilient, after all the health issues my family and I had faced. I kept a positive attitude. I rediscovered that resolve in the face of adversity could help me locate my inner strength. Next, I developed a severe sinus infection with large chunks of blood clots coming out of my nose and throat. This was because I had to keep my head down for so long. I drove to a nearby Carle Clinic again and a strong antibiotic treated the problem.

During this time, I could see faint light giving me hope that my eye was healing well. I saw a few weird images and black floaters flying in front of me. One Saturday, however, after I woke up from sleep, I saw a very large number of small black fly-like floaters blocking whatever scanty vision I had. I became nervous and contacted Dr. Tsipurski, who immediately decided to come to the hospital. Dora's nephew Tamim Khan, a graduate student at UIUC, living with us at the time drove me and Dora to the hospital. We hurried to the retina department, after a short wait. Dr. Tsipurski opened the door and motioned to me to go to a treatment room and have a seat. After checking my eye, he said that he didn't see any problem. Feeling somewhat relieved I came back home. I was functioning with one eye. After about a month, I started seeing things progressively better albeit very slowly. Over time my vision improved, and I saw fewer floaters. I managed to administer and grade the final exam for my course. As it happens, I was not out of the woods though, next I developed double vision.

This made driving difficult. Dora used to drive a lot, but after her renal transplant she developed a neurological problem with her feet, possibly as a reaction to anti-rejection drugs, and stopped driving. I had been always independent and didn't want to bother anybody on a routine basis. On the road, I would close my affected eye, so I could see single images. This worked, but the condition continued for a few days. The doctor could not give a good explanation of it. I assumed that perhaps my brain was calibrating my newly regained vision after surgery.

It so happened that Murad came to visit us, and he brought a movie for us to watch. I had some difficulty watching it but tried my best. At that time, I got a call from my sister Shahid Ara in Canada enquiring about my health. Miraculously, as I was telling her about my double vision, I started seeing two images of an object merge. I told her as we spoke. The next morning, my condition improved and from then onward, I began to see things normally.

It was already January 2015, and the winter semester began. I decided to teach to stay active and thought of maybe continuing to teach for the long term. However, our two daughters urged us to move to Chicago, so we could be close to them. They assured us that they would take care of finding a house for us and for moving us. Chicagoland was not new to us, as we started our life in America in this large city and had a real fondness for it. Dora and I finally agreed and decided to move close to our daughters. It was through the efforts of Jinat that we contracted a builder to build a new home in a suburb called Naperville. We left Champaign on November 6. Ifat contributed to the interior design, with paint color, curtains, and more. We were given a farewell party by the local community. After that we also threw a dinner party for the community before we left. After staying at Jinat's home overnight we moved into our new home on November 7 in the morning and started our new life.

We liked it immensely as Chicago was familiar and we enjoyed the company of our daughters, fine sons-in-law, and more importantly, our three grandchildren. We also reconnected with some old friends and met new people. But we missed Urbana-Champaign, the UIUC campus life and our friends there. We had lived there for almost 31 years, the longest that I had lived anywhere.

Jinat's MBA graduation, (L to R: Seated: Dora, Ifat, Mike;
Standing: Me, Murad, Jinat, Byron), Chicago, IL 2003

Dora and me, Cairo Museum 2007

My first camel excursion, Cairo, Egypt 2007

Lunch reception in my honor in Malta where I was on Fulbright mission
at the U.S. Ambassador's residence 2008

My three grandchildren (Talia, Rasim & Jayna)
with me in my home in Savoy, IL 2010

Dora and me in Turkey 2010

My family at Murad's wedding in Dallas, TX, July 2010

With Professor Kathy Anthony, friend and colleague,
at the Bombay Indian Grill in Champaign, IL 2013

My 70th birthday with daughters Ifat and Jinat in Champaign, IL 2014

Muirwoods Park near San Francisco, October 2018

My nephew Tarek and me before Holud occasion as prelude to Murad's wedding, a traditional Bengali custom, Dallas, TX, July 2010

Dora and me next to the Mediterranean Sea, Alexandria, Egypt 2007

Speaking at the fundraising dinner in New York, NY for Fazlur Rahman
Khan Chair at Lehigh University, November 1997

Dora and me at Stanford University Campus,
Palo Alto, CA, October 2018

Dora and me at the Sphinx in Giza on the outskirts of Cairo, Egypt 2007

A group of engineer friends at a dinner party hosted by A. Mannan;
(L to R: Aminul Karim, me, Mansurul Haque Ahmed, Jamilur Reza
Choudhury, Nurul Ambia Chowdhury, Ferdous Chowdhury),
Lake Forest, IL , September 2018

Murad, Mike and me visiting my newborn
grandson Rasim, Chicago IL 2007

My first grandchild Talia 2006

With engineering classmates and friends at the office of DDC
Consultants; A.K.M. Rafiquddin, founder and Managing Director
of the firm is to my left, Dhaka 2006

With my fourth grandchild Leila 2017

A group picture of my entire family 2017

PART FOUR
FULFILLMENTS

CHAPTER 14

MY BOOKS

Living My Dream

The ups and downs of my life helped me develop patience and resilience in the face of adversity. I never blamed my environment, or any person, and took responsibility for my own life. Fortunately, most of the setbacks were overcome by my efforts and my destiny. I didn't allow grief and sadness to consume me, there is no point in that. I knew events in life naturally came and went in cycles. Happiness and sadness interspersed, like light and darkness. Professor H. Leipholz, Dean of Engineering, gave me this advice when I went to see him before I left the University of Waterloo, after finishing my doctoral studies.

Fortunately, I was able to compartmentalize my professional and personal lives. When I had to focus on work or studies, I could handle life's difficulties. Life has never been easy for me. But it came together in the delightful moments between hardships. Like securing a job at SOM, my quick promotion to full professor and publication of my books. Writing relieves me from worldly and personal issues. Writing, whether books or articles, keeps me engaged with concepts and intellectual exercises. If my writing influences or benefits someone else, then I would consider that an accomplishment. Seeing my own books published has been a source of boundless joy, as I was able to live out my dream of authorship.

During my years at UIUC, I wrote and edited a few books, even at times through personal adversity. As a child and in my teenage years I wrote short stories. I composed some Bengali poems while in my native country and after I immigrated to Canada. I also wrote an essay in English about the political situation of East Pakistan before leaving the country. When I left Dhaka for Waterloo in 1970, I was in the middle of writing a Bengali novel which fell by the wayside and was never completed because of the move. There's a story behind each book that I authored or edited. Of course, I wrote many papers and articles in diverse areas: from structural engineering, flood control, transportation, low-cost housing, tall buildings, urban design, to Islamic architecture. I didn't necessarily seek out book projects, but circumstances induced me to become author or editor.

Architecture of Tall Buildings (1995)

In 1988 I had an opportunity to meet Dr. Lynn S. Beedle, the founder of CTBUH. He was the chief guest, invited by the Bangladesh Association of Chicago, where I met him first. He was fundraising for the proposed Fazlur Rahman Khan Chair that he conceived of to be established at Lehigh University. I told him I wanted to meet him one day as I knew so much about him through readings about the CTBUH and his crucial role. I volunteered to contribute as I had a strong interest in tall building research. Upon my return to Urbana-Champaign, where I lived, I received a letter from the CTBUH stating that I had been appointed Chairman of the Committee on Architecture. The committee was composed of 33 members from around the world. There were several architects, both professionals and academic, and included such famous names as Henry J. Cowan,

Myron Goldsmith, Bruce Graham, and Ken Yeang, among others.

As committee chairman, my job was to coordinate with the members regarding the latest research and developments in the field of tall building architecture. I would also be responsible for developing a Monograph, as one of a series of monographs, prepared under the sponsorship of CTBUH. An earlier Monograph, Volume PC: Planning and Environmental Criteria of Tall Buildings, was published in 1981, in which a chapter on architecture was included.

The committee I chaired decided there was a need to produce a new Monograph that would encompass the issue of architecture in a comprehensive manner. The scope of the Monograph focused on the specific issues affecting and shaping the design of tall buildings in a complex and rapidly changing world. I was responsible for the primary conceptual and editorial work of the Monograph. I was in touch with my committee members from time to time to seek their opinions. We endeavored to preserve the in-depth nature of the subjects we had chosen. I contacted about 50 architects, engineers and urban planners inviting them to contribute to the Monograph in their respective areas of expertise. I got many commitments; eventually followed by 32 written contributions on tall building architecture from the perspective of the leading professionals of Australia, Canada, India, Italy, Japan, Malaysia, Spain and the U.S., several of whom were star architects and academics.

The Monograph was compiled deliberately with an international scope. This unique international work was poised to examine the many issues that must be considered when designing tall buildings as part of the urban habitat. The tall building design process is collaborative. Professionals must be supported by the most up-to-date technology, research, and innovative thinking regarding tall building architecture in this endeavor.

Initially, I was on my own for some time, carrying out this major project. I was looking for an editor to assist me. At the recommendation of my colleague Professor Johann Albrecht, I invited Professor Paul Armstrong, an assistant professor at the time, to be the editor responsible for comprehensive editing. He readily accepted my invitation. I took the lead in preparing an outline of 12 chapters on diverse topics. I spent an immense amount of time corresponding with the contributors in different countries via mail as emails were still not in place.

Upon receiving several contributions, I realized that editing for non-native English speakers would be a major challenge. I discussed this with Paul and decided to apply for a research grant from the UIUC Research Board, which was approved. We hired two research assistants Jennifer Salen and Douglas Shoemaker, both of whom were graduate students in our school and turned out to be excellent and dedicated workers. We also got a room and a computer dedicated to the project in Flagg Hall, one of the buildings of the School of Architecture. I contributed large sections of the book and so did Paul Armstrong.

The editing process continued under my overall supervision. I was fortunate to have Paul Armstrong, as he was thorough and dedicated to the project. This process continued for a few years. Throughout the process, I coordinated with Dr. Beedle for guidance about the direction of the project, counting upon his vast experience and clout. When working on the book became a drag, he encouraged me and continuously appreciated my leadership and work. His leadership style was courteous, he motivated volunteers by gentle persuasion. He also reviewed the entire manuscript. At a later stage, CTBUH asked me to add a full segment at the end of the text with the title of "Current Questions, Problems, and Research Needs" which I almost single-handedly did. I was also asked to add a Nomenclature containing a glossary of terms used in the Monograph and a Building Index of the tall buildings cited. We hired Aparna Bapu and David Eilken as research assistants for short-time assignments on these items.

I organized and chaired a workshop session "Architecture of Tall Buildings" at the Fifth World Congress on Tall Buildings in Amsterdam, The Netherlands, in May 1995 with the purpose of gaining additional insights into the subject from accomplished architects from around the world. Finally, the book was published by McGraw-Hill the same year. When I got a few complementary copies, I felt immense gratification at producing my first book -- a book of such magnitude for the first time. I also felt that my sustained hard work had paid off. The project was going full swing in late 1992 but stalled when I had a heart attack. Even in my hospital bed, while thinking of my mortality, I was concerned about the future of the book if I didn't survive.

The 750-page book was unique in scope and content. I didn't initially envision that it would be so exhaustive, but ultimately it was. In addition to the entire architectural design process, it provided comprehensive coverage of feasibility studies, urban development and zoning, tall buildings of varied occupancies, form and aesthetics, psychological aspects of tall buildings, integration of facade design and structural elements, design and construction automation, to name a few. It explored innovative building materials, high-efficiency environmental systems, and a host of other topics, making it an essential reference tool for architects, engineers, and developers. Throughout the sourcebook the narratives were abundantly illustrated. It highlighted the valuable contributions of some of the world's most famous architects. Their views and insights, collected into a single book, was a rarity. The book offered the concept, the philosophy, the art; in short, it allowed a journey of the reality of building tall.

This book was the first of its kind. It was set a course for my career as I benefited from it in multiple ways. By contributing major chapter sections and editing the entire manuscript, I developed heightened awareness, understanding, and skill in the art of writing. We had to incorporate different contributions as sections in chapters, at appropriate places, and ensure that they blended in with other contributions in keeping with the theme.

I became well connected with many international contributors and learned how they envisioned the architecture of tall buildings in general and in their own respective countries. The many case studies were instrumental to my learning in diverse areas. Although I am a structural engineer, I always aspired to have a wider view of tall buildings and understand how people debated tallness from various perspectives. I quickly learned the architectural vocabulary that helped me write many papers and articles.

This facilitated better communication with architectural faculty members at my own school, with the students in classroom and design studio settings and with professional architects at other venues. My relationship with my colleague Paul cemented through this association, propelled us to work together again later, on other papers and another book. Our collaboration became an example at the school about how a structures professor could collaborate with an architectural design counterpart.

Bangladesh Floods: Views from Home and Abroad (1998)

After the devastating floods in 1987 and 1988 in Bangladesh, I took the lead in establishing an organization called Bangladesh Environment and Flood Committee (BEFCA). I initially invited some of my friends whom I thought were interested to a meeting held in Chicago. Two international conferences on flood problems in Bangladesh were subsequently organized by BEFCA and the Institute of Flood Control and Drainage Research (IFCDR) of Bangladesh University of Engineering & Technology (BUET).

The first conference was held at UIUC in Champaign during April 2-4, 1993. The objective of this conference was to examine the multidisciplinary issues related to the recurring flood problem of Bangladesh with special emphasis on the Bangladesh Flood Action Plan (FAP) that was launched after two disastrous floods. A total of 22 papers were presented in 7 sessions in the conference.

Soon after the conference, a catastrophic flood hit the upper Mississippi River basin. This devastation called for more innovative flood plain management in the U.S. It inspired BEFCA to think that the lessons learned during and after the Mississippi flood could provide valuable insight into the modification and enhancement of the FAP in Bangladesh. To fulfil this goal, a second international conference was organized jointly by BEFCA and IFCDR in Dhaka, Bangladesh during May 25-27, 1995. A total of 11 papers were presented in this conference.

In both conferences, papers were presented by specialists and experts from both Bangladesh and the U.S. I edited the proceedings of the 1993 conference, which were published by The Center for International Business Education and Research of UIUC. The 1995 conference proceedings were published by the University Press Limited (UPL) in Bangladesh. Both conferences were broadly publicized in the U.S. and Bangladesh.

BEFCA and IFCDR thought that some selected papers from both conferences could be published in a book that offered a cumulative account of the experts' insights. An editorial committee consisting of Mir M. Ali and Salim Rashid from BEFCA and M. Mozzammel Hoque and Rezaur Rahman from IFCDR was formed. Selection was made by the committee for nine papers from the 1993 conference presented in Part I and 11 papers from the 1995 conference included in Part II of the book. Each paper was presented as a chapter, thereby making the 285-page book a total of 20 chapters long. The book was published by University Press Ltd. (UPL) in 1998.

The Editorial Statement in the book stated the core objective and future expectation stemming from the initial compilation and editing:

"The present attempt to publish some selected papers from both proceedings in the form of a book was conceived in 1995, when it was thought that the papers on such an important issue should be better documented to reach a much wider audience. The papers taken together represent a broad spectrum of topics related to floods and indicate the present state of the art. In some cases, papers have been updated by the authors.

...It is hoped that this book will serve to time-bind this generation of scholars and professionals to future generations who will still seek a "permanent" solution to the almost eternal flood problems of Bangladesh and USA."

I was delighted by the outcome when we established BEFCA in Chicago with a small but devoted group. I had no idea we could accomplish so much. When the book was published, Bangladesh was in the process of preparing a national water management plan. The consensus of the conferences and associated workshops emerged from multiple viewpoints expressed by different experts, in an apolitical climate. Experts agreed that emphasis should be on management and mitigation rather than structural solutions. Building extensive embankments could adversely affect Mother Nature. Our efforts may have influenced the decision makers, as river basin management became the core principle driving the flood control policy of Bangladesh.

The deliberations of the conferences were valuable for the researchers, environmentalists and decision-makers of other countries facing flood-related challenges. I also benefited from the collaboration of many individuals from Bangladesh and the

U.S. and developed friendships with several people that has lasted for many years.

Although I was not the sole editor of the book and its publication was possible because of the collaborative efforts of all of the co-editors, I took pride in it. I viewed it as the fruit of BEFCA's efforts in collaboration with IFCDR. It represented an important documentation of papers of varied content, a treasure trove for future researchers on floods in Bangladesh.

Art of the Skyscraper: The Genius of Fazlur Khan (2001)

When I had been working as a project engineer at SOM in Chicago from1980-84, I had the opportunity of working on two projects with Fazlur R. Khan, who was the partner-in-charge. The second project was a tall building called Pacific Plaza in Los Angeles. As mentioned previously, I also came to know him on a personal level, through the Bangladeshi cultural events hosted by the Bangladesh Association of Chicago, which he had founded in 1980, the same year that I joined SOM.

While at SOM, I heard him speak in an in-house seminar and realized the extensive research and professional work that he carried out. I noticed that he would come to office early and leave late. Following his untimely death in 1982, all the organizations and media related to the building industry reacted in grief and showered their praise and appreciation of his work and innovations. He was variously referred to as the "Einstein of Structural Engineering," as "philosophical engineer," as "gentle giant," "towering personality" and so on. A top construction magazine, the *Engineering News-Record (ENR)*, identified him as "master builder" and "thought leader" and called him "one of the century's most eminent structural engineers" and *Newsweek* called him "the man at the top." Such admiration for him left a remarkable impression on me. I realized how he revolutionized the structural design of tall buildings. Even after I moved to Singapore and then Urbana-Champaign, I continued to study his work as I had been undertaking tall building research. I found out more about him from the literature. I had already collected plenty of materials on his life and work from various sources for future reference. Also, after being associated with CTBUH, of which he was a co-founder, I learned even more about him. So, I thought I had enough material to write a book. But after working very hard for a few years on the establishment and operation of BEFCA and the two flood-related conferences, and the CTBUH Monograph *Architecture of Tall Buildings*, I was not thinking seriously about writing again right then.

Shortly after Dr. Khan's death, Professor Lynn Beedle conceived the idea of establishing a Chair in his honor at Lehigh University. I was appointed a member of the Fazlur Rahman Khan Chair Advisory Committee, and soon I joined the fundraising effort by Lynn Beedle as a volunteer. I contacted many acquaintances. In November 1997, the Bangladeshi community in New York organized a fundraising dinner there, spearheaded by Dr. Sufyan Khondoker, whom I had contacted earlier about the Khan Chair. I visited there with Dora and stayed in a friend's home in New Jersey. My host and friend Dr. Ashfaq Hossain took me to his office at Lucent Technologies one weekend. He showed me a few pictures in the main lobby of the office of innovators in his field of computer engineering.

During the conversation, the name of Dr. Fazlur R. Khan came up as one of the innovators in tall buildings. When asked, I briefly explained the innovations that made Dr. Khan so renowned in the tall building industry. He looked at me and said, "You know so much about his work and knew him personally...why don't you write a book about him?" I replied, "Great suggestion! I will think about it." He strongly urged me to do it. I then felt a powerful impulse to write a book as I had collected so much information on Dr. Khan and worked with him personally.

After I returned to Champaign, I got busy with my family and work, but his impromptu suggestion kept ringing in my ears. It rekindled a flickering flame. I was holding off this wish for many years hoping someone else would do it as I had been hearing rumors that several individuals were planning to. I started thinking more seriously about this. With my editorial and writing experience I felt confident I could do it. I realized it would be a lot of hard work, but it would be worthwhile to begin this new journey of a writing project without delay. I prepared an outline of several chapters. I knew from experience that writing a book started with writing a chapter, remaining determined and focused, and making progress. Once I started and had gone some distance, I couldn't quit.

I decided to write the book with two main goals; first, to provide a biography of a memorable life, and secondly, to describe his projects and accomplishments. My combined professional and academic backgrounds in structural engineering and architecture, coupled with the fact that both of us were from Bangladesh, were helpful for critiquing his projects and appreciating his design philosophy and motivation.

With Dora's support and cooperation, I began to write the book. I never learned professional typing. Thus far, I had been writing by hand. My handwritten papers were then typed by Jane Cook, at our School's word processing center. This book was no exception. I went to libraries for his journal and magazine articles, and even to the Ryerson and Burnham Libraries at the Art Institute of Chicago, where many documents related to him were archived at the behest of his wife, Liselotte Khan. I visited CTBUH headquarters at Bethlehem, PA to research his activities with that organization. Lynn Beedle organized an event there at Lehigh University where I delivered a seminar on the life and work of Dr. Fazlur Rahman Khan.

I also interviewed many people personally, foremost among those were his advisor Professor Chester Seiss and co-advisor Professor Narbey Khachaturian, from academia; Lynn Beedle, his colleague and founder of CTBUH, Bruce Graham, his architectural partner, Hal Iyengar his closest structural associate and an icon in his own right, and John Zils, his protégé and my former boss at SOM, from the profession; Joseph Colaco, a prominent structural engineer, President of CBM Engineers in Houston, TX and a close former associate of Khan at SOM; Chandra Jha, a developer and owner of PSM International, Chicago and his closest friend; Mark Fintel, a professional from Portland Cement Association and his friend; and Jane Quinn, his secretary. I also interviewed several people on the phone including Professor Ralph Peck, a collaborator with Professor Karl Terzaghi (the father of Soil Mechanics) and a giant of soil mechanics in his own right; and Probhash Nag and Hem Gupta, his Indian friends. I was fortunate to interview so many distinguished people. I also interviewed a few students of his from Illinois Institute of Technology (IIT) where he was an adjunct professor. There were several others whom I mentioned in my book.

In 1999, I went on sabbatical leave and visited Bangladesh where I also interviewed a few people, foremost among them were Musharraf Hossain, retired professor of Economics at Dhaka University and a close friend of Khan; Abul Faraz Khan, Superintending Engineer of Public Works Department; Bashirul Haq, a reputed architect; Zillur Rahman Siddiqui, husband of Khan's cousin; and Zeaul Huq, Khan's cousin. My friend A.K.M. Rafiquddin, Managing Director of Development Design Consultants Ltd., who arranged a seminar on Dr. Fazlur Rahman Khan at his office on October 13, 1999, which was attended by many architects and engineers. I also received information from some Bangladeshis in the U.S. and Bangladeshis who knew him well, foremost among them were Professor Aminul Karim and Dr. M. Sirajullah M.D. in Chicago and Dr. Jamilur Reza Choudhury in Dhaka.

As I began writing the first chapter, which was an overview of his life, I felt the urge to write more and gather more information. Initially, I had planned for a few chapters but eventually the book totaled 16 chapters. Dr. Khan rose to fame mainly because of his success with the innovative design of Chicago's John Hancock Center and the Sears Tower (renamed Willis Tower). Dr. Beedle suggested that I add a chapter on the Tall Building Council as Dr. Khan had a prominent role in the shaping of the Council. Also, I added a chapter on the Haj Terminal in Jeddah, Saudi Arabia as it was a major project, being the largest fabric roof structure and the largest "permanent" tent structure of the world. He developed the design concepts, although it was not a tall building structure.

Although he was a structural engineer by training, he grew into a complete designer and a master builder, integrating aesthetics, construction, technology, and the building services systems. I covered these in the book, which also addressed the humanistic side of him as a philosopher- engineer. His love for many cultures and his interest in people were described. Also portrayed was his deep concern and feelings for the U.S., and the world at large, as well as his own roots in Bangladesh. His death and the circumstances surrounding his death were described. Recognitions granted posthumously, especially focusing on the establishment the Fazlur Rahman Khan Chair at Lehigh University were covered as a separate chapter.

I attempted to assess the impact that he made on the design and construction industries, as well as society at large. His enormous success during his rather short life was due to his own brilliance and acumen, but also the loyalty, support and collaboration of his colleagues and associates. The huge success of his projects was possible because of teamwork and collaboration with his fellow architects and engineers, that was part of his genius. I credited the contributions by others in my book wherever possible.

I devoted a full chapter to his humanistic side, chapter 13, "A Lover of Humanity." He was more than a technical man, but also a devotee of humanity. On December 14, 1983 after Dr. Khan's death in 1982, a plaque was installed in the front lobby of the Onterie Center building in Chicago, which was his final project. It was designed and made by the French-born artist Juan Gardy Artigas. A quotation from Dr. Khan was inscribed on the plaque:

> The technical man must not be lost in his own technology;
> he must be able to appreciate life, and life is art,
> drama, music, and most importantly, people.

He liked classical music and his native Bengali music. The Bengali language, spoken by about 250 million people, in Bangladesh and the Indian province of West Bengal, has a rich heritage. During the Liberation Movement of Bangladesh in 1971, *Time* magazine called Bengali a "singsong language." The language has been immensely enriched by Rabindranath Tagore and Kazi Nazrul Islam, two great poets amongst so many other literary greats. Khan was very fond of Tagore's songs. One song he often sang to himself opened with:

Tomar holo shuru, amar holo shara
Tomaye amaye meelay emni bahey dhara

Translation:
>   This is your beginning and my end
>   The flow (of life) continues mixing both of us.

In the book, I also portrayed him as cultured, international citizen, who was sensitive to ethnic differences in a respectful way. Because of his untimely death at the age of 52, I devoted an entire chapter to the circumstances leading to his death. Complying with his wife's request, he was buried in Chicago's Graceland Cemetery where many renowned architects, engineers and Chicago's many luminaries are buried. He led a life of unique quality and greatness that I captured in the book in a couplet written by the renowned Pakistani poet and philosopher Dr. Mohammad Iqbal:

>   Live your life in such a way that,
>   should death be eternal,
>   God should be ashamed of that.

Towards the end of the book, I recounted how several posthumous recognitions were bestowed on him and how his spirit lived on.

Echoing the sentiment of many about the endeavors of future engineers, I concluded my book with these words:

>   They may well reach much greater heights of buildings
>   than what we can imagine. Khan laid down the path for
>   them.
>   He will always remain the guiding spirit.
>   Future giants of skyscraper design will undoubtedly
>   stand on his shoulders and look upon his work seriously.
>   Students of tall building design ... will appreciate his
>   constant search for structural logic and truth in architecture.

...Sure, future designers will be humbled by his insights
relating to society and to humanity at large.
Together, these will be Khan's lasting legacy.
Meanwhile, his great structures will continue to
soar into the sky and gleam in the sun.

The amply illustrated 240-page book was published by Rizzoli
International Publications, Inc. in 2001. It got wide publicity. It
was released in November 2001, shortly after the tragic event in
New York on September 11. Because of this it received additional
attention as the book dealt with tall buildings. I was immediately
invited to a book signing event at the Prairie Avenue Bookshop
in Chicago, IL on November 14. The large lecture hall was full,
where I spoke for an hour about the book with a lecture title
"Skyscrapers, Technology, Art and a Vision: Insights of an Innovator." The book was well received.

In 2003, when I visited Bangladesh, I was invited to give a
lecture on the book at the Engineers' Institution of Bangladesh,
Dhaka on July 8. The large auditorium was full. The size of the
audience in Chicago in 2001 and Dhaka in 2003 demonstrated
how popular Dr. Khan was in the building industry in both the
U.S. and Bangladesh. I donated a copy of my book to the Institution's library and another copy to the library of BUET. The
book was subsequently translated into the Korean language by
a Korean publisher. A Bangladeshi publisher saw me in Urbana-
Champaign and wanted to publish a Bengali version of the
book. However, this never materialized.

Catalyst for Skyscraper Revolution: Lynn S. Beedle – A Leg-
end in His Lifetime (2004)

This book came out of nowhere. The idea of preparing this book
was conceived and initiated by a few friends of Dr. Lynn S. Beedle who had known him and worked with him for many years,

led by Professor Ryszard Kowalczyk from Poland. The Initiative Group consisted of: Ryszard Kowalczyk (Group Leader), Sabah Al-Rayes, Mir M. Ali, Henry J. Cowan, Manfred Hirt, R. Shankar Nair, and Gilberto do Valle.

The purpose of this proposed book was to advance the Council's cause and legacy by shedding light on the achievements and dedication of Dr. Beedle. We sought to document his will to transform the Council into a prestigious and authoritative international and interdisciplinary organization. Dr. Beedle was recognized for his efforts and as the founder of the Council through the Award Dinner and the establishment of the Lynn S. Beedle Achievement Award.

The Initiative Group thought the Council could do more. They believed that while he was known to all previous members of CTBUH, new incoming members should be acquainted with his contributions. This could be done through documenting his life and work in a book. The Initiative Group prepared a proposal and presented it to CTBUH. Ron Klemencic, the Council Chairman embraced the idea and Sabah Al-Rayes offered a generous gift to fully finance its production.

Ryszard Kowalczyk, on behalf of the Initiative Group, invited me to be the editor, which I accepted. I realized that this would demand a lot of hard work collecting materials, compiling, and editing. Despite this, I decided to take it on as a "labor of love", simply because of my immense respect for Dr. Beedle. It was an entirely voluntary project for me, but I didn't mind it. Instead of going to an outside publisher, I decided to produce it at UIUC and get it published by CTBUH, an idea embraced by CTBUH. An Editorial Committee was set up with Ryszard Kowalczyk (Chair), Sabah Al-Rayes, Mir M. Ali, Henry Cowan, Ron Klemencic, and R. Shankar Nair.

Dr. Lynn Beedle's active career with Lehigh University, the Structural Stability Research Council (SSRC) and CTBUH spanned a half century. He received his highest recognition at Lehigh University where he was named University Distinguished Professor. He transformed the Column Research Council (renamed SSRC) into a highly successful research organization with a much broader scope. His close association with the famous Fritz Laboratory as its long-time director helped him in this regard. It also propelled him to the position of top authority in the field of plastic design of steel structures in the U.S. He transformed the Joint Committee on Tall Buildings into CTBUH, which continues to flourish even now and impact the urban fabric and environment of cities around the world.

He was far more than a talented structural engineer -- he was a thinker, a prolific writer, and a practical manager. He was keenly interested in people, in the arts, in politics, in athletics, in spirituality, and in music. An eternal networker, he believed in collaboration during his entire career. He had strong opinions but was willing to listen to others with an open mind and to accept new ideas. It was not easy to depict the many facets of his persona and achievements over a long period of time.

Before starting the book, I called him. He was driving at that time but instead of cutting me off while he was on the road, he moved to a parking lot and asked me why I was calling. I gave him the news about the book. He didn't hide his joy upon hearing this unexpected news and told me, "Knowing you, you will do a good job." To get a rare glimpse into the workings of the mind of this august personality who evoked reverence and admiration, I asked him if I could interview him later for his thoughts and opinions. He agreed. He also obliged to give me documents, pictures and more to use for the book. To gather information about his parents, family, and childhood I contacted some of his family members.

In the first chapter, which was a biographical, I wrote about his early childhood, youth, education, marriage, his active career and achievements, and retirement. Beedle's thoughts and opinions constitute the subject matter of the second chapter. In the next chapter I discussed the history and his involvement in CTBUH. The next two chapters were focused on the events surrounding the Award Night to honor him and the many tributes that I sought from people. The speeches given during the Award Night and congratulatory letters from his friends and well-wishers were recorded in one chapter. All the tributes were presented in a separate chapter. I resisted including my own tribute in this chapter and instead offered it in the "Afterword".

Dr. Beedle worked tirelessly to establish the Fazlur Rahman Khan Chair at Lehigh University to honor Dr. Khan and his legacy. I was involved in the program as I have written elsewhere. Unfortunately, because of the time crunch and my wish to publish the book in his lifetime, I rushed the project. I was working overtime, mainly alone on this voluntary undertaking, and in the process, through oversight, I didn't include his efforts in this regard in a separate chapter. I take some satisfaction in knowing that I had covered his contribution, in detail, in my book *Art of the Skyscraper: The Genius of Fazlur Khan,* where I explained Dr. Beedle's total dedication to the establishment of the Fazlur Rahman Khan Chair.

The tragic news of his terminal illness shocked his relatives, friends and colleagues worldwide. He informed them himself via an inspiring letter he emailed to them. He titled it "Free Ball." The letter showed the inner strength and positive attitude that he possessed. As I knew and observed him, he was an eternal optimist and his life had indeed been a celebration of the human spirit. I included his letter and the messages from several people in response to this letter in the last chapter. I am reproducing his letter here as I feel it is a very special one.

Free Ball

We think we're going to be here forever. Then suddenly we realize, firsthand, that there are limits. This week the doctor told me I had pancreatic cancer and that the tumor is inoperable (from both 2nd and 3rd opinions).

The good news is that I don't have to take the chemo/radiation treatments that can be so debilitating. The doctor says, "They don't prolong life expectancy enough to compensate for loss in quality of life." In my case, the time perspective is six months, or a year, or two years. As every doctor has said, "Attitude means so much." We saw that dramatically when our grandson Lynn waged war against testicular cancer and was soon back playing championship hockey at Norwich University.

I have been fortunate. During the several life-threatening situations I've experienced, I never had a fear of not coming through. And I felt ready if I didn't. It's at times like this that I'm thankful my parents started me on the path to a personal belief in a Higher Power.

And let me tell you a story: When my oldest son Lynn saw me for the first time after my 1989 heart attack (which I survived only due to Ella's speed in contacting the Dewey Fire Company Ambulance) here's what he said: "Dad, do you remember those old pinball machines? ... and if you were lucky you got a free ball? Well, you got one."

I've played the free ball for 14 years. And what wonderful things have happened during this time: the annual family vacations...watching the children and grandchildren grow, mature, and succeed ... enjoying their accomplishments and those occasional awards. ... The amazing recognition I received from professional societies. ...

I am going to keep on playing that free ball. I feel great!

Lynn
May 1, 2003

In this last chapter I covered the health condition leading to his death. Dr. Beedle continued his normal work schedule despite his failing health and even went to the office of CTBUH and spent some time there. During this time, he continued his conversations with me on the phone about the book and gave me valuable information. He died peacefully in his sleep after midnight on October 30, 2003 at the age of 85. Sadly, for me he could not see the book before his death. The news of his death spread like wildfire and was widely reported in the media and newspapers, including the *New York Times* and *Los Angeles Times*.

He prepared a collection of "Notes for Living" with 379 entries, beginning in the late 1970s. He had the notes taped to the wall and to the file cabinet. Then he thought of a booklet and completed the compilation in October 2002. The material came from scriptures, hymn books, articles in *Guideposts*, the *Reader's Digest*, from technical articles and from conversations overheard in the elevators. These notes gave him courage and support for the day – a "one a day" brand of spiritual vitamin, as he called it in the Preface of the Notes. Before his death, he sent me the original for my use, which was a blessing for me as I could learn from these. I also felt that he liked me and felt close to me, as this was like a gift to me from him. In the Notes, I found entry number 1 by Ruth Stafford Peale, wife of Norman Vincent Peale published in *Guidepost*. I thought this must have been so reassuring for Beedle before his death. So, I ended the main text of the book with this entry:

There are times when I forget
And permit me to think that
I am in the midst of death.
But this is not so.
It is *life* that surrounds me. Life.
No, the Lord's promise

Is not for those who give up,
But those who forge ahead.
He has promised:
'Fear not I will help thee.'

The remaining portion of the 210-page book was filled with his travels, musings, letters, original hand-written notes, selected papers, etc.

As I mentioned, he provided me with a lot of information for this book during the critical stage when he was fighting for his life. Just a few days before his passing, he called me to discuss a historic picture of him in a crowd holding the eastern support of an arch. The picture was taken during the opening of the Golden Gate Bridge in 1937. I decided to exclude it from the book as it was a very old fuzzy picture, but he insisted that I should include it and gave the instructions about how to do it. I honored his request. After the book was published by CTBUH in 2004, his wife Ella wrote me a letter expressing her appreciation of my work and wrote to me that Her husband liked working with me, and this book kept him engaged during his end stages, as it was the last project of his life.

I was personally delighted that I could work on these two books on Dr. Fazlur R. Khan and Dr. Lynn S. Beedle and successfully complete them. Despite my overtime and very hard work, my experience was joyful. Through these books, I could bring the life and work of these two giants of the tall building industry to the attention of the international community. The book was well received in the profession and stated by the American Institute of Steel Construction (AISC) in the13th edition of AISC Steel Construction Manual, which was dedicated to the memory of Dr. Lynn S. Beedle, a rare honor.

The Skyscraper and the City: Design, Technology, and Innovation (2007)

CTBUH was initially focused on the tall building since its founders, Dr. Lynn Beedle and co-founder Dr. Fazlur R. Khan, Leslie Robertson, and a few others were structural engineers. However, the demolition of the Pruitt-Igoe Housing Project in St. Louis in 1972, led the Council to recognize other important concerns and consequences related to tall building typology, including livability, economics, planning, as well as social and environmental problems. Pruitt-Igoe was plagued with social problems and also the energy crisis of 1973 brought the issue of energy consumption in high-rise buildings into the fore. Such considerations led Dr. Beedle to teach a special course at Lehigh University in the early 1980s covering such diverse topics.

Looking back on the origin of the book, in early 2001 he had a proposition for me. He said that he had given a series of lectures for the special course he offered at Lehigh University. He had prepared handwritten lecture notes for the course. He was closely familiar with my work on the *Architecture of Tall Buildings.* He also knew that I finished my book *Art of the Skyscraper: The Genius of Fazlur Khan,* which he reviewed and was about to be published. His proposal was for us to co-author a book based on his lecture notes. At the time I was still in the final stages of finishing my latter book, so, I had reservations about taking on another book project. But I simply couldn't decline, out of my respect for him and the wonderful opportunity to work with him. He, however, made it clear that at his age, he could not do much other than review my work. In other words, I had to take full responsibility for this ambitious project. It would be a comprehensive book on tall buildings and the urban habitat. Once I agreed, he sent me all his notes. I reviewed the notes and had some difficulty with some parts of it as some of the materials required updating and some needed additional materials to make meaningful chapters. Occasionally, I had difficulty comprehending some of the ideas. I started communicating back and forth with him by writing down my feedback comments on a copy of the lecture notes, piecemeal, and following this up with phone calls after he had a chance to review my comments.

While this communication was going on, my younger brother in Cincinnati, OH passed away unexpectedly as I described before. I got busy taking care of his family. After losing my brother who was so close to me, my spirits were down, and I found it impossible to work on the book project in that mental state. I called Dr. Beedle and explained my situation. I told him clearly that I couldn't do it under my present circumstances. He was disheartened but understood my predicament. I returned all his original lecture notes and felt relieved of the responsibility of developing a new book. By 2002, as I described before, I got involved in working on a new book about him that was subsequently published in 2004.

While I was still working on the book on him, he became ill and died in October 2003. A few weeks before his death, he called and earnestly requested that I take his lecture notes back and develop the book we discussed in 2001. He told me to do it whenever and in whatever way I wished. I didn't have the heart to decline the request from a man who was terminally ill and whom I deeply revered. Without hesitation, I just said, "Please send me those notes again. I will certainly do it once I finish the book on you." I sensed a feeling of comfort and relief from him. After the conversation, I felt good that I could make him happy while he fought for his life. I made a solemn promise to myself that I must begin the task and get it published no matter what. Soon I got the notes. Once the pending book was published in 2004, I turned my full attention to the new book that I had promised to him.

I wanted the book to contribute to the extant body of knowledge on tall buildings. Although a structural engineer, as a professor in a School of Architecture I expanded my horizons to include architecture and design more broadly. This satisfied my desire to combine the interests of both my left and right brain. I had been always equally comfortable with both arts and science. My committee work with CTBUH dealing with engineers, architects, urban planners, environmentalists, sociologists, and others opened me to seeking broad perspectives.

While working on the integration of physical systems in tall buildings, I was moved by the thought that tall buildings are essentially vertical cities and as such, an extension of the cities on the ground. They share similarities in their facilities and functionalities, except at two different scales. The main theme of the book would be to logically bring together the horizontal and vertical scales of the city. Dr. Beedle had a similar vision as I found from his notes; so, my job was to update and substantially expand upon the contents of those notes, in every chapter, with the latest research, since so much had changed during the intervening period.

To keep pace with most recent developments I decided to create a few new sections with new contents nested in his notes and added four new chapters on structural framework; sustainability of tall buildings and cities; safety, serviceability and security; and megacities and megastructures.

I spent time thinking about how to frame the outline of the book. I recognized that neither urban architecture nor urban habitat could be considered in isolation. Together they defined the urban civilization that humankind had so tenaciously built and nurtured throughout history. I realized that The book might be the first of its kind and would essentially be two books in one. There were many books both on tall buildings and on cities, but none that I knew of combined the two. The diversity of the topics in the book stemmed from the relationships between architecture, urban design, contemporary engineering and technology, and societal issues. These seemingly disparate disciplines must be interlocked in order to realize a large-scale project like a skyscraper and enhance the urban fabric in which it was located. The book was written during a period of complexity and confusion caused by many conflicting events, one of which was the September 11, 2001 collapse of the World Trade Center in New York, that added a new dimension to the subject.

The aftershock of that catastrophic event involving skyscrapers was still palpable. Many questions and concerns were raised and the viability of tall buildings and their role in cities was being debated by the professional community. So, I wanted to address these in the book. The mushrooming world of the Internet and the World Wide Web (www), the impact of shifting economic centers to Asia and the Middle East, and the ramifications of the changing global culture, introduced new challenges to skyscraper design. The emerging information society precipitated unprecedented shifts that shaped our thinking and lifestyle. We were in the midst of a brave new world, in a new millennium. We were living in thought-provoking times, dealing with climate change, terrorism, ethnic turmoil, religious upheaval, war and destruction, nuclear proliferation, major natural disasters, rising energy costs, and worldwide political tension – all occurring at the same time and continuing at this writing. However, on the positive side, cities continued to grow, and new iconic skyscrapers continued to flourish. Rapid proliferation of digital, wireless and satellite technologies has made business and commerce more efficient, also impacting the design of tall buildings.

In the Introduction to the book, I wrote about the symbiotic relationship between the skyscraper and the city:

The tall building represents the quintessential modern building type, therefore the need for combining the skyscraper and the city in any discourse is compelling. Just as hydrogen and oxygen molecules combine to create water, there would be no water and no life on earth without both components interacting with each other. Drawing an analogy, we may say that without tall buildings located within the urban core, the city would be stagnant, creating no interest in major conglomerates. Without a vibrant economy created by the corporations and the city government, the city would be a 'place-less place' with no incentives for people to migrate to the urban community. This relationship works the other way. If cities did not exist, there would be no need for tall buildings, which require proximity to their urban infrastructure and a certain amount of density. The combination of tall buildings and urban environment is an interdependent relationship because one helps define the other. Skyscrapers give specific cities an identity, while cities determine how a skyscraper will be viable and be constructed and give it a meaning.

The dominant theme throughout the book was the fusion of the city, its tall buildings, and each of their components acting together as a single unit. It was emphasized that the skyscraper was merely a vertical expansion of the city for sky-high living and working.

My original plan was, as desired by Beedle, to be his co-author, a book by "Beedle and Ali" quoting him. At the start, however, I realized quickly that this book project would demand a lot of work, time, and effort as I had to cover many assorted topics. I decided to include my colleague Paul Armstrong, who had worked with me on the previous book *Architecture of Tall Buildings* and co-authored a few papers with me. I told him he would be the third author of the book. He gladly accepted. I showed him my book outline and sought his input. I asked him to write the initial draft of some chapters that were theoretical in nature with additional thoughts revolving around Dr. Beedle's notes, as Paul was proficient in architectural theory and design.

The book, when completed, consisted of 15 chapters and 774 pages with many illustrations; but because of the diverse topics covered and the length of the manuscript it was divided into Book 1 and Book 2 following the advice of the publisher Edwin Mellen Press. It was published in 2007. Once this book was published, we made it the textbook for the "High-Rise and Habitat" course. I felt very gratified that I succeeded in publishing it and keeping my promise to fulfill the last wishes of my mentor and good friend.

The Future of the City: Tall Buildings and Urban Design (2013)

In late 2007, I got an email from the Fulbright Foundation asking if I would be interested in going to Malta in the summer of 2008 and conduct a study on high-rise buildings there. I agreed and took it as an opportunity for visiting a new country, experiencing a new culture, and above all working on a project related to my keen interest. Later, I heard from my team in Malta that the Malta Environmental and Planning Authority (MEPA) requested the U.S. State Department to identify an expert on tall buildings in the U.S. This expert would conduct a study on the feasibility of high-rise buildings in Malta. Two such experts were identified, and MEPA selected me. The Fulbright Award was conferred on me to work with MEPA and the School of Architecture of the University of Malta. The overarching purpose of the project was to offer expert advice to MEPA and provide policy guidelines on the siting, use, and design of tall buildings in appropriate locations in Malta. Such policy planning became necessary as MEPA received many applications for construction permits for high-rises from builders and developers and they realized that the old permit requirements needed updating.

In the summer of 2008, I arrived in Malta on May 14 accompanied by Dora. I liked the project and was very engaged. Toward the end of the project, in June, I went to Amman, Jordan with Dora, at the invitation by the Jordan Association of Engineers to give a keynote speech at a high-rise conference. After the conference, in a plenary session, I gave my opinion about the feasibility of constructing new and future high-rise projects in Amman and the problems the country faced in this regard. Interestingly, I found a parallel between the challenges encountered by Malta and Amman.

Upon my return to Malta, I completed my study and focused on preparing a report for MEPA. This project initially posed some challenges for me as I was trained as a structural engineer, but this was an urban design project. Fortunately, my academic career in the School of Architecture at UIUC, my long-term association with CTBUH in leadership positions and the book *The Skyscraper and the City: Design, Technology and Innovation* offered me a good understanding of the cityscape.

A news reporter in Malta asked me about my formal education in structural engineering and if I was qualified to work on an urban design project. I had no difficulty in answering that question to her satisfaction. During my stay in Malta, I attended 18 meetings with administrators, architects, faculty members of civil engineering and architecture at the University of Malta, urban planners, an economist, several NGO representatives, and a social anthropologist. My experience through this project made me even more at ease with the complexities of urban life and its relationship with high-rise buildings. Further, realizing the nature and extent of the relationship between tall buildings and cities, it was not difficult for me to envision similar challenges for other cities around the world where new tall buildings were being built. The idea started fomenting about how I could translate the lessons for the benefit of the profession.

After I finished my draft report for MEPA, I had a few days of free time. I was in a reflective and contemplative state, and decided I should write another book, so that all my ideas were not lost. I sat down and quickly prepared an outline for a new book. During this time my daughter Ifat, who had a master's degree in urban planning, came to visit us from Chicago. I showed her the book outline and asked for her opinion. She correctly commented, "Dad, it will need a lot of work. You should get someone else to work on this book with you as a co-author. Kheir, who is a faculty member in urban planning at the University of Illinois at Chicago, may be a good choice since you knew him as a student at Urbana-Champaign." I took her suggestion seriously.

Upon my return to campus, I completed the formal report entitled "Urban Design Strategy Report on Tall Buildings in Malta" in July 2008 and dispatched it to MEPA. I focused on my new book and invited Dr. Kheir Al-Kodmany to be my co-author. He gladly accepted and came to Urbana-Champaign to discuss the book. We discussed the pros and cons of the topics that I had outlined.

After my classes started in the fall, I got busy for a while. Not much was being done on the book. In September, I went to Skiathos, to present at a conference on urban regeneration. My paper discussed how tall buildings could make a city sustainable. Earlier, I met the organizer of the conference, Dr. Carlos Brebbia, whom I met at an earlier conference. After hearing my presentation, he approached to ask me if I planned to write a book. WIT Press, which he led could publish one if I did. I didn't make any commitment other than saying that I would think about it and let him know. But that gave me the stimulus to write the book sooner than later, and upon my return, I expanded the outline for each chapter and brainstormed the main ideas. I entered into a contract with WIT Press with me as the first author and Kheir as second author.

After we signed it, Kheir was getting ready to face the challenge of working on the book project. I started writing but by March 2009, I felt some discomfort in my chest that led to the placement of four stents. Soon after I felt better, I started writing again thinking that I had to do most of the writing as the first author. After writing for a short while I felt stressed and tired. Dora's kidney function was declining rapidly, and I felt I should prioritize her care and my health. I reluctantly decided to drop the project and inform the publisher of my decision to annul the contract on health grounds. I made the decision and informed my co-author. I thought he would agree with my decision and feel relieved that he didn't have to go through the tedious demanding and time-consuming project.

But I was wrong. When I informed him of my decision, it was a bombshell for him. He told me that the book was such a good project and that we should not abandon it, and that he would do much more work under my direction. I realized he had been building hopes for collaborating on this book but not fully prepared to dive into the lead role. After he assured me that he would take the lead, we agreed that he would be the first author and I would be the co-author. I informed the publisher of this change. Now that he had taken major responsibility for the book, I found he was working very hard and he started writing, with some oversight provided by me. We corresponded through emails and he would frequently visit Urbana-Champaign over the weekends to sit with me at home for all-day meetings and discussions. Out of the 12 chapters of the book I took the responsibility of writing five, the Introduction, and the Preface, and he took responsibility of preparing the draft for seven chapters for me to review, along with getting pictures and developing sketches.

Our book project went smoothly. Kheir worked hard and passionately. I wrote my chapters and edited his work. The book took a global perspective on urban development and growth that encompassed skylines, regulatory aspects, the logic of vertical density, and the integration of tall buildings with their neighborhood. We asked important questions necessary to encourage smart growth, and often presented both sides of an issue. We came up with many sketches and pictures. He was very skilled in graphics and photography. I observed that whatever I told him he absorbed like a sponge. When we had almost completed the manuscript, in one of our meetings at my home I told him, "Look, this will be a great book as many ideas are introduced here. It would be really nice if we could add pictures from different cities with tall buildings to illustrate the concepts." He didn't say anything in response.

A few days later, he called me saying that he was in New York and wanted to know what kind of pictures I would like him to take for the book. After that, he not only visited several cities in North America, but also Europe and Asia. Initially, the publisher wanted the pictures in black and white to reduce cost, but after seeing a profusion of excellent pictures they decided to include color pictures. The 445-page book was published by WIT Press in 2013. Broad and deep in its scope, the beautifully illustrated book is a definitive reference source for those engaged in vertical urban design in the new century.

During this period, Dora was enduring kidney dialysis since June 2011 until March 2013, when she finally got a donor transplant. My work on this book was helpful, as it kept my mind temporarily diverted. Once the voluminous book was published, I felt delighted even in the midst of a family crisis. I was pleased the book idea that I conceived in Malta, based on my work and insights, had finally came to fruition. This was indeed possible because I had an excellent collaborator like Kheir, who also made many good contributions to the book in his areas of expertise.

Kabitamala (Necklace of Poems)

This is a book that contains poems by my brother Mosaddeq. I mentioned it in an earlier chapter. Although it is not my book, I include it here because I spent time in compiling, editing and aiding in the production of the book. Mosaddeq was a talented mechanical engineer with General Electric, designing aircraft engines. His talent didn't stop there; he loved music and loved to sing. Another remarkable quality was his fondness for poetry.

During our college days, we would discuss his practice of writing poems. I read some of them and found that he had great mastery of the Bengali language and literature. Poets often mentally travel to surreal worlds for the duration of composing a poem. After seeing, hearing or sensing something, poets get into a mood of elation and start writing a poem as if in a trance. The emotions are captured in poetic words, rhymes, and rhythms. Since I wrote a few poems, a practice that I later abandoned to focused on my career and professional writing, I experienced the exhilaration of such romanticism when my mind drifted into a dreamlike world.

The poems that Mosaddeq wrote were from his adolescence and early youth. I knew he wrote a few poems but stopped after moving to the U.S. becoming busy with study, career, and family. After his sudden death in 2001, I discovered that he had in fact written many poems. Perhaps he put these aside and was thinking of publishing them later. I was surprised at how prolific he was at a tender age. Moreover, these poems had deep embedded meaning. I knew they should be published.

During a visit to Bangladesh in 2003, I took the original handwritten poems with me. I organized the materials, written at different times, and developed a format suitable for publication. I noted that the poems could be classified in three categories, timewise. The first was from March to October of 1963.

Mosaddeq was about 16 years old. Therefore, his writing had not matured yet. However, during this short period he wrote many poems. The next category spanned from June 1964 to March 1968. During this period, his writing showed a noticeable expansion in style and thoughts. He started writing again after a hiatus beginning in December 1976. Only a few poems were composed after that. His handwriting was very artistic. I noted the influence of Rabindranath Tagore in his writing, especially during the earlier period, and of Jibananda Das, and perhaps some contemporary poets in later stages.

I selected a total of 100 poems that I thought were the best for the publication. His wife Tora funded the publication of the book. We distributed the hardbound book to our relatives and his friends. Tora also donated copies to Dhaka University Library and Patuakhali Public Library. I placed a full-page picture of him in the beginning of the book before the Preface. I designed the front cover with the picture of a chain of flowers under the book title. On the back cover, I placed another one of his pictures, under which I put an excerpt from his poem, *Bhagno Hridai Samity* (Association of Broken Hearts). Here is my English translation of it:

I need to be someone
In whom everybody will find love
Who will be shelter for all;
Whether they are rich or poor, happy or unhappy.

Towards the end stage of his writing he wrote a poem that struck me titled *Ebar Palatay Chai* (Let Us Run Away Now). The poem expressed his yearning for a peaceful independent life free from the trammels and brusqueness of modern-day fast paced life. This reminds me of a similar poem of Tagore's yearning for the independent life of an Arab Bedouin, with open sky over him and hot desert under him. He composed it in Dhaka in 1976. I present my English translation of the poem below:

Let Us Run Away Now

Let us go and live in Papua New Guinea,
Where the silent coconut trees on the seacoast
Can hear with their spread-out leaves;
Hear my loud call:
I know you and only you.

This city is too crowded for me.
The roads, alleys, walls, and barbed-wire fences
Always hear with their ears
Just like men and women.
Any event gets arrested in cameras
Press releases go out everywhere in no time.
All words are spread with fanfare.
I am wounded by the reactions to all these actions.

I want to move away from here
Taking you with me.
I want to go to Papua New Guinea.
There I can loudly say without hesitation –
I know you and only you.

You will see those coconut trees will
Passionately agree with me;
And will the exotic birds, the rolling ocean waves
And the half-naked natives there.
And I will keep saying –
I know you and only you.

So, let us run away from here
And go to Papua New Guinea.

The 160-page book was printed by Aroma Printing Publications in Dhaka. I dedicated the book to our parents. Once it was published, I felt a great sense of satisfaction and relief in that I had done something for my departed brother. It was my "labor of love" for him.

CHAPTER 15

RESEARCH AND EXPLORATIONS
Questioning and Seeking Answers

I am curious by nature. My first taste of satisfying my curiosity through research came when I was an undergraduate student. I worked on a classical structural analysis method called column analogy. I had asked a question of my teacher Dr. Wahiduddin Ahmed, who was the head of the Civil Engineering Department at EPUET. I noted that the method he was teaching was applied to hinged (that can rotate but not slide) and fixed (that can neither rotate nor slide) supports only, but not roller (that can rotate and slide) supports. I asked him "Sir, why isn't the method applied to rollers?" He was disconcerted at my question and asked me to see him after class. Later, he and I started brainstorming about and I started working earnestly, I couldn't get the question out of my mind. Eventually I found a solution to the problem under his guidance.

From my early student days in engineering, I would tackle the most difficult practice problems at the end of the textbook chapters. I thought if I could do those hard ones, I could do the easy ones too. Every now and then I got stumped but instead of giving up, I would stay awake at night until I solved them. I would say to myself, "I got it!" This tenacity paid off for my exams. In my later professional engineering career, when I solved difficult problems for a project – and this happened many times – I felt the same way.

The profession of engineering demands problem-solving skills. Even though engineers excel in problem-solving they are not sufficiently recognized for the important work they do behind the scenes. There is a joke: "First God created the world, and then created engineers to do the rest." Engineers are rarely in the limelight for what they do for the welfare of mankind, yet they are happy people because of a feeling of gratification. Incidentally, I wrote an essay much later on this topic titled, "Are Engineers Happy People?" for a *Civil Engineering* Magazine, 1982 essay contest, in which I got an honorable mention, and my essay was published in August 1983.

I can categorize my professional research efforts in two ways, applied research and theoretical research. My applied research relates to finding innovative and creative solutions to practical problems. This research was developed for projects that I worked on during my employment and consultancies. I published papers based on some of them. Now, I will briefly review my theoretical research, although there may be some occasional overlaps with applied research.

Although I have carried out research and published in diverse areas including the blast resistance of concrete structures, wind-resistant design of cyclone shelters, flood mitigation, low-cost housing, Islamic architecture, post-Katrina rehabilitation, and more, my principal focus has always been on all aspects of tall buildings. My academic career in the School of Architecture and my long-time association with CTBUH, gave me a foothold for multi-disciplinary research. As a result, I developed a broad, 360-degree view of issues as they related specifically to tall buildings. I worked in several of these areas and published papers, but I focused on a few topics that interested me most, in addition to structural systems -- my core area of interest. I hope my general readers will excuse me for using technical language to describe my research work, particularly for my master's and doctoral research.

Limit Design of Reinforced Concrete Structures

Fortunately, I got good grounding in research working on my master's and doctoral theses at the University of Waterloo, a reputed research university in Canada known for engineering, mathematics, and computer science. I faced intellectual challenges and overcame daunting tasks by solving original problems. I approached my research as if I were carefully untying knots and exploring uncharted territories.

Unlike steel, a ductile and elastoplastic material, reinforced concrete (R.C.) is a composite material consisting of brittle concrete and ductile reinforcing steel. Elastoplastic behavior of a material means the material can elongate or shorten under load, but can return to its original state if the load is removed; but at higher loads beyond a threshold, called yield point, the material continues to deform and, if unloaded, does not return to its original state. Steel structures can form "plastic hinges" at critical locations when steel undergoes inelastic or plastic deformation beyond the yield point. However, R.C. structures can't form plastic hinges because of the brittleness of concrete. Elastic hinges can rotate freely. Plastic hinges can also rotate but face resistance, analogous to a rusted hinge.

The application of inelastic theory to R.C. structures was initially proposed by Professor A.L.L. Baker in the 1950s. This was at the core of limit design principles, that accounted for inelastic behavior of R.C. structures. Subsequent work by Professors V. Petcu, M.Z. Cohn, G. Macchi, H.A. Sawyer and others in the 1960s and 1970s provided fresh ideas and enriched the area of limit design and made this design philosophy a popular area of research.

The merit of this method was that it was based on rational concepts representing the actual behavior of the structures; it results in better performance of structures; and significant savings in material consumption. It accounted for the plastic adaptability of the structure under ultimate or collapse loads, and the occurrence of moment (that is, a rotational force) redistribution in the structure. Structures must be safe and serviceable, that is, functional under routine loads. They also must be strong and deformable. These structural performance criteria must be ensured for any structure. The limit design methods that were developed by various researchers, however, needed iterations in design, as all the required performance criteria for safety and serviceability, in terms of strength and deformability of the structure, could not be satisfied in a single design formulation without avoiding laborious trial and error procedures.

My master's thesis research aimed at developing a general method that would satisfy both strength and deformability requirements throughout the structure at both service (i.e., when routine loads are applied) and ultimate (i.e., when the structure reaches the failure or limit state) for all anticipated load patterns and deformation profiles. In the method that I developed, the design requirements were simultaneously satisfied at the ultimate and the service load levels, for all load patterns and deformation profiles in a single formulation.

To accomplish this objective, I introduced a bilinear elasto-plastic behavior, originally conceived by Professor H. Sawyer in conjunction with the partial locking behavior of R.C. beyond the yield point, to account for strength and deformation of the structure, respectively. Here is a simple way to understand locking: take some compressible material in a jar and apply compressive pressure; initially it gets compressed but at some point, this stops, and the material becomes "locked." The elastoplastic behavior originates from the ductile reinforcing steel whereas the locking behavior arises from the concrete in compression and together they define the bending behavior of R.C. members. Similar to the notion of collapse mechanisms for steel structures consisting of plastic hinges, I introduced the notion of "locking modes" as counterparts of collapse mechanisms and "locks" in locking modes as counterparts of plastic hinges.

I also optimized the design to minimize the material consumption. This led to conceptual complexity and the mathematical formulation became a nonlinear programming (NLP) problem. This comprehensive design formulation applied primarily to continuous beams and simple rigid frames made from R.C. A limitation of this method that I developed, was that it could not easily be applied to multi-bay, multistory building frames.

The work was so fundamental and extensive in nature that one of the thesis reviewers, Professor E.F.P. Burnett, commented that it could qualify for a doctoral thesis. My work was published in a paper entitled "Reinforced Concrete Design for Strength and Deformability" in the *ASCE Journal of the Engineering Mechanics Division* in October 1974. The publication, among others, had the following important features: (a) the minimum combined cost of concrete and steel was the guiding objective for design; (b) deflection serviceability was explicitly satisfied within the design formulation; and (c) cross-sectional member dimensions and steel percentages were directly found by the design. I pushed my imagination as far as it could go; I worked very hard on the thesis and this was my first taste of doing rigorous original research.

My doctoral study was aimed, firstly, at extending the previous method to multistory and multi-bay framed building structures and, secondly, and more extensively, at developing an alternate method of design with broad application to both continuous beams and frames to simplify the design. An advantage of this alternate method was that it provided for direct design control at service, which, in practice, should be more important to the designer as the structure is subjected to routine service loads during its lifetime vs direct design control at ultimate. Another advantage is that the concept of collapse mechanisms and locking modes is no longer required, as these tend to become prohibitive in terms of computational time.

The alternate method, which I developed for my doctoral dissertation, employed a totally new formulation also minimizing the cost of concrete and reinforcing steel. It was similar to the previous method and led to an NLP design formulation. I carried out a mathematical investigation into the uniqueness, and existence of the solution, for my NLP problem.

A study of uniqueness involves investigating the global versus local optimality of solutions. At the time of my investigation no general NLP algorithm had yet been developed that would guarantee an absolute global optimum solution. At best, given an initial starting point, existing algorithms guaranteed a local optimum, i.e., the best solution in the region of the solution space containing the starting point. I chose a numerical example from the alternate method as the basis of investigation for the uniqueness and existence of solution. After a detailed mathematical investigation, I concluded that the solution to the NLP problem was not unique, i.e., a global optimum was *not* guaranteed and a solution to the NLP problem *did* exist. This is adequate since in practical structural design problems conservative, i.e., safe, but economic solutions are acceptable. That provides a margin of safety and therefore exact solutions are not necessary.

I also published a paper on the alternate method entitled "Nonlinear Design of Reinforced Concrete Frameworks," in the *ASCE Journal of Structural Engineering*, October 1986 while I was a faculty member at UIUC. I presented a few papers at conferences on the two methods in the U.S. and in China.

Although the limit design method as a whole was very realistic and economical, it was not accepted by the practicing profession because of the complications of both the concepts and the formulations. The American Concrete Institute (ACI) Code for buildings didn't adopt it or even encourage its use, although it recognized the concept implicitly, by allowing for moment redistribution, a basic principle of limit design, through empirical provisions. As a result, the method lost its popularity in the profession. However, the method has since morphed into Limit State Design (LSD) or Load Resistance Factor Design (LRFD) considering the ultimate and serviceability limit states and still prevails in academic deliberations.

Masonry Mechanics

After completing my doctoral studies, when I was working in Timmins, Ontario during 1977-78, I had been involved in a few masonry structures projects both in terms of new design and investigation of existing structures. I observed that masonry was a very commonly used structural material for buildings, made of concrete blocks and occasionally bricks. As I never took a course in structural masonry design -- and such courses were rarely offered in engineering or architectural schools -- I discerned that the code procedure for unreinforced masonry design was empirical, based on experimental results and observations.

I assumed that this was so because of the complex mechanics of the behavior of a composite material, composed of two dissimilar materials, put together in complicated patterns, with horizontal bed and vertical head joints. It was either too intricate and not well understood, or it was neglected by researchers as it was often used for smaller structures. This seemed awkward to me since masonry had been a popular material since ancient times. I started wondering about the performance of two completely different materials, i.e., stones, bricks, or concrete blocks combined with mortar in the joints to create a composite material like masonry. To complicate the behavior further, the shape and size of the bricks or concrete blocks and their laying patterns influence the interaction of the two materials significantly.

The was a large bookstore in a mall in Timmins, Ontario, that often attracted me like a magnet, I entered the store to explore. Suddenly, I saw a thick 1969 book titled *Designing, Engineering and Constructing with Masonry Products* edited by F.B. Johnson that had several articles on masonry written by different professionals and researchers. I was not expecting to find a book like this in a small remote city with no university. Turning the pages, I found an article titled "An Investigation into the Failure Mechanism of Brick Masonry Loaded in Axial Compression" by H.K. Hilsdorf. It immediately grabbed my attention as this was exactly what I was looking for. I bought the book to read this article and other articles at home*.

After studying this article by Hilsdorf, I got some ideas about the behavior of structural masonry, especially the mechanics of masonry. I read a few other articles in the book to gain more insights. Having grasped the fundamentals of the topic I started my own research at home and started writing a paper. After I moved to Sudbury from Timmins in 1979 and then to Chicago in 1980, I completed two papers on masonry and presented them at the Second Canadian Masonry Symposium at Carleton University in Ottawa, Ontario in 1980 and

---

* I may note here that since the time of my investigation more subsequent research studies of masonry mechanics have advanced the understanding of masonry behavior. Such research efforts are still continuing. Use of "engineered masonry" for the structural design of masonry structures is now common.

Canadian Congress of Applied Mechanics (CANCAM-81) at the University of Moncton in Moncton, New Brunswick in 1981.

The first paper was on failure investigation of masonry structures and was based on my own investigations of damaged or failed masonry structures. The latter paper was specifically on masonry mechanics, which was received well by the attending delegates, particularly by Dr. Sherbourne, a senior civil engineering professor for the University of Waterloo and Dr. Grierson, adviser of my master's and doctoral theses. Both papers were published in the respective conference proceedings.

Before sending my paper to the CANCAM-81 congress I shared the paper with Dr. Fazlur R. Khan in his SOM office in Chicago, who reviewed it in my presence. Then he commented, "This is good. But this is a theoretical paper. If you can do something practical such as finding a good shape for a brick to make the masonry stronger, that could make your work useful and valuable to people." Clearly, the practical side of his mind was working, and his emphasis was on real-world applications for people's benefit.

Heeding his advice, I started working on different shapes of bricks and concluded that the best shape to maximize the strength was a honeycomb form and the other form was a triangle, which would create honeycomb and triangular patterns in the masonry. This conclusion matched my intuition, but two questions came to my mind, both related to the shape: 1. How much would the labor cost increase for laying these newly shaped bricks? and 2. How could a theoretical investigation into its mechanics be conducted? I started thinking about these issues. But because of the intervention of unexpected circumstances in my career, I could not develop these ideas further and I moved to other imminent things.

Engineering Education

After joining the School of Architecture at UIUC in 1985 I continued research on my doctoral work for some time, but soon turned my attention to other research areas, lingering interests from my industrial and other experiences. Meanwhile, I learned two things at the School. First, most architects recognized that technology, which to them encompassed structures, HVAC, plumbing, electrical systems, etc. was a part of architecture. Despite the fact that design conception and technical knowledge were intertwined and went hand in hand during the design process, some failed to appreciate the importance of technical erudition in the building design process. As a result, they had a general misconception about the significant role that engineering plays in the design process. Engineers were considered support professionals who assisted with architects' design goals by providing calculations and technical expertise. Being a structural engineer myself I was well acquainted with the bias in our profession as well. Engineers often mistook architects as lightweights in the area of structures, materials and mechanics. To them, architects were concerned with site analysis, indoor layout, circulation, color scheme and aesthetics. It was the engineers that erected the buildings and kept them safe. Second, being in an architectural school, it was very difficult to get major funding from the National Science Foundation (NSF), the foremost funding source for researchers from engineering schools to carry out engineering and technical projects. NSF preferred engineering schools and had little interest in architectural schools.

On the first point, I realized that I needed to integrate architecture and engineering in my teaching and research efforts. I found most design professors warm and friendly, conversational, and easy to get along with. I had an easy time uniting the two professional disciplines as I liked both engineering and architecture, and therefore, in fact, the new direction was a good fit for me.

However, I was not very satisfied with the implications of the second point. It meant I could not get major funding for my research, other than small grants primarily through the campus Research Board. Compounding the problem was the absence of any Ph.D. program in place in the School, although efforts were being made to initiate one. This hindered any serious and durable research by doctoral students under my supervision. Since architecture is a highly practice-oriented profession, only a handful of American architectural schools had Ph.D. programs. I started thinking about going into the job market again to work for a civil engineering school. Then I thought of how another move would affect my family. I also thought that by going to an engineering school my interest in art and architecture would be lost. I liked my colleagues and they liked me. Moreover, I was tenured in two years in 1987 and promoted to full professor in another two years in 1989. So, the School had treated me well and recognized my accomplishments.

I developed interests in several areas of structures, architecture, sustainable design, and urban design, particularly focusing on tall buildings. I worked on papers based on special directed research projects and independent study courses taken by graduate students under my supervision as well as my own research. Subsequently, a Ph.D. program was introduced in which the topic of architectural structures was included under the specialization "Technology and Environment."

Meanwhile, I focused on engineering education, particularly, architectural engineering education. Architectural engineering deals with structural and building services systems, i.e., mechanical, electrical, plumbing and associated technical systems, in which the structure defining the building's skeleton occupies a dominant place. With my engineering background, I initially started my new research on engineering education to infuse fresh thought into it. I wrote my first paper on the subject "Unity in Diversity: Search for a New Dimension in Engineering Education," that I presented at the Fifth Canadian Conference on Engineering Education, University of Western Ontario, London, Ontario, Canada in May 1986.

My emphasis was to encourage diversification of engineering education away from purely technical aspects to the extent the curriculum would permit. Learning from my industrial experience, later I started working on two papers, one on developing a suitable undergraduate program in architectural engineering and the other on bringing together industrial and academic research in architectural engineering. I presented both papers at a conference on engineering education of the American Society of Engineering Education (ASEE) in Reno, Nevada in June 1987. The same year in October I presented a paper titled "From Intuition to Induction: Promoting Creativity in the Classroom," at the Frontiers in Education Conference held at the Rose-Hulman Institute of Technology, Terre Haute, Indiana. Also, I published an invited paper on how computers could impact architectural engineering education and research in the *International Journal of Applied Engineering Education* in 1988.

Structural Art

Whether it is clearly recognized or not there exists something called the art of engineering. I knew from my own experience that there was definitely art in structural engineering called structural art, a term coined by Professor David Billington of Princeton University, who pioneered the discipline of structural art, which appraises the artistic manifestation of structures while meeting the practical requirements of engineering. In his book of 1983 *The Tower and the Bridge: The New Art of Structural Engineering*, he wrote the following words in the opening paragraph of its preface to set the tone of the book:

The Eiffel Tower and the Brooklyn Bridge became great symbols of their age because the general public recognized in their new forms a technological world of surprise and appeal ... that the tower and the bridge are only two of the numberless works of recent engineering that constitute a new art form, structural art, which is parallel to and fully independent of architecture.

Professor Billington identified three fundamental ideals of structural art: efficiency, economy, and structural elegance. He also identified three pairs of criteria to be met for achieving structural art: thinness and safety; integration and cost; and contrast and affinity. Generation of structural form does not necessarily require that it be totally subservient to the scientific laws of mechanics. Great structural artists – Robert Maillart, Pier Luigi Nervi, Antoni Gaudi, Felix Candela, Fazlur R. Khan and others – believed in their freedom to choose what system was rational structurally and most fitting aesthetically.

This is what lies at the core of structural art. They applied structural art, wittingly or unwittingly, to the design of their buildings and bridges because they thought that the structure should be the architecture, or in other words, structure and architecture should be one and the same. Billington's work stimulated a group of scholars and redefined the consideration of great works of engineering, from bridges to buildings. It motivated me and inspired me to work in this area. Later at my invitation he and his daughter Sarah Billington contributed a chapter on the topic to the book *Architecture of Tall Buildings*.

Structural art or the art of structural engineering entails an aesthetically pleasing and meaningful arrangement of structural elements, that demonstrates precision in the application of a system of rules and principles to facilitate a skilled engineering accomplishment. A building should be simple, orderly, and pleasant. Structural artists believe that structures can be considered art and objects of art. Thus, an in-depth understanding and appropriate application of structural principles should lead to the creation of elegant forms. Structural artists use mathematical analyses for their structure but are not restricted by them. They believe in the freedom to choose what system is logical structurally, and most fitting aesthetically. They can apply their skills to identify the optimal force flow throughout the structure and arrange the structural components to conform to this flow. By doing so they harmonize nature's laws and material properties with the inherent artistry of design.

These considerations led to my first conference paper on the topic titled "The Forgotten Half of Design: Structural Art Form," that I presented at the Association of Collegiate Schools of Architecture (ACSA) West Regional Meeting held at UIUC, Champaign, IL in 1986. Subsequently, I studied the related concept of structural expressionism in depth, as an important attribute of tall buildings, and wrote papers on the subject. I also covered this topic in a few books of mine on tall buildings. In particular, I devoted an entire chapter to this topic in my book *Art of the Skyscraper: The Genius of Fazlur Khan*.

Earthquake-Resistant Design

An important area of my research was earthquake-resistant design of buildings. While working at SOM, because of my experience in designing a 60-story tall building in Los Angeles, in a severe seismic zone, I became keenly interested in seismic research. I realized that the nature of dynamic seismic forces and the buildings response were complex to comprehend unless thoroughly studied. Knowledge of structural dynamics was essential, but I had no prior education in the subject.

So, I began intense self-study on how it was applied to earthquake engineering. Seismic loads are dynamic loads originating from underground and need special consideration. I performed the dynamic analysis of the 60-story building structure using the Response Spectrum Method. A building can oscillate or vibrate in different ways during an earthquake, known as modes of vibration. Initially it vibrates in its first or fundamental mode, in which it bends in a single curvature. Then the higher or subsequent modes become progressively more complex but less critical, with multiple curvatures and modes look like whiplashes. However, to capture the total behavior, all the modes should be combined. This is an arduous task, and often a few early modes are considered for structural analysis.

I was not content with this conventional approach, as this seemed too inaccurate to me. I decided to carry out an investigation for the tower that I was working on to find out how many modes I should consider for achieving convergence of the results. Assisted by a junior engineer in the office, Joseph Burns, who was helping me on the project, I developed an analytical procedure which allowed me to conclude that for the 60-story building in question I needed 33 modes to get an accurate outcome by the method of analysis that I employed. A paper titled "Dynamic Analysis of Tall Buildings" covering this research was published in the Proceedings of the ASCE Structural Division Specialty Conference at the University of Houston in1983. I followed up my research on other aspects of seismic design of tall buildings in a paper titled "Seismic Design of Tall Steel Buildings" published in the Proceedings of the 3rd US National Conference on Earthquake Engineering in Charleston, South Carolina, in August 1986. I continued my work on seismic design of tall buildings and other aspects of buildings subsequently.

One such aspect was the seismic design of foundations. During my sabbatical leave in 1993, I had been working at the office

of Portland Cement Association (PCA) in Skokie, Illinois. Dr.
S.K. Ghosh suggested that I might conduct research on foundation design in seismic zones. I agreed and found that this was
a topic that had little information available in the literature or
building codes for the practical design of foundations in seismic zones. Usually, designers focus their primary attention to
the structure above ground. I started researching the subject
and recommended guidelines recognizing that more research
was desirable. Two papers emerged from my research: "Earthquake-Resistant Design of Foundations," in the Proceedings
Seventh Canadian Conference on Earthquake Engineering,
Montreal, Canada, June 57, 1995; and "Design of Foundations
in Seismic Zones" in the *Concrete International*, American Concrete Institute (ACI), January 1997.

Teaching in the School of Architecture, my attention naturally turned to the effect of earthquakes on the architectural
configuration of buildings. Following my intense research on
the subject I presented a paper on "Influence of Architectural
Configuration on Seismic Response of Buildings," published in
the Proceedings of the 5th Canadian Conference on Earthquake
Engineering at Carleton University, Ottawa, Canada, July 1987.
Later, I continued to work on this area for my lecture notes on a
graduate course I taught on seismic design. I was invited by the
UIUC Civil Engineering Department to lecture on the topic in a
campus honors course. On December 2, 2004 I guest lectured on
"Architectural Seismic Design Concepts" at `Seismic Overview
Seminar`, co-sponsored by Mid-America Earthquake Center,
University of Illinois Facilities and Services, American Institute
of Architects, American Society of Plumbing Engineers, American Society of Heating, Refrigerating, and Air-Conditioning
Engineers (ASHRAE), and Illinois Capital Development Board,
in Urbana, IL. The seminar was attended by a large audience of
engineers, architects, and other interested professionals.

Structural Expressionism, Aesthetics and Form

Many tall buildings draw on their exposed structure or readily visible mechanical systems. They may also champion technology, exploration, or innovation by embodying certain physical forms. The proliferation of new structural systems and advanced technologies combined with Modernism's principles of structural clarity, helped to give birth to the movement of Structural Expressionism. It is aligned with the Modern movement in design, that sought to break away from stylistic and historical links to the past, often flamboyant, eclectic architecture. The Modern movement began in the 1960s and flourished throughout the 1970s, and then tailed off in the 1980s during the architectural period known as Late Modernism. Many Modernist high-rises carry the trait of structural expression. They were built in an era that vigorously espoused "honestly" in exhibiting their structure.

However, in Structural Expressionism, the notion of aesthetic has been redefined to emphasize the role of new structural systems and innovative building materials. In this way, structural expression dominates the design of façades, becoming synonymous with the architectural expression of the building as a whole. Such expression was also fully compatible with the International Style that arose during the Modern era.

Although structural expression was still an emerging form, it manifested in several projects at the time. These projects were the harbingers of what was to follow in the 1960s and 1970s, when structural engineer Fazlur R. Khan and architect Bruce Graham designed a number of structurally expressive buildings in steel and concrete. Chicago architect Mies van der Rohe had a profound influence on Khan, who had himself helped to define the concept of tall buildings as art forms. As mentioned, he developed tubular structural design, achieving these conceptual breakthroughs at the high point of Modernism, in the late 1970s.

Aesthetics and the form of tall buildings always fascinated me. So, I got into researching this topic. This was difficult terrain to tread. Aesthetic quality could only be judged but not measured. The aesthetic appeal of a building could be elusive to the architectural designer but critical to the success of the design. A tall building's response to the environment, and its visual impact on the observer, affect both the acceptance and the success of the building.

Aesthetics of buildings is a very imprecise field of study. It encompasses a broad sense of beauty and harmony in a structure or object and the perception of the viewer. What delights one person may be just interesting to someone else or may not delight another person at all. Thus, beauty is subjective and emotional. I soon discovered that past attempts at developing aesthetic rules or laws, were essentially baseless and failed to stand the test of time. The designer just relied on instincts and artistic sense rather than on hard and fast rules, since it was difficult to formulate such rules in the field of art *versus* engineering.

Rather than rules, I attempted to develop some guiding principles. In addition to some subsequent papers, I presented my findings in a complete chapter titled "Aesthetics and Form" in the book *Architecture of Tall Buildings* (except a section "Search for a Skyscraper Style" in the chapter contributed by my colleague Paul Armstrong). I also included a section on this topic in the chapter "Structural Framework" in the book *The Skyscraper and the City: Design, Technology, and Innovation.*

In the design of tall buildings, the basic need for providing lateral resistance to wind and earthquake loads prevails during the structural design process. This also impacts the architectural planning and the selection of materials and structural system. My assertion was that although aesthetic quality of buildings was admittedly in the domain of the architects, the fact that for tall buildings, form-giving was intertwined with the lateral load-resisting system of the structure, the overall aesthetic quality must be determined by both architectural and structural perspectives.

Pursuing this notion, I identified nine characteristics from an *architectural* viewpoint: plan view; elevation; external appearance; balance and simplicity; proportion and scale; relationship of spaces; visual impact; style; and ornamentation and décor. I observed that these attributes provided a spectrum of reference points against which a building's aesthetics and form could be compared and could be treated as a checklist for a qualitative and candid aesthetics assessment.

Likewise, I identified seven characteristics from a *structural* viewpoint: shape and size; dimensions; strength and stability; stiffness; efficiency and economy; simplicity and clarity; and lightness and thinness. I took the John Hancock Center in Chicago for a case study to apply these two checklists. I may mention here that this building is an example of structural expression in which the façade honestly displays the structure of the building and thus merges with the architectural expression of the building creating a distinctive expression. In other words, the structural expression is the architectural expression. My most recent paper on the subject co-authored with K. Al-Kodmany entitled "An Overview of Structural Developments and Aesthetics of Tall Buildings Using Exterior Bracing and Diagrid Systems" published in the December 2016 issue of the *International Journal of High-Rise Buildings* covered the topics of aesthetics and structural expression with several illustrations.

Integration of Physical Systems

A principal area of my research was the integration of tall building's various physical systems. Although the structural form and facade describe the overall presence of a tall building, the building's hidden systems are the "guts", which insure function and habitability. One important design goal is to optimize the performance of each component, system and subsystem. Maximum performance can be achieved if careful attention is given to integrating the various functional components and building systems. This integrated approach throughout the design stage can open the door to creative, synergistic solutions.

For a better understanding of integration, I will draw this often-repeated analogy. In a basic way, a high-rise building can be compared to the human body. It has a complex system of interdependent functions similar to the human body. The physical systems of a building can be understood as follows: structure-*skeleton*; mechanical-*internal organs*; electrical-*nerves*; plumbing-*circulation*; building envelope-*skin*, etc. In both cases, that is, the building and the human body, each part cannot function alone; integration of systems is needed for proper functioning of the whole. Integration is fundamentally based on the principle of "systems thinking."

Interestingly, early on in the School some professors were having a conversation about how building projects in the design studios could apply the concept of integration. As the large School had a deep pool of faculty members with expertise in several technical disciplines. I arrived at this idea of integration when I gave a seminar "Integration of Architectural and Structural Concepts for Building Design" at BUET, Dhaka in August 1989 so I was fully supportive of the effort in the School. As discussions were ongoing, I wrote an article titled "Integration of Structures/Building Technology and Architectural Design in Design Studios" in the student newsletter *Rickernotes* in its October 19, 1992 issue. It was republished in *Connector* in its Fall 1993 issue. Following this, the students arranged a panel discussion to address the topic and invited me as a panelist.

While I worked in the industry, particularly at SOM, a firm with a large engineering staff, I observed that architects and engineers collaborated on projects and organically carried out integration. It was by no means a deliberate or coordinated strategy but seem to just happen. I drew upon that private sector experience and started to think about how to train students to engage systematizing and optimizing the design process. Undoubtedly, a successful efficiently functioning building, with integrated systems could offer peak performance as well as save time and money during construction and over the life of the building.

I thought that these considerations were even more important for tall buildings, given their scale and impact on the cityscape. Tall buildings are enormous urban artefacts. The design process is complex and needs to integrate many highly specialized fields. From labor to materials to construction scheduling, all the steps leading to building assembly require a very high level of organization and coordination. Importantly, liability issues can increase if the architect and the engineer fail to communicate, collaborate and integrate the building's main physical systems, right from the design phase.

With these important considerations in mind, I focused on tall buildings and published the paper "Interdisciplinary Approaches to Tall Building Design" in the 1995 Collected Volume entitled *Habitat and the High-Rise: Tradition and Innovation*, a special publication of CTBUH. The same year I made contribution to Chapter 8: "Building Systems Automation and Integration" in the book *Architecture of Tall Buildings*. I began more detailed research into the subject along with Paul Armstrong, an architectural design professor, as collaborator. Because of our respective engineering and design backgrounds, I feel our partnership mirrored the objectives of collaboration in design. The exploration was thus even more meaningful.

The central question regarding integration facing contemporary societies, as I write this, is how to make sense of the increasingly technological world around us. In my research I argued that even though the initial cost of systems integration might be higher than conventional incomplete integration, this cost was recovered in a few years and in fact there was a long-term cost premium for incomplete integration. Integration deals with the complex relationship amongst architectural, structural, mechanical, electrical, and plumbing systems.

After thoroughly investigating the topic we developed a schematic chart, conceived by me, called the "integration web". It clearly showed the interrelationship of the components of integration, as well as the associated sub-systems, demonstrating how integration worked. We presented this research at a few conferences. I attended and presented our work at the Research Summit of the American Institute of Architects (AIA) held in March 2007 in Seattle, WA. An updated paper including building sustainability entitled "The Role of Systems Integration in Sustainable Tall Buildings," was also published in the *International Journal of Sustainable Building Technology and Urban Development* in its December 2010 issue. I devoted the entire Chapter 11: "Physical Systems and Integration" to this topic in the book *The Skyscraper and the City: Design, Technology and Innovation*.

As mentioned before, a building's physical systems, like the physiological systems of a human body, cannot function to their optimal level without the careful integration and coordination of one system with another. Integration demands human dexterity and ingenuity and is more of an art than science. In a tall building project, different professionals work from conceptual design to completion and commissioning of the building. The different phases of the project follow a certain timeline, usually sporadic target dates for the completion of different segments of the project. Different professions and trades set their own deadlines, sometimes overlapping. An optimal and effective timeline including all the segments of the project, allows the building to be efficiently completed, on time, which is good for both the owner and other participants in the project.

I spent some time thinking this over and conceived a chart to systematize the entire process, along with a timeline. I developed a diagram similar to the one used in the construction industry's Critical Path Method (CPM) for planning and management. I planned to undertake a research project for this. However, it was not to be, as I was consumed with other impending tasks and interruptions.

Structural Systems

Although I published a few papers on limit design, seismic design, and dynamic analysis of structures, I always had the intention of conducting research on structural systems. Since my work at SOM, I had a keen desire to work on structural systems of tall buildings. Having designed, analyzed and investigated many structures during my long career, I developed a strong affinity to structures, particularly the loads on them, how and where stresses developed, and how they deformed. My interest in other areas prevented me from focusing my research on this topic to the degree I would have liked. The subject was not a major shared priority in an architectural school setting.

In the late1990s, because of my interest in history, I decided to conduct research on the structural history of tall buildings and hired a graduate research assistant to help me. It turned out to be a fruitful effort as I was able to collect a history of how structural systems for tall buildings evolved, from their inception in 1885, with the 10-story Home Insurance Building in Chicago.

I composed a timeline beginning with this 1885 building, which employed a skeletal metal frame up to until 2004 construction, when many alternative structural systems were in vogue. I had been planning to write a paper or even a book on this topic but sadly, it never materialized for various reasons. However, it was displayed as "Timeline for the Structural History of Skyscrapers" at the exhibition *The Dream of the Tower* at the NRW-Forum

Kultur and Wirtschaft Ehrenhof 2, Dusseldorf, Germany on November 5, 2004. I was invited by the organizers to participate in the exhibition, but I could not make it due to time conflict. Later, I included it as an entire section in Chapter 3: Skyscraper Evolution in the book *The Skyscraper and the City: Design, Technology and Innovation.*

In 2001, at the CTBUH Congress in Melbourne, I distributed a draft paper on concrete tall buildings to the participants of a workshop session. The editor of an Australian journal who was there later contacted me and invited me to submit a paper on this topic. This led to the publication of my paper "Evolution of Concrete Skyscrapers: From Ingalls to Jin Mao" in the *Electronic Journal of Structural Engineering,* May 2001. The paper narrated the developments of structural systems for concrete tall buildings. These buildings were becoming more popular worldwide than those in steel, as concrete technology had been rapidly advancing and outstripping steel technology. Following this, I got an invitation from the editor of a reputed Indian journal to submit another paper, which I obliged and the paper "Rise of Concrete High-Rise" was published in the *Indian Concrete Journal* in August 2001. At the invitation of the editor of a Czech Republic journal *BETON TKS Journal,* I published two papers titled "Emergence and Growth of Concrete High-Rise Construction," October 2008 and "Evolution of Concrete Skyscrapers: From Ingalls to Burj Dubai," December 2008.

In 2007 I was invited to write a paper on the structural systems of tall buildings from the editor of the *Architectural Science Review Journal* published from Australia. This gave me an opportunity to write a comprehensive paper on structural systems. The beginning of computer technology, in conjunction with the construction boom following the Great Depression and World War II, facilitated the development of new structural systems and forms.

During my research on the structural history of tall buildings, I realized that although there were different types systems, an organized classification was absent in the literature; a paper treating this topic would be a good contribution. I also recognized that Dr. Fazlur R. Khan had already pioneered this effort with his revolutionary concepts on tall building design. He discovered that as buildings become taller, there is a "premium for height" due to lateral wind force. Lateral wind force really drives the structural design of tall buildings. Consequently, as a building gets taller, there is more lateral wind load to consider, the total material consumption increases and demands on the structural system dramatically increase, as well.

This observation led to a breakthrough replacing the traditional application of a rigid frame system, in favor of other economic and efficient structural systems for building to greater heights. He innovated his signature tubular design for tall buildings and applied it as a basic framed tube, to the 43-story DeWitt Chestnut Apartment Building in Chicago in 1965. In the late 1960s he developed height-based structural systems charts for steel and concrete tall buildings, relating the systems to the number of stories. The advent of computers to analyze different complex systems facilitated the development of even more innovative systems. The absence of digital technology was the primary reason for why the conventional rigid-frame system was the prevalent structural system for tall buildings up until then.

In the 1960s, the notion of aerodynamics, finite element analysis, computational fluid dynamics, etc. related to the aircraft industry was an up-and-coming exploration for application to tall buildings. Moreover, it was also the high point of Modernism. As a result, the structural systems charts were conceived in terms of the basic forms that were rectilinear in plan. Since the first development of Dr. Khan's charts followed by his modification of the charts later in 1973 and 1974, a few new structural systems for supertall buildings appeared on the scene. However, to my knowledge, no new classification of height-based structural systems was made for many years. It, therefore, became necessary to develop state-of-the-art charts. I decided to develop comprehensive charts updating the structural systems charts developed by Dr. Khan with a broader classification system.

As I was very busy with my teaching, administrative, in-house and external committee work, and other research and writing activities, I invited Kyoung S. Moon, a former student of mine, to be a co-author the paper with me. He had recently joined our Structures Division as a faculty member. We worked together and wrote a paper entitled "Structural Developments in Tall Buildings: Current Trends and Future Prospects" that included the structural systems prevalent up to 2007. The paper classified the systems broadly based on height of the buildings, as *interior* and *exterior* systems to reflect where the primary lateral load-resisting system is employed. Instead of classifying the charts in terms of steel and concrete, these charts included steel, concrete, and composite (mixed steel-concrete) in interior or exterior systems chart. In addition to these the paper covered several other aspects, particularly a detailed narrative of damping systems frequently used in supertall buildings to minimize building vibrations caused by wind and earthquake forces. The paper further gave innovative ideas for future research on structural systems of tall buildings. The paper was published in the journal in its September 2007 issue and was very well received by the research community worldwide and continues to be read and used for related research.

In 2018 I got an invitation from the guest editor of *Buildings Journal* to contribute a paper on tall building structures to its upcoming special issue. I decided to write a paper on the latest developments and advancements of structural systems for supertall (greater than 300 meters tall) and megatall (greater than 600 meters tall) buildings. Like our previous paper Kyoung S. Moon then at Yale University, once again joined me as a co-author. We decided to upgrade our structural systems charts from 2007 as many new tall buildings of enormous heights had appeared on the skylines of world cities.

The paper titled "Advances in Structural Systems for Tall Buildings: Emerging Developments for Contemporary Urban Giants" was published in the journal in August 2018. We maintained the same broad classification of interior and exterior systems but included new systems and additional examples of tall buildings. We further introduced the modifications of existing systems that had recently taken place, as well as interpretations and characterizations of these systems and the newer systems. We also added a new concept for the structural system of a mile-high tower. The paper presented facts and figures on the "race for height" that is an ongoing phenomenon. Regarding the possibility of a mile-high building often dubbed the "Mile-High Dream" here was our observation:

Though the current tallest building (Burj Khalifa) and the soon-to-be tallest (Jeddah Tower) are still astonishing in their achievements, they provide occupiable spaces only up to about two-thirds height of the buildings. Therefore, though it is said by many that we are now very close to reaching mile-high towers, perhaps we have reached only a fraction toward it yet in terms of occupiable height. Nonetheless, with the pride, drive, and ambition of the owners, the vision and creative artistry of the architects, and ingenuity and skill of engineers, mile-high dream may be realized in the foreseeable future. Clearly, technological prowess, innovative materials, energy efficiency, occupant comfort, fire safety, as well as re-creation of a ground-like natural environment and ecosystem at dizzying heights, etc. will be some of the determinants of the enormous height of future skyscrapers.

The paper concluded with the following last words:
In the very long architectural history, tall buildings, with their short history of about 150 years, are still one of the most recent building types. Nonetheless, tall buildings as a building type is most rapidly evolving, very much advanced technology-driven, and most significantly impacting our built environments in urban, regional and even documented timely updates on their various aspects are continuously required to help many related people including architects and engineers keep track of and better understand the most up-to-date status of this quintessential building type now and for the future. Structural systems have certainly been one of the most fundamental technologies for tall buildings and are lately evolving fast to address ever increasing design requirements and global density problem. No other building type needs frequent updates on reviews and predictions of its structural systems like tall buildings. As our precedents tell us, we will see more advances in structural systems for tall buildings during the coming years. It is expected that the next update will be carried out whenever a meaningfully increased number of these urban giants appear in cities.

Sustainable Tall Buildings and Cities
The concept of sustainable development or sustainability did not first emerge from academic discourse. Rather from an international concern for the future of human habitats. Following this, global political attention turned to all aspects of the environment, emphasizing sustainability. In 1987 the United Nations published *Our Common Future* also known as Brundtland Report that anchored environmental issues firmly as a global agenda item and aimed to treat environmental concerns with development as a single integrated issue. It put the international community on a sustainable development path.

At our School in the early 1990s Director Alan Forrester made sustainability a principal agenda item in a session that I co-moderated at the annual faculty retreat. Faculty carried out intense deliberations and searched for ways to include environmentally oriented building design in our curriculum. The goals were to save energy consumption, reduce the use of resources and reduce carbon emissions as some of the elements of sustainable design. The term sustainable design eventually became used interchangeably with the expression "green design." This led to a worldwide "green" movement.

I readily embraced this new design approach and began to study the topic with vigor. The expression "sustainable architecture" describes an approach to building design that is concerned, at its core, with minimizing resource consumption thus prolonging the availability of natural resources. It correctly asserts that no manmade micro-environment can survive independently of the larger global natural environment or ecological systems. This concept continues to be developed and incorporate new dimensions and broader horizons.

My first exploration into sustainability was in the area of recycling concrete. Once a concrete building, pavement, or object is demolished, instead of throwing the material away as debris, I thought it could be reused in some way for new applications and began an investigation. This led to a publication titled "Concrete Change" in *Civil Engineering* in its February 1998 issue.

Soon after, concrete recycling became the topic of my rigorous research, with special focus on tall buildings.

In the early 2000s I undertook an elaborate investigation on the sustainability of tall buildings in collaboration with my architectural design colleague Paul Armstrong. I realized that designing a tall building required a 360-degree view of the entire building enterprise. Our work led to numerous seminars and publications. I will mention a few: "Sustainable Tall Buildings: Recent Developments and Future Trends," Proceedings of the AIA Illinois Symposium on Critical Practice for the 21st Century, Peoria, IL, November 2006; "Integration of Physical Systems in Sustainable Tall Buildings, AIA Research Summit, Seattle, WA, March 2007; "Overview of Sustainable Design Factors of High-Rise Buildings," Proceedings of the CTBUH 8th World Congress: Tall and Green – Typology for a Sustainable Urban Future, Dubai, March 2008; "The Role of Systems Integration in Sustainable Tall Buildings," *International Journal of Sustainable Building Technology and Urban Development*, December 2010; "Sustainable Technologies and the Tall Building: Emerging Trends and Future Challenges," *National Building Materials & Construction World (NBM&CW)*, India, Vol. 17, July 2011.

For decades, climate scientists had promoted their contention that uncontained, man-made global warming would inflict mayhem on human civilization. Average global temperatures had been slowly rising and at some point, if it crossed a threshold temperature rise of 56.3°F (1.5°C) the earth would experience a massive climate change, precipitating the destruction of ecosystems, changes in the weather patterns, and cause some island nations and low-lying lands to sink under water. It is frightening to think that the earth is gradually approaching this threshold temperature rise.

Buildings, especially tall buildings, emit plenty of greenhouse gases and are partly responsible for global warming. Armed with this understanding, I carried out intensive research that leading to two publications. The first paper was "Energy-Efficient Architecture and Building Systems to Address Global Warming," *Leadership and Management in Engineering Journal*, ASCE, Special Issue, July 2008. In this paper I acknowledged that increased carbon admissions arise from human activity, including emissions by tall buildings. These increased emissions contribute to global warming (now more accurately referred to as global climate change). I suggested how emissions could be mitigated with appropriate design. The paper concluded that designers of the next generation of buildings, whether residential, commercial, or institutional, should set "zero energy" targets, in which no energy would be drawn from a region's power grid. In this approach, I argued, the climate and environment were leveraged together, rather than being treated as adversaries and buildings would become sources of energy -- like batteries -- which in turn supply electricity to a city's power grid.

All my research up to this point, was related to overall architectural sustainability. This changed during a casual conversation over lunch, with renowned architect Ken Yeang. He was a strong proponent of environmentally conscious "bioclimatic" green design. As we sat in a restaurant in Champaign, it occurred to me that structural design could have a significant impact on the overall sustainability of a building and moreover, the structure of a building could also be made sustainable. He agreed to this line of thinking. He floated the idea of writing a book together on the subject. I felt that it would be a great idea to pursue it collaboratively, but knowing my workload and schedule, as well as what it meant to the write a book on this new topic, I hesitated. I decided to conduct research in this area to get a sense of scope.

My literature survey on the subject showed that prevailing structural practice had only just begun to address these issues. This encouraged me to further pursue the topic, which resulted in my writing a paper applicable to all buildings, tall or otherwise, titled "Structural Sustainability of High-Performance Buildings". I presented the paper at the 5th International Structural Engineering and Construction Conference: Challenges, Opportunities and Solutions, Las Vegas, NV, September 2009 and it was published in its Proceedings. This paper demonstrated how structure could be a catalyst for achieving sustainable buildings. It emphasized that the sustainability of a structure could be considered with respect to the embodied energy of structural materials, durability, design flexibility, optimality, and deconstruction, to name a few. It showed how the structure could promote achieving overall sustainability of buildings.

As the population of cities grows, increasing the density and consequently raising land prices, real estate market conditions generally drive the height of tall buildings. When we discuss a tall building in terms of its setting and context we first think of neighborhood, then a district and finally the city. The relationship between tall buildings and major cities is always complementary, and one defines the other.

My long-term connection and leadership roles with CTBUH and my relevant experience led me to the idea of tall buildings being extensions of a city. That is, a major tall building is a vertical city representing a microcosm in a larger city with analogous physical systems. On a macro-scale, a sustainable city means a livable city in which the past is preserved, while ensuring the interests and aspirations of future generations also remain viable. In such a city the urban systems and the infrastructure are planned and designed with long-term requirements in mind. The city ought to be viewed as an "ecosystem" or a "biological system" which is complex and dynamic. Thus, since tall buildings and cities are integral to each other, I turned my attention to research on cities, particularly sustainable cities. My research yielded two papers: 1. "The Role of Tall Buildings in Sustainable Cities," Proceedings of the Fifth International Conference on Urban Regeneration and Sustainability: The Sustainable City 2008 Conference, Skiathos, Greece, September 2008 and 2. "Sustainable Urban Life in Skyscraper Cities of the 21st Century," The Sustainable City VI: Urban Regeneration and Sustainability, C.A. Brebbia, S. Hernandez and E. Tiezzi, editors, WIT Press, Southampton, U.K., 2010.

I wrote a complete chapter titled "Sustainable Tall buildings and Cities: Turning Ideas for Survivability into Reality" for the 2007 book *The Skyscraper and the City: Design, Technology, and Innovation* that reflected much of my research on the subject. Later, an updated chapter on the same topic was included in the 2013 book *The Future of the City: Tall buildings and Urban Design.*

Another related topic that I investigated was dealing with the suburbs of major cities and how they could be made more sustainable with high-rises, a rather controversial topic. In this regard I wrote a couple of papers, one of them with Paul Armstrong titled "Overcoming Unsustainability: Retrofitting American Suburbs with High-Density Built Environment" presented at the International Conference on Sustainable Cities 2012, Ancona, Italy, May 2012 that appeared in the conference proceedings. I also gave a group presentation together with two others titled "The Growth of High-Rise Buildings in the U.S. Suburbs: Will Suburban Tall Promote Sustainable Development?" at the Makeover Montgomery Innovative Strategies for Rethinking America's Suburbs conference, Silver Spring, Montgomery County, MD, April 2011.

My segment of the presentation was on sustainable tall buildings in suburbs and how suburbs can be made sustainable After researching, I promoted the following ideas: concentrated high-density complexes in the form of green high-rise buildings are an appropriate typology for the suburbs; density creates efficient land use, pedestrian-friendly mixed-use suburban hubs; high-rises in suburbs will reduce walking/biking distances between amenities and promote small energy footprint, among other notions.

This kind of thinking is not always liked, particularly not by those who are opposed to tall building construction. I once talked about sustainable suburbs, proposing the idea of green high-rises at Judson University in Elgin, IL but was vehemently opposed by someone. There are a few who are also opposed to tall buildings in general and I encountered some of them. As far as opponents of tall buildings are concerned, they oppose tall buildings anywhere. When asked what alternative they have in mind to accommodate a growing urban population worldwide, they simply didn't have a clear answer. It is because there is no answer.

Thermal Mass of Concrete Buildings

At a CTBUH conference in Chicago in October 2009 on the evolution of skyscrapers I met Richard Tomasetti, a principal of the internationally renowned structural engineering firm Thornton Tomasetti. We had a brief conversation about impending issues on structural engineering for tall buildings. He mentioned over the course of conversation, that the thermal mass property of concrete structures was an area that warranted research. I took that suggestion seriously. Upon my return to UIUC, I hired a graduate student Amir Ghoreishi to assist me in this research. He worked as my research assistant for a year.

The thermal mass is the heat capacity of a material, a measure of how much heat a material can absorb and hold. Concrete has thermal mass and can be employed to improve a building's energy performance and reduce heating and cooling loads thereby leading to sustainability, especially in locations with extreme climate. We investigated the thermal mass effect of concrete in comparison with masonry and steel.

For the purpose of this research, three major parameters including height, occupancy, and location of buildings in six U.S. climate zones were considered and maximum cooling load was chosen as the main measuring index of building energy performance. This work led to a paper titled "Contribution of Thermal Mass to Energy Performance of Buildings: A Contemporary Analysis," published in the *International Journal of Sustainable Building Technology and Urban Development*, September 2011.

While Amir had been working on this, he was looking for an adviser for his doctoral research. Consequently, he started his doctoral work with me. He extended the previous work with me and he continued to carry out independent research under my supervision. During the work we published another paper "Parametric Analysis of Thermal Mass Property of Concrete Buildings in U.S. Climate Zones," published in the *Architectural Science Review Journal*, November 2012. In addition to energy performance he continued to work on thermal comfort and life cycle performance related to thermal mass to complete his doctoral thesis.

Most tall and supertall buildings worldwide are built at present using concrete as the primary structural material. This research on thermal mass of concrete is expected to be of benefit to designers who are thinking in terms of energy efficiency and thermal comfort of occupants.

Urban Design

I had been working the book *The Skyscraper and the City* and trying to incorporate the chapter on urban habitat originally handwritten by Dr. Lynn Beedle as class lecture notes. I had to expand on the notes to make it a complete book chapter. Over the course of my research, I developed an interest in the idea of fashioning a city which is very much intertwined with the built environment. I studied the subject further. As Group Leader of the Group Planning and Criteria committee of CTBUH I had been overseeing eight topical committees covering a broad range of topics related to the city that broadened my horizons. These offered a deeper look into the urban fabric. However, the real impetus came when I was awarded a Fulbright grant to study the feasibility of tall buildings in Malta in 2008. It was essentially an urban design project. While in Malta I took the mission as a unique opportunity to dig deeper and work on a hands-on project to apply my acquired knowledge on urban design.

When we talk about tall buildings in terms of their setting and context in a city, we invariably step into the professional discipline called urban design. A cursory review of the literature on cities reveals that arriving at a definition of urban design is difficult. It is an allied discipline with both architecture and urban planning. Some scholars argue that the main role of urban design is to provide functional and attractive urban spaces. Others argue that its key role is to facilitate environmental stewardship, social equity, social justice, and economic efficiencies. Thus "urban design" can be defined as an interdisciplinary field that shapes high quality urban spaces while engaging with the socio-economic, environmental, and political realities of a city and its residents.

In Malta, the Malta Environmental and Planning Authority (MEPA), together with University of Malta, who jointly organized the project, had a small library with some limited literature on urban design, and I carried some reading materials with me from Urbana-Champaign. I studied the subject in more depth while there and successfully completed my mission. I prepared a report on my Malta project entitled "Urban Design Strategy Report on Tall Buildings in Malta," in July 2008. The Malta project led me to start writing a book and I co-authored the book *The Future of the City: Tall Buildings and Urban Design* with Kheir Al-Kodmany.

CHAPTER 16

CONTRIBUTIONS TO THE
MOTHERLAND
Paying Back

A majority of my life has been spent learning, living and loving my adopted lands, Canada and especially the U.S. This book will be incomplete however, without sharing my equally deep attachment to Bangladesh. I take great pride in whatever contributions, big or small, I could make to the land of my birth. In 1970 when I was enroute to Canada, I felt the pang of separation, leaving my parents, pregnant wife and baby daughter Ifat behind, but also the land where I was born and raised. Catching an aerial view of my homeland, the buildings, houses, rivers and gentle rural landscape, I felt as if a strong rope was keeping me connected, yet I knew, for the moment, I had to struggle forward.

Despite my wish, always in the back of my mind, factoring into each of my life's major decisions, a permanent return was not to be. I became engrossed in life and studies, worked in the industry, and entered academia. I felt quite settled and started thinking instead, about how to contribute from afar. Bangladesh had given me an almost free education and I felt a great debt of gratitude. At EPUET I received two scholarships, one from there and the other from the Education Board; these paid most of my expenses. I received a great education in engineering, allowing me to progress in my field, far beyond what I had imagined as a young student. Opportunities to pay back my debt in some small ways was soon to come.

United Nations TOKTEN Fellowship

In late 1988 on vacation in Bangladesh with my family, I stayed in Dhaka for a while where I met Mr. Abul Faraz Khan, a superintending engineer of the Public Works Department (PWD) of the Government of Bangladesh. I was introduced to Mr. Khan by Mr. Nazrul Islam, a diploma engineer who knew him well. Mr. Khan arranged my visit to the City of Comilla where I gave a seminar in January 1989 to engineers on earthquake-resistant design of buildings.

After I returned to the U.S., Mr. Khan sent me a summary of what I presented there. He contacted me again through Mr. Nazrul Islam, who acted as a facilitator, and informed me that I was sponsored by PWD for a United Nations TOKTEN Fellowship to visit Bangladesh and give a series of seminars primarily on tall buildings, as well as conduct training and workshop sessions for PWD engineers. The fellowship dates were July-August 1989. Dhaka had been experiencing a boom in the construction of high-rise buildings and it was a timely topic for deliberations. This fellowship was administered by the United Nations Development Program (UNDP).

I arrived in Dhaka and stayed in Sonargaon Hotel, the most luxurious hotel in the city at the time, funded by the fellowship. During my earlier visits, I would stay with my relatives. This was the first time I had ever stayed in a hotel in my home country. I availed the opportunity to focus without much distraction. Invited by different institutes and organizations, I gave nine seminars and a PWD-sponsored highly attended general lecture in Dhaka at different venues, one seminar in

Joydevpur, and two seminars in Barisal and Khulna. I covered different topics, although most of the seminars were on tall buildings.

Some other topics that I covered were design of masonry structures, prestressed concrete and its use in high-rises, wind-resistant design of houses in cyclone-prone coastal areas, integration of architectural and engineering concepts in building design, and earthquake-resistant design. I emphasized that the maximum height for tall buildings in Dhaka should be 50 stories, although much taller buildings could be built at a high cost premium. I advised that uncontrolled growth of high-rises should be discouraged without master planning. Dhaka, being in a moderate seismic zone, buildings there should be designed with seismic considerations.

I was able to see certain cities, townships and rural areas of the country that I had never seen before and I really enjoyed the visits. Driving through the beautiful green countryside afforded breathtaking views. In particular, I was able to visit *Sagardari* village in Jessore, the birthplace of legendary poet Michael Madhusudan Dutta, known for (among other works of extraordinary Bengali literature) his epic *Meghnath Bodh Kaibbyo*. I also visited the *Laloner Aakhra* (Lalon's meeting place) in the village of *Chiuria* in Kushtia, of Lalon Shah, a thinker-philosopher, who influenced the most famous Bengali poets Rabindranath Tagore and Kazi Nazrul Islam, and who was the most well-known poet-practitioner of the *baul* music tradition, a form of mystical and spiritual music and songs.

I also conducted a workshop/training session on high-rise design and construction in Dhaka at the PWD Headquarters for the engineers and architects. I reviewed the conceptual design of the proposed 24-story Benevolent Fund building in Dhaka and offered guidance to the engineers for the preliminary design of the building.

My seminars were published in a book entitled *Tall Structures: Design and Allied Topics* edited by Abul Faraz Khan and published by PWD Technical Training Institute in 1989. While in Dhaka on this mission, I collected data on Dhaka's high-rise construction. Subsequently, I wrote an article titled "High-Rise Construction in Dhaka" giving my suggestions and observations, which was published in two parts on August 21 and 22, 1992 in the local daily newspaper *The Bangladesh Observer.*

Bangladesh Flood and Environment Committee in America (BEFCA)

In 1987 and 1988 catastrophic floods swept through most of Bangladesh. The 1988 flood had been described as a "once- in-a-century event" which caused extensive damage to properties, livestock and the infrastructure. The loss was estimated at nearly $2 billion, in addition to rendering about 35 million people homeless. Although the death toll was limited to about 2,000 because of the relocation of residents to higher grounds, the suffering of the people was immeasurable. The floods engulfed about three-fourths of the country and even caused disruption of the capital city of Dhaka, where two-thirds of the city was flooded. The floods were shown on American televisions, and worldwide as these floods caught the attention of the international community. I watched these scenes of devastations and human suffering and was immediately moved. I asked myself, being a civil engineer with knowledge and education in flood mitigation, could I help? I consulted with Dora and she encouraged me to do something.

I invited Rezaur Rahman, a doctoral student in civil engineering in the area of hydraulics and water resources to my home to get a better understanding of the different rivers and waterways and the topography of Bangladesh. We drew sketches of the rivers and discussed the specific causes of the floods in the Ganges River Basin. My civil engineering background allowed me to easily assess the technical issues and together we brainstormed different approaches the challenges that Bangladesh faced.

These massive floods prompted many Bangladeshis living in America and in Bangladesh, to think about a long-term solution. I realized that the best way to coordinate a response was to form a viable group of a few devoted individuals, establish a committee and develop a mission plan. I first contacted my friends Salim Rashid, Economics professor at UIUC and Aminul Karim, an electrical engineer and Vice President of Illinois Technical College, Chicago. Both of whom strongly supported my idea and extended all necessary cooperation. We agreed that we Bangladeshis couldn't simply accept offers of financial assistance from abroad when natural disasters hit Bangladesh. We could also rely on ourselves by implementing durable solutions to alleviate the recurring flood problem.

Then I invited Rezaur Rahman and Monzurul Hoque, who received a doctoral degree in Economics from UIUC and joined the Loyola University in Chicago as a faculty member. Others who were contacted were Atik Rahman, a Chicago architect, Munirul Islam, a Chicago engineer, and Mosleh Uddin Ahmed, a physicist, all of them living in Chicago. Mosleh Uddin Ahmed was very active initially but later moved away from Chicago preventing him from participating easily.

In October 1988, we held a meeting in Chicago and established the Bangladesh Flood Committee of America, subsequently renamed as Bangladesh Environment and Flood Committee in America (BEFCA), acknowledging that the long-term solution to the flood problem entailed dealing with related environmental issues. I was very fortunate that I could bring together all these qualified individuals from diverse backgrounds. I was elected president of the committee, with Aminul Karim, vice president, Operations and Salim Rashid as vice president, Research. Monzurul Hoque was elected the Secretary. Others were elected executive members with various responsibilities. I was struck by noticing how passionate all the members were to help their motherland. Mukit Hossain, a Chicago resident, joined the group at a later stage and was elected Treasurer/Newsletter Editor of the committee. Also, Belayet Khan, a professor of Geography at Eastern Illinois University, Charleston, Illinois and Abdul Qayyum Khan, a hydraulic engineer living in Champaign were subsequently added to the committee as executive members.

With zeal for their motherland, BEFCA members quickly moved to action. I met Glenn E. Stout, a hydrologist at UIUC and president of the International Water Resources Association and discussed the issue with him. He assured me that we would get all the help we needed and gave me some contacts of experts at UIUC campus and in other areas of the U.S. During December-January of 1988-1989, I visited Dhaka and met with several flood experts beginning with Professor Muhammad Shahjahan of Bangladesh University of Engineering and Technology (BUET), who later became the Vice Chancellor of the university in 1991. He was one of my professors during my student days. I also met Professors Mohib Uddin Ahmed and Jahiruddin Chowdhury of the Institute of Flood Control and Drainage Research (IFCDR), a research unit of BUET. Both of them emphasized collaboration between IFCDR and BEFCA. Mohib Uddin Ahmed, the Director of IFCDR was a classmate and friend of mine. I called on Mr. B.M. Abbas, a retired Chief Engineer of Water and Power Development Authority (WAPDA)and a renowned expert on Bangladesh flooding. He suggested the following:

(i) pursue the issue of international collaboration
(ii) follow through on the idea of building dams in Nepal or India to control flood originating from upstream, ideally in Nepal. A dam in the Brahmaputra was a possibility, but its site at Meghalaya was disputed territory

between India and China. Moreover, it was in an earthquake-prone region

(iii) establish contact with the Government of Bangladesh
(GOB)

I visited Dhaka again in July-August of 1989 on the UN TOKTEN mission described earlier. This gave me an opportunity to contact more Bangladeshi experts. I began my visit by contacting again B.M. Abbas, who was the Flood Minister of Bangladesh. I met Md. Amjad Hossain Khan, Chairman of the Bangladesh Water Development Board (BWDB), who told me about an old report, never realized, but authored by the World Bank. The report recommended the construction of a dam in Nepal accompanied by mitigation efforts within Bangladesh. I again met Mohib Uddin Ahmed, who re-emphasized the need for collaboration. I also met Professor Ainun Nishat, a Civil Engineering professor of BUET to gain further understanding of the flood problem.

Aminul Karim conducted many operational and administrative activities and promoted BEFCA's vision and activities to other organizations. Salim Rashid and Rezaur Rahman attended a symposium on Bangladesh floods in Montreal in May 1989, organized by the International Society of Bangladesh in Canada and both were involved in a panel discussion. On August 13, 1990 Salim Rashid presented a paper at a symposium in Dhaka organized by the Institution of Engineers, Bangladesh. He also presented a paper on September 5, 1992 at the Sixth North America Bangladesh Convention in Chicago, where Monzurul Hoque arranged a panel discussion on the flood issue.

Atik Rahman and Munirul Islam prepared letters introducing BEFCA and seeking collaboration, sent to different key individuals, international organizations and newspapers in the U.S. and Bangladesh. Mosleh Uddin Ahmed attended the 3rd North American Bangladesh Convention in Boston in September 1989, where he promoted our organization and presented a position paper written by Rezaur Rahman. In November 1991, I presented a paper on the management of natural disaster in Bangladesh at a seminar organized by Canada-Bangladesh Forum at Carleton University in Ottawa. My article on long term policy planning was published serially, in the Dhaka daily newspaper *Bangladesh Observer* from January 12-14, 1992.

Meanwhile, on May 9, 1991, the news program "Nightline" on ABC Network in the U.S., broadcast the aftermath of a cyclone that hit Bangladesh. Professor Garett Hardin, an ecologist from the University of California at Santa Barbara blamed overpopulation in Bangladesh as the primary cause of the large number of deaths. He suggested that the U.S. government should not continue to help Bangladesh unless Bangladeshis addressed population control modify their ideals and culture. Adrienne Germain, Vice President of the International Women's Health Coalition in New York, who was a guest of the same "Nightline" program, debated this notion. After discussing with BEFCA members, I wrote a letter on July 2, 1991 to Professor Hardin and contested his viewpoint.

Soon we found that this issue was being deliberated by many people and organizations. The unusual severity and magnitude of the 1988 floods resulted in four major international proposals. Although all of them supported the general idea of non-structural and mitigation measures through flood forecasting and early warning, flood preparedness, topographical mapping, flood-proofing pilot project, among others. There was, however, a difference of opinion on the issue of a structural solution calling for the construction of embankments along major rivers. These plans were formulated in such a way that they could be implemented wholly within the borders of Bangladesh, ruling out a highly desirable regional solution, in order to avoid possible political disputes among co-basin countries.

The Bangladesh Flood Policy Study prepared by the GOB and UNDP and French proposal, prepared by the French Engineering Consortium (FEC) supported the structural solution embodying the notion of "Countering the Floods," popularly known as "Controlled Flooding" by constructing large scale embankments. During my visit to Dhaka, I was told that the French report was partially based on GOB/UNDP report. The USAID proposal known as Eastern Water Study on the other hand, was opposed to the idea of embanking the rivers, while a Japanese proposal also cautioned against the construction of long and continuous embankments, at enormous cost, without in-depth studies of their environmental consequences and recommended localized polder-type projects to regulate floodwater levels. The last two reports constituted the non-structural solutions to the problem and promoted the concept of "Living with the Floods." The World Bank reviewed these proposals and prepared an overarching Flood Action Plan (FAP) comprising a set of guidelines that included the recommendations by various agencies, primarily endorsing the UNDP and French proposals, which were prepared in collaboration with GOB.

The FAP activities were designed to explore all possible options for a range of flood control actions. The G-7 countries in a summit meeting in London in December 1989 endorsed the GOB/UNDP and French proposals and agreed to fund further studies along these lines. Although initially BEFCA had been supporting this approach, it started deliberating these issues further and realized that the non-structural approach deserved further consideration. Meanwhile, with the funding from the G-7 countries, some studies were being conducted in Bangladesh and it was reported that BWDB was carrying out the implementation of some of the embankment projects with the funding from GOB.

This information alarmed us since if such structural solutions were executed even partially without considering the long-term environmental and socio-economic consequences, irreparable adverse effects might result. Despite their occasional fury, floods also have a beneficial effect on crop production, fishery, natural ground water discharge, and the ecosystem. Strong arguments on both structural and non-structural solutions should therefore be deliberated in the best interest of Bangladesh. During a private discussion between Salim Rashid and me, he floated the idea of organizing a conference to debate this matter, which I immediately embraced. I informed other members of this and they all agreed and assured me of any help that might be needed.

Once again, my civil engineering background made it easy for me to write a grant proposal for funding an international conference at UIUC campus from the National Science Foundation (NSF). I took the primary responsibility of going through the process of securing funds. I contacted Osman Shinaishin of NSF to discuss this matter. He encouraged me to proceed. I was the Principal Investigator with Salim Rashid as the Co-Investigator for the grant application. The review and approval process took some time, but at the end we got it. Additional funding for the conference was given by Louis Berger International and POUSH, USA. Salim Rashid took the primary responsibility of organizing the conference.

We invited a number of prominent American and Canadian experts and some Bangladeshi experts from BUET, BWDB and GOB. We wanted to get a few other specialists from the Bangladeshi public. To achieve that, we placed an advertisement in a Dhaka newspaper inviting people to apply for funding their round trip to Champaign, IL by submitting an abstract of their proposal. We received a large number of applications and selected a few winners. The conference time was fixed for April 2-4, 1993. Salim Rashid took the lead in managing contacts with the speakers and arranged their visits. He also coordinated with the UIUC authorities to reserve a conference venue and arrange a banquet for the participants. Mukit Hossain took the responsibility of publishing a newsletter for the occasion. As president of BEFCA I led the overall efforts in collaboration with Salim Rashid and others. I also took the responsibility of editing and publishing the proceedings of the conference. We were all excited and had been looking forward to the event and seeing the fruit of our labor.

Most of the specialists from Bangladesh came to Champaign by bus on the same day. It was a cold wintry day with some snow, which the visitors had not foreseen in April, coming from a tropical country. They came by bus and some of them were able to buy jackets at Chicago's O'Hare Airport, while others were shivering in the cold. The conference on "Bangladesh Floods: An Interdisciplinary Analysis of Alternative Solution Strategies" went well and smoothly. Following the end of the presentation of papers, we had an intense discussion on several topics moderated by Glen Stout and myself. A cordial exchange of ideas occurred on both structural and non-structural solutions, the FAP, and other allied topics.

Lunches were arranged for the participants and a dinner at Beckman Institute on one night and a banquet at Peabody Hall on another night, both venues being a part of the UIUC campus. Meals were prepared by the families of most local Bangladeshi residents. Although no immediate firm conclusions were drawn from the conference, discussions pointed to a non-structural approach as a preferable solution and thus leaned towards the idea of "Living with the Floods". We wanted the Bangladeshi experts, including policymakers, to take away ideas and review their ongoing actions and frame their future long-term policy on floods, keeping the proceedings discussions in mind. Assisted by Nurul Amin, a graduate student in the department of accounting at UIUC, I edited the Proceedings of the conference papers and notes on the discussions, which was published in August 1993 by the Center for International Business Education and Research (CIBER), an affiliated body of UIUC.

While we were done with our conference at UIUC, another major flood had been brewing in the American Midwest. The Mississippi River and its tributaries were swollen after torrential rainfalls beginning in April. A devastating flood, dubbed the Great American Flood of 1993 – the worst in American history, occurred from April to October resulting in major damages. The toll was in loss of human lives, dislocation of people, livestock, failure of levees, and more. The estimated cost of the damages was $15 billion. The unusual devastation caused by this flood called for more creative flood plain management in the U.S. We immediately thought that the lessons learned during, and in the wake of the Mississippi flood, could also be applied to the formulation of an appropriate FAP for Bangladesh. With this broad goal in mind, we conceived of another conference, this time in Bangladesh.

I drafted a new proposal for another conference funded by a grant from NSF comparing the flood control approaches for 1987-88 Bangladesh and 1993 American floods. Like the last one, I was the Principal Investigator and Salim Rashid was the Co-Investigator for the project. Our application was approved, and we received the funds to arrange the second international conference on "Comparative Evaluation of Flood Control Approaches for Bangladesh and the Mississippi River Basin," which was held in Dhaka during May 25-27, 1995. University Press Limited (UPL) of Bangladesh provided additional support for the conference.

Meanwhile, I didn't want to be the lifetime president of BEFCA, so we shuffled our positions. Aminul Karim was elected as president and I became the vice president, operation and Salim Rashid remained as vice president, research. Atiqur Rahman and Belayet Khan were elected as secretary and treasurer, respectively. The remaining three members of the BEFCA Board of directors were Munirul Islam, Monzurul Hoque, and Rezaur Rahman.

Initially, plans were made to hold the conference at BUET campus, but because of some student unrest, it was arranged at Hotel Purbani. IFCDR took an active role in organizing the event locally, with the active coordination by Salim Rashid on behalf of BEFCA. Papers were presented by both Bangladeshi and U.S. specialists and experts. The principal goal of this conference was for these specialists to learn from each other's experience. Proceedings of this conference were published by UPL. Both the proceedings of 1993 conference in the United States and 1995 conference in Dhaka were widely circulated among various persons and organization and publicized in both the U.S. and Bangladesh. *ASCE News* briefly featured an article of our activities in its September 1995 issue under the heading "U.S. and Bangladesh Engineers Trade Tips on Flood Control."

All this was possible through the collaboration between BEFCA and IFCDR, who agreed that we should publish a book combining the papers of both conferences as a document and source material for researchers and policymakers. The book entitled "Bangladesh Floods: Views from Home and Abroad" was published in 1998 by UPL. I discussed the details of the book in a previous chapter.

The conclusion that stemmed from both conferences was that floods should be eased through local management rather than implementing large-scale structural solutions, interfering with nature and causing disruption to the ecological balance. Our efforts were vindicated as this notion might have helped in guiding the flood policy of Bangladesh. During my journey through this process, it also became clear to me that another serious challenge was looming over the region. Population growth would inevitably lead to global water shortages and future wars over the finite resource and its distribution amongst neighboring countries. During the writing of this book major floods took place in Bangladesh, India and Nepal in 2017. The same year in late August, a catastrophic and historic flood took place in Texas hitting the city of Houston hard, in the wake of Hurricane Harvey and unusually heavy rainfall. Indeed, we humans and other creatures on earth are all vulnerable to natural disasters also known as Acts of God!

A new problem in Bangladesh, groundwater contamination by arsenic, came to the attention of the international community in 1995. In several areas of Bangladesh, this contaminated drinking water from deep tube wells began to create public health problem. Plenty of discussions were going on in Bangladesh and West Bengal in India about this new hazard and how to mitigate it. Pictures of sick people affected by arsenic poisoning emerged in newspapers and other media outlets. Some researchers were investigating the development of filters and other means of resolving this widespread and deadly problem. Once BEFCA was more or less done with the flood issue, this new problem drew my attention. I realized that we could do something about this too. Yet again, my civil engineering background dealing with hydrology and public health gave me the confidence to tackle it. I started researching the matter and prepared a grant proposal for a conference. Salim Rashid and other BEFCA colleagues fully agreed. I was the Principal Investigator and Salim Rashid was the Co-Investigator for the grant application to NSF.

In September 1999, while on sabbatical, I visited the headquarters of CTBUH at Lehigh University in Bethlehem, PA. I met the head of the Civil Engineering department, who was from West Bengal, and had been conducting research on arsenic contamination of drinking water in West Bengal. He mentioned that he had also traveled to Bangladesh. I gained some new insights from him in this matter.

In October, I visited Bangladesh where I met a few people with expertise or knowledge to get a better understanding of the problem. I set up a meeting with Quadiruz Zaman, Chairman of the Public Health Department of GOB, whose office was located in *Kakrail*, Dhaka. I talked with a few engineers there as well who explained the nature and extent of the problem. I was looking for a possible venue for the conference and asked Quadiruz Zaman for input. He showed me the nice auditorium of the department, which I thought would be perfect for the conference. Upon my return, I finalized the grant application, after running it by some local experts in hydrology and submitted it to NSF. We applied on behalf of BEFCA as the acting facilitator and host to other international experts to deliberate the matter. Unfortunately for us, our request for funding was denied as one reviewer commented that we didn't have experts in our group. We were disheartened at this outcome, but still felt good about our earnest efforts to serve our native motherland.

On the whole, whatever success we had through BEFCA, were possible because of the collective commitment and hard work of all its members. Although the organization was my brainchild, I owe gratitude to all the members, particularly Salim Rashid and Aminul Karim, whose clout and continued partnership, active participation and focus on the cause made the efforts worthwhile.

Mass Rapid Transit (MRT) for Dhaka
In 1978 on my first trip back to Dhaka, I observed a major increase in street traffic in the newborn country of Bangladesh. At the time I left, Bangladesh was still East Pakistan. In 1984 when I returned again to Dhaka after leaving Singapore en route to the U.S., I noticed Dhaka streets were even busier than before with increased traffic jams. On both occasions, I didn't think much of it as I was busy visiting relatives. Later in the summer of 1989 when I was in Dhaka on a TOKTEN mission, I stayed at the

opulent Sonargaon Hotel for the entire period funded by UNDP. Being on my own in a hotel gave me the opportunity to consider the horrendous traffic problem. Before I'd retire for the night, I tried to picture Dhaka from the point of view of a foreign consultant.

When I was in Singapore in 1984, they were building a subway there. There were many cities in the world with subways that eased the load of street transportation. Suddenly, I had a mental flash of a subway system in Dhaka. I was busy with my work related to the TOKTEN mission, but the idea stayed on my mind. A subway was complicated and there were many questions and challenges to be addressed before I could form an opinion. My civil engineering background allowed me to take a serious look at this issue upon my return to the U.S. In 1990 Dora visited Dhaka and reported the excessive amount of traffic in Dhaka's streets. She urged me to do something about the problem. At the time, I didn't have enough knowledge and realized I needed to investigate the topic in great depth. I wondered why (to the best of my knowledge) no one in Bangladesh brought this up publicly or even wrote about it.

Initially, I took a serious look at existing conditions. According to a UNDP report at the time, the growth of Dhaka from a population of only 250,000 in 1950 to 6 million in 1990 represented an accelerated population explosion in the city. The corresponding density of population had increased from 3,200 per square kilometer to 7,720 per square kilometer, that is, an increase of 140 per cent. The city also expanded in land area during this time. Along with other urban maladies, Dhaka's street transportation had dramatically deteriorated. During peak office hours, traffic was excruciatingly slow, resulting in a waste of time and wracking the nerves of city dwellers. The large number of rickshaws exacerbated the problem together with other slow-moving modes for transporting goods, push carts, bullock carts, etc. and the often-intimidating trucks and lorries made the traffic pattern even more complex.

The many advantages of a massive number of rickshaws, however, were that they were non-polluting, employed more than 200,000 people, eliminated fuel consumption, were affordable by low-to-middle income city dwellers, and they were readily available. A principal disadvantage was that their large number caused congestion and slow speed contributed to traffic jams. It was hard for private cars, buses, and other faster modes of traffic to move around them in the chaotic environment.

Because of the prevailing conditions, and population pressure on the city's street network, there was no room for lateral expansion. The main reason for the accelerated population growth was the reliance on a central urban hub that provided job opportunities and livelihood. The center city was drawing an influx of people to Dhaka from other parts of the country. Also, other cities and smaller towns didn't have some of the basic facilities and amenities that were available in Dhaka. The number of vehicles was significantly increasing every year, but not the roads to support them. The economic cost due to lost fuel and time, as well as the negative environmental effects were magnifying drastically.

Dhaka could no longer afford the economic and environmental loss due to severe traffic congestion on its streets. Above all, there was no mass rapid transit (MRT) system for moving a large volume of people within the city. I felt an underground tunnel system could mitigate the problem as most large cities of the world had resolved their own problems with such systems. I also thought of overhead light rail or heavy rail transportation as an alternative. I was wondering though why underground transportation was more popular than overhead in major cities of the world. At this time, I was also working on the flood problem of

Bangladesh together with my colleagues of BEFCA as well as the book *Architecture of Tall Buildings*.

In 1991, I presented a paper on "Disaster Management in Bangladesh: Need for a Long-Term Policy," at the Canada-Bangladesh Forum at Carleton University, Ottawa, Canada as part of my efforts to promote our concern and activities on behalf of BEFCA. At the conference, I met Mr. Tanwir Nawaz, an architect and urbanist, who was concerned about Dhaka's urban malaise. Because of our common interest, I bonded with him quickly and invited him to contribute to my book *Architecture of Tall Buildings*, a section on urbanization of cities in developing countries, mainly focusing on Dhaka. He wrote a thought-provoking article in the *Daily Star*, a prominent newspaper in Dhaka, published on June 28, 1991, entitled "Dhaka: 2000 A.D. and Beyond, an Urban Black Hole or a Livable World City." In this article he portrayed a bleak future for the city and its living conditions unless some needed actions were taken. He argued that transportation was a matter of utmost concern. I read the article and took the message to heart. It only reinforced what I was already thinking and inspired me to do something about it. It was possible that someone might have thought of some action plan before, but I was certainly not aware of it.

I invited Shawkat Ali to my home. He was a doctoral student in geotechnical engineering at UIUC, who had previous industrial experience in soils and foundations. My purpose was to get a better understanding of Dhaka's soil and ground water conditions to determine if these conditions were amenable to underground tunnel construction, without excessive cost. He gave me a good account of the soil conditions in Dhaka and gave me some documents to read. He also gave me information on the city's ground water level. The information he gave me was reliable as I confirmed it later from other sources.

UIUC had, and still has one of the largest libraries of the country. I spent time there and borrowed books on subways and tunneling. I read the fascinating history of underground tunnels in major cities, rivers, the English Channel, etc. I particularly enjoyed reading about the history of construction of underground tunnels in New York, in Detroit River connecting Detroit to Windsor, Ontario, Thames tunnel, and Tokyo subway tunnels. The 31-mile (50-kilometer) Channel Tunnel connecting England and France by rail is still a great wonder. About 25 miles (40 kilometers) of the tunnel lies under the sea. At its lowest point, it is 250 feet (74 meters) below the seabed and 377 feet (115 meters) below sea level. Its construction started in 1988 and eventually it was opened in 1994. The earliest known tunnel in recent era for transportation is the 188-mile (300-kilometer) Thames Tunnel built at 75 feet (23 meters) below the river surface at high tide and was built between 1825 and 1843.

My research yielded that constructing subterranean tunnels was definitely technically feasible. Most Asian cities such as Tokyo, Hong Kong, Singapore, Manila, Kolkata, and Taipei had built the underground tunnels to alleviate the massive transportation problem. So, I asked myself: why not Dhaka? To find the answer I needed to "dig" deeper into this subject. I absorbed myself in the pros and cons of the engineering behind tunnel construction.

Most of Bangladesh is underlain by flood-plain deposits laid by ancient and recent rivers. Dhaka's soil is made up of brown to light brown clay and silty clay belonging to the Madhupur Soil Group, about 30 feet (9 meters) deep with fine dense sand at lower strata below the clay layer. The ground water table in Dhaka was 27 feet (8 meters) to 40 feet (12 meters) below ground surface during peak periods and 40 feet (12 meters) to 52 feet (16 meters) during dry season.

I was convinced that the technology of tunnel construction was quite well advanced and could be utilized for Dhaka for a subway project. Basically, the principal methods of tunnel construction are Cut-and-Cover method, Shield Method, Caisson method, Submerged Tunnel method, and Freezing method, the first two being the most popular. The Cut-and-Cover method is the most suitable for Dhaka considering the city's ground conditions and the method's cost-effectiveness. Issues related to the feasibility study, alignment, networking, and operation and maintenance needed to be addressed. I wrote an article entitled "Mass Rapid Transit System for Dhaka City," that was published in the daily newspaper *Bangladesh Observer* on August 30, 1993. The article outlined my thoughts and treated the subject in depth. In its last section I concluded the article by writing the following:

An underground mass transit system is certainly capital intensive. The issues of technical and economic feasibility need to be addressed. But a main advantage is that it does not affect the surface traffic and it can move a large volume of people in a short time.

...Unless the Bangladesh intelligentsia both in Bangladesh and abroad as well as the Government of Bangladesh start seriously thinking about it now and take some immediate steps to face this gigantic challenge head on, it may be too late and much more complex as well as cost intensive to meet the tremendous burden of handling this problem at a later time. Any delay in planning and executing such a project will only cause more problems for the future.

At this time, I was busy with activities related to BEFCA, focusing on the two conferences on floods, at Champaign in 1993 and Dhaka in 1995. However, I continued reading about mass rapid transit, tunneling, and overhead rail construction and kept track of developments around the world. To understand the issue better I contacted Parsons Corporation in the U.S., who are well known for diverse types of engineering and construction services. They had been designing subways and tunnels as part of their many transportation projects globally. They referred me to their topmost tunneling expert Irshad Ahmed. I talked with him a few times and came away with the conclusion that subway was a feasible option. He explained to me how to deal with floods and earthquakes in the design, and how to construct tunnels under existing high-rise buildings that had long piles under them.

I soon came to the realization that I needed to go to Dhaka and share my insights with prominent decision makers. That opportunity came when I was on sabbatical leave in 1999 and visited Bangladesh in October for a few weeks. I met two locally prominent former classmates and friends like A.K.M Rafiquddin, Managing Director of Development Design Consultants Ltd., the topmost consulting engineering firm in Bangladesh and S.M. Kamaluddin, founder and Managing Director of Concord Engineers and Construction, the largest construction firm in Bangladesh.

I then met my other classmate and friend General Mustafizur Rahman, Commander-in-Chief of Bangladesh Army, who was reportedly a close relative of Sheikh Hasina, the Prime Minister at the time. I was hoping to see the Prime Minister and make a case to her about the construction of a subway system in Dhaka. My friend was unable to arrange such a meeting. I approached a relative of mine, Khondoker Mahbub Rabbani, a retired civil servant of Pakistan (CSP), who had good connections. He arranged a meeting with the Communications Secretary, who listened to my narrative. During my discussion, he mentioned that an underground pedestrian tunnel had been constructed across a busy street in the Motijheel commercial area. It was not very successful, as it became a place for vagrants, beggars, and petty criminals. I explained to him that a subway system was entirely different and would be gated and guarded by security people. At the end, he wished me success with my efforts and assured his cooperation if needed.

I then turned to academics. I went to BUET and met Professors Jamilur Reza Choudhury, a structural engineer and Mujibur Rahman Alamgir, a transportation engineer, and some other faculty members in a meeting at BUET. I explained my ideas and they were receptive. I sensed this idea was new to them as nobody mentioned anything about any previous effort in this area. I also separately met Professor Sarwar Jahan of the Urban Planning Department at BUET and briefed him, he was very appreciative of my efforts. During many of these discussions the prospects of building flyovers in some parts of Dhaka and overhead rail system for mass rapid transportation came up. I didn't like the idea of flyovers as they were temporary "Band-Aid" solutions that didn't address the movement of large volumes of people and were not a long-term solution to the problem.

Likewise, I didn't like the idea of overhead rail system as these are noise-intensive, they would affect the environment with fuel emission, needed regular maintenance, could affect the privacy of homes and other facilities, and could create other social problems. They might be acceptable in the city's outskirts but not in the crowded city. An underground system would be more expensive than overhead system, but tunnels were a more durable solution as they could last for centuries without much maintenance as they were naturally protected from the ravages of external weather conditions. It is for similar reasons that overhead construction was discarded in favor of tunnels in New York, Bangkok and Cairo. Although the initial cost of tunneling would be more, the overall life cycle cost would be less. I even found out from my research how the cost of construction of the tunnels could be met through a BOT (build, operate, and transfer) scheme and possible resources from donors and local resources. In fact, I wrote an article while in the U.S. updating my earlier article published in 1993. It was titled as "A Rapid Transit Subway System for Dhaka and Suburbs" published in two parts on November 3 and 4 in the daily *The Bangladesh Observer.* Covering more insights that I gained from my visit to Dhaka, I wrote another article upon my return to the U.S., which was entitled "Going Subterranean" and published in the Dhaka newspaper *The Daily Star* on January 28, 2000.

My next visit to Dhaka was in 2003 in connection with a conference on tall buildings organized by the architecture department at BUET. I connected with Tanwir Nawaz, architect and urbanist from Ottawa, Canada, who had been living in Dhaka at the time where he established an architectural and development firm. He was passionate about a solution to Dhaka's transportation problem. In a lunch meeting with him we discussed the matter at length. He was very supportive of my ideas. Then I met Dr. Sarwar Jahan, Professor and head of the urban and regional planning department at BUET, who told me that he would arrange a seminar on the topic. Accordingly, he graciously spearheaded a major seminar at BUET, inviting many distinguished local professionals, faculty members, and government officials. Mr. Nazmul Huda, who was the Communication Minister of Bangladesh under the government of Prime Minister Khaleda Zia, was invited as the Chief Guest. Professor Golam Rahman, former Vice Chancellor of Khulna University and an urban planner, chaired the seminar which was held on July 4 at the BUET Auditorium. I gave a PowerPoint presentation titled "Underground Mass Rapid Transit System for Dhaka." I was excited to see the huge audience filling the large auditorium, confirming to me the interest of the local people to overcome this major problem and improve their quality of life.

My presentation was very detailed and as convincing as I could make it. I prepared it with all the facts, data, sketches, etc. from my research of a few years. I took great pains to make a high

-quality presentation, since this was my opportunity to promote the idea to an audience of decision makers and stakeholders. I sensed from my 1999 trip that the idea of underground construction for Dhaka was unfamiliar. It would take time for people to digest and overcome their resistance to the unfamiliar.

I covered the causes of traffic congestion and repercussions, as well as answered questions on why a subway system was needed and why it was better than an overhead system. I detailed the history of tunneling and gave examples of other world cities that opted for subway systems including Kolkata, Dhaka's closest neighbor. I outlined the soil and water conditions of Dhaka, economic viability, constructability, flood protection, etc. I proposed a 50-feet (15-meter) wide tunnel accommodating two rail tracks, with sidewalls 23-feet (7-meter) high and the crown of the top arch at 30 feet (9 meters) below ground level – all shown on a sketch labeled with the dimensions. I suggested that a masterplan of routes should be made, connecting Karwan Bazar, Motijheel, New Market, Old Dhaka, and then extending to Gulshan, Mirpur, Uttara, and other outlying areas. I showed this proposed route on a map. I proposed to start the subway over a 10-kilometer stretch and then build the rest in phases. In conclusion I stated the following, which were essentially my recommendations:

- A subway system was a must to alleviate the traffic gridlock ... the question was not whether but when;
- The Bangladesh government and Dhaka City administration should act fast in a concerted way;
- Give the subway project top priority as a national project;
- Educate the public through the press and broadcast media; and
- Raise funds and secure Build, Operate and Transfer (B.O.T.) agreement with the builder.

After I finished, the Communication Minister spoke. After a few nice comments, he gave his own perspective which was at odds with what I presented. To my great surprise, he said he didn't see any traffic problems on Dhaka's streets. I could not believe what I heard. He said he lately visited China and was impressed by the Maglev trains, and he was determined to build a Maglev train line between Dhaka and Chittagong first. I then realized that he was committed to the thought and wanted to put aside any idea of building and MRT system for Dhaka.

As the seminar drew to a close and I was leaving, Quamrul Islam Siddique of the Local Government Engineering Department (LGED) approached me. I met him once when I was a TOKTEN fellow in 1989, when I gave a seminar on masonry structures, held at his LGED office. He was a very decent man with impeccable reputation for competence, honesty, and passion for doing great things for Bangladesh. He told me that he would locally pursue this matter with the government despite the minister's naysaying, cooperate with me and try to do as much as he could because he believed this was a very pressing issue that needed attention and action. The seminar was well publicized on local media.

Upon my return to the U.S., I worked on an article entitled "Mass Rapid Transit Options: Problems and Prospects" updating the topic of MRT and subway and conducted research on Maglev trains. It was published by the *Daily Star* in Dhaka on October 17, 2003. In the article, I re-emphasized the need for underground construction and gave reasons why Bangladesh was not yet ready for Maglev trains.

It came to my knowledge that Quamrul Islam Siddique, Jamilur Reza Choudhury and a few other prominent professionals convinced the government of Prime Minister Khaleda Zia to set up an Advisory Committee for Strategic Transportation Planning (STP) through the Dhaka Transportation Coordination Board (DTCB). Their task would be to formulate a plan for Dhaka's ground transportation. On December 22, 2003, Prime Minister Khaleda Zia sought Russian assistance for launching underground railway services in Dhaka, through the Russian Ambassador Oleg S. Malginov, which was a welcome sign. I suppose nothing transpired from it.

In 2004, however, the government approached the World Bank to fund the preparation of the Strategic Transport Plan (STP). The Advisory Committee consisting of professionals, academics and government officials for STP 2004-2024, charged with developing a 20-year plan was established in 2004. Dr. Jamilur Reza Choudhury chaired the committee. I was included as the only expatriate member. Louis Berger Group Inc. was retained as a consultant. Bangladesh Consultants Ltd. was retained as local consultant.

I wrote another article titled "Integrated Transportation in the Built Environment," which was published in the *Executive Times*, Dhaka in its July 2004 issue. In this article, I went into further details and concluded by saying that the notion of transportation planning must encompass the entire city and the outlying areas. It must include all aspects of civic infrastructure within the framework of a grand scheme, keeping in mind the projected growth of the city 30 to 50 years down the road, so our future generations would not be burdened with problems of our creation. If Dhaka were to remain a livable, balanced city, this challenge along with other urban problems must be faced squarely by the government and the people of Bangladesh. The sooner this was done, the better.

As a committee member, I was kept apprised of all the deliberations of the Advisory Committee. I communicated with the committee by emails. After many meetings and considerations, a draft urban transport policy report for Dhaka was prepared. I was not at all satisfied with it as it eventually recommended in 2005 a Bus Transit System (BRT) and didn't emphasize the urgent need for an MRT. I got a clear sense that there was a feeling on the part of the American consultant, that Bangladesh was a poor country and not yet ready for an MRT. I was made aware by Mr. Quamrul Islam Siddique, of some comments, including from one Mr. Lloyd Wright reacting to an article on Kolkata Metro. They held that the MRT system was a luxury for an impoverished country like Bangladesh. After reviewing the report, I sent my review comments, vehemently opposing the idea of BRT to the STP Advisory Committee as follows:

The Draft Urban Transport Policy was prepared by the Louis Berger Group Inc. and Bangladesh Consultants Ltd. to provide the Government of Bangladesh (GOB) with the basis for future action to resolve the burgeoning problem of transportation in Dhaka City. The report has 15 sections dealing with various issues. Section 2 lists 15 key policy issues. It appears to be comprehensive and touches upon many facets of urban transportation but has some flaws that need to be addressed.

The report recognizes that the present population of 12 million in "Greater Dhaka" will reach 35 million in 20 years. Yet, this alarming trend of population explosion and its consequences are not addressed adequately. The intimate relationship between the physical infrastructure of the city and its projected urban form will necessitate tomorrow's transportation systems to include tomorrow's needs in their planning, implementation and operation. Livable communities and open space will be the focus of future transportation. Also, transportation's ability to shape urban density and promote efficient use of energy through mass transit solutions should be duly recognized.

At present, there is no Mass Transit System in Dhaka. The report recognizes the need for a future system. The report is uncertain about what will be the best option. However, it seems to place emphasis on buses without recognizing that right now there are already a large number of buses and fewer roads to sustain them. Buses will be always crowded in a city like Dhaka and passengers will need to spend a lot of travel time. Creating more roads will be difficult in existing densely populated areas and they will eat up more open space if there is any left now. While buses are inevitable, they are not the solution. Dhaka needs something better. Time has come for building underground subway lines. They are out of sight, do not take up surface space in a crowded city environment, and can carry many passengers at high speed because they are heavy rail. Overhead light rail and monorail systems are obstructive and are justifiable for moderate passenger loads. New York had demolished much of its overhead systems almost a century ago and Boston is doing it now-- in both cases in favor of subway.

Subways are expensive. The high cost comes from the digging or boring of tunnels, the concrete linings and the need to relocate utility lines. However, for large cities, the high cost of a subway is justified in densely populated areas, where large number of people can be moved by the system. Also, the long-term cost is not high. Its benefits are immense. The report should prioritize what is essential for solving the city's acute transportation problem. Cost of it is the concern of GOB.

There is a sense of urgency in the matter. Seeing the burgeoning transport problem of Kolkata, the visionary Chief Minister of West Bengal, Dr. B.C. Roy conceived for the first time the idea of underground railway in as early as 1949. Subsequently, a Metropolitan Transport Project (Rly) was set up in 1969 who had prepared a Master Plan in 1971 envisaging construction of five rapid transit lines totaling a length of 97.5 km, out of which priority was given to the 16 km Dum Dum-Tollygunge line. Construction started in 1973. After some initial setbacks and hurdles a 3.45 km segment was completed in 1984. More segments were done in stages of about 2 to 4 km, and the entire stretch was completed in 1995. I recount the history of our neighboring city here to show how long it takes to realize such a project. Surprisingly, the Urban Policy Document does not emphasize the *dire need* for mass transportation other than some general references to it, although it recognizes that Dhaka's population will skyrocket to 35 million in only 20 years.

Regarding systems integration, I would point out that this is an important issue. Not only people come to Dhaka by highways and waterways, but also by railways. Any Master Plan should consider how these transportation systems must be integrated with the city's Mass Transit System. Also, such a system must effectively integrate with the adjoining civic infrastructure.

To sum up, Dhaka needs an underground Mass Rapid Transit System. Planning and feasibility studies should be conducted as soon as possible. The challenge of Dhaka's traffic malady must be linked to achieving the goal of sustainable development. The focus must be on the redevelopment of today's Dhaka City that can transition into a city in balance with its growing and changing population.

I then read the detailed reply from Mr. Lloyd Wright, which was sent to me by Mr. Ashraf Sarkar, to which I reacted by sending the following letter to the STP Advisory Committee:

My comments of September 18 were based on an email from Mr. Q.I. Siddique forwarding brief comments by one Mr. Lloyd Wright. In another email forwarded by Mr. Ashraf Sarkar on September 20, I could see Mr. Wright's detailed comments reacting to an article on Kolkata Metro. Therefore, I would like to elaborate upon my previous comments.

I find Mr. Wright's comments opinionated, not based on the reality of the situation. He advises against holding Kolkata as an example for Dhaka or any other city on four counts: infrastructure costs, operating costs, ridership numbers and fare affordability.

Regarding infrastructure costs, initial costs of many mega-projects purported to solve problems on a long-term basis are high, but if the life-cycle costs are low and the projects are immensely beneficial for the suffering public, the initial costs are justifiable because they can be recovered over the long haul. I am not sure if Mr. Wright took a hard look at this point. Also, governments all over the world have to subsidize many essential projects that serve the public. When citizens face enormous hardships, governments have to step in to alleviate the sufferings. Nothing meaningful can be accomplished in a society without the sacrifice of the people and the government of a country.

In another note he sent to "Karl", he wrote, "The main problem is that Kolkata (like Dhaka) sits on a very wet river delta, and thus the water table is quite high". According to my sources, top 9 meters of Dhaka's soil is light brown clay and silty clay of Madhupur soil group, and the lower strata comprise fine dense sand, the water table being at 12 to 16 meters below ground during dry season and 8 to 12 meters below ground during peak season. These are very good conditions for subway construction when we compare them to many other cities. Tunnels have been built under seas, rivers and lakes. The city of Amsterdam is under sea water level and I took a ride in the subway there, which was quite comfortable. Regarding ridership, I am surprised to hear from him that that it is poor. All people I talked with say that the metro in Kolkata is very popular. Recently I talked with Dr. Nani Gopal Bhowmik, Principal Scientist and Head of the Hydraulic Division (retired) of the Illinois Water Survey (nbhowmik@uiuc.edu). He is originally from Bangladesh and many in the steering committee may know him. He visits Kolkata every year and went there as recently as last February. He tells me just the opposite... that the subway is very popular and comfortable. He had taken rides in it. The somewhat elevated cost of ridership with respect to bus transportation is amply justified by the fact that people don't have to get held up in traffic gridlock and can thus save time. For working people time is money. They don't mind paying this somewhat increased fare greatly. According to him, many people owning cars take the subway for saving time which in turn reduces street traffic. Dr. Bhowmik did not see any notable water problem in the subway. Right now, construction on the extension of the 16-kilometer Dumdum-Taliganj line is going on. I presume more of this will happen in the future. I wonder wherefrom Mr. Wright got some of his information.

I agree with him that the monorail system, while may be viable in limited applications, is not generally a suitable system for densely populated areas. Such light rail cannot transport people on a mammoth scale and may create future problems in areas where population density will drastically increase. I also agree with him on his comments about integration of transit modes and fare structures as well as integration of associated physical and urban systems. This should be carefully looked into for any planning for metros.

About Mr. Wright's observations on the politicians, my impression about our Bangladeshi politicians on the particular issue is different from what he suggested. We may blame politicians for many things but not on this one. Tunneling technology started in the first half of the 19th century. In my opinion, it is not high technology anymore. Unfortunately, Mr. Wright does not see the benefits of technology transfer and sustainable infrastructure development in all this.

His reference to the Madrid Metro is worth looking into, but then he takes it away from us because it is in a "western European city." I take his findings as a whole with a grain of salt. I think Mr. Wright's comments are based more on his perception than reality on the ground. I don't see the reason why South Asian cities cannot have integrated metro systems that included subways when much of the world has them.

Given this scenario, I assume my opposition got through to the committee members and may have swayed the consultants as they finally changed their recommendations, stating in their final report of 2006 that out of the six BRT lines which they had identified, three would be MRTs and the remaining three BRTs could be converted to MRTs in the future. Moreover, the MRTs would be either over-ground or underground.

I was delighted to see the outcome of the concerted efforts of the STP 2004-2024 Advisory Committee. This report was sent to the Communication Minister for approval and further action. However, I came to learn from reliable sources that sadly no action was being taken there at his office. In late 2006, political instability ensued over a lingering dispute between the ruling Bangladesh National Party led by Khaleda Zia and the opposition party Awami League led by Shaikh Hasina. The dispute was about how to conduct a free and fair general election, as the end of ruling party's term was impending.

During this time, I was invited to deliver a keynote paper on tall buildings at the 18th CAA Conference on Society, Architects & Emerging Issues organized by the Commonwealth Association of Architects (CAA) and Institute of Architects Bangladesh (IAB), Dhaka, Bangladesh. The conference was canceled because of the political turmoil. At the time, I was on a sabbatical leave so, I decided to go to Dhaka anyway. Knowing that I was in Dhaka, Tanwir Nawaz spearheaded a meeting for me to address some key people. Professor Golam Rahman, former Vice Chancellor of Khulna University, who was in the group, proposed a seminar on MRT.

I was invited to be a keynote speaker at a seminar on "Strategic Transportation Plan for Dhaka: The Way Forward," which was sponsored by the Bangladesh Urban and Municipal Forum (BUMF) and Dhaka Urban Forum (DUF), and LGED. It was held at LGED Bhaban, Dhaka, on December 24, 2006 and was chaired by Jamilur Reza Choudhury. Quamrul Islam Siddique was the Chairman of LGED and took a very active role in arranging the seminar along with others. In my speech, attended by many local influential people, I reiterated my position about the urgency of building a Metro Rail system and gave examples of the system in our neighboring cities like Kolkata, Delhi, and Bangkok. I stressed that the traffic jam of Dhaka was becoming a horrific problem for city dwellers day by day and flyovers were only temporary solutions for automobile traffic and not for the mass movement of the general public. I passionately urged the policymakers to pursue the implementation of the STP report. The audience was generally receptive.

The seminar was publicized by the local media. Tanwir Nawaz was the other keynote speaker giving details of the STP's findings. After I returned to the U.S., on January 11, 2007 the military took over the country's power and set up a Caretaker Government consisting of civilians. This new government announced its official intent to build a Metro Rail system in Dhaka.

By this time, I had no further involvement or contribution to the subsequent developments but kept my interest in it from a distance. In 2008 the caretaker government approved the STP report. That was welcome news. A general election was held in 2009 in which during the election campaign Awami League leader Shaikh Hasina promised a Metro Rail for Dhaka. She won the election and became the Prime Minister of Bangladesh.

To make it cost effective, it was decided to build an overhead rail system. This is a great start and should somewhat ease the traffic jam in the foreseeable future. A few flyovers were built to provide some relief but did not significantly resolve the issue. Eventually, an underground system will be necessary for the most crowded segments of the city. Meanwhile, a Revised Strategic Transportation Plan (RSTP) for 2016-2035 that included some revisions of the original STP (2004-2024) was formulated.

I retrieved the following abridged text at this writing from Wikipedia on October 3, 2019:

The Dhaka Metro is an approved metro rail system under construction in Dhaka. Together with a separate Bus Rapid Transit (BRT) system it has been long called for to solve the extreme amount of traffic jams ... that occur throughout the entire city on a daily basis, one of the heaviest in the world. It is a part of the Strategic Transport Plan (STP) chalked out by the Dhaka Transport Coordination Authority (DTCA), a governmental agency.

Currently the metro rail system consists of one line referred to as the MRT (Mass Rapid Transit) Line-6, with other metro rail lines going to be added in the future.

The Dhaka Metro Rail Line-6 consists of 16 elevated stations each of 180m long and 20.1 km of electricity powered light rail tracks. All of Line-6, save for the depot, as well as some of its accompanying BRT, will be elevated above current roads primarily above road medians to allow traffic flow underneath, with stations also elevated.

Construction began on 26 June 2016 with an inauguration ceremony presided over by the reigning prime minister Sheikh Hasina. The civil work is being done by the Italian-Thai Development Public Company Ltd. and Sinohydro Corporation Ltd. JV and a Tokyo-based construction company is developing the depot's land.

The problem of traffic jams is getting worse by the day. The intelligentsia and city dwellers who suffered the most must mobilize their efforts to press upon the GOB to act fast. Not only in the areas of BRT and overhead rail systems but also a subway system, in the crowded part of the city. As city population continues to grow, constructing a comprehensive transportation network in the unused subterranean space is the ultimate long-term solution.

CHAPTER 17

TALL BUILDING COUNCIL AND THE KHAN CHAIR

Fulfilling a Dream

O n account of my many moves as a student and profession-al, it was not until I joined UIUC that I could think of doing any voluntary work in my field. Once at UIUC and I felt settled, I looked for committee work in the profession. Since my research area at the time was in concrete and I had a special in-terest in concrete, I soon joined two committees of the American Concrete Institute (ACI): Committee 120 - History of Concrete and Committee 124 - Concrete Esthetics. I chose Committee 120 as I was interested in structural history. I chose Committee 124 to pursue my interest in art and architecture. I attended a meet-ing of Committee 120 in Seattle but didn't like how the meeting was conducted. I found the intellectual atmosphere rather stag-nant and the thinking seemed entrenched, unable to encourage ideas from newcomers. I continued my membership but didn't actively participate. Similarly, I also gradually lost interest in the other committee, as I didn't agree with their approach. The opportunity of doing committee work in a creative way, with freedom to infuse my ideas came when I joined CTBUH.

Council on Tall Buildings and Urban Habitat (CTBUH)

My primary affiliation in the U.S. was with CTBUH dating back to1988. Before that I was involved in American Society of Civil Engineers (ASCE) and American Concrete Institute (ACI) as member. I developed a fascination for tall buildings ever since seeing the urban giants in Toronto and New York and later, Chicago. These colossal towers soared high in the sky toward heaven, defying the pull of gravity. To me they represented a triumph of extreme engineering. These out-of-human-scale vertical artifacts in the hustling business districts of great cities captivated me and stimulated my imagination. I wondered how such mammoth structures were holding themselves together, standing serenely in static equilibrium. I wondered how they were erected to such great heights. Being a structural engineer, obviously I wanted to understand the mechanics and conceptualize the interplay of resisting internal forces in response to the brutal natural forces of vertical weights, high winds, and earthquakes. I had a powerful fantasy of someday designing these buildings myself.

Through SOM and the honor and opportunity of working with Dr. Fazlur R. Khan, who forever revolutionized the structural design of tall buildings, and his closest associate Hal Iyengar, another great structural engineer who left his mark in his own right with his innovations. Such associations helped me fulfill my aspirations. My accidental meeting in Chicago with Lynn S. Beedle in 1988, the founder of CTBUH - and himself a giant of tall buildings - drew me further toward tall buildings.

CTBUH is an international organization dedicated to research and dissemination of information related to tall buildings and their impact on the urban environment. The members of the Council are professional specialists in the areas of planning, designing, constructing, and operating tall buildings. It does not promote tall buildings, but where such buildings are feasible as a solution to urban needs, it encourages the use of the latest information and makes it available to its membership and other interested parties. The Council's Headquarters were initially located at Lehigh University in Bethlehem, PA, where Dr. Lynn Beedle was a professor of structural engineering. Subsequently, after his death in 2003, the Headquarters was moved to Chicago at the Illinois Institute of Technology and then to a downtown office building on Michigan Avenue. The Council fulfills its mission of technology transfer through publications, congresses and conferences worldwide, and its databases and membership resources are intended to provide answers to questions.

One of the Council's major strengths was its series of monographs published periodically. The monographs were prepared by the topical groups and were aimed at documenting the state-of-the-art of various aspects of tall buildings and the urban habitat. The first five monograph volumes were published by ASCE during 1978-81. This would be followed by the McGraw-Hill Series after the Steering Group of the Council decided to publish monographs prepared by individual topical committees rather than groups. It was in 1990 when I was appointed Chairman of the Council's Committee 30–Architecture (1990-1998). In that role, I was actively involved in spearheading the preparation of a monograph on tall building architecture during 1990-95 and found it to be an amazing experience.

As I mentioned before in the chapter on my books, I found it gratifying to be able to connect and work with committee members, and particularly, the 32 contributors to the monograph from around the world. Such contacts, together with the tasks of compiling and editing the book enriched my understanding of architectural trends and the regional and local socio-cultural traditions around the world. Unquestionably, these settings where I interacted with prominent architects, urban planners, and engineers of the world, offered me an opportunity to broaden my horizons and stay informed on the ideas and developments on tall buildings worldwide.

Another major strength of the Council was the convening of World Congresses at five years intervals in major world cities. I participated in all of them as well as the international conferences during my active years. At the Congresses, I organized and led workshops in Hong Kong, Amsterdam, and Melbourne. These events drew people from different countries and offered me an opportunity to exchange ideas, immensely benefitting my professional career and personal growth. Furthermore, my frequent contacts with Dr. Beedle, the Council's founding father, who held the position of the Director of the Council and who was revered internationally, also elevated my understanding of issues and widened my vision, both at professional and personal levels.

In 1998, I was appointed by CTBUH to be Chairman of the newly formed Group PA- Planning and Architecture to oversee eight topical committees (1998-2005). I was also appointed at the same time, as a member of the Council's Steering Group (1998-2005). This group recommended all major policy matters for the approval of the Executive Committee, the final decision-making body. I was instrumental in proposing new names for topical committees to reflect the latest trends in the building industry in their respective fields, in a joint meeting of the Executive Committee and the Steering Group. All my proposals were adopted by the Executive Committee. I attended most of the Executive Committee and Steering Group meetings. I also served on the following CTBUH committees: Committee 3-Structural Systems (1990-2000); Committee 14-Analysis and Design; Advisory Council for Lynn S. Beedle Achievement Award and Fazlur R. Khan

Medal (2004); Height and Data Committee (2004-2005); the Council's Advisory Group (2008-2011).

At the Amsterdam World Congress in 1995, we had a discussion on the Council's newsletter *The Times,* which was very brief and rudimentary but gave a rundown of the Council's events and disseminated news to the Council's members. Our discussions were aimed improving and broadening its scope. The idea of a bulletin emerged from the deliberations in which Shankar Nair, a prominent structural engineer and Vice President at Teng & Associates in Chicago, and an active member of the Executive Committee, played an important role. I also wholeheartedly embraced it.

Invited by Beedle, I wrote a piece "On My Mind ..." in the newsletter *The Times* in its August 1995 issue. I devoted the entire article to justifying and promoting the idea of the bulletin, which was never published but the dormant idea turned into reality in the form of an online publication, *CTBUH Review Journal* which was approved by the Executive Committee in 1998 in a meeting in New York. I was appointed the first editor of the journal. As I was the founding editor, it became a major undertaking for me to set it up. I invited my colleagues Paul Armstrong to be associate editor and Abbas Aminmansour as managing editor. Abbas was skilled in computers and his services were helpful in creating a web site for the new journal. I was leading the team and contacting prospective contributors for the new, as-yet-unknown journal. I took the lead in editing assisted by Paul, while Abbas primarily worked on the management of the web site, formatting, and other related matters.

Funded by CTBUH, we launched the journal in 1999 with its first issue of *CTBUH Review,* subtitled "The Professional Journal of the Council on Tall Buildings and Urban Habitat" released in May 2000, volume 1 issue 1 in which I made an announcement explaining why this journal was long overdue. It contained a foreword by the founder and the then-Director Emeritus of CTBUH Lynn S. Beedle, "CTBUH: A Historical Sketch," as well as research papers by architect Ken Yeang on ecological design, structural engineer Shankar Nair on structural design in difficult locations along the Chicago River, and by others. It was available electronically on the CTBUH web site. It was scheduled to be published bi-annually, with all papers receiving a peer review and editor's scan before publication.

After withstanding the growing pains of this new venture, we were able to place the journal on firm footing. It was all voluntary work for me and my associates. Volume 1 issue 2 appeared in February 2001. The journal continued under my editorship until August 2002 when a new editor's name was announced. I decided not to continue as it had been taking a lot of my time. The journal continued to be published as *CTBUH Review* and went through some stages of periodic but irregular publication. Regular publication resumed in 2008 under the title of *CTBUH Journal* and has been successfully being published, with major improvements as of this writing. At this writing Daniel Safarik has been a long-time editor of the journal. I had been on its editorial board for many years. I continue to review its papers.

I may mention here that CTBUH has expanded tremendously under the leadership of current Chief Executive Officer, Dr. Antony Wood, a networker and an energetic person.

In 2004 a book titled *Catalyst for Skyscraper Revolution: Lynn S. Beedle – A Legend in His Lifetime,* that I edited was published by CTBUH. I discussed this book in some detail in the earlier chapter on my books.

I remained on the CTBUH Advisory Committee as an active member until 2011 when I resigned as Dora required kidney dialysis and I realized that I could not continue as an active participant anymore. However, I continued on the editorial board of the *CTBUH Journal.* In 2009 I was made a Fellow of

CTBUH in an award ceremony held at the Crown Hall of Illinois Institute of Technology, Chicago. I have remained engaged in some of the journal-related activities and review of conference papers and research proposals until now. In February 2019 I was invited to be a member of the steering committee for the symposium on "What is the First Skyscraper of the World?" as a segment in the World Congress celebrating the 50th Anniversary of CTBUH held in October 2019 in Chicago. The Home Insurance Building of 1885 designed by William Le Baron Jenney is generally recognized as the first skyscraper. But there are some who disagree. I wrote a paper titled "The First Skyscraper: The Case for the Home Insurance Building in Chicago" with my co-author Dr. Kyoung Sun Moon, which I presented at the October Symposium.

Fazlur Rahman Khan Chair

Following the untimely death of Dr. Fazlur R. Khan in 1982 Lynn Beedle envisioned the idea of establishing a Chair in his honor. He worked with Khan at CTBUH and knew him intimately. He spearheaded the program for establishing the Fazlur Rahman Khan Chair at Lehigh University, where he found immediate support. All agreed it was a fitting consummation of the efforts of the man who had chaired CTBUH headquartered at Lehigh University at the time of his death. Thus, the program, with a goal of $1.25 million for a fully funded Chair, was established in 1982. The entire amount for the endowment was to be acquired through direct appeals. Beedle assumed the role of Coordinator of the Khan Chair and began his long-term efforts. For him, it was a noble mission -- a labor of love for Fazlur R. Khan. He told Nadine Post of *Engineering News-Record,* a well-known American construction magazine in 1989, "I'm struck with the breadth of the man's abilities and the regard that people had for him." This was probably the first time an American had initiated the major task of establishing a Chair to honor a person of South Asian origin, especially with donor funds.

Dr. Beedle, known for his interpersonal skills, networking, and as a "polite pusher," began his fundraising drive by going almost door to door to potential donors all around the world using his international connections and personal clout, particularly focusing on those who had known Dr. Khan. He used his warmth and charisma to influence people and even mobilize a small group of volunteers to work with him, with Chandra Jha, President of PSM International, a development firm in Chicago and a very close friend and admirer of Dr. Khan, as its leader. I was recruited as such a volunteer in the summer of 1988 soon after I met Dr. Beedle. Together with Aminul Karim, an academic administrator and Chicago resident, who also worked with me in BEFCA, we raised funds from Bangladeshis living in America. The eventual goal of this endeavor was to honor Khan by establishing a Fazlur R. Khan Scholarship (later renamed Fazlur Rahman Khan Prize) to be awarded to a meritorious Bangladeshi student studying at Lehigh University, as a component of the Fazlur Rahman Khan Chair program.

The Chair's Advisory Committee was formally established in 1990 with Chandra Jha as its chairman and the following members: Muhammad Ridzuan Saleh from Malaysia, Sabah Al Rayes from Kuwait, Zuhair Fayez from Saudi Arabia, Jamilur Reza Choudhury from Bangladesh, and Aminul Karim and Mir M. Ali from the U.S. The principal mission of the Chair was to honor a world-famous American engineer originally from Bangladesh. The main goal was to perpetuate Dr. Khan's philosophy: to use the finest technology, remember that building design is for people, and ensure a better life for urban dwellers through improving the built environment. Other core objectives were identified: to foster state-of-the art teaching and research, stimulate closer ties with universities around the world, develop close ties with professionals, encourage the application of new knowledge to practice, and accelerate the development of computerized databases. It was determined that the Fazlur Rahman Khan Professor – the faculty member occupying the Chair – would be a member of the Lehigh faculty. The duties and responsibilities of the Khan Professor were also identified.

In addition to the Fazlur Rahman Khan Prize at Lehigh University, a "Bangladesh Program" under the umbrella of the Chair was developed. Under this program, a center named the "F.R. Khan Center for Study of the Built Environment" would be established at Bangladesh University of Engineering and Technology (BUET) a counterpart of the Chair program at Lehigh. The Bangladesh Program was aimed at raising adequate funds so that every year the Khan Professor could spend up to a month in Bangladesh and conversely, a faculty member from BUET would be a visiting scholar at Lehigh University.

Dr. Beedle received major donations from several large companies in the industry. He also secured major contributions from the governments of Saudi Arabia and Malaysia because of the generosity of his Royal Highness Prince Sultan bin Abdul Aziz, Minister of Defense, Saudi Arabia and Mohamad Mahathir, Prime Minister, Malaysia. Dr. Beedle contacted some 20 countries with his efforts. He even went to Dr. Khan's and my native country Bangladesh. The Secretary of Industries of the Bangladesh government, A.K.M. Musharraf Hossain, arranged a meeting of him with President Hussain Muhammad Ershad, in 1989.

He explained to President Ershad how the Khan Chair would directly benefit Bangladesh and bring recognition to the country through tributes being paid to one of its most illustrious sons. President Ershad was persuaded and made his intention clear to pledge for $100,000. However, by the time the matter was under active consideration, Bangladesh was immersed in sudden political instability. Beedle was formally notified by the Secretary of Industries. The political instability resulted in the departure of President Ershad. The successive governments of Prime Minister Khaleda Zia and Sheikh Hasina didn't act on the pledge by President Ershad. During these times, I had been in frequent contact with Jamilur Reza Choudhury, a member of the Chair's Advisory Committee and my contact person in Dhaka. Sadly, nothing further materialized on this and the pledge was never fulfilled by the Bangladesh government.

Meanwhile, in the U.S., Aminul Karim and I initiated a vigorous fundraising campaign. I drafted a letter in consultation with Aminul Karim tot individual donors. We mailed the letter to different Bangladeshis and some others in the U.S. I personally went to the SOM office in Chicago once and approached my acquaintances there to seek donations from them. All these efforts, although well intended, didn't meet our lofty expectations. But we didn't relent. A major donation was given by Bangladesh Association of Chicago (BAC), the organization that Dr. Khan founded. We got another break when I contacted Dr. Sufyan Khondoker, a civil engineer in New York, who was a leader of the American Association of Bangladeshi Engineers and Architects (AABEA). I knew him from the Second International Conference on Floods in Bangladesh held in Dhaka organized by BEFCA where he presented a paper. He was a very active person and organized a fundraising dinner in New York on November 15, 1997. Many Bangladeshi professionals and businessmen participated in the dinner meeting. Dr. Beedle, Aminul Karim and I spoke, urging the audience to donate money for a distinguished Bangladeshi structural engineer, who had put "Bangladesh on the map" through his groundbreaking innovations in the tall building industry.

The meeting produced $10,000 in a single night -- thanks to Dr. Khondoker, his associates, and the Bangladeshi donors of New York. Aside from the generosity of individual donors, the two major contributions from BAC and AABEA expedited the matter for us. My role as a volunteer ended after that but I continued to be a member of the Chair's Advisory Committee. The Chair was finally established in the Department of Civil and Environmental Engineering at Lehigh University in 2007. The founding of the Chair was only possible by the tireless and selfless efforts of a big-hearted man like Dr. Beedle. I am glad I was a part of it.

CHAPTER 18

MY CONSULTANCIES
Design Adventures

During my professional and academic career, I had the opportunity to work on many consultancy projects – large and small. I did these projects as overtime work outside my regular jobs with the consent of my employers. Apart from some extra money, I did them primarily to experience the excitement of purposeful real-world projects and to enrich my professional skills. For the most part, my consultancies were thrilling and thought-provoking as every project was distinctive with unique challenges. I took each of them as a new adventure and immensely relished the work.

Mr. Abdul Halim, Dhaka, Bangladesh
This project on a residence in Gulshan, Dhaka, was neither a major nor significant one, but I include it here because this was the very first consultancy of my career. It gave me my first experience dealing with a construction project and a client on my own.

It was in 1967 when I was the Assistant Executive Engineer with State Bank of Pakistan in Dhaka, that I was retained for this project. Mr. Saleem Thariani, a prominent architect in Dhaka was the architect-of-record of the new State Bank of Pakistan building under construction in Motijheel Commercial Area and the classy Deputy Governor's Bungalow in Gulshan. I became intimately connected with this incredibly competent, sharp, likeable, and wise architect.

One day, an engineer from his office, Mr. Yusuf, called me and asked me to see Mr. Thariani at his office. I thought it was related to a Bank project that I was supervising, and probably something serious had happened, requiring a face-to-face meeting. He told me that one Mr. Abdul Halim, an Income Tax Commissioner, was looking for an engineer who could supervise the construction of his large new residence, designed by Mr. Thariani, who thought I would be a good fit. He asked me if I could do it and I gladly accepted. I knew that there was a great deal of responsibility involved in this project as it was a masonry structure with reinforced concrete (R.C.) floor and roof slabs and columns. Concrete is a brittle material, highly vulnerable to cracking unless the structural design is done correctly and, more importantly, the construction is properly carried out and overseen.

I met the client -- a very nice man – with whom I discussed my fees and the scope of my work; I also met the contractor. My overall supervision went well. There was, however, one challenge. The residence had a moderately long verandah in the front and designed with beams placed under the reinforced concrete slab, along its perimeter. Mr. Halim didn't like the placement for aesthetic reasons. He asked me if the beams could be removed and the slab designed without any beams running along the long direction. I contacted Mr. Thariani, who requested that I handle the urgent matter myself since Mr. Yusuf was the only structural engineer in the office and was already swamped with work.

It was not easy for me, but after some brainstorming, I redesigned the slab in an unconventional way, by supporting the slab at the ends on short beams, spanning the width of the verandah and keeping the long side at the front flush, without any beam. With appropriate calculations assuming that the one-way slab spanned in the long direction, I placed the main reinforcing steel in the long direction. Typically, loads are distributed in the short direction in a one-way rectangular slab and the main steel is placed in the short direction accordingly. To meet the clients wishes, I transposed the loads to take a path in the long direction, assuming that since there was no beam, and therefore no support, along the long direction, loads would find their way in the long direction instead of the natural short direction. It was a bold and risky assumption for me at the time. Structures have a "mind" of their own and in reality, they behave as they want, creating their own natural load path, regardless of how the designer wants them to behave. In this case I had to "force" the slab to follow a path that I chose.

I was still thinking "Will the slab comply with my design alteration deviating from the conventional design approach?" After the concrete was poured, I was anxious about what would happen once the scaffolds and the formwork were removed. If the slab collapsed, I would run into a big problem and my reputation – whatever I developed by then – would be on the line. Once the formwork was removed, after two weeks, to my great relief, nothing happened; no catastrophic collapse occurred nor did any cracks appeared. The rest of the supervision went well, and I tried my best to remain vigilant and kept on monitoring the slab over the verandah. Until the end of the project and beyond, I didn't hear of any problems. I felt satisfied and encouraged, more confident in my skills.

Mining Corporation, Timmins, Ont., Canada

Immediately upon completing my doctoral degree in 1977, I joined a consulting engineering/architectural firm in the small mining town of Timmins, Ontario. The mining company there had many ongoing projects that needed the technical expertise of a structural engineer. There were only two consulting firms in structural engineering at that time: Stewart Smith and Associates and B. H. Martin and Consultants Ltd. Mining Corporation (Canada) Ltd., whose head office was in Salt Lake City, Utah, USA. They approached me to work as a private consultant helping them with their mining structures.

I never had any experience nor an iota of awareness about what the design of such structures entailed, but I felt excited at the thought of doing something different and getting exposed to a new area of structural engineering. It was like an adventure in design for me. I thought that the fundamental structural engineering principles are the same regardless of the type of structures and I should be able to handle the design problems. I discussed this opportunity with my boss Barry Martin for his consent. He encouraged me to do it by saying, "Mir, go ahead. This city needs the services of a qualified engineer like you." I assured him that I would do it only during nights and weekends. For my consultancy work I was assigned by the mining company to a very competent, collaborative, and levelheaded senior mining engineer, Mr. Ramesh Mondol.

My consultancy with this company lasted from 1977 to 1979 the duration of my stay in Timmins. During this time, I was involved in the design of different types of mining structures, such as: bulkheads, heavy equipment foundations, mill buildings, ore bins, jaw crusher foundations, an ultra-high retaining wall, and underground reclaim feeder structures. I had never even heard of such structures. Several of the structures were underground as could be expected in a mining industry. Each structure I designed or worked on was thus a challenge for me. There was no computer at that time there, so I had to do all my calculations manually, longhand. There was no university in

Timmins, but only a small community college library that didn't have a big collection on the subject. There was no Internet or Google then. So, I had to learn about the function of these structures from Mr. Mondol, to get a sense of their nature and the loads that they were subjected to.

All the structures were usually massive, carrying heavy loads, both static and vibratory, unlike commercial and residential building structures. The good thing for me was that mining engineers were less concerned about costs and more about safety. So long as the structures behaved adequately and safely, I could overdesign the massive structures. err on the side of using approximations in the absence of sophisticated analytical tools. As many of my designs were based on gut feelings and certain assumptions in the absence of any well-defined design guidelines, I added 15 to 20 per cent additional material, Mr. Mondol didn't mind. Although most mining structures were challenging for me, I will mention only a few, where I faced enormous challenges. I also realized that mining engineers didn't have the depth and breadth of structural knowledge because of their focused education and training on mining.

The Ore Bins project was one in which I carried out the structural design of large steel ore bins of various sizes. The project also included a 40-foot (12-meter) high reinforced concrete retaining wall that I designed. It retained the backfill material on its back and had also to support the heavy surcharge loads of large trucks carrying large pieces of rock, that would be dumped below on low ground onto the exposed front side of the wall.

I learned as a student how to design much shorter retaining walls, but the maximum height was about 20 feet (6 meters). To give an idea it was roughly the height of a three-story apartment building. The scale of this wall was enormous from a design point of view as the lateral soil pressure on the back face of the wall increased downward in a triangular fashion. No ordinary retaining wall would work for such exceptional conditions. I felt I was helpless as I couldn't consult with anyone in town who had the needed expertise. Fortunately, I brought a structural design handbook with me from Waterloo, that had different types of structures including a discussion on tall retaining walls. The section gave some concise ideas and guidelines. But even that was not enough, as it was the high soil pressure acting on the wall, amplified by the surcharge load from the top that made the problem more complex for me. After a lot of consideration, I employed several counterfort walls on the backside. These acted as ties connecting the tall wall to the foundation. On the front side of the wall, I employed several robust buttressed walls connecting the tall wall to its foundation. I had to use a large amount of steel reinforcement everywhere.

The ores dumped from the top were carried to a Jaw Crusher building nearby. Here the ores were crushed by heavy machines with large "jaws" that would crush them. I also designed the foundation for this building. It had to withstand the heavy vibrations from the ore crushing machinery. I used my judgment in designing the heavy foundation, which was new experience for me. I played extra safe using a large safety factor for my design because of the uncertainties involved.

The Reclaim Feeder Structure was another very challenging project for me. I completely designed an underground reinforced concrete mining structure, the top elevation of which was at 30 feet (9 meters) below the ground level. In addition to this soil overburden, an ore dump with a maximum height of 60 feet (18 meters) would be occasionally placed close to it on the ground above. For whatever reason, the company placed this system underground. It conveyed ores to a storage structure. This project had been running through my mind for a couple of days. Since the structure would be buried deep into the ground, the amount of load that would be carried by the structure compared to how much would go into the foundation, was a complicated question for me to answer. Design of this structure entailed a heavily reinforced, thick slab and special foundation design considerations. I don't remember the details now, but what I remember is that using my best intuition and judgment, I must admit, I managed to overdesign it to my satisfaction, given that it was uncharted territory for me. As a structural engineer, I was trained to design a structure to service adequately and be safe against failure. I think my research training helped shape my thoughts and give me confidence, which in turn helped me in gaining the trust of the mining company.

National Iron & Steel Mills, Singapore

Toward the beginning of my stay in Singapore, Professor Chen, Dean of Engineering at NTI (now NTU), offered me a local consultancy project on tall buildings. He knew about my experience in tall building design from my credentials. I gladly seized this opportunity. I was confident in my ability to handle such a task. As advised by Dean Chen, I contacted National Iron & Steel Mills, Ltd., a manufacturer of reinforcing steel for concrete, and I was retained by the company for the project.

I met a topmost administrator at the company's office to learn the scope of the project, negotiate my fees and sign a contract. The objective of the project was to carry out unbiased research to determine which structural material, steel or concrete, was more economical for tall buildings in Singapore and produce a report. Singapore, like many other countries of the world, was a concrete country and most buildings, including tall ones were built in concrete. Japan at that time was pushing very hard to promote structural steel as a building material for tall buildings in Singapore. I investigated three tall buildings of different heights in concrete and steel by analyzing and designing them. Dean Chen suggested that I should have a local faculty member to work with me and he recommended Paul Ang, a lecturer. He had no experience in tall buildings but was a very nice man and followed my instructions and helped me when I needed him.

I had to work very hard on this project at night after dinner until midnight and often beyond as I didn't have any time during the day when I was busy with my teaching duties. Initially, I developed an economic feasibility study technique for a comparative study of cost-effectiveness of tall buildings in steel and concrete. I did the approximate structural analysis and preliminary design of three concrete tall buildings of different heights, 25, 40, and 60 stories, employing hand calculations. Following this, I repeated the calculations for three steel buildings of the same heights and plan dimensions. Then, based on the prevailing market prices for materials and labor, I did the cost analysis in detail using a computer program for which Paul Ang's computer skills were put to great use. I plotted two curves on a graph paper, one for concrete and the other for steel, with number of stories versus cost. The two curves that were nonlinear and convex at top with different gradients intersected at a break-even level (BEL). The BEL determined the number of stories that I was seeking, which was 58.

Thus, I successfully completed the project and concluded that for Singapore's market conditions and existing local infrastructure for concrete and steel, concrete buildings would be cost effective for tall buildings up to 58 stories. Beyond that height, steel buildings would be more economical. I learned a lot about local real estate market conditions and building economics from this project. During the process I visited some sites where tall buildings were under construction and talked with the contractors and construction foremen.

I prepared a detailed report documenting the research methodology, the design process, structural design, factors affecting building economy, cost analysis, tables, bills of material, figures, computer programs, computer output, and the findings of the study. I submitted the report to National Iron & Steel Mills Ltd. I gave a presentation to the managing director and other to officials. The results garnered wide attention and publicity in the local press of Singapore. It so happened that the completion of my report coincided with an international conference on tall buildings held in October 1984, in Singapore. The deadline for submitting the conference papers had already passed. I called the conference chairman, explained the project and requested him to accept a paper even though it was late. He accepted my request with the condition that I had to submit my paper in three days.

I wrote feverishly with Paul Ang as my co-author and presented at the conference. In addition, I published two other journal articles on the topic, one while I was there and one later after I returned to the U.S. The work was cited in 1985, at an international conference on steel structures in Chicago, in a paper "High-rise Steel Buildings in the Far East" by N. Krishnamurthy and S. H. Lim. As another outcome of the study, while I was a faculty member at UIUC, I carried out a similar study for Chicago in 1988 using the same methodology and found that the BEL was 45 stories. I published a paper on this topic for the international conference on high-rise buildings held in Nanjing, China in March 1989.

U.S. Army Corps of Engineers, Champaign, IL

I had a consultancy project with Construction Engineering Research Laboratory (CERL) in Champaign, Illinois, a research wing of the U.S. Army Corps of Engineers. Part of the mission of the research and development program was to acquire and impart innovative technologies to the Department of Defense, the U.S. Army and many other customers, while simultaneously supporting research and development in engineering, civil works, and military engineering. CERL directed its research efforts toward increasing the Army's ability to efficiently design, construct, operate and maintain its installations and facilities and to ensure environmental quality and safety at a reduced life-cycle cost. CERL and UIUC had a collaborative relationship in the former's research activities.

James Simon, chairman of our Structures Division, called me to his office one day in the fall of 1986 to discuss the opportunity. I eagerly met with him. He told me that CERL was looking for a structural engineering professor from our School whom they could retain for a research project, but he didn't give me any further information. He gave me the contact information of a senior official at CERL, whose name I can't remember. I contacted and me the individual then met Mr. Thomas R. Napier, who would be the liaison.

The project entailed evaluating two emerging and innovative structural systems that the Army was considering employing for its facilities. It sounded exciting and I expressed my willingness to work on it and signed a contract for a fixed fee. Sadly, when I called CERL about the project after that, I came to learn that the senior official had collapsed suddenly in the office and died after suffering a massive heart attack. I met Tom Napier to discuss the full scope of the project, the meeting schedule and other pertinent details. I realized the project was extensive, so I hired a graduate student by the name of R.R. Anway, as my research assistant for a year. I was fortunate to get him, a very hardworking, tenacious, and dedicated student who carried out my instructions diligently and with the rigor that I was expecting. Because of this I remember him as an especially gifted student, out of the many research assistants who worked with me.

In the beginning, I did some general analysis and realized that the outcome of my evaluation should be quantitative. Because of my engineering training I never believed in speculative or qualitative evaluation of physical entities. I established a methodology to follow and conduct the project. It involved the development of an appraisal technique for innovative or emerging building structures. I applied this technique to the two pre-selected structural systems that were considered innovative and evolving at that time.

I prepared a detailed outline of a step-by-step procedure. I conducted a thorough literature survey after acquiring many CERL documents and other outside publications and books. Then I established a rating system for the two structural systems as test cases. These could be applied to any system, not only to the test cases I was given. The rating scheme consisted of a few attributes of the structures for which I apportioned points. I contacted some outside professionals to seek their assessment of the selected attributes. I visited fabrication and manufacturing plants in some locations, particularly in Florida and California to see some of these systems first-hand and talk with the fabricators and manufacturers. I recall my visits in Florida and California. I enjoyed being exposed to manufacturing plants for the first time. These unique opportunities through consultancy projects were always enriching.

In May 1988, I prepared and submitted a comprehensive technical report entitled "Building Technology Forecast and Evaluation of Structural Systems" describing the evaluation technique, field investigation, and review of construction regulations and building codes. I was told that this evaluation technique would be employed to other future military construction projects. The results were subsequently published in CERL's official document. Finally, I wrote a paper with Tom Napier as my co-author titled "Evaluation Technique of Concrete Structural Systems," which was published in the American Concrete Institute's *Concrete International* magazine in July 1989.

Wickersheimer Engineers, Champaign, IL

Soon after I joined UIUC in 1985, David Wickersheimer, a colleague of mine, and president of a small local firm offered me a consulting position. I always enjoyed consulting and I accepted despite the limited size of projects and lower fee. I cheerfully seized this opportunity that just happened to come my way. I continued doing consultancy there with projects involving new construction, additions, as well as investigation and renovation for many years. David is an experienced and competent engineer with expertise in the projects. I was fortunate to work with him as he occasionally guided me and offered suggestions during the design process. After my heart attack un 1992, and after being appointed Chairman of the Structures Division in August 1993, I ceased doing consulting with this firm. During these years I worked on many projects.

During 1985-86 I was fully engaged in the Public Safety Complex in Muncie, Indiana. It was a three-story prison building, housing a courthouse in steel and masonry. I appreciated the use of euphemisms in the U.S. Instead of calling it a prison or jail it was called the Public Safety Complex. Structural design involved composite steel beams supporting concrete floors. I designed many large girders (large beams supporting other beams or columns from above) to support transfer columns. The hefty building covered a large area, and because of the pentagonal shape of the building I had to develop special connection details. The very thick perimeter walls were hollow concrete block masonry filled with grout (a fluid form of concrete to fill gaps or holes) and steel reinforcement.

While working on this project I got a glimpse of what an American prison looked. I found that the prison that I worked on had a library, televisions and a gym for exercise. I visited the site during construction and resolved some field problems. Unfortunately, the building had some construction defects and the architect, engineers, and the contractor were sued by the prison authorities. As a result, my firm had to submit all my calculations for the project to the court who appointed an independent investigator to review all calculations. It was a tense time for David Wickersheimer in terms of any potential liability arising from the lawsuit. Despite being confident of my work, I was concerned about my professional reputation should any error or oversight come to light. Fortunately, our firm was cleared, and we were relieved.

Trade Center South at the corner of Kirby Road and Neil Street in Champaign was a multistory building project. It utilized light-gauge metal studs to create efficient resistance of the exterior curtain walls to wind, as well as structural tubing to resist wind loads at large window openings at the ground floor. The owner of the building hired a Chicago structural engineering firm to design the main structural system. Curtain walls are usually proprietary items, the structural framing of which is designed by the engineers for the fabricators. However, to save money the owner retained Wickersheimer Engineers to design the structural framing system for the curtain walls. I had never designed anything like this before, so I took it as a challenge. I used steel braces supported at the floor structure above to buttress the vertical studs and sized them for the code-specified wind pressure for Champaign.

For the large window openings, I employed vertical hollow steel tubing that carried the wind forces. After the building construction was completed and the building was commissioned and occupied, some functional problem arose. Rainwater and snowmelt penetrated the windows and started dripping into the interior. The owner sued the architect, engineers and the contractor. Like the Muncie, Indiana project, Wickersheimer Engineers had to turn in all my calculations to the court for review by the independent investigators. Once again, it was a tense time.

Finally, we learned that the problem was with the window caulking, which had been improperly mixed; this was revealed by a chemical analysis. It was a relief for us.

I may mention that I have investigated many buildings before with defects or inadequacies. So, I knew how important it was to work on projects thoroughly and leave no room for mistakes. I would emphasize this in my class lectures and would tell my students to do the design calculations and prepare construction drawings carefully and revise just as carefully, assuming someday these calculations and drawings might end up in court. Also, I told them to record all design assumptions because later they might have to retrieve these should any question arise in the future. At a later phase of the project I also designed a steel bridge connecting the building to a newly built hotel at an upper floor level.

Lando Mall Addition in Champaign, Illinois was a unique project. It was not a large job, but it posed several challenges. I conducted the design of a three-story steel building that would function as a bookstore within the atrium of a commercial-residential complex. On the street side, it was flanked by a mall, and on the other three sides it was surrounded by apartments. The building was designed for the heavy floor loads associated with bookshelves. Since no X-bracing was permitted by the architect to stabilize the building, I designed its skeleton as rigid frames in both directions with complex moment connections. The foundation system comprised 2-foot (0.6-meter) diameter drilled caissons (heavy poured concrete piles) to avoid any vibratory impact that could damage the existing surrounding structures. Some unexpected and complex field problems were revealed during the construction that demanded I come up with innovative solutions.

Pakistan Agricultural Research Center, Islamabad, Pakistan was a project that was being handled by architect James Miller, who was retained by the U.S. Department of Agriculture and U.S. Agency for International Development. Miller was professor at our School and had a design firm in Urbana. He hired Wickersheimer Engineers for the structural design component of the project involving the design development, review and approval of construction documents in connection with Phase 2 of the project. The building located in a seismic zone employed concrete framed construction. Islamabad was in a location equivalent to America's Uniform Building Code major seismic zone designated as Zone 3. My review involved major changes in design that I recommended which would comply with ACI 318-83 building code regulations of the American Concrete Institute (ACI) for seismic design. Many of the changes were in the foundation, I added tie beams connecting the footings of columns.

I faced new challenges working on the Lantz Gymnasium for Eastern Illinois University, Charleston, Illinois. The building was abutting an existing building on one side. I completed the steel structure with complex horizontal and vertical configuration, a running track hung from the roof structure on the upper floor, a large basketball court, two small basketball courts, and other exercise/gym areas were adjacent to an existing building. The stability of the building was ensured by providing knee braces to columns, masonry shear walls and horizontal steel trusses in the plane of the suspended running track. The foundation of the two-story tall steel columns supported with knee braces posed a challenge for me as these were carrying not only vertical weights but also lateral wind forces. A 110-foot (33.5-meter) long and 14-foot (4.3-meter) deep steel truss was employed to support a mechanical room above one of the basketball courts. The foundation system for the large sunken basketball court comprised tall concrete retaining walls that were supported on augured piles. I spent time designing drag ties in the thin metal roof deck that were necessary to introduce diaphragm action of the roof to resist wind forces.

In addition to the above projects I worked on two interesting church projects. Such projects were not new to me as I worked on some in Canada for my employers there. The first project was the existing United Methodist Church in Tuscola, Illinois, a small town about 25 miles (33.5 meters) south of Champaign. The building's sidewalls were bulging out and my investigation revealed that the 100-year old and 52-foot (16-meter) long wood scissor trusses supporting the roof were distressed and had been slowly spreading outward over time causing problem at the two ends. To save the building from further distress necessitated major repairs to the trusses. I conducted a thorough computer analysis of the existing roof structure and developed repair techniques involving the installation of post-tensioned wire ropes between truss supports and steel gusset plates at truss joints to prevent any further movement of the walls. Special details were developed by me to combine the gussets and the wire rope anchorages.

The other project was the First United Methodist Church, Rantoul, Illinois, a small town about 20 miles (32 kilometers) to the north of Champaign. This church had a school and some other spaces for cultural activities. Major structural repair needed to be done to the floors and roof of the Education Wing Building. The 50-year-old church had some floor cracking, symptomatic of progressive floor diaphragm failure due to inadequacy of the lateral load resistance system. There were fewer than necessary structural walls in the ground floor that could act as shear walls to transfer wind forces; new masonry shear walls were added. Drag struts in conjunction with special connections were introduced to transfer loads from the floor diaphragm to the shear walls.

I found a few other structural deficiencies over the course of my investigation, particularly in the roof sheathing that was made of some synthetic material. This material had very low in-plane strength as a diaphragm to transfer wind forces to the structural shear walls. Roof diaphragm action was developed by introducing horizontal trusses at the roof level attached to perimeter walls on all four sides of the building. In addition, I investigated the steel roof trusses in the Sanctuary area of the church and found some minor deficiencies which were fixed. The church board requested that I plan the building upgrades with a schedule and methods that would allow church functions, including the school to remain in place without disruption. This added a new challenge for me, and I had to plan the design of new structural components and develop a schedule for the contractors for how repair work should proceed.

For both above church projects I had the opportunity of interacting with a few individuals from the Christian communities. I met with the board members for discussions. In both cases, I alerted them of the projected cost of expensive repair work. They gladly embraced my ideas and told me this (paraphrased): "Please do whatever is necessary. Don't worry about the cost. We have many rich church members willing to donate for a good cause. They will gladly donate because they feel that it was their religious obligation to help the church." I felt delighted on two accounts: First, they showed their confidence in me and trusted my judgment; second, they gave me the latitude to do whatever was necessary without worrying about the cost. Of course, as a structural engineer safety and cost-effectiveness had always been the two basic principles of structural design. My master's and doctoral research on optimal design also trained me to implement these core principles in structural design.

Innovators Consulting Engineers, Jeddah

During 2006-2007 I was engaged in a major consultancy project with a firm in Jeddah, Saudi Arabia. Mr. Muneeb Rahman, a structural engineer and employee of Innovators Consulting Engineers contacted me on behalf of Mr. Sameer Mansouri, Managing Director of the company to invite me to be a consultant on a tall building project in Addis Ababa in Ethiopia. The building was called City Center Development Complex. A wealthy Saudi developer was going to build a 32-story multi-use concrete building which was a challenging project for a few reasons. First, it was located in a severe earthquake zone, categorized by the International Building Code (IBC) as Seismic Category D, in which structures must be designed to withstand very strong shaking. Second, the building had an elliptical (oval) plan with two stand-alone columns at the two ends of the building supporting large areas of the floors above. Third, it was on a sloped site making the foundation retaining walls (around the basement) of variable height from outside, which caused design complexity for the foundation in a seismic zone.

If I accepted the offer, I would be contracted to guide the overall structural design, review computer-aided structural analysis and design calculations performed by the firm, as well as review the design drawings. I would correspond through emails, occasional phone calls, and if needed, visit Jeddah. At that time, I was already busy teaching, writing papers and books, and administrative work. Clearly, I thought this would be demanding on my time and stressful. But I couldn't resist working on an irregularly shaped tall building on tilted terrain in a severe earthquake zone. I thought it would be fun with my interest, background, and experience with tall buildings and seismic design. I accepted the offer on a fixed-fee basis.

Once I started the project and interacted with my client, I realized the engineers at the firm had little experience in earthquake-resistant design of a tall building. I would have to guide the coordinating engineer remotely and review the work. Because of my experience with seismic projects, particularly a 60-story building in a high-risk earthquake zone in Los Angeles, and the fact that I had been teaching a graduate course on Seismic Analysis and Design at UIUC for many years, as well as my research on seismic design of foundations during my sabbatical leave in 1993, I was confident and comfortable working on the project despite its several design challenges, including the foundation design. During my time with the firm, I faced a number of perplexing issues related to the structure itself and the foundation. As I already knew, every major project has unique complexities that have to be resolved in real time, I carried out my own research to resolve the issues. This project was completed successfully with technical expertise and good communication.

Christo and Jeanne-Claude, New York

In 2007, I was invited as one of four structural engineers to propose a conceptual structure for a monumental project in the United Arab Emirates (UAE) called Mastaba (the Arabic word for bench). I was invited by the celebrated and legendary New York artists Christo and Jeanne-Claude for this international competition. Two other European structural engineers from the United Kingdom and Switzerland and someone from Japan were also invited. This invitation was an enormous honor and came by way of my colleague Abbas Aminmansour, an associate professor at our School. He was a campus committee member, where he was approached by a UIUC professor on that same committee, who inquired about my availability. The professor was in contact with the artists' representative who was seeking out an American structural engineer to work on preliminary structural design. My background on tall buildings made me his natural choice. Abbas asked me if I was available and interested in this project.

We went to that professor's home in Champaign to discuss and better understand the scope. After he briefed us on the project, I accepted the unique opportunity. Abbas also wanted to work with me on the American team, as we were called, which I led. Our team was invited to join the process after the European and Japanese teams got to work.

We met Mr. Johannes Schaub, the artists' representative at Chicago's O'Hare Airport on September 6, 2007 to discuss the details of our involvement. Our role was to prepare two options for the Mastaba structure and prepare sketches, drawings, and models for presentation in New York at the studio of the artists. We were responsible for providing a preliminary cost estimate and subsequently signed a contract with the artists later that month to carry it out.

The artists who first conceived of the Mastaba in 1977 for UAE near Abu Dhabi – a dream that was never realized, got a nod from the Emir of Abu Dhabi to proceed with design and construction. But construction of the Mastaba was placed on hold indefinitely until the appropriate time and resources were available. In recent years, the artists pursued efforts to build the highly anticipated monument. During this time, in about 2007, the regional economic climate was healthy, which perhaps encouraged the Emir to proceed. A Mastaba resembles a truncated pyramid flat at the top with two vertical walls and two inclined walls on the sides. The proposed Mastaba structure of UAE measured 492 feet (150 meters) in height and 984 feet (300 meters) by 738 feet (225 meters) in plan at the base. It was large enough to house the largest Egyptian pyramid inside it.

The artists designed the proposed behemoth monument as an enclosure only, with no occupational or other utilization of the space inside at any time. The Mastaba was to be covered on all four sides as well as the roof with about 400,000 horizontally placed 55-gallon steel oil barrels of solid brilliant colors acting as façade and roof. Given that the entire Mastaba was a work of art, the laying patterns of barrels and their colors were established by the artists. The proposed monument was to stand alone with no other facilities in the vicinity of the structure.

Assisted by Abbas and a graduate student acting as a research assistant I developed two options for the artists' consideration in New York. In the meantime, I gave an initial presentation to Mr. Schaub in Champaign in presence of Abbas at our UIUC campus. He traveled to Champaign for the presentation. He liked our work and gave his feedback suggesting a few changes in the drawings to make them clearer.

A number of factors and client requests were taken into consideration. We selected reinforced concrete as the construction material based on local construction practices as well as availability of the necessary material and workforce. All surfaces of the Mastaba were to be covered by barrels only and no penetrations through the walls or roof were to be made. Barrels were to be accessible from behind, i.e., from inside the Mastaba for repair or replacement. Access to the inside of the Mastaba was to be through underground ramps. Six elevators were placed inside the space for access to different elevations for repair and maintenance. The space inside the Mastaba was to be ventilated, but not conditioned.

Because of the enormous size of the structure and the many restrictions imposed on the design, the design was complex. Option 1 of our design consisted of a series of closely spaced columns and beams making up the enclosure. The beams and columns were flush from outside creating a smooth outer wall surface but had different inward depths. Beam and column sizes were different over each third of the structure's height, named upward as Tiers I, II and III. A series of shear walls (that carry wind and seismic forces) were placed perpendicular to the four walls from inside. In addition, a series of horizontal floors or "shelves" were placed on the inside of the outer walls. The shelves braced the shear walls and would provide a platform area for access to, and maintenance of, the barrels. The roof was flat and supported by a grid system of beams and girders which were in turn supported by a series of arches. The arches spanned between the inclined walls (parallel to the vertical walls) near the top and were supported in the middle by tubular mega-columns reaching from the ground to the arches supporting the roof. A beam spanning between the top ends of mega-columns braced them at that level.

Option 2 utilized a grid-like wall system with constant thickness within each third tier of the Mastaba's height. On the inside, a series of structural members formed a three-dimensional truss providing support for the walls. The structure supporting the roof consisted of the same system as Option 1, including the mega-columns.

The site was vulnerable to earthquakes adding complexity to the design. Computer analyses of Option 1 were conducted for gravity, wind and seismic loads using a SAP2000 software. A total of seven cases were considered. Case 1 was based on member sizes originally conceived by rough approximations. In each of the following cases, dimensions of certain structural members were adjusted based on the results of the previous computer analyses. In addition to the self-weight of the structure, the weight of the barrels and the substructure supporting them were included in the analysis. The latest version of IBC was used for the analysis and design of the structure. For Option 2 we expected similar outcome and didn't find any strong reason to perform additional analysis for the preliminary design. Interestingly, the analyses revealed that it was the gravity load, not wind or seismic loads, that controlled the design as excessive lateral deformations in the form of bulging of the walls were observed under gravity loads. Member sizes were adjusted to control these deformations. For this preliminary design we did not carry out any structural design of the foundation but suggested heavy piles connected by a continuous pile cap. Two research assistants worked on this part of the project helping us.

We visited New York in 2008 and I presented our work to the artists in their studio. They seemed to like it. Questions were raised primarily by Jeanne-Claude. I prepared a preliminary estimate of the cost at $300 million for the entire reinforced concrete structure using lightweight concrete. Incidentally, the artists' web site stated, "It is indeed logical to expect that the construction of the Christo and Jeanne-Claude's Mastaba of the UAE can only be financed by the ruler if he wishes to have an option to build, and take care of the maintenance of a structure which is larger and taller than the largest pyramid in Giza, Egypt." We were treated with hospitality by our gracious hosts who took us to an evening dinner. During conversation Jeanne-Claude, who was Jewish, told us "I have lived in Arab countries for many years. I like these people as they are very nice and hospitable. I was also in Afghanistan. To me, they are the most beautiful people. Their facial features are the best that an artist can have for painting human portraits." We met there the artists' long-time photographer since 1972, Wolfgang Volz, whom they would affectionately call Wolfie.

We were later told that we could proceed with a more detailed design as the next phase. I realized that this was a major project and it would not be possible without the help of a consulting firm as we didn't have the facilities at UIUC to carry this out this very private project. I knew Ron Klemencic, we worked together at the Tall Building Council. We contacted Magnusson Klemencic Associates and met David Eckman, the firm's head in its Chicago office, who was my former student. I gave them a presentation, but it was not to be. Soon after the project was cancelled as the economy turned severely. Lehman Brothers in the U.S.

collapsed, and a deep economic recession ensued that impacted the world economy. It resulted in a period of global economic downturn and uncertainty. The artists' long-time wish remained unfulfilled.

A year after we met the artists, sadly, Jeanne-Claude died in New York City on November 18, 2009, from a brain aneurysm. It was a delight for me to work on this project, I felt fortunate to work with two world-class artists, a romantic couple who provided me a rare glimpse into the world of artists. I was able to visit their studio where they created numerous unique and beautiful works of art. To document our work, I wrote a joint paper coauthored with Abbas on the project entitled "Preliminary Design of a Special Monumental Structure" which was presented by Abbas at the April 30-May 2, 2009 SEI 2009 Structures Congress of ASCE in Austin, Texas, as I couldn't go because of my other preoccupations.

As a footnote to this, later in 2018 a smaller Mastaba was built in London in the Serpentine Lake of the famous Hyde Park, fulfilling the dream of the couple. But Christo is not done yet. At this time, he still cherishes the couple's old dream of building the larger Mastaba in Abu Dhabi someday.

Malta Environmental and Planning Authority, Malta

In the summer of 2008, I was in Malta on a Fulbright Mission. J. William Fulbright Foreign Scholarship Board (FSB) funded the project and the Council for International Exchange of Scholars (CIES) co-sponsored by the Department of State of the U.S. Government. This prestigious award is bestowed upon a U.S. expert. I mentioned the background of this project before. Although this was a Fulbright mission, it was not a theoretical research undertaking like many Fulbright assignments, but a practical project in which I would give my expert opinion for the benefit of the Malta Environmental and Planning Authority (MEPA) who could use my recommendations for formulating their policy on high-rise construction in Malta. The goal was for me to offer advice to MEPA planning professionals and provide policy guidance on the siting, use, and design of tall buildings in appropriate locations in Malta. So, this was really a consultancy project for me, and I was known by the MEPA employees and others there as a Fulbright consultant.

MEPA received many building permit applications from developers for high-rise construction in Malta. They wanted my expert guidance on whether these buildings were feasible at the locations they earmarked for such construction. More specifically, the detailed goals of the project were to:

- Assess the existing situation related to high-rise construction in Malta;
- Evaluate the locations earmarked for tall buildings by the 2006 Planning Policy of MEPA;
- Select specific locations and carry out an appraisal of them for their characteristic features;
- Study and comment on the architectural style and construction of tall buildings in Malta;
- Draft an urban strategy report for the selected locations; and
- Promote and disseminate information about the design strategy of tall buildings to others.

The program of the mission involved a series of site visits and meetings. Mr. Joseph Scalpello, an urban planner, was MEPA's Team Manager and coordinator for me. He was a first-rate professional with great relationship skills and an excellent guide for me through every step. He led me through meetings, site visits and other activities. The schedule of my meetings with different people and organizations was intense with a total of

18. The first meeting was on May 19, 2008 with MEPA Director General Godwin Cassar, the second meeting on May 20 was MEPA's Chairman Andrew Calleja, Director of Planning Chris Borg, and Assistant Directors Sylvio Farrugia and Frans Mallia. Subsequently, I held meetings with other MEPA's Directors, Managers and professional staff. Additional meetings were with several local architects who had designed high-rises, the Chamber of Planners, the Chamber of Architects, NGOs, an economist, a social anthropologist, as well as Professor Alex Torpiano, Dean of the Faculty of Architecture and Civil Engineering and Professor Franco Montesin from the Department of Civil Engineering. These meetings were extremely useful for me to gain insights into the local conditions from different perspectives. The minutes of these meetings were recorded by Mr. Scalpello, who was present in each meeting.

I was shown six earmarked locations by Mr. Scalpello. I carried out visits to Tinge and Gzira on May 20, Qawra on May 28, and Pembroke, Paceville, and Marsa on June 4. I revisited Paceville and Marsa on June 16 to get a better understanding of these two sites. Each site had its own pros and cons for possible tall building construction. I took pictures of these sites and later analyzed them in my office at MEPA Headquarters.

From my meetings and site visits I formed some broad impressions about this island city-state. For example, people of Malta were generally conservative, inward-looking and protective of their heritage and culture. They were insulated from and apprehensive of modern-day forces of globalization and many of them were not open to the idea of constructing new high-rises as they considered them intrusive to their traditions and innovations from outside. Neither commercial nor residential high-rises were justifiable as the economic growth was stunted and there was no demand in the rental market. Developers were proposing to build high-rises to make quick money taking risks in a speculative market, and the outcome was uncertain. I also noted that there existed no mass rapid transport (MRT) or bus rapid transport (BRT) system in the city. Based on my research I found that Malta might be lagging in environmental performance compared to many other cities of the world, a concern that was confirmed by the local NGOs and other environmentalists I met.

I developed a list of 17 criteria for selecting appropriate sites for tall buildings. For each earmarked site, I studied their suitability by checking them against these criteria. Finally, I prepared a set of detailed guidelines and recommendations for MEPA covering different aspects of planning, siting, design, operation and upkeep, management, transportation, environment, to name a few on the basis of my findings. Overall, I recommended a master plan for Malta before any tall building construction. I submitted a rough draft of my report to MEPA Chairman and gave a Power-Point presentation to the MEPA Board on June 19. I responded to several questions posed.

My draft copy was distributed to Board members by MEPA Chairman before my presentation. I promised that I would send a final report of my findings and recommendations upon my return to the U.S. Then I gave a PowerPoint presentation to MEPA authorities and staff at large and gave some additional perspectives. During this event, I presented the book titled *The Skyscraper and the City: Design, Technology, and Innovation* that I co-authored with Lynn Beedle and Paul Armstrong to MEPA Chairman as a gift to the MEPA Library.

Upon my return to Champaign, I completed the final report titled "Urban Design Strategy Report on Tall Buildings in Malta" and sent it to Joseph Scalpello. I offered 16 guidelines and recommendations. In item 12, I wrote, "My recommendation is to carry out more detailed studies on not only the economic and social factors, but also master planning. MEPA should proceed slowly and take more time. Lack of a master plan results in uncontrolled developments and unpredictable impacts on urban life...Future tall building developments should not be considered without further studies and master planning." I ended the report with the following two-paragraph remarks:

In the final analysis, it is up to the political leadership and the people of the country to decide if their future vision is for a modern, progressive and forward-looking port city in a strategic location or for maintaining their old way of life and culture. Both of these have positive and negative impacts on the country. The choice is theirs to make.

Good architecture and urban design do not necessarily depend on tall buildings and there should not be any illusion that a city can achieve great urban status only by building many tall buildings. Actually fewer, but better clusters of tall buildings should be the aim. Tall buildings alter the urban scale and cannot be avoided in our times. The choice for the inhabitants of Malta is whether to control them or put up with their future growth.

During my stay in Malta, I was honored with a lunch at the U.S. Embassy, attended by many distinguished professionals and people including a staff reporter from an influential local newspaper. She interviewed me and later published excerpts of the interview. Other local media subsequently quoted me from the report.

I enjoyed working on the project immensely. For me it was a combination of vacation with business. It opened up a new area of urban design for me as it relates to tall buildings thereby enriching my career. As I wrote before, it led to a new book on tall buildings and urban design, *The Future of the City: Tall Buildings and Urban Design*.

PART FIVE
LAST WORDS

CHAPTER 19

BACK TO THE WINDY CITY

My Vision of Life After Career

I n late 2010, I had to make a major life decision about retirement. I was still a full-time professor and the chairman of the Structures Division. Only one professor other than me, William Erwin, was left out of the eight in this division when I originally joined the School of Architecture. All others were either deceased, retired, or left. Across the School, only a few of my contemporaries were still teaching. I knew that the time was ripe for me to consider retirement. Professor James Simon, a colleague of mine, told me upon his retirement, "You will know Mir when the best time for you to retire is," when I had asked him why he was retiring so early since he could have continued for a few more years.

I saw the writing on the wall, I was pretty sure that after I retired, the Structures Division as we knew it, a separate autonomous entity, would be eliminated. I had been struggling to hold on to it, with success, for many years. But I also questioned if it was important for me or even my responsibility to stay and hold on to it. Professor Erwin was also ready for retirement. Once he retired, I would miss all my old colleagues with whom I had bonded so well. Dora's health condition was deteriorating, certainly heading for dialysis, and she was getting weaker by the day. She needed more time of me to take care of her. With retirement, I could spend more time with my family. There would be no more pressure from work except for the self-imposed kind. My three grandkids in Chicago were growing up fast and it would be good to watch them grow. I could move there and be close to them and my two daughters or my son in Alexandria, Virginia if I wanted (now he lives in Fairfax, Virginia). But, alas, I loved to teach, wanted to keep doing it as long as I could.

I had built up a moderate nest egg, thanks to the late Dr. Azizul Islam of Urbana-Champaign who repeatedly advised me to do so and prepare for my senior years. The State of Illinois that controlled our university had a good pension plan. I already reached the full benefit level for retirement. So, financially I should be fine. But the money situation, although important, was only part of my retirement planning. There were some emotional aspects; for example, as a new retiree I thought I would have "me-time." How would I fill this time in a productive way though? I realized that no matter what I had accomplished in my working life, and even if I had fulfilled the American Dream the way I interpreted it, an extended time after retirement would redefine me. How could I shape a new identity, accounting for my welfare and happiness outside of my formal career? I had been an active person and a workaholic all my life, how could I truncate that active life abruptly? Would that create an emotional hole for me for the rest of my life? I was thinking about the pros and cons of retirement and searching for an answer.

During this time, it so happened that the university was experiencing some ongoing financial crisis. To cut cost, the authorities decided to offer incentives to prospective retirees through attractive retirement packages. This gave me the nudge I needed, as I recognized the importance of timing, and I needed to take care of Dora. I retired in May 2011 at the age of 67 but continued to teach part-time.

The School Director David Chasco requested that I continue as the chairman of the Structures Division, appropriate since I would be teaching part time, and therefore, be a faculty member. I declined the offer telling him I wanted a retired life but would continue to teach part time because of my love for teaching young students with aspirations and dreams. I taught for another four years during a period of family crisis, while Dora underwent kidney dialysis beginning in June in 2011 immediately after my retirement. I was able to manage my teaching duties and other affairs despite this prolonged and grueling ordeal. In March 2013 Dora received a kidney transplant and I continued to teach part time.

Against the backdrop of my own unexpected health issues, including retinal tears (mentioned in detail previously), I also realized Dora and I needed to be close to our children and the three grandchildren. My granddaughters Talia (born on March 1, 2005) and Jayna (born on October 1, 2009) and a grandson Rasim (born on August 31, 2007) had been growing up fast and we wanted to have them near us. With the help of my two daughters we moved to a newly built home in Naperville, a suburb of Chicago on November 6, 2015 and soon settled in there. Our son Murad and his wife Rashmee could see us more frequently since flying directly from Washington D.C. to Chicago, was much easier than getting to Champaign. They were blessed with a daughter Leila on January 7, 2017.

While living in Champaign, a former student of mine had an interesting conversation with me that included my health and lifestyle. At one point the question arose about what I was going to do after retirement. I replied "I will spend time with my family, take care of my and Dora's health and keep reading and writing. I added that God had endowed me with the gift of being inquisitive. There were so many things I didn't know and yet don't fully understand. I learned something new every day. My curiosity would keep me active and well." Sure, as I write this, my curiosity and spirituality still help me overcome occasional setbacks in life and keep me happily sailing through turbulent times. I understand that I need to be brave, create my own world and live through my remaining years.

I met some old friends in Chicago, notably Mr. Aminul Karim with whom I had a longtime friendship even when I lived in Urbana-Champaign and Dr. Monzurul Hoque and Ranga Monzur. Others include Nurul Ambia Chowdhury, Ashraf Ali, and Atik Rahman. I met some new ones notably Dr. Shamsul Islam Chowdhury, whom I knew before, Dr. B.D. Khan, Dr. Ahmed Khan, and Mr. Monsurul Hoque Ahmed. I also developed friendship with some of my neighbors. I was invited by Mr. Ruknul Islam, president of Bangladesh Association of Chicago to deliver the Keynote Speech on the night of March 25, 2017 celebrating Bangladesh Independence Day. I also met many other Bangladeshis, both engineers and non-engineers. I met Mr. Iqbal Kabir, president of BUET Alumni Group. In February 2017 I was invited to a social evening gathering of CTBUH members marking the occasion of moving the office to a prestigious and pricey location on Michigan Avenue in downtown Chicago. The office had previously been in Crown Hall, IIT. I met many professionals and several former students of mine there.

However, my socializing was restricted because of Dora's health. She had been weakened because of the strong steroids and anti-rejection drugs following her kidney transplant. Her health took a sharp turn for the worse in late 2018 causing mobility issues. At this time, I am her constant and devoted caregiver.

Once I fully retired and moved to Chicagoland, settling in kept me engaged and then I quickly got back to my other work commitments. Meanwhile, in early 2016 after seeing my new cardiologist, Dr. Mark Ottolin at Edward Hospital, he ordered a nuclear scan of my heart that revealed two new blockages in my arteries. Both were at difficult locations. He strongly urged me to treat these. I was aware of these two blockages from before. However, my previous cardiologist from Carle Hospital in Champaign who had treated me for many years told me not to do anything as my heart was functioning adequately. It was a major dilemma for me.

I declined to undergo treatment and Dr. Ottolin, a compassionate doctor, called me again and passionately urged me to reconsider. I decided to go ahead. Because of the complexity of the blockages he stented them on two occasions on April 28 and May 24. This brought the total number of stents to six. Then on September 11, 2017 I had profuse bleeding from my urinary passage in the morning that led me to the Emergency. A scan revealed that I had a growth in my bladder which was surgically removed on October 25 by my urologist Dr. Robert Seo at Edward Hospital and was found to be benign. In December the same year I had retinal detachment of my left eye. Having the experience of the surgery of my right eye in 2014 in Urbana-Champaign, I rushed to see the retina specialist. Eye surgery was carried out by Dr. Jon Geiser on December 12 at the Wheaton Eye Clinic. This time I had to keep my head down for only four hours post-surgery as opposed to seven days and my eyesight was restored in two weeks instead of two months like in 2014. I believe it was so because I immediately saw the doctor.

In Bangladesh, when people retire, they are not congratulated as they are considered less vital and powerful, as well as poorer. The retirees, by and large, feel the same way and many of them have feelings of inadequacy, being of no more use to society. This attitude has shifted now, as many people continue to work at private organizations long after retirement, to make extra money and to stay engaged. In the U.S., on the other

hand, people are congratulated and told they deserved retirement. Most people look forward to retirement, although I never
did. Retirement is the last chapter of the book on our life stories. It feels very incongruous writing about the retirement of a
lifelong workaholic like me. All signals from society assert that
70 is old and naturally that's a depressing thought. As I mentioned before, I formally retired at the age of 67 and continued
teaching part time until age 71. The idea of fully retiring didn't
sink in until after we moved to Naperville.

During this period of retirement, I took a trip to San Francisco.
The city was once destroyed by the 1906 Great San Francisco
Earthquake, when 3000 people died and 80% of the city was
destroyed. Although I visited most large cities of America for
various reasons, but not this one. I include it here as it was unlike
any other visit and I found that San Francisco was unique among
other American cities. Our three children organized a party in
Chicago and a short trip to celebrate our 50th wedding anniversary on March 3, 2018. The trip was the second part of the celebration, but because of a schedule conflict the trip was postponed until October 19 when, accompanied by Ifat and Murad,
we flew from Chicago to San Francisco. Ifat planned the trip
well.

We stayed at a hotel near the intersection of Van Ness Avenue
and Lombard Street. I was amazed to see the hilly terrain of
the city. The next day I went for a walk with Murad on Lombard Street, a famous crooked way for visitors. By climbing the
street uphill and descending downhill I had an invigorating
experience. Then we reached a winding segment of the street
and walked uphill and downhill again. The street was flanked
by flower plants and beautiful foliage as well as some expen-

sive homes. Murad suggested that we might call a taxi for the return trip because he thought I might be exhausted by then, but I declined and decided to walk back. Since I wasn't feeling strained, and did all these activities without much effort, I felt reassured that I was fit, and that my heart was functioning well.

We then proceeded to the Marina District. We parked at Fisherman's Wharf, the central tourist area. From there we went on the San Francisco Bay Boat Cruise. We boarded the large ferry boat shortly after noon. I stayed on the uppermost deck throughout the cruise to take in the San Francisco skyline and all the buildings on the shore and the San Francisco Bay. A highlight for me was seeing the Golden Gate Bridge and the Bay Bridge. Our boat went under both bridges and I was able to look at both from the underside. The boat also circled around the Alcatraz Prison, a maximum-security prison on a small island in the Bay that is no longer in use.

I viewed the many buildings of the city including the sky-scrapers and felt reassured by how much structural engineers had accomplished in the field of seismic design. These amazing buildings could stand up to staggering natural forces unleashed by earthquakes. Later, we drove through the Union Square, the financial district where I had a close look at the TransAmerica Pyramid on Montgomery Street, a harbinger of the iconic tall buildings that we are so familiar with today. We saw historic Chi-natown, and the famous "Painted Ladies," a group of historic and colorful Victorian-style houses near the Alamo Square. At the Square I walked uphill to stand on high ground and get a pan-oramic view of the visible part of the city. It was a thrilling expe-rience for me. Many of the buildings that I saw in San Francisco had Mediterranean architecture. I noticed many apartment and commercial buildings with bay windows reminding me of Malta.

Another memorable visit was to Muir Woods National Monu-ment, on a hilltop 16 miles (26 kilometers) away from San Francisco. Murad drove us through steep, winding roads hugging the mountainous terrain. Once we checked in at the Visitor Center at the entrance and rested a while, we walked the trail. The place is a forest with ultra-tall California redwoods reaching up to a maximum of about 250 feet (76 meters). Some of the trees have unbelievably huge girths. I asked an official narrator of the trees about the age. He replied, "800 to 1,000 years old." The average age of redwood trees is normally between 500 and 800 years, but some live even longer. I felt like we were in a different world, away from the din and bustle of cities and other human habitats. The trees are so dense that in some locations, sunlight could barely peek through. I ventured a hike with Murad but once the way became very steep and narrow, we returned.

I wanted to visit the University of California at Berkeley campus but at the suggestion of my daughter Jinat changed my mind and visited the Stanford University campus about 50 miles (80 kilometers) south of Muir Woods instead. I am glad I had a chance to see the very picturesque campus. We walked around and enjoyed the well-maintained beautiful landscape. During my long career I have visited many campuses, but this one was really striking to me. The buildings' architecture is exotically different. I visited the engineering section of campus, going through an arcade and walkways flanked by flowerbeds. We then proceeded to nearby Palo Alto and visited the nice residential areas to get a sense of the place. Overall, the San Francisco trip was enjoyable. Passing through on the highway, I was able to see a part of what is known as the famous Silicon Valley and the headquarters of some major corporations.

Yes, I am retired now but remain fully active. I was always passionate about helping my students to get a quality education. I prided myself in helping them get the best technical and practical knowhow so when they moved from the academic to the professional world, they were well prepared to accept the challenges. I got correspondences occasionally from some of them, they told me they consulted my lecture notes when faced with a structural design problem.

I thought, abruptly shifting from regular work mode to my own schedule was going to be an interesting and different new life stage. I would have more time for family and friends, I could pursue my passions that I developed after my heart attack in 1992, that is regular walking and stretching exercises and meditation, later extended to strength training, yoga, and swimming. I thought I would have more time to just do whatever I liked. Not so... honestly, I stay so busy with different things that I barely have time to do any of that. I have little time to dedicate to the reading and writing that I love so much. Of course, I would still like to teach somewhere but for now Dora needs me to be with her.

Despite my very full and busy post-retirement life, I was able to write an invited paper for a journal on the latest advances of structural systems for contemporary supertall and megatall buildings. My former student Dr. Kyoung S. Moon, who is a faculty member at Yale University, was my co-author. I cherish the hope of continuing to write, if God permits. I remain active reviewing papers for journals and conferences. In May 2018 I was interviewed by WildBear TV of Australia for a documentary series "Building to the Sky" on May 7, 2018; the interview was released in January 2019. As mentioned before, I have written another paper with Kyoung about the Home Insurance Building in Chicago, historically known as the first skyscraper of the world. My presentation was on October 31, 2019 in Chicago.

I am proud of my three children who are well established in society. Ifat has a master's degree in urban planning and policy

studies and is a Director of Research in the Mathematics department of the University of Illinois at Chicago. She is dutiful, social,
responsible and very organized. Jinat has a master's degree in
journalism from the Medill School of Journalism, Northwestern
University in Chicago and an MBA degree from the University of
Chicago. She was a TV reporter for many years and now raises
her three children. She is social, friendly and can complete a
complex and challenging task whenever she puts her mind to it.
Murad has an MBA from the Smith School of Business, University of Maryland at College Park and is a Regional Director of
Thyssen Krupp, a multinational elevator/escalator company. He
is personable, social, and caring. All three of them are loving,
independent in nature, and good communicators.

Who says retirement is monotonous? I have found a tremendous balance in life. I am retired from my job but not from work.
I still read and write at home when I find time. Going to the gym
is a routine task for me, again, when I find time. I take care of
my beloved wife Dora who has been suffering from the many
long-lasting and debilitating side effects of steroids. I know my
curiosity will carry me through to the end. But I am not in denial
as, yes, I am not as vigorous as a 40- or 50-year old. Yes, I must
deal with aches and pains as well as occasional ailments. I need
to take medicines that have side effects which affect my life. It
is my fundamental belief that there is wisdom to be found in
celebrating life right now. With the benefit of advanced medical
technologies and the amenities of modern times, we have the
power to live life on our own terms, of life that our ancestors
didn't have. We can make good choices that our predecessors
couldn't. A positive attitude and thoughtful philosophy are the
master keys to happiness. My near-death experience in 1992
taught me that every day since then has been a gift for me. I have
been living on borrowed time since then and I need to make the
best use of it each day.

And who says there is no delight in senior ages? One thing we can't avoid is the roller-coaster ride to the end of life as we age. Aristotle warned, "Beware of old age." Our strength declines; our pleasure and satisfaction from foods and other things dwindle; our world becomes constricted; our circles of relatives and friends get smaller. However, I believe my happiness lies very much within me. This happiness begins from serenity, fulfillment and gratitude to God. It comes from my children and grandchildren who will live on beyond me. The world can and will continue if I am not around. It is best to enjoy my remaining years and be happy.

The lesson from my wise father's story, told to me as a young boy, remains with me: a life that looked outwardly happy was not necessarily so, and happiness is not an outward thing, it rests inside us. With my advanced age, weathering the storms and even hurricanes during my life's voyages with health, career, and family, I have developed more wisdom and judgment, I learned to manage my resources more carefully, I can see the obvious, quickly, and most of all I feel free. Only a feeling of self-worth, being able to contribute to society, and leading a purposeful life can give us inner strength and true happiness. In the final analysis, I believe the definition of a happy and successful life lies in the ability to be calm, fulfilled, and joyful till one reaches the finish line of life's racetrack, no matter how long or short.

CHAPTER 20

GOD BLESS AMERICA AND GOLDEN BENGAL

Dreams and Reality

When I came to New York from Ottawa by Greyhound bus in October 1970, shortly after I landed in Canada, I was imagining the America I was about to enter. I read so much about this country, for me it was a dreamland. I didn't know the full meaning of the expression "American Dream," but the notion took shape in my subconscious. When I reached Manhattan, I felt a spark in me at seeing the skyscrapers. It was an exhilarating experience and a genuine "wow" feeling burst forth. Following this short first visit, in November that year I returned to America a second time and stayed with my brother in Muncie, Indiana over a period of about two months. I saw cities like Indianapolis and Detroit -- no match for New York -- but appealing to me. With my civil engineer's mindset, I thought of the people who built this great country.

Despite historic departures from the ideals of this nation, and serious issues related to the doctrine of manifest destiny, brutal human slavery, and U.S. imperialism, I must say, the

America that I was introduced to as a young boy was a generous one. I recalled that after cyclones devastated my hometown and the coastal region of East Pakistan, America would send aid in the form of butter oil, milk powder, blankets, and clothing. My mother, who was the Vice President of the All Pakistan Women's Association (APWA) and her associates would distribute these to the needy and affected. I fell in love with the technological triumphs of this country and admired the people who built such a great urban civilization.

At a much later time, I visited Washington DC and New York with my family in 1988 for a vacation. I saw the White House and Capitol Hill, the seats of American power and democracy that dominate the world stage. I also saw the Washington Monument and Lincoln Memorial and wondered about the positive visions of the politicians represented by the monuments. Indeed, the history of America includes some lingering contradictions but, in my estimation, the resilience and ingenuity of the people and their leaders allowed America to rethink such debacles.

We visited the Statue of Liberty on Liberty Island, a national monument representing America. The torch of liberty was held high by Lady Liberty, a gift by the French government to the U.S. It was a symbol commemorating the human potential for success and freedom of people inspired by the American Declaration of Independence. It also became a symbol for immigrants from around the world to come here to enjoy freedom and achieve their dreams of success through dedication and hard work. It represents a beacon of hope for immigrants from around the world seeking opportunities for betterment. This country was built by the toil of immigrants, from diverse backgrounds working hard to fulfil their dreams while exercising their inalienable rights to life, liberty, and the pursuit of happiness. These immigrants fueled the U.S. economy. How nicely and thoughtfully such words were framed in the founding document! The

Statue of Liberty is an iconic symbol of the American Dream. At a later date, I visited Independence Hall in Philadelphia, PA where the pronouncement of the United States Declaration of Independence was adopted at a meeting on July 4, 1776 and the new republic was born. I also visited the site of the Liberty Bell that remains an iconic symbol of American independence.

When the nation of America was born, it was formed as an idea, made of an awkward assemblage of incompatible colonies that eventually coalesced and rose to become a political, economic and military superpower. It was shaped by the wisdom, vision and efforts of the founding fathers like George Washington, Thomas Jefferson, Benjamin Franklin et al., and later visionaries including Abraham Lincoln, a wise personality revered worldwide for his unswerving convictions and courage in the face of calamity during the American Civil War.

Throughout the relatively young American history, this country, known as a melting pot, has run on the power spawned by competing ideas, complex arguments and while calibrating a balance between privacy and protection, freedom of expression and responsible behavior, individual rights and common good. Americans are united under a common mantra of pursuing happiness and prosperity. They are committed to the notion that the rights of one should not hinder those of another; they agree to be governed by an elected democratic body, with a hierarchy of representatives and a check-and-balance system made from three coequal branches of government, instead of monarchs, a group of elders, oligarchs or aristocrats.

These lofty ideals have been broadly and repeatedly embraced by generations of immigrants, seeking the freedom to shape their own future. The country was refined by the feelings and viewpoints of visionaries, thought leaders, and mavericks alike. To function as a great nation, it still requires the shared stewardship of ideals like inalienable rights, equality and the inviolability of liberty and happiness for all. This is the spirit of a country defined not by religion, race, or ethnicity but instead by a lofty ideal.

People worldwide have heard about the American Dream. The idea of this dream was rooted in the Declaration of Independence that affirmed that "all men are created equal" with the right to "life, liberty and the pursuit of happiness." The pursuit of happiness became the driver of the entrepreneurial spirit that defines the free market economy. In his 1931 book *The Epic of America,* historian James T. Adam first coined the term "American Dream" and defined it when he wrote,

…that dream of a land in which life should be better and richer and fuller for everyone, with opportunity for each according to ability or achievement…It is not a dream of motor cars and high wages merely, but a dream of social order in which each man and each woman shall be able to attain to the fullest stature of which they are innately capable, and be recognized by others for what they are, regardless of the fortuitous circumstances of birth or position.

The Statue of Liberty on Liberty Island of New York is an iconic symbol of freedom welcoming immigrants to America, the land of opportunity, to fulfil the American Dream. However, this dream is universal and applies not just to immigrants but also to each subsequent generation of American citizens.

Others have variously defined the American Dream; in fact, there is no single definition anymore. For some, it is the dream of having a decent job, and owning a home and a car. For others it may be fulfilled with ambition, inspiration and accomplishments, whether academically, professionally or in business. Another interpretation is that those who could enrich subsequent generations of their family, by securing wealth and assets for posterity have accomplished the American Dream. Yet one other simple elucidation of the American Dream is that one has achieved it by steadily improving one's quality of life. Collectively, upward social and financial mobility, that is, the increase in per capita income is a measure of the American Dream. The dream is also reimagined from one generation to another. It is an ethos replete with attitudes and conceptual aberrations. But we all have a certain sense of what it is, since we are all dreamers and have our own hopes hovering surreally in the not too distant future. To many however, the American Dream is only a myth, not reality.

In a book titled *Tailspin*, Steven Brill, an eminent lawyer and journalist, wrote about the faded glory of the American Dream. For most Americans it's been smothered by an entrenched nobility, developed steadily over the last five decades. This idea was also spelled out by Professor Daniel Markovits at the graduation ceremony of the Yale Law School for the class of 2015. He pointed out that billionaires have taken over control of America, shattering the American Dream for the common people. The result this produced is a divided country, with the privileged few, on the one side, as the winners, who don't need government for much, and the unprotected masses on the other. Markovits commented that American meritocracy has become precisely what it was intended to combat, a mechanism for the dynastic transmission of wealth and privilege across generations. Meritocracy, according to him, now constitutes a modern-day aristocracy. Thus, the idea of the American Dream has indeed become a myth for the vast majority of working-class and underprivileged people. Of course, I believe that at some point there will be a pushback, and the story is not over yet.

There is yet another dimension to the American Dream. What is the American Dream today as I write this in these uncertain times in America? Does the Statue of Liberty still welcome all immigrants? Ask a Latin American, a Muslim, or an African American. Ask a Hindu, a Sikh, or an Asian, or for that matter any minority immigrant group. Why do some political leaders no longer welcome others as before? Why do divisive leaders have huge bases of support? What happened to America? What happened to this great country where immigrants have been keeping the wheels of service rolling and the economy thriving? Has the American Dream evaporated and become the American Nightmare because of errant politics and policies that hold people back? These are serious, big questions and I am optimistic that we will find the answers. American history has witnessed times of turmoil before and will continue to in the future. This is the nature of a government of, by, and for, the people.

The Founding Fathers' proclamation, underscoring the equality of opportunities for all still holds a powerful truth. The American Constitution and the Bill of Rights continue to guide the nation's long tradition of democracy and its institutions, keep this great country stable, vibrant, and strong. This is a country where people of all faiths can worship freely. Fortunately, I have never directly encountered any discrimination as an immigrant due to my race, color, or religion. That doesn't mean others didn't or don't. This is a country of dreamers and immigrants who have changed the world with their innovations and their hopeful, clever, creative tinkering. This is a country of law and order. Immigrants hold the American framework together. A clear majority of Americans is comprised of decent people whose origins are from elsewhere.

If the American Dream vanishes, then inevitably, America will begin to crumble. This is because the American Dream represents the essence of the Founding Fathers' vision for this new, vast and resourceful citizenry. If the dream shatters, the American economy will in my opinion take a nosedive and the country will spiral into anarchy and disintegration. There is much at stake. But I firmly believe that America is large, strong, and resilient enough to restore the hobbled American Dream. Americans continue to hold the spirit of innovation and productivity. The country's intellectual, technological, and entrepreneurial bents have sustained it even through harder times than this.

Despite the occasional setbacks in the political and economic arenas, the country will survive on the strength of its institutions. No lasting damage can be done to the country by incompetent and erratic leaders or politicians. The political system enshrined in the constitution ensures a stable democracy and periodic elections, to remove erratic leaders and replace them with sensible ones.

Despite the attitudes and actions of some contemporary politicians, who dislike immigrants as the country becomes browner, the moving arrow of events cannot be stopped, let alone reversed. But immigrants need to integrate with American society at large, while simultaneously maintaining their native culture -- a tall order particularly for those who live in smaller communities. As for me, I love being a Bangladeshi Muslim living in America and I have evolved into a well-adjusted cultural mix. I feel that I strive to be a complete Bangladeshi and a complete American.

Now comes the great question. Has my own American Dream been fulfilled? Did I manage to meet my aspirations after migrating to this land from Bangladesh, via another great country Canada, where I lived for about 10 years? Lucky for me, I can confidently say that I have realized my personal dream in this country, the dream of working, teaching, and being able to conduct academic research without any impediment. Although financially I have had some moderate success as well, I am comfortable with what I have. What I love are the great cities and their tall towers hugging the sky and universities and institutions of education. Being able to work on skyscrapers and walking the hallowed halls of learning, in turn as a student, teacher, mentor, administrator and finally, life-long learner, is certainly proof of my American Dream, fulfilled.

I have always had a compulsive urge for visiting university campuses, and still do, when I visit a new city. Throughout my domestic travels I've found the vast majority of American people are courteous and friendly. I always enjoy talking to them, as in my experience, most of them are refined, open-minded, and have a sense of humor. I like the country's spirit of discovery and scientific endeavor, and the abundance of art and music. Groundbreaking scientific breakthroughs, inventions and innovations by Americans include elevators, automobiles (mass production and the assembly line were invented here), steel fabrication, skyscrapers, airplanes, telephones, air conditioning, light bulbs, fluorescent light, cinematography, medicines and medical technologies, high-speed computers, internet, GPS, smart phones, space technology, to name only a few. The first man on moon in 1969 was an American, which was possible because of the American president John F. Kennedy's vision, the hard work of American engineers and scientists, and of course the steadfast courage and risk-taking character of Neil Armstrong, who walked as the first man on the moon. The list can go on in other fields. I like the American transportation systems, the hospitals where patients are treated courteously, the time-consciousness of people, and the racial, religious, and cultural diversity. I always felt and still do that I have been judged on my personal and professional merits, by how efficient and competent I have been at work, how I interacted with my associates and colleagues, what I did and what I said, and not by my ethnicity. Of course, I know others may feel differently, but I can only speak for myself and hope that my story is not so miraculous or unique and others have also come to love their own American experiences.

I had the advantage of working in a large architectural company like Skidmore, Owings & Merrill (SOM) under a highly respected mentor and fellow countryman from Bangladesh, and I worked in a large engineering company, Sargent & Lundy, both populated by employees of many ethnicities. I of course also worked in the multinational academic environment of UIUC for much of my career in the U.S. and thus might have been insulated from many negative experiences. I always recognized that I was part of a minority community, but I also noticed that it didn't operate as a barrier, as I always tried to integrate with my colleagues of diverse backgrounds at work and with the local multi-national communities.

I feel fortunate that I was able to avail the opportunities that the country extended to me. I also gave this country all of what I could, at my places of employment in various capacities. I am so grateful that I had the liberty and resources to explore and experience the world, write, and do what I wanted to do without much hindrance. Despite my inherent longing and love for Bangladesh where I was born and raised, I am so thankful to God that I have spent the major portion of my life in America, the land of opportunities, where I came to realize who I am. In America, it's not where you were born but where you end up that matters. Living in America (and Canada) allowed me to look deep inside myself to uncover the East and the West in me, and blend both harmoniously.

Despite the gains I made by being in America, personal and professional, I feel I have also lost a part of me in terms of my eastern heritage – my native values and culture. I unwittingly allowed my children to be confused victims of biculturalism. And of course, I suffer from ongoing nostalgia, being separated from my native land and people. If I went back to Bangladesh, I could have contributed to my native land in whatever way I could within the constraints there. I was far away from my parents during their old age when I should have been there to serve and comfort them.

Now let me put my mind to another dream; I will call it the Bangladeshi Dream. This is a national dream. The country of Bangladesh was born on March 26, 1971 when independence was formally declared while the Pakistan Army launched a brutal assault on the Bengali people and the country was still under their occupation. Victory was achieved on December 16 in the same year after a bloody civil war in which countless Bangladeshi freedom fighters and civilians lost their lives at the hands of a marauding Pakistani Army. The new nation's dream was to achieve a metaphorical *Sonar Bangla* (Golden Bengal). Bangladesh was created from the erstwhile East Pakistan, the eastern wing and onetime province of Pakistan. Echoing the definition of the American Dream, the ethos of the Bangladeshi Dream can be stated as "…that dream of a land in which life should be better and richer and fuller for everyone, with opportunity for each according to ability or achievement…It is not a dream of motor cars and high wages, but a dream of social order in which each man and each woman shall be able to attain the fullest stature of which they are innately capable, and be recognized by others for what they are, regardless of the fortuitous circumstances of birth or position. The new nation should be precious, stunning and durable, like gold." The last sentence is entirely mine, added to James T. Adam's definition of the American Dream.

Like the American Dream, the Bangladeshi Dream was an idea. I will now give an expository narrative of the genesis of this idea. During British rule, the Greater Bengal was the large region combining Assam and Bengal. After the partition of India in 1947, Bengal was divided into East Bengal that became a province of Pakistan and became known as East Pakistan, and West Bengal became a province in India. Bengal under British rule was divided once before. The majority of Muslims in Bengal were poor, less educated or illiterate. This was true for the entirety of India and by extension other Muslim lands that were colonized by the West. A main reason was that Muslims balked at accepting Western education imported by the new colonizers. In India, the Hindus, who were under Muslim rule for hundreds of years, on the other hand, readily accepted Western education and became more educated and prosperous than Muslims.

Most of the wealthy *zaminders* (landlords) in Bengal were Hindus, of which Rabindranath Tagore, the Nobel Laureate poet, was one. To mitigate this condition and to accelerate the growth of Muslims in terms of education and employment, a renowned Muslim *zaminder* of Dhaka, Nawab Sir Salimullah, and a few other prominent Muslim leaders appealed to the British government to partition Bengal into Muslim East Bengal including Assam and Hindu West Bengal.

After a thorough investigation, the British government complying with that request and for administrative reasons, decided to divide Bengal into two provinces in 1905 with East Bengal and Assam with a Muslim majority and West Bengal, Orissa and Bihar with a Hindu majority. During this time Dhaka High Court, Curzon Hall, Dhaka Medical College and a few other historic buildings were constructed. Viewing this, the privileged Hindu *zaminders* who had their land holdings in East Bengal but lived in West Bengal primarily in Kolkata, became outraged as they anticipated the partial or full loss of their unlimited control and influence in East Bengal.

Moreover, they saw this as a "divide and rule" tactic to split the Bengalis. They spearheaded a movement to annul the partition of Bengal and restore their control and influence. To make this movement successful and mobilizing a larger population, they started a literary and cultural drive by creating the catch-phrase of Bengali nationalism under the rubric of *Swadeshi* Movement. In the backdrop of this, Rabindranath Tagore, who was a prominent participant in this movement, composed a poem "*Amar Sonar Bangla, ami Tomaye bhalobashi....*" (My Golden Bengal, I love you ...). Thus, the expression *Sonar Bangla* was coined during and because of the movement. The will of the Hindus was so fierce that the British Government was compelled to rescind the partition in 1911. This poem turned into a song, and many decades later, in 1971, was adopted as the national anthem of the newly born country of Bangladesh.

Despite the fact that Tagore was a *zaminder* living in Kolkata and might have a vested interest in this movement, I believe this poet-philosopher didn't join the movement for personal material gains. Also, he was a unitarian Hindu believing in the oneness of *Brahma,* the four-headed singular god of creation. He believed in total absorption in God and avoided religious orthodoxy. I believe he supported the movement against partition not due to any anti-Muslim prejudice as he was a lover of humanity and Nature. He did it because he didn't want to see the partition of Bengal which he loved so much as his thoughts were amply reflected in this poem. Needless to say, Bengal was partitioned again in 1947 when India and Pakistan became independent from British rule. This time though, the Hindu Bengalis supported the partition of Bengal for fear of Muslim domination in combined Bengal where Muslims formed the majority. Assam was excluded from East Pakistan and became a province of India.

At present, Bangladesh has achieved a great degree of economic uplift and remains on this trajectory for more than a decade. But political instability and bickering have plagued this young country. Now, this Bangladeshi Dream or *Sonar Bangla* still remains unfulfilled for most people there after half a century of its birth. For the American Dream the history of modern America is fairly recent and short; it began after European invaders conquered the land from the Native Americans and colonized it. Bangladesh, on the other hand, is an ancient land with a very old history and has been an integral part of the ancient land of the Indian Subcontinent. The land has Hindu, Buddhist and Islamic influence from the past and has a rich cultural heritage.

Its more recent history was nicely described in a book *Bangladesh: Reflections on the Water* by James J. Novak. He argued that Bengal was an affluent land but the widespread Bengal Famine of 1943* in which 2 to 3 million people perished, hurt the country's economy badly and broke the spirit of the people. The famine took place after Japan occupied Burma next to Bengal during World War II and the indifference of the British colonists to the alarming food shortage of Bengal. He, however, offered a sympathetic positive and hopeful assessment for the country's future. I also share that hope.

The country was born at the expense of countless martyrs who gave their lives and women who were dishonorably robbed of their dignity during the Liberation War with Pakistan, a country suffering from political instability since its inception. The hope for Bangladesh was that people would realize their dream of living in the Golden Bengal. It was a collective dream, the impassioned hope of all Bengalis, including me, when the for-

---

* Known in Bengali as *Ponchaches Monnontor* (Famine of the Fifty, referring to the year 1350 in the Bengali calendar). *Foreign Service Journal* commented on the book thus: "This is a love story based on the author's ongoing affair with an exotic land.... (Novak) captures the reader's attention, admiration and sympathy and then describes straightforwardly the external and internal elements of thinking and policy that are detrimental to the country's survival."

mer East Pakistan became independent Bangladesh. The country has all the ingredients needed to be successful. It has fertile land and massive manpower to develop and sustain the economy. People are intelligent and hardworking, the population is racially, religiously, and culturally homogeneous speaking the same language, and more than 90 percent of the people share the same faith. Yet two important elements are missing in all these -- the cohesiveness of the people and their collective vision for working towards the same goal. Dhaka has to be a livable city, attractive to foreign investors and tourists, while at the same time decentralized and more specifically decentralized concentration should be the cornerstone of overall development of the country. Meaning simply that all the various towns and cities of the country outside Dhaka should be uniformly developed with identical opportunities.

Politically, the absence of a liberal democracy in which people can vote freely prevails at this writing because of political wrangling, intolerance of any opposition, and above all the compelling craving for power by major political parties. Bengalis have shown their mettle twice during the Language Movement and the Liberation War. I have faith that they will eventually correct course in an effort to achieve the as yet unrealized Bangladeshi Dream – the dream of Golden Bengal.

I love Bangladesh, my native land and America, my adopted land. I am indebted to both. I also love and feel indebted to Canada, a peaceful and welcoming country where I lived for a decade. After coming to the West my worldview changed as for the first time, I met people of different races, ethnicities and cultures. I still identify myself with Bangladesh and take interest in things Bangladeshi and I identify myself with America and take interest in things American. My hometown in Bangladesh is still in full memory. My parents are buried in Bangladeshi soil. My school and the colleges that gave me a fine education in

Bangladesh are still there. How can I detach myself from those? But now I live on American soil. I hope my children and grand-children never forget our roots. I like both Eastern wisdom and passion, and Western rationality and technology. To me, it is in these complements where we find our humanity and creativity, similar to my liking for science and engineering in parallel with art and architecture. The East and the West can learn from each other. Our global society needs to sustain both. I know I can live with and love both Bangladesh and America. May God bless both America and Golden Bengal. In my mind I can travel freely over the invisible bridge spanning the East and the West whenever I want and can see dreamers at both ends.

CHAPTER 21

HUMAN FRAME AND THE ART OF LIVING

Health is Wealth

This is a different kind of chapter standing out from the rest in the book. Before I decided to write this chapter, I wondered whether to write it at all, as it might seem to be out of context. But my health is a very important part of my life; so, I couldn't resist writing about it. The information on maintaining good health and lifestyle are available ubiquitously in medical literature, books, magazines, and on the internet for anyone who cares. However, I thought I have gained much insight through self-study and can summarize my observations and provide insight. I have struggled with my own health trials and by God's infinite grace have reached the mature age of my mid-70s by addressing and treating my health challenges. By opening up my private health encounters, it may help others. In addition to my own major health blows, I had and still have to deal with Dora's health conditions as her caregiver. Since I was able to bounce back from all my ailments, I can look ahead with hope and still generally feel well.

I was sent to Dhaka from my hometown Patuakhali for medical treatment twice once as an infant and then as a child. I had been suffering from frequent allergy attacks and acute sinusitis since my teenage years. Between my teenage years and later in my 30s and early-to-mid-40s I generally enjoyed a healthy life. Later, I developed issues with my heart, prostate, urinary bladder, and both of my eyes. I also developed back pain beginning in my mid-30s, making me immobile at times, which then became chronic even though I tried to do the right things such as physical therapy a few times, seeing a spine specialist, a chiropractor, and exercising. I don't have any pains anymore. If I get occasional pains these days, the intensity is less, and they subside quickly. I also developed mild joint and muscle pains when I was in my 50s. I became pre-diabetic at the age of 62 and remain so until now despite my best efforts. Topping all my ailments is life-threatening advanced coronary disease that I developed in my late 40s which forced me to investigate the subject and develop an individualized plan. While health is to me a form of science dealing with the anatomy and organ functions of the body, how we manage it is, I believe, an art.

In our lives we are sure about two things; first, we are growing and second, we will one day face death. Many people live beyond the century mark. I believe our body was designed by God, the Grand Designer, to live up to about 100 years, give or take, under normal circumstances barring accidental death or death caused by incurable preexisting genetic conditions. Our intervention in the form of taking good care or neglect and witting or unwitting abuse of our body and mind influences our longevity. Death is waiting for all of us at some unknown distance and we approach it through illness, when our immunity to fight disease diminishes and ultimately our bodies fail. Most diseases are essentially caused by chronic inflammation in different forms as well as toxicity. Our body is a fort that protects us from invasions from foods, water, air, and innumerable bacteria and viruses that can wreak havoc. We must let the body persevere, strengthen, and heal itself by cooperating with it. As a general rule, we can either be our body's best friends and treat it compassionately with care, or our own worst enemies and treat it inhospitably with neglect. The choice is ours to make.

I am a heart attack survivor, after having had a brush with death in 1992 at the age of 48. I often asked myself, particularly after the death of my younger brother of a heart attack at the age of 54 later in 2001, "Why did God spare me in November 1992 when I prayed to Him frantically to save me in the hospital room in Chicago?" Fortunately, I got medical treatment immediately and my heart muscles were not damaged. Also, I was not diabetic. These conditions worked in my favor. I also loved life in all its aspects and my work and had a will to live to contribute to society. Because I was relatively young when I had a heart attack, I felt I had not achieved enough in my life yet, so I needed to live longer. My wife and young children needed me. Moreover, the world is a fun, beautiful place so I wanted to stick around as long as I could. I always felt the main culprit of my heart disease was stress. It weakened my resistance to fight the disease. This event forever changed my perspectives and perceptions. My parents and most of my uncles from both my father's and mother's sides lived long lives without heart disease, diabetes or cancer. They lived organic lives and that was a big plus for them.

Like me, two of my brothers who lived in the U.S. also developed heart disease. I believe it is not merely due to genetics. Genes certainly had a latent role to play. It is easy to blame our genes and hard to blame ourselves. It is possible that I had genetic susceptibility to heart disease as there are some markers that we inherit, and of course this is a problem. But we can take those problems as surmountable challenges. I never blame my genes and look at this matter this way: since I didn't do things that my father or uncles did, that could be a cause for my health challenge. I must have done something they didn't do. What did I then do wrong? Admittedly, yes, I had been a good eater, enjoying foods and I was sedentary much of the time in my adolescent and later years. Although I ate a variety of foods, I didn't eat too much junk or processed foods during my early age. They were not even available at that time in my native country. It is usually believed, heart disease is exacerbated by bad eating, lack of exercise and physical activities, stress and poor living habits. The medical profession usually focuses on cholesterol, blood pressure, and a few other markers that are quantifiable through lab tests. Stress can't be quantified but only the associated symptoms can be recognized. Yes, I know I didn't take preventive measures early on because of an erroneous assumption that my parents and most of my uncles lived long and hadn't experienced heart disease. If I had a history of heart disease in my family, I would certainly have paid attention early on and be proactive.

I am not a medical doctor, but because of my health conditions I studied medical literature extensively. So, I'll provide my findings from my own research which may or may not always be fitting or accurate but represents my own opinion as an informed patient. I may add that I dealt with many medical doctors, a naturopathic doctor and have investigated not just mainstream medical literature but also that related to alternate medicine such as naturopathic, homeopathic, and integrative. I asked doctors many questions. I have respect for all of them and what they do to help patients with adverse health conditions, but I occasionally disagree with them. I also studied the basics of vitamins and supplements to the best of my ability. My opinion is based on research in these disciplines and my overall judgment to combat heart disease.

The heart is a biological pump associated with the circulatory system. It beats about 100,000 times a day pumping more than 2,000 gallons of blood through miles of blood vessels -- an incredible feat indeed. Therefore, it needs to be strong and have a lot of energy since it rests only momentarily between beats throughout our lifetime. Blockages in arteries generally caused by bad cholesterol and high blood pressure can lead to heart attacks, strokes, clots in other locations of the body, etc. Since blood is a dynamic liquid traversing through the body delivering life-giving oxygen to all its nooks and corners, the cardiovascular system plays a vital role keeping us healthy.

The human frame with all its auxiliary components is a complex and tangible biological entity. But we have thoughts which are intangible, this adds further intricacy to our human form. Despite all the advances in understanding how our body functions we still don't fully know how all the parts interact with each other. I took a casual interest in knowing why and how our God-given, supposedly well-designed body occasionally turned against us. Curiosity about my own health issues, Dora's major health crisis in Canada before we moved to the U.S., while both of us were still in our 30's, and my reading, *How to Stay Healthy with Natural Foods* by Edward Marsh (described briefly in a previous chapter) had a great impact on me. It was because of my own major health crisis in 1992 that I decided to examine the whole issue more thoroughly.

My heart attack at the young age of 48, changed everything for me and, but it was a blessing in disguise as it made me stronger. I understood the significance of mortality and realized that longevity was not guaranteed so I should utilize every moment of my remaining time pursuing productive activities. I thought it best to learn as much as I could, including about health and nutrition, to go forward.

Our heart receives blood supply from the coronary arteries. These arteries and their branches supply all parts of the heart muscles with blood. The left main artery branches into the circumflex artery and left anterior descending (LAD). There is another important artery called right coronary artery (RCA) that branches into right marginal artery and posterior descending artery. A complete blockage at the beginning zone of either the left main artery or the LAD leading to a heart attack is almost always fatal without immediate treatment and is a condition known as a "widow maker." Here I'll give a brief history of the progression of my own heart disease to the best of my understanding.

In my heart attack in 1992 in Chicago and the subsequent collapse of my angioplasty (stents were still not available then) in Urbana, carried out by Dr. Nelson in early January 1993, another, complete blockage occurred near the beginning of the RCA. This blockage completely cut off blood supply to the heart muscles via the RCA. However, the dormant collateral arteries branching out around it became active and started delivering blood to the affected areas.

My cardiologist Dr. Nelson at Carle Hospital in Urbana, IL advised me to exercise for rest of my life to keep these collaterals active. In March 2009 my LAD developed a few blockages at several locations and four stents were placed throughout the artery by Dr. Mehta at Carle Hospital to fully open that blood vessel, except the tail end of the artery where it was not needed. He however found partial blockages in that tail end of LAD and the Circumflex but decided not to do anything. In 2016 two more stents were placed by Dr. Ottolin at Edward Hospital in Naperville, IL, one in April in the tail end of LAD and the other in May in the Circumflex arteries where the previously detected, partial blockages progressed further. This makes a total of six stents and all arteries are open. Dr. Ottolin characterized my heart disease as "advanced" and told me that I was still hanging around because of my diet and exercise.

So, what causes heart disease from a physiological point of view? The medical profession assumes the main offender is high blood cholesterol levels. Cholesterol is a fat chemically classified as a *sterol*. Of course, we need cholesterol for proper bodily functions since cells need it for the membranes. I came across the word "cholesterol" for the first time in Sudbury, Ontario when in 1980 I saw Dr. Takatch for my severe back pain. That day for whatever reason he ordered a blood test and after reviewing results he said my total cholesterol was175, which was fine. I asked him "What is cholesterol?" He told me "It is a type of blood fat and if you have too much of it you could develop heart disease." I asked him "How can you reduce it?" His simple reply was "You have to starve." I didn't ask him any more question and thought in my mind that I didn't have to worry about it as my cholesterol level was fine.

The earlier stages of heart disease were known as early as in 1850 to Dr. Rudolph Virchow, who described it in his book *Cellular Pathology*. Further studies produced the cholesterol theory of narrowing of arteries, which appeared during the mid-1930's. In 1951 Dr. John Gofman and his colleagues published a book *The Low-Fat, Low-Cholesterol Diet* which described how low-fat and low-cholesterol diet prevented heart disease. Following this a few more studies in the 1950's and 1960's confirmed the position, although not without controversy. In the 1970's the controversy began to gradually melt away. In the 1980's the medical community formally accepted the connection between cholesterol and heart attacks.

The full details of cholesterol chemistry and metabolism are complex. I will summarize it here for interested readers. Cholesterol is produced in the liver. In simple terms, there are three types of cholesterol, low-density lipoprotein (LDL), the "bad" cholesterol, high-density lipoprotein (HDL), the "good" cholesterol, and very-low-density lipoprotein (VLDL), the "ugly" cholesterol. Current conventional thinking is that LDL and VLDL play major role in atherosclerosis or narrowing of arteries caused by plaque build-up. LDL transports cholesterol to the cells whereas HDL transports cholesterol away from the cells. In simple words, LDL causes plaque build-up and HDL prevents it. Studies have shown that excessive LDL is a major risk factor for heart disease. However, more recent studies show that there are two different LDL particle sizes, of which the larger size is difficult to oxidize like HDL cholesterol and is protective. The smaller LDL particle size is easy to oxidize and is a major cause of atherosclerosis.

The oxidized LDL sets up an inflammatory process in the arteries leading to the build-up of plaque. Some believe that the small particles are caused by excessive sugar and refined carbohydrates rather than fat. The total cholesterol is not a good marker for heart disease. When the total cholesterol by itself is high, chances are the small-size LDL is also high and then the probability of heart disease increases. But if the small-size LDL is low, the high total cholesterol is not as meaningful. It is also accepted by the medical profession that saturated fat causes excess LDL. A high value of triglyceride, a fat in the blood released in bloodstream and produced by VLDL in the liver, is another player in causing heart disease and is caused by snacking on sweets and refined carbohydrates as well as excess alcohol. There is no simple way to measure VLDL and is calculated as a percentage of measurable triglyceride (approximately 20%). Another important factor is the ratio of LDL and HDL and of total cholesterol to HDL, as well as a few other lipid ratios.

Doctors normally order blood tests to determine the LDL and HDL cholesterol and triglyceride levels. However, there are other advanced blood tests that doctors don't normally order except in very acute cases. These are: C-reactive protein (CRP) for measuring inflammation; homocysteine which defines a type of metabolism; Lipoprotein (a) or Lp(a) which is a special sticky type of blood lipid and believed to be hereditary; fibrinogen for determining how easily blood clots; HDL particle map test for determining HDL metabolism; cholesterol balance test to determine the need for inhibiting high cholesterol absorption in the intestine, etc.

Often proper diet and lifestyle modifications as well as statin drugs are adequate for most abnormalities. Our bodies naturally produce about 75% of cholesterol and the remaining 25% is acquired from foods. Statin drugs block the synthesis of cholesterol in the liver, but they don't address intestinal sources of cholesterol in which the intestine absorbs the cholesterol from food sources and sends it into the blood stream. What is not absorbed is excreted in feces. Eating plenty of fibers, such as Metamucil, will reduce the absorption of cholesterol in the intestine. Plant *sterol,* the equivalent of cholesterol in plants, is believed to reduce the absorption as well. In severe cases when the absorption is very high additional medical treatment becomes necessary.

It is not easy to know what exactly causes the blockage in heart arteries as there are many actors at play in the human body. There is a general agreement with the overarching fact that a high LDL cholesterol and low HDL cholesterol, or high triglyceride level, or a combination of them cause this disease. While a small part of heart disease is hereditary, it is mostly triggered by poor dietary and lifestyle habits. Some other factors that cause or aggravate it are diabetes, smoking, high blood pressure, stress, caffeine, sedentary lifestyle, etc. This is by no means a complete list.

In 1955 Nathan Pritikin, an engineer and inventor from Chicago, was diagnosed with heart disease at the age of 40. This motivated him to become a longevity researcher and formulate a diet and exercise program for himself. Based on his research genre on nutrition he considered food along with exercise as medicine and created a low-fat diet that was high in unrefined carbohydrates like fruits, vegetables, and whole grains, in conjunction with moderate aerobic exercise. His dietary and exercise regime is known as the "Pritikin Diet." Following his 1985 death at age 69 from an unrelated cause, the autopsy revealed no blockage in arteries and no compromise of his heart's pumping efficiency. His pioneering work stimulated the medical and nutritional research communities to continue deliberating the matter further.

In 1990 a groundbreaking book entitled *Dr. Dean Ornish's Program for Reversing Heart Disease* by Dr. Dean Ornish, a celebrity cardiologist, further examined the presumption that heart disease was irreversible. Earlier, Nathan Pritikin's autopsy result already pointed in that direction, and demonstrated that the presumption was false. Dr. Ornish's probing research offered scientific evidence that modifications in lifestyle could actually stop and then reverse the progression of the formation of plaques in the coronary arteries. His book focused on prevention and reversal of heart disease through diet.

The Reversal Diet for those with heart disease already, eliminates animal products except egg whites and nonfat dairy products, no added oils or concentrated fats are allowed. Foods with fat and cholesterol should be avoided. He thinks the 75% of cholesterol that the body produces should be enough for us and there is no need for additional cholesterol from foods. He also argued that even the dietary cholesterol (different from saturated or trans fats) that we get directly from food has an independent effect on heart disease over and above its effect on blood cholesterol. Moderate amounts of sugar, alcohol and salt are allowed but caffeine and other stimulants are not. High amounts of proteins are discouraged. He recommends plant-based protein such as from beans. There is no particular restriction on carbohydrates as people have to satisfy their appetite with food.

The Prevention Diet for those who have not developed heart disease allows somewhat higher amounts of fat and cholesterol. He also suggested among other things, stress management techniques including stretches, breathing techniques, progressive relaxation, meditation and directed imagery, good communication skills and intimacy techniques. He prohibited smoking. He recommended walking at least one-half hour per day or for one hour three times a week. I had the opportunity to hear Dr. Ornish's lecture in Urbana, sponsored by the local Carle Hospital and Busey Bank, when he visited Urbana after my heart attack in 1992.

In a 2007 book entitled *Prevent and Reverse Heart Disease,* a best seller, Dr. Caldwell Esselstyn, Jr., a cardiologist from Cleveland Clinic took Dr. Ornish's stringent diet recommendations a notch further. He reasoned that coronary heart disease is a food-borne illness which need never exist or progress. He made the case for a low-fat, whole foods and plant-based diet that avoids all animal products and oils, as well as reducing or avoiding nuts, soybeans and avocados. He advocated that any living creature that has a face is bad for heart patients, meaning any animal-based food is forbidden.

This diet has been embraced and advocated by President Bill Clinton. Dr. Esselstyn developed his groundbreaking program based on a prolonged, evidence-based 20-year study and asserted that his plant-based and oil-free diet and nutrition program could actually cure heart disease. Although his program could immensely benefit those in critical or very advanced stages of heart disease, it's an extremely restrictive plan, rather hard for most people to follow. Dr. Esselstyn's entire focus was on food intake and not on other factors like exercise and stress management. I feel his program is excellent for prevention and reversal but not practical for a vast majority of heart patients.

Meanwhile, the 1972 book *Dr. Atkins Diet Revolution* by Dr. Robert Atkins, a cardiologist and nutritionist, promoted the idea of a low-carb and high-protein diet. After putting on weight he came across a publication in the *Journal of the American Medical Association* advocating a low carbohydrate diet to lose weight. Dr. Atkins pursued this approach and eventually wrote his landmark book on diet, primarily targeting weight loss. He subsequently wrote a follow-up book *Dr. Atkins New Diet Revolution* in 1992 and 1999, that became a bestseller, selling millions of copies. His diet also cuts out processed foods, refined carbohydrates, trans fats, and alcohol but allows red meat, butter, cream and cheese, fruits and vegetables.

The underlying concept of Dr. Atkins diet is that when the carbs you eat are limited, your body seeks another fuel to function, that is fat, and starts burning it. Reducing carbohydrates forces the body to burn both body fat and natural fat from foods. When a person is overweight the fat in the body demands more food multiplying the fat cells. Employing fat as an alternative fuel source for energy steadily lowers food cravings, which could make a difference in losing and maintaining weight.

Dr. Atkins insisted that his program could prevent and even reverse heart disease. Critics of this diet program pointed out that this low carb diet had some adverse effects and that the high amounts of fat, particularly saturated fat, and protein could lead to increased cholesterol and hence heart disease and loss of kidney function. Some people following the diet reported lack of energy, dry mouth, dizziness, constipation, and nutritional deficiencies.

Following his 1992/1999 book, Dr. Atkins appeared on television and became famous. In 2002 *Time* magazine named him one of the ten most influential people. In that same year, he suffered cardiac arrest due to coronary artery disease. Many of his critics took this episode as evidence that his low-carb, high-protein diet was harmful. In numerous interviews, however, Atkins stated that his cardiac arrest was not the result of poor diet but was rather caused by a chronic infection.

Interestingly, Edward Marsh, who was not a physician and not a household name, whom I mentioned before, in his book *How to Be Healthy with Natural Foods*, published in 1967 suggested that high protein and high fat diet was good for many diseases including heart disease. Thus, to me, as Nathan Pritikin was a forerunner of Dr. Dean Ornish; likewise, Edward Marsh was a forerunner of Dr. Robert Atkins.

Another book I read was, *10% Solution for a Healthy Life* by Raymond Kurzweil, himself a computer scientist, he published the book in 1993. Based on his study he recommended a maximum of 10% caloric fat intake out of the total rather than the conventional 30% advocated by American Dietetic Association and American Heart Association. Kurzweil also claims that such a low-fat intake increases energy and leads to a generally happier life. Moreover, he recommends exercise, suggesting walking, because it is low-impact, and easy to do. However, I recall reading a book with a similar title that I found while sorting through a stack of inexpensive books spread over a Chicago downtown sidewalk sale.

To the best of my memory it was in the early 1980's, while I was living in Chicago. It was not very detailed and was written by an engineer whose name I don't remember. The book didn't make waves, and I couldn't find any reference to it, despite my internet searches. The book not only recommended 10% caloric fat intake but also 10% sugar and 10% salt intakes compared to what was typically recommended to prevent disease and maintain a healthy life. That made sense to me. Salt indeed is considered a risk factor for heart disease although pink Himalayan salt and to a lesser extent sea salt, is considered acceptable and less harmful compared to processed common salt.

Other diet programs primarily to reduce weight appeared on the scene such as South Beach diet, Paleo diet, and Mediterranean diet. Currently, many people find benefits in the Mediterranean diet which is portrayed in a Mediterranean Diet Pyramid. In this pyramid, fruits, vegetables, whole grains, olive oil, nuts and seeds, beans, etc. are placed at the base and meats and sweets at the apex. Other foods are placed in between. This food scheme is recognized by Mayo Clinic and recommended by the renowned integrative physician Dr. Andrew Weil, M.D., a nutrition and wellness guru and known for Dr. Weil Anti-Inflammation Diet.

There is an inflammation theory of heart disease. The human body has 92 minerals which can get oxidized by foods that are processed or foods that contain pesticides or herbicides as well as chemicals, fried foods, sugar and simple carbohydrates, inflammatory foods, etc. The process of oxidation causes inflammation in the inner lining of the heart's arteries. Cholesterol, which acts as a curative agent, rushes there, carried by the bloodstream, to heal the inflammation and forms the blockage. Therefore, foods that are antioxidants and anti-inflammatory are essential to prevent heart disease.

There are other serious researchers who promote integrative and functional medicine. The general premise is that conventional medical treatment is expensive and often unnecessary. The pharmaceutical companies (Big Pharma) push for more and more medicines through their lobbying efforts. These medicines have severe side effects and cause long-term damage to the body. Some of the doctors who seem to espouse integrative medicine are: Dr. Sherry Rogers, M.D., Dr. Russel Blaylock, M.D., Dr. Joseph Mercola, D.O., Dr. Al Sears, M.D., and Dr. Mehmet Oz, M.D., a renowned television personality in America, among others.

As can be seen, there is a wide range of opinions, all based on sincere studies carried out by proponents of each dietary scheme. So, like many heart patients the question arose for me, "What should I do?" I had to choose from the many opinions, but I will come to that soon. Let me go through a few other often-debated issues related to food. These are fats, oils, and eggs.

Saturated fats are tightly packed fats that are soaked with hydrogen molecules. They are typically solid or semi-solid at room temperature as in butter or animal fat. When we eat foods laden with these fats, they increase the LDL cholesterol and therefore contribute to plaque formation in coronary arteries. Unsaturated fats are of two types: monounsaturated and polyunsaturated fats. Good sources of monounsaturated fats are olive oil, most nuts, and avocadoes. There are two types of polyunsaturated fat; omega-3 and omega-6 fats. Heart healthy omega-3 is present in fish, particularly salmon, tuna, and sardines; chia and flaxseed; walnuts, etc. Omega-6 is inflammatory and is believed to be not good for heart disease unless it is properly balanced by enough omega-3 fat. Monounsaturated fats and omega-3 fats are good for the heart. Some cardiologists suggest that all fats are bad and should be avoided. Dr. Esselstyn is the greatest proponent of this notion. Dr. Ornish excludes foods high in saturated fat such as avocadoes, nuts, and seeds, although he allows a small quantity of up to 10 % of calories from fat, mostly consisting of unsaturated fats.

Another type of fat, trans fat, often used commercially in foods such as hydrogenated vegetable oil, is the worst kind of fat for heart disease. Naturopathic and integrative doctors, however, think good fat is not really that bad. In extreme cases some doctors even think that the bad fats (saturated and trans), if they are from plant sources, are acceptable. Even mainstream medicine does not totally prohibit fat (except for trans-fat and saturated fat) as fat is essential for the body. My take on this is that we need healthy fats for neurological and certain organ functions; they also help in digestion and improve immunity. It is important to always choose unrefined, plant-based sources of fat and exclude animal fat as much as possible. I believe these kinds of fat are natural and easier to absorb. While eliminating fat from our diet may help our heart, on the flip side, we may develop other ailments if we avoid fat entirely.

Oil is essentially a fat, but I am describing it separately as it demands attention and discussion in its own right. Finding the best oil for cooking, an oil that is conducive to heart health is a daunting task. Some of the commonly used fat for food preparation are canola, olive, corn, peanut, soybean, safflower, and sunflower. These have more unsaturated fats than saturated fats. Each has its own pros and cons. Coconut oil and palm oil have a large fraction of saturated fat and are not recommended by the medical and nutritional professionals. Hydrogenated vegetable oil is totally forbidden for heart patients. There are other healthy specialty oils like grapeseed oil, avocado oil, rice bran oil, sesame oil, and algae oil that could be good choices. I realized that I needed to conduct independent research on oil as it is something we need for cooking and has negative effects on heart. I understood well that saturated fat in the oil could be harmful for heart patients like me. Opinions are as diverse as the variety of cooking oils.

Regardless of whatever oil we consume, when food is fried at high temperature the oil becomes harmful, leading to an increased risk of heart disease. One important factor to consider when assessing oil, is the smoke point. Also called flash point, it is the temperature at which oil burns and starts to smoke, producing toxic fumes and harmful free radicals making the oil unhealthy. For high temperature cooking, oils with a high smoke point is best. Considering different factors, for my own use I shortlisted four oils: avocado, coconut, grapeseed, and olive.

Avocado oil is one of the healthiest oils with great healing properties. Of all oils it has the highest smoke point of 520° F (271° C) and a high 65% heart-healthy monounsaturated fat. Coconut oil is loaded with saturated fat and has a low smoke point of 350° F (177° C). However, it is rich in medium-chain triglycerides and is the most healthful type of saturated fat. It is packed with antioxidants, moisturizing fatty acids, and has antibacterial, antiviral, and antifungal properties. Integrative doctors highly recommend it and its popularity is increasing steadily among consumers. For regular low-to-medium heat cooking it is a very healthy cooking oil.

Grapeseed oil has a high smoke point of 485° F (252° C) and is a heart-healthy alternative. Olive oil is widely recognized as a healthy oil and is extensively used by health-conscious people. It is the most commonly used oil in the countries around the Mediterranean and the people in those regions have a low incidence of heart disease. It is an essential component of the Mediterranean diet.

Extra virgin olive oil has a low smoke point of 331° F (166° C). Although it is healthy in raw form or for low-heat cooking, I would not use it for high-heat cooking. The refined (light) olive oil has a smoke point of 428° F (220° C). It has a very high monounsaturated fat of 78% and a lower saturated fat of 14%. However, the processing of the oil takes away some of the health benefits. So, I prefer just olive oil for high heat cooking or extra virgin olive oil for low heat cooking and considering all factors, I have been using this oil for cooking. Cold pressed oil is the best process since using heat for processing reduces the quality of the oil.

Algae oil is new on the market and has very low saturated fat and high monosaturated fat and hence is a great option. Moreover, its smoke point is 485°F (252°C), an added benefit. But since it is new and not well tested yet, I am not using it for now. I think though any of my shortlisted four oils is good for heart health. Moderation is of course important. Fried foods, especially deep-fried foods, are extremely bad for heart disease as many studies have shown regardless of which oil is used.

Eggs have been a big issue for both heart patients and those who take preventive care. Egg have been a wonderful food since ancient times. They provide a complete protein of the highest quality and taste great. The yolk is packed with many useful nutrients and antioxidants. The problem for heart patients is the nutritious and delicious yolk, is laden with cholesterol. Because of this, eggs got a bad name for having dietary cholesterol and were abandoned by many heart patients and even other people being cautious about preventing heart disease.

I did the same thing, particularly after reading Dr. Ornish's book and following the recommendations of the American Heart Association. But I ate eggs once a while as I felt somehow that such a great thing could not be totally bad if eaten in small quantities. When I asked my naturopathic doctor about it, he said, "The medical profession is far behind on this. The entire egg is a healthy food and you should eat it regularly." As of this writing, eggs with their yolks are back on the menu, albeit in a controlled manner. It is believed that when you eat dietary cholesterol, the natural cholesterol production of the liver slows down, and the added cholesterol does no great harm. The cholesterol caused by trans and saturated fats from animal sources is the real villain. But many integrative and naturopathic doctors believe that plant-based saturated fat does not cause any harm either.

Benjamin Franklin once said, "One should eat to live, not live to eat." Prophet Mohammad said that we should never fill our stomach more than one-third food, one-third water and one-third air. He recommended that we fast once or twice a week. In terms of a healthy diet I firmly believe we should never entirely cut out any natural and wholesome food from our diet unless there is a compelling reason to. A balanced diet and portion control are the key to a healthy diet. A balanced diet is not only about eating diverse foods containing protein, good carbs, and good fats but also allowing diversity within each category of foods. Commercially produced processed food or food-like substances, saturated fat from animal sources, refined carbs and foods with high glycemic index, and refined sugar should be eliminated from our diets completely, if possible. Also, most foods that we eat in restaurants are not conducive to good health. The focus there is on preparing delicious foods, attracting customers, maximizing profit, not on our health. It is our responsibility to preserve our own health.

Some health challenges could be related to chronic inflammation. Consuming inflammatory foods can lead to a variety of conditions and symptoms including musculoskeletal and digestive systems, headaches and tiredness, eczema and psoriasis, to name a few. Although the inflammatory foods may have some health benefits, they cause or trigger sensitivity reactions in some people. The list of such foods is long, and it is hard to avoid some of them in our routine foods. For example, oranges, wheat, milk, beef, eggplant, peanuts, potatoes, tomatoes, etc. are some of the examples. The inflammation concept primarily believed by alternative medicine practitioners suggests that the so-called leaky gut caused by inflammatory foods allows harmful bacteria to penetrate into the blood stream through the permeable intestine causing inflammation throughout the body.

Some nutritionists and health professionals recommend low-calorie food. I think when we become undernourished our immunity decreases the same way it would by overeating. Regarding natural food choices, I started using a blender in the early 2000's for making smoothies with various vegetables and fruits as well as some protein and foods like soy lecithin, wheat germ, brewer's yeast, etc. recommended by Edward Marsh in his book on natural foods. I experiment with different foods and keep changing and assessing new options.

—⊰⊱—

Based on my experience, it is often hard to get patient-centered care in America. When the doctor asks, "How are you?" say, "I have a health issue." Don't say, "I am fine" simply out of nicety. Then you better explain fast, what your ailment is before he/she cuts you off. This is not what we deserve or want.

When we enter the healthcare system, we often find ourselves powerless. Many doctors don't spend time on your case before seeing you, but instead take time out of your appointment, to look up your details and then ask you questions. Most patients have little medical knowledge and go by what the doctor prescribes, despite not getting a good explanation about the diagnosis or the treatment.

These days, some physicians stare incessantly at their computer screen while they are "listening" to you, without making direct eye contact nor engaging in normal human interactions with you. One of the biggest problems I see in the medical profession today is the erosion of the doctor-patient relationship. Due to reimbursement methods and schedules, set by insurance companies, doctors have less time with patients, they look at keyboards and computer screens and patients end up having a very impersonal experience. Doctors are not exclusively at fault. They are pressured by hospitals, clinics, and medical groups that are owned by private, profit-driven corporations. Also, some unethical doctors make money by suggesting medical procedures that may not be essential.

Then there are the politicians and health care lobbyists, insurance companies, pharmaceutical companies, and other stakeholders who also directly or indirectly control the health-care system. Most physicians have little time to read and stay on top of the latest developments in the medical field and thus their knowledge is fossilized. They follow medical protocols set by the medical associations leaving no room for independent and creative thinking. Moreover, doctors get desensitized after seeing unhappy people day in and day out. A doctor's sunny disposition and kind words of encouragement mean a lot to sick and anxious patients. Many times, doctors feel threatened or an assault on their authority if they are asked pointed questions. Of course, I have met some compassionate and communicative doctors. Also, I recognize dealing with a living complex human body and trying to cure it is hard and challenging. Over the years, I realized I have to take the doctor's advice, but I must have some knowledge and the final decision is mine, it is my body.

Doctors are firefighters, not fire-proofers, so it's me that has to take the latter role, so I don't need to see the doctor as frequently. Upon reviewing the writings of many authorities, I concluded that we have not heard the final word on the subject of health and wellness. Based on my self-study I composed and follow a definite lifestyle and diet plan for myself. I wholeheart-edly believe that we are responsible for our own health and ail-ments. We only get once precious God-given body and we must maintain and cherish it. I believe in balance in our life. When the body goes out of balance, we develop health problems. We need good protein, good carbohydrates and good fat for proper nutrition in each meal if possible. I try my best to eat mostly plant-based high-quality protein, complex carbs, and good fat from plant sources. I do not eliminate completely any natural food item from my diet, not knowing fully what blessing may lie in that food. I just minimize the bad ones and maximize the good ones.

My studies led me to another important nutrition-related insight, that is, nutritional supplementation. Indeed, I live in an affluent country with plenty of diverse foods, readily available and affordable. Unfortunately, despite having so much food around us, we are not getting enough nutrients. We often get hollow calories from processed foods like soda, sweets and desserts. Our indulgence, wittingly or unwittingly, undermines our wellbeing and depletes our body. As we grow older, we need a full spectrum of vitamin and mineral supplements that are properly manufactured, in balanced and well-absorbable forms.

In the 1950s Dr. Evan Shute, M.D. from the University of Western Ontario, London, Ontario conducted thorough research on Vitamin E and promoted the idea that it could cure many diseases, particularly cardiovascular diseases. Dr. Linus Pauling, a chemist, educator, a Nobel Prize Winner in chemistry in 1954 and Nobel Peace Prize Winner in 1962, was a pioneer of the natural health movement employing vitamins that led to a vitamin revolution. He promoted vitamins to cure diseases, with high doses of Vitamin C as a cure for many of our major illnesses including heart disease. I read his popular and comprehensive book *How to Live Longer and Feel Better* and learned a lot about our health in general and heart disease in particular. Unfortunately, the work of both researchers was either sidelined or rejected by the medical profession. Supporters of naturopathic or alternative medicine argue that since vitamins are cheap and don't generate enough profit for drug manufacturers, they are not included as a serious treatment option for disease. One among other reasons, hardly any research funding is available in the area of naturopathic, vitamin-based treatments or regimens. There is, I believe, some truth in the naturopathic approach to health particularly for wellness and preventive care.

There is no magic bullet to maintain good health; it is only through targeted nutrition and the right supplements that we can try to prevent illness and maintain good health. My thinking was focused on how to optimize my health. After thoroughly studying the vitamins and supplements, I had decided to take multivitamin and several other nutritional supplements for my specific needs. Most medical practitioners don't encourage vitamins except a very few like Vitamins D3, B6, B12, etc. perhaps due to their training bias and narrow focus on human anatomy, diseases and drug-based treatment. I am a sincere believer in vitamins and supplements though.

Later in my life my son-in-law Dr. Byron Johnson, M.D., boosted my belief in vitamins. He is a radiologist and a believer in drug-free integrative and holistic medicine in the form of natural foods and nutritional supplements. He also takes supplements and vitamins himself.

I often refer to a book titled *The Real Vitamin & Mineral Book: Using Supplements for Optimum Health* by Shari Lieberman and Nancy Bruning, which is a practical guide to nutritional supplements. As supplements are not monitored or regulated nor evaluated by the Food and Drug Administration, I buy them from reputed manufacturers. However, although I take a large number of supplements, because of my chronic health issues, I also maintain regular contact with my primary care physician, cardiologist and urologist, and continue to take prescribed medications.

The role of exercise is very important in keeping the body and mind healthy. My naturopathic doctor once told me, "Exercise is the best supplement you can have." Research shows that physical weakening and reduced functions associated with aging are to a large extent caused by inactivity, as the saying goes, "Use it or lose it." Sedentary living leads to degenerative diseases. For cardiovascular disease and diabetes exercise is particularly important. Exercise gives us a better physique, stronger muscles and bones, it also bestows many health benefits allowing us perhaps to live longer and enjoy a better quality of life as we age. It has a direct bearing on age-related muscle loss and insulin sensitivity. I realized after my heart attack that I must exercise regularly throughout my life. Exercise has three fitness components: aerobic, strength training, and stretching. Although aerobic exercise is essential for cardiovascular and metabolic health, all three are needed for good health.

Since my childhood days I have always that heard that exercise is a good thing for the body. But because I was two years younger and therefore smaller in size and weaker than most of my classmates at Dhaka College, during my adolescent and early teenage years, I couldn't really keep pace with them physically. This effectively ended my interest in sports and athletics. Despite this, before my heart attack in 1992, I was somewhat conscious of the importance of physical activity and started walking around the neighborhood occasionally. However, following the heart attack I started walking regularly at the UIUC Armory. Dora accompanied me there regularly. In summer I would take long walks around my neighborhood in the morning or late afternoon. I thought I should perhaps do more, so I visited the university gym and saw a few people working with weights and machines, but that didn't impress me. I thought it was an artificial replacement for natural exercise, and in a confined environment.

In 2006 Dora and I visited Murad who lived in a downtown Philadelphia apartment. He was new to his job and single. We went there to help him settle in. One day when he was leaving for work, he took me to a small gym on the ground floor of the apartment complex and said, "Dad, you can spend some time here if you want. During working hours, nobody is around." I made note of the possibility and one early afternoon, while reading a book, it occurred to try out the treadmills and some of those machines to kill time. Once there, I found to my surprise, that I liked it. I used the machines regularly while I was there. I always thought gyms were facilities artificially reproducing what our ancestors did naturally. I still feel somewhat like that and believe that nothing can replace walking outdoors or activities in a natural environment. But going out is not always possible and so it's better to exercise in gyms than leading an inactive life indoors.

Upon my return, I joined the university gym and exercised there. In the gym I engaged in all three components of exercise and started appreciating the equipment. I saw a large Olympic-size swimming pool and felt the urge to swim. Swimming is great aerobic exercise. Initially I was weary since I hadn't done it in about five decades. I wasn't too keen on the hassle of getting wet in a pool let alone swimming.

One day, however, I made up my mind to give it a try and slid into the indoor pool. I felt like I couldn't float well at first and became nervous, but soon was able to overcome the nerves, I was just a bit out of practice, after all I swam a lot as a child. By the time a few days passed, I started swimming and enjoying it. I also added occasional sauna sessions to encouraged natural sweating, with my cardiologist's approval. Then I started yoga regularly in group fitness classes.

These habits have stayed with me now in Chicagoland, although less frequently because of other time commitments. Although I use machines at the gym for stretching needs, I stretch at home as well. I learned different postures from physical therapists for my aches and pains at different times. Specifically, when I was in Malta, where I developed debilitating back pain, the physical therapist taught me a few excellent stretching poses and advised me to do them every day in the morning upon waking up, a practice I follow to date.

Another extremely important part of maintaining good health and increasing longevity is stress management. Stress is intangible and cardiologists can't really measure it. Although stress causes or contributes to the development of most diseases, heart disease is particularly prone to exacerbation from stress. I know it well, as deep in my heart -- pun intended -- I feel that stress was the major cause of my heart attack in 1992.

As a structural engineer I have been dealing with stress in structural materials throughout my education, professional and academic career. When an object or structure is subjected to an external force it develops internal stresses to resist it*. The object or structure gets damaged or fails when the respective carrying capacity to withstand the external force falls short. This also happens when excessive or frequent (cyclic) forces are applied. Drawing an analogy, our body and psyche can normally withstand stresses caused by external events, up to a certain capacity. When the capacity is exceeded, our body is overstressed leading to diseases of the body and mind. Stress is not the actual event in our life but is the *reaction* to those events by our body and mind.

In a structure, stress is needed, even just from its own weight, to keep it stable. Likewise, we need a stress response to keep us stable when facing the challenges of life. When we are faced with a stressful situation our body produces a stress response by releasing hormones from the hypothalamus, pituitary and adrenal glands. These call in and boost our reserve energy to help us deal with the situation. Once the stressor goes away, our body and mind return to a stable and normal state. During a highly stressful event, the body often responds by shaking, exhibiting elevated blood pressure, rapid heartbeat, dry mouth, headache, nervousness, etc. If the stress response is excessive or is triggered too frequently, our body and mind go out of balance, depleting energy reserves. If we carry the stress for a longer period, it will lead to many new health problems, chronic diseases, and aggravated health hazards.

---

* This follows directly from Newton's third law of motion that states: *To every action in nature, there is an equal and opposite reaction.*

Studies show that people who sleep seven to eight hours, at regular times are generally more relaxed and energetic, healthier, and live longer than those who sleep fewer hours. Nothing is better than going to bed and sleeping most instead of tossing and turning or sitting up and worrying. Practicing relaxation techniques helps manage stress. During relaxation, we channel our thoughts away from our problems and concentrate on pleasant, enjoyable and peaceful thoughts and feel calm. Those of us who love music, listening to soft and classical music can certainly soothe our minds and make us feel peaceful.

Viewing natural landscapes from time to time is another way to relax our minds. Other relaxation techniques include deep breathing, yoga, Tai Chi, dhikr or zikr (a form of Islamic/Sufi meditation, usually invoking the names and attributes of God), directed imagery, mindful meditation, massage therapy, etc. that can all help in reducing physical and emotional tension. Relying on pleasant memories as virtual touchstones, can relax our body and mind and help manage stress. Availing oneself of leisure time can also bring great fulfilment and relief. Resting for a few minutes daily is a great way of rejuvenating the body and mind. It is not always possible to carry out all these practices everyday but trying to do as much as possible is the key and has immense benefits.

Above all, nothing beats having a positive attitude towards life and while dealing with others. It is easy to be paranoid, cynical and detached from other things in this world, one that is often perceived to be imperfect, unreasonable and unjust. Acceptance is key. We need to count our blessings first and focus on fixing our own shortcomings. This is the process through which we can eventually be of service to society to others.

To help my body combat progressive heart disease, enlargement of prostate, and my prediabetic condition, at this writing my daily routine is as follows: In general, I have an optimal diet i.e., low-fat, low-sugar, low salt, high-fiber. I also follow an exercise routine. I developed a supplement plan for myself, which I follow diligently. In the morning, I do regular full body stretches, then I eat my breakfast: first a little juice with three brazil nuts and a handful of pumpkin seeds. Next, I drink a warm glass of water mixed with a tablespoon of organic apple cider vinegar and a teaspoon of organic lemon juice. Following this, I eat a bowl of oatmeal cereal and unsweetened almond milk or flaxseed milk with a banana, flaxseeds, hemp hearts, and occasionally, blueberries. Almost every day, I eat an egg omelet or boiled egg. The omelet is made with one organic egg and three tablespoons of organic egg whites. Occasionally, I eat toast and jam with the egg. I finish my breakfast with a cup of black or green tea.

During mid-morning I eat a fruit usually a nectarine, pear, orange, apple or plum. Then, a few times a week I go to the gym for cardio and/or strength training exercise wrapped up with stretching. On some days I go to yoga classes or swimming instead of the other exercises. I also get a one-hour full body massage once a month. I rest for at least two days a week and avoid any type of strenuous physical activity. Because I am now a caregiver of Dora, I can't do these things as frequently.

In the late morning, I make a smoothie of water, juice, or almond milk and a few vegetables and fruits. I add frozen berries and about 20 mg of a vegan or whey protein powder to my smoothie My lunch is usually vegetarian. I drink a cup of organic green tea after lunch when time permits. Later, I rest and meditate when I find time.

My dinner is typically a small amount of rice, vegetables, lentil, fish, and meat (mostly chicken). Two days in a week, I try to go vegetarian for dinner. For dessert I eat half a cup of nonfat Greek yogurt sweetened with a date. I throw a few walnuts, almonds, or other nuts into it. I occasionally finish my evening meal by drinking a cup of organic green tea.

After breakfast, lunch and dinner I take a large number of dietary supplements, focused on each of my specific ailments and general health. I avoid calcium supplements as they may calcify my heart's arteries.

We have all heard the expression "broken heart." To me the literal meaning refers to the biological pump in our body that can be damaged or broken. It needs repair to restore and maintain its function as long as we live. The metaphorical meaning points to the heart as the repository of our feelings and emotions, with the brain as the source. To prevent the metaphorical heart from breaking, it must not be stressed with excessive or chronic emotional loads. Like the physically broken heart, an emotionally broken heart can also be mended and restored through soul-searching, reflection, and the right attitude of hope, faith, love, and giving.

I will add to all that I have written here that I am a profound believer in God, and I believe that God has created us, so we can worship Him, and play a role in this world. I feel that people of genuine faith are more prepared than others to follow a path to peace, wellness and happiness. Because of my steadfast faith in the Almighty and trust in His unbounded generosity, love and mercy, and my submission to His Will, I have established more self-discipline in my life – both spiritual and physical – through regular prayers, fasting, and charity.* I have also developed hope and vision for the future, and a purpose in life larger than myself.

---

* I take inspiration from these inspiring words: Whoever submits his whole self to God, and is a doer of good, has grasped indeed the most trustworthy handhold: and in God rests the End and Decision of (all) affairs. (Holy Qur'an: 31:22)

CHAPTER 22

BRIDGING NATIONS AND
IDEOLOGIES

Then and Now

I feel like I am a product of both the East and the West. I love both and look upon myself this way. My younger, formative years were spent in the East. My sense of character, the foundations of my values about work, education, honesty, diligence and responsibility, were established in, and by, Bangladesh and the myriad cast of characters that populated my experiences there. But just as much of who I am today is the result of the life I've made in the West. Canada and the U.S. are my adopted countries and home to the "wonder years" of my young adulthood. Curious and inquisitive, I learned about myself, my profession, the world and universe, in the libraries, on the sidewalks, the hallowed halls, meeting rooms and living rooms of the West.

Looking back, I explored my surroundings in the West, and let them shape me. While they were shaping me, I in turn shaped it. Like many immigrants of my generation, I occupy the interstitial space, between East and West. My life, outlook and perspectives are a composite material, reinforced by the steely values of my youth, gleaned from enduring lessons of my parents and the hard knocks of life. The formative years of my life in former East Pakistan were shaped not only by my parents, family and community, but by the history of that place itself. It's equally true that the history of the U.S. has also shaped who I am today.

Before writing this last chapter of the book, I looked back to when I first envisioned writing it. I pondered over the main theme. That is to say, I wondered what was so remarkable in my life that warranted the writing of a book? After some soul searching, I found out that a theme emerged after all. It is the process of transformation that was taking place as I traveled, regularly, back and forth across the bridge, between East and West. This transformation was running in the background of my life, like an operating system of sorts. As I review my life so far, I can say that this theme deserves special attention. So, in keeping with this thought, I have reviewed and reflected upon my composite life, from this perspective. A perspective that I could not fully unlock before, as I had many other aspects of my life to cover.

During high school, we read short stories in English class the story of Rip Wan Winkle stood out to me. Washington Irving's very imaginative story, written in 1819, is set during the American Revolution and the main character is a Dutch American, Rip Van Winkle. He lived at the foot of New York's Catskill Mountains and would often roam the mountains with his dog to escape his nagging wife.

On one such occasion, he came across a few men playing nine-pins, got drunk and fell asleep. When he woke up, he was surrounded by shocking changes all around, he had gotten older and grown a long beard. To his surprise, the men and his dog were long gone. He proceeded to his village and saw many unfamiliar people who didn't recognize him either. He had no idea that he had slept through the entire American Revolution, his ignorance of which almost got him in deep trouble with the villagers. An elderly woman finally recognized him as the long-lost Rip Van Winkle. He realized that he had slept for 20 years and his wife was dead. He was taken in by his daughter and quite simply, resumed his usual life. What I took away from this story at my tender age, was the fact that change is inevitable, society and surroundings evolve with the passage of time.

We humans reminisce about the past, live in the present and look forward to the future. We have no control of our past, have direct control of our actions in the present, and have little control on our future. Childhood and adolescence are periods when we engage the new world around us with the thrill of exploration and wonder. In our senior years, when we reach the end zone, we have acquired experience and wisdom. These two periods are the bookends of our lives. For me, these two book ends were crafted and carved over time and space, across cultures and traditions, separate histories, and my experience in the two places where I lived the most – my native homeland and my present adopted country.

I recall the day when I left East Pakistan in September 1970 from Dhaka Airport at Tejgaon about half a century ago as of this writing. This long period of time, the backdrop of my hectic life, has passed very fast. Although I wasn't sleeping, looking back now, the events feel like a series of dreams, as if, upon waking I decided to write this chapter. I vividly remember the land of the Royal Bengal Tiger far away where I lived, before I left for the West. I developed a hidden love, mostly through reading, about the distant land called America. Now that I have been a long-time resident of the West and a keen observer here, I keep the love of my native land alive as well, following news and events there.

I grew up as a conscious child and teenager, in the tumultuous years of young, East Pakistan. I was born in the province of Bengal under British India at the tail end of World War II and the aftershock of that devastating war was still shaking the world. In August 1947, when I was only three years old, I knew nothing of the grand plans for my country, taking shape in the halls of power. Nevertheless, some of my earliest memories include hearing snippets of stories and anecdotes by grownups around me with keywords like Hitler, Japanese bombing, Churchill, atom bomb, etc. Not knowing what the meaning or substance of these words or expressions they made a lasting impression.

Occasionally I went to my father's office chamber, next to our house where he would sit with his clients. There I heard the prevalent theories of how Pakistan's Prime Minister Liaqat Ali Khan was assassinated. I heard about the Kashmir problem and how it might be solved. Other discussions were about the Indian Congress and Muslim League. I heard about Jinnah Saheb and Gandhiji. I also heard about President Eisenhower and speculations about how he might help Pakistan. Then came the language movement in 1952, triggered by the killing of several people in Dhaka on February 21, at a student demonstration who were protesting the imposition of Urdu as the only state language of Pakistan excluding Bengali, the native language of the East Pakistanis, who were the majority among the population of Pakistan at the time.

The Muslim League Party was formed on the notion of a new Muslim homeland, Pakistan, being carved out of India. In 1954 it lost hold in East Pakistan in a general election when a newly formed *Jukto Front* (United Front), launched a successful challenge. Jukto Front was a group of a few parties brought together by their common goal of defeating Muslim League. Muslim League was already losing popularity among Bengalis following the bloody event of 1952. A new constitution was composed and promulgated by the Pakistani government in 1956, declaring Pakistan as an Islamic Republic in which Major General Iskandar Mirza became the president. The Pakistanis were not, however, ready to govern and made one mistake after another leading to continuous instability in its political order. This culminated in the imposition of military rule in 1958 by General Muhammad Ayub Khan that was warmly welcome by people who were fed up with the instability of the country's government. I heard one person, an out-of-the box thinker, Mr. Shamsuddin, a Moktar (a licensed legal practitioner in the lower courts dealing with criminal cases), who said that he didn't like it as the General might stay in power indefinitely. I was 14 years old then.

The history of a country is intertwined with its society and prevailing politics, these dynamics must be examined side by side to get an accurate view. I will delve into the history of Bangladesh and occasionally analyze and share my thoughts. Bangladesh is a secular country with a cosmopolitan population of Muslims, Hindus, Buddhists, and Christians, the vast majority of over 90 percent being Muslims adhering to Sunni Islam. There are some tribal populations of Chakma, Garo, and Manipuri descent. Being a part of the larger Indian sub-continent, Bangladesh history is intertwined with Indian and cannot be truly understood without a brief history of India being told.

Since antiquity, India has been a highly diverse land, ethnically and linguistically. It has been frayed by infighting and conflict between large number of tribes and kingdoms, and by periodic power turnovers stemming from foreign incursion. The first foreign invasion was by the Aryans who settled in India and established the Indo-Aryan faith later known as Hinduism. The second turnover was with Muslims, who settled there. The third was a takeover by the British who just colonized the land and extracted resources without settling. When I studied Indian history in my high school years, this history was categorized along a timeline as the Hindu, the Muslim and the British periods.

The earliest civilization of India is known as the Indus Valley civilization of which Harappa and Mohenjo-Daro are the most famous cities, located in present-day Pakistan. It was a very sophisticated early world civilization comparable to Egyptian and Mesopotamian civilizations. I visited the Mohenjo-Daro site in 1963. Although the decline of this civilization has been ascribed to many factors, the frequent flooding of the Indus River, eroding the land and weakening the agricultural economy was a major one. The final devastation was probably caused in the second millennium BCE when the Aryan tribes from the northwest invaded the land. The better armed Aryans, led by a warrior aristocracy, pushed the local native Dravidians inhabiting the region to the south. The Aryan society is believed to be based on social classes of worriers, priests, artisans, and slaves, which was introduced in India later in the form of the caste system of Hinduism. The caste system became a hereditary classification of people. It also became a specifically religious institution. Beyond the spectrum of the Aryan society were the degraded untouchables and outcastes, their contribution to society limited to unclean and menial tasks. Out casting was a form of permanent exclusion from Aryan society employed as a punishment for serious violations of caste prohibitions.

Conformity to the caste system was not just a social structure but also a religious obligation. The Aryans worshiped a number of glorified deities personified in natural objects and phenomena and representing lofty ideals of human qualities and virtues. These morphed into the deities of Hinduism. This was followed by the struggle for control between the leaders of the Aryan-Hindu and a new group instilled with the teachings of Gautam Buddha, the founder of Buddhism, as well as Mahavir, the founder of Jainism. Both Buddha and Mahavir were from non-Aryan heritage and vehemently opposed to violence and the caste system and promoted the idea that people's status should be judged not by their birth but by their deeds.

In the fourth century BCE a Mauryan state emerged. The third and most renowned Mauryan king, Asoka, witnessed the bloodbath of thousands of soldiers killed in the War of Kalinga, and converted to Buddhism. Asoka promoted the non-violent doctrine of Buddhism in his vast empire and sidestepped the caste system.

During the following era, the Hindu Guptas came to power and established the Gupta Empire. The most notable ruler of this era was Samudragupta, who firmly reestablished Hinduism. Some other notable rulers of the ancient time after that are Kanishka and Harshavardhana. Occasional invasions by Greeks, Kushans, Huns, etc. reinforced Hindu vitality as the impact of those invaders didn't last too long and was marginal. The Hindu faith and social order find their true origins in the early foreign Aryan invasion; but the events and processes of transformation took place over such a long period of time, so long ago, that these roots grew blurry in the memory of most people in India. Most Hindus don't have a vivid recollection of their alien cultural and religious origin; they consider their faith and culture as unquestionably indigenous now.

Bengal in the eastern flank of India had been ruled by many dynasties and rulers. Shashanka, a major figure in Bengali history, reigning in the 7th century, became the first independent king of a unified state in the Bengal territory, with his capital in Gaud (present-day Murshidabad in West Bengal). After his death his empire collapsed, and an uncertain situation was created resulting in lawlessness that lasted for about 150 years. Bengal became fragmented and the state of lawlessness and infighting reached a peak when the people of Bengal elected a feudal king Gopal who founded the Pala dynasty followed by the Sena dynasty.

Next came the Muslim turnover, beginning in the eighth century, which initiated the Muslim rule in the sub-continent until the mid-19th century. It began with the Arab conquest of Sindh in 712 by Muhammad bin Qasim. However, later, following a few raids by Sultan Mahmud Ghazni whose purpose was to gather wealth from India to support his battle expeditions in Central Asia, the Delhi Sultanate was established after the invasion of India in 1192 in which Muhammad Ghori of Turkic origin defeated the Hindu Rajput king Prithviraj Chauhan.

This phase of the Muslim rule came to be known as the Delhi Sultanate that was firmly established and that expanded to the east to Bihar province. Lakshman Sen of Bengal, the Hindu king of the ruling Sena Dynasty, became apprehensive of Muslim onslaughts there. It is said that the astrologers told him that he would be defeated and killed by the conqueror of Bihar, that is, Muhammad Bakhtiar Khilji. In 1204 Bakhtiar Khilji entered the capital Nadia in an unconventional way and attacked King Sen's palace with a battalion of 18 advanced soldiers. The king thought the capital had fallen and without putting up a fight escaped through the backdoor never to be seen again. This was the beginning of Muslim rule in Bengal.

After the dynastic rule of a few Turkic Sultans, the most notable rulers of Bengal were of the Husain Shahi Dynasty that reigned from 1494 to 1538. The most glorious period of Muslim rule in India was during the Mughal rule of India. The most famous ruler of this period was Emperor Akbar the Great in the 16th century whose grandson Emperor Shah Jahan, a great builder, built the Taj Mahal as the tomb of his beloved wife Mumtaz Mahal. Full information about the Muslim rule in India can be readily found in the literature and I don't want to repeat it here.

In 1757 the independent Muslim ruler of Bengal, Bihar, and Orissa, Nawab Siraj ud-Doula, whose capital was in Murshidabad in present-day West Bengal, was defeated by British Major General Robert Clive in the Battle of Plassey in Bengal. This created an opening for the British who first came to India as merchants under the rubric of the East India Company with the ulterior motive of colonizing India. Nawab Siraj ud-Doula, who was very young, deputed his uncle Mir Jafar Ali Khan for the battle against Robert Clive. However, Mirjafar, as he is commonly known, conspired with the British against his nephew with the hopes of gaining power and ascending the throne. By prematurely withdrawing from the battlefield he allowed the British opponent to win and declare victory. His dethroned nephew, while trying to escape was assassinated in a preplanned plot.

Once Mirjafar became the Nawab, soon he realized he would not have any real power nor control resources and would just be a figurehead. He objected to this to his British patrons and was replaced by his son-in-law Mir Qasim, who vigorously fought the British but was defeated. Robert Clive amassed enormous wealth and adopted dubious means for which he was later put on trial in London. Warren Hastings was subsequently sent in 1765 as the Bengal Governor of the East India company to be the de facto ruler. Mirjafar's name has since then become synonymous with the term "traitor" in Bengali folklore and literature.

There are many instances of such collusion with the enemy in self-interest, by other historical figures, yet they are not perhaps as scorned as Mirzafar as he was instrumental in creating the foothold for the British to eventually vanquish the rest of India and establish prolonged British rule. The last Mughal emperor, Bahadur Shah, was defeated by the British in 1857. Throughout the world the once dominant Islamic forces had been losing power at the time as the Islamic spirit, intellectual and religious tradition was breaking. There ensued widespread complacence, dereliction of administrative responsibilities on the part of the rulers, and a general failure of institutions to engage with, reconcile or participate in the world of science and technology in which Europe excelled. All this and more, led to the sun setting on Muslim civilization worldwide.

Unlike the British, the Muslims never considered India a colony. Instead they settled in the new land and made it their home. Although Muslims ruled India for many centuries and Islam is a missionary religion, interestingly, the vast majority of Indians didn't convert to Islam despite its message of universal brotherhood and equality in a caste-ridden society openly promoting inequality. I can suggest a number of reasons for this.

First, the Muslim rulers were more interested in acquisition of land and ruling and not demanding faith conversion. This is amply demonstrated by the fact that the Hindus always constituted the majority population around Delhi and in the heartland of India despite the location of the Muslim Sultanate also being in Delhi. The Muslims population had been larger in the far-flung regions that today make up Pakistan and Bangladesh, the reason for which I will explain later.

Second, Hinduism being a product of the long established ancient Indo-Aryan creed was deeply engrained in the Indian population. This yielded a closed society with strong Indo-Aryan and Sanskritic civilizational and cultural associations, impervious to new ideologies. Anyone who converted was considered an outcast violating the purity of Hinduism. Islam was mostly spread by the many Sufi saints and preachers who came from other Muslim lands as merchants, travelers and students.

Third, India is a vast country of forests, wetlands, and rivers where communication was very difficult, and transportation was very slow in those days. The natural topography may have prevented the preachers from moving about easily and proselytizing the faith to people in remote areas.

Fourth, there were tribes in different regions of society. Unlike the nomadic people who survived with tribal support in climatically harsh environments, these tribes were primarily agrarian with a large fragmented population, not ubiquitously tribal in nature. Islam was often more successful in nomadic lands with sparse populations, among a proliferation of tribes with strong central authority. The tribal chiefs would determine the religious destiny of the tribes.

⋙⋘

I will now explore the conversion to Islam by the indigenous people in Bengal. This is very important as present-day Bangladesh is a Muslim majority country in the Hindu majority Indian subcontinent. At the present time Bengal has one of the largest Muslim populations in the world (about 180 million in Bengal combining Bangladesh and West Bengal). This fact first came to be recognized in the census of 1872. It was revealed then that contrary to popular belief about Bengal being the principal domain of Hindus, Muslims constituted 48 per cent.

In 1901 the Hindu-Muslim population became equally split. At the time of this writing, Muslims constitute about 70 per cent of the total population of combined Bengal. The revelation of 1872 led to a debate among historians and social scientists about the origin of the great body of Muslims in Bengal. Several theories have been floated since then to explain this out of which four have been well scrutinized. These are the immigration theory, "religion of the sword" theory, political patronage theory, and the social liberation theory.

The immigration theory suggests that Bengal was populated by Muslims during the Turkic and Mughal times. Although some Muslims might have migrated and settled there in small numbers, this theory is illogical, however, as it doesn't explain the large Muslim population, unless one assumes the fact of mass conversions following a small migration of Muslims to the area.

The sword theory was proposed by some historians who hold anti-Muslim bias and as a result a common misconception in India is that Hindus were forcefully converted. This theory has been questioned by historians like P. Hardy, Sir Thomas Arnold, and Richard Eaton. Hardy has observed that those who argue forced conversion theory, failed to define either the "force" or "conversion" and left us to presume that a society could and would simply agree to change its religious identity under threat of violence. The practical working of this theory has never been spelled out, nor are there examples, to substantiate this. Over the course of many centuries, in such a vast area as the Subcontinent, it is possible that some rulers with religious bias and dreams of grandeur, gained converts by intimidation; but it is generally recognized that the extent is limited. Arnold argued that the conversion force played no part and the only influences at work were the teachings and persuasions of peaceful missionaries. He reasoned in the last decade of the 19th century thus:

How little was effected towards the spread of Islam by violence on the part of the Muhammedan rulers may be judged from the fact that even in the center of Muhammedan power, such as Delhi and Agra, the Muhammedans in modern times in the former district hardly exceeded one-tenth, and in the latter they did not form one-fourth of the population.

Similarly, Eaton wrote explicitly in his well-publicized volume *Islam and the Bengal Frontier, 1204-1760:*

If Islamization had ever been a function of military or political force, one would expect that those areas exposed most intensively and over the largest period to rule by Muslim dynasties – that is, those that were most fully exposed to the "sword" – would today contain the greatest number of Muslims. Yet the opposite is the case, as those regions where the most dramatic Islamization occurred, such as eastern Bengal or western Punjab, lay on the fringes of Into-Muslim rule where the "sword" was weakest and where brute force could have exerted the least influence. In such regions the first accurate census reports put the Muslim population between 70 and 90 per cent of the total, whereas in the heartland of Muslim rule in the upper Gangetic plain – the domain of the Delhi fort and the Taj Mahal, where Muslim regimes had ruled the most intensively and the longest period of time -- the Muslim population ranged from only 10 to 15 per cent. In other words, in the subcontinent as a whole there is an *inverse* relationship between the degree of political penetration and the degree of Islamization.

The "political patronage" theory suggested that upper class Indians converted to receive favors in terms of getting better social and political status and material advantages from the ruling religious class. This theory, apparently sounding adequate, does not explain the massive conversions to Islam of the peasants and cultivators in rural areas taking place in Bengal.

Historical records show that the "social liberation" theory appears to be most logical. A large number of preachers coming from other Muslim lands, many of them warrior Sufi saints, were instrumental in taking up the cause of the most persecuted communities. The Sufis gained many converts through their sympathy and readiness to serve the downtrodden and those identified as inferior for generations. The Sufis welcomed them into a universal brotherhood based on equality of all. To lifelong outcasts or inferior caste people, this message was thrilling. Out of these preachers, some were great organizers and leaders mobilizing locals to clear the woodlands and forests and create arable land.

The most prominent among the preachers was Shah Jalal who came to Sylhet in about 1300 and was able to convert locals in massive numbers. He settled in Sylhet. The International Airport in present-day Dhaka has been named in his honor. Many other Sufis and preachers throughout Bengal, particularly East Bengal, settled in this region and left their mark in many districts of Bangladesh and are still revered by the locals. As I mentioned before my ancestors also came to India from Iraq to preach Islam and settled in Bengal. Moreover, Arab traders had been accessing the coastal regions of India since the beginning of Islam in the 6th century. On their way to the "Spice Islands" (Malacca, Sumatra, etc.) many of them rerouted through the Bay of Bengal and turned to being preachers and became settlers. They contributed to the increasing number of Muslim populations in the Bengal delta.

Yet another proposition has been floated more recently[*]. In the middle of eighth century, the rule of the Buddhist Pala kings was established in northern and western Bengal which continued with various changes for about four centuries. Both Buddhist and Hindus flourished in Bengal. In the middle of 12th century the Hindu Sena dynasty rose to power and took control of Bengal completely. The Senas, unlike the Palas, were not Bengalis; they were South Indians and were upholders of the Brahmanical system. Under Hindu Sena rule, Buddhism fell victim to degeneration within itself and the process of decline set in. The differences between Buddhism and Brahmanism gradually faded, and many Buddhists adopted Brahmanical manners while still retaining the original connections to Buddhism. Foreign travelers and the Muslim invaders didn't often distinguish between Brahmanical Hindu and Buddhist religions. Buddhism became the religion of the suppressed masses. Thus, the Buddhists who constituted a large proportion of the population could easily welcome the Muslims and joined hands with them by converting. Many Bengali Hindus would refer to Muslims as "Nere", a derogatory use of the word meaning clean-shaven, a reference to Buddhist monks who typically shave their heads.

⇒╬⇐

---

[*] See, for example, the essay "Conversion to Islam in Bengal: An Exploration" by Abdul M. Choudhury in *Bangladesh: Volume One - History and Culture,* edited by S.R. Chakravarty and Virendra Narain, South Asian Publishers, New Delhi, 1986.

An important event affecting Bengal in the 19th century, during the British period, is the Sepoy Mutiny in 1857. Some call this event the beginning of the War of Independence. It started in Barrackpore in Bengal in which the last Muslim Mughal emperor, Bahadur Shah and the Hindu Queen of Jhansi, joined together to fight the British. The founding of the Fort William College in Kolkata, the first capital of the British in India, led to the growth and rise of English-educated Bengali – generally Hindu -- scholars and intelligentsia.

The Indigo business was a booming in India during the Mughal period but was curtailed in the early 17th century and later became unpopular. It was not a profitable business in India during the 19th century. However, the profit-hungry European Indigo planters continued to cultivate the low yield crop and oppress their local workers, resulting in several rebellions. In 1861 the "Blue Mutiny" took place in Bengal in which the Indigo farmers rebelled.

Kolkata's educated community came out in protest against the tyranny of the European planters to show their support for the workers. A drama "Nil Darpan" meaning the "Indigo Mirror" was a well-written drama based on the miserable life on indigo plantations and the associated cruelties perpetrated on the indigo cultivators. The play was staged at Jorasanko in Kolkata on December 7, 1872. It was a historical event that impacted Bengali history as I heard about it in the 1950s as a teenager, the story having been told and still retold.

The British colonized India but never settled there as the rulers were more interested in extracting wealth to enrich their homeland. They instituted a divide and rule policy amongst the Hindus and Muslims. This rule was instituted after 1857 when Muslims and Hindus jointly rebelled against the British. Hindus became more prosperous after that as they cooperated with and were favored by the British and the Muslims looked upon the British with disdain as usurper of their past glory as India's rulers.

In the 1860s Bankim Chatterjee, an accomplished Bengali writer wrote anti-Muslim invectives arousing feelings of anti-Muslim prejudice in some Hindus and came up with a nationalistic poem called *Vande Mataram*. It was later used as a lyric for a song that became popular throughout India. By the early part of the 20th century a new Hindu nationalist movement took root. The Rashtriya Seva Sangh (RSS) was founded in 1925 and adopted an ideology espousing the need for a "Hindu nation" promoting Hindutva (Hindu-ness). Other organizations with parallel ideology such as Hindu Mahasava and Arya Samaj also grew around that period. A number of Hindu-Muslim riots took place around this time. Hindus blamed Muslims for these events and Muslims blamed Hindus. Muslims were particularly offended when Hindus deliberately conducted loud processions, playing music in honor of their deities, passing near mosques during prayer times.

Christopher Jaffrelot pointed out the theme of "stigmatization and emulation" in the ideology of the RSS along with Hindu Mahasava and Arya Samaj. Muslims and Christians were considered as "foreign bodies" implanted on the Hindu nation. Ironically, the Aryan invaders were also foreign bodies that were implanted in the one-time Dravidian nation of India. Like the Aryan invaders Muslim invaders settled in India and became Indians.

The Hindu extremists proposed that all Muslims should leave India and go to Mecca, and Christians should go to Jerusalem. Even though Muslims were natives of India they were considered "converts" by these extremist Hindus and thus classified as foreign. Again, the ideology disregarded the obvious contradiction of Hindus themselves being converted by the foreign Aryans. Similarly, broadly speaking, one could argue that Jews were converted by Moses, Buddhists by Buddha and his descendants,

Christians by St. Paul, and by and large, the first Arabs were also converted to Islam from pagan idolatry. In other words, no religious adherents nor their ancestors, were originally attached to the religions they hold now.

Many Hindus, Muslims, Jews, Christians, Buddhist, or Sikhs, etc. have hardly read their own scriptures or understand them. This ignorance can incite fervor among co-religionists often provoking the most base, tribal instincts. This holds true for organizations like RSS, who also preached strength, discipline and fierceness in their followers. The inciting activities of the RSS culminated in the1948 assassination of Mahatma Gandhi who they accused of a pro-Muslim stance. He was protesting the destruction of a mosque by Hindu fanatics, he preached Hindu-Muslim unity. He was one of the three rare avatars of peace and non-violence that India had ever produced, the other two being Gautam Buddha and Emperor Asoka. Gandhi was assassinated by Nathuram Godse, a member of Hindu Mahasava and a past member of RSS.

It was against this backdrop of the rise of Hindu nationalism in the 1920s that another counter movement later rose among Muslims. Muslims were fearful that an independent India with majority Hindu population would oppress them as a minority. They believed the only solution was a separate independent homeland of their own. This eventually culminated in the creation of Pakistan in 1947 under the leadership of Muhammad Ali Jinnah.

I may mention here that following the partition of Bengal in 1905, the All India Muslim League was spearheaded and formed in Dhaka under the leadership of Dhaka's Sir Khwaja Salimullah in 1906. Muslim leaders from all over India participated in this event. The Muslim League was instrumental in the creation of Pakistan after Mr. Jinnah assumed leadership of the organization. The Pakistan Resolution (also called Lahore Resolution) was presented by a Bengali leader Mr. A.K. Fazlul Huq in Lahore in 1940 setting the stage for the Pakistan Movement.

Although there were valid reasons for Muslims to seek a new country, the prospect was not thoroughly studied, and its long-term ramifications were not, in my opinion well thought through. The Muslim League led by Mr. Jinnah announced the Direct-Action Day on August 16, 1946 that led to communal riots in Calcutta to prove the two-nation theory as evidence for why Hindus and Muslims must be two separate nations. The new country was created in haste, to get the British colonists out of India in a very politically charged environment. I, however, think the partition of 1947 was problematic. The British were good at partitioning regions under their control in Africa and the Middle East. Here are the reasons why I think the partition was not a good idea.

First, Pakistan was created to encompass two far-flung regions. East and West Pakistan were separated by about 1,000 miles (1,600 kilometers) with the massive geographic and political entity of India in the middle. People of the east and west, shared a race and were longtime cohabitants of the subcontinent and co-religionists but they had different languages, customs, traditions, cultures, dress, and food habits.

These distinctions, in the setting of a new, post-partition political order, were bound to be the downfall of Pakistan, as was demonstrated later in 1971. A merciless and bloody civil war took place, in which the Pakistani army adopted a scorched earth policy. The army's indiscriminate killing of fellow Muslims and of Hindus, catalyzed a strong sense of Bengali nationalism. It also left a lasting scar on the Bangladeshi history and psyche, as evidenced in the literature, media, and culture of Bangladesh. I would also argue that Mr. Jinnah's two-nation theory was inherently flawed since if religion was a criterion for nationality, then language could easily be another. In fact, the two nations of Pakistan and Bangladesh were created primarily on the basis of language.

Second, a massive economic disparity was entrenched from the outset. West Pakistan got mostly arid and barren lands, deserts, hills and unproductive mountains. East Pakistan got low-lying cyclone- and flood-prone squelchy lands. India on the other hand, got territory that was productive, arable, resource rich and they were bequeathed the industrial heartland.

Third, both East and West Pakistan got the downstream portions of the major rivers. This would allow India to control the supply of river water that constituted a lifeline to Pakistani citizens, as became painfully clear later.

Fourth, most of the Islamic cultural and historical centers were in Delhi and Agra and the ownership of these places fell entirely in Hindu India's domain. Muslims thus being a small minority in India became powerless to retain control of their own history, architectural assets and cultural hubs, thereby relegating the remarkable contributions of Islam in India to the partitioned Hindu-majority India.

Fifth, Muslims in the subcontinent were fragmented, and the Muslims left behind in Hindu majority India became an even much smaller minority with little influence on Indian politics. A proper conception for a separate Muslim homeland, should have included all Muslims, a prospect that was improbable, if not impossible, given the volume of population distributed in the vast geography in question.

Sixth, partition created a problem of princely states like Hyderabad and Jammu & Kashmir. Kashmiris are still agitating for freedom and the exercise of their right to self-determination. This problem has also caused another layer of bitter enmity between India and Pakistan that continues to this day. The hasty decision to leave the fate of Kashmir unclear has led to consequences that continue to reverberate today. The cost is in people's lives, progress and democratic aspirations.

Seventh, during the partition in 1947 massive communal riots and casualties were suffered among the Hindus, Muslims, and Sikhs creating intense hatred and generational religious and ethnic tension. Moreover, the partition resulted in the largest mass migration in history among the communities, most enduring unspeakable miseries along the way. The list can go on.

The opposing viewpoint is that the creation and independence of Pakistan in 1947, have benefited the people of both countries in terms of education, job opportunities, and social uplift compared to the Muslims in India. This is so despite the political turmoil, the failure to establish a legible liberal democracy with strong opposition parties in both Pakistan and Bangladesh.

Some argue that in a united India the economy and political power would be in Hindu hands and the subjugated Muslims who were less educated than Hindus would never thrive. However, I doubt if this is true. In the long run, with about 40 per cent Muslims making up the combined population of India, Pakistan, and Bangladesh at this time, Muslims would constitute a very large voting bloc. Moreover, the strong military in the Muslim heartland that is now Pakistan would have a dominant role in a united India. However, this is an analysis of water under the bridge. Decisions taken, cannot now be undone. Establishing lasting peace in the region depends on current political action and will.

One way to create a united Subcontinent is for India to allow self-determination to Kashmiris. This will eliminate the main point of contention and remove bitterness and enmity with Pakistan. After that, the countries are free to forge ahead to create a friendly rapport in the subcontinent because of the reduction of tension. I recognize that at the moment, this seems like wishful thinking or merely a pipe dream. Exacerbating the issue, the Indian government has removed the special autonomous status of Kashmir as of August 6, 2019 as I write this, making a resolution even more hard to come by. I must admit that looking at the Hindu nationalist government's present activities and mistreatment of the Muslim minority in India, a perpetual tension between these two communities is likely and the unified India of 1947 in some form is now unthinkable.

As a child I grew up in Patuakhali, a small coastal town, surrounded by rivers where there was no electricity and no automobiles. The only travel route to Dhaka was by water. We didn't have much of modern-day amenities, and technologically, we were far behind other developed countries. There was no television in those days. I used to stay outdoors playing with my friends and I kept close touch with the outside world through reading. Life was so simple. From the newspapers and books that I read at home and later in Dhaka during my college and professional years I knew in a cursory way about America and the West. I knew about the Cold War between America and the Soviet Union.

While living in Dhaka I always kept abreast of news and world events. A number of important events took place in the 1960s before my departure for Canada. I read about Russian astronaut Yuri Gagarin's first orbiting in the space in 1961. President John F. Kennedy spearheaded the moon landing program by U.S. astronauts. We got a TV for the first time in our student dorm in Dhaka in 1964. In December 1968 three U.S. astronauts with their Apollo 8 mission ventured out to the moon and became the first human beings to orbit 10 times around our nearest heavenly neighbor. A picture was taken of the moon's surface with a TV

camera and beamed to viewers below on earth. A beautiful picture, the "Earthrise," of our blue planet was also taken.

A "giant step for mankind" was taken by American astronaut Neil Armstrong in July 1969 in the Apollo 11 mission which
landed allowing him to walk on the moon. As a young man I
admired from a distance this unusual achievement by America.
In January 1968 the Viet Cong began the massive Tet Offensive
that killed 35,000 on both sides. Three other major events took
place in the same year. In April Rev. Martin Luther King was
assassinated and in June Senator Bobby Kennedy was assassinated. I was wondering about what was going on in that country.
The Soviet military tanks rolled into Czechoslovakia in July.

During my childhood and subsequent years in Dhaka, I witnessed continuous political instability and turmoil in Pakistan
that made me believe my grown-up countrymen couldn't manage the challenges of a new country. The most tragic event that
I recall and that I mentioned before was the killing of some protesters and bystanders by the police in Dhaka on February 21,
1952 when they were peacefully demonstrating against the imposition of Urdu as the only national language of Pakistan. Most
Bengalis loved their own poetic and rich language and didn't
know or speak Urdu. The Pakistani authorities misread the Bengali mind and committed the fatal mistake of carrying out this
violence against peaceful demonstrators. Bengalis in East Pakistan started to realize that West Pakistanis were strange bedfel-
lows despite their common faith, upon which the new country
was founded.

Then came the economic exploitation and exclusion of Bengalis in political positions and in the bureaucracy that made the
Bengalis feel that they were essentially being colonized by the
West Pakistanis. Shortly after leaving my country for Canada in
1970 the Pakistanis committed the second fatal mistake of carry-

ing out a large-scale massacre of Bengalis. That not only created the new country of Bangladesh but also a lasting contempt for Pakistan in the Bengali mind. Pakistan has still not apologized for its past actions.

The lesson from the above is that people forming a significant population of a country cannot be ruled against their wishes. They will soon come to resent and rightfully reject, the economic, political, and socio-cultural exploitation and disparity. Rule of force, guns on their necks may work for a while but not in the long run in an age of information and consciousness of the human right to self-determination.

I will now turn my attention to America, my country now. I wish to begin by concisely delving into a bit of America's formative history, the way I did for Bangladesh. I don't need to get into too many details as America is a relatively new and well-known country with a short history and plenty of well-recorded information is available in the literature and likely known to most readers.

The earliest colonial settlements were by the Spanish, French, Dutch, and the British. In 1620 the Pilgrims who wanted to practice their faith in freedom made a famous voyage from England in a ship called the *Mayflower* to escape from the National Church of England. They established the Plymouth Colony in New England. These people were puritanical in their religious views and are known as Puritans. The Puritan migration was comprised mainly of entire families, and the way of life they established in the colonies was marked by intense devotion.

More Europeans started arriving after that. The nomadic Native Americans didn't pay much attention to this initially as there was abundant vacant land and the Europeans cleared the forests to settle. Often, they even aided the settlers. However, the colonists had mixed feelings about the "primitive" natives. Conquest was in the back of their minds. Eventually after many wars and battles the heroic but poorly armed natives were vanquished.

Prevailing against the British, after the Revolutionary War of independence, on July 4, 1776, the Americans under the leadership of George Washington and other founding fathers composed a constitution that came into force in 1789. It remains the most notable American document till now and forms the basis of the supreme law of the country. Other important documents in connection with the constitution are *The Federalist Papers* consisting of 85 essays written by James Madison, Alexander Hamilton and John Jay. It was published in 1788. The authors of this document wanted to influence voters to ratify the constitution. These essays portray some of the fundamental premises of the constitution and reflect the intellectual depth and vision of the authors, with insight about how the new country should be governed.

The Trans-Atlantic slave trade was rampant in those days. A significant event of American history was the American Civil War fought during 1861 to 1865 between the north and the south in which the secessionist Southern Confederate states of the Union were defeated by the northern Federalist Army. This happened during the presidency of Abraham Lincoln who led the nation during the war and issued the Emancipation Proclamation on January 1, 1863. By this proclamation the slaves of the Confederate states were freed. However, the war continued until 1865.

Later, the process of racial segregation was enforced in southern states by way of Jim Crow laws enforced at the state and local level in the late 19th and early 20th centuries. The laws expanded to some states in the north. Following the Civil Rights Movement in 1964 president Lyndon B. Johnson signed the Civil Rights Act which ended Jim Crow laws. Although these laws officially ended, the racial tension due to disparity between whites and blacks still prevails today in many sectors of the American society.

Lincoln was assassinated in April 1865. He remains the most revered American president domestically and around the world. A series of assassinations took place a century later first with the assassination of President John F. Kennedy in November 1963, Malcolm X in 1965, and Rev. Martin Luther King Jr. in April 1968, and Senator Robert F. Kennedy in June 1968. In March 1981 President Reagan survived an assassination attempt. Mass shootings and gun violence have been commonplace in America.

During my half a century of living in North America, four decades in the U.S., I have developed a perspective for this country but have never lost sight of Bangladesh. Present-day Bangladesh is quite different now from when I left the country. The population has swelled from 70 million in 1971 to about 170 million and Dhaka has become a megacity. Greater Dhaka has about 20 million people. Despite the large population of the country, surprisingly, there is hardly any starvation. People are healthier, wealthier, more educated, and better dressed. U.S. Secretary of State Henry Kissinger called Bangladesh in 1974 a "a bottomless basket" when Bangladesh as a new country was experiencing its growing pains. He was wrong and clearly underestimated the Bangladeshis, who were intelligent and hardworking people. The GDP growth rate is about 7 per cent at this writing. Use of digital technology is commonplace. As part of the geopolitical environment in Asia, Bangladesh is on the move economically. The NGOs, remittance by Bangladeshis from overseas, rise of private entrepreneurship, and the intelligence and drive of the people have all contributed to the economic development.

In addition to numerous colleges, there are about 40 public and 100 private universities in Bangladesh with varying degrees of academic standards. In the health sector there are a few thousand hospitals and clinics although the quality of service varies dramatically. The country has electricity in rural areas; and all cities, towns and villages are well connected through extensive communication networks and infrastructure.

Bangladesh has initiated numerous world-class innovations: microcredit, oral rehydration in the treatment of diarrhea, an effective set of cooperatives in managing electrical power in rural areas, etc. Despite all the strides Bangladesh has made there exists major income inequality. There are 28 television channels and numerous newspapers and magazines in the country. Most people have mobile telephones and many people use the social media. At this writing, Padma River Bridge, the largest project that Bangladesh has ever undertaken is under construction. When completed, it will provide a direct link between the central and southwestern regions of the country and facilitate the socio-economic and industrial development of the region inhabited by over 30 million people.

Notwithstanding the above, Dhaka, the political, economic, and cultural nerve center of the country, remains an unsustainable city out of balance. Traffic gridlock in the streets continues to be unbearable despite the construction of a few flyovers. I discussed this issue in some detail in a previous chapter. At present an overhead metro rail is under construction from Uttara to Motijeel. The city's infrastructure is also inadequate to cater to the needs of the increasing population of this megacity. Sanitation remains a major problem. Uncontrolled construction of buildings causes problems of light and air and is a grave concern for public health and safety. Fire regulations for buildings are rampantly disobeyed resulting in frequent deaths from fire events. Slums can be seen all around in the city. A major problem is the absence of concentrations of decentralized economic hubs in other cities and townships. People from different places of the country continue to migrate to Dhaka as the only main hub for employment opportunities.

While Bangladesh has advanced economically, on the political front the country is in a state of what I call unstable stability. Following the assassination of Bangabandhu Sheikh Mujibur Rahman, the founding father of the new nation, Major Ziaur Rahman took over the leadership after a period of turmoil and instability. Sheikh Mujibur Rahman had introduced a one-party rule by his newly created party called Bakshal, leading to his assassination by a group of disillusioned military personnel and their cohorts. Ziaur Rahman brought stability and framed a new constitution. After President Ziaur Rahman was assassinated, General Muhammad Ershad staged a coup and became the new ruler. This clearly demonstrated the new country had been experiencing growing pains.

Once President Ershad was ousted by a popular movement, democracy was established and Begum Khaleda Zia of BNP (Bangladesh Nationalist Party), the party founded by President Ziaur Rahman, was elected. After that, power was held by Begum Zia, wife of deceased Ziaur Rahman and Sheikh Hasina, daughter of deceased Sheikh Mujibur Rahman by rotation but with considerable bickering by both parties. I may add here that because of lack of trust and possible voter fraud, at the behest of Awami League, Bangladesh introduced a new concept of a neutral caretaker government comprised of technocrats who would assure free and fair elections.

Such a short-term government was in place in 1996 and 2001 to considerable success. Because of political turmoil and disagreements between the Awami League and BNP, particularly when BNP was trying to set up its own partisans in the caretaker government, a temporary caretaker government backed by the

Army was installed in 2006 that lasted until 2008. Sheikh Hasina and her Awami League party won the elections that year with a majority in the parliament, and expectations were high that, finally, the country would establish democratic practices.

That didn't, however, happen. The Awami League party who wanted such a caretaker government before annulled the provision of such a government by a constitutional amendment in 2011. The major opposition party, BNP protested and made a wrong strategic decision to boycott the forthcoming 2014 elections and staged a violent movement that resulted in several casualties making the party unpopular.

This offered Awami League an opportunity to take full control of the election process. Sheikh Hasina asked Khaleda Zia to stop the violence and invited her to a dinner. It didn't work out as Khaleda Zia showed indifference. Then Sheikh Hasina offered to form a joint interim government with both Awami League and BNP people while remaining as the Prime Minister. That did not go well for BNP because of its distrust of the Awami League. As BNP boycotted the election, the Awami League took advantage of this situation and easily won the election by default and acclamation.

In the 2018 election in which BNP participated under the umbrella of *Oikko Front* (United Front) led by Dr. Kamal Hossain, Awami League received 96 per cent of the electoral votes, an election that many have criticized as fraught with irregularities and widespread voter fraud. The opposition leader Begum Zia was incarcerated on charges of corruption before the election and a large number of the BNP members and activists were also allegedly put in jail. Awami League is now in near-total control of the country's destiny. The 2014 and 2018 elections have resulted in the obscurity of the political opposition.

BNP had their own problems of miscalculation. The danger now is that there is no accountability for the ruling party which is troubling as the maxim goes: absolute power corrupts absolutely. It is hard to forecast when a liberal democracy with a strong opposition party will return to the country unless a sudden mass upheaval takes place in the future. This is sad as so many Bengalis sacrificed their lives and limbs to gain independence from Pakistan. They hold aspirations of achieving a democratic and secular society where people can vote freely and choose their leaders. The Bangladeshi Dream of achieving the Golden Bengal thus remains to be realized. If the ruling Awami League can turn Bangladesh into the promised Golden Bengal during its rule over a long period, the party will create a legacy allowing people to ignore its political faults.

A recent happening affecting Bangladesh has been the forcible eviction of Rohingya Muslims from their homeland in the Rakhine province of Myanmar where they form a majority. The Myanmar military burnt their homes, set babies on fire, raped women, and terrorized people until they fled from their homes. The Myanmar government evicted them before, and Bangladesh gave them shelter, but this time it was unabashed ethnic cleansing. The government of Myanmar inspired by some fanatic Buddhist monks continued their persecution of the Rohingyas claiming that they belonged to Bangladesh as their ancestors migrated from there many centuries ago.

Lately, the Rohingyas have been stripped of their citizenship making them stateless. The oppressed Rohingyas started an insurgency in response to these unjust actions of the Myanmar authorities. Using this as a pretext, the Myanmar government executed its plan of perpetrating horrific atrocities and forced expulsion of about one million Rohingyas who migrated en masse to neighboring Bangladesh in 2017. The government of Bangladesh accepted them on humanitarian grounds and put them in camps near Cox's Bazar, a coastal town in Chittagong.

Bangladesh's response to this tragedy was rather tepid other than calling it a genocide, but no complaint of genocide was lodged to the International Criminal Court for war crimes. Diplomatic efforts are continuing. When under pressure by the international community, using that old tactic Myanmar promises to take back many of the migrants but never implements it by dragging its feet. The stalemate continues.

⊷⊶

I will now focus on present-day America. Clearly, it has greatly changed since I migrated to this country in 1980 after living in Canada for 10 years. This is undoubtedly a great country with diverse landscapes, races, ethnicities, religions, and more. It has been a beacon of hope offering successful career and job opportunities for aspiring and hardworking people from around the world. Despite many setbacks in its political and economic history, surprisingly, America has always bounced back showing the resilience of its citizens. The country is fortunate to have a large mass of land, abundant natural resources, and a skilled talent pool drawn from all around the world.

At this time when I am writing this, a few things have happened on the political front. A two-year investigation under special counsel Robert Mueller wrapped up about any possible conspiracy and collusion between Russia and the current President Donald Trump. There were questions brought up during the presidential election of 2016 about the possibility of obstruction of justice. In 2016 election Hillary Clinton, Democrat, won the popular vote by over three million more votes, but Trump, Republican, defeated her through gaining more electoral votes. Mueller's report was ambiguous and inconclusive in that it didn't clearly recommend any action for any possible wrongdoing. Of course, Mueller didn't have the authorization to do it as he explained. This gave rise to partisan politics. At this writing, the House with a majority of Democrats who took control of the House in the 2018 midterm election, has impeached President Trump following an impeachment enquiry regarding his attempt to influence the 2020 U.S. election in his favor with the help of a foreign country, Ukraine. This has led to a confrontational situation between the White House and the Congress. Since the Senate is controlled by Republican majority, he was promptly acquitted by the Senate by partisan votes without holding a formal trial.

Another recent crisis is at the U.S.-Mexico border where migrants have been trying to enter America from Central American countries to escape from poverty, violence, and utter instability. America mostly had generally a humane and open-door policy for asylum seekers and immigrants. But currently there is a concerted movement, promoted by some nationalists against immigration. The country has become very polarized and divided. This is not a good sign for the country's future. The present government has gradually withdrawn from world affairs including from the international climate change pact. Gun violence is widespread and there are no strict gun control laws for criminal background checks before purchase. The two major parties, the Democratic and Republican, have major policy differences about tax cuts, abortion, same-sex marriage, climate change, gun control, health care, size of government, immigration, etc. The country's deepening polarization along racial, religious, socio-cultural, and economic lines is continuing. Resentment against immigrants and people of color stoked by political opportunists is on the rise. Polarization is however not new in American history and hopefully this present cycle of polarization will also pass.

The country has a well-thought-out political system and a great constitution, as well as strong governing institutions. These are what allow the U.S. to enjoy the stability it has. Despite this, I have a few misgivings. As I see it, the President has too much power. If a president behaves erratically and abuses power, it could be a major problem for the country, as it is very difficult to remove him/her. The provision of impeachment of the president could be divisive and needs bipartisan support, which is generally difficult as often politicians vote along party lines without considering their conscience. The real threat to constitution may come from an abusive, demagogic and despotic President aided by large masses of supporters following his divisive rhetoric and by his own party. Such a President can overrule the constitution exploiting its loopholes and become a despotic leader with devastating consequences. The present safeguard in the constitution in my opinion is not enough to stop it.

The electoral college, which essentially ratifies the election results, is based on electoral votes rather than popular votes; this is another problem. In recent times George W. Bush won over Al Gore and Donald Trump won over Hillary Clinton by securing 270 electoral votes although the losers earned more popular votes. Democratic elections should be based on one person one vote.

In my opinion the judiciary should be totally independent, but it isn't quite so. This is particularly critical for the Supreme Court where the justices often hold liberal or conservative views and are likely to apply their personal bias rather than remaining neutral and objective in delivering their judgment. The Supreme Court that is the ultimate decider of all judicial cases and controversies should be free from politics and the justices should not necessarily be loyal to the Republican or Democratic President who nominated them. Also, the justices should have term limits even though these limits can be long to avoid frequent turnovers.

The limits of free expression are not well defined in the First Amendment leaving room for hateful, inciting, irresponsible, and tasteless expressions. The original intent of the framers centuries ago regarding the Second Amendment, needs reexamination under present-day circumstances of frequent gun violence and mass killings of innocent people using advanced and destructive weapons.

Humans have not found a better system than democracy to establish freedom and assurance of citizens' rights. Its competitor is absolute rule in the form of dictatorship, authoritarianism, or shall I say strongmanship, that seems to be spreading globally at this time. These are not great days for democracy as the United Nations and regional alliances have been weakening. Books like *How Democracy Ends* by David Runciman and *Fascism: A Warning* by former U.S. Secretary of State Madeleine Albright highlight a pessimistic future. Chances are that there are more dictators and autocrats waiting in the wings. Some countries have illiberal democracy that is virtually authoritarianism in disguise. Absolute rule suppresses institutional growth and freedom of press and media and is unsustainable in the long run.

Democracy has shortcomings too though and this applies to all countries of the world. The democratic process is messy by nature where group decisions are needed, and this often leads to chaos, deadlock and delay. For less stable countries people lose patience with bickering politicians and want strong and decisive leaders, thus paving the path for invasive strongmen promising stability as well as quick and decisive corrections. Regarding democracy, I have a few doubts. I believe the world community has not still devised a perfectly functional system to run a government. It is ultimately the quality of the people that can make democracy work. With the current age of uncontrolled internet and social media platforms, as well as partisan television and media, democracy has become even more weak. Admittedly, there is no better system at present than democracy, but in addition to being untidy it has its other faults. There are many shapes and forms of democracy that must fit socio-economic as well as cultural norms and traditions of a country. It is not a fool-proof system. Here are some of the problems of democracy as I see it:

- It is subject to manipulation -- people's biases or emotions to be specific -- when they vote. Many times, voters make decisions without analyzing the whole political system believing in the candidates based on their charisma, looks, demagoguery, and promises rather than judging them by substance. In general voters like strong candidates with clarity, conviction and a mission -- whether right or wrong. With rare exceptions, political candidates are motivated by their longing for power and self-interest rather than for helping the people. Even sincere ones who want to help people, seem corrupted by power and are influenced by the political environment around them. They get addicted to power and privilege. They become like other politicians in the prevailing political climate. Political stagnation continues.

- Most voters vote blindly on the basis of party policies, association or loyalty to their party rather than whether a candidate is the best fit to be in power. Thus, voters really belong to political tribes and vote without being objective or using their conscience and sensible judgment. This happens because primitive tribal nature is an inherent instinct in humans.

- Politicians in power vilify opponents to undermine them. Democracy does not work when the main opposition party is weak and hence their criticism of the ruling party does not matter to the stronger ruling party. This discourages negotiation and conciliation and encourages unilateralism.

- When a party is in power and has a majority in the legislative assembly the political leader becomes authoritarian. They are surrounded by self-seeking cronies and oligarchs and end up behaving like a monarch or dictator without making efforts to compromise with opposing viewpoints. In this case there are no checks and balances on power. Free expression and institutional development are suppressed. Democracy, the nemesis of authoritarianism, is thus vulnerable to fail in achieving its true spirit.

At present democracy is not achieving its highest ideals, as it should, in most countries. Nationalism/nativism, identity politics leading to racial, religious, and ethnic tension, as well as authoritarianism are gripping the world. Having said that, America has always remained a marketplace of ideas and still is. The country remains the beacon of hope for the world. The democratic ideal established by the founding fathers continues to remain high despite occasional lapses. The democratic practice, however, needs periodic review and updating. In today's America many millennials are losing faith in capitalism and drifting towards "democratic socialism."

Another issue gripping the world today is climate change. A majority of scientists have, for decades, recognized that the earth's atmosphere is heating up, resulting in climate change and humans are causing it. Already arctic ice caps are melting due to the warming of ocean water and with more warming we may see the catastrophic effects of climate change on the planet including the inundation of low-lying and island nations and the destruction of world's coral reefs and other delicate habitats. People worldwide notice a shift in known climate patterns. Young activists have begun to raise their concerns as they will be the potential victims of the consequences of climate change. However, the rift between the two major political parties in America means that even this scientifically sound truth, falls along party lines.

⊷⊶

America was built on immigration from other countries and is very culturally diverse in many cities. The original Native American culture has been re-shaped by the English who first colonized, by Africans slaves, Latin Americans, Asians and migrants from all over the world. The country is truly a melting pot to which different cultures have added their own distinct flavors. The people who have come from all over continue to shape the country in important ways. Generations of American-born citizens, with immigrant roots, are vital contributors to the fabric of this country.

Interestingly, as many immigrants have influenced the American culture, American culture has also been exported to other countries, whether in clothing, fashion, food, English language, music, television shows, movies, and more. The exchange has been facilitated mostly by globalization, but also by connections between families living in different countries. For example, Valentine's Day on February 14, which was obscure elsewhere, is now celebrated in most countries in various forms. In Bangladesh they call it *Bhalobasha Dibosh* or Love Day. And Mother's Day and Father's Day are called *Ma Dibosh* and *Baba Dibosh*, respectively. The American TV show "American Idol" has been and continues to be imitated in different forms and settings on local televisions worldwide. In Bangladesh when people talk in Bengali, a large number of English words are unwittingly interspersed in the conversation.

One thing I truly love about America is the ingenuity and innovative quality of the people. Science and technology have been flourishing here since the days of America's industrialization in the 19th century and following World War II technology has been thriving rapidly giving rise to many inventions. The digital revolution, artificial intelligence (AI), internet, and a host of other technological advances have been rooted and developed here and have impacted the entire world. The rapid proliferation of technology in every field and how it impacts the society begs a serious debate. America fosters innovations and is at the forefront of most of the recent ones in science and technology, and the rest of the world keeps up or follows suit.

I have strong feelings about technology that usually originates from America and the rapidly expanding role it plays worldwide. People who are against technology, but use it anyway, feel that it is leading us to a superficial and unnatural life. They feel it has created murderous monsters like war machines and weapons of mass destruction. Technology in the form of automation and robotics will be responsible for the rise of unemployment, although it has not happened yet. They argue that industrialization has caused global warming and threatens impending human disaster and that technology is tampering with the natural environment and ecosystem. Humans are playing god by making test tube babies, cloning, and genetic engineering and modifications of plants, animals and people.

On the other hand, people who are for technology, argue that technology is helping us in many ways. Medical technologies help cure and treat diseases, unthinkable a few decades ago. They are increasing longevity and improving the quality of life. Use of AI and nanotechnology has many possibilities in the medical field. Apple developed a watch that can monitor our heart with an instant ECG. Similar devices by tech companies are wireless blood pressure monitor, Bluetooth-enabled glucose monitor, and others.

Renewable energy technologies and clean coal technology for sequestering greenhouse gases can reduce global warming and hence mitigate the adverse effects of climate change. In the agricultural field, genetically modified crops are increasing crop production and saving millions from starvation. Development of educational technology has allowed more lessons to be taught in classrooms and has facilitated online distance learning. Skype has allowed distance video communication.

Other benefits are in the area of transit and navigation/GPS technologies. Satellite technologies have been applied in many areas of communication. In the area of communication, the internet has revolutionized the world. Wireless applications, information technology (IT), the mobile phone with all its apps allows us the benefit in ways too long to list. Banking has become easier and faster. Bills can be paid online. In my own professional field, the construction of long span bridges and supertall and megatall skyscrapers has been possible due to many technological applications in design, construction, and monitoring. Frequently, I feel I am living in a totally different world than the world I lived in before I left my native homeland.

I feel the proliferation of technology is a blessing, as life has become easier on many fronts. We can travel faster, communicate instantly, carry out fast business transactions from a distance, get better medical care; we can enjoy recreation at home and with the internet can get access to countless pieces of information. We have now driverless cars, home security systems and monitoring from a distance, and other incremental improvements to mobile phones with each passing day. All we need to connect with the rest of the world are a laptop computer and a smart phone, a device invented by Steve Jobs, who put the technology in the palm of our hands. He was an American, the biological son of a Syrian man, and founder of Apple. We live in a world of tech giants like Facebook, Twitter, Instagram, Snapchat, Google, Bing, Uber, Airbnb, Xoom, to name a few.

But then it is also a curse as we are getting more and more immersed and lost in man-made technology. We are in danger of losing physical touch and the simple human chemistry between one another. I recall a wedding ceremony that Dora and I attended, sharing the table with a professor, his wife, two daughters, and a son. At one point I noticed all five of them were looking at something on their mobile phones.

The internet has been instrumental in promoting pornography worldwide, corrupting society. The social media platforms like Facebook, Instagram, Snapchat and Twitter have inherent privacy concerns and many cultural problems including broken marriages, extortion, crimes, mass killings, political turmoil, misinformation, radical ideologies, hate speech and trolling are rampant. Online platforms despite their many benefits can promote extremism, hatred, bigotry, racial and religious tension, conspiracies, fake news and create global social chaos. They lead to social and political polarization, populism and extremist nationalism. We don't have any privacy anymore as our uncontrolled internet use is captured, stroke for stroke, on multiple databases.

Cyber hacking is another major problem. We become victims of online scams and the activities of the Dark Web. It's an untamed beast that can't be controlled. Many people make the case that social media platforms like Facebook, Twitter, etc. are addictive, particularly for millennials. For all these negativities, though, technologies can't alone be blamed. Discretion is up to the users.

Young kids are busy with their iPads, mobile phones, and video games that make them self-absorbed. Throughout my many road trips, I would look up the road atlas and follow the map. In a city I would look at landmarks to locate places. When I saw a cluster of tall buildings, I knew this must be the city's downtown. I used my brain to think, navigate and orient myself to the place I was in. I engaged my analytical skills, power of observation and imagination. Now, GPS tells me where to go and when I have arrived at my destination.

For music lovers like me music tapes are gone, even CDs are on their way out; now songs can be downloaded off the internet. VCRs are extinct and have been replaced by DVDs. Parents have a difficult time raising their children in this age of social media, YouTube, Google, Facebook, etc. and undesirable television shows. The list can go on. We are becoming human robots enslaved by technology instead of making technology our slave. Technology is dumbing society down. Or, does it? Proponents of technology assert that it is making us smarter, and our thinking process is faster and more efficient. Things can be argued both ways. But this is the world we live in. This brings me to the next questions.

Where are we heading with our technology? What is the future of technology? I believe we will see more wars over ideas for innovations. Advances in medical, agricultural and biological sciences and technologies are ongoing. Space technology and space travel will increase and additional advances in communication technology are expected. Humans will find new sources of energy. America will likely take the lead in these. I predict America will be the vanguard of most future innovations. Based on what I have witnessed during the last few decades I can't fully imagine what the world will be like a few decades from now. I for sure am living in a different world. I can't entirely foresee the future. What I can imagine is that humans will change because of advances in computer technology and engineering achievements. It is hard for me to know anything beyond now as the pace of technological change is dizzying. It is also hard to predict which side will win the debate, for or against technological proliferation. Some other questions are:

- Will technology result in social good or ill?
- Will technology really dehumanize and dumb down society?
- How do we balance our best hopes and worst fears?
- How do we prevent eventual self-destruction of mankind?

These are difficult to answer as no one has a crystal ball. But I believe that open-minded and secular approaches, however praiseworthy they may be, can't ultimately offer solutions to the moral and ethical dilemmas of technological societies. Only moral values and a belief system under Divine Guidance, can help us distinguish right from wrong.

The future depends upon how technology is used. It can be used for benevolence or abused for social ills and degradation impacting everyone in this globalized world. Technology itself is not evil and can't be blamed for anything. It can make society better, smarter and more efficient if used properly. In the final analysis, mankind will determine the outcome of technological proliferation. If excessively used or abused and unconditionally relied upon, it will dumb down society. I shudder to think that even our minds and bodies could be modified in the future through genetic engineering. The day when technology will surpass human ingenuity and interaction will be a sad day, and the world will have a generation of people imprisoned by technology. To avert this, a defensible boundary must be drawn between beneficial and harmful uses of technologies.

We must avoid playing god as science and technology don't guarantee the future. Technology will continue to advance but values and ethical guidelines must be established to protect the human race. We must recognize that humans are inherently infirm and weak and have little or no power against the infinite forces of Nature. We humans are creative and resilient, but also can be violent towards others and therefore self-destructive. Our destiny depends upon our own responsible behavior. The ruling elite, politicians, and corporate profiteers, who control and determine social outcome, bear a great responsibility. Therefore, people must be enlightened and vigilant, and elect strong, good, sensible and wise politicians who value the democratic process instead of intellectually hollow demagogues with Machiavellian mindsets. Democracy is the best system humans have devised for political governance, but it is not a panacea for society's wellbeing unless it is cherished and nurtured, and citizens are watchful.

⋙⋘

This book was conceived as my life's account, covering the events and experiences of my life from East and the West, while I have maintained a connection to both sides of the ocean. I have put my thoughts in this book to the extent that is possible, as candidly as possible revealing a lot about myself. I recognize my own imperfections and have dealt with those in other people. I have learned that nobody is likely to take care of my interest unless I do it myself. Others are often motivated by their self-interests. True selflessness is rare.

In the East I learned more about my duties. In the West I have learned more about my rights.

At school we are not taught about our dealings with the opposite sex, children, nor human relationship skills or financial planning, so, we have to learn these from the occasional hard knocks of life. Like history, our life follows its own course despite our plans. The earth is an unstable planet geologically, socially, economically, and politically. The strong want to control and subjugate the weak. The poor and the weak often suffer at the hands of the rich and powerful. Most people are impressed by the powerful and wealthy, instead of the wise and those with impeccable character. Most people admire the strength and ferocity of lions and tigers above all the animals in the world, even though they are killers and they lord over the other animals.

If you belong to a minority community in any country, you are disadvantaged; you better be on good terms with the majority. You alienate them at your own peril. I noticed that while Bangladeshi culture encourages too much reliving of the past, the Americans on the other hand, like to forge ahead often, quickly.

People love winners and the losers are forgotten fast everywhere. Winners and those in power control and determine the course of history and the way it is portrayed. What I find intriguing is that history eventually follows its own course, like a river. Historians analyze past events, but many are biased. History is what a historian thinks, with prejudgment and not necessarily based on reality or what was. Of course, there are rare exceptions.

Knowledge of history is essential to make political judgments. One has to study history objectively to understand the past and present and extrapolate the future. Reading history written by different historians helps us see opposing views to determine the truth. History itself is not judgmental, people are. Many people love rumormongering and conspiracy theories. They love myths and not truths. They quickly judge people outwardly. They love quickly negating others without trying to understand any opposing views. This is why there are so many sects and divisions in every religion and other spheres of life. They are driven by their own desire rather than reason.

Partisanship in politics leads to subjective assessments of a political platform and people blindly follow. People should have different viewpoints. But when people get addicted to excessive partisanship, they demonize the opposition, and show blind loyalty to their own party. They show disdain for the opposite party without thinking rationally and become entrenched in polarization and society suffers. This is true for both Bangladesh and America and for the entire world at large. A country's leadership ultimately determines if the nation will rot away or achieve prominence. To elect the right political leaders, people need to educate themselves with an open mind and use good judgment. If they end up getting bad leaders who only care for themselves and people of their own party and not for all citizens, a country will inevitably become unstable and degraded.

Finally, I have thought of myself as a citizen of the world, but I also think of myself as a tiny living being in our galaxy and by extension the universe. I have always wondered about the God of Creation and Life and how to connect to Him more frequently rather than rarely. I have realized that when people leave this world, they are forgotten except a few who have made a big impact. What we do with our time, for ourselves and others on the planet, matters to us now, not when we join the countless others who have departed this world. In fact, accountability of our earthly actions in the afterlife is on a personal basis. I, like many others, of course believe in afterlife, but it is a belief without any proof. Nobody has returned from that world to tell the living what it is like. Without the religious explanation of the Higher Power, I can't find any real meaning and enduring purpose in life. I am thankful to God and my parents who brought me into this world. I am glad I have lived in this world so far with all its joys, fears, occasional setbacks, and hopes. I look forward to enjoying my life in this beautiful world for as long as I can.

EPILOGUE

With $20 Canadian cash in my pocket and a beat-up suit-case, I headed across continents and oceans to a start a new life. It has been a complicated ride as it is for most self-starters. I hope my descendants will recount that I was their first Bangladeshi ancestor to set foot on American soil. Because of my life's trek, I paved the way for them toward prosperity and freedom of thought. I saved them the pain of visa applications, deportation threats, and immigration status struggles, gifting them established citizenship.

While I weathered many hardships, the net effect will inevi-tably be a dilution of Bangladeshi heritage and religious adher-ence. We only have influence over the generation directly after our own. Children must contend with the greater society which has dissimilar, if not completely opposing norms and mores. The only way to preserve a culture, heritage or faith practice is if mar-riages take place between individuals who share those in com-mon. I can't picture the demographic of my progeny. But even in as little as one to two generations, minority groups will include children of mixed race, interfaith or no faith at all. This is a reality of immigration to any foreign land. If we stabilized our own home countries and made them livable and economically prosperous, we wouldn't have to face the uncertain cultural future that immigration brings.

With every hard knock and every roadblock, I stayed the course and relied on my faith and determination to pull me through. When I reflect on my life, I realize I became battle-hardened and thick-skinned. The lessons I learned came from a series of uncoordinated events mostly beyond my control. In turn, these led to a series of fateful decisions where sometimes I was proactive and sometimes reactive. I was sent to earth to serve, so I have a couple of regrets in that regard. First, I was not able to take care of my parents during their old age; and second, I wish I could have given more quality time to my children when they were very young, but I was still struggling to establish myself financially and in my career.

It was also the support and mentorship of key individuals who helped me to get to where I am. This was possible because of relationships with several people including teachers, associates, relatives, and friends. Most of all the influence of the following people was paramount in shaping my career: my strong and loving mother Azifa Ali, who implanted in me the value of education and morality. She was ahead of her time. My wise and saintly father Mir Muazzam Ali, whom I consider a gentle giant who taught me humility, honesty and finding a path to pursue my worldly objectives. My oldest brother Dr. Mir Maswood Ali displayed elevated thinking and was an intellectual, and I frequently sought his advice. He would also go out of his way to help others. Dr. Fazlur Rahman Khan, whose magnitude was so undetectable as he was very down to earth. He viewed structural engineering as an art form, and revolutionized tall building design as his legacy; and Dr. Lynn S. Beedle, a Renaissance man, an eternal networker and visionary who founded the Council on Tall Buildings and Urban Habitat (CTBUH). His brainchild CTBUH has flourished into a continuing global force in creating and improving urban life. They are no longer with us, but their memory is etched in my consciousness. Finally, my wife Dora's sustained encouragement and everlasting calm under pressure, secured me in the knowledge that I could overcome life's occasional setbacks. I have also learned from my three children who have occasionally helped me to make decisions and have shown how invaluable they are to me.

My father once said "The world is like a mirror. It laughs when you laugh and cries when you cry." I have experienced this firsthand during blissful and calamitous times. Most of my life events are important not because they forecast my remaining years on earth, but because they offer me a sense of proportion for my present. I judge my present in reference to what I've dealt with before. I see myself as a fusion of East and West.

ACKNOWLEDGMENTS

Following my retirement from the University of Illinois at Urbana-Champaign (UIUC) in 2011, I continued to teach part time until 2015. When I fully concluded my teaching career that year, one day my good friend Dr. Salim Rashid (professor emeritus of Economics at UIUC) asked me, "Now that you have retired, what are you going to do next?" I replied, "I intend to write some books that I have been thinking of for a while." He suggested, "Why don't you write an autobiography?" I didn't respond positively. He noticed that I was not very excited about it and he insisted on his suggestion. I paused and thought to myself: who is going to read my life story other than my children or some relatives and close friends? After all, my children have grown up in my household; if I have experienced or learned anything in my life, I've shared it with them from time to time, that is good enough. A book is not essential to tell them who I am because they know a lot about me already, including my idiosyncrasies, but then again, maybe not everything. The idea of a book started hatching.

Later, my sister-in-law (younger brother's wife) Moshira Ali (Tora), also encouraged the idea. She lived with us in Urbana-Champaign for a few years after the tragic premature death of my younger and dearest brother Dr. Mir Mosaddeq Ali from a massive heart attack. She had dealt with and observed me closely while I cared for her and her two children, one of them was a minor child with special needs, after my brother's death. I told her that I planned to do it after writing another book that I had in mind. She insisted that I should write the autobiography first. Her older son Tarek, a student at the time, who had been living with us then, also suggested the same.

Then one day when I was talking with my brother-in-law Dr. Ehsanes Saleh (my sister's husband and professor emeritus of Statistics at Carleton University, Ottawa, Canada), this topic came up when he asked me what I had been doing in my retired life. When I told him the embryonic thought about writing an autobiography, he gave me a further nudge by saying, "You should prioritize writing this book. As you had a very interesting and struggle filled life in the past, this may be a good example for others who may be striving in their lives. Young people need role models." I thought perhaps there was some truth in it. Without delay I prepared an outline of the book in early 2016 after I moved to Chicago in November 2015 and started writing.

After I finished writing a few chapters my friend Dr. Salim Rashid volunteered to review the chapters. As I finished each new chapter, he reviewed it and thus completed reviewing and offering valuable comments and suggestions on the entire manuscript. Then my friend professor Aminul Karim of DeVry University, Chicago, whom I contacted for his review referred me to Dr. Maris Roze, a professor emeritus of English and author who after reviewing the manuscript offered me some general comments and important suggestions. Dr. Ahmed Khan, another professor, who is a writer and book reviewer, reviewed the entire manuscript thoroughly and made several critical comments. I am grateful to all of them.

Dr. Kyoung Sun Moon, a professor at Yale University and my former student at UIUC helped me with the family tree. Professor Taher Saif (professor of Mechanical Engineering at UIUC) and Dr. Muhammad Al-Faruque (former librarian at UIUC) reviewed a few chapters and offered useful comments. I am thankful to both. I am also thankful to Saadia Shah for copyediting and proofreading the entire manuscript.

My daughter Ifat and nephew Tarek helped me gather some old pictures for this book. My daughter Jinat helped me immensely with editing and collating pictures and offered insightful feedback to enrich my story. Ifat and my son Murad were very helpful in working on the book's publishing process. At the end the book became a family project.

Finally, I am grateful to my dear wife Morsheda Ali (Dora) for allowing me to write this book mainly at night, despite her poor health.

APPENDIX I

MEDIA COVERAGE AFTER 9/11

Here is an incomplete list of interviews that immediately followed this catastrophic event:

- *Daily Illini,* September 11 (published September 12)
- *Chicago Daily Herald,* September 11 (published September 12)
- Illinois Radio Network, Springfield, IL, September 12
- *Chicago Sun Times,* September 11
- Don and Carla Radio Talk Show, San Simon, Arizona, September 12
- *Architectural Record* Magazine, September 13 (published in the October issue)
- *New York Times,* September 14 (quoted in article "Defending Skyscrapers Against Terror," September 18; also, quoted in *AsiaWeek,* September 18)
- *Rickernotes,* School of Architecture, UIUC, September 17 (published September 24)
- UIUC News Bureau, September 17 (posted on UIUC News Website, October 1)
- *Toronto Star,* September 18 (published September 19)

- Space.com (a syndicate of MSNBC), September 18 (posted September 19)
- *Milwaukee Journal Sentinel,* September 24 (published article on World Trade Center and my book on skyscraper, October 7)
- Powderhouse Productions for skyscraper segment of "Engineering the Impossible" of a television program on the Discovery Channel, October 9
- WILL AM Radio, Champaign, IL, October 15 (interview also broadcast on Public Radio International and National Public Radio)

There was some additional coverage of my interview and invited lectures on the topic around that time:

- Feature article "Urge to Build Skyscrapers Will Endure, Scholar Says," *Inside Illinois,* Vol.
- 21, no. 8, October 18, 2001.
- Invited speaker at the book signing event, "Skyscrapers, Technology, Art and a Vision: Insights of an Innovator," Prairie Avenue Bookshop, Chicago, IL, November 14, 2001.
- Invited speaker at the `Know your University' 2002 spring lecture series on "Designing the Impossible in the Aftermath of the World Trade Center Collapse," University YMCA, Champaign, IL, January 29, 2002.

APPENDIX II

50TH WEDDING ANNIVERSARY

During our 50th Wedding Anniversary on March 3, 2018, our second daughter Jinat composed a tribute, my granddaughter Talia framed it and gave it to us as one of the gifts from our three children. It nicely captures my life. Dora and I liked it very much and I reproduce it here.

5 0 G O L D E N Y E A R S

March 3rd, 1968
A day we celebrate
A definitive event took place
The Union of our parents by God's grace
Their story began in faraway Patuakhali
Two fathers, both juris docs, were colleagues
Negotiated terms of the betrothal
As they were both prominent families in Barisal

Mother, a stunning beauty, noted for her looks
Hailed from a clan of well-renowned cooks
Father was brilliant and set his sights on a PhD
This landed him overseas

You can well call their story "dreamers"
Immigrants who planted roots far from their birth country
Welcomed by the Home of the Brave and the Land of the Free
In a distant culture with foreign values
Yet to themselves they remained true
Maintaining their identity and beliefs too

A family further bonded them
First came Ifat, then Jinat and a much wished for Murad
The birth of the baby boy
Brought the family so much joy
While dad advanced his career at rapid pace
Mom dedicated herself to keep her children safe
Cleaning up day after day and toiling over a stove
The aroma of amazing dishes was our home sweet home
Mom is a culinary master like no other
Our family was well fed, both sisters and brother
Mom's exquisite meals define our childhood
Just an evening math session with dad would

Our family lived through moves from Canada to Asia to Cham-
    paign
The pinnacle of Dad's career shaped there, to much acclaim
The University of Illinois is where Dad built his distinguished
    career
Even in retirement his scholarly pursuits are abundantly clear
Spending their "Golden Years" where the Chicago skyline looms
After all, the Windy City brought us here when 1980 was in full
    bloom
Mom and Dad found parenting full of wear and tear
Feisty, strong willed children can make you lose your hair
Together they struggled when times were lean but Ultimately
    achieving wealth

But they're the first to tell there is no price on good health
Having powered through a share of health crises and conditions
Now, they're experts on fitness and nutrition
We wish you a long and prosperous life
You've lasted half a century as husband and wife
A legacy of your 1968 marriage are the children you bore
Who now have given you another generation to adore
You give all of us hope, direction and sage advice
To work hard, practice self-care and enjoy life
You remind us to pray everyday
Foster good relations with the family; they are here to stay
We are so fortunate to have you both model for us the righteous
    way
So, a huge thank you to both of you for our DNA

Happy 50th Anniversary. We love you!

APPENDIX III

LESSONS OF LIFE

I 've learned and indeed, applied these lessons throughout my
life. Each theme is culled from my many life experiences. It is
intended for my children, grandchildren and other descendants,
but other readers can benefit from the notions as well.

ON HEALTH
Take care of health as without it nothing really matters.
If you eat less, you eat longer and more.
Eat real foods, not food-like substances.
The foods you eat now determine how healthy you will be later.
Eat less, exercise more for good health.
Read, walk, eat natural food, drink water, and breathe fresh air.

ON WEALTH
Manage your money well as it is hard to save and easy to spend.
Poverty can shatter a life whereas wealth is a great equalizer.
Money does not give happiness but gives security.

ON LOVE
Avoid making enemies as life is too short.
There is no better feeling than to love and be loved.

Love is the outcome of love.

Marriage works well when both people respect and understand each other.

We can forget everything except hurt feelings.

Love needs to be cherished and nurtured.

ON CURIOSITY

Everything is interesting if you take interest.

Listen to music, it is the tranquilizer for the soul.

Take interest in different things, it will make you well-rounded.

Beauty cannot be measured but only recognized.

A beautiful scene or object is like frozen music.

The world is a fun place and so feel the wonder.

ON HAPPINESS

Happiness lies in the arduous climb to the perfect summit of life.

One key to happiness: Giving has its pleasure, expect little in return.

Happiness comes from the feeling of self-worth.

Avoid bickering with your family members.

A happy family means happiness for all.

ON SELF AND OTHERS

Don't criticize others before seeing yourself in the mirror.

Control your own behavior, not that of others.

One's problem starts in the head, where its solution lies too.

The tongue is your worst enemy or best friend depending on how you use it.

Accept imperfect behavior of others since humans are not perfect.

Democracy works best when people are conscious and think independently.

Before criticizing others try to understand their background and
 culture.
Avoid giving unsolicited advice to others.

ON WISDOM
Don't mess with dirt, it will make you dirtier.
You don't need to be the center of attention.
It takes at least two to quarrel and fight.
Mindful meditation gives us solace and composure.
If you are angry, don't let it linger, extinguish it quickly.
Forgiveness is the apex of virtues.

ON DILIGENCE
Don't start something that you can't finish.
If you already started something finish it, as finishing is winning.
Do things in order of importance and priority.
Common sense is not as common as it seems.
Life is difficult; try to make it easy.
Work hard and smartly; rewards just happen.
Paying attention is intelligence and it makes you smarter.
Try to see yourself as others see you.
Stop talking when nobody is listening.

ON INTELLIGENCE
Continue to educate yourself lest you stagnate.
Avoid generalizing or stereotyping others from a few examples.
Smartness means you are self-reliant and can defend yourself.
Intelligence and wisdom are different things.
A wise person knows what to ignore.
Think for yourself but take advice from experienced people.
If you want to learn and be informed read many books.
Science is not always perfect but believe in it as it strives for truth.

ON PERSPECTIVE

You see what you want to see.

Live in the present but try to foresee the future.

Forget the past but learn from it.

Always try to see the big picture.

Crisis makes you recognize and reinvent yourself.

The right attitude will make you; the wrong attitude will break you.

Life is full of complexity; so, seek patience and ease.

Don't waste your time as it is the best resource you have.

The best word in English is "Serene."

APPENDIX IV

ANCESTRAL HISTORY

Genealogy of the Mir Families of Indrakul and Dharandi in Patuakhali District, Bangladesh (until approximately 1910)

Preface

This account of the two Mir families rooted in Indrakul and Dharandi having the same origin was developed from what was told to me by the last living members of each families. The story of ancestry was orally handed down to them from their forefathers. Some specific information was gathered by A.T.M. Obaidullah, son of Mir Wajed Ali, and Mir Mosaddeq Ali, youngest son of Mir Muazzam Ali. Mir Mosaddeq Ali collected the information directly from his father. Some of the information from both sources was not fully verifiable. Mir Alauddin Ahmed, son of Mir Motahar Ali, who lived in Dhaka, was the longest surviving member of the present-day Mir clan until his death in June 2019. He took the initiative to initially document the ancestral history and requested that I, Mir Maqsud Ali, third son of Mir Muazzam Ali, edit it and compose a narrative.

Mir Alauddin Ahmed provided me with brief written material on the family tree while living in Chicago. I had an alternative family tree prepared by my brother Mir Mosaddeq Ali and had myself heard some stories about ancestors from my parents as well. I exerted my best efforts to carry out diligent investigation, screening out doubtful and inconsistent materials after comparing the different pieces of available information, based on these sources. I compiled this chronology in consultation with Mir Alauddin Ahmed to develop this history of the ancestry covering eight generations up to 1910 including my father's generation. The account that I developed was reviewed by my elder brother Mir Masoom Ali. Since family titles are traditionally determined by men's titles, only men are included here. In any case, the names of female ancestors were unavailable. Information is presented here with as much accuracy as was possible in the absence of recorded documents from the ancestors.

Lineage
The earliest known ancestor, Syed Noor was from Baghdad in Iraq and lived in late 17th century. Not much is known about his family or occupation. He traveled to present-day Saudi Arabia most likely to perform the hajj and then moved to Khorasan, a historical region that lay mostly in parts of modern-day Afghanistan, Iran and Turkmenistan. He decided to settle there. His son was Syed Nasir, who had a son named Syed Bashir, whose son was Syed Abbas. Historically, many Syeds considered descendants of Prophet Mohammad (peace be upon him) traveled from the Middle East to the Indian Subcontinent, Southeast Asia and Central Asia primarily to preach the Islamic faith. Syed Nader Ali, the eldest son of Syed Abbas, was one such preacher. To preach the religion, he and his two brothers Syed Kamar Ali and Syed Omar Ali travelled from Khorasan to Dhaka via Delhi and other Indian cities in early 19th century when India was ruled by an emperor of the declining Mughal Empire and Bengal was under the rule of the British colonists.

Syed Nader Ali's son Syed Nezamat Ali, who was also a preacher, grew up in Dhaka and developed a rapport with Dhaka's famous Nawab family. Because of his amiable and spiritual nature, one of the reigning Nawabs, either the patriarch of the family Khwaja Alimullah or his philanthropic son Nawab Abdul Ghani, who was pleased with him, allotted him in the mid-19ᵗʰ century a tract of land from their estate in Indrakul, a rural wooded area in the then Bakergonj district. It later fell into the Barisal district and then into the Patuakhali district. He moved and established a new settlement in Indrakul after clearing the forest there for his family and became the forerunner of a new clan there. His two uncles also joined him and settled in Indrakul. Syed Nezamat Ali had three sons. It is not known why he changed the family title for his sons from Syed to Mir. It is likely that, as was customary then, once he fulfilled his Islamic requirement of preaching his faith as a Syed and settled in Indrakul, he wished to absolve his sons of that obligation and let them hold the new equivalent title Mir instead of Syed. His oldest son was Mir Emran Ali, who took the job of an administrator of the Nawab Family's estate in the area. As part of his responsibilities he used to travel in the area and surrounding regions.

Circa 1900, Mir Emran Ali visited a village called Dharandi. There was a well-established Khan family in that area who had many landed properties. He met the wealthy patriarch of the Khan family, who had two daughters and no son, and who requested Mir Emran Ali to marry his elder daughter Jamila, so she could have a husband from a respectable Mir family of Indrakul. After due consideration, Mir Emran Ali agreed and took her as his second wife and let her stay in her parental home by agreement. He would continue to live in Indrakul but would visit her from time to time. Two sons were born to Jamila: Mir Muazzam Ali and Mir Mohsen Ali. My father Mir Muazzam Ali was born in 1901. Mir Emran Ali had six sons from his first marriage.

Mir Emran Ali's second brother Mir Anwar Ali later married the other sister of Jamila and settled in Dharandi. Mir Anwar Ali had the job of local honorary magistrate. These two marriages by the two brothers created the foothold of the second Mir family in Dharandi originally hailing from Indrakul. Later, Mir Sakhawat Ali, one of the sons of Mir Emran Ali from his first marriage, also voluntarily moved to Dharandi and settled there. Thus, the Mir family became well established, influential and well known in this village.

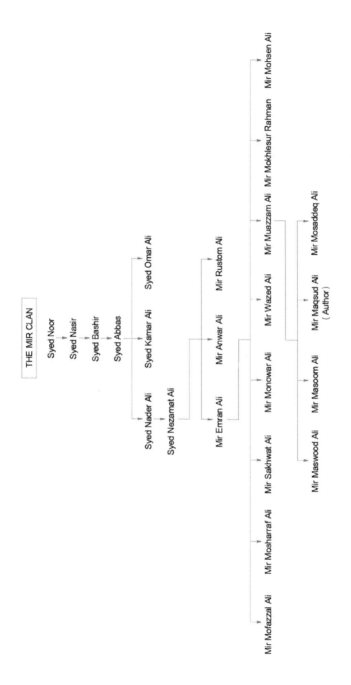

THE MIR CLAN

Syed Noor
Syed Nasir
Syed Bashir
Syed Abbas
Syed Kamar Ali
Syed Omar Ali
Syed Nader Ali
Syed Nezamat Ali
Mir Emran Ali
Mir Anwar Ali
Mir Rustom Ali
Mir Mofazzal Ali
Mir Mosharraf Ali
Mir Sakhwat Ali
Mir Monowar Ali
Mir Wazed Ali
Mir Muazzam Ali
Mir Mokhlesur Rahman
Mir Mohsen Ali
Mir Maswood Ali
Mir Masoom Ali
Mir Maqsud Ali
(Author)
Mir Mosaddeq Ali

Made in the USA
San Bernardino, CA
04 June 2020